Basic Accounting
Concepts, Principles, and Procedures
Second Edition

Volume 2

Applying Principles
and Procedures

03/15/20

Basic Accounting
Concepts, Principles, and Procedures
Second Edition

Volume 2

Applying Principles and Procedures

Gregory Mostyn
Mission College

Worthy & James
PUBLISHING

Worthy & James Publishing

Before you buy or use this book, you should understand . . .

© 2017 Worthy & James Publishing

Cataloging-in-Publication Data
Mostyn, Gregory R.
    Basic accounting. Volume 2, Applying principles and
procedures / Gregory Mostyn.
        p. cm.
        Includes index.
        "Concepts, principles, and procedures."
        LCCN 2006939188
        ISBN-13: 978-0-9914231-1-8
        ISBN-10: 0-9914231-1-9
        Previous edition cataloged as follows:
        1. Accounting.   I. Title.

    HF5636.M67 2007   657'.042
                                       QBI07-600131

Worthy & James Publishing
P.O. Box 360215
Milpitas, CA 95036
www.worthyjames.com

Suggestions, questions, comments, criticism? Use: inquiries@worthyjames.com

*To my parents, Bob and Melita, who by word and deed
have taught me the value of lifelong learning*

And

*Daisy, who has always been exactly right about
the importance of long walks in the park*

BRIEF Contents

Contents

Preface

Basic Accounting Concepts, Principles, and Procedures provides a new pedagogical approach for introductory accounting. The content does not begin with a focus on the accounting profession and introductory accounting procedures. Instead, the text first explains the basic concepts and structure of a business to create a meaningful context for the accounting concepts that follow. The conversational, relaxed approach is built on a research-based instructional design that improves comprehension and retention, and minimizes stress. The system's special design becomes immediately apparent by viewing the appearance of the material.

As any experienced accounting instructor can relate, accounting knowledge is very much a building-block architecture. Accounting skills rest on the foundation of critical basic concepts. Instructors know that introductory accounting students who miss the early concepts seldom successfully complete a course. ***Basic Accounting Concepts, Principles, and Procedures***, particularly Volume 1, is specifically designed to address this weakness in traditional texts, in which *early foundation concepts receive no greater emphasis than later content*. These two volumes provide the reader with guidance that strongly reinforces key foundation concepts, particularly those that beginning students often find most difficult. Volume 1, for example, places great emphasis on building a clear understanding of transaction analysis. In Volume 2, each type of adjusting entry is reinforced in a separate appendix to the adjusting entries, Learning Goal 4. This approach provides special emphasis for key concepts as well as for difficult concepts and is applied to all topics. In our experience, this builds the confidence that assures future progress and creates curiosity about the value (and shortcomings) of accounting. At the same time, the flexibility of the design allows readers to move quickly through the parts of the material with which they are comfortable.

Particularly in Volume 2, Applying Principles and Procedures, the reader will also benefit from real-world practical help. Some examples are: what to do if a bank reconciliation will not balance, how to handle partial payments, a checklist for an accounting software purchase, and how to identify the hidden costs of accounting software.

Basic Accounting Concepts, Principles, and Procedures is a complete self-study package. The two volumes contain full coverage of the traditional first accounting principles course plus a complete first-course coverage of corporate accounting and financial statements analysis. The importance of ethics in business and accounting is reinforced by exposition as well as by articles and questions, including Internet exercises. Volume 2 contains two complete merchandising practice sets with solutions. The disk included with each volume contains detailed solutions to all learning goal questions and problems, a complete basic math review with problems and solutions, and templates that provide an unlimited supply of various types of accounting paper, worksheets, journals, and ledgers.

About the Author

Greg Mostyn is an accounting instructor at Mission College, Santa Clara, California. He is a member of the American Accounting Association and American Institute of Certified Public Accountants. He has served as accounting department chairman and has extensive experience in accounting curriculum design and course development. He has authored several books and published articles in the areas of learning theory and its application to accounting instruction, textbook use, and accounting education research.

Acknowledgments

No book can ever be written alone. I wish to especially acknowledge the following individuals for their excellent suggestions, useful criticism, and creative ideas. They have fixed mistakes and generously shared their wisdom in more ways than I can describe.

William Bernacchi, CPA, MBA
William E. Bjork, JD, CPA, MBA
Randy Castello, CPA, MBA
Jennifer Chadwick, CPA, EA, MBA
Betty Paine Christopher, CMA, CFP, EA, MBA
George Dorrance, CPA, MBA
Magdy Farag, Ph.D., MBA
Richard Hobbs, MA
John Hui, CPA, MPA
Ching-Lih Jan, Ph.D., MAS, MBA
John Koeplin, Ph.D., CPA, MA, MBA

Christopher Kwak, CPA, MBA
Shellie Mueller, MBA
Jose Nava, CPA, MBA
Ernestine Porter, CPA, MBA
Howard Randall, CPA (retired), MBA
Diana Smith, CPA, MBA
Teresa Thompson, CPA, MBA
James Van Tassel, Ph.D., MBA
Guoli Zhang, MA, MS

Cover Design: David Ruppe, Impact Publications
Interior Design: Mark Ong
Typesetting: MPS Limited

Cover Images

Skyline: Stockbyte/Getty Images
Basketball Players: Jim Cummins/Taxi/Getty Images
Office: Stockbyte/Getty Images
Golden Gate Bridge: Andrew Gunners/Digital Vision/Getty Images
Market: David Buffington/Photodisc/Getty Images

How to Use This Book

MANY RESOURCES FOR YOU

"Overviews" and "quick reviews"

- Each *section* has an overview to direct you to the parts of the book that are most important for you. Be sure to read each section "overview" when you come to it.
- Each *learning goal* has a short overview of the content of the goal. Read this overview before you begin. Then, after you study a learning goal, read the "quick review" and "vocabulary."

Answers to questions and problems

All the learning goal questions and problems in this book (except for Internet exercises and instructor-assigned problems) have detailed solutions. These solutions are in the computer disk that is located on the inside back cover of this book. **Tip:** Whenever you want to have extra examples, you can always use the problems with their solutions as more examples, as well as for practice. **Solutions are also available at www.worthyjames.com**

Cumulative tests

This book includes cumulative tests with answers after each test. Each test also has a **Help Table.** After you check the answers, use the **Help Table** to specifically identify your strong and weak knowledge areas. Use this for review.

Accounting paper

The disk at the back of the book contains a complete selection of all types of accounting paper that you can use for the solution of any problem type in the book. You can print out an unlimited supply of accounting paper by using the disk. **Accounting paper is also available at www.worthyjames.com**

Complete basic math review

The disk at the back of the book also contains a comprehensive, step-by-step math review beginning at the most basic level. The review contains many types of problems, all with solutions. The review begins with Volume 1 and continues on the disk for Volume 2 with fractions, ratios, and basic algebra.

R E V I E W	# The Essential Accounts for a Corporation

The Accounts For a Corporation

The Accounts For a Corporation

Equity Accounts

Overview

In volume 1, we began the study of accounting by using the proprietorship form of business as our model. We continued this through Learning Goal 27. After that point, we began a detailed study of corporations. In this book, we continue our study of accounting using the corporate business model. However, if you did not study corporations in volume 1, it is not necessary to review that material. For the purposes of this book, you will only need to understand the essential accounts that are always used by corporations. These are illustrated below and in the balance sheet on page 3.

Comparison of Proprietorship and Corporation

The key accounting difference between a proprietorship and a corporation is the manner of reporting the owners' equity. The word "equity" refers to the owners' claim on the business assets (business wealth). The owner's claim in a proprietorship is called *owner's equity*. Owner's equity consists of both an owner's capital account which contains the owner's investments, and revenue and expense accounts which together result in either net income or net loss. For reporting purposes, the net income or loss is combined with the owner's capital account balance and reported as a single amount. This amount is usually identified with the owner's name, such as "Bill Smith, Capital". If an owner withdraws any assets from the business, this is recorded in a withdrawals account. Withdrawals reduce the capital.

In a corporation, the equity is called *stockholders' equity*. In a basic corporation such as we use in this book, the stockholders' equity consists of the balances of two accounts. These are the *common stock* and *retained earnings* accounts. Common stock is the amount of the owners' investment, resulting from their purchase of shares of stock in the corporation. Any kind of stock is often referred to by the general name of *paid-in capital*. Retained earnings is an account that records the cumulative amount of net income or net loss resulting from revenues and expenses, since the corporation was created.

Distributions of cash or other assets to the owners (stockholders) of a corporation are called *dividends*. Dividends are like withdrawals in a proprietorship, and are often recorded in a separate dividends account. Dividends act as reductions to retained earnings.

Illustration: Proprietorship Compared to Corporation Equity

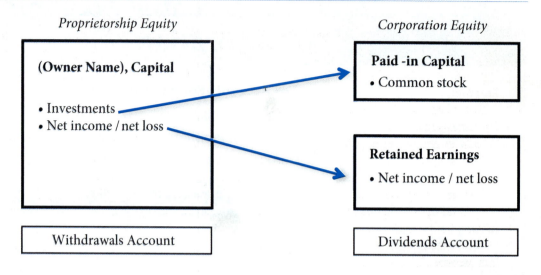

Proprietorship Equity

Corporation Equity

(Owner Name), Capital

• Investments
• Net income / net loss

Paid -in Capital
• Common stock

Retained Earnings
• Net income / net loss

Withdrawals Account

Dividends Account

**Debit and
Credit Rules**

In a corporation all the debit and credit rules remain the same as what you have studied. All the accounting principles, such as the accounting equation, remain the same. The table below compares debits and credits in the specific equity accounts.

Transaction	Recorded With A . . .	Proprietorship Account Name	Corporation Account Name	Section on Corporate Balance Sheet
Investment	Credit	Capital	Common Stock	Paid-in Capital
A sale	Credit	Revenue	Revenue	Becomes part of retained earnings
An expense	Debit	Expense	Expense	
Payment to owner	Debit	Withdrawals	Dividends*	

* It is also acceptable to debit a retained earnings account.

Corporate Financial Statements: Quick Review

Financial statements combine and summarize individual account balances. A basic corporate income statement, statement of retained earnings, and balance sheet are illustrated on the next page. **Notice the stockholders' equity on the balance sheet**. Notice that the term "Inc." follows the name in each heading. This is a frequently used abbreviation that means "Incorporated". Another common term is "Corp." for "Corporation".

Corporate Financial Statements: Quick Review, *continued*

Watson Consulting Services, Inc.
Income Statement
For the Month Ended May 31, 2017

Revenues		
Consulting service revenue..		$12,900
Operating expenses		
Salaries and wages expense..	$4,100	
Rent expense	2,500	
Advertising expense...	1,300	
Utilities expenses...	800	
Total operating expenses...		8,700
Income before tax...		4,200
Income tax expense..		1,000
Net income		$3,200

Watson Consulting Services, Inc.
Statement of Retained Earnings
For the Month Ended May 31, 2017

Retained earnings, May 1	$71,200
Add: net income	3,200
Less: dividends..	(1,500)
Retained earnings, May 31	$72,900

Watson Consulting Services, Inc.
Balance Sheet
May 31, 2017

Assets

Cash...		$83,500
Accounts receivable...		26,300
Supplies		1,800
Equipment..		32,000
Total assets		$143,600

Liabilities and Stockholders' Equity

Liabilities		
Notes payable..		$31,000
Accounts payable...		14,700
Total liabilities		45,700
Stockholders' equity		
Paid-in capital		
Common stock..	15,000	
Retained earnings	72,900	
Total stockholders' equity		87,900
Total liabilities and stockholder's equity		$143,600

Corporate Financial Statements: Quick Review, *continued*

Income Statement

The income statement reports revenues and expenses for the purpose of calculating net income in a specific period; in this example, the current period is the month of May. Net income is the combination of revenues minus expenses. Revenues increase net income. Expenses decrease net income. Net income is also reported as an increase on the statement of retained earnings. Here, the net income of $3,200 increases reported retained earnings as shown in the next statement.

Note that a corporation pays income tax. A corporation is a separate legal entity. Therefore you see a line item for income tax expense, which does not appear on an income statement of an unincorporated business such as a proprietorship.

Statement of Retained Earnings

A retained earnings account accumulates every period's net income or loss. The statement of retained earnings explains the changes and shows the balance of retained earnings. The changes in the statement occur over the same time period as the income statement. The first line on the statement of retained earnings shows the prior balance as of the beginning of the period (May 1). Net income (loss) increases (decreases) retained earnings. Dividends decrease retained earnings. The last line shows the final (May 31) balance of $72,900, which is reported in stockholders' equity on the balance sheet.

(Note: a statement of stockholders' equity is a more comprehensive disclosure. This is discussed in Volume 1, but is not necessary here.)

Balance Sheet

The balance sheet reports assets, liabilities, and stockholders' equity as of a specific date (May 31). This date is normally the ending date of the current income statement reporting period. You can think of a balance sheet as a flash photograph of a company's wealth (assets) and the claims on that wealth (liabilities and stockholders' equity) at a point in time. A corporate balance sheet is based on the fundamental accounting equation of:

$$\textbf{Assets = Liabilties + Stockholders' Equity}$$
or:
$$A = L + SE$$

Statement of Cash Flows

Not shown here is the fourth required financial statement: the statement of cash flows. This statement explains the changes in a company's cash balance. Volume 1 introduces this statement and Learning Goal 21 in this volume covers the preparation and analysis of the statement in detail.

Adjusting the Accounts

LEARNING GOALS

LEARNING GOAL 1	# Explain the Meaning of "Accounting Period"

In Learning Goal 1, you will find:

Overview of Accounting Periods

Introduction

A long time ago, I had an accounting professor who loved to trick most of his students (including me) with this question: "When is the only time you can be completely certain of the profit or loss of a business?"

Correct answer: Only when the business is sold or ceases to exist. Only then, when all the debts are paid, can you compare the value of the assets left over plus what you withdrew along the way to the cost of everything you invested.

Example of the Problem

The Kaufman Delivery Service began business in 1967 with an investment of $20,000 by the owner & stockholder, Jerry Kaufman. In 2017, Jerry retires and sells the business and receives $4,000,000 after business debts are paid. During all the years he owned the business, the corporation paid out $1,500,000 of dividends to Jerry.

1967	Withdrawals for 51 years: $1,500,000	**2017**
$20,000		$4,000,000

After the business is finally sold, we know that the total profit of the business is:

Remaining proceeds of sale	$4,000,000
Dividends	1,500,000
Less: Invested	(20,000)
Total Profit	$5,480,000

Overview of Accounting Periods, *continued*

No One Wants to Wait!

Problem: No one is going to wait the entire life of a business to find out how well a business has performed! Owners, managers, investors, lenders, taxing authorities, and many other stakeholders in a business need to evaluate the progress of a business frequently and regularly. Therefore, a business prepares financial statements at frequent, regular intervals. However, as we will soon see, doing this also creates problems, difficulties, and traps for the unwary.

The Need to Measure Change

Time-Period Assumption

Even though business operations are a continuous process, accountants assume that the life of a business is divided into regular, fixed time intervals. This assumption is called the **periodicity assumption** or the **time-period assumption**. Financial statements are prepared at the end of each time period. This is the only way that the financial changes can be measured at regular intervals.

Example of Time Periods

The diagram below illustrates the balance sheets and income statements that are prepared at the end of time intervals of one *calendar year*, for years 2015, 2016, and 2017.

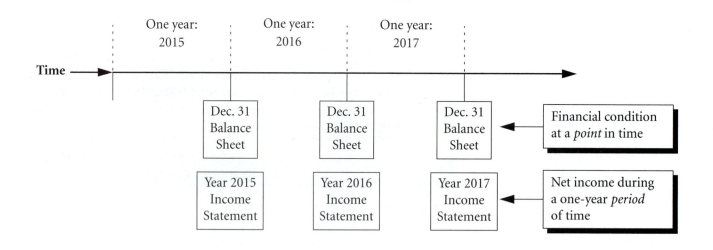

The Need to Measure Change, *continued*

Timeliness

Net income can only be calculated for a period of time. Dividing the life of a business into equal, fixed time periods such as years, quarters, or months makes it possible to measure income over shorter periods than the entire life of a business. When information is frequently available like this, it has the quality of **timeliness**. Timeliness is a quality that makes financial information more relevant and useful. Timeliness is especially important to the owners and managers of a business.

By using the *equal periods* of time, such as the years 2015, 2016, and 2017, the income statements also become comparable to one another. As you can see from the diagram on page 8, managers can easily compare the annual income of one year to the annual income of another year.

Accounting Periods

The fixed time intervals into which a business life is divided are called **accounting periods**.

Why Accounting Periods Are Needed

The table below summarizes why accounting periods are needed.

Condition Measurement (balance sheet)	The condition of a business needs to be checked at regular intervals.
Income Measurement (income statement)	Net income or loss can only be determined for a specified *period* of time.
Timeliness	Financial information is needed frequently and regularly.
Comparability	By making time periods equal, financial reports can be compared to analyze changes.

Fiscal Years

All companies prepare financial statements at the end of an accounting period of one year, called a **fiscal year**. A company that has seasonal variations in its operations usually selects a fiscal year that ends just after the busy season is over. For example, department stores often choose January 31 as the end of their fiscal year, after Christmas sales and returns are completed.

continued ▶

The Need to Measure Change, *continued*

Typical Periods

Although every business prepares financial reports at least once a year, some companies also use shorter accounting periods to measure progress more often. Financial reports that are prepared for periods shorter than one year are called *interim statements*.

Here are some typical accounting periods:

Fiscal year	Any consecutive 12-month period of time
Calendar year	A fiscal year that begins on January 1 and ends on December 31
52–53 week year	A year that always ends on the same day of the week that is closest to the last day of a calendar month (*Example*: the Saturday closest to January 31)
Quarter	A consecutive three-month period
Month	A calendar month (January, February, etc.)

The Tremendous "Side Effects" of Accounting Periods

When you first think about it, dividing the life of a business into regular time periods does not seem like a big deal. You would think that it should not be especially difficult to calculate a company's progress one year at a time (or quarterly, monthly, etc.). Really, how complicated can that be?

Answer: Unfortunately, very complicated.

By simply dividing the life of a business into regular time periods, profound and complex issues are created. Also, the possibility for error and fraud becomes much greater. Many traps are created for the careless accountant.

Issues Created

The rest of Section I explains the following important issues that result from dividing the life of a business into time periods:

- What is the *best way to measure* the progress of a business each period?
- What elements are needed to measure progress (revenues and expenses)?
- When should a revenue or expense be recorded?
- How can we be sure that all revenues and expenses really do get recorded in the proper periods?

The Best Way of Measuring Financial Change

The Best Way to Measure

The purpose of dividing the life of a business into regular time periods is to measure the progress of the business at regular intervals. However, trying to do this creates the most basic questions immediately: What is the best way to measure the "progress" after each period?

Naturally, there are different ways to measure progress, such as observing the ability to pay debts as they become due (called *solvency*) or the change in the number of customers. However, over many years, managers and accountants have agreed that:

> The single most important measure of business progress each period is *the effect that business **operations** have on the **stockholders' equity.***

Definition: Operations

Operations are the actions of a business that create something of value (services or products) and that make sales to customers.

Operations Has Two Important Elements

"Operations" consists of two basic elements:

1. consuming resources to create something of value, and
2. selling what was created (services or products)

Definition: Revenue

Revenue is an *increase in stockholders' equity caused by making a sale* of services or products to a customer. The amount of the revenue is the dollar amount of the sale.

Why Revenue Increases Stockholders' Equity

A revenue *always* makes either assets increase or liabilities decrease. When this happens, to keep the accounting equation in balance, stockholders' equity increases. (Revenues increase net income, which increases retained earnings, and retained earnings is part of stockholders' equity. See balance sheet on page 3.)

Examples of Revenue

- Jones Company sells a $950 computer to Johnson. Jones Company has $950 of revenue.
- Smith Company provides $400 of repair service to Johnson. Smith has $400 of revenue.

Examples That Are NOT Revenues

- Borrowing money—because no sale is being made
- Collecting money owed—because no sale is being made
- Receiving an advance payment from a customer—because there is no sale yet

continued ▶

The Best Way of Measuring Financial Change, *continued*

Definition: Expense	*Expense* is a *decrease in stockholders' equity caused by using up goods or services in operations to create revenues.*
Why Expenses Decrease Stockholders' Equity	An expense *always* makes either assets decrease or liabilities increase. When this happens, to keep the accounting equation in balance, stockholders' equity decreases. (Expenses decrease net income, which decreases retained earnings, and retained earnings is part of stockholders' equity. See balance sheet on page 3.)
Expense Synonym	Expense is sometimes called **expired cost**.
Examples of Expense	■ Using $800 of cash to pay the rent ■ Using up $200 of office supplies ■ Using an advertising service ■ Using employee services
Examples That Are NOT Expenses	■ Paying a loan—because money is not being used up in operations ■ Buying equipment—because one asset is simply exchanged for another
How Revenue and Expense Affect Stockholders' Equity	If we subtract expenses from revenues, the result is the net effect of the operations on stockholders' equity. This net effect is called *net income* or *net loss*. Net income is the excess of revenues over expenses. Net loss is the excess of expenses over revenues. Net income increases stockholders' equity during a period. Net loss decreases stockholders' equity during a period.

Summary of Effects of Revenues and Expenses

Revenue Examples

A revenue can either increase an asset or decrease a liability, depending on the transaction. At the same time, the accounting equation will always show an increase in stockholders' equity because revenues increase net income, which is reported as part of retained earnings, an element of stockholders' equity.

	A $\uparrow$	=	L	+	SE $\uparrow$
Revenue increases an asset	+ Accounts Receivable		------		+ Service Revenue

	A	=	L $\downarrow$	+	SE $\uparrow$
Revenue decreases a liability	------		– Unearned Revenue		+ Service Revenue

Summary of Effects of Revenues and Expenses, *continued*

Expense Examples

An expense can either decrease an asset or increase a liability, depending on the transaction. At the same time, the accounting equation will always show a decrease in stockholders' equity because expenses reduce net income, which is reported as part of retained earnings, an element of stockholders' equity.

	$A\downarrow$	=	L	+	$SE\downarrow$
Expense decreases an asset	– Supplies		------		+ Supplies Expense

	A	=	$L\uparrow$	+	$SE\downarrow$
Expense increases a liability	------		+ Accounts Payable		+ Repairs Expense

VOCABULARY

Accounting periods: fixed periods of time for which a company prepares financial statements (page 9)

Balance sheet (corporation): A statement that shows assets, liabilities, and stockholders' equity (page 3)

Calendar year: a fiscal year that begins on January 1 and ends on December 31 (page 8)

Expense: a decrease in owner's equity caused by using up resources to create revenues (page 12)

Expired cost: another name for expense (page 12)

Fiscal year: any consecutive 12-month period of business activity (page 9)

Income statement: A statement that shows revenues, expenses, and net income or loss. (page 3)

Interim statements: financial statements prepared more often than annually (page 10)

Operations: all the business activities to create and sell something of value (page 11)

Periodicity assumption: the assumption that the life of a business is divided into regular, fixed time intervals (page 8)

Revenue: an increase in owner's equity caused by making a sale of services or products to a customer (page 11)

Solvency: accumulating enough cash to pay debts when they are due (page 11)

Statement of retained earnings: A statement that shows the beginning and ending balances and changes in retained earnings.(page 3)

Stockholders' Equity: Stockholders' claim on the value of corporate assets (page 1)

Timeliness: making information available frequently (page 9)

Time-period assumption: another name for periodicity assumption (page 8)

PRACTICE   Learning Goal 1

Solutions are in the disk at the back of the book and at: www.worthyjames.com

Learning Goal 1 is about accounting time periods. Use these questions and problems to practice what you have learned about accounting periods.

Multiple Choice
Select the best answer.

1. The periodicity assumption, or time-period assumption, states that:
    a. similar accounting periods must be used for similar businesses.
    b. the economic life of a business is divided into regular, fixed time periods.
    c. income must be reported periodically using the income statement.
    d. none of the above.
2. The purpose of using a regular, fixed accounting period includes:
    a. creating a standard, fixed time interval over which to measure business income.
    b. creating a time period that can be compared to other time periods of equal length when analyzing net income or net loss.
    c. making information available to stakeholders in a timely manner.
    d. all of the above.
3. If a company's annual accounting period always ends on March 31, when does its accounting period always begin?
    a. March 1 of the preceding calendar year
    b. February 28 of the preceding year
    c. April 1 of the preceding calendar year
    d. April 1 of the current calendar year
4. An accounting period one year in length that does not necessarily end on December 31 is usually called a:
    a. calendar year.
    b. 52–53 week year.
    c. fiscal year.
    d. none of the above.
5. The most important measure of the progress of a business each period is:
    a. the effect that operations have had on stockholders' equity.
    b. the increase or decrease in cash.
    c. the change in the amount of debt owed.
    d. the increase or decrease in the number of customers.
6. The only time you can be absolutely sure of the total profit or loss of a business is when · · · · · · · ·. However, to measure progress and provide financial information more quickly, the life of a business is divided into regular · · · · · · · ·:
    a. it is terminated / fiscal years.
    b. financial reports are prepared / cycles.
    c. it is terminated / accounting periods.
    d. tax returns are prepared / projections.
7. One of the side effects of dividing the life of a business into accounting periods is having to choose the best way to measure the change in a business. To do this, accountants use:
    a. revenues, which increase stockholders' equity.
    b. expenses, which decrease stockholders' equity.
    c. net income, which combines the effects of revenues and expenses.
    d. none of the above.

PRACTICE   Learning Goal 1, continued

Solutions are in the disk at the back of the book and at: www.worthyjames.com

Reinforcement Problems

LG 1-1. Why does the life of a business need to be divided into regular, equal accounting periods? What issues are created by doing this?

LG 1-2. On September 10, a company paid for a two-year insurance policy that began on September 10, 2017. The company has a fiscal year that begins on July 1. In what fiscal years will the insurance policy provide some insurance coverage?

LG 1-3. Greg's Company and Rosie's Company both had net incomes of $12,000 in their most recent accounting periods. The accounting period of Greg's Company is annual, but the accounting period of Rosie's Company is monthly. Are both companies equally profitable?

LG1-4. Effect of revenues and expenses on the accounting equation / balance sheet Complete the following:
- A revenue can either increase an .... or decrease a .... but always **increases/ decreases**............
- An expense can either increase a .... or decrease an .... but always **increases/ decreases**..........

LG1-5. Prepare basic corporate financial statements. The table below shows, in random order, the account names and final account balance information for Sonora Company Corporation for the year ended December 31, 2017. The beginning balance of retained earnings is also included. *Instructions:* Prepare an income statement, statement of retained earnings, and balance sheet for the year ended December 31, 2017.

Accounts Payable	$27,390	Unearned Revenue	$3,000	Service Revenue	$475,200
Cash	82,440	Salaries Expense	269,220	Dividends	25,000
Income Tax Expense	15,620	Utilities Expense	26,130	Accounts Receivable	69,330
Advertising Expense	42,750	Office Supplies	5,600	Common Stock	10,000
Equipment	101,300	Rent Expense	48,400	Repairs Expense	11,100
Retained Earnings, Jan. 1	181,300				

Instructor-Assigned Problem

If you are using this book in a class, this review problem may be assigned by your instructor for homework, group assignments, class work, or other activities. Only you instructor has the solution.

IA1-1: Assume that the following amounts are revised in LG1-5 above: Service revenue: $481,950; Salaries Expense: $277, 320; Rent Expense: $51,300; Dividends, $33,000; Equipment: $90,000. Income tax expense is 20% of income before tax. *Instructions:* Prepare an income statement, statement of retained earnings, and balance sheet for the year ended December 31, 2017.

LEARNING GOAL 2

Explain the Basic Principles for Recording Revenues and Expenses

In Learning Goal 2, you will find:

Accrual Basis Accounting

Overview of Accrual Basis

Continuing from the Prior Learning Goal . . .

When we left off in the prior learning goal, we were discussing the issues that are created by dividing the life of a business into accounting periods. We now continue with two remaining issues:

- *when to recognize* (record) revenues and expenses, and
- *how to make sure* that *all* revenues and expenses get recognized in the correct periods.

Overview of Accrual Basis, *continued*

Why Correct Recognition Is Very Important

To *recognize* means to record a transaction. If we recognize the correct amount of revenues each period and the correct amount of expenses each period, we will correctly report the full effect of the business operations on the stockholder's equity.

In other words, we will correctly determine the net income or loss.

Example of Bad Recognition

Imagine that I own a business. Part way into the year 2018, my computer parts business is in desperate need of cash, and I am trying to get you to invest $50,000 in my business. Here is the actual amount of the revenue of my business in each of the past three years:

2015	2016	2017
$475,000	$390,000	$355,000

I am so desperate that I decide to lie to you and defraud you. I tell you that my business is very successful. I say that you will see that revenue has been increasing every year! I prepare financial statements for you to look at. However, when I prepare the financial statements, I purposely group some of the sales invoices together from the wrong years, like this:

- I take $50,000 of 2015 sales and include them with the year 2016 sales.
- I take $100,000 of current year (2018) sales and include them with 2017 sales.

Now, when you look at the financial statements, here is the revenue you will see:

2015	2016	2017
$425,000	$440,000	$455,000

continued ▶

Overview of Accrual Basis, *continued*

Result

The business looks a lot more successful, doesn't it? Revenue appears to be increasing every year! And I did all this with actual revenue—I can show you all the actual sales invoices. I simply recorded some of the revenue in a *different period* than when it was actually earned.

I could do the same kind of thing with the expenses and make the expenses appear to be decreasing over a selected time period. By the time you find out the truth . . . too late, I have your money!

"Oh yes, my business is earning more revenue every year!"

To prevent these kinds of misstatements, accountants have developed some very important rules for when to record revenues and expenses.

Accrual Accounting Principles

Revenue and Expense Recognition Rules

Under Generally Accepted Accounting Principles (GAAP), two rules tell us the correct time to record ("recognize") revenues and expenses. These are the rules:

> ■ **Revenue—the *revenue recognition principle* (also called the *revenue principle*):** A revenue must be recorded in the same accounting period in which it was earned.
> ■ **Expense—the *matching principle*:** An expense must be recorded in the accounting period in which it helped to create revenue.

Definition: Accrual Accounting

Accountants use many different techniques to make sure that the two principles above are put into effect. Together, all the techniques for implementing the revenue recognition and matching principles are called **accrual basis accounting**. Accrual basis accounting records all revenue and expense transactions according to the two rules above.

Accrual Accounting Principles, *continued*

Summary of the Principles

The table below summarizes these two very important GAAP principles:

Accrual accounting is the application of the . . .	that tells accountants . . .
revenue recognition principle	when to record revenue.
matching principle	when to record expense.

Required by GAAP

Accrual accounting is the most accurate kind of accounting, and it is required by GAAP (Generally Accepted Accounting Principles).

Applying the Revenue Recognition Principle

Rule

The correct application of the revenue recognition principle is to record revenue in the period in which the revenue is *earned*.

When Revenue Is Earned

Revenue is earned when all three conditions are met:

- The price is agreed upon.
- A customer receives the goods or services agreed upon.
- The customer can reasonably be expected to pay, or has paid.

Receive Some Asset

When a sale is made, a business will have received some asset, usually cash or accounts receivable.

The timing of when cash is received has nothing to do with when revenues are recorded. A revenue is recorded when it is earned, and cash is not always received at the same time.

Caution!

It is NOT necessary for a business to receive cash at the time of the sale in order to recognize revenue. The customer can promise to pay later or could have already paid in advance.

continued ▶

Applying the Revenue Recognition Principle, *continued*

Examples   The table below shows you examples of correct revenue recognition.

If this happens . . .	then revenue . . .	because . . .
Central Piedmont Company receives $250 from a customer who *pays in* advance, *before* the service is provided,	is *not* recognized,	the services have not yet been performed, so revenue is not *earned*. It does not matter that cash has been received from a potential customer.
In *January*, Sandhills Corp. performs services for a customer who paid $500 in advance *in November*,	is recognized in the amount of $500 in *January*,	the services were performed in January, so revenue is *earned* in January (not in November).
Fayetteville Ventures delivers $1,000 of merchandise to a customer on June 25, and the customer promises *to pay later* (an account receivable for Fayetteville),	is recognized when the sale is made, (delivery completed) on June 25,	the merchandise was delivered to the customer on June 25, so a sale is made (revenue is earned). The asset accounts receivable is recorded.
Johnston, Inc. paints an office building in June and receives $25,000 cash in June from the customer,	is recognized in the amount of $25,000 in *June*, when services provided	the painting service was provided in June, so this is when the revenue is *earned*. Receiving the cash in June has nothing to do with recognizing the revenue in June.

Applying the Matching Principle

Overview   A business incurs expenses—that is, uses up resources—to create revenue. Therefore, there is a natural cause-and-effect relationship between expenses and revenues. When expenses are correctly matched against (subtracted from) revenues, the result is correct net income.

Matching is accomplished by following the matching principle. The ***matching principle*** tells accountants to record expenses *when resources are used up* and *help produce revenues*. (The time when cash is paid is ignored and does not affect when the expense is recorded.)

Rule   To apply the matching principle, record an expense in the same accounting period in which it helped to create revenue.

Guideline   How do we know when an expense helps to create revenue? We observe when a resource is being consumed (property or services), and then we try to identify any revenue that results from the resource consumed.

Applying the Matching Principle, *continued*

How to Apply the Rule

How the matching principle is applied depends on whether or not a particular expense can be identified with a particular revenue. Here is the method:

If . . .	Then . . .
a particular expense *can* be identified with a particular revenue that it helped to create . . .	record the expense in the same period as the revenue is recorded.
a particular expense *cannot* be identified with a particular revenue that it helped to create . . .	record the expense in the accounting period that *received a benefit from the expense* (even if there is no revenue in that period).

Expense recognition is easy if you can see a direct connection between an expense and a revenue. However, often there is no direct connection between a particular expense and a particular revenue.

Examples: Expense Identified with a Revenue

- A car salesman, who is paid by commission, makes a sale in May for a car dealership (sales services consumed). The car is not delivered to the customer until June. The commission expense should be deferred until June, when the revenue is recorded from the sale.
- In July, a furniture company uses $500 of materials to build a chair. The chair is sold in November. The $500 of materials becomes part of the asset "chair" until it is sold in November, at which time an expense is recorded when the chair goes to the customer (an asset used up).

Examples: Expense Not Identified with a Revenue

- $3,000 was paid for the December rent (rental service consumed). It is impossible to know what part of the rent for the whole month is connected with any particular revenue in this month or any other month. The rent expense is recorded as a December expense (December benefit).
- In October, Raleigh Advertising Agency uses computer repair services (repair services consumed) costing $1,000, but it does not pay for them until December. October was the period receiving the benefit of the repairs, so the expense is in October because the expense is not identified with any particular revenue (October benefit).
- Raleigh Advertising Agency pays $3,000 in October for a fire insurance policy that covers October, November, and December. Because three months receive the benefits of the policy (insurance services consumed), record $1,000 expense in each of the three months of October, November, and December (October, November, December benefit).

Check Your Understanding

Write the completed sentence on a separate sheet of paper. The answers are below.

The revenue recognition principle requires that revenue be recorded in the same period in which it was · · · · · · · ·. This will happen whenever a · · · · · · · · is made.

For example, if services are performed in June and cash is received in July, then the revenue should be recognized in · · · · · · · ·. Or, if a cash advance is received in April and the product is delivered in May, then revenue should be recognized in · · · · · · · ·.

The matching principle tells accountants when to record · · · · · · · ·. "Matching" means subtracting · · · · · · · · from the · · · · · · · · that they created. Correct matching requires two steps. First, see if an · · · · · · · · can be identified with a particular · · · · · · · ·. If this cannot be done, then record the · · · · · · · · in the accounting period that received a benefit from the resources consumed.

Answers

The revenue recognition principle requires that revenue be recorded in the same period in which it was earned. This will happen whenever a sale is made.

For example, if services are performed in June and cash is received in July, then the revenue should be recognized in June. Or, if a cash advance is received in April and the product is delivered in May, then revenue should be recognized in May.

The matching principle tells accountants when to record expenses. "Matching" means subtracting expenses from the revenues that they created. Correct matching requires two steps. First, see if an expense can be identified with a particular revenue. If this cannot be done, then record the expense in the accounting period that received a benefit from the resources consumed.

Cash Basis Accounting— A Simplified Alternative

Overview of Cash Basis

Definition: Cash Basis Accounting

Cash basis accounting is a type of accounting in which noncash transactions are ignored. Revenue is recognized *only* if cash is received. Expense is recognized *only* if cash is paid.

Note: "Cash" does not literally mean only currency. It includes checks and money orders.

Not Acceptable Under GAAP!

Cash basis accounting is not acceptable under GAAP. Why? Because cash basis accounting does not accurately record net income. This is because cash basis uses only the receipt and payment of cash to identify revenues and expenses.

- Cash basis accounting will miss revenue that is earned if cash is not received (*example:* sales on account).
- Cash basis accounting will also miss expenses that are incurred if cash is not paid (*example:* expenses involving accounts payable).
- Cash basis accounting sees revenue when cash is received in advance— even though services are not yet performed (*example:* unearned revenue).
- Cash basis accounting sees expense when prepayments are made, even though an item is not yet used up (*example:* buying prepaid insurance).

A final problem with cash basis accounting is that it is very easy to manipulate the amount of expenses for any accounting period by simply deciding to write a check before, during, or after the period. Often, it is also possible to manipulate the receipt of cash and thereby manipulate revenues.

Why Use Cash Basis?

- Cash basis is simple. It is much easier to learn than accrual accounting. Cash basis is a simplified method that is generally used by small service businesses and individuals. Most people can easily see when cash is received or paid.
- Cash flow is important. Cash basis focuses on cash flow instead of income measurement.
- If outsiders such as investors or lenders are not involved, it may not be necessary to prepare the more accurate accrual basis financial statements.

No Adjusting Entries

Accrual basis accounting requires adjusting entries because it recognizes non-cash revenues and expenses as well as cash transactions. However, cash basis accounting recognizes revenues and expenses only when cash is received or paid. Therefore, adjusting entries are not required for cash basis accounting.

How to Apply Cash Basis

Rules

Here are the rules for recording revenue and expense for cash basis accounting:

- **Revenues:** A revenue is recorded only when cash is received from a customer.
- **Expenses:** An expense is recorded only when cash is paid for goods or services.

  Note: Many cash basis systems make an exception for assets lasting longer than one year, and they properly record them as long-term assets rather than expenses. This is called "modified cash basis." The assets become expenses as they are used up.

Revenue Comparison

The table below compares revenues recorded on a cash basis to revenues properly recorded on an accrual basis.

Transaction	Cash Basis Revenue	Accrual Basis Revenue
Pitt Company sells $500 of merchandise in December 2016 (revenue actually earned). The customer pays in February 2017.	$500 in February 2017	$500 in December 2016
Surry Company receives a $750 advance from a customer in April. The company performs the services in June.	$750 in April	$750 in June

Expense Comparison

The table below compares expenses recorded on a cash basis to expenses properly recorded on an accrual basis.

Transaction	Cash Basis Expense	Accrual Basis Expense
Robeson Company receives a $450 telephone bill for September (actually incurred in September). The bill is paid in October.	$450 in October	$450 in September
In June, Haywood Company pays $350 for supplies. The supplies are used in July.	$350 in June	$350 in July

Illustration of Cash and Accrual Method Differences

Revenues

Example

Suppose that a business provides $500 of consulting services to a client. Cash can be received at three possible points:

- Client pays in advance, before services are provided.
- Client pays at the time services are provided.
- Client pays after the services are provided.

The illustrations below show the journal entries that would be made for each method at the three possible points at which cash can be received. Notice that cash basis records revenue at whatever point the cash is received. Accrual basis only records revenue at the point at which it is earned, regardless of when the cash is received (before or after the revenue).

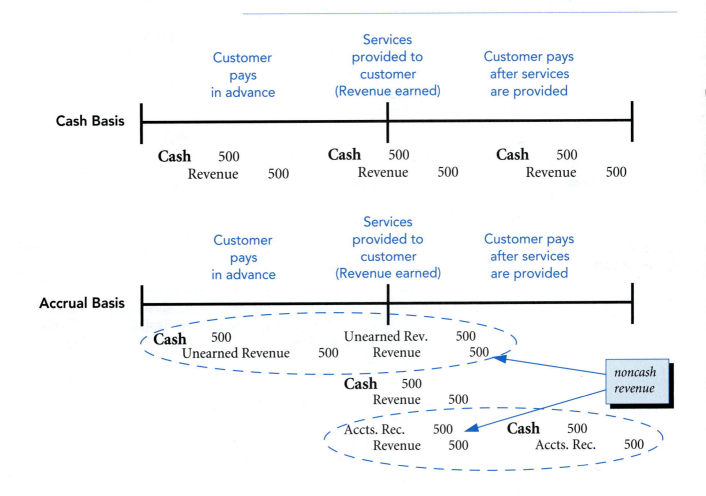

Expenses

Example

Suppose that a business uses $300 of advertising services. Services can be paid for at three possible points:

- Payment in advance, before expense is incurred
- Payment at the time the expense is incurred
- Payment after the expense is incurred

The illustrations below show the journal entries that would be made for each method at the three possible points at which cash could be paid. Notice that cash basis records expense at whatever point the cash is paid. Accrual basis only records expense at the point at which the expense is incurred, regardless of when the cash is paid (before or after the expense).

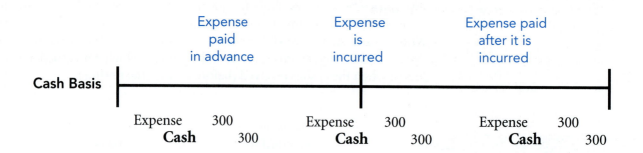

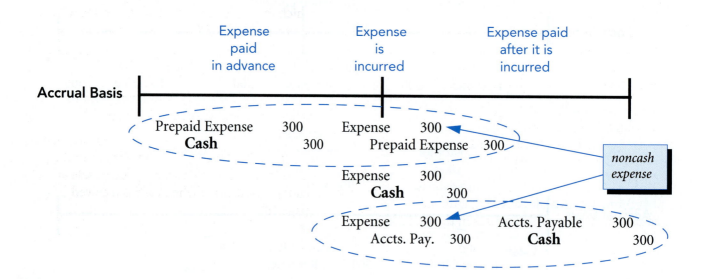

QUICK REVIEW

- Accrual basis accounting is the accountant's answer to the problem of deciding in which period revenues and expenses should be recorded.

- In accrual basis accounting, revenues are recorded in the period in which they are earned. Expenses are matched against the revenues that they created. It does not matter when cash is received or paid. Accrual basis accounting is applied by following these two principles:

  - *The revenue recognition principle:* Record a revenue when it is earned.
  - *The matching principle:* Record an expense in the period(s) in which it helped create revenues.

- GAAP requires the use of accrual basis accounting.

- Cash basis accounting is a simplified method of recording transactions. It only recognizes revenue when cash is received and only recognizes expenses when cash is paid. Cash basis is not acceptable under GAAP, but it is often used by small service businesses.

- Adjusting entries are not required for cash basis accounting.

VOCABULARY

Accrual basis accounting: the method of accounting that records the effects of all transactions (both noncash transactions and cash transactions) by applying the revenue recognition and matching principles (page 18)

Cash basis accounting: the method of accounting that records only the effects of cash transactions. Revenues and expenses are recorded only when cash is received or paid (page 23)

Matching principle: a rule that directs accountants to record expenses in the period in which they helped produce revenues regardless of when cash is paid (page 20)

Recognize: to record a transaction, particularly a revenue or expense (page 17)

Revenue principle: another name for the revenue recognition principle (page 18)

Revenue recognition principle: a rule that directs accountants to record revenues in the period when they are earned (when a sale is made) regardless of when cash is received (page 18)

TIP

This book has many practice problems and questions with solutions. Whenever you want extra examples, you can always use the problems with their solutions as more examples, as well as for practice.

PRACTICE   Learning Goal 2

Solutions are in the disk at the back of the book and at: www.worthyjames.com

Learning Goal 2 is about accrual basis accounting. Use these questions and problems to practice what you have learned about accrual basis accounting.

Multiple Choice
Select the best answer.

1. The purpose of accrual basis accounting is to:
    a. determine the correct amount of business income in each accounting period.
    b. include noncash revenues as well as cash revenues in business income.
    c. include noncash expenses as well as cash expenses in business income.
    d. all of the above.
2. An "expired cost" is:
    a. an unrecognized expense.
    b. an unconsumed asset.
    c. another description for expense.
    d. none of the above.
3. The two rules that must be applied to correctly determine net income are:
    a. the periodicity (time-period) assumption and the matching principle.
    b. the periodicity (time-period) assumption and the revenue recognition principle.
    c. the periodicity (time-period) assumption and the business principle.
    d. the revenue recognition principle and the matching principle.
4. GAAP:
    a. allows either accrual or cash basis accounting.
    b. requires that only accrual basis accounting be used.
    c. requires that only cash basis accounting be used.
    d. does not relate to the determination of net income or loss.
5. Which basis of accounting measures business income the best?
    a. Cash basis, because it includes all receipts and payments of cash.
    b. Accrual basis, because only a little judgment is required.
    c. Cash basis, because it is simple.
    d. Accrual basis, because it includes both noncash revenues and noncash expenses recorded in the correct periods.
6. Which basis of accounting is the most difficult to use?
    a. Cash basis, because it is hard to know when cash is received or paid.
    b. Accrual basis, because identifying when noncash revenues and expenses occur requires training and good judgment.
    c. Cash basis, because cash is easy to steal.
    d. Accrual basis, because it is harder to learn.
7. What guideline do accountants use to know when to record revenues in accrual basis accounting?
    a. the matching principle
    b. the cash flow guideline
    c. the revenue recognition principle (also called the revenue principle)
    d. the materiality constraint

PRACTICE   Learning Goal 2, continued

Solutions are in the disk at the back of the book and at: www.worthyjames.com

8. What guideline do accountants use to know when to record expenses in accrual basis accounting?
   a. the matching principle
   b. the time-period assumption
   c. the revenue recognition principle (also called the revenue principle)
   d. the cost principle
9. Which statement is *false*?
   a. The matching principle says that expenses must be matched with cash receipts.
   b. Accrual basis accounting is required by GAAP.
   c. Under cash basis accounting, expenses are paid in cash before being recorded.
   d. Accounts receivable and accounts payable only appear on the balance sheet of a company that uses accrual basis accounting.

Reinforcement Problems

LG 2-1. Explain how the revenue recognition and matching principles are related to the periodicity (time-period) assumption.

LG 2-2.
   a. On a cash basis, do you think that accounts receivable and accounts payable should appear on the balance sheet? Explain your answer.
   b. For accrual basis accounting, is it necessary to receive cash in order to record revenue? Should all cash receipts be recorded as revenues? Explain your answers.
   c. For accrual basis accounting, is it necessary to pay cash in order to record an expense? Should all cash payments be recorded as expenses? Explain your answers.
   d. You are an accountant for a computer parts supply company. It is December 31, and the management needs to record more revenue for the year. There is a $50,000 order from a customer that is almost completed, but will not actually be shipped until early January. A manager directs you to record $50,000 of revenue on December 31 because "the order is practically finished and is as good as delivered." Is she correct?

PRACTICE   Learning Goal 2, continued

Solutions are in the disk at the back of the book and at: www.worthyjames.com

LG 2-5. Practice cash basis accounting. Using the same information in LG 2-4, complete a worksheet like the one shown below, assuming that Lopez Marketing Solutions uses cash basis accounting.

Revenues	November	December	January
	(Reminder: Use a separate sheet of paper to complete the table.)		
Expenses			
Net Income (Loss)			

LG 2-6. Comparing cash basis and accrual basis revenue events. Each transaction that you see below involves revenue and/or the receipt of cash.

Instructions: Analyze each event for its correct classification (account name), valuation (amount), and timing (date) assuming that you are using cash basis accounting. Then repeat the procedure assuming that you are using accrual basis accounting. Then use a separate piece of paper to create a table like the one you see below. For each event, enter the date and then record the journal entry (based on your classification and valuation analysis). Record the journal entry in one the three columns: use column 'A' if the transaction occurs before the revenue is actually earned, use column 'B' if the transaction occurs and revenue is earned, and use column 'C' if the transaction occurs after the revenue was actually earned. Accounting periods are monthly.

Events:

a. On June 3, a customer pays $900 that was owing on account for services provided on April 8.
b. On November 12, Jane Lott invested $5,000 in her business (a corporation).
c. Services in the amount of $750 are performed on May 8, and the customer immediately pays.
d. $10,000 is borrowed from a bank on August 31 by signing a note payable due December 31.
e. Services in the amount of $500 are provided on March 5. The customer will pay sometime later.
f. On October 23, your business receives a $1,000 advance payment from a customer for services to be performed later in November.

	Method	Date	(A) Before Revenue Is Recorded	(B) Revenue Is Recorded	(C) After Revenue Is Recorded
a.	Cash Basis		(Reminder: Use a separate sheet of paper to complete the table.)		
	Accrual Basis				
b.	Cash Basis				
	Accrual Basis				

Solutions are in the disk at the back of the book and at: www.worthyjames.com

LG 2-7. Comparing cash basis and accrual basis expense events. Each transaction that you see below involves expense and/or the payment of cash.

Instructions: Analyze each event for its correct classification (account name), valuation (amount), and timing (date) assuming that you are using cash basis accounting. Then repeat the procedure assuming that you are using accrual basis accounting. Then use a separate piece of paper to create a table like the one you see below. For each event, enter the date and then record the journal entry (based on your classification and valuation analysis). Record the journal entry in one the three columns: use column 'A' if the transaction occurs before the expense is actually incurred, use column 'B' if the transaction occurs and expense is also incurred, and use column 'C' if the transaction occurs after the expense was actually incurred. Accounting periods are monthly.

Events:

a. On September 5, an account payable in the amount of $450 is paid for the August telephone expense.
b. On January 30, David Sing, the sole stockholder, withdrew $4,000 from his business (a corporation).
c. Repairs expense of $825 is incurred and is immediately paid on February 11.
d. A $15,000 note payable for money previously borrowed is fully paid on April 9.
e. On October 3, we received a $300 bill for September 20 advertising expense. The bill will be paid later.
f. On June 28, paid 12 months of prepaid insurance costing $1,200 for coverage beginning on July 1.
g. On May 2, a business paid $800 to purchase office supplies.
h. On May 31, a business determined that it had used up $300 of office supplies during the month of May.

	Method	Date	(A) Before Expense Is Recorded	(B) Expense Is Recorded	(C) After Expense Is Recorded
a.	Cash Basis		(Reminder: Use a separate sheet of paper to complete the table.)		
	Accrual Basis				
b.	Cash Basis				
	Accrual Basis				

PRACTICE   Learning Goal 2, continued

Instructor-Assigned Problems

If you are using this book in a class, these review problems may be assigned by your instructor for homework, group assignments, class work, or other activities. Only your instructor has the solutions.

IA2-1. **Apply revenue recognition and matching principles.** Ashland Enterprises designs and installs computerized accounting information systems. The company uses accrual accounting and completed the transactions that are shown below.

Instructions: Draw a table similar to the table in problem LG 2-5. For the accounting periods, use column titles of March, April, and May. Enter the names of the revenue and expense items and the amounts of revenues and expenses in the correct accounting periods. Calculate the net income or loss for each period.

Revenue Events:

a. On March 8, the business received an $8,500 advance payment from Jones Company for a system that was installed on April 20.

b. On April 11, a contract was signed with Smith for a system that was installed on May 25. The contract amount was $12,000 and was paid in advance on April 11.

c. Ashland Enterprises has a service contract with Mayberry Company, which pays $1,800 per month for the service.

d. On May 17, Ashland Enterprises completed a consulting job for Sunnyvale Company, a new company (a "start-up" company), and sent a bill to the company for $5,200.

Expense Events:

a. The company employs a sales staff that is compensated by commissions. The Jones Company contract was signed in March and the commission was $2,500. The Smith Company contract was signed in April and the commission was $5,000. A commission is paid when a job is completed.

b. Employees were paid wages as follows: $4,900 in March and in April; $8,900 in May. $4,000 of the May wages were directly related to an Acme Company consulting job. The job was started in May but not completed. The $4,000 wages were recorded as deferred wages.

c. Computer service charges were paid as follows: March, $950, of which $250 was for the Jones Company job; April, $1,900, of which $700 was for the Smith Company job; May, $1,500, of which $1,000 was for the Acme consulting job. Computer service charges paid prior to jobs completed are recorded as deferred items until the related jobs are completed.

d. Telephone bills were as follows: March, $200; April, $300; May, $175. The telephone bills are paid in the month following the service.

e. On April 3, the company purchased $600 of supplies on credit. The bill was paid in June. On April 30, $400 of the supplies had been consumed, and $50 of supplies remained on June 30.

IA2-2. **Cash basis.** *Instructions:* Using the information from problem IA2-1 above, prepare a table using cash basis accounting.

PRACTICE   Learning Goal 2, continued

IA2-3. Ethical issues and accounting methods. *Instructions:* There are four independent situations below. Questions "a" and "b" both apply to each situation. Question "c" applies to all the situations.

Questions:
a. What will be the effects on the income statement and the balance sheet in the current period and in the next period?
b. Use the following ethical guidelines to analyze the situation: 1. Decide if there is the moral issue of a potentially wrongful act that might result in loss, injury, or damage. 2. List all the facts 3. List the possible alternatives 4. Evaluate the possible outcomes of each alternative. 5. Make your decision and justify by: 1) What does the most good or least harm? 2) Is everyone treated fairly, regardless of outcome? Explain.
c. After answering "a" and "b" for each situation, do you feel that technical accounting knowledge (such as you needed to answer part "a") is by itself sufficient to provide reliable financial information?

1. Acme Company, Inc. operates a business in which profits and losses can change quickly from one year to the next. This year, the company is having a very good year. The company decides to take advantage of this by over-estimating the amount of its vacation pay liability to employees. The excessive estimate this year means that next year the company can under-estimate the liability if necessary. This would help create a smoothly increasing net income (next year higher than this year) which investors and lenders usually like to see. The company records vacation pay by debiting vacation pay expense and crediting vacation pay payable.

2. Baker Company, Inc. is also having a very good year. Baker Company receives many advance payments from customers, and properly records these by crediting unearned revenue. The company then reduces unearned revenue and records revenue when goods are shipped to customers. This year at year-end, the company decides to slightly delay shipping some of the goods so that some of the revenue can be recorded next year.

3. John's consulting service uses cash basis accounting with a December 31 year-end. At the end of October, John offers his customers an extra discount if they pay him before the end of the year. The business also delays paying all outstanding bills until early January.

4. Mega Corporation has been losing money for several years. Management decides to "restructure" the company by closing some operations, thereby selling assets at a loss, making layoff payments, and incurring legal fees. Management plans to have all these losses and expenses recorded in a single year, with the result that later years will look better by comparison.

INTERNET EXERCISES

Search for financial information on the Internet. Select a well-known company that interests you. Follow this procedure for your search: 1) Go to **finance.yahoo.com** and then enter the company name in your search. 2) Search the company name with the term "investor relations" 3) Go to **morningstar.com** and search using the company name. 4) Go to **sec.gov** and search under the company name.

a. Summarize the types of information that were available by following website links.
b. What was most useful to you?

LEARNING GOAL 3	# Explain the Concept of Adjusting Entries

In Learning Goal 3, you will find:

Overview of General Features

Overview of Adjustment Types

Overview of General Features

Summary

Essential Features

The concept of *adjusting entries* consists of some general features that you need to understand. Here is a summary of these features, which are further explained in this learning goal:

- What they are
- Why they are needed
- The kinds of transactions that cause them
- The common qualities of adjustments
- The five causes of the five adjustment types

What Are Adjusting Entries?

Definition:
Adjusting Entries

Adjusting entries are journal entries that are made at the end of an accounting period to make sure that:

- all revenue that belongs in that period is recorded in that period, and
- all expense that belongs in that period is recorded in that period.

Why Adjusting Entries Are Needed

Revenues and Expenses in the Correct Periods

Adjusting entries are needed because at the end of an accounting period, significant revenues and expenses are often unrecorded for various reasons. **Adjusting entries ensure that the correct revenues and expenses are recorded in the correct accounting periods.**

Adjusting entries are part of accrual basis accounting. Cash basis accounting does not use adjusting entries, because revenues and expenses are recorded only with cash receipts and cash payments.

The Common Qualities of Adjusting Entries

Overview

The adjusting entries you will study all have some qualities in common. A review of these features will help you to better understand what adjusting entries do and to recognize adjusting entries when you see them.

Adjusting entries:
- Record previously unrecorded revenues and expenses
- Are *recorded* together at the end of an accounting period
- Are actually calculated *after* an accounting period is over
- Affect at least one income statement and one balance sheet account
- Do not affect the cash account

Quality 1

- **Adjusting entries record previously unrecorded revenues and expenses.**

Examples of unrecorded revenues and expenses:
- Supplies used up have not been recorded because there was not enough time.
- Income was earned but has been overlooked because cash was not received.
- Expense was incurred but is still unrecorded because cash was not paid.

continued ▶

The Common Qualities of Adjusting Entries, *continued*

Quality 2

■ **Adjusting entries are recorded together at the end of an accounting period.**

Here are the reasons why:
- It is usually more efficient to record all the adjusting entries at one time at the end of a period, just before the financial statements are prepared.
- A second important reason for recording adjustments at the end of a period is to ensure that no more transactions will take place after the adjustments.

Quality 3

■ **Adjusting entries are actually calculated after an accounting period is over.**

Accountants wait a short time after an accounting period is over before they begin to actually make the calculations for the adjustments. However, even though the adjustments are actually calculated after the end of an accounting period, the entries themselves are always recorded and dated *as of the last day* of the period to which they apply.

Quality 4

■ **Adjusting entries always affect at least one income statement account and one balance sheet account.**

Examples:
- At the end of the period, accountants for the Henry F. Company record $300 of office supplies that have been used up. This requires a debit to Supplies Expense (an income statement account) and a credit to Office Supplies (a balance sheet asset account).
- At the end of the period, accountants for Muskegon, Inc. record $1,000 of revenue for services that were provided to clients but were not yet billed or recorded. This requires a debit to Accounts Receivable (a balance sheet asset account) and a credit to Fees Earned (an income statement revenue account).

The Common Qualities of Adjusting Entries, *continued*

Quality 5

"It says here . . . you will not adjust the cash account!"

■ **Adjusting entries do not affect the cash account.**

When doing an adjusting entry, you should *not* record a debit or credit to the cash account. This is because an adjusting entry will either:

• update a transaction for which the cash was *already* paid or received, or
• record a transaction for which the cash will be paid or received *later*.

Exception: If you were doing a reconciliation of the cash account, then cash might be affected by an adjustment. However you are *not* doing a cash reconciliation in any situation here.

TIP

Other kinds of entries are also called *adjusting entries*. This can be confusing because sometimes people use the word "adjustment" very loosely to mean *any* change that needs to be made to an account. When people use the term adjusting entries in this more general way, the entry they are referring to will not always have the same specific qualities listed here.

Examples:
■ Hamilton Company purchases supplies on account but *wrongly* records the transaction as a purchase of land for cash. When the accounts in this entry are *corrected*, some people might call it an *adjustment*, even though it is really a correction of an error.
■ Kirkwood Company converts financial statements that only record cash receipts and payments into GAAP accrual basis financial statements. The accountant might call the conversion changes by the name *adjustments*.

How Do I Know Which Account Needs Adjustment?

The general approach, which we will practice, is to do two things:

1. Look for revenue and expense events that have occurred, but have not been recorded. Recording the transactions would be called making adjustments.

2. Review balance sheet accounts that are usually connected with revenues and expenses. Recording changes in these accounts will usually result in revenues or expenses, and these would also be called adjustments. Typical accounts are receivables, supplies, prepaids, payables, and unearned revenue.

Overview of Adjustment Types

The Five Causes of the Five Adjustments

Overview

In the learning goals coming up, you will study each of the five basic types of adjusting entries. The table below gives you a quick summary of the five types of transactions that cause the five basic types of adjustments. What the five transaction types have in common is that they are all sources of potentially unrecorded revenues and expenses.

Category	Transaction Type
Prepayments (also called **deferrals**)	■ **Prepaid expenses:** Cash payments for *future expenses* that are recorded as assets at the time of payment and used up later ■ **Unearned revenues:** Cash receipts for *future revenues* that are recorded as liabilities at the time of receipt and earned later ■ **Depreciation:** Using up of plant and equipment assets
Accruals	■ **Accrued revenues:** Revenues earned but cash not yet received ■ **Accrued expenses:** Expenses incurred but cash not yet paid

TIP

■ **For prepayments (deferrals):** Cash flows first, revenue or expense recorded later
■ **For accruals:** Revenue or expense recorded first, cash flows later

Classification, Valuation, and Timing

Review

In Volume 1, we emphasized that every transaction should be analyzed for three elements: classification, valuation, and timing. Classification means selecting the correct accounts for a transaction. Valuation means recording the correct dollar amounts for the accounts. Timing means recording a transaction in the correct accounting period.

Prepayment and Accrual Adjustments Focus on Timing

This three-part analysis should be applied to all transactions, including adjusting entries for the prepayments and accruals in the table on page 40. However, the focus here is on correct timing. This is because the adjustments for these items result from the application of the revenue recognition and matching principles, which are all about correct timing. "In what period should revenue be recorded?" "In what period should expense be recorded?" These essential questions must be asked about prepayments and accruals.

Of course, the correct accounts and the correct amounts are still involved, and they also play important roles. However, you will see that the focus on timing dictates the choice of accounts and the calculation of amounts.

Re-valuation—Another Kind of Adjustment

To complete our discussion, you should also be aware that another kind of event requires another type of adjusting entry—a valuation adjustment. This event occurs when GAAP requires a change in the recorded value of an asset because it has lost or gained monetary value. This is different from timing adjustments that result from prepayments and accruals. Valuation adjustments are discussed later, when we study specific kinds of assets.

Now, we will concentrate on timing adjustments from prepayments and accruals.

Check Your Understanding

Write the completed sentences on a separate piece of paper. The answers are below.

These are some common features of all adjusting entries.

- Adjusting entries are used to record previously · · · · · · · revenues and expenses.
- Adjusting entries are recorded as of the (beginning/end) · · · · · · · · of an accounting period, just before the · · · · · · · · · · · · · · · · · are prepared.
- The calculations for adjusting entries are actually done shortly after the (beginning/end) · · · · · · · of the accounting period to which the adjustments will apply, to be sure that all bills and other information have been received.
- Adjusting entries always affect at least one · · · · · · · · · · · · · · · · · account and one · · · · · · · · · · · · · · · account.
- Adjusting entries do not affect the · · · · · · · account.

Answers

Adjusting entries do not affect the cash account.
Adjusting entries always affect at least one balance sheet account and one income statement account.
The calculations for adjusting entries are actually done shortly after the end of the accounting period to which the adjustments will apply, to be sure that all bills and other information have been received.
Adjusting entries are recorded as of the end of an accounting period, just before the financial statements are prepared.
Adjusting entries are used to record previously unrecorded revenues and expenses.
These are some common features of all adjusting entries.

QUICK REVIEW

- Adjusting entries are needed because revenues and expenses are often not properly or fully recorded in the correct accounting period for various reasons.

- Adjusting entries are required in accrual basis accounting, but not cash basis accounting.

- All adjusting entries have important qualities in common.

- Five basic transaction types create the need for adjustments.

LEARNING GOAL 4

Analyze Accounts and Prepare Adjusting Entries

In Learning Goal 4, you will find:

How to Know Which Adjustment to Do

Overview of the Process

How to Use the Book for This Topic

Learning to analyze accounts and prepare adjusting entries usually requires extra time and effort. However, doing this will clarify your understanding, improve your confidence, and show you examples of the procedures that businesses regularly need to do to.

Learning Goal 4 discusses each of the 5 types of adjusting entries. If you feel that you want **more explanation or more practice** for any type of adjustment, use the **Appendix to Learning Goal 4**. The appendix is divided into five parts, one part for each type of adjustment. Each part offers detailed discussion and practice.

Prepaid Expenses (Deferred Expenses)

Definition

A **prepaid expense** is an advance payment for goods or services that is recorded as an asset. When the goods or services are used up—usually within a year—an expense is recorded. The expense is said to have been "deferred."

Example 1:
Office Supplies

Office Supplies is an asset account that consists of items such as paper, envelopes, pens, and various computer-related supplies. Office Supplies items are recorded as assets when purchased. Although supplies could be recorded as expenses daily when used, it is easier to wait until the end of an accounting period to record the entire amount used as a single adjustment.

The December 31 trial balance of Oakville Computer Repair Services shows the Office Supplies asset account with a balance of $1,200. A physical count of the office supply items indicates an actual balance of supplies in the amount of $750. Although it would be possible to record an expense each time the asset is used, it is easier to record the whole amount of expense for the entire period at one time, at the end of the period. Therefore, the amount of the adjustment to record the supplies used up is:

Trial balance amount	$1,200
Actual amount	750
Used up (adjustment)	$ 450

Supplies will have to be reduced (credited) and Supplies Expense will have to be increased (debited).

The adjusting journal entry is:

Dec. 31	Supplies Expense	450	
	Supplies		450

T accounts would show:

	Supplies		Supplies Expense	
Bal.	1,200			
Dec. 31 Adjustment		**450**	450	
Adjusted Balance	750		450	

Prepaid Expenses (Deferred Expenses), *continued*

Example 2:
Prepaid Insurance

Most businesses purchase various kinds of insurance that pay a business for losses such as fire, theft, or business liability lawsuits. Payments for insurance (called premiums) are usually made in advance. For example, on November 1, Oakville Computer Repair Services paid $1,500 for a one-year fire insurance policy. As of December 31 year-end, the trial balance shows a $1,500 balance in the Prepaid Insurance asset account.

As of December 31, an adjustment is required because two months' of the insurance have been used up. Insurance expense must be increased (debited) and Prepaid Insurance decreased (credited). The amount of the adjustment is $1,500/12 = $125 per month × 2 = $250. The adjusting journal entry is:

Dec. 31	Insurance Expense	250	
	Prepaid Insurance		250

T accounts would show:

	Prepaid Insurance		Insurance Expense	
Balance	1,500			
Dec. 31 Adjustment		**250**	**250**	
Adjusted Balance	1,250		250	

Notice That . . .

- No cash is involved with the adjustments. Cash was paid earlier when the supplies were purchased and when the insurance was purchased.
- Without the adjustments, assets would be overstated on December 31 and expenses would be understated. Understating expenses also overstates net income, which overstates stockholders' equity.

More Help

If you would like more detailed explanation and help with adjustments for prepaid expenses, go to Part I of the appendix for this learning goal.

Unearned Revenues (Deferred Revenues)

Definition

An **unearned revenue** is an advance payment from a customer for future product or services. It is recorded as a liability when the payment is received. The unearned revenue becomes revenue later as goods or services are provided.

Example

Many companies receive advance payments from customers. Advance receipts for items such as rent, insurance, magazine subscriptions, travel, and professional services are common. On October 10, Oakville Computer Repair Services received a $5,000 advance payment from a customer. This was properly recorded as a debit to Cash and a credit to Unearned Revenue. As of December 31 year-end, analysis indicates that the revenue earned for services provided to the customer is $3,000. At that time, the trial balance still shows $5,000 of Unearned Revenue.

Although it would be possible to reduce the liability as the revenue is earned, the company finds it easier to record all the revenue in a single adjustment at the end of the period. This entry reduces (debits) unearned revenue liability and increases (credits) revenue. The adjusting journal entry is:

Dec. 31	Unearned Revenue	3,000	
	Service Revenue		3,000

T accounts would show:

	Unearned Revenue		Service Revenue	
Balance		5,000		
Dec. 31 Adjustment	**3,000**			**3,000**
Adjusted Balance		2,000		3,000

Notice That . . .

- No cash is involved with the adjustment. Cash was received on October 10 when the customer made the advance payment.
- Without the adjustment, liabilities will be overstated by $3,000, and revenue will be understated by $3,000. Understating the revenue will understate net income, which will understate stockholders' equity.

More Help

If you would like more detailed explanation and help with adjustments for unearned revenues, go to part II of the appendix for this learning goal.

Depreciation

Definition

Depreciation is the process of allocating the cost of a plant and equipment asset into expense, during the asset's estimated useful life.

Estimated Useful Life

Plant and equipment assets provide many years of service. To calculate depreciation, the years of service life must be estimated at the time an asset is acquired because the number cannot be known exactly. The details of depreciation calculations are discussed in the appendix, Part III, page 139.

Overview

Most businesses own long-term productive assets such as buildings, land, vehicles, furniture, and equipment. Except for land, all of these assets eventually lose their usefulness because they wear out or become obsolete. The matching principle requires that as these assets provide benefits, a portion of their cost should be reported as an expense each accounting period. This is similar to adjusting a prepaid expense that has been used up, except that depreciation is *an estimated amount* and is for plant and equipment assets, that last many years.

Example

Oakville Computer Repair Services purchased $10,000 of equipment at the start of the year. Based on the equipment's cost and an estimated useful life of 10 years, the adjusting entry for the year's depreciation expense is:

| Dec. 31 | Depreciation Expense ($10,000/10) | 1,000 | |
| | Accumulated Depreciation | | 1,000 |

T accounts would show:

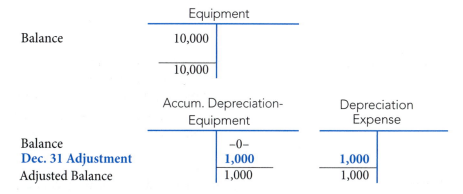

Accumulated Depreciation-Equipment is a *contra-asset* account. A contra-asset account is an account that acts as an offset to the balance of a related asset account. Contra-asset accounts have credit balances. On the balance sheet, a contra-asset balance is subtracted from the balance of its related asset. In the example above, the difference between the asset cost of $10,000 and the accumulated depreciation of $1,000 is $9,000 and is called *book value*. Book value is the undepreciated cost of an asset.

continued ▶

Depreciation, *continued*

Notice That . . .

- The amount of the depreciation is an **estimate** based on useful life.
- No cash is involved in the adjustment.
- Without the adjustment, assets are overstated by $1,000 and expenses are understated by $1,000, which overstates net income and stockholders' equity.

More Help

If you would like more detailed explanation and help with adjustments for depreciation, go to Part III of the appendix for this learning goal.

Accrued Revenues

Definition

An *accrued revenue* is a revenue that has been earned but no cash has been received. An accrued revenue *adjustment* is required if an accrued revenue would remain unrecorded at the end of an accounting period. It always requires a debit to a receivable and credit to revenue.

Example

Austin Advertising Agency performed $900 of advertising services for a client on November 5; however, no cash was received and the bookkeeper forgot to record the accrued revenue. The company has monthly accounting periods. At November 30 month-end, this adjustment is needed:

Nov. 30	Accounts Receivable	900	
	Service Revenue		900

T accounts would show:

	Accounts Receivable		Service Revenue	
Balance	4,500			31,000
Nov. 30 Adjustment	**900**			**900**
Adjusted Balance	5,400			31,900

Notice That . . .

- No cash is involved with the adjustment. Cash is received later when the customer pays the receivable.
- Without the adjustment, assets will be understated by $900. Revenue also will be understated by $900, understating net income and stockholders' equity.

More Help

If you would like more detailed explanation and help with adjustments for accrued revenues, go to part IV of the appendix for this learning goal.

Accrued Expenses

Definition

An **accrued expense** is an expense that has been incurred but no cash has been paid. An accrued expense *adjustment* is required if an accrued expense would remain unrecorded at the end of an accounting period. It always requires a debit to an expense and a credit to a payable.

Example

Omaha Co. received an $850 utility bill for December services that will not be paid until January. The accounting period ends on December 31.

| Dec. 31 | Utilities Expense | 850 | |
| | Accounts Payable | | 850 |

Example

Austin Advertising Agency has monthly accounting periods and a five-day workweek. Wages were last paid on Friday, May 25. Wages are paid every two weeks and the next payday will be Friday, June 8. Wages are $4,000 per week ($800 per day).

May		F	S	S	**M**	**T**	**W**	**T**
. . . .		(25)	26	27	**28**	**29**	**30**	**31**

June		1	2	3	4	5	6	7
		(8)	. . . .					

Unless an accrued expense adjustment is made, the last four days of May wages expense will remain unrecorded on the May financial statements. The following adjusting entry is needed:

| May 31 | Wages Expense (4 × $800) | 3,200 | |
| | Wages Payable | | 3,200 |

T accounts would show:

	Wages Expense		Wages Payable	
Balance	15,200			–0–
May 31 Adjustment	**3,200**			**3,200**
Adjusted Balance	18,400			3,200

Notice That . . .

- No cash is involved with the adjustments. Cash is paid later.
- Without the adjustment, liabilities will be understated. Expenses also will be understated, overstating net income and stockholders' equity.

continued ▶

Accrued Expenses, *continued*

More Help

If you would like more detailed explanation and help with adjustments for accrued expenses, go to part V of the appendix.

The Simple System

The Basic Idea

"Simple!"

Whenever an event has created a revenue or an expense that has not been recorded by the end of the period, an adjustment will be needed.

*How to Know
If an Adjustment
Is Needed*

The table below shows you a simple system for deciding if you need to do an adjustment and, if so, what kind. **The most important part of the system is to be alert for situations when any revenue or expense has not been recorded.**

IF . . .	Look For . . .	THEN the adjustment is for . . .
revenue was earned, but there is no indication that the revenue was recorded	a cash advance was previously received from the customer,	unearned (deferred) revenue
	no cash (or other asset) has been received	accrued revenue
expense was incurred, but there is no indication that the expense was recorded	a noncash asset was used or consumed,	■ prepaid (deferred) expense and supplies or ■ depreciation (long-term)
	no cash (or other asset) has been paid or consumed	accrued expense

The Standard Forms of Adjusting Journal Entries

The Standard Form of Each Adjusting Entry

After you have *identified* a particular type of transaction that needs to be adjusted, you need to know the form of adjusting entry. The table below shows the standard form of each type of adjusting entry.

Adjustment for . . .		The form of the adjusting entry is . . .
Prepaid Expense	Dr. Cr.	Expense ↑ Prepaid Expense ↓
Unearned Revenue	Dr. Cr.	Unearned Revenue ↓ Revenue ↑
Depreciation	Dr. Cr.	Depreciation Expense ↑ Accumulated Depreciation ↑
Accrued Expense	Dr. Cr.	Expense ↑ Payable ↑
Accrued Revenue	Dr. Cr.	Receivable ↑ Revenue ↑

Note: These standard forms assume that prepaid and unearned items were entered in balance sheet accounts, which is what you have studied. Alternative methods are also available. You can study these in the disk at the back of the book.

Other Special Entries: Reversals and Corrections

Reversing Entries

Overview

Reversing entries, particularly for accruals, are a frequently-used technique in practice. Reversing entries are a time-saving device that are recorded on the first day of a new accounting period after adjusting entries are completed and the books have been closed for the prior period.

See Disk at the Back of This Book

The disk at the back of this book contains extensive explanation, examples, and illustrations of reversing entries for both accrual and deferral balances.

Correcting Entries

Overview

Corrections are not always needed, but are not unusual. Two types of correction situations can occur. First, corrections may be required at any time during the current accounting period, whenever an error is detected. In this circumstance all that is required is an entry that corrects the error in the account balances. In the second circumstance, the error is discovered after the books have been closed. In this case, a different type of correction will be required in the following accounting period.

> Note: Do not confuse correcting entries with adjusting entries, which are a normal part of the accounting cycle, and occur at the end of an accounting period. Correcting entries can affect any account balances and be needed at any time.

See Disk at the Back of This Book

The disk at the back of this book contains extensive explanation, examples, and illustrations of correcting entries.

QUICK REVIEW

There are five types of adjustments categories:

- Prepaid expense
- Unearned revenue
- Depreciation
- Accrued expense
- Accrued revenue

The table on page 51 will help you remember how to record the adjusting entries, however, you should first understand why each adjustment is needed and what would happen it the adjustment was not made.

- Review the table on page 50: "How to Know if an Adjustment Is Needed."
- If you need more explanation and practice, use the appendix to this learning goal.

VOCABULARY

Accrued Expense: An expense that has been incurred but no cash has been paid (page 49)

Accrued Revenue: A revenue that has been earned but no cash has been received (page 48)

Book Value: Cost of an asset minus accumulated depreciation of the asset (page 47)

Contra-asset: An account that acts as an offset to the balance of an asset account (page 47)

Depreciation: The process of allocating the cost of a plant and equipment asset into expense during the asset's estimated useful life (page 47)

Prepaid Expense: An advance payment for goods or services that is recorded as an asset (page 44)

Unearned Revenue: An advance payment from a customer for future revenue that is recorded as a liability when the payment is received (page 46)

PRACTICE   **Learning Goal 4**

Solutions are in the disk at the back of the book and at: www.worthyjames.com

Learning goal 4 is about identifying what type of adjustment is required and knowing how to make that adjustment. Answer the questions and problems below to practice what you have just read.

Multiple Choice
Select the best answer.

1. The purpose of adjusting entries is to:
   a. make sure all cash receipts and payments have been recorded.
   b. make sure the revenue recognition and matching principles are fully applied.
   c. make the necessary daily corrections in accounts that frequently change.
   d. record expenses in the correct period.

2. In July, Delhi Company received $500 cash for revenues accrued in June. The company also recorded $500 of unearned revenue that had been earned in July. The effect of these two transactions on July revenue is:
   a. decrease $500.
   b. They offset each other.
   c. increase $500.
   d. increase $1,000.

3. Which of the following could not be an example of an accrual?
   a. wages unpaid and owed to employees
   b. advance payment of a one-year insurance policy
   c. interest owing on a loan
   d. fees earned but not yet billed to client

4. Which of the following could not involve a deferral (prepayment) transaction?
   a. paying the balance owed in Wages Payable
   b. receipt of an advance payment from a customer
   c. using up supplies
   d. deferred interest revenue

5. Adjusting entries for accrued expenses affect what kinds of accounts?
   a. revenues and expenses
   b. assets and liabilities
   c. revenues and assets
   d. expenses and liabilities

6. Adjusting entries for accrued revenues affect what kinds of accounts?
   a. revenues and expenses
   b. assets and liabilities
   c. revenues and assets
   d. expenses and liabilities

7. Adjusting entries for prepaid expenses affect what kinds of accounts?
   a. revenues and expenses
   b. assets and expenses
   c. assets and liabilities
   d. revenues and liabilities

8. Adjusting entries for unearned revenues affect what kinds of accounts?
    a. revenues and expenses
    b. assets and expenses
    c. assets and liabilities
    d. revenues and liabilities

9. Failure to make an adjustment to record unearned revenue that had been earned would result in what errors on the financial statements?
    a. assets understated and revenues understated
    b. liabilities overstated and revenues understated
    c. liabilities understated and revenues understated
    d. assets overstated and revenues overstated

10. Failure to make an adjustment to record accrued revenue that had been earned would result in what errors on the financial statements?
    a. assets understated and revenues understated
    b. liabilities overstated and revenues understated
    c. liabilities understated and revenues understated
    d. assets overstated and revenues overstated

11. Failure to make an adjustment to record prepaid advertising expense that had been used would result in what errors on the financial statements?
    a. assets understated and expenses overstated
    b. liabilities overstated and expenses understated
    c. liabilities understated and expenses understated
    d. assets overstated and expenses understated

12. Failure to make an adjustment to record accrued advertising expense would result in what errors on the financial statements?
    a. assets understated and expenses overstated
    b. liabilities overstated and expenses understated
    c. liabilities understated and expenses understated
    d. assets overstated and expenses understated

13. Failure to make an adjustment to record depreciation would result in what errors?
    a. assets understated and expenses overstated
    b. liabilities overstated and expenses understated
    c. liabilities understated and expenses understated
    d. assets overstated and expenses understated

14. Before year-end adjustments on December 31, the total revenues on the trial balance are $55,000 and the total expenses are $47,000. If the following adjustments are needed, what is the correct net income (or loss) for the year ended December 31?
    - Accrued insurance expense at December 31: $4,700
    - Prepaid insurance consumed: $2,000
    - Unrecorded and unpaid rent expense at December 31: $3,500
    a. Net loss: ($2,200)
    b. Net income: $4,800
    c. Net income: $2,500
    d. Net loss: ($10,200)

15. Which sequence of events correctly describes a prepaid expense?
    a. pay cash, consume the service, make the adjustment
    b. consume the service, make the adjustment, pay cash
    c. make the adjustment, consume the service, pay cash
    d. pay cash, make the adjustment, consume the service

16. Which sequence of events correctly describes an accrued expense?
    a. pay cash, consume the service, make the adjustment
    b. consume the service, make the adjustment, pay cash
    c. make the adjustment, consume the service, pay cash
    d. pay cash, make the adjustment, consume the service

17. Which sequence of events correctly describes unearned revenue?
    a. receive cash, earn revenue, make the adjustment
    b. earn revenue, make the adjustment, receive cash
    c. make the adjustment, earn revenue, receive cash
    d. receive cash, make the adjustment, earn revenue

18. Which sequence of events correctly describes accrued revenue?
    a. receive cash, earn revenue, make the adjustment
    b. earn revenue, make the adjustment, receive cash
    c. make the adjustment, earn revenue, receive cash
    d. receive cash, make the adjustment, earn revenue

19. On August 1, Chen Company paid $3,000 in advance for six months of advertising service. What adjustment should the company make on August 31?
    a. debit Advertising Expense and credit Cash for $3,000
    b. debit Prepaid Advertising and credit Cash for $500
    c. debit Advertising Expense and credit Prepaid Advertising for $500
    d. debit Advertising Expense and credit Prepaid Advertising for $3000

20. Blakeslee Corporation completed a carpet installation job for $5,500. At year end, the bill has not yet been sent to the customer. What adjustment should be made?
    a. debit Accounts Receivable and credit Unearned Revenue $5,500
    b. debit Accounts Receivable and credit Installation Revenue $5,500
    c. debit Cash and credit Unearned Revenue $5,500
    d. debit Unearned Revenue and credit Installation Revenue $5,500

21. On January 3, Aviles Enterprises purchased a new computer system. It was estimated that the Depreciation Expense for the year would be $3,000. On December 31:
    a. debit Depreciation Expense and credit Accumulated Depreciation $3,000
    b. debit Computer Equipment and credit Cash $3,000
    c. debit Depreciation Expense and credit Cash $3,000
    d. debit Depreciation Expense and Computer Equipment $3,000

22. Cash basis accounting will require adjusting entries to be done:
    a. the same as accrual basis accounting.
    b. at the option of the accountant.
    c. only if cash has been paid or received.
    d. never.

23. An adjusting entry could include all of the following except:
    a. debit to Accounts Receivable.
    b. credit to Accounts Payable.
    c. debit to Unearned Revenue.
    d. debit to Cash.

24. On January 27, 2018, Rivas Enterprises collected $35,000 from a customer for which it had accrued a $27,000 account receivable on December 31, 2017. Rivas Enterprises had no other accounts receivable. The revenue from this customer was:
    a. $27,000 in 2017 and $35,000 in 2018.
    b. $27,000 in 2017 and $0 in 2018.
    c. $27,000 in 2017 and $8,000 in 2018.
    d. $0 in 2017 and $35,000 in 2018.

PRACTICE   Learning Goal 4, continued

Solutions are in the disk at the back of the book and at: www.worthyjames.com

Discussion Questions and Brief Exercises

Answer the following questions:

1. The types of adjusting entries we have discussed are recorded in order to apply two important GAAP principles. What are these two principles and what do they require?

2. Why are adjusting entries recorded at the end of an accounting period?

3. If revenue was earned, but there is no indication that it was recorded and a cash advance was previously recorded from a customer, what type of adjusting entry will be needed? What kind of account will be debited and what kind of account will be credited?

4. If expense was incurred, but there is no indication that the expense was recorded and a short-term noncash asset was used up, what type of adjusting entry will be needed? What kind of account will be debited and what kind of account will be credited?

5. If expense was incurred, but there is no indication the expense was recorded and a plant and equipment asset was being used, what type of adjusting entry will be needed? What kind of account will be debited and what kind of account will be credited?

6. If revenue was earned, but there is no indication that it was recorded and no cash (or other asset) has been received, what type of adjusting entry will be needed? What kind of account will be debited and what kind of account will be credited?

7. If expense was incurred, but there is no indication the expense was recorded and no cash (or other asset) has been paid or used, what type of adjusting entry will be needed? What kind of account will be debited and what kind of account will be credited?

8. What is the purpose of the two accounts "Depreciation Expense" and "Accumulated Depreciation"? What are their normal balances? Where do they appear on financial statements?

9. At the end of June, the Wages Expense account has a balance of $29,000, and the unrecorded Wages Payable is $3,500. What amount of Wages Expense should be recorded on the monthly income statement for June?

10. Our company hired a consultant in May. In June, our company paid $15,000 cash to the consultant for full cost of the completed job, and we recorded $5,000 of this as a June expense. What was the adjusting entry that we recorded on May 31?

11. What was the May 31 adjusting entry recorded by the consulting company in #10 above?

12. On a trial balance, total debits equal total credits. Does this mean that adjusting entries will be not be necessary? Explain your answer.

13. On January 25, a company paid $3,800 for repairs expense. $1,000 of this amount had been accrued on December 31. What is the entry to record the payment in January?

14. A company accrued $500 of revenue and $300 of expense at the end of the current year. What would the effect have been if these accruals had not been made?

15. Joe thinks that adjusting entries only affect the income statement. Mary believes that adjusting entries affect both the income statement and the balance sheet. Is one of them correct?

16. Dennison Company owes $20,000 on a note payable. On the first day of each month, the company makes a payment to repay the amount owed plus interest. Should Dennison Company make an adjustment on December 31, year end? Explain.

17. Depreciation is the process of recording the loss of value of a plant and equipment asset. Do you agree? Explain.

18. For each of the separate items below, part of an adjusting entry is shown. What is the other part of the entry? In some cases, there may be more than one possibility.
   a. debit Depreciation Expense
   b. credit Office Supplies
   c. credit Service Revenue
   d. debit Rent Expense
   e. debit Accounts Receivable

PRACTICE Learning Goal 4, continued

Solutions are in the disk at the back of the book and at: www.worthyjames.com

Reinforcement Problems

Learning Goal 4 is about adjusting entries. Use these questions and problems to practice what you have studied.

LG 4-1. Recognizing what kind of adjustment is needed. You cannot correctly do an adjustment unless you can first recognize what kind of adjustment is needed. In this exercise, we do not care at all about actually calculating the adjustment. What is important here is training yourself to *recognize the situation* when an adjustment is needed.

Instructions: Use a separate sheet of paper to complete the table. For each independent situation, if an adjustment is needed, identify what kind of item requires an adjustment, as either:

- prepaid expense
- unearned revenue
- accrued expense
- accrued revenue
- depreciation

Then show what accounts would be debited and credited. The first item is an example. Some situations might not require adjustments. Do not assume a revenue or expense was recorded unless explicitly stated.

	Situation	Adjusting for what?	Adjusting accounts at end of period
a.	On May 1, Holyoke Company paid $12,000 for a three-year insurance policy. Holyoke Company has a June 30 year end.	prepaid expense	Dr. Insurance Expense Cr. Prepaid Insurance
b.	In November, Middlesex Company earned one-fourth of the amount that had been advanced by a customer in September.	(Reminder: Use a separate sheet of paper to complete the table.)	
c.	An inventory count shows $520 of office supplies on hand at year end. The beginning balance was $1,000.		
d.	Cape Cod Enterprises performed $7,000 of services for customers during December that remained unrecognized at year end.		
e.	Burdett Enterprises shows $15,000 of Office Equipment and $105,000 of Automotive Equipment on the balance sheet.		
f.	This year, Massasoit Company paid for 18 months of magazine subscriptions, and at year end seven months' worth is still in force.		
g.	Kinyon Company records show utility expenses unrecorded and unpaid of $350.		
h.	Campbell Corporation paid a utility bill that was owing in the amount of $240.		
i.	In June, Springfield Company completed negotiations, signed a contract and received $25,000 in advance. By year end, the company had performed $5,500 of services on the contract.		
j.	North Shore Inc. has a six-day workweek and pays employees weekly, each Saturday. June 30, year end, is on a Tuesday.		
k.	Bristol Enterprises signed a contract to perform $30,000 of future services.		

PRACTICE   Learning Goal 4, continued

Solutions are in the disk at the back of the book and at: www.worthyjames.com

LG 4-1, *continued*

Situation	Adjusting for what?	Adjusting accounts at end of period
l. The Supplies account of Northern Essex Enterprises shows a beginning balance of $700 and purchases of $1,200. The ending inventory shows $150 still unused.	(Reminder: Use a separate sheet of paper to complete the table.)	
m. Three Rivers Corporation received a $50,000 advance from a customer for 2,500 switching devices, all at the same fixed price. By year end, 520 of the switches had been shipped.		
n. In April, Manchester Company made an $8,500 deposit with a security services company. At year end on September 30, there were $7,200 of charges against the deposit.		
o. The trial balance of Hartford and Hartford Partnership shows a note payable of $10,000. Principle and interest are not payable until next year.		
p. The trial balance of Mitchell Company shows Unearned Fees of $11,000. Fees still unearned at the end of the period are $2,200.		
q. In April, Naugatuck Services, Inc. received an advance from a client for 10 months' services at a monthly fee of $1,000. The date of the trial balance is December 31.		
r. At year end, a tenant of the Bridgeport Company owes two months of unpaid rent, which has not been recorded.		
s. In September, Housatonic Company prepaid for 500 hours of computer maintenance services. At December 31, year end, 390 hours would be used in the following year.		
t. Northaven Company has $1,500 of advertising expense incurred but unpaid at year end.		
u. Waterbury Company has $440 of earned but uncollected service revenue at year end.		
v. The trial balance of Boston Company shows a balance of $1,800 in Prepaid Insurance.		
w. The Norwich Company makes semiannual insurance payments. At year end, the Prepaid Insurance account shows debits of: beginning bal. of $900, and March 1 and Sept. 1, $1,800 each.		
x. A corporation calculates at year end that it owes $100,000 of income tax.		

LG 4-2. Identifying the journal entry. To do an adjustment, it is necessary to know the correct form of the journal entry and to understand what the entry is doing. One of the best ways to practice this is to look at adjusting entries that have already been prepared. Then, interpret what kind of entries they are and what they are doing.

Instructions: Use a separate sheet of paper to complete the table. The table below shows a series of unrelated journal entry items. If an item is an adjusting entry, identify what kind of adjustment it is. Also explain what the entry is recording.

The five adjusting entries are:

- prepaid expense
- unearned revenue
- accrued expense
- accrued revenue
- depreciation

Use the first item as an example. (All prepayments are recorded in balance sheet accounts.)

Journal Entry Item			What kind of adjustment is it?	What is the adjustment recording?
a. Utilities Expense Accounts Payable	Dr. 820	Cr. 820	accrued expense	a utilities expense that is unpaid
b. Accounts Receivable Fees Earned	Dr. 1,100	Cr. 1,100	(Reminder: Use a separate sheet of paper to complete the table.)	
c. Unearned Revenue Subscriptions Revenue	Dr. 200	Cr. 200		
d. Depreciation Expense Accumulated Depreciation—Truck	Dr. 2,500	Cr. 2,500		
e. Cash Accounts Receivable	Dr. 1,100	Cr. 1,100		
f. Rent Expense Prepaid Rent	Dr. 500	Cr. 500		
g. Rent Expense Rent Payable	Dr. 500	Cr. 500		
h. Accounts Receivable Service Revenue	Dr. 950	Cr. 950		
i. Unearned Revenue Service Revenue	Dr. 950	Cr. 950		

PRACTICE   Learning Goal 4, continued

LG 4-2, *continued*

Journal Entry Item			What kind of adjustment is it?	What is the adjustment recording?
	Dr.	Cr.	(Reminder: Use a separate sheet of paper to complete the table.)	
j. Supplies Expense	200			
Supplies		200		
	Dr.	Cr.		
k. Supplies	200			
Accounts Payable		200		
	Dr.	Cr.		
l. Advertising Expense	3,000			
Accounts Payable		3,000		
	Dr.	Cr.		
m. Wages Expense	10,000			
Wages Payable		10,000		
	Dr.	Cr.		
n. Insurance Expense	700			
Prepaid Insurance		700		
	Dr.	Cr.		
o. Unearned Sales Revenue	2,000			
Sales Revenue		2,000		

LG 4-3. Review: analyzing accounts. It is not unusual to be asked to calculate some part of an account other than the ending balance. Use these exercises to practice analyzing an account.

a. The Supplies account had a beginning balance of $150. During the period $3,530 of supplies was purchased. The supplies on hand at the end of the period were $420. What is the adjusting journal entry to record the amount of supplies used?

b. On a separate sheet of paper, complete the table.

Item	Prepaid Insurance	Prepaid Rent	Prepaid Travel	Prepaid Subscriptions
Beginning balance	$1,000		$5,000	$300
Payments/purchases made	$5,050	$ 850	$3,000	
Expense for the period		$4,100	$3,250	$750
Ending balance	$ 700	$ 500		$100

c. The beginning balance of Prepaid Insurance was $9,500, and the ending balance was $8,450. During the period, $12,200 was paid for additional insurance. What was the insurance expense for the period?

d. During the period, the balance of Unearned Revenue increased by $26,000 to $41,900. Also, $84,100 of Unearned Revenue was recorded as earned. What was the amount of cash advance payments received during the period?

LG 4-4. Each of the following independent events occurred during the quarter ended June 30 for Joseph City, Inc., which prepares quarterly financial statements.

Instructions: record the necessary June 30 adjustments.

a. On April 1, the balance in the supplies account was $4,950. $2,800 of supplies were purchased during the quarter. A physical count of supplies inventory as of June 30 indicated a balance of $1,710.

b. $10,300 wages expense is paid weekly on each Friday for a 5-day workweek. June 30 quarter-end was a Wednesday.

c. Advance payments from Page Company during the quarter were $25,000 and were credited to unearned revenue. The company estimates that 70% of the services have been provided to the client. The balance of unearned revenue at the beginning of the quarter was $2,750. The work for these services was completed during the quarter.

d. Annual depreciation for office equipment is $9,000 and for automotive equipment is $11,400.

e. On June 30, $3,100 was billed to a client but remains unrecorded.

f. On July 7, a bill for $800 of advertising expense was received for June advertising.

g. The unadjusted Prepaid Insurance account is presented below:

Prepaid Insurance	
Bal. March 31	1,875
April 2	9,000
Bal. June 30	10,875

Insurance is paid in advance for eight months. The March 31 balance is the remaining amount of an October payment.

LG 4-5. *Instructions*: Record the appropriate period-end adjusting journal entry for each of the following independent situations.

a. Baton Rouge, Inc. records $35,000 of weekly payroll for a 5-day workweek that ends on Saturday. The current accounting period ended on a Wednesday, September 30.

b. Wichita Falls Company received a $3,800 bill for computer repair services on January 3 for prior month services. The company has a December 31 year-end.

c. Ogden Company started business on May 1 of the current year and needs to record depreciation expense on equipment at December 31, year-end. The depreciation expense is based on a 12-year equipment life. The cost of the equipment is $128,000, with no residual value.

d. Detroit Company received an advance payment of $18,000 on June 1 for 500 pounds of landscaping material. At July 31 year-end, 300 pounds had been delivered.

e. The prepaid insurance account balance at September 30 year-end shows a balance of $18,000. The only policy still in force at year-end is from a one-year prepayment made on June 1 in the amount of $12,000.

f. Brooklyn Enterprises signed a $500,000 3-year consulting contract on December 1 of the current year. The current accounting period ends on December 31.

g. Lorain Enterprises completed work on a $45,000 project on January 14 of the current year, which ends on January 31. Cash of $45,000 was received on January 27 and has not yet been recorded. The company had properly billed the customer for $20,000 of the work on the prior December 31.

LG 4-6. Prepare adjusting entries.

Allegheny Tennis School, Inc.
Trial Balance
December 31, 2017

Account	Dr.	Cr.
Cash	$63,040	
Accounts Receivable	2,730	
Prepaid Insurance	4,000	
Office Supplies	1,750	
Tennis Supplies	2,000	
Notes Receivable	14,500	
Equipment	50,500	
Unearned School Revenue		1,800
Taxes Payable		2,700
Common Stock		1,000
Retained Earnings		4,595
Tennis School Revenue		206,925
Wages Expense	49,000	
Rent Expense	22,000	
Advertising Expense	3,500	
Utilities Expense	1,500	
Insurance Expense	500	
Income Tax Expense	2,000	
Total	$217,020	$217,020

Additional information:

The company prepares annual financial statements with a December 31 year end.

a. The prepaid insurance is one year's insurance paid on March 1.
b. Office supplies unused at year end are $225.
c. Tennis supplies were purchased on January 2 and were used up at the rate of 5% per month.
d. Equipment was purchased on July 1, 2017, and is estimated to have an eight-year life and $7,300 residual value.
e. The school pays wages of $1,000 per five-day week ending on Saturday. December 31 is a Thursday.
f. The company has earned but not yet received $500 of interest on a loan.
g. The school received an $1,800 payment for three months of classes on November 1.

Instructions: Prepare adjusting journal entries. For journal paper, use the template in the disk at the back of the book, or at worthyjames.com (student info.).

PRACTICE   Learning Goal 4, continued   *Solutions are in the disk at the back of the book and at: www.worthyjames.com*

LG 4-7. Prepare adjusting entries.

Rainforest Research Technology Company, Inc.
Trial Balance
June 30, 2017

Account	Dr.	Cr.
Cash	$258,815	
Accounts Receivable	7,300	
Supplies	500	
Prepaid Insurance	2,400	
Office Equipment	30,000	
Accounts Payable		1,920
Notes Payable		15,000
Interest Payable		750
Unearned Revenue		15,000
Common Stock		10,000
Retained Earnings		89,930
Dividends	23,000	
Consulting Fees Revenue		276,700
Research Revenue		49,400
Rent Expense	25,200	
Utilities Expense	2,750	
Supplies Expense	1,475	
Interest Expense	2,010	
Wages Expense	103,250	
Income Tax Expense	2,000	
Total	$458,700	$458,700

Additional information:

The Rainforest Research Technology Company prepares annual financial statements with a June 30 fiscal year end.

a. Unbilled at year end is $4,500 of consulting services to Megawatt Industries, Inc.
b. A physical inventory count determined that $650 of supplies is still on hand.
c. The company received its June telephone bill in early July. The amount was $900.
d. Prepaid Insurance still in force on June 30 is $500.
e. On May 1, the company received a payment from the Brazilian government for $15,000 for one year of research.
f. Depreciation on the office equipment is $5,000.

Instructions:
1. Prepare adjusting entries. For journal paper, use the template in the disk at the back of the book.
2. For each adjusting entry, identify the analysis elements of classification, valuation, and timing.

LG 4-8. **Prepare adjusting entries.**

Midway Charter Service Company, Inc.
Unadjusted Trial Balance
June 30, 2017

Account	Dr.	Cr.
Cash	$51,650	
Prepaid Insurance	4,900	
Office Supplies	1,150	
Aircraft Supplies	37,950	
Aircraft	480,000	
Accumulated Depreciation—Equipment		$45,000
Unearned Charter Revenue		47,700
Notes Payable		241,000
Common Stock		25,000
Retained Earnings		51,000
Charter Service Revenue		221,000
Wages Expense	29,000	
Equipment Rent Expense	21,500	
Insurance Expense	500	
Utility Expense	2,050	
Income Tax Expense	2,000	
Total	$630,700	$630,700

Additional information:

Midway Charter Service Company has a year end of June 30. The company provides sightseeing helicopter and aircraft tours around the scenic Midway Island area. The charter company requires all tours and charter service to be booked and paid for in advance.

a. In April, a whale-watching group paid $25,000 for 200 hours of flight time. This was recorded as Unearned Charter Revenue. So far, 42 hours of flight time have been provided. The rest of the balance in the Unearned Charter Revenue is from other receipts during the year, and is 40% still unearned.

b. The aircraft was purchased during the prior fiscal year and is estimated to have a useful life of 10 years.

LG 4-8, *continued*

   c. The company has a six-day workweek ending on Saturday. The two employees each earn $1,260 per week and are paid on the Monday following the end of the workweek. This year, June 30 falls on a Tuesday.

   d. The prepaid insurance consisted of two policies:
- Policy R173: $1,800, term 9 months, paid on May 2.
- Policy JRX22: $3,100, term 20 months, paid on January 30.

   e. The company also leases (rents) other aircraft as the need may arise. In early July, the company received a bill in the amount of $4,400 for aircraft rental charges in June.

   f. On June 30 an inventory showed $500 of office supplies unused and $19,900 of aircraft supplies unused. All of the supplies had been purchased in July, 2016.

Instructions:

1. Prepare the adjusting entries. For journal paper, use the template in the disk at the back of the book.
2. What is the correct net income of the company after the adjustments are prepared?
3. Assuming there were no payables or receivables at the beginning of the year, what would the net income have been if the company had used cash basis accounting? (See Learning Goal 2.)

LG 4-9. Calculate adjustment amounts. Refer to Problem LG 4-1.

   a. For each separate situation, calculate the amount of the adjustment if there is sufficient information and if an adjustment is required.

   b. If there is not sufficient information to calculate an adjustment or if an adjustment is not required, indicate what information you would need and how you would use it to determine the amount of the adjustment, or why an adjustment is not required.

Instructor-Assigned Problems

If you are using this book in a class, these review problems may be assigned by your instructor for homework, group assignments, class work, or other activities. Only your instructor has the solutions.

IA 4-1. Each of the following independent events occurred during the year ended December 31 for Portland Enterprises. *Instructions:* Record the necessary adjusting journal entries at year-end.

   a. Depreciation expense for the year is $19,200.

   b. On December 28, a bill for $11,600 was sent to a customer, but is still unrecorded.

   c. The company received $20,000 of advance payments during the year from Vancouver Company for a consulting project. Approximately 35% of the work was completed but is unrecorded.

   d. The company incurs $20,000 of wages expense for a 5-day week ending on Fridays. This year December 31 year-end was a Thursday.

   e. The January 1 balance of Prepaid Insurance is $3,000. Each payment of $4,500 is for the following three months. Payments were made on March 1, June 1, September 1, and December 1. No adjustment was made to Prepaid Insurance during the year.

   f. The company received a $700 utilities bill on January 2 for the month of December.

IA 4-2. Prepare adjusting entries. The trial balance of Dubuque Internet Consulting Company after its first month of operations:

Dubuque Internet Consulting Company, Inc.
Trial Balance
November 30, 2017

Account	Dr.	Cr.
Cash	$4,500	
Accounts Receivable	9,350	
Supplies	1,400	
Prepaid Travel	5,000	
Office Equipment	38,000	
Unearned Revenue		$9,100
Common Stock............................		19,350
Retained Earnings........................		32,070
Consulting Revenue		12,800
Wages Expense	11,100	
Utilities Expense.........................	470	
Advertising Expense......................	2,500	
Income Tax Expense......................	1,000	
Total	$73,320	$73,320

Other information:

a. At the end of the month, the company completed $1,100 of consulting services; however, as of November 30, a bill had not been sent to the client.

b. A November invoice in the amount of $950 from an Internet service provider was received on December 4.

c. The Prepaid Travel account consists of ten airline tickets at the same price, of which six have been used.

d. The amount of supplies not yet used is $330.

e. As of November 30, $7,200 of the Unearned Revenue account was not yet earned.

f. The office equipment was purchased on November 1. It is estimated to have a five-year life with no residual value.

g. Wages are $3,500 and paid weekly, Monday through Friday. November 30 is a Wednesday.

Instructions: Prepare the November 30, month-end adjusting entries. For journal paper, use the template in the disk at the back of the book.

PRACTICE   Learning Goal 4, continued

IA 4-3. Part I Prepare adjusting entries. The trial balance of Mayaguez Enterprises at September 30, the end of the fiscal year:

Mayaguez Enterprises, Inc.
Trial Balance
September 30, 2017

Account	Dr.	Cr.
Cash	$17,990	
Accounts Receivable	27,500	
Supplies	1,400	
Prepaid Insurance	6,000	
Office Equipment	24,000	
Accumulated Dep'n—Office Equipment		$ 1,440
Land	150,000	
Unearned Revenue		4,490
Notes Payable		100,000
Common Stock		15,500
Retained Earnings		57,220
Service Revenue		289,410
Wages Expense	215,100	
Utilities Expense	5,800	
Repairs Expense	11,350	
Rent Expense	7,820	
Income Tax Expense	1,100	
Total	468,060	468,060

Other information:

a. The balance in the Prepaid Insurance account is the cost of a 12-month fire insurance policy purchased on February 1 of the current fiscal year.
b. The amount of supplies still on hand is $250.
c. $2,500 of the balance recorded in Unearned Revenue has been earned.
d. Interest expense accrued for September is $750.
e. At the end of September, the company completed $900 of services, but the amount is still unbilled.
f. Current employee wages are $4,200 per week, Monday through Friday. September 30 is a Thursday.
g. Monthly depreciation for office equipment is $200.

Instructions: Prepare the September 30 year-end adjusting entries. All adjustments are made at year end. For journal paper, use the template in the disk at the back of the book.

Part II Financial Statement Review: *Instructions:* a) Create T accounts, enter beginning balances, and post adjustments into accounts. b) Prepare an income statement, statement of retained earnings, and report form balance sheet from account balances.

PRACTICE   Learning Goal 4, continued

IA4-4. Each of the following independent events occurred during the year ended December 31 for Clearwater, Inc. Instructions: Record the necessary adjusting journal entries at period-end.

a. On December 30, $7,500 was billed to a client but is unrecorded.

b. Office equipment of $47,000 is being depreciated over a 10-year useful life, with no residual value. $12,000 of new testing equipment was purchased on November 2. The equipment has an estimated 5-year useful life with $500 residual value.

c. The company incurs $24,300 of weekly wage expense for a six-day week, Monday through Saturday. Wages are paid on the following Monday. December 31 year-end was a Thursday.

d. The unadjusted balance of Prepaid Rent at year-end is $34,000. Each prepayment of $18,000 is made at nine-month intervals. The last payment was made on September 1.

e. Analysis of completed jobs shows that the Unearned Revenue account should increase by $12,800 for the year. The company received $21,000 of advance payments during the year. Reduction to the account is made only at year-end as an adjustment.

f. On January 8, the company received a $350 telephone bill for December.

g. The beginning balance of the Supplies account is $4,600, which increased by $700 during the year. A count of supplies on December 31 shows a balance of $2,950.

INTERNET EXERCISES

Ethics—analyze cases. Go to the Carnegie Mellon Tepper School of Business, Arthur Andersen Case Studies in Business (at web.tepper.cmu.edu/ethics/aa/arthurandersen.htm).

Select at least three mini-cases that interest you. Do not look at the teaching notes yet. (Use bookmark/favorites to save the location in an Accounting References folder.)

a. Read each case, then write down the name of the case. If you are using Volume 1 in this set, apply the ethics discussion and guidelines in Learning Goal 10 to analyze the case. If you are not using Volume 1, do the following: 1) Identify the facts and the parties involved. 2) Determine if there a moral issue of a possibly wrongful act.

b. Make a decision or take a position. Write a paragraph to explain how you reached your decision or position.

c. Compare your answer to the teaching notes. Do you agree with the notes? Would you change them or add more?

Your Questions?

It is *very* important to be aware of what you need to understand better. What do you need to understand better about this learning goal? On a separate piece of paper, write the questions that you want to discuss with your classmates, instructor, or supervisor. Try to be very specific about what is bothering you, such as explanations that you do not fully understand.

APPENDIX PART I

Appendix Part I
to Learning Goal 4

In Part I, you will find:

A Closer Look at Prepaid Expenses

Identify Prepaid Expenses

Overview

There are five basic adjustment types. This part is about:

Prepaid Expense	Unearned Revenue	Depreciation	Accrued Revenue	Accrued Expense

Definition

A *prepaid expense* is an advance payment for a future expense that is recorded as an asset at time of payment. (Debit prepaid expense, credit cash.) When the asset is used up later—usually within a year—an expense is recorded.

Synonym

A prepaid expense is also called a **deferred expense**.

Why a Prepaid Expense Is an Asset

Do not be fooled because the word "expense" is in the term "prepaid expense." A prepaid expense is always an asset. A prepaid expense is an asset because it will provide future benefits when some amount of the asset is later used up. All prepaid expenses are used up because of either:

- the passage of time, or
- physical consumption, or
- services received.

Only when the asset is *used up* does an expense need to be recorded.

Examples

The table below shows you examples of common prepaid expense items.

Cash is paid now in order to . . .	and an *asset* is recorded that is called . . .	which is later used up because of . . .	so an *expense* adjustment will be needed, called . . .
purchase one year of fire insurance,	Prepaid Insurance,	the passage of time,	Insurance Expense.
purchase office supplies,	Office Supplies,	physical use— consuming the supplies,	Supplies Expense.
prepay 50 hours of computer training,	Prepaid Employee Training,	services received— the training,	Training Expense.

Identify Prepaid Expenses, *continued*

Examples That Are NOT Prepaid Expenses

- Debt payment, because the payment is reducing debt, not paying an expense in advance
- Purchase equipment, because equipment is used up over many years
- Pay current wages expense, because nothing is paid in advance—the expense is current

TIP

The word "expense" is sometimes added to the word "prepaid" as the name of the asset account. However, the item is still really an asset. *Remember:* If you ever see the word "prepaid" in front of the word "expense," the item is an asset.

Examples:

- Prepaid Insurance Expense
- Prepaid Rent Expense
- Prepaid Interest Expense

How a Prepayment Becomes an Expense

Debit Expense, Credit Asset

Any amount of a prepaid item that has been used up becomes an expense. The expense is recorded by making an adjusting entry at the end of the accounting period when you know how much of the asset has been used. Sometimes, the use of a prepaid item occurs over one, two, or more accounting periods. At the end of each accounting period, before the financial statements are prepared, the adjustment is recorded for the amount of the asset used up:

Asset	Expense
$ adjustment	$ adjustment

Assets ↓ = Liabilities + Stockholders' Equity ↓

Check Your Understanding

Recognize a prepaid expense situation. Answers are on page 75.

To do an adjustment for a prepaid expense, you must be sure that you can *recognize a prepaid expense* when you see one. On a separate piece of paper, create a table like the one below. For each transaction that creates a prepaid expense, complete the table. Use the first transaction as an example. *Careful:* Not all the transactions involve prepaid expenses!

Cash is paid in order to . . .	and an asset is recorded that is called . . .	which is later used up because of . . .	so the asset is credited and an expense is debited, called . . .
purchase one year of fire insurance,	Prepaid Insurance	the passage of time,	Insurance Expense.
pay rent four months in advance,	(Reminder: Use a separate sheet of paper to complete the table.)		
pay accounts payable,			
loan money,			
prepay six months' of consulting service,			
buy spare parts for the equipment,			
pay wages expense,			
buy paper for the copier,			
purchase airline tickets three months in advance,			

Answers

Cash is paid in order to . . .	and an asset is recorded that is called . . .	which is later used up because of . . .	so the asset is credited and an expense is debited, called . . .
purchase one year of fire insurance.	Prepaid Insurance	the passage of time,	Insurance Expense.
pay rent four months in advance.	Prepaid Rent	the passage of time,	Rent Expense.
pay accounts payable,	Not a prepayment—you are paying a debt, not paying for a future expense.		
loan money,	Not a prepayment—this expenditure will be repaid, so is not a future expense.		
prepay six months' of consulting service,	Prepaid Consulting Service	the passage of time,	Consulting Expense.
buy spare parts for the equipment,	Parts Supplies	physical use—using up the parts,	Parts Expense.
pay wages expense,	Not a prepayment—this is a current expense, not a future one.		
buy paper for the copier,	Office Supplies	physical use—using up the paper,	Office Supplies Expense.
purchase airline tickets three months in advance,	Prepaid Travel Expense	services received—airline flight	Travel Expense.

"Mon Dieu! If only we had known it was a prepaid expense!"

How to Adjust Prepaid Expenses

The Two Objectives

Introduction

At this point, we assume that you have learned what a prepaid expense is and why it often needs to be adjusted. If you do not feel sure about this, it would be best to review the prior material (starting on page 44).

The Two Objectives

The adjustment procedures for prepaid expenses are done with the intention of completing two objectives:

1. Prepare the adjusting journal entry.
2. Determine the new balances of the accounts affected.

Sometimes you may be asked to complete only the first objective, or sometimes both of them. The detailed procedures for the two objectives are presented as separate topics in the material that follows this discussion.

Overview of the Two Objectives

The following two tables show an overview of the steps that accomplish the two objectives. (Upcoming pages discuss each step.)

Objective I Overview: Prepare the Adjusting Journal Entry		
Step	**Action**	**Example**
1	Identify the key information type.	Any of these types: ■ The asset cost remaining ■ The asset cost used up ■ The cost per unit of the asset
2	Calculate the asset cost used up.	Calculation depends on the type of information given.

3	Prepare the adjusting journal entry.	*Example:* $500 used up
		
		                     Dr. **Cr.**
		Expense 500
		   Asset 500

The Two Objectives, *continued*

Objective II Overview: Determine the New Balances of the Accounts Affected		
Step	**Action**	**Example**
1	Identify the adjusting journal entry.	From Objective I
2	Set up T accounts with the account names and the unadjusted account balances.	Asset Expense $$ \| $$ |
3	Debit the expense and credit the asset, and calculate the new account balances.	Asset Expense $$ \| $$ | | 500 500 | $$ \| $$ |

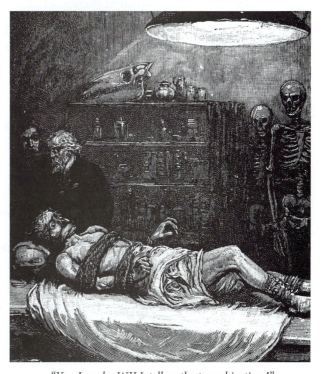

"Yes, Igor, he WILL tell us the two objectives!"

Objective I: Prepare the Adjusting Journal Entry

Step 1: Identify the Key Information Type

Overview of the Three Information Types

The single most important step in doing the adjustment calculation is identifying the key information type. You will not always be given the same kind of information about prepaid expenses. Three possible types of information concerning prepaid expenses might be given to you:

1. The asset cost remaining
2. The asset cost used up
3. The cost per unit of the asset

Your job is to correctly use whatever kind of information is given to you when you calculate the adjustment. Each of the information types is discussed below.

Type 1: The Asset Cost Remaining

- **What it means:** "The asset cost remaining" means the cost of the asset *actually remaining at the end of the accounting period*. It is the cost of the prepaid item that is still unused. This means the amount of the prepaid item that actually still exists, regardless of what the accounting records might show.

- **"Clue" words:** The following descriptive words are frequently used to refer to the cost of an asset actually still remaining:

  - unexpired
  - unused
  - still in force
  - actual
  - left over
  - remaining

  - in effect
  - available
  - on hand
  - for next . . .
  - ending inventory

  Examples:

  - "The unexpired prepaid insurance is $750."
  - "The prepaid insurance still in effect is $750."
  - "The supplies on hand were $3,000."
  - "Of the $5,000 balance in the Prepaid Rent account, $3,000 is for next month."

Step 1: Identify the Key Information Type, *continued*

Type 2:
The Asset Cost
Used Up

- **What it means:** "The asset cost used up" means the dollar cost of the prepaid item that was consumed or used up during the current accounting period. This can be part of or all of the prepaid item, regardless of what the accounting records might show.

- **"Clue" words:** The following descriptive words are frequently used to refer to the cost of the prepaid item that was used up:

  - expired
  - used
  - used up
  - consumed
  - utilized

  - received
  - provided
  - expense
  - incurred
  - charged against

- **Two ways it can be given:**

  1. *The cost used up is given directly, as a dollar amount.*

     Examples:

     - "The expired insurance cost is $250."
     - "The trial balance shows $900 in Prepaid Advertising, but $180 of that amount had actually been charged against the account."
     - "The company provided $3,000 of fringe benefits to employees."
     - "The insurance expense for the period was $9,500."

  2. *The cost used up is given indirectly, as a fraction or percent.*

     Examples:

     - "One-fourth of the $1,000 cost of Prepaid Insurance was consumed."
     - "The trial balance shows $900 in Prepaid Advertising, but 20% had actually been charged against the expense account."
     - "The company incurred rent expense of one-third of the balance in the Prepaid Rent account."

continued ▶

Step 1: Identify the Key Information Type, *continued*

Type 3:
The Cost Per Unit
of the Asset

- **What it means:** "The cost per unit of the asset" refers to allocating an equal amount of the asset cost to each unit of the asset. Cost per unit is really another way of showing the cost used up, but it is easier to see cost per unit as a separate information type.

- **Two ways it can be given:**

  1. *The cost per unit is given directly.* Key words like "at the rate of," "per," and "for each" indicate cost per unit. Also, "weekly," "monthly," etc.

     Examples:

     - "The asset was used up at the *rate of* $500 *per* month."
     - "*For each* job finished, the insurance expense was $800."
     - "The *monthly* insurance expense was $200."

  2. *Information is given so you can calculate cost per unit.* Instead of cost per unit being directly given to you, sometimes information is given to you so that you can calculate it. **You always know you have cost per unit information when:**

     - you are given a *total dollar cost for what was purchased*, and
     - you know *how many units* of goods or services were purchased.

The "units" can be physical units, job units, or time units.

The table below shows you examples of the two ways cost per unit can be given.

For cost per unit, you can be given . . .	
the direct cost per unit . . .	. . . or information that allows you to calculate the cost per unit
■ "The cost of the magazine subscription is $10 per issue." (units of issues)	■ "The cost of the 12-issue magazine subscription is $120." (units of issues)
■ "The service contract charged $100 for each service call." (units of service calls)	■ "The company paid $2,000 for a service contract that provided 20 service calls." (units of service calls—jobs)
■ "The cost of the prepaid insurance that expired during December was $1,000." (units of time—in months)	■ "On December 1, the company prepaid $5,000 for five months of fire insurance." (units of time—in months)

Step 1: Identify the Key Information Type, *continued*

No Particular Order

If you are doing a problem in which you think several prepaid expense accounts might need adjustment, you can select any account first. When looking for key information, or when deciding which prepaid expense account might need adjustment, there is no particular order.

Check Your Understanding

Find the "clue" words. Each of the phrases below is taken from quiz and test questions about making adjustments to prepaid expense accounts. See if you can find the identifying "clue" words in each phrase. The first phrase of each information type is underlined for you as an example. Answers are on page 82.

Type 1: The asset cost remaining

- "As of the end of the month, ending inventory of office supplies was $200."
- "At the end of the month, the amount of the prepaid rent that was still in force was $3,000."
- "On the date of the trial balance, the unexpired insurance premium was $750."
- "On the date of the trial balance, spare parts on hand totaled $1,100."
- "At year end, there was $250 of unused supplies."

Type 2: The asset cost used up

- "Orem Company determined that $500 of supplies were used up during the month."
- "Bryce Company failed to record $950 of prepaid insurance that had expired."
- "An advance deposit payment of $5,000 was made for future equipment servicing. During the period, there were $3,500 of charges against the deposit."
- "For the year, the supplies consumed totaled $4,400."
- "During the year, one-fourth of the $5,000 in the supplies account was used up."
- "On November 3, the company paid $2,100 for prepaid insurance. At year end, 25% had expired."

Type 3: The cost per unit of the asset (Underline the words that give cost per unit or that give the information to calculate cost per unit.)

- "On July 1, the business made a $3,600 payment for one year of insurance coverage."
- "Prepaid insurance expires at the rate of $300 per month."
- "The prepaid service contract costs $5,000 and is for 50 service calls."
- "Salt Lake Company paid $7,500 in advance for magazine advertising. The prepayment was for advertising in 10 issues of a magazine."
- "The automotive lubricating oil supplies are used up at the rate of 8 quarts per 10,000 miles."

"Just look for the key words."

Answers

Type 1: The asset cost remaining

- "As of the end of the month, <u>ending inventory</u> of office supplies was $200."
- "At the end of the month, the amount of the prepaid rent that was <u>still in force</u> was $3,000."
- "On the date of the trial balance, the <u>unexpired</u> insurance premium was $750."
- "On the date of the trial balance, spare parts <u>on hand</u> totaled $1,100."
- "At year-end, there was $250 of <u>unused</u> supplies."

Type 2: The asset cost used up

- "Orem Company determined that $500 of supplies were <u>used up</u> during the month."
- "Bryce Company failed to record $950 of prepaid insurance that had <u>expired</u>."
- "An advance deposit payment of $5,000 was made for future equipment servicing. During the period, there were $3,500 of <u>charges against the deposit</u>."
- "For the year, the supplies <u>consumed</u> totaled $4,400."
- "During the year, <u>one-fourth</u> of the $5,000 in the supplies account was <u>used up</u>."
- "On November 3, the company paid $2,100 for prepaid insurance. At year end, <u>25% had expired</u>."

Type 3: The cost per unit of the asset

- "On July 1, the business made a <u>$3,600 payment for one year</u> of insurance coverage." (*units of time*)
- "Prepaid insurance expires at the rate of <u>$300 per month</u>." (*units of time*)
- "The prepaid service contract cost <u>$5,000 and is for 50 service calls</u>." (*units of service calls*)
- "Salt Lake Company paid <u>$7,500</u> in advance for magazine advertising. The prepayment was for advertising in <u>10 issues</u> of a magazine." (*units of magazine issues*)
- "The automotive lubricating oil supplies are used up at <u>the rate of 8 quarts per 10,000 miles</u>." (*units of miles*)

Check Your Understanding

Identify information types. In the table below, situations involving the three different key information types for prepaid expenses are given to you. On a separate piece of paper, make a list of which information type is being described. Each description refers to only one of the three types. The answers are below.

Description	Information Type
1. New Orleans Company has $1,000 of fire insurance still in force.	(Reminder: Use a separate sheet of paper to complete the table.)
2. A physical inventory of the supplies account of Bossier Company shows that $375 of supplies has been consumed.	
3. Shreveport Enterprises spent $9,000 to prepay six months' rent.	
4. At year end, the Lake Charles Company has $1,100 of office supplies still on hand, although the Office Supplies account shows a different balance.	
5. Baton Rouge Corporation prepaid $5,000 for magazine advertising for five monthly issues.	
6. 80% of prepaid insurance of Chalmette Enterprises expired during the year.	
7. Lafayette Company paid $2,500 for a computer repair service contract. The contract is for 25 service calls.	
8. Prepaid insurance was purchased in June. On June 30, the end of the period, the balance in the Prepaid Insurance account relates to the period June 1 through October 31.	

Answers

Description	Information Type
1. New Orleans Company has $1,000 of fire insurance still in force.	The asset cost remaining
2. A physical inventory of the supplies account of Bossier Company shows that $375 of supplies has been consumed.	The asset cost used up
3. Shreveport Enterprises spent $9,000 to prepay six months' rent.	The cost per unit of the asset
4. At year end, the Lake Charles Company has $1,100 of office supplies still on hand, although the Office Supplies account shows a different balance.	The asset cost remaining
5. Baton Rouge Corporation prepaid $5,000 for magazine advertising for five monthly issues.	The cost per unit of the asset
6. 80% of prepaid insurance of Chalmette Enterprises expired during the year.	The asset cost used up
7. Lafayette Company paid $2,500 for a computer repair service contract. The contract is for 25 service calls.	The cost per unit of the asset
8. Prepaid insurance was purchased in June. On June 30, the end of the period, the balance in the Prepaid Insurance account relates to the period June 1 through October 31.	The cost per unit of the asset (June 1 through October 31: 5 months)

"And now on to Step 2!"

Step 2: Select the Proper Method to Calculate Cost Used Up

Introduction

In the previous topic starting on page 78, you learned how to *identify* the key information type (Step 1). In the upcoming discussion, you will learn the second step in the procedure—how to *calculate* how much of the prepaid item that was used up (Step 2).

Calculation Depends on Key Information

The kind of calculation that you do is not the same every time. The kind of calculation that you do *depends upon which type of key information* is given to you.

Before You Begin . . .

Select any prepaid expense item that you are thinking about adjusting (order is not important) and verify that it has been recorded as an asset.

Step 2: Select the Proper Method to Calculate Cost Used Up, *continued*

Calculation Procedures Table

Each key information type may require you to consider several actions before calculating the cost used up. To see the actions that can apply to each information type, use the table below. Look down the column under the "yes" that applies to each information type. A "✓" marks an action that you must do or consider.

Detailed explanations for each item can be found on the referenced pages.

IF the key information type is . . .				. . . see page
Type 1: The asset cost remaining (given or calculated)	yes			78
Type 2: The asset cost used up (given or calculated)		yes		79
Type 3: The cost per unit of the asset (given or calculated)			yes	80

Then, to calculate the adjustment amount . . .				. . . see page
subtract the asset cost remaining from the unadjusted account balance.	✓			86
sometimes you first might have to calculate the unadjusted account balance or the asset cost remaining.	✓			87
the dollars of cost used up is given to you—no further calculation.		✓		90
sometimes you might have to calculate the portion of the asset cost used up.		✓		90
multiply cost per unit × units used up.			✓	93
sometimes you first might have to calculate the cost per unit.			✓	93

■ Using Information Type 1: The Asset Cost Remaining

If the key information is . . .	then to calculate the asset cost used up . . .
the asset cost remaining,	subtract the asset cost still remaining from the unadjusted account balance of the prepaid expense account.

Example

"The balance of prepaid insurance in the trial balance on December 31, year end, is $3,000. There is $300 of insurance still in force at year end."

Calculation:

$3,000 (unadjusted balance) − $300 (asset cost remaining) = $2,700 used up

Sometimes You Have to Calculate the Unadjusted Account Balance

Normally, after you have identified the asset cost actually remaining as the key information, you look for the unadjusted account balance from which you subtract the actual remaining cost. But sometimes you cannot find the unadjusted account balance! Instead, you are given information about the activity in the account.

Example:

"At the beginning of the year, the balance of the Prepaid Insurance account was $250. On March 3, $1,950 of prepaid insurance was purchased. On September 5, another $800 was purchased. At year end, $300 of insurance remained unexpired."

Solution:

Use the formula below to calculate the account balance.

Formula

> **beginning balance + purchases recorded
> − uses recorded = ending balance**

From the information above:
$250 + ($1,950 + $800) − 0 = $3,000 (unadjusted balance)

TIP

During a period, purchases are usually recorded, but often uses are not. A company will wait until the end of a period to record the total uses as a single adjustment to decrease the account. Notice in the example above that the company had not recorded any prepaid insurance used up during the period.

■ Using Information Type 1: The Asset Cost Remaining, *continued*

Sometimes You Have to Calculate Asset Cost Remaining	Sometimes a problem does not directly tell you what the actual cost remaining is. Instead, information is given to you so you can calculate what portion of the asset is actually still remaining.

What Is a "Portion"?	The "portion" of the asset actually still remaining means some single, lump-sum part of the asset. You can think of a portion as a piece or "chunk" of the asset that is still unused. This will usually be presented to you as

- a fraction of the asset that is still unused, or as
- a percent of the asset that is still unused.

Example

This example shows a situation in which you have to calculate *both* the unadjusted account balance *and* the portion of the asset cost actually remaining.

Details of the supplies account for Vasco Company are shown below as of December 31, year end. The company has an actual ending balance of one-eighth of the unadjusted balance. What is the amount of the adjustment?

	Supplies
Jan. 1	1,275
Jan. 31	1,155
Sept. 30	1,850

- Unadjusted balance: $1,275 + $1,155 + $1,850 = $4,280
- Actual ending balance: The portion 1/8 of $4,280 = $ 535
- Adjustment: The difference of . . . $3,745

Example of No Adjustment Required

If the actual balance of the prepaid item is the same as the unadjusted account balance, then no adjustment is required! The entries needed have already been done and the account balance is correct.

Example:
"On November 1, Capizzi Company paid $2,400 for 12 months of prepaid insurance. On December 31, the unused amount of prepaid insurance remaining was $2,000. On the trial balance, the Prepaid Insurance account shows a balance of $2,000."

"*I say!* **Type 1** *(asset remaining) calculations to try.*"

Check Your Understanding

Calculate the amount of the adjustment for each of the Type 1 information (asset actually remaining) situations below. Answers are on page 89.

Description	Answer
1. The Office Supplies account of Greenbriar Company had a January 1 balance of $3,720. During the year, $7,815 of supplies were purchased. At year end, supplies on hand were $1,900.	(Reminder: Use a separate sheet of paper to complete the table.)
2. The June 30 unadjusted trial balance of Bluefield Enterprises showed a balance of $4,755 in the Prepaid Advertising account. Of this amount, $2,500 remains to be used in the next fiscal year, beginning on July 1.	
3. Shepard Corporation has three manufacturing buildings, and maintains one Spare Parts account for all the buildings. At year end, the unadjusted trial balance shows a balance of $10,500 in the Spare Parts account. A physical count shows $1,525 of spare parts on hand in Building 1, $275 remaining in Building 2, and $750 unused in Building 3.	
4. On January 1, the beginning balance in Prepaid Insurance was $3,000. On April 5, $2,250 was paid to Jones Insurance Agency, and on September 3, $17,150 was paid to Smith Agency. At year end, one-fourth of the current year payments remains still in force.	

Answers

Description	Answer
1. The Office Supplies account of Greenbriar Company had a January 1 balance of $3,720. During the year, $7,815 of supplies were purchased. At year end, supplies on hand were $1,900.	$3,720 + $7,815 − 0 = $11,535 unadjusted account balance $11,535 − $1,900 = $9,635 adjustment
2. The year-end unadjusted trial balance of Bluefield Enterprises showed a balance of $4,755 in the Prepaid Advertising account. Of this amount, $2,500 remains to be used in the next fiscal year, beginning on July 1.	$4,755 − $2,500 = $2,255 adjustment
3. Shepard Corporation has three manufacturing buildings, and maintains one Spare Parts account for all the buildings. At year end, the unadjusted trial balance shows a balance of $10,500 in the Spare Parts account. A physical count shows $1,525 of spare parts on hand in Building 1, $275 remaining in Building 2, and $750 unused in Building 3.	$10,500 − ($1,525 + $275 + $750) = $7,950 adjustment
4. On January 1, the beginning balance in Prepaid Insurance was $3,000. On April 5, $2,250 was paid to Jones Insurance Agency, and on September 3, $17,150 was paid to Smith Agency. At year end, one-fourth of the current year payments remains still in force.	$3,000 + ($2,250 + $17,150) − 0 = $22,400 unadjusted account balance. ($2,250 + $17,150) × 1/4 = $4,850 (portion of the asset still unused). Therefore, $22,400 − $4,850 = $17,550 adjustment. (Notice that you had to calculate *both* the unadjusted account balance *and* the actual balance before you could subtract!)

■ Using Information Type 2: The Asset Cost Used Up

If the key information is . . .	then to calculate the asset cost used up . . .
the asset cost (the prepaid expense) already used up in the current period,	use the dollar amount given as the cost asset used up.

Example

■ "The amount of the prepaid insurance expired during the year was $2,700."

Calculation:
There is no calculation. The cost used up is the dollar amount given: $2,700.

■ "The $2,700 payment for Prepaid Insurance on February 12 was for the remainder of the current year."

Calculation:
There is no calculation. At year end, the cost used up is the dollar amount given: the full $2,700.

Calculate the Portion of Asset Cost Used Up

The prior two examples *directly* indicate the amount of cost used up as a given dollar amount. Sometimes cost used up information is presented indirectly, as a portion of an asset.

The "portion" of asset cost used up means some single, lump-sum part of the asset, expressed as a fraction, a percent, or information about the account balance. You can think of a portion as a single piece or "chunk" of the asset.

Note: Usually, the portion is less than the entire amount of the asset. However, occasionally it may even be the entire asset.

■ Using Information Type 2: The Asset Cost Used Up, *continued*

How Do I Identify a "Portion"?

Information that indicates a portion may be presented to you as a fraction, a percent, or an account balance. *Remember:* What is common in all of the ways is that the information refers to some single piece or "chunk" of the asset. (See table below.)

To identify a portion used up . . .		
Look for information presented as a . . .	**Portion Information**	**Calculation**
fraction used up.	"$3,000 for prepaid insurance was paid on April 1. By year end, 9/10 of the insurance had been used up."	$3,000 × 9/10 = $2,700 cost used up
percent used up.	"$3,000 for prepaid insurance was paid on April 1. By December 31, 90% of it had been used up."	$3,000 × .9 = $2,700 cost used up
beginning or ending account balance, that is partially or fully used up.	■ *Beginning balance example:* "The January 1 balance in Prepaid Insurance was $1,100. This was the balance from a one-year prepayment made in the prior year." ■ *Ending balance example:* "On the year-end June 30 trial balance, the $1,700 balance of Prepaid Insurance represents the insurance for May and June." ■ *Ending balance example:* "On the year-end June 30 trial balance, the $1,800 balance of Prepaid Insurance represents the insurance for May, June, and July."	■ A balance from last year will fully expire this year if it was for a year or less. Cost used up is entire $1,100. ■ Because June 30 is the year end, any amount for May and June must have fully expired. Cost used up: entire $1,700. ■ Two-thirds of $1,800 has been used for May and June. $1,800 × 2/3 = $1,200

Check Your Understanding

On a separate piece of paper, calculate the amount of the adjustment for each of the Type 2 information (asset used up) situations below. Answers are below.

Description	Answer
1. The records of Waukesha Partnership show that $12,000 of prepaid advertising was consumed during the past fiscal year.	(Reminder: Use a separate sheet of paper to complete the table.)
2. At year end, the unadjusted trial balance of La Cross Company showed $15,900 of Prepaid Insurance. A study of the policies indicates that 40% of the insurance was used up.	
3. On the December 31 unadjusted trial balance of Baraboo Company, $4,500 of the balance in the Prepaid Rent account represents the rent for the period September 1–December 31.	
4. On January 1, the balance in Prepaid Insurance was $3,000. On April 5, $2,500 was paid to Jones Insurance Agency, and on September 3, $17,150 was paid to Smith Agency. At year end, three-fourths of the unadjusted account balance had been used.	

Answers

Description	Answer
1. The records of Waukesha Partnership show that $12,000 of prepaid advertising was consumed during the past fiscal year.	$12,000 adjustment
2. At year end, the unadjusted trial balance of La Cross Company showed $15,900 of Prepaid Insurance. A study of the policies indicates that 40% of the insurance was used up.	$15,900 × .4 = $6,360 adjustment (portion of the asset used up)
3. On the December 31 unadjusted trial balance of Baraboo Company, $4,500 of the balance in the Prepaid Rent account represents the rent for the period September 1–December 31.	$4,500 adjustment (portion of the asset used up)
4. On January 1, the balance in Prepaid Insurance was $3,000. On April 5, $2,500 was paid to Jones Insurance Agency, and on September 3, $17,150 was paid to Smith Agency. At year end, three-fourths of the unadjusted account balance had been used.	$3,000 + ($2,500 + $17,150) – 0 = $22,650 account balance $22,650 × 3/4 = $16,988 (rounded) adjustment (portion of the asset used up)

■ Using Information Type 3: The Cost Per Unit of the Asset

Introduction

Cost per unit is really just a different way of determining the cost used up. However, it is easier to see cost per unit as a separate information type.

If the key information is . . .	then to calculate the asset cost used up . . .
the cost per unit of the asset, or information you can use to calculate the cost per unit,	determine units used up, then (cost per unit) × (units used) is cost used up.

Note: If you need to calculate the cost per unit, the calculation is:

total $ cost of units purchased / total units purchased = cost per unit

Examples: Using Cost Per Unit to Calculate Total Expense

■ **Cost per unit of the asset is given.**
"From April 1 to December 31, the company used up prepaid insurance in the amount of *$300 per month*. What is the adjustment on December 31, year end?" (We know the cost per unit is $300 per month—units of time.)

Calculation of total expense:
April 1 to December 31 is 9 units (9 monthly units)
$300/month × 9 months = $2,700

■ **You have to calculate cost per unit.**
"On April 1, the company paid $3,600 for 12 months of fire insurance. It is now December 31, year end."

Calculation of cost per unit:
$3,600 (cost of units purchased)/12 months (units purchased is months of coverage) = $300 per month

Calculation of total expense:
April 1 to December 31 is 9 units (9 monthly units)
$300/month × 9 months = $2,700 total cost used up

continued ▶

■ Using Information Type 3: The Cost Per Unit of the Asset, *continued*

*Identifying the
Kind of Units*

Assets provide different kinds of benefits. These benefits are measured in different kinds of units. You will see three basic kinds of units:

Goods:
■ Physical units (things you can feel or see)

Services:
■ Job units
■ Time units

To use the key information correctly, be sure that you understand exactly what kind of units is being used up as the prepaid item expires.

Examples of units:
■ **Physical units:** Supplies used up, meals consumed
■ **Job units:** A car wash job, a theater performance, a repair job
■ **Time units:** Months of interest, weeks of rent, hours of repair service, days of gardening service, months of insurance coverage

TIP

Things that are provided or supplied are often called "deliverables." A *deliverable* can be either goods or services, measured in any kind of units.

Check Your Understanding

On a separate piece of paper, calculate the amount of the adjustment for each of the Type 3 information (cost per unit) situations below. Answers are on page 96.

Description	Answers
1. In February, Hastings Partnership prepaid for 100 service repair visits. So far this year, 32 service visits have been charged against the account, at a cost of $250 per visit.	(Reminder: Use a separate sheet of paper to complete the table.)
2. On March 1, Omaha Company paid $324 for a 12-month magazine subscription, beginning in March. At year end, December 31, the Prepaid Subscription account still shows a balance of $324.	
3. At December 31, the Prepaid Insurance account of Scottsbluff Enterprises shows the following: Prepaid Insurance Jan. 1 3,750 Sept. 30 1,800 The January 1 amount represents the balance from a payment made last year that, on January 1, had 15 months remaining. The September 30 payment is for a 24-month insurance policy.	
4. Lincoln Company uses 1.5 gallons of lubricating oil for every 100 hours of machine operation. During the month, the machines operated 1,200 hours. Lubricating oil costs $22 per gallon.	

"Aim over there . . .
Type 3 (cost per unit)
prepaid expense
calculations!"

Answers

Description	Answers
1. In February, Hastings Partnership prepaid for 100 service repair visits. So far this year, 32 service visits have been charged against the account, at a cost of $250 per visit.	32 visits ("jobs") × $250 = $8,000 adjustment
2. On March 1, Omaha Company paid $324 for a 12-month magazine subscription, beginning in March. At year end, December 31, the Prepaid Subscription account still shows a balance of $324.	$324/12 magazines = $27 per magazine $27 × 10 magazines = $270 adjustment
3. At December 31, the Prepaid Insurance account of Scottsbluff Enterprises shows the following: Prepaid Insurance Jan. 1 3,750 Sept. 30 1,800 The January 1 amount represents the balance from a payment made last year that, on January 1, had 15 months remaining. The September 30 payment is for a 24-month insurance policy.	For the beginning balance, $3,750/15 = $250 per month For 12 months, $250 × 12 = $3,000 adjustment For the September 30 payment, $1,800/24 = $75 per month For three months (October, November, and December), 3 × $75 = $225 Total adjustment: $3,000 + $225 = $3,225
4. Lincoln Company uses 1.5 gallons of lubricating oil for every 100 hours of machine operation. During the month, the machines operated 1,200 hours. Lubricating oil costs $22 per gallon.	1.5 gallons of oil costs a total of 1.5 × $22 = $33. This will be the cost for 100 hours of machine time, or $33/100 = $.33 per hour. 1,200 hours × $.33 = $396 adjustment

■ Using Combinations of Information Types

Overview

You may encounter accounts in which there are:

- multiple items of the same information type, or
- multiple items of different information types.

Although this results in multiple items to evaluate for one account, the methods for dealing with the individual information types are exactly the same.

■ Using Combinations of Information Types, *continued*

Examples

■ **Actual cost remaining for three items:** "The Prepaid Insurance account shows that during the current year ending December 31, three different insurance policies were prepaid as follows:

- January 12: $2,500
- April 27: $750
- November 15: $2,700

At year end, the unexpired balances are:

- from January 12: $500
- from April 27: –0–
- from November 15: $1,250."

■ **Combination of Type #2 and Type #3:** The Prepaid Repairs account shows the following:

	Prepaid Repairs
Balance Jan. 1	3,000
May 1	900
Nov. 30	1,500

"The beginning balance of $3,000 is for a one-year repair service contract that was prepaid last year. The May 1 item is a nine-month repair service contract, and the November item is for a 10-month repair service contract. The current accounting period is the year ending December 31."

Rule

Using the same methods you have learned, determine the cost used up for each information item *individually*. Then add the individual costs used up to get the total cost used up for the entire account.

continued

■ **Using Combinations of Information Types,** *continued*

Examples of Applying the Rule

The first example on the prior page has three different items for Information Type 1. Following the usual procedure for this information type, we subtract the actual ending balance from the account balance for *each* item:

Cost used up:

$2,500 – $500   = $2,000
$750 – $0   = $750
$2,700 – $1,250 = $1,450
                       $4,200   **total cost used up**

In the second example, you need to recognize that the January 1 balance is a beginning balance that is fully used up (Information Type 2—the asset cost used up). The May 1 and November 30 are Type 3—items for which you can calculate the cost per unit of the asset.

Cost used up:

Jan. 1:	$3,000	(fully consumed in the current period)
May 1:	$800	= $100 × 8 months ($900/9 months = $100 per month)
Nov. 30:	$150	= $150 × 1 month ($1,500/10 months = $150 per month)
	$3,950	**total cost used up**

"Cool! Combined information types."

Step 3: Prepare the Adjusting Journal Entry

Overview	After the amount of the adjustment (the asset cost used up) has been calculated, the journal entry can be prepared.

Journal Entry Format

The basic format of the adjusting journal entry is:

	Dr.	Cr.
Expense	$$$	
Prepaid Expense		$$$

Example with Prepaid Insurance (page 93)

$$A \downarrow \quad = \quad L \quad + \quad SE \downarrow$$

Prepaid Insurance		Insurance Expense
− 2,700		+ 2,700

Journal entry:

December 31	Insurance Expense	2,700	
	Prepaid Insurance		2,700

Note: Adjusting a prepaid expense recorded as an asset always makes the asset decrease and an expense increase.

If the Adjustment Is NOT Done . . .

If the prepaid expense adjustment is not done, the financial statements will be incorrect.

Balance sheet:
- ↑ **Assets** will be overstated because some of the prepaid item has been used up, but it was not recorded.
- ↑ **Stockholders' equity** will be overstated because net income will be overstated.

Income statement:
- ↑ **Net income** will be overstated because some expense has not been recorded.

"If the adjustment is NOT done . . ."

continued ▶

Step 3: Prepare the Adjusting Journal Entry, *continued*

Verify the Asset Balance Whenever Possible . . .

If you used key Information Type 2 or Type 3, see if you have enough information so you can verify the final asset balance after the adjustment is done. For example, on page 91 you read: "$3,000 for prepaid insurance was paid on April 1. By December 31, 90% of it had been used up." The adjustment amount was $2,700.

Here, you have enough information to verify what the asset balance should be:

If 90% was used, there should be **10% remaining** after the adjustment, or $3,000 × .1 = $300. The adjustment must result in this final asset balance. If it does not, you must change the amount of the adjustment so the asset account shows the actual amount—the $300—that is remaining.

Summary of All Objective I Steps

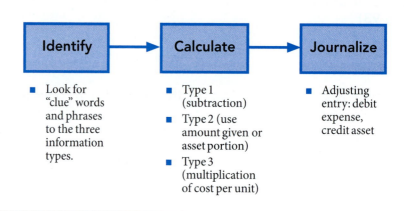

Identify	Calculate	Journalize
■ Look for "clue" words and phrases to the three information types.	■ Type 1 (subtraction) ■ Type 2 (use amount given or asset portion) ■ Type 3 (multiplication of cost per unit)	■ Adjusting entry: debit expense, credit asset

Objective II: Determine the New Balances of the Accounts Affected

Three Easy Steps

Overview

It is often important to know what the final account balances will be for the accounts, after the adjustments have been made.

Step 1: Identify the Adjusting Journal Entry

Suppose that the Prepaid Insurance and Insurance Expense accounts have been adjusted to record using up $2,700 of prepaid insurance. You identify the adjusting journal entry as the following:

Insurance Expense	2,700	
Prepaid Insurance		2,700

Step 2: Set Up T Accounts with the Account Names and the Unadjusted Account Balances

Locate the Prepaid Insurance account and the Insurance Expense account in either the trial balance or the ledger. On a separate piece of paper, draw T accounts with the names and unadjusted balances of these accounts.

Assume that these two accounts have the following unadjusted balances:

Prepaid Insurance		Insurance Expense	
3,000		–0–	

Step 3: Debit the Expense and Credit the Asset, and Calculate the New Account Balances

Enter the debits or credits from the adjusting entry into the accounts. Here, a debit of 2,700 is entered in Insurance Expense, and a credit of 2,700 is entered in Prepaid Insurance.

Prepaid Insurance		Insurance Expense	
3,000		–0–	
	2,700	2,700	
300		2,700	

Result: The new balance of Prepaid Insurance is $300, and the new balance of Insurance Expense is $2,700.

PRACTICE   Learning Goal 4 Appendix, Part I

Solutions are in the disk at the back of the book and at: www.worthyjames.com

Appendix Part I is about making adjustments for prepaid expenses (also called deferred expenses). Use these questions and problems to practice what you have learned.

Reinforcement Problems

Instructions: On a separate piece of paper, complete the table below. For each separate example, write in the middle column which one of the three key types of prepaid expense information is being given to you. Next, in the right column, explain what kind of calculation you need to do, without actually doing the calculation. Use the first item as an example.

LG A4-1.

Information Example	The key information type is . . .	To determine the cost used up, you need to . . .
1. On April 1, Madison Company prepaid $1,750 for five service repair calls. On June 30, the trial balance shows a balance of $1,750 in the Prepaid Repairs account, after three repair jobs have been done.	the cost per unit of the asset (5 service jobs)	calculate the cost per unit of the asset (in units of jobs)
2. The balance of the Spare Parts Supplies account on the trial balance is $14,550. A physical count shows $1,500 of the supplies remaining at year end.	**(Reminder: Use a separate sheet of paper to complete the table.)**	
3. On October 1, Fox Valley Company purchased a 12-month fire insurance policy for $9,000. The year-end trial balance on January 31 shows $9,000 of Prepaid Fire Insurance. The trial balance also shows $2,500 of Insurance Expense, which does not include the cost of any fire insurance.		
4. Wisconsin Grand Hotel provides each guest with a complimentary bar of soap. The unadjusted trial balance shows $17,500 of soap supplies at year end. At year end, a physical count shows $3,500 of soap supplies actually remaining. (Soap Expense is recorded only at year end.)		
5. Blue Mountain Corporation has a December 31 year end. On December 31, year end, an analysis of the unadjusted balance of the Prepaid Insurance shows: Policy Type / Date Purchased / Amount Fire / July 10 / $5,000 Liability / May 1 / $2,100 Flood / Oct. 20 / $7,500 The insurance agent verifies that $900 worth of the fire policy is still in force, as well as $1,000 of the liability policy and $2,750 of the flood policy.		

PRACTICE

Reinforcement Problems, *continued*

LG A4-1, *continued*

Information Example	The key information type is . . .	To determine the cost used up, you need to . . .
6. On June 30, year end, the trial balance of Milwaukee Company showed an ending balance of $2,110 in the Prepaid Rent account. This represents the rent for May and June.		
7. On December 31, year end, the Prepaid Insurance account of Moraine Park Company shows: **Prepaid Insurance** Beg. Bal. Jan. 1 2,500 Oct. 1 9,000 The beginning balance is the unexpired part of a one-year policy purchased in the prior year. The October amount is for a three-year policy.		
8. At the beginning of the year, the Prepaid Rent account had a balance of $1,300, and during the year $10,700 of additional prepayments were made. The amount of Prepaid Rent in force at year end is $3,000.		
9. At year end, the Prepaid Rent account balance shows as $12,000. 75% of this balance expired during the year. The remaining 25% will be used next year.		
10. The June 30 trial balance of Waukesha Company shows prepaid interest of $5,000 for money borrowed on June 1. Interest expense is incurred at $1,500 per month. No interest expense has been recorded.		
11. Springfield Company, which has a December 31 year end, shows the following in the Prepaid Advertising account: **Prepaid Advertising** Jan. 1 2,000 May 1 4,500 Nov. 1 4,500 The advertising is purchased semiannually.		

PRACTICE

Solutions are in the disk at the back of the book and at: www.worthyjames.com

LG A4-2. Do the adjustment and verify new account balances. After you check the answers for items 1 through 11, on separate piece of paper, for each item:

- Calculate the amount of the adjustment.
- Make the journal entry.
- Determine the new balances of the accounts affected.

Your Questions?

It is *very* important to be aware of what you need to understand better. What do you need to understand better about this learning goal? On a separate piece of paper, write the questions that you want to discuss with your classmates, instructor, or supervisor. Try to be very specific about what is bothering you, such as explanations that you do not fully understand.

APPENDIX PART II

Appendix Part II to Learning Goal 4

In Part II, you will find:

A Closer Look at Unearned Revenue

Identify Unearned Revenues

Overview

There are five basic adjustment types. This part is about:

Prepaid Expense	Unearned Revenue	Depreciation	Accrued Revenue	Accrued Expense

Definition

An *unearned revenue* is an advance payment received from a customer for future goods or services and is recorded as a liability at the time cash is received (debit cash, credit unearned revenue). An unearned revenue becomes a revenue later, when the goods or services are provided—usually within a year.

Synonym

An unearned revenue is also called a *deferred revenue*.

Why an Unearned Revenue Is a Liability

Do not be fooled because the word "revenue" is in the term "unearned revenue." An unearned revenue is always a liability. An unearned revenue is a liability because, until the business provides the goods or services, there is an obligation to return the money. Later, when the goods or services are actually provided, the liability is reduced and revenue of the same amount is recorded.

Examples

The table below shows you examples of common unearned revenue items.

Cash is received because . . .	and a *liability* is recorded that is called . . .	which is later eliminated when . . .	so a *revenue* adjustment will be needed, called . . .
a magazine publisher receives $120 for a 12-month subscription,	Unearned Subscription Revenue,	magazines are delivered monthly and $10 per month is earned,	Subscription Revenue.
a landlord receives six months' rent in advance,	Unearned Rent,	time passes and the rent is earned,	Rent Revenue.
an airline receives $750 for a round-trip flight two months from now,	Unearned Passenger Revenue, (unless the ticket is nonrefundable, in which case it would be revenue)	the customer travels on the airline,	Passenger Revenue.

Identify Unearned Revenues, *continued*

Examples That Are
NOT Unearned Revenue

- *Borrow money:* The loan must be paid back in cash—the bank is not a customer.
- *Stockholders' investment:* There is no obligation to provide anything back unless the business is liquidated.
- *Receive payment from customers for this month's services:* Nothing is paid in advance—the cash has already been earned.

TIP

Do not let the word "revenue" fool you. Whenever you see the word "unearned" in front of the word "revenue," the item is always a liability.

How the Liability Becomes a Revenue

Debit Liability,
Credit Revenue

Whenever unearned revenue (a liability) has been earned, it must be reduced and recorded as revenue. The revenue is recorded by making an adjusting entry at the end of the accounting period, when you know how much of the unearned revenue has been earned.

Also, it is possible that the earning process may take place over one, two, or more accounting periods. In this case, at the end of each accounting period before the financial statements are prepared, an adjustment is recorded. The adjustment always reduces the unearned revenue liability by the amount that has been earned:

Unearned Revenue		Fees Revenue	
$ adjustment			$ adjustment

Assets = Liabilities ↓ + Stockholders' Equity ↑

How to Adjust Unearned Revenues

The Two Objectives

Introduction

At this point, we assume that you have learned what an unearned revenue is and why it often needs to be adjusted. If you do not feel sure about this, review the prior material on page 106.

The Two Objectives

The adjustment procedures for unearned revenue are performed with the intention of completing two objectives:

1. Prepare the adjusting journal entry.
2. Determine the new balances of the accounts affected.

You may be asked to complete only the first objective or both of them. The detailed procedures for the two objectives are presented as separate topics in the material that follows this discussion.

Overview of the Two Objectives

The following two tables show an overview of the important steps that accomplish the two objectives. (Forthcoming pages discuss each step.)

Objective I: Prepare the Adjusting Journal Entry		
Step	**Action**	**Example**
1	Identify the key information type.	*Any* of these: ■ The unearned revenue actually remaining ■ The unearned revenue that was earned ■ The unearned revenue per unit
2	Calculate the revenue earned.	Calculation depends on the type of information given.

3	Prepare the adjusting journal entry.	*Example:* $300 of liability earned
		
		                         Dr. Cr.
		Liability 300
		    Revenue 300

continued ▶

The Two Objectives, *continued*

	Objective II: Determine the New Balances of the Accounts Affected	
Step	**Action**	**Example**
1	Identify the adjusting journal entry.	From Objective I
2	Set up T accounts with the account names and the unadjusted account balances.	**Liability** **Revenue** \$\$ · · \$\$
3	Debit the liability and credit the revenue, and calculate the new account balances.	**Liability** **Revenue** \$\$ · \$\$ **300** · **300** \$\$ · \$\$

"Wait a minute . . . aren't these the same two objectives as for prepaid expenses?"

Objective I: Prepare the Adjusting Journal Entry

Step 1: Identify the Key Information Type

Overview of the Three Information Types

The single most important step in doing the adjustment procedure is identifying the key information types. You will not always be given the same kind of information about unearned revenues. Three possible types of information concerning unearned revenues might be given to you:

1. The unearned revenue actually remaining
2. The unearned revenue that was earned
3. The unearned revenue per unit

Your job is to correctly use whatever kind of information is given to you when you calculate the adjustment. Each of the information types is discussed below.

Type 1: The Unearned Revenue Actually Remaining

- **What it means:** "The unearned revenue actually remaining" means the unearned revenue that is *actually still remaining at the end of the accounting period.* It has not yet been earned. Therefore, it is still a liability. This is the amount of the unearned revenue item that actually still exists, regardless of what the accounting records might show.

- **"Clue" words:** The following descriptive words are frequently used to refer to the amount of unearned revenue liability actually still remaining:

  - actual
  - still outstanding
  - still owing
  - remaining
  - will be earned in (next year, next month, etc.)
  - not yet earned
  - still unearned
  - liability for
  - deferred
  - unexpired

  Examples:

  - "The remaining amount of unearned rent is $1,000."
  - "The amount of rent still unearned is $1,000."
  - "The $1,000 balance of unearned rent will be earned in the next fiscal year."
  - "The deferred rent revenue as of year end is $1,000."

Step 1: Identify the Key Information Type, *continued*

Type 2:
The Unearned
Revenue That
Was Earned

■ **What it means:** "The unearned revenue that was earned" means how much the unearned revenue should be reduced. The unearned revenue is reduced because goods or services were provided to the customer that had made the advance payment.

■ **"Clue" words:** The following descriptive words are frequently used to refer to the amount of the liability that was earned:

- earned
- provided (to)
- performed
- sold
- supplied

- shipped
- completed
- revenue from
- income from
- billed

■ **Two ways it can be given**

1. *The revenue amount is given directly, as a dollar amount.*

Examples:

- "Atlanta Company received a $1,500 advance payment from a customer for consulting services. Two weeks later, the company performed $750 of services for the customer."
- "Albany Enterprises earned $500 of the Unearned Advertising Revenue."
- Jamestown Company, which had received an advance payment of $12,000, billed the customer for $3,000 of services provided.

2. *The revenue amount is given indirectly, as some fraction or percent.*

Examples:

- "Atlanta Company received a $1,500 advance payment from a customer for consulting services. Two weeks later, the company performed *one-half* of services for the customer."
- "Columbus Company received a $10,000 advance payment for merchandise. If Columbus Company shipped *20%* of the merchandise, what should the adjustment be at year end?"
- "Jamestown Company, which had received an advance payment of $12,000, provided *25%* of the services and billed the customer."

continued ▶

Step 1: Identify the Key Information Type, *continued*

Type 3:
The Unearned
Revenue Per Unit

■ **What it means:** *The unearned revenue **per unit** refers to allocating an equal amount of the unearned revenue to each unit of service or product that the customer has paid for.*

■ **Two ways it can be given:**

1. *The unearned revenue per unit is given directly.* Key words like "at the rate of," "per," and "for each" indicate an amount per unit. Also, "weekly," "monthly," etc.

   Examples:

   - "The unearned revenue was earned at the rate of $100 per month."
   - "The liability for unearned revenue decreased $250 for each job performed."
   - "The company signed a contract for a $300 monthly fixed fee."

2. *Information is given so you can calculate unearned revenue per unit.* Instead of unearned revenue per unit being directly given to you, sometimes information is given so that you can calculate it. **You always know you have unearned revenue per unit information when:**

   - you are given a *total dollar amount of the customer advance*, and
   - you know *how many units* of goods or services are to be provided. The "units" can be physical units, job units, or time units.

The table below shows examples of the two ways unearned revenue per unit can be given.

Examples

For unearned revenue per unit, you can be given . . .	
The unearned revenue per unit . . .	**. . . or information that allows you to calculate unearned revenue per unit**
■ "The amount received in advance for the magazine subscription is $10 per issue." (units of issues) ■ "The advance payment received for the service contract is for $100 for each service call." (units of service calls) ■ "The unearned insurance revenue earned monthly was $1,000." (units of time—in months)	■ "The subscription for the 12 issues of magazines is $120." (units of issues) ■ "The company received $2,000 for a service contract and agreed to provide 20 service calls." (units of jobs) ■ "On December 1, an insurance company received $5,000 for five months of fire insurance coverage." (units of time—in months)

continued ▶

Step 1: Identify the Key Information Type, *continued*

No Particular Order

If you have a situation in which you think several unearned revenue accounts might need adjustment, you can select any account first. When looking for key information, or when deciding which unearned revenue account might need adjustment, there is no particular order. You can select any unearned revenue account and look for information about that account.

Check Your Understanding

Find the "clue" words. Each of the phrases below is taken from quiz and test questions about making adjustments to unearned revenue accounts. See if you can find the identifying "clue" words in each phrase. The first phrase of each information type is underlined for you as an example. Answers are on page 114.

Type 1: The unearned revenue actually remaining
- "As of the end of the month, the amount of unearned rent still unearned was $750."
- "At the end of the month, the amount of the unearned rent remaining was $3,000."
- "On the date of the trial balance, the remaining deferred fees were $900."
- "On the date of the trial balance, the liability for unearned service revenue was $5,000."
- "As of year end, $3,500 of unearned insurance revenue will be earned in the next period."

Type 2: The unearned revenue that was earned
- "Jacksonville Company earned $300 of the unearned revenue it had received."
- "Gainesville Company forgot to record a $950 decrease in unearned revenue for services it had performed."
- "Winter Haven Furniture Company received an advance payment of $5,000 for office furniture, which was shipped to the customer before the end of the accounting period."
- "At the beginning of the year, the Pensacola Company ledger balance showed $8,000 of unearned revenue. During the year, the company provided $7,000 of services."
- "On September 12, Panama City Partnership received a $900 advance payment for advertising services. On October 31, year end, one-third of the services had been completed."

Type 3: The unearned revenue per unit (underline the words that indicate revenue earned per unit or that give the information to calculate revenue earned per unit)
- "On July 1, the insurance company received a $3,600 payment for one year of insurance coverage."
- "Unearned revenue expires at the rate of $300 per month."
- "On March 1, $1,800 was received as prepaid rent for the months of August through January."
- "The advance payment received for the service contract was $5,000 for 50 service calls."
- "Riverside Company received $7,500 for 750 hours of prepaid advertising services."
- "The weekly fixed fee was $350."

Answers

Type 1: The unearned revenue actually remaining
- "As of the end of the month, the amount of unearned rent <u>still unearned</u> was $750."
- "At the end of the month, the amount of the unearned rent <u>remaining</u> was $3,000."
- "On the date of the trial balance, the <u>remaining</u> deferred fees were $900."
- "On the date of the trial balance, the <u>liability for</u> unearned service revenue was $5,000."
- "As of year end, $3,500 of unearned insurance revenue will be <u>earned in the next period</u>."

Type 2: The unearned revenue that was earned
- "Jacksonville Company <u>earned</u> $300 of the unearned revenue it had received."
- "Gainesville Company forgot to record a $950 decrease in unearned revenue for services it had <u>performed</u>."
- "Winter Haven Furniture Company received an advance payment of $5,000 for office furniture, which was <u>shipped</u> to the customer before the end of the accounting period."
- "At the beginning of the year, the Pensacola Company ledger balance showed $8,000 of unearned revenue. During the year, the company <u>provided</u> $7,000 of services."
- "On September 12, Panama City Partnership received a $900 advance payment for advertising services. On October 31, year end, one-third of the services had been <u>completed</u>."

Type 3: The unearned revenue per unit (underline the words that indicate revenue earned per unit or that give the information to calculate revenue earned per unit)
- "On July 1, the insurance company received a <u>$3,600 payment for one year</u> of insurance coverage."
- "Unearned revenue expires at the <u>rate of $300 per month</u>."
- "On March 1, <u>$1,800</u> was received as prepaid rent for the months of <u>August through January</u>."
- "The advance payment received for the service contract was <u>$5,000 for 50 service calls</u>."
- "Riverside Company received <u>$7,500 for 750 hours</u> of prepaid advertising services."
- "The <u>weekly</u> fixed fee was $350."

"Just look for the key words."

Check Your Understanding

Identify information types. In the table below, situations involving the three different key information types for unearned revenue are given to you. On a separate piece of paper, write which information type is being described. Each description refers to only one of the three types. Answers are below.

Description	Information Type
1. Van Nuys Company has $1,000 of unearned revenue still unearned at year end.	(Reminder: Use a separate sheet of paper to complete the table.)
2. Los Medanos Company earned $3,750 of the advance payments received from customers.	
3. Merced Enterprises received $9,000 from a tenant who prepaid six months' rent.	
4. At year end, the Evergreen Company has $5,000 of unearned revenue that will be earned next year.	
5. The $500 beginning balance in the Unearned Revenue account of Glendale Corporation represents advances for 50 weekly issues of magazines.	
6. 25% of the Unearned Service Revenue of Gavilan Corp. was earned during the year.	
7. Sylmar Airlines received $2,500 for advance ticket purchases. The purchases are for 10 flights.	
8. E. Z. Finance and Bank Company received $7,000 from a borrower for interest paid in advance. The advance payment was for three months.	

Answers

Description	Information Type
1. Van Nuys Company has $1,000 of unearned revenue still unearned at year end.	The unearned revenue actually remaining
2. Los Medanos Company earned $3,750 of the advance payments received from customers.	The unearned revenue that was earned
3. Merced Enterprises received $9,000 from a tenant who prepaid six months' rent.	The unearned revenue per unit (monthly units)
4. At year end, the Evergreen Company has $5,000 of unearned revenue that will be earned next year.	The unearned revenue actually remaining
5. The $500 beginning balance in the Unearned Revenue account of Glendale Corporation represents advances for 50 weekly issues of magazines.	The unearned revenue per unit (magazines)
6. 25% of the Unearned Service Revenue of Gavilan Corp. was earned during the year.	The unearned revenue that was earned
7. Sylmar Airlines received $2,500 for advance ticket purchases. The purchases are for 10 flights.	The unearned revenue per unit (units of airline flights)
8. E. Z. Finance and Bank Company received $7,000 from a borrower for interest paid in advance. The advance payment was for three months.	The unearned revenue per unit (monthly units)

Step 2: Select the Proper Method to Calculate the Revenue Earned

Introduction

In the previous topic, you learned how to *identify* the three types of key information that determine the method of calculation (Step 1). In the upcoming discussion, you will learn the second part of the process: how to *calculate* the amount of the unearned revenue liability that is decreased and recorded as revenue (Step 2).

Calculation Depends on Key Information

The kind of calculation you do is not the same every time—*it depends on which type of key information* is given to you.

Step 2: Select the Proper Method to Calculate the Revenue Earned, *continued*

Calculation Procedure Table

Each key information type may require you to consider several actions before doing the calculation. To see the actions that can apply to each information type, use the table below. Look down the column under the "yes" that applies to each information type. A "✓" marks an action that you must do or consider.

Detailed explanations for each "✓" can be found on the reference pages.

IF the key information type is . . .				. . . see page
Type 1: Unearned revenue actually remaining (given or calculated)	yes			110
Type 2: Unearned revenue that was earned (given or calculated)		yes		111
Type 3: Unearned revenue per unit (given or calculated)			yes	112

Then, to calculate the adjustment amount (the revenue earned) . . .				. . . see page
subtract the unearned revenue actually remaining from the unadjusted liability account balance.	✓			118
sometimes you first might have to calculate the unadjusted account balance or the portion of the unearned revenue actually remaining.	✓			119
the dollars of unearned revenue that were earned is given to you—no further calculation.		✓		121
sometimes you might have to calculate the portion that was earned.		✓		121
multiply the unearned revenue per unit times the units provided.			✓	124
sometimes you first might have to calculate the unearned revenue per unit.			✓	124

■ Using Information Type 1: The Unearned Revenue Actually Remaining

If the key information is . . .	then to calculate the decrease in the liability . . .
the unearned revenue actually remaining,	subtract the unearned revenue actually remaining from the unadjusted balance of the unearned revenue account.

Example

"The balance of unearned service revenue in the trial balance on December 31, year end, is $3,000. There is $300 of unearned revenue still unearned at year end."

Calculation:
$3,000 (unadjusted balance) − $300 (unearned revenue actually remaining) = $2,700 earned ($2,700 is the decrease in the liability)

Sometimes You Have to Calculate the Unadjusted Account Balance

Normally, after you have identified the unearned revenue actually remaining as the key information, you look for the unadjusted account balance. Then you subtract the amount actually remaining. But sometimes you cannot find the unadjusted account balance! Instead, you are given information about the activity in the account.

Example:
"At the beginning of the year, the balance of the Unearned Revenue account was $250. On March 3, a $1,950 customer advance was received. On September 5, another $800 was received. At year end, $300 of unearned revenue remained unearned."

Solution:
Use the formula below to calculate the account balance.

■ Using Information Type 1: The Unearned Revenue Actually Remaining, *continued*

Formula

> **beginning balance + advances recorded
> – decreases recorded = ending balance**

From the information above: $250 + ($1,950 + $800) – 0 = $3,000 balance.

TIP

During a period, receipts are usually recorded, but often decreases are not. A company will wait until the end of a period to record the total earned as a single adjustment to decrease the unearned revenue account. Notice in the example above that there *had not* been any reductions in unearned revenue during the period.

Sometimes You Have to Calculate the Unearned Revenue Remaining

Sometimes a problem does not directly tell you what actual remaining unearned revenue is. Instead, information is given so you can calculate what portion or "chunk" actually remains.

Examples

■ "During the year, Sammi and Bobbi partnership received $21,000 of advance payments. At year end, one-fifth of this amount was still unearned."

$21,000 × 1/5 = $4,200 still unearned

■ "Big Bear Corporation does earthquake retrofitting and requires a $50,000 advance payment for each job. During the year, it received $500,000 of advances, and at year end, seven jobs remain uncompleted."

$50,000 × 7 = $350,000 still unearned

Example of No Adjustment Required

If the actual balance of the unearned revenue item is the same as the unadjusted account balance, then no adjustment is required! The entries needed have already been done and the account balance is correct.

Example:
"On November 1, Mission Enterprises received $3,000 for six months of consulting services. On December 31, the actual balance still unperformed was $2,000. On the trial balance, the Unearned Revenue account shows a balance of $2,000."

Check Your Understanding

Using a separate piece of paper, calculate the amount of the adjustment for each of the Type 1 information (unearned revenue actually remaining) situations below. Answers are below.

Description	Answer
1. At month end, January 31, the Steamboat Springs Ski Lift Company has $12,300 in the Unearned Revenue account. The actual balance of unexpired ski lift tickets at that date is $2,400.	**(Reminder: Use a separate sheet of paper to complete the table.)**
2. During the year, Denver Insurance Company received $350,000 in advance payments for liability insurance policies, which were credited to Unearned Premiums Revenue. At year end, $291,000 worth of the payments was still unearned.	
3. On October 19, Greeley Advertising Company received 12,000 as an advance payment for advertising services to be provided. At year end, the company estimated that one-third of the services paid for in advance had not yet been earned.	
4. The Unearned Commission Revenue account of Littleton Real Estate Company at year end shows a beginning balance of $15,050 and receipts during the year of $112,450. (There were no debits against the account during the year.) Company records show $14,500 in commissions still unearned at year end.	

Answers

Description	Answer
1. At month end, January 31, the Steamboat Springs Ski Lift Company has $12,300 in the Unearned Revenue account. The actual balance of unexpired ski lift tickets at that date is $2,400.	$12,300 − $2,400 = $9,900 adjustment
2. During the year, Denver Insurance Company received $350,000 in advance payments for liability insurance policies, which were credited to Unearned Premiums Revenue. At year end, $291,000 worth of the payments was still unearned.	$350,000 − $291,000 = $59,000 adjustment
3. On October 19, Greeley Advertising Company received $12,000 as an advance payment for advertising services to be provided. At year end, the company estimated that one-third of the services paid for in advance had not yet been earned.	$12,000 × 1/3 = $4,000 (portion still unearned). $12,000 − $4,000 = $8,000 adjustment
4. The Unearned Commission Revenue account of Littleton Real Estate Company at year end shows a beginning balance of $15,050 and receipts during the year of $112,450. (There were no debits against the account during the year.) Company records show $14,500 in commissions still unearned at year end.	$15,050 + $112,450 − 0 = $127,500 unadjusted account balance. $127,500 − $14,500 = $113,000 adjustment

■ Using Information Type 2: The Unearned Revenue That Was Earned

If the key information is . . .	then to calculate the decrease in the liability . . .
the amount of the liability that was earned in the current period,	use the dollar amount earned that is given to you.

Example

"The amount of the unearned revenue earned during the year was $2,700."

Calculation:
There is no further calculation. The decrease in the unearned revenue liability is the dollar amount given to you: $2,700.

Calculate the Portion Earned

The prior example *directly* indicates the amount of revenue earned, as a dollar amount. However, sometimes revenue earned information is presented indirectly, as a portion of the liability, service, or product to be provided.

The "portion" means some single, lump-sum part of a liability, service, or product, expressed as a fraction, a percent, or information about an account balance. You can think of a portion as a single piece or "chunk" earned during a period.

> *Note:* Usually, the portion is less than the entire amount of the liability. However, occasionally it may even be the entire liability.

How Do I Identify a "Portion"?

Information that indicates a portion may be presented to you as a fraction, a percent, or an account balance. *Remember:* What is common in all the ways is that the information refers to some single piece or "chunk" of the obligation.

continued

■ Using Information Type 2: The Unearned Revenue That Was Earned, *continued*

To identify a portion earned . . .		
Look for information presented as a . . .	**Information example**	**Calculation**
fraction earned.	"$3,000 unearned rent was received from a tenant on April 1. By year end, 9/10 of the amount had been earned."	$3,000 × 9/10 = $2,700 amount earned
percent earned.	"$3,000 of unearned rent was received from a tenant on April 1. By December 31, 90% of it was earned."	$3,000 × .9 = $2,700 amount earned
beginning or ending account balance that is partially or fully earned.	■ *Beginning balance example:* "The January 1 balance in Unearned Rent was $1,100. This was the balance from a one-year prepayment received in the prior year." ■ *Ending balance example:* "On the year end June 30 trial balance, the $1,700 balance of Unearned Revenue was for services provided in May and June."	■ A balance from last year will be fully earned this year if it was for a year or less. Amount earned is the entire $1,100. ■ Because June 30 is the year end, any amount for May and June must now be fully earned. Revenue: entire $1,700

Check Your Understanding

Using a separate piece of paper, calculate the amount of the adjustment for each of the Type 2 information (unearned revenue that was earned) situations below. Answers are on page 123.

Description	Answer
1. During the year, Reno Antique Store calculates that it has earned $27,900 of the unearned revenue advances from customers.	(Reminder: Use a separate sheet of paper to complete the table.)
2. On June 25, Las Vegas Company received a $15,000 advance payment for consulting services. At year end, the company estimates that 75% of the services were provided.	
3. At December 31, year end, the unadjusted trial balance of Carson City Corporation shows $8,000 in the Unearned Rent account. $5,000 of this amount represents rent income for November and December, and the balance is for next year.	
4. On October 19, Truckee Advertising Company received $12,000 as an advance payment for advertising services to be provided. At year end, the company estimated that two-thirds of the services paid for in advance had been earned.	

"Look! Earned revenues!"

Description	Answer
1. During the year, Reno Antique Store calculates that it has earned $27,900 of the unearned revenue advances from customers.	$27,900 adjustment
2. On June 25, Las Vegas Company received a $15,000 advance payment for consulting services. At year end, the company estimates that 75% of the services were provided.	$15,000 × .75 = $11,250 adjustment (portion earned)
3. At December 31, year end, the unadjusted trial balance of Carson City Corporation shows $8,000 in the Unearned Rent account. $5,000 of this amount represents rent income for November and December, and the balance is for next year.	$5,000 adjustment (portion earned)
4. On October 19, Truckee Advertising Company received $12,000 as an advance payment for advertising services to be provided. At year end, the company estimated that two-thirds of the services paid for in advance had been earned.	$12,000 × 2/3 = $8,000 adjustment (portion earned)

■ Using Information Type 3: The Unearned Revenue Per Unit

Introduction

"Unearned revenue per unit" is really just a different way of determining the revenue that was earned. However, it is easier to see unearned revenue per unit as a separate information type.

If the key information is . . .	then to calculate the amount earned . . .
the unearned revenue per unit or information you can use to calculate the unearned revenue per unit,	■ determine the units provided, then ■ (unearned revenue per unit) × (units provided) is the amount earned.

Note: If you need to calculate unearned revenue per unit, the calculation is:

total $ of customer advance/total units to be provided to customer = unearned revenue per unit

Examples: Using Unearned Revenue Per Unit to Calculate Amount Earned

■ **Unearned revenue per unit is given.**
"From April 1 to December 31, the company earned advertising revenue in the amount of *$300 per month*. What is the adjustment on December 31, year end?" (We know the unearned revenue per unit must be $300 per month—units of time.)

Calculation of total amount earned:
April 1 to December 31 is 9 units (9 monthly units)
$300/month × 9 months = $2,700

■ **You have to calculate unearned revenue per unit.**
"On April 1, the company received $3,600 from a customer for 12 months of advertising services. What is the adjustment on December 31, year end?"

Calculation of unearned revenue per unit:
$3,600 (total advance received)/12 months (monthly units of service to be provided) = $300 per month

Calculation of total amount earned:
April 1 to December 31 is 9 units (9 monthly units)
$300/month × 9 months = $2,700

■ Using Information Type 3: The Unearned Revenue Per Unit, *continued*

Identifying the Kind of Units

Businesses receive advance payments from customers for many different kinds of goods or services. These goods and services are measured in different kinds of units. You will see three basic kinds of units:

Goods:
- Physical units (things you can see or feel)

Services:
- Job units
- Time units

To use the key information correctly, be sure that you understand exactly what kind of units are being used up as the prepaid item expires.

Examples of units:
- **Physical units:** Supplies used up, meals consumed, miles operated
- **Job units:** A car wash job, a theater performance, a repair job, telephone service
- **Time units:** Months of interest, weeks of rent, hours of repair service, days of gardening service, months of insurance coverage

"What kind of units did you have in mind?"

Check Your Understanding

On a separate piece of paper, calculate the amount of the adjustment for each of the Type 3 information (unearned revenue per unit) situations below. Answers are below.

Description	Answer
1. On July 31, Baytown Company received an advance payment of $7,000 for eight months of janitorial services. What adjustment is required at year end on December 31?	**(Reminder: Use a separate sheet of paper to complete the table.)**
2. Laredo Legal Corporation received an advance payment (called a "retainer") of $50,000 from a client to provide 200 hours of legal services. At the end of the current accounting period, 115 hours had been billed to the client.	
3. On August 31, Plano Aquarium Company signed a contract to provide 300 fish tanks. When the contract was signed, the company received $96,000. At year end, 130 of the fish tanks had been shipped to the customer.	
4. On November 1, Sherman Theater Company signed a contract to present 40 performances of "Macbeth" for a fee of $250,000. This was recorded as unearned revenue. By December 31, year end, 25 performances had been completed.	

Answers

Description	Answer
1. On July 31, Baytown Company received an advance payment of $7,000 for eight months of janitorial services. What adjustment is required at year end on December 31?	$7,000/8 = $875 per month. $875 × 5 months (August–December) = $4,375 adjustment
2. Laredo Legal Corporation received an advance payment (called a "retainer") of $50,000 from a client to provide 200 hours of legal services. At the end of the current accounting period, 115 hours had been billed to the client.	$50,000/200 = $250 per hour 115 hours × $250 = $28,750 adjustment
3. On August 31, Plano Aquarium Company signed a contract to provide 300 fish tanks. When the contract was signed, the company received $96,000. At year end, 130 of the fish tanks had been shipped to the customer.	$96,000/300 = $320 per fish tank 130 tanks shipped × $320 = $41,600 adjustment
4. On November 1, Sherman Theater Company signed a contract to present 40 performances of "Macbeth" for a fee of $250,000. This was recorded as unearned revenue. By December 31, year end, 25 performances had been completed.	$250,000/40 = $6,250 per performance (a "job") $6,250 × 25 = $156,250 adjustment

Check Your Understanding

Identify information types. In the table below, situations involving the three different key information types for unearned revenue are given to you. On a separate piece of paper, list which information type is being described. Each description refers to only one of the three types. Answers are below.

Description	Information Type
1. The balance in the Unearned Rent account of Louisquisset Pike Company is $3,600. The amount is a prepayment from a customer for three months' rent.	(Reminder: Use a separate sheet of paper to complete the table.)
2. The amount of Warwick Company's customer advances still unearned at December 31 is $12,300.	
3. During the month, Providence Enterprises performed $10,000 of services for a customer who had paid in advance.	
4. On June 1, Middletown Consulting Service received a $4,800 advance from a customer for 32 hours of consulting service. As of June 30, no services had yet been provided.	
5. On December 31, year end, the Pawtucket Company received an $800 advance from a customer for a job to be performed in January.	

Answers

Description	Information Type
1. The balance in the Unearned Rent account of Louisquisset Pike Company is $3,600. The amount is a prepayment from a customer for three months' rent.	the unearned revenue per unit
2. The amount of Warwick Company's customer advances still unearned at December 31 is $12,300.	the unearned revenue actually remaining
3. During the month, Providence Enterprises performed $10,000 of services for a customer who had paid in advance.	the unearned revenue that was earned
4. On June 1, Middletown Consulting Service received a $4,800 advance from a customer for 32 hours of consulting service. As of June 30, no services had yet been provided.	the unearned revenue per unit (per hour)
5. On December 31, year end, the Pawtucket Company received an $800 advance from a customer for a job to be performed in January.	the unearned revenue actually remaining

Step 3: Prepare the Adjusting Journal Entry

Journal Entry Format

The basic format of the adjusting journal entry is:

	Dr.	Cr.
Unearned Revenue	$$$	
Revenue		$$$

Example

Suppose that an insurance company had received an advance payment in the amount of $3,000 of which $2,700 has now been earned:

December 31	Unearned Revenue	2,700	
	Insurance Revenue		2,700

An adjustment to an unearned revenue recorded as a liability always makes a liability decrease and a revenue increase.

$$A \quad = \quad L\downarrow \quad + \quad SE\uparrow$$

A	=	L ↓	+	SE ↑
		Unearned		Insurance
		Revenue		Revenue
		−2,700		+2,700

If the Adjustment Is NOT Done . . .

If the unearned revenue is not reduced, financial statements will be incorrect.

Balance sheet:

↑ **Liabilities** will be overstated because some of the unearned revenue has been earned, but the decrease in the liability was not recorded.
↓ **Stockholders' equity** will be understated because net income will be understated.

Income statement:

↓ **Net income** will be understated because some revenue has not been recorded.

"If the adjustment is NOT done . . ."

Step 3: Prepare the Adjusting Journal Entry, *continued*

Verify the Liability Balance Whenever Possible . . .

If you used key Information Type 2 or Type 3, see if you have enough information so you can verify the final liability balance after the adjustment is done. For example, on page 124 you read, "On April 1, the company received $3,600 from a customer for 12 months of advertising services. What is the adjustment on December 31, year end?" The adjustment was $2,700.

Here, you have enough information to verify the liability balance:

If nine months' worth was earned, there should be **three months remaining** after the adjustment, or $300 × 3 = $900. The adjustment *must* result in this ending liability balance. If it does not, then you must change the amount of the adjustment, so the unearned revenue account shows $300 remaining.

Summary of Objective I Steps

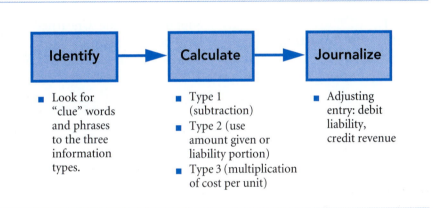

- Look for "clue" words and phrases to the three information types.

- Type 1 (subtraction)
- Type 2 (use amount given or liability portion)
- Type 3 (multiplication of cost per unit)

- Adjusting entry: debit liability, credit revenue

Objective II: Determine the New Balances of the Accounts Affected

Three Easy Steps

Overview

It is often important to know what the final account balances will be for the accounts that are adjusted. Why?

■ You may wish to know what certain account balances are before actually preparing the financial statements.
■ You may wish to know certain ledger account balances before the journal entries are all posted into the ledger.

Step 1:
Identify the Adjusting Journal Entry

Suppose that the Unearned Revenue and Insurance Revenue accounts have been adjusted to record the earning of $2,700 of unearned revenue. You identify the adjusting journal entry as the following:

Unearned Revenue	2,700	
Insurance Revenue		2,700

Step 2:
Set Up T Accounts with the Account Names and the Unadjusted Account Balances

Locate the Unearned Revenue account and the Insurance Revenue account in either the trial balance or the ledger. On a separate piece of paper, draw T accounts with the names and unadjusted balances of these accounts.

Assume that these two accounts have the following unadjusted balances:

Unearned Revenue	Insurance Revenue
3,000	–0–

Note: Sometimes account activity information may be given to you instead of the account balances. In this case, you can compute the unadjusted balances by using the simple formula in the prior discussion (see page 119).

Three Easy Steps, *continued*

Step 3:
Debit the Liability and Credit the Revenue, and Calculate the New Account Balances

Enter the debits and credits from the adjusting entry into the accounts. Here, a debit of $2,700 is entered in Unearned Revenue and a credit of 2,700 is entered in Insurance Revenue.

Unearned Revenue	
	3,000
2,700	
	300

Unearned Revenue	
	–0–
	2,700
	2,700

Result: The new balance of Unearned Revenue is $300 and the new balance of Insurance Revenue is $2,700.

Comparing the Two Deferrals

Prepaid Expense Compared to Unearned Revenue

Comparison

The table below compares the adjustments for prepaid expenses and unearned revenues that were recorded as assets and liabilities.

An adjustment to a prepaid expense always . . .	An adjustment to an unearned revenue always . . .
makes at least one asset account go down and one expense account go up	makes at least one liability account go down and one revenue account go up
has this affect on the accounting equation:	has this affect on the accounting equation:
$A \downarrow = L + SE \downarrow$ – Prepaid Expense + Expense	$A = L \downarrow + SE \uparrow$ – Unearned Revenue + Revenue

and has a journal entry that looks like this:
    (name) Expense $$$
        Prepaid Expense $$$
	and has a journal entry that looks like this:
	    Unearned Revenue $$$
	        (name) Revenue $$$

PRACTICE

Learning Goal 4 Appendix, Part II, continued

Solutions are in the disk at the back of the book and at: www.worthyjames.com

Reinforcement Problems

Which kind of information do you have? How do you use it? In Step 1 of the journalizing objective, it is very important to understand what kind of information you have about an account and how to use that information. Each of the descriptions below gives a key type of information about an unearned revenue item.

Instructions: On a separate piece of paper, complete the table. For each example, write in the middle column which one of the three key types of unearned revenue information is being given to you. In the right column, explain what kind of calculation you need to do, without actually doing the calculation. Use the first information item as an example.

LGA 4-3.

Information Example	The key information type is . . .	and to determine the total revenue earned (to decrease the liability) . . .
1. On April 1, Adirondack Rental Company received $1,750 for five months of equipment rental. The June 30 year-end trial balance shows a balance of $1,750 in the Unearned Rent Revenue account.	the unearned revenue per unit,	<ul><li>calculate the unearned revenue per unit (per month)</li><li>multiply by the number of units provided</li></ul>
2. The trial balance of Manhattan Company shows the balance in the Unearned Sales account as $4,040. A review of sales invoices shows that 75% of these orders was shipped.	(Reminder: Use a separate sheet of paper to complete the table.)	
3. On October 1, Erie Insurance, Inc. received a $9,000 payment for a 12-month insurance policy. The year-end trial balance on January 31 shows $9,000 of Unearned Revenue.		
4. The ledger of La Guardia Enterprises showed $25,000 of Unearned Service Revenue as a beginning balance. This is a balance from the prior year for six months of services. During this year, La Guardia received $52,000 of advance payments and earned $40,000 of them.		
5. The Nassau Company sells computer service contracts. Each $1,500 contract is good for 10 service repairs calls. All contracts sold are recorded as Unearned Revenue. During the quarter ended September 30, Nassau Company made 710 service calls.		
6. Suffolk Printing Partnership received a $10,000 advance payment on February 1, to print 5,000 calendars. By December 31, year end, 3,500 calendars were supplied to customers who made the prepayment.		

PRACTICE

LGA 4-3, *continued*

Information Example	The key information type is . . .	and to determine the total revenue earned (to decrease the liability) . . .
7. Queensborough Corporation's Unearned Revenue account showed an $8,000 balance at year end. $7,000 of the amount is for the last seven months' rent. The remainder is a deposit for the last month's rent that expires next year.		
8. On September 1, Kingsborough Banking Company made a loan that required the customer to prepay six months' interest in the amount of $9,000. On December 31, year end, the Kingsborough ledger showed: **Deferred Interest Revenue** | 9,000 **Interest Revenue** | 200,000		
9. On March 22, Suny Consulting Company received a $14,000 advance payment from a client. By June 30, year end, $1,500 of the advance was still not earned.		
10. On March 22, Suny Consulting Company received a $14,000 advance payment from a client. By June 30, year end, $12,500 of the advance had been earned.		
11. At year end, Hudson Valley Test Labs, Inc. has a Deferred Revenue account that shows a beginning balance of $50,000 from a prior year's five-month service contract. During the current year, the company received an advance payment of $200,000 to test 1,000 units. This was also recorded in Deferred Revenue. The company tested 212 units.		

LGA 4-4. Do the adjustment and verify new account balances. After you check the answers for items 1 through 11, on a separate piece of paper, for each item:

- Calculate the amount of the adjustment.
- Make the journal entry.
- Determine the new balances of the accounts affected.

APPENDIX PART III	# Appendix Part III to Learning Goal 4

In Part III, you will find:

A Closer Look at Depreciation

Overview of Depreciation

Overview

There are five basic adjustment types. This part is about:

Prepaid Expense	Unearned Revenue	Depreciation	Accrued Revenue	Accrued Expense

Definition: "Depreciation"

Depreciation is the process of allocating the cost of plant and equipment assets into expense, during their estimated useful lives, in a systematic and rational way.

Reason for Depreciation

Except for land, plant and equipment assets are used up and become expenses. The amount of the expense is the cost of the asset that is used up. However, the useful life of a plant and equipment asset will span many accounting periods. How do we record the expense of an asset that is used up over many accounting periods? We allocate some expense into each accounting period during the asset's useful life.

Overview of Depreciation, *continued*

Matching Principle	Depreciation is a good example of applying the ***matching principle***. The matching principle requires that the cost of any asset that is being used up must be recorded as an expense in each period that the asset helped to generate revenue.
Estimating the Life of an Asset	*There is a problem:* It is impossible to predict exactly what the useful life of a plant and equipment asset will be. For example, over how many years will the copy machine be used up and become an expense? Four years? Four and one-half years? Five years? More than that? Accountants can only make educated guesses based on past experience. Therefore, the cost of plant and equipment assets that is allocated to expense is based upon an *estimated* useful life for each asset.
Residual Value	Sometimes an asset will still have some value after the business is finished using it. Some small part of the original cost will be left over, and therefore should not be depreciated. This is called ***residual value***, or ***salvage value***. If possible, this amount should be estimated and not included in the depreciation. On the other hand, sometimes residual value cannot be estimated.

TIP

Do not make the common mistake of confusing accounting or financial depreciation with the everyday meaning of the word "depreciation." In everyday language, depreciation means loss of *value*. If you say, "When you buy a new car, it will depreciate $500 after the first day you own it," you are actually saying that the car will sell for $500 less—it has $500 less value.

However, in accounting, depreciation means the process of *matching expense against revenues*. The purpose is to record how much of the original cost of the asset is being used up each period as the asset helps the business to generate revenue. *This has nothing to do with whatever value an asset could be sold for.*

Overview of Plant and Equipment

Definition: "Plant and Equipment"	***Plant and equipment*** assets are tangible assets that have useful lives of more than a year. Often the useful lives may be many years.
Synonyms	Plant and equipment assets are also called ***plant assets, property, plant, and equipment*** or ***fixed assets***.

continued ▶

Overview of Plant and Equipment, *continued*

Definition: "Useful Life"	The **useful life** of an asset is the period of time that the asset can provide benefits and be useful to a business.
Definition: "Tangible Asset"	A **tangible asset** is one that can be touched—that has physical substance, like a desk. Unlike plant and equipment, some assets are **intangible assets** (for example, prepaid rent is the legal right to occupy space). A legal right is an asset, but it is not tangible.
Compare to Prepaid Expense	Just like prepaid expenses, plant and equipment assets are purchased first and then are used up in the future. The essential difference is that plant and equipment is used up over many years, whereas prepaid expenses usually last for less than a year. *Exception:* Land is normally not used up.

Examples of Plant and Equipment

- Building
- Truck
- Drilling equipment
- Aircraft
- Tools
- Computer
- Furniture
- Copy machine
- Boat
- Land (Land is not generally used up.)

Examples That Are NOT Plant and Equipment

- Supplies, because they are used up quickly (in less than a year)
- Prepaid insurance, because it is intangible (and is usually used up in less than a year)
- A patent, because it is intangible

Calculating Depreciation and Making the Adjusting Entry

Calculating the Amount of Depreciation

Overview

Depreciation can be calculated in various ways. (Learning Goal 19 discusses this in more detail.) However, the most common and simplest way to calculate depreciation is shown on page 140. It is called the ***straight-line depreciation***. With this method, an equal amount of depreciation expense is allocated to each period in the asset's estimated useful life.

Procedure

The table on page 140 shows you the three-step procedure for calculating the amount of straight-line depreciation for each accounting period.

continued ▶

Happy times for accountants: Calculating depreciation.

Calculating the Amount of Depreciation, *continued*

Step	Action	Example
1	Estimate the useful life of the asset in whatever length of accounting period is being used (usually years or months). *Note:* Choose the shortest time that it will take for the asset to be either used up, to deteriorate, or to become obsolete.	The Fine Cookware Company buys a new computer. The company prepares annual financial statements. The computer can continue to operate for 7 to 10 years, but it will probably be obsolete in 5 years. The accountants choose 5 years as the estimated life. (If the company prepared monthly statements, the accountants would convert the 5 years into months: 5 years × 12 months per year = 60 months.)
2	Divide the cost of the asset by the estimated useful life. (If there is estimated residual value, subtract this from the cost.)	*Formula:* (Asset Cost − Residual Value) / Estimated Useful Life = Depreciation Expense The Fine Cookware Company paid $3,600 for its new computer, which will be worthless at the end of five years. Therefore, the depreciation expense per annual period is $720. ($3,600 − 0)/5 years = $720 per year *Note:* For monthly financial statements, the depreciation would be $3,600/60 = $60 per month.
3	In any accounting period in which the asset is not owned during the entire period, reduce the depreciation to correspond to the time actually owned.	Assume the year end is December 31. If the company bought the computer on November 1, the correct depreciation expense at year end is for 2 months: November and December. $720 × (2/12) = $120 (or $60/month × 2 months = $120)

What if the actual life of an asset is different from its estimated life? We discuss this in Learning Goal 19.

Making the Adjusting Entry

The Entry Looks Like This

Just like other expense adjustments, depreciation expense is a noncash adjustment. For example, if the Fine Cookware Company had owned the computer the entire year, the adjusting entry for depreciation expense would be:

December 31:		
Depreciation Expense—Computer	720	
Accumulated Depreciation—Computer		720

Accumulated Depreciation

Notice that an account called Accumulated Depreciation—Computer is credited instead of the Computer Equipment account. Accumulated depreciation is called a contra asset account. Accumulated depreciation is a *cumulative* account. It shows the entire accumulated depreciation of an asset.

Definition: "Contra Asset" Account

A *contra asset* account is an account that:

- is an offset against the balance of an asset account, and
- has a normal credit balance.

Examples

The table below lists some typical contra asset accounts.

This contra asset account . . .	offsets the balance in this asset account . . .
Accumulated Depreciation—Computer	Computer
Accumulated Depreciation—Trucks	Trucks
Accumulated Depreciation—Building	Building
and so on . . .	

A "contra" account always has a balance that is the opposite of its companion account. There are many different kinds of contra accounts, sometimes called "allowance accounts."

continued ▶

Making the Adjusting Entry, *continued*

***Example Using
T Accounts***

The T accounts below show how the $720 depreciation adjusting entry would appear in the accounts.

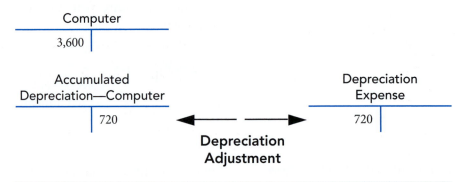

***Effect on the
Condition***

The T accounts make it clear that we put the $720 credit entry in the Accumulated Depreciation account, not into the asset account. Total assets are reduced because the contra account Accumulated Depreciation acts as an offset to the balance in the Computer account.

$$\text{Assets} \downarrow \quad = \quad \text{Liabilities} \quad + \quad \text{Stockholders' Equity} \downarrow$$

Accumulated		Depreciation
Depreciation + 720		Expense + 720
(Cr. balance)		(Dr. balance)

***Why Accumulated
Depreciation Is Used***

The Accumulated Depreciation account is used for two reasons:

1. The accumulated depreciation will not be mixed up with the cost of the asset. If the $720 credit had been entered as a credit in the asset account, it might look like the company had disposed of a $720 part of the computer. By keeping the credit for accumulated depreciation out of the asset account, the Computer account will show only the actual cost of an asset.

2. By using a separate Accumulated Depreciation account, we can clearly see how much depreciation has accumulated on any particular asset. The Accumulated Depreciation account makes it easy to see the *cumulative amount* of depreciation that has been recorded for any asset. For example, this is how the Computer account and the Accumulated Depreciation—Computer account would appear after four years:

Computer		Accumulated Depreciation—Computer	
3,600			720
			720
			720
			720
			2,880 bal.

Making the Adjusting Entry, *continued*

If the Adjustment Is NOT Done . . .

If the adjusting entry for depreciation is not done, the financial statements will be incorrect.

Balance sheet:
↑ **Assets** will be overstated because the accumulated depreciation was not recorded.
↑ **Stockholders' equity** will be overstated because net income is overstated.

Income statement:
↑ **Net income** is overstated because the expense was not recorded.

Book Value

Definition and Examples

Definition: "Book Value"

Book value means the cost of the asset that is still undepreciated. Book value is always calculated as asset cost minus accumulated depreciation. Book value has nothing to do with what an asset might sell for.

Example of Book Value

Using the amounts in the T accounts on page 142, the book value of the computer after four years is: 3,600 – 2,880 = 720.

Synonyms for Book Value

Other names for book value are ***carrying value*** and ***net property and equipment***.

continued ▶

Definition and Examples, *continued*

Appearance on the Balance Sheet

The balances from the asset account and its companion Accumulated Depreciation account will appear in the asset section of the balance sheet that shows the plant and equipment assets. For example, the two T accounts balances on the bottom of page 142 would appear in the asset section of the balance sheet like this:

Computer equipment	$ 3,600
Less: Accumulated depreciation	(2,880)
Net equipment	$ 720

You might also see this presentation:

Computer Equipment, net of accumulated depreciation of $2,880:	$720

"Reserve" for Depreciation

Occasionally, accumulated depreciation is called "reserve for depreciation." This phrase is misleading and gives the false impression that there may be a cash fund associated with a plant asset. Use of the word "reserve" is not recommended. Be cautious wherever you see "reserve" used with a non-cash asset.

QUICK REVIEW

- Plant and equipment assets are different than prepaid expense assets because plant and equipment assets usually have useful lives of greater than one year and the useful lives must be estimated for the purposes of depreciation. Also, plant and equipment assets are tangible.

- Depreciation is not a valuation method. It is a process of allocating cost into expense over an asset's estimated useful life.

- The simplest method for calculating depreciation expense is:
  - $ cost − residual value/estimated useful life = depreciation expense
  - If the asset was not owned for a full period, the expense must be reduced.

- The journal entry to record depreciation always takes this form:

  Depreciation Expense $$$
      Accumulated Depreciation $$$

- The Accumulated Depreciation account is known as a contra asset account because it will offset the balance of a companion asset account.

VOCABULARY

Book value: the cost of a plant asset minus its accumulated depreciation (page 143)

Carrying value: another name for book value (page 143)

Contra asset: an account that is an offset against the balance of an asset and has a normal credit balance (page 141)

Depreciation: the process of allocating the cost of plant and equipment assets into expense, during their estimated useful lives, in a systematic and rational way (page 136)

Fixed assets: another name for plant and equipment (page 137)

Intangible assets: assets not having physical substance (page 138)

Matching principle: the principle that directs accountants to record expenses in the period that the expense helped to generate revenue (page 137)

Net property and equipment: another name for book value (page 143)

Plant and equipment: tangible assets having a useful life of more than a year (page 137)

Plant assets: another name for plant and equipment (page 137)

Residual value: the remaining value of a depreciable asset at the end of its useful life (page 137)

Salvage value: another name for residual value (page 137)

Straight-line depreciation: a depreciation method that allocates an equal amount of depreciation expense into each period of an asset's estimated useful life (page 139)

Tangible assets: assets that have physical substance (page 138)

Useful life: the period of time that an asset can provide benefits and be useful to a business (page 138)

Part III is about making the adjustment to record depreciation. Answer the questions and problems below to practice what you have just read.

Multiple Choice
Select the best answer.

1. Long-lived (more than a year) tangible assets are called:
   a. plant assets or plant and equipment.
   b. plant and equipment or fixed assets.
   c. plant assets or fixed assets.
   d. any of the above.

2. An adjusting entry to record depreciation for equipment would take this form:
   a. Depreciation Expense—Equipment
          Equipment
   b. Depreciation Expense—Equipment
          Accumulated Depreciation—Equipment
   c. Depreciation Expense—Equipment
          Accumulated Depreciation Expense—Equipment
   d. Accumulated Depreciation Expense
          Depreciation Expense—Equipment

3. Book value is
   a. asset cost minus accumulated depreciation.
   b. the same dollar amount as accumulated depreciation.
   c. asset cost minus current depreciation expense.
   d. depreciation expense plus accumulated depreciation.

4. If a transaction is recorded in the "Depreciation account," this means it was recorded in:
   a. Depreciation Expense.
   b. Accumulated Depreciation.
   c. both (a) and (b).
   d. There is no such thing as a "Depreciation" account.

5. Properly recording the depreciation adjustment has the following effect on financial statements:
   a. increases total liabilities and decreases net income
   b. decreases net income and increases total assets
   c. decreases total assets and decreases net income
   d. increases total assets and increases net income

6. Failing to record a depreciation adjustment would have the following effect:
   a. overstate total assets and understate net income
   b. understate total assets and understate net income
   c. understate total liabilities and overstate net income
   d. overstate total assets and overstate net income

7. Which of the following is a contra asset account?
   a. Depreciation Expense
   b. Withdrawals
   c. Accumulated Depreciation—Trucks
   d. Accounts Payable

8. The Office Equipment account of Trocaire Company shows a normal balance of $17,500. The Accumulated Depreciation—Office Equipment account shows a normal balance of $3,500. If all the other assets add up to $100,000, what will the balance sheet show as total assets?
   a. $114,000
   b. $100,000
   c. $117,500
   d. $121,000

9. The accumulated depreciation account is what kind of account?
   a. a liability
   b. an offset against an asset
   c. an expense
   d. a revenue

10. Which of the following kinds of transactions would you consider the most difficult if you are trying to properly apply the matching principle?
   a. the expiration of part of the two-years' prepaid insurance
   b. using up office supplies
   c. depreciating a new air-conditioning system for the office
   d. paying for computer repairs when they are provided

11. The basic formula for calculating depreciation expense is:
   a. cost × useful life = current period expense.
   b. (cost – residual value)/useful life.
   c. useful life/cost = current period expense.
   d. original cost minus what the asset will sell for today.

12. On April 1 of the fiscal year ended December 31, St. Louis Company purchased a new truck for $27,000. This purchase was unusual because the truck normally sells for $32,000. The company estimated that the truck will have a useful life of five years and have no residual value. The depreciation expense for the truck for the current fiscal year is:
   a. $4,800.
   b. $6,400.
   c. $4,050.
   d. none of the above.

Reinforcement Problems

LG A4-5. Distinguish between accounts. What is the difference between accumulated depreciation and depreciation expense?

LG A4-6. Explain accumulated depreciation. When depreciation is recorded, why is an accumulated depreciation account used, instead of crediting the asset account directly?

LG A4-7. Make the journal entry. The depreciation for office equipment is $1,500. Record the journal entry on a separate piece of paper.

PRACTICE **Learning Goal 4 Appendix Part III, continued** *Solutions are in the disk at the back of the book and at: www.worthyjames.com*

LG A4-8. **Calculate the depreciation and make the journal entry.** Record the year-end adjusting entry for the correct amount of depreciation in each of the following independent situations. For general journal paper, you can make copies from the template in the disk at the back of the book.

a. On January 2, Tompkins Company purchased a computer for $12,250. The useful life of the computer is estimated at five years. Tompkins Company has a December 31 year end.

b. On April 1, Tompkins Company also purchased drilling equipment for $35,000. The equipment is estimated to have a 10-year useful life and a $1,000 estimated residual value.

c. Schenectady Corporation purchased a new truck for $54,000 on January 2 of this year. The truck is estimated to have a five-year useful life and no residual value. The corporation has a June 30 year end.

LG A4-9. On September 30 of the fiscal year ending on December 31, Kathy's Company purchased some equipment with an estimated useful life of 10 years and with no residual value. On December 31, after all adjustments are completed, the accumulated depreciation for this equipment is $12,000. What is the cost of the equipment? (Straight-line depreciation is used.)

INTERNET EXERCISES

Locating and analyzing sources of business information. Do an Internet search for 10 sources of business information as if you were an investor. Look at the current news and information concerning specific companies. Include in your search the following sources of information: Bloomberg, Yahoo finance, Reuters, CNBC, Businesswire, Hoovers, New York Times online and Security & Exchange Commission. (Use bookmark/favorites to save the locations in an "Accounting References" folder.)

a. For each source, how would you describe the kind of information available—detailed financial information or general information or both? Does much of the information consist of forecasts and opinions?

b. Is there any good way to judge the reliability of this information?

c. Did you find a source called "PR newswire"? What do you think this is? Do you think that a company might release a favorably biased news report for the purpose of making the company appear more successful?

d. Select two large companies. Using your 12 sources, identify the following for each company:
- what the company does
- the company's main competitors
- whether the company has had net income or net loss for the past several years
- recent news about the company within the last two months

Your Questions?

It is *very* important to be aware of what you need to understand better. What do you need to understand better about this learning goal? On a separate piece of paper, write the questions that you want to discuss with your classmates, instructor, or supervisor. Try to be very specific about what is bothering you, such as explanations that you do not fully understand.

APPENDIX PART IV

Appendix Part IV to Learning Goal 4

In Part IV, you will find:

Overview of Accruals

Accrued Revenues and Accrued Expenses

Definition:

The word *accrual* (pronounced *uh-croo-ull*) means a transaction in which:

- a revenue is earned but no cash has been received, or
- an expense is incurred, but no cash has been paid.

Examples

- **Accrued revenue:** Rochester Services Company provided $100,000 of accounting and financial services in October, but the customers did not pay until November. Because the revenue was earned in October and no cash was received then, the company has $100,000 of accrued revenue at the end of October. The company should record this as October revenue.
- **Accrued expense:** Brooklyn Partnership incurred $3,300 of utilities expense in July but did not pay for this until August. Because the expense was actually incurred in July and no cash was paid then, the partnership has $3,300 of accrued expense at the end of July. The partnership should record this as a July expense.

Examples That Are NOT Accrued Revenue

- If the customers of Rochester Services Company had *paid in October*, there would be no accrual because cash was received *when the revenue was earned*.
- If the customers of Rochester Services Company had paid an advance to the company *before October*, there would also be no accrual because cash was received *before the revenue was earned*.

Examples That Are NOT Accrued Expense

- If Brooklyn Partnership had *paid in July*, there would be no accrual because the expense was paid for in cash *when the expense was incurred*.
- If Brooklyn Partnership had prepaid the utility company *before July*, there would also be no accrual because the expense was paid for in cash *before the expense was incurred*.

Accrual Adjustments

Why Are Accrual Adjustments Important?

When there is an accrual transaction, revenue is earned without cash being received, or an expense is incurred without cash being paid. Non-cash transactions like these are very easy to overlook. However, *all* revenue and expense transactions must be recorded in each accounting period. Accrual adjustments are used to record these types of unrecorded revenues and expenses.

Accrual Adjustments, *continued*

Definition: Accrual Adjustment	An ***accrual adjustment:*** ■ records an accrued revenue that is not recorded by the end of a period, or ■ records an accrued expense that is not recorded by the end of a period.

Examples	■ Dundalk Company provided $2,000 of consulting service in November but did not record revenue because it had not yet received cash or billed the client by December 31, year end. A year-end accrual adjustment is necessary to record this revenue. ■ Frederick Company received a $500 utility service bill in late December but did not record the expense because it had not yet paid the bill by December 31, year end. A year-end accrual adjustment is necessary to record this expense.

A Closer Look at Accrued Revenues

Identify Accrued Revenues

Overview	There are five basic adjustment types. This part is about:

Prepaid Expense	Unearned Revenue	Depreciation	**Accrued Revenue**	Accrued Expense

Definition: Accrued Revenue	An ***accrued revenue*** is a revenue that has been earned but no cash has been received. You have already learned how to record revenue "on account" in volume 1 and in previous learning goals.

Why an Adjustment Is Needed	■ Accrued revenues are not new for you. You have already learned how to record revenue "on account" in previous learning goals. However, an accrued revenue *adjustment* is needed whenever an accrued revenue has not been recorded. If an accrued revenue is missed, then the total revenue on the income statement will be understated. Usually this happens because a company has not yet sent out a bill or has not received cash from a customer. Another reason that accrued revenues might not be recorded is that many companies find it easier to wait until the end of a period to record all accrued revenues at one time.

continued ▶

Identify Accrued Revenues, *continued*

**Examples of
Accrued Revenue
Adjustments**

- Sullivan Company performed $500 of painting services in June, and forgot to send a bill to the customer. No cash was received in June. Does Sullivan Company have an increase in wealth when the revenue is earned in June, even though no cash is received? Yes! In June, the company earned a $500 asset called Accounts Receivable—the legal right to collect money. A June 30 adjustment is needed to record the revenue and receivable.
- Caldwell Company, which prepares monthly financial statements, rented a computer to a customer during October. The monthly rental is $150. Even if the bill was not sent until November, Caldwell Company must accrue $150 of revenue at the end of October because the revenue was earned in October.

**Example That Is
NOT Accrued Revenue**

- Jamestown Concrete Pumping Service performs a job and bills the customer $750. The customer pays immediately. Cash is received, so there is no accrued revenue.
- Rockland Flight Services provided $500 of pilot instruction. The client had already made an advance payment for the instruction, which Rockland previously recorded as an unearned revenue.

How to Adjust for Accrued Revenues

The Two Objectives

**The Two Objectives
of the Adjustment**

The adjustment procedures for accrued expenses are performed with the intention of completing two objectives:

1. prepare the adjusting journal entry
2. determine the new account balances

Sometimes you may be asked to complete one of these objectives or both of them. The detailed procedures for the two objectives are presented as separate topics in the material that follows this discussion.

The Two Objectives, *continued*

**Compare the
Two Objectives**

The following two tables show an overview of the important steps in accomplishing the two objectives.

Objective I Overview: Prepare the Adjusting Journal Entry		
Step	Action	Example
1	Identify the key information types.	*Both* of these conditions exist: ■ A revenue has been earned but is unrecorded, and ■ no cash (or other asset) has been received.
2	Select the proper method to calculate the revenue earned.	The calculation depends on the type of information given.
3	Prepare the adjusting journal entry.	*Example:* $250 revenue 　　　　　　　　　　Dr.　Cr. Account Receivable　250 　Revenue　　　　　　　　250

Objective II Overview: Determine the New Account Balances		
Step	Action	Example
1	Identify the adjusting journal entry.	From Objective I, above.
2	Set up T accounts with the account names and the unadjusted account balances.	A/R　$$　｜　Revenue　｜$$
3	Debit the receivable and credit the revenue, and calculate the new account balances.	A/R: $$ / 250 / $$　　Revenue: $$ / 250 / $$

Objective I: Prepare the Adjusting Journal Entry

Step 1: Identify the Key Information Type

What the Key Information Does

The key information tells you if an accrued revenue has not yet been recorded. If you find such a transaction, then you need to do an accrual adjustment.

Two Conditions Required

The key information must show two conditions about a transaction, if an accrued revenue adjustment is indicated:

1. a revenue has been earned but has not been recorded, and
2. no cash (or other asset) has been received.

You will only do an accrual adjustment if **both** conditions are met.

Descriptive Key Words

The following words are frequently used to describe accrued revenue transactions:

- accrue(ed)
- unbilled/not (yet) billed
- owes/owing
- unpaid

- on account
- unrecorded
- payment not received
- not (yet) recognized

Examples

- "Fees earned but unbilled are $5,000."
- "Washington Enterprises accrued $2,000 of revenue."
- "Revenue earned but not yet recognized was $350."
- "Services performed on account but still unpaid by the customer were $11,000."

Check Your Understanding

The table below shows information about various separate revenue transactions. On a separate sheet of paper, if the transaction satisfies the two key information requirements, place a mark in the box under the column titled "Accrual Required." If an adjustment is **not** required, place a mark under the column that indicates which of the two qualities is missing. (Answer on next page)

Transaction Information	Accrual Required	Missing Quality	
		Revenue earned but not recorded	Cash not received yet
1. Ponce Consulting Company provided $2,000 of consulting services on May 3. At year end on May 31, the client had not yet been billed.	(Reminder: Use a separate sheet of paper to complete the table.)		
2. Bayamon Products, Inc. shipped merchandise to a customer. The customer had made an advance payment.			
3. San Juan Services, Inc. did $1,500 of computer repair work in early December. This was recorded as December revenue although the customer has not yet paid.			
4. Aguadilla Roofing Company constructed a new roof for $20,000. The customer paid immediately.			
5. Rio Piedras Enterprises completed the first part of a contract that will not be billed until the contract is completed.			
6. Utado Corporation signed a contract to perform future advertising services. As of year end, no services have been performed.			
7. Arecibo Painting Company completed a job in June, but as of June 30, the bookkeeper had forgotten to record the transaction.			
8. Carolina Company received $50,000 for services provided. The company has not received $5,000 for other services provided in the current period. The owner also invested $4,000. Carolina Company shows revenue of $50,000.			

Answers

Transaction Information	Accrual Required	Missing Quality	
		Revenue earned but not recorded	Cash not received yet
1. Ponce Consulting Company provided $2,000 of consulting services on May 3. At year end on May 31, the client had not yet been billed.	✓		
2. Bayamon Products, Inc. shipped merchandise to a customer. The customer had made an advance payment.			✓
3. San Juan Services, Inc. did $1,500 of computer repair work in early December. This was recorded as December revenue although the customer has not yet paid.		✓	
4. Aguadilla Roofing Company constructed a new roof for $20,000. The customer paid imediately.		✓	✓
5. Rio Piedras Enterprises completed the first part of a contract that will not be billed until the contract is completed.	✓		
6. Utado Corporation signed a contract to perform future advertising services. As of year end, no services have been performed.		✓ No revenue	
7. Arecibo Painting Company completed a job in June, but as of June 30, the bookkeeper had forgotten to record the transaction.	✓		
8. Carolina Company received $50,000 for services provided. The company has not received $5,000 for other services provided in the current period. The owner also invested $4,000. Carolina Company shows revenue of $50,000.	✓ $5,000 accrual		

Step 2: Select the Proper Method to Calculate the Revenue Earned

Overview

If the key information in Step 1 indicates that an accrual is necessary, then your next step is to determine the correct amount to record in the accrual adjustment.

Procedure

The table below shows you the procedure for calculating the amount to accrue.

Step	Procedure	Examples
1	Determine if the amount of the adjustment is given to you. ■ If not, go to **STEP 2**.	■ "Fees earned but unbilled are $1,000." ■ "Services provided but unrecorded were $800." ■ "Interest earned but not received was $250." ■ "Accrued revenue is $750." ■ "$1,500 of services were provided, and the client paid $500" (accrual is $1,000).
2	*Calculate* the amount of the accrued revenue by: ■ prorating, or ■ revenue per unit. *Note:* Which one you do depends on what information is given.	■ **Pro-rate (allocate) the amount:** "Baruch Company earned one half of a $2,000 contract that would be completed and billed later." *Calculation:* 1/2 × $2,000 = $1,000 ■ **Revenue per unit times units provided:** "Ulster Enterprises sold 700 units of merchandise at $25 per unit, and the buyer will pay later." *Calculation:* 700 × $25 = $17,500 "Rent is $450 per month, and the tenant owes our company two months' rent." *Calculation:* 2 (monthly units) × $450 = $900

Prorating Calculations

To *pro-rate* means to allocate or apportion part of a total amount. This is done either by multiplying by a fraction or by a percent. If you want to learn more about multiplying with fractions, review "Essential Math for Accounting" in the disk at the back of this book. If you want to learn more about multiplying with percents, refer to the "Essential Math for Accounting" in the disk with Volume 1.

Check Your Understanding

On a separate sheet of paper, identify the amount of revenue that must be accrued for each of the separate events below. Note: Not all events require accrual. Answers are below.

Event	Amount to Accrue
1. Drake Sailing Supplies sold $1,000 of anchor chain on account.	
2. Clinton Enterprises provided $500 of TV repair services. The client will be billed later.	
3. Cazenovia Graphic Designs has completed and billed three-fourths of a $1,000 service contract. (Billed does not mean recorded.)	
4. Orange County Company performed $750 of accounting services for a client who made a prepayment before the services were provided.	
5. As soon as Taylor Company performed $2,500 of consulting services, the client paid for $500 of the services.	
6. South Bend Company completed 85% of a $5,000 executive training program but has not yet billed the client.	

Answers

Event	Amount to Accrue
1. Drake Sailing Supplies sold $1,000 of anchor chain on account.	Accrue $1,000.
2. Clinton Enterprises provided $500 of TV repair services. The client will be billed later.	Accrue $500.
3. Cazenovia Graphic Designs has completed and billed three-fourths of a $1,000 service contract.	Accrue $750.
4. Orange County Company performed $750 of accounting services for a client who made a prepayment before the services were provided.	Nothing to accrue—already paid
5. As soon as Taylor Company performed $2,500 of consulting services, the client paid for $500 of the services.	Accrue $2,000.
6. South Bend Company completed 85% of a $5,000 executive training program but has not yet billed the client.	Accrue $4,250. It does not matter if the client has not been billed. The services were provided.

Step 3: Prepare the Adjusting Journal Entry

Standard Entry

When a revenue is accrued, the journal entry always takes this basic form:

	Dr.	Cr.
Receivable	$$$	
Revenue		$$$

The effect on the condition of the business looks like this:

$$A \uparrow \qquad = \qquad L \quad + \quad SE \uparrow$$
Receivable   Revenue

If the Adjustment Is NOT Done . . .

If the revenue is not accrued, the financial statements will be incorrect.

Balance sheet:
- ↓ **Assets** will be understated because the receivable was not recorded.
- ↓ **Stockholders' equity** will be understated because net income is understated.

Income statement:
- ↓ **Net income** is understated because the revenue was not recorded.

"If the adjustment is NOT done . . ."

What is interest revenue? Interest is the *rental charge* for the use of money. A borrower pays this charge, and a lender records the payment as revenue.

If the borrower has not paid but the revenue has been earned, the lender debits Interest Receivable and credits Interest Revenue, which is an interest revenue accrual. Interest is accrued at the end of an accounting period.

---

continued ▶

Step 3: Prepare the Adjusting Journal Entry, *continued*

Examples of Journal Entries

The table below shows you two examples of adjusting journal entries that record accrued revenue.

Example of information . . .	the accounts needed are . . .	and the adjusting entry is . . .
Beginning on December 12, Monroe Investments has earned $50 per day of interest revenue on a note receivable that is not due to be paid until February X. Year end is December 31.	Interest Receivable Interest Earned (always a receivable and a revenue)	**Dec. 31** Interest Receivable 1,000 Interest Earned 1,000 A ↑ = L + SE ↑ Interest Interest Receivable Earned +1,000 +1,000
Broome Internet Consulting Company worked 35 hours for a client at the rate of $100 per hour. As of June 30, year end, the client has not yet paid.	Accounts Receivable Service Revenue (always a receivable and a revenue)	**June 30** Accounts Receivable 3,500 Service Revenue 3,500 A ↑ = L + SE ↑ Accounts Service Receivable Revenue +3,500 +3,500

Objective II: Determine the New Account Balances

Three Easy Steps

Overview

Often, after someone has prepared an adjusting journal entry, that person wants to know what the final account balances will be for the accounts that are affected by the adjustment. This can be easily done by using T accounts without actually having to record the adjustment in the journal or ledger.

Step 1

The first step is to identify the accounts in the adjusting entry.

Example

In the second example on page 160, we saw that Broome Internet Consulting Company accrued $3,500 of revenue. By looking at the journal entry, we see that:

- Accounts Receivable increased by $3,500.
- Service Revenue increased by $3,500.

Step 2

Set up T accounts for the accounts you identified in Step 1.

Example (continued)

Continuing with Broome Internet Consulting Company, suppose that we open the ledger (or look on the trial balance) and find out that the *unadjusted account balances* are:

- Accounts Receivable: $5,000
- Service Revenue: $80,300

Now we can draw the T accounts and enter the unadjusted account balances:

Accounts Receivable		Service Revenue	
5,000			80,300

continued ▶

Three Easy Steps, *continued*

Step 3	Calculate the new account balances.

Example (continued)

To determine the new account balances, enter the debits and credits from the adjustment into the T accounts:

Accounts Receivable			Service Revenue	
5,000				80,300
3,500				**3,500**
8,500				83,800

If the journal entry is approved, entered into the journal, and posted to the ledger, then we know that the final ledger account balance for Accounts Receivable will be $8,500 and for Service Revenue it will be $83,800. These same balances will appear on the financial statements.

What Happens in the Period After the Accrual?

Examples

Overview

In the next accounting period, cash will be received from the customer in payment of the receivable. However, there is no revenue. The revenue was *already recorded by the adjustment* in the prior period. When cash is received, the entry is simply to eliminate the receivable in return for the cash:

Cash	$$$	
Receivable		$$$

Examples

Each of the next three examples shows you what happens in the next accounting period to Bronx Company, Monroe Investments, and Broome Internet Consulting Company from the prior accrual examples.

 Receiving cash is not part of the accrued revenue adjustment procedure. The cash is received later.

Examples, *continued*

Bronx Company accrued $500 of revenue on December 31 and the customer paid this in January (or later).

First	Dec. 31	Later
— the adjustment —		— the $ collection —
December		**January (or later)**

Accounts Receivable	500	Cash	500
Sales Revenue	500	Accounts Receivable	500

A ↑	=	L	+	SE ↑		
Accounts				Sales		
Receivable				Revenue		
+500				+500		

A ↓ ↑	=	L	+	SE	
Accounts					
Receivable	−500				
Cash	+500				

Monroe Investments accrued $1,000 of interest revenue on December 31, and the company collected this amount on January 2.

First	Dec. 31	Later
— the adjustment —		— the $ collection —

Interest Receivable	1,000	Cash	1,000
Interest Earned	1,000	Interest Receivable	1,000

A ↑	=	L	+	SE ↑		
Interest				Interest		
Receivable				Earned		
+1,000				+1,000		

A ↓ ↑	=	L	+	SE	
Interest					
Receivable	−1,000				
Cash	+1,000				

continued ▶

Examples, *continued*

Sometimes a company accrues revenue at the end of one period and continues to earn revenue from that same customer into the next period. Then the customer pays the entire amount owing for both periods.

Example: Broome Internet Consulting Company, which prepares monthly reports, worked for a client in June and continued working for the client until July 9. The company earned $3,500 in June and $2,000 in July from this same client. The client paid the full amount due of $5,500 on July 15.

Notice in the right panel that $3,500 of the cash collection in July is to eliminate the account receivable for accrued revenue in June. Then, $2,000 of the cash collection is for the revenue earned in July. (This could be done in two entries but is usually combined into one as you see here.)

First		June 30	Later	
— the adjustment —			— the $ collection —	
June			**July**	

		Cash	5,500
Accounts Receivable	3,500	Accounts Receivable	3,500
Service Revenue	3,500	Service Revenue	2,000

A ↑ = L + SE ↑	A ↑ ↓ = L + SE ↑
Accounts Service	Accounts Service
Receivable Revenue	Receivable −3,500 Revenue
+3,500 +3,500	Cash +5,500 +2,000

Check Your Understanding

Write the completed sentences on a separate sheet of paper. Answers are below.

An accrued revenue is a revenue that has been earned, but no · · · · · · · · has been received. If this transaction is not recorded, then an accrued revenue · · · · · · · · becomes necessary.

When doing an adjusting entry to record an accrued revenue, you will always debit a · · · · · · · · account and always credit a · · · · · · · · account.

On a separate sheet of paper, answer the following question:

1. What are the two key information items you must identify to know that you will need to do an adjustment for an accrued revenue?

Make the necessary journal entry for each situation:

2. Advertising services provided to customers, but unbilled on December 31, were $500.

3. In January of the following year, the bill was mailed and the customer paid the $500 in full.

Answers

An accrued revenue is a revenue that has been earned, but no <u>cash</u> has been received. If this transaction is not recorded, then an accrued revenue <u>adjustment</u> becomes necessary.

When doing an adjusting entry to record an accrued revenue, you will always debit a <u>receivable</u> account and always credit a <u>revenue</u> account.

1. ■ Revenue is earned but not recorded.
   ■ No cash (or other asset) has been received.

		Dr.	Cr.
2.	Accounts Receivable	500	
	Revenue		500
3.	Cash	500	
	Accounts Receivable		500

(Practice is at the end of Part V)

APPENDIX PART V	# Appendix Part V to Learning Goal 4

In Part V, you will find:

A Closer Look at Accrued Expenses

Identify Accrued Expenses

Overview

There are five basic adjustment types. This part is about:

Prepaid Expense	Unearned Revenue	Depreciation	Accrued Revenue	**Accrued Expense**

Identify Accrued Expenses, *continued*

Definition: Accrued Expense	An *accrued expense* is an expense that has been incurred but no cash (or other asset) has been paid or used.

- An accrued expense always creates a new payable.
- An accrued expense is usually for services.

Accrued Liability	The liability that results from an accrued expense is called an *accrued liability*.

Why an Adjustment Is Needed

Accrued expenses are not new for you. You have already practiced recording expenses "on account" in previous learning goals.

However, an accrued expense *adjustment* is needed whenever an accrued expense has not been recorded. If this expense is missed, total expenses on the income statement will be understated. Usually this happens because a company has not yet received a bill or delays paying cash for the services it has received. Also, many companies find it easier to wait until the end of a period to record accrued expenses.

Example of Accrued Expense Adjustment

Villa Maria Company prepares monthly financial statements. During October, the company began renting a computer system from a computer rental company. The monthly rental cost is $150, and Villa Maria did not receive the October bill until November 5. When the bill is received in November, the company must accrue $150 of rental expense for the period ending on October 31, because the expense was incurred in October but not yet recorded.

Example That Is NOT Accrued Expense

- On December 29, Raritan Valley Ventures received a bill for $950 of consulting expense incurred in December. The company immediately paid the bill.
- Cittone Construction Partnership incurred a $200 expense for cleaning services during the month. The company had made an advance payment for the services, which was previously recorded as a prepaid expense. This is a prepayment, not an accrual.
- Hackensack Company received a bill for advertising services on December 11. The accountant debited advertising expense and credited accounts payable. No adjustment is needed at December 31 year end because the accrued expense has been recorded.

How to Adjust for Accrued Expenses

The Two Objectives

The Two Objectives of the Adjustment

The adjustment procedures for accrued expense are performed with the intention of completing two objectives:

1. Prepare the adjusting journal entry.
2. Determine the new account balances.

You may be asked to complete one of these objectives or both of them. The detailed procedures for the two objectives are presented as separate topics in the material that follows this discussion.

Compare the Two Objectives

The two tables on page 169 show an overview of the important steps in accomplishing the two objectives.

*"Don't worry John . . . it could happen to anyone . . .
its easy to forget to accrue revenues and expenses."*

The Two Objectives, *continued*

OBJECTIVE I: PREPARE THE ADJUSTING JOURNAL ENTRY		
Step	**Action**	**Example**
1	Identify the key information type.	Both of these conditions exist: ■ An expense has been incurred but is unrecorded, and ■ no cash (or other asset) has been paid or used.
2	Select the proper method to calculate the expense.	The calculation depends on the type of information given.

3	Prepare the adjusting journal entry.	*Example:* $800 expense
		
		              Dr. **Cr.**
		Expense 800
		    Accounts Payable 800

OBJECTIVE II: DETERMINE THE NEW ACCOUNT BALANCES		
Step	**Action**	**Purpose**
1	Identify the adjusting journal entry.	From Objective I, above.
2	Set up T accounts with the account names and the unadjusted account balances.	Expense A/P $$ \| \| $$
3	Debit the expense and credit the payable, and calculate the new account balances.	Expense A/P $$ \| \| $$ **800** | | **800** $$ \| \| $$

Objective I: Prepare the Adjusting Journal Entry

Step 1: Identify the Key Information Type

What the Key Information Does

The key information tells you if there is an accrued expense that has not yet been recorded. If you find such a transaction, then you need to do an accrual adjustment.

Two Conditions Required

The key information must show two conditions about a transaction, if an accrual expense adjustment is indicated:

1. an expense has been incurred but has not been recorded, and
2. no cash (or other asset) has been paid or used

You will only do an accrual adjustment if **both** conditions exist.

Descriptive Key Words

The following words are frequently used to describe accrued expense transactions:

- accrue(ed)
- unbilled/not (yet) billed
- owes/owing
- unpaid
- on account

- unrecorded
- payment not made
- not (yet) recognized
- amount due
- accumulated expense

Examples

- "Coalinga Company accrued 3 days of wages expense at year end."
- "Atwater Enterprises accumulated $12,000 of unpaid advertising expense by the end of the quarter."
- "Suisun Company has $3,000 of accrued utilities expense."
- "Ventura Corporation owes $6,500 for unpaid rent expense."

Check Your Understanding

Use a blank sheet of paper to complete the table. The table below shows information about various separate expense transactions. If the transaction satisfies the two key information requirements, place a mark in the box under the column titled "Accrual Required." If an adjustment is **not** required, place a mark under the column that indicates which of the two qualities is missing. (Answers on next page)

Transaction Information	Accrual Required	Missing Quality	
		Expense incurred but not recorded	Cash (or other asset) not paid or used
1. Chattanooga Service Company received a utility bill for $350 on June 5. At year end on June 30, the bill had not been paid.	(Reminder: Use a separate sheet of paper to complete the table.)		
2. Motlow Enterprises, Inc. received a utility bill for $500 on June 7. The bill was immediately paid.			
3. Memphis Ventures prepaid nine months of fire insurance on September 1. By December 31 year end, four months of insurance had been used up.			
4. Draughon Company had computer repair work done, which was still unbilled by the company that did the work.			
5. Gallatin Partnership purchased $1,000 of office supplies, which were received but not yet paid for. The supplies are still unused			
6. Gallatin Partnership (#5 above) used up the supplies, and this has not been recorded yet. The $1,000 owing for the supplies still has not been paid.			
7. Jackson Company's payroll period ends each Friday, at which time the employees are paid. However, the current year end occurs on Thursday, December 31. The wages total $400 per day.			

Answers

Transaction Information	Accrual Required	Missing Quality	
		Expense incurred but not recorded	Cash (or other asset) not paid or used
1. Chattanooga Service Company received a utility bill for $350 on June 5. At year end on June 30, the bill had not been paid.	✓		
2. Motlow Enterprises, Inc. received a utility bill for $500 on June 7. The bill was immediately paid.		✓ Expense recorded	✓
3. Memphis Ventures prepaid nine months of fire insurance on September 1. By December 31 year end, four months of insurance had been used up.			✓
4. Draughon Company had computer repair work done, which was still unbilled by the company that did the work.	✓		
5. Gallatin Partnership purchased $1,000 of office supplies, which were received but not yet paid for. The supplies are still unused		✓ No expense	
6. Gallatin Partnership (#5 above) used up the supplies, and this has not been recorded yet. The $1,000 owing for the supplies still has not been paid.			✓ Supplies used up
7. Jackson Company's payroll period ends each Friday, at which time the employees are paid. However, the current year end occurs on Thursday, December 31. The wages total $400 per day.	✓		

Step 2: Select the Proper Method to Calculate the Expense

Overview

If the key information in Step 1 indicates that an accrual is necessary, then your next step is to determine the correct amount to record in the accrual adjustment.

Step 2: Select the Proper Method to Calculate the Expense, *continued*

Procedure

The table below shows you the procedure for calculating the amount to accrue.

Step	Procedure	Examples
1	See if the amount of the adjustment is given to you. ■ If not, go to **STEP 2.**	■ "Expenses incurred but unbilled are $1,000." ■ "Interest owed but not paid was $250." ■ "Accrued wages expense is $750." ■ "Advertising expense owing not yet recognized is $10,000."
2	*Calculate* the amount of the accrued expense by: ■ prorating, or ■ expense per unit. *Note:* Which one you do depends on what information is given.	■ **Pro-rate (allocate) the amount:** "Roane Enterprises signed an advertising contract and agreed to pay $7,000 for advertising services. So far, 20% of the advertising has been provided but is unbilled." *Calculation:* .2 × $7,000 = $1,400 ■ **Multiply expense per unit times units used:** "Walters Company wages are $5,000 per week, and the payroll period ends each Friday. The current accounting period ends on a Wednesday." *Calculation:* $5,000/5 = $1,000 per day (daily units) $1,000 × 3 days = $3,000 ■ "Interest expense is $1,000 per month, and the company owes two months of unpaid interest." *Calculation:* 2 (monthly units) × $1,000 = $2,000

Calculating Accrued Interest

Often a business incurs interest expense that has not yet been paid at the end of an accounting period. This needs to be accrued. If you want to learn how to calculate simple interest on a loan, refer to Learning Goal 17 or "Essential Math for Accounting" in the disk at the back of the book.

Step 3: Prepare the Adjusting Journal Entry, *continued*

Examples of Journal Entries

The table below shows you three examples of adjusting journal entries that record accrued expense.

Example of information . . .	the accounts needed are . . .	and the adjusting entry is . . .

On March 3, Odessa Company received a bill from the utility company for $500 of utility services. By year end on March 31, the bill remained unpaid.	Utilities Expense
	Accounts Payable
	
	(always an expense and a payable)
		March 31
		Utilities Expense 500
		    Accounts Payable 500
		
		A = L ↑ + SE ↓
		      Accounts Utilities
		      Payable Expense
		      +500 +500

Amarillo Enterprises owed $750 for interest on a note payable but the payment was not due until after December 31 year end.	Interest Expense
	Interest Payable
	
	(always an expense and a payable)
		December 31
		Interest Expense 750
		    Interest Payable 750
		
		A = L ↑ + SE ↓
		      Interest Interest
		      Payable Expense
		      +750 +750

On December 31 year end, the Laredo Company had wages accrued but unpaid (and unrecorded) of $5,000. The payroll period ends in early January.	Wages Expense
	Wages Payable
	
	(always an expense and a payable)
		December 31
		Wages Expense 5,000
		    Wages Payable 5,000
		
		A = L ↑ + SE ↓
		      Wages Wages
		      Payable Expense
		      +5,000 +5,000

Objective II: Determine the New Account Balances

Three Easy Steps

Overview	Often, after someone has prepared an adjusting journal entry, that person wants to know what the final account balances will be for the accounts that will be affected by the adjustment. This can be easily done by using T accounts without actually having to record the adjustment in the journal or ledger.
Step 1	The first step is to identify the accounts in the adjusting entry.
Example	In the third example on the prior page, we saw that Laredo Company accrued $5,000 of wages expense. By looking at the adjusting journal entry, we see that:

- Wages Expense increased by $5,000.
- Wages Payable increased by $5,000.

Step 2	Set up T accounts for the accounts you identified in Step 1.
Example (continued)	Continuing with Laredo Company, suppose that we open the ledger (or look on the trial balance) and find out that the *unadjusted account balances* are:

- Wages Expense: $85,000
- Wages Payable: $–0–

Now we can draw the T accounts and enter the unadjusted account balances:

Wages Expense		Wages Payable	
85,000			–0–

Step 3	Calculate the new account balances.

continued ▶

Three Easy Steps, *continued*

Example
(continued)

To determine the new account balances, enter the debits and credits from the adjustment into the T accounts:

Wages Expense		Wages Payable	
85,000			–0–
5,000			**5,000**
90,000			5,000

If the journal entry is approved, entered into the journal, and posted to the ledger, then we know that the final ledger account balance for Wages Expense will be $90,000, and for Wages Payable it will be $5,000. These same balances will appear on the financial statements.

What Happens in the Period After the Accrual?

Examples

Overview

In the next accounting period, cash will be paid to the creditor in payment of the payable. However, there is no expense. The expense was *already recorded by the adjustment* in the prior period. When cash is paid, the entry is simply to eliminate the payable in exchange for the cash that is paid:

Payable	$$$	
Cash		$$$

Examples

Each of the next three examples show you what happens in the next accounting period to Odessa Company, Amarillo Enterprises, and Laredo Company from the prior accrual examples.

Examples, *continued*

Odessa Company made an accrual adjustment for $500 of utilities expense on March 31 and then paid the bill in April.

	First	March 31	Later
	— the adjustment —		— the $ payment —
	March		**April (or later)**

Utilities Expense	500		Accounts Payable	500
Accounts Payable		500	Cash		500

A = L ↑ + SE ↓
Accounts   Utilities
Payable   Expense
+500   +500

A ↓ = L ↓ + SE
Cash   Accounts
−500   Payable
          −500

Amarillo Enterprises accrued $750 of interest expense on December 31, and the company paid this amount on January 2.

	First	December 31	Later
	— the adjustment —		— the $ payment —

Interest Expense	750		Interest Payable	750
Interest Payable		750	Cash		750

A = L ↑ + SE ↓
Interest   Interest
Payable   Expense
+750   +750

A ↓ = L ↓ + SE
Cash   Interest
−750   Payable
          −750

continued ▶

Examples, *continued*

Sometimes a company accrues an expense at the end of one period and continues to incur that same kind of expense owing to the same creditor into the next period. Then the company pays the entire amount owing for both periods to the creditor.

Example: Laredo Company had incurred $5,000 of wages expense by December 31 year end. However, the two-week payroll period did not end until January 4, at which time Laredo Company paid the entire amount of wages owing to the employees for the prior two weeks. On January 4, the company paid the employees $7,000.

Notice in the right panel that $5,000 of the cash payment in January is needed to eliminate the wages payable that was recorded in December. Then, the rest of the cash paid ($2,000) is for the wages expense for the part of the payroll period that fell into January. (This could be recorded in two entries, but it is usually combined into one as you see here.)

	First	December 31	Later
	— the adjustment —		— the $ payment —
	December		January

Wages Expense	5,000		Wages Payable	5,000		
Wages Payable		5,000	Wages Expense	2,000		
			Cash		7,000	

A =	L ↑	+	SE ↓		A ↓	=	L ↓	+	SE ↓
	Wages		Wages		Cash		Wages		Wages
	Payable		Expense		−7,000		Payable		Expense
	+5,000		+5,000				−5,000		+2,000

Corporations and Accrued Taxes

Most accrued expenses are the same for any business entity. However, one kind of accrued expense happens only with corporations: accrued income tax expense. Proprietorships and partnerships do not record or accrue income tax expense. Learning goals 28–31 in volume 1 discuss corporations in more detail.

Examples, *continued*

Comparison:
Both Sides of an Accrual

The table below illustrates both revenue and expense accrual journal entries for a provider of services and the user of the services that have not yet been paid.

Transaction	Provider (Seller) of Service	User (Buyer) of Service

Repair Services	Accounts Receivable 500
	  Service Revenue 500
		Repairs Expense 500
		  Accounts Payable 500

QUICK REVIEW   Appendix Parts IV and V

- An accrual is a noncash transaction in which either:
  - a revenue is earned without being recorded, and no cash (or other asset) has been received, or
  - an expense is incurred without being recorded, and no cash (or other asset) has been paid or used.

- An accrued revenue adjustment is needed when an accrued revenue remains unrecorded at the end of an accounting period. Two accounts always increase: a receivable and a revenue.

- An accrued expense adjustment is needed when an accrued expense remains unrecorded at the end of an accounting period. Two accounts always increase: an expense and a payable.

- The two objectives of doing accrual adjustments are:
  - Prepare the adjusting journal entry.
  - Determine the new account balances.

- Cash is received or paid and recorded in the period after the accrual.

VOCABULARY   Appendix Parts IV and V

Accrual: a transaction in which either a revenue is earned or an expense is incurred, which has not been recorded, and no cash (or other assets) are received, paid, or used (page 150)

Accrual adjustment: an adjusting entry that is used to record an accrued revenue or an accrued expense that has not yet been recorded at the end of an accounting period (page 151)

Accrued expense: an expense that has been incurred but is unrecorded, and no cash (or other asset) has been paid or used (page 167)

Accrued liability: another term for accrued expense (page 167)

Accrued revenue: a revenue that has been earned but is unrecorded, and no cash (or other asset) has been received (page 151)

LG A4-10, *continued*

Item		Accrued . . .		Not an accrual
		Revenue	Expense	
m. Rent Expense 8,000				
Rent Payable 8,000				
n. Rent Expense 8,000				
Prepaid Rent 8,000				
o. The trial balance shows a balance of $2,500 in the Prepaid Rent account.				
p. The trial balance shows a balance of $4,000 in the Unearned Service Revenue account.				

LG A4-11. **Prepare accrual adjustments.** From the information given as of September 30, year end, prepare the year-end accrual adjusting entries. Each item is separate and independent from the other items. Journal paper templates are available in the disk at the back of the book.

Information:

a. Wages of $5,000 have been earned by the employees but not yet recognized in the accounts.
b. Fees earned but unbilled are $4,400.
c. Accrued interest on the mortgage payable is $2,500.
d. Sage Company has accrued service revenue of $800.
e. $3,000 of consulting services were provided to the client, but only one-third of the services have been billed.
f. Rent in the amount of $4,000 is owing to the landlord.
g. Pace Company has a five-day workweek, Monday–Friday. The end of the current accounting period is September 30. On Monday, October 4, the company paid the wages from the prior workweek in the amount of $4,500.

LG A4-12. **Prepare accrual-related journal entries.** Concord Enterprises, Inc. has a December 31 year end.

Instructions:

From the information below, prepare the correct journal entry for each item. (For journal paper, you can make general journal copies from the template in the disk at the back of this book.)

a. On August 28 of the current year ending December 31, the company signed a contract to provide financial advisory services totaling $38,000 to Lexington Company. As of year end, Concord Enterprises had provided 20% of these services. No bill has been sent to the customer, and no cash has been received.
b. On December 31, the company received a bill for Internet Services in the amount of $4,500. This bill was not immediately paid.

LG A4-12, *continued*

c. Each payroll period is 14 days, and as of December 31, year end, 8 days remained in the current payroll period. The total wages are $2,100 per day.

d. On December 6, the company signed a monthly lease agreement for new computers. The lease (rental) charge is $1,550 per month.

e. Two years ago, Concord Enterprises loaned $25,000 to Rochelle Development Company. The monthly payments to Concord from Rochelle are made on the first day of each month. The January 1 payment is $220 dollars, of which $180 is interest.

f. Last year, Concord Enterprises signed a franchise contract with a large, well-known insurance company. This contract allows Concord to use the name and resources of the insurance company to attract new clients. At year end, the insurance company charges Concord 25% of insurance policy revenue for the year, payable by January 15. The contract also requires Concord to make an advance payment of $12,000 each February 1, which Concord records as Prepaid Franchise Expense. For the current year, Concord recorded insurance premium revenue of $136,800.

g. On January 9, Concord paid the employees for the payroll period ending January 8.

h. On January 11, Concord Enterprises completed the work for Lexington Company, which paid in full.

Prepare and Use an Adjusted Trial Balance

In Learning Goal 5, you will find:

The Adjusted Trial Balance

Overview of the Adjusted Trial Balance

Introduction

We discussed the trial balance in Volume 1. Here we return to the trial balance again, as we prepare a second trial balance after completing the adjusting journal entries and posting them into the ledger.

Adjusting entries are posted into the ledger accounts in the same way as all other journal entries. After the adjusting entries have been posted, it is necessary to prepare another trial balance, called the *adjusted trial balance*.

Definition: "Adjusted Trial Balance"

An adjusted trial balance is the trial balance that is prepared after all adjusting entries have been journalized and posted into the ledger accounts. Because all necessary adjustments are completed, the ledger accounts will show correct final balances. These final balances are the amounts used in an adjusted trial balance.

Why It Is Prepared

An adjusted trial balance is prepared for the reasons:

- The adjusted trial balance is a test to verify that the the total of account debit balances in the ledger equals the total of the credit balances, *after the adjustments are posted.*
- Because all the ledger account balances are correct final balances (assuming posting is correct), the adjusted trial balance is the source of the financial statements.

Overview of the Adjusted Trial Balance, *continued*

Financial Statements

Financial statements are prepared after accounts are adjusted. This can be done by using an adjusted trial balance (next page) as the source of final account balances. We will discuss this in more detail in Learning Goal 7 when we use a worksheet.

Prepare Financial Statements from the Adjusted Trial Balance

Example

For the purpose of comparison, a trial balance and an adjusted trial balance are shown side by side. In the adjusted trial balance, the account balances in bold print are the ones that have been changed by the adjusting entries.

Note: Remember that the balances in the trial balance are taken from the final account balances in the ledger.

Schuylkill River Rowing and Sailing, Inc.
Trial Balance
December 31, 2017

Account	Dr.	Cr.
Cash	$24,620	
Accounts Receivable	2,730	
Prepaid Insurance	5,500	
Office Supplies	2,250	
Boating Supplies	12,000	
Equipment	145,700	
Accum. Depreciation— Equipment		80,500
Unearned Revenue		1,800
Accounts Payable		15,300
Common Stock		10,000
Retained Earnings		45,000
Dividends	25,000	
Boat Rental Revenue		331,200
Teaching Revenue		29,300
Wages Expense	206,500	
Rent Expense	32,000	
Insurance Expense	35,000	
Utilities Expense	18,300	
Income Tax Expense	3,500	
Totals	$513,100	$513,100

Schuylkill River Rowing and Sailing, Inc.
Adjusted Trial Balance
December 31, 2017

Account	Dr.	Cr.
Cash	$24,620	
Accounts Receivable	2,730	
Prepaid Insurance	**2,500**	
Office Supplies	**1,250**	
Boating Supplies	**4,150**	
Equipment	145,700	
Accum. Depreciation— Equipment		**88,800**
Unearned Revenue		**300**
Accounts Payable		15,300
Common Stock		10,000
Retained Earnings		45,000
Dividends	25,000	
Boat Rental Revenue		**332,700**
Teaching Revenue		29,300
Wages Expense	206,500	
Rent Expense	32,000	
Insurance Expense	**38,000**	
Utilities Expense	18,300	
Office Supplies Expense	**1,000**	
Boating Supplies Expense	**7,850**	
Depreciation Expense	**8,300**	
Income Tax Expense	3,500	
Totals	$521,400	$521,400

continued ▶

Prepare Financial Statements from Adjusted Trial Balance, *continued*

Schuylkill River Rowing and Sailing, Inc.
Adjusted Trial Balance
December 31, 2017

Account	Dr.	Cr.	
Cash	$24,620		Use these accounts for the balance sheet.
Accounts Receivable	2,730		
Prepaid Insurance	2,500		
Office Supplies	1,250		
Boating Supplies	4,150		
Equipment	145,700		
Accum. Depreciation— Equipment		88,800	
Unearned Revenue		300	
Accounts Payable		15,300	
Common Stock		10,000	
Retained Earnings		45,000	Use these accounts for the statement of retained earnings.
Dividends	25,000		
Boat Rental Revenue		332,700	Use these accounts for the income statement.
Teaching Revenue		29,300	
Wages Expense	206,500		
Rent Expense	32,000		
Insurance Expense	38,000		Then put the net income or net loss in the statement of retained earnings to complete the calculation of the ending balance of retained earnings. Also put this balance in the balance sheet.
Utilities Expense	18,300		
Office Supplies Expense	1,000		
Boating Supplies Expense	7,850		
Depreciation Expense	8,300		
Income Tax Expense	3,500		
Totals	$521,400	$521,400	

On the next page, you can see all the completed financial statements.

Prepare Financial Statements from Adjusted Trial Balance, *continued*

Schuylkill River Rowing and Sailing, Inc.
Income Statement
For the Year Ended December 31, 2017

Revenues		
Boat rental revenue	$332,700	
Teaching revenue	29,300	
Total revenues		$362,000
Operating expenses		
Wages expense	$206,500	
Insurance expense	38,000	
Rent expense	32,000	
Utilities expense	18,300	
Depreciation expense	8,300	
Boating supplies expense	7,850	
Office supplies expense	1,000	
Total operating expenses		311,950
Income before tax		50,050
Income tax expense		3,500
Net income		$46,550

Schuylkill River Rowing and Sailing, Inc.
Statement of Retained Earnings
For the Year Ended December 31, 2017

Retained Earnings January 1, 2017	$45,000
Add: Net income	46,550
Less: Dividends	(25,000)
Retained Earnings, December 31, 2017	$66,550

Schuylkill River Rowing and Sailing, Inc.
Balance Sheet
December 31, 2017

Assets

Cash		$24,620
Accounts receivable		2,730
Office supplies		1,250
Boating supplies		4,150
Prepaid insurance		2,500
Equipment	$145,700	
Less: Accum. depreciation	(88,800)	56,900
Total assets		$92,150

Liabilities

Accounts payable	$15,300
Unearned revenues	300
Total liabilities	15,600

Stockholders' Equity

Paid-in capital	
Common Stock	10,000
Retained Earnings	66,550
Total stockholders' equity	76,550
Total liabilities and Stockholders' equity	$92,150

PRACTICE   Learning Goal 5

Solutions are in the disk at the back of the book and at: www.worthyjames.com

Learning Goal 5 is about preparing and using the adjusted trial balance. Answer the questions and problems below to practice what you have just read.

Multiple Choice
Select the best answer.

1. An adjusted trial balance is prepared:
   a. as soon as the adjusting entries have been prepared and posted.
   b. before the adjusting entries have been prepared and posted.
   c. after the financial statements have been prepared.
   d. none of the above.

2. The purpose of the adjusted trial balance is to:
   a. verify the equality of debit and credit balances of the ledger accounts after the adjusting entries have been posted.
   b. serve as a source of account balance information for the preparation of financial statements.
   c. both a and b.
   d. none of the above.

3. Which of the following accounts would probably show a higher balance on the adjusted trial balance than on the trial balance?
   a. Prepaid Insurance
   b. Insurance Expense
   c. Cash
   d. Supplies

4. Which of the following accounts would probably show a smaller balance on the adjusted trial balance than on the trial balance?
   a. Supplies
   b. Insurance Expense
   c. Service Revenue
   d. Accumulated Depreciation

5. Financial statements are usually prepared in the following order:
   a. income statement, balance sheet, statement of owner's equity
   b. income statement, statement of owner's equity, balance sheet
   c. balance sheet, income statement, statement of owner's equity
   d. balance sheet, statement of owner's equity, income statement

6. The source(s) of the account balance numbers used in an adjusted trial balance is (are) the:
   a. unadjusted trial balance.
   b. final balances of the individual ledger accounts after adjusting entries have been posted.
   c. prior financial statement balances.
   d. general journal adjusting entries.

7. The sequence of the accounts that appear in a trial balance is determined by
   a. each account's chart of accounts number.
   b. the size of each account's balance.
   c. a decision of each individual preparer.
   d. GAAP.

| LEARNING GOAL 6 | # Review the Accounting Cycle |

The Accounting Cycle Procedures

Cycle of Regular Procedures

In most businesses, accounting activity occurs in a regular, sequential kind of pattern. This sequential pattern of accounting activity is known as the *accounting cycle*. The cycle consists of analyzing, processing, and communicating.

What You Should Know at This Point

The parts of the cycle that you should understand so far are:

- **Analyze:** During the period, events are analyzed to determine if they should be recorded as transactions. Analysis is also done at the end of the period to determine how adjustments should be recorded.

- **Process:** Processing refers to recording, organizing, adjusting, and correcting procedures. So far, you have learned:
  - Recording (journalizing) transactions (Volume 1)
  - Posting (Volume 1)
  - Preparing a trial balance (Volume 1)
  - Journalizing and posting the adjusting entries
  - Preparing the adjusted trial balance

- **Communicate:** Communication refers to the preparation of financial reports and disclosures and interpretations. So far, you have practiced preparing three reports:
  - The income statement
  - The statement of retained earnings
  - The balance sheet

You will learn more about the remaining processing steps in upcoming sections.

Some Variations

Not every business and not every accountant are exactly the same, so you can expect some small differences in the exact steps of the accounting cycle. However, a useful overview of the cycle is shown on the next page for you to study.

The Accounting Cycle Procedures, *continued*

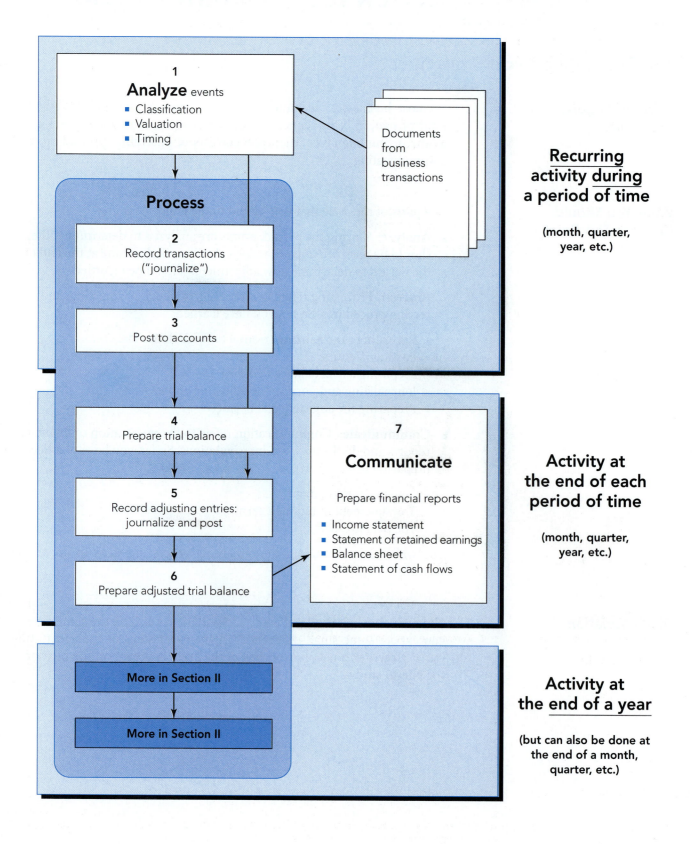

1

Analyze events
- Classification
- Valuation
- Timing

Documents from business transactions

Recurring activity during a period of time

(month, quarter, year, etc.)

Process

2
Record transactions ("journalize")

3
Post to accounts

4
Prepare trial balance

5
Record adjusting entries: journalize and post

6
Prepare adjusted trial balance

7

Communicate

Prepare financial reports

- Income statement
- Statement of retained earnings
- Balance sheet
- Statement of cash flows

Activity at the end of each period of time

(month, quarter, year, etc.)

More in Section II

More in Section II

Activity at the end of a year

(but can also be done at the end of a month, quarter, etc.)

CUMULATIVE VOCABULARY REVIEW

This is a vocabulary review for Learning Goals 1 through 6. On a separate piece of paper, match each description with the term that it describes. The answer for each term is in the right column. (Suggestion: Cover the answers in the right column as you test your vocabulary.)

Term	Description	Answers
1. Revenue	a. Another name for expense.	1l
2. Matching principle	b. The assumption that the life of a business can be divided into regular, fixed time periods. Also called the periodicity assumption.	2h
3. Unearned revenue	c. A fiscal year that begins on January 1 and ends on December 31.	3t
4. Deliverable	d. The accounting method that records the effects of both cash and noncash transactions by applying the revenue recognition and matching principles.	4k
5. Accounting period	e. A rule that directs accountants to record revenue in the period in which it is earned.	5n
6. Accrual adjustment	f. An asset account used to record a near-term future expense for which cash was paid.	6y
7. Expense	g. The cost of a plant asset minus its accumulated depreciation.	7z
8. Accrued expense	h. A rule that directs accountants to record expenses in the period in which they helped to create revenue.	8x
9. Accrual basis accounting	i. Financial reports prepared more frequently than annually.	9d
10. Deferral	j. To record a transaction.	10w
11. Calendar year	k. The specific goods or service that will be provided.	11c
12. Contra asset	l. An increase in stockholders' equity caused by making a sale of goods or services.	12r
13. Accrued revenue	m. Journal entries that are done to make sure that revenue from a transaction is recorded in the correct periods and that expense from a transaction is recorded in the correct periods.	13s
14. Time-period assumption	n. A fixed period of time used to measure the progress of a business.	14b
15. Cash basis accounting	o. Allocating the cost of plant and equipment assets into expense.	15v
16. Revenue recognition principle	p. The period of time that an asset will provide benefits and be useful to a business.	16e
17. Expired cost	q. Having enough cash to pay debts as they become due.	17a
18. Prepaid expense	r. An account that acts as an offset against an asset account.	18f
19. Interim statement	s. A revenue that has been earned but no cash has been received.	19i
20. Recognize	t. A liability account used to record the amount of a near-term future revenue for which cash has already been received.	20j
21. Adjusting entry	u. Any consecutive 12-month period of business activity.	21m
22. Book value	v. An accounting method that records only the effects of cash transactions.	22g
23. Fiscal year	w. A transaction in which cash is either paid in advance or received in advance for a near-term future expense or for a near-term future revenue.	23u
24. Depreciation	x. An expense which has been incurred but no cash has been paid.	24o
25. Useful life	y. An adjusting entry that is used to record an accrued revenue or an accrued expense that has not yet been recorded.	25p
26. Solvency	z. A decrease in stockholders' equity caused by consuming goods or service resources to create revenue.	26q

CUMULATIVE TEST — Learning Goals 1–6

Time Limit: 60 minutes

Instructions

*On a separate sheet of paper, select the best answer to each question. Do **not** look back in the book when taking the test. (If you need to do this, you are not ready.) After you finish the test, refer to the answers and circle the number of each question that you missed. Then go to the **Help Table** (on page 203) to identify your strong and weak knowledge areas by individual learning goal.*

Multiple Choice

Select the best answer.

1. In accrual accounting, the rule that tells accountants when to record revenues is called the ········ recognition principle, and the rule that tells accountants when to record expenses is called the ········ principle.
   a. matching/expense
   b. revenue/matching
   c. matching/revenue
   d. revenue/accrual

2. Adjusting entries are needed because:
   a. in cash basis accounting, some transactions create unrecorded expenses or revenues.
   b. in accrual basis accounting, some transactions create unrecorded expenses or revenues.
   c. they ensure that accrual basis accounting includes all noncash revenues and expenses.
   d. both b and c.

3. Brainard Company properly recorded the receipt of a $1,500 advance payment from a customer into unearned revenue. If the company later failed to prepare an adjusting entry for the revenue earned from this transaction, the result would be:

	Assets	Liabilities	Net Income
a.	understated	overstated	overstated
b.	no effect	understated	understated
c.	no effect	overstated	understated
d.	overstated	overstated	overstated

4. Alexandria Company failed to prepare an adjusting entry for revenue that it had earned, but had not yet billed to the customer. The result of this error would be:

	Assets	Liabilities	Net Income
a.	understated	overstated	overstated
b.	understated	no effect	understated
c.	no effect	overstated	understated
d.	overstated	no effect	overstated

5. The normal balance of a depreciation expense account is a ········, and the normal balance of accumulated depreciation is a ········. The greater the accumulated depreciation, the ········ the book value of an asset.
   a. debit/credit/greater
   b. credit/debit/lower
   c. debit/credit/lower
   d. debit/debit/greater

6. Which of the following journal entries is an accrual adjusting entry?
   a. Depreciation Expense $$
          Accumulated Depreciation $$
   b. Cash $$
          Service Revenue $$
   b. Unearned Revenue $$
          Service Revenue $$
   d. Accounts Receivable $$
          Service Revenue $$

7. For the accounting cycle, which of the following sequence of events is in the correct order?
   a. analyze, journalize and post adjustments, journalize transactions
   b. journalize transactions, prepare financial statements, prepare adjusted trial balance
   c. journalize transactions, prepare adjusted trial balance, prepare financial statements
   d. prepare financial statements, journalize and post adjustments, prepare adjusted trial balance

8. The periodicity (time-period) assumption means that:
   a. the calculation of net income should be deferred until a business is sold.
   b. one transaction can only affect one accounting period.
   c. the economic life of a business can be divided into time periods.
   d. businesses should be audited periodically.

9. Which of the following is *not* a correct description of accrual basis accounting?
   a. Accrual basis accounting is applied by the use of the revenue recognition and matching principles to determine net income.
   b. It is necessary to record revenue when sales are made even though no cash is received.
   c. Expenses can occur with or without a cash payment.
   d. Revenue should not be recorded until all cash is actually received from a customer.

10. An adjusting entry is:
    a. an important technique used only in accrual basis accounting to apply the revenue recognition principle.
    b. an important technique used only in accrual basis accounting to apply the matching principle.
    c. an important technique used only in accrual basis accounting to apply both the revenue recognition and matching principles.
    d. used both in accrual basis and cash basis accounting.

11. On December 1, Central Company paid $9,000 for four months' rent. On December 31, year end, the balance in the Prepaid Rent account should be:
    a. $6,750.
    b. $2,250.
    c. $9,000.
    d. none of the above.

12. Metro Company has a five-day workweek that ends on Fridays. The weekly payroll is $24,000. If the last day of the year falls on a Thursday, the adjusting entry should be:
    a. Wages Expense, debit $24,000; Wages Payable, credit $24,000.
    b. Wages Expense, debit $19,200; Wages Payable, credit $19,200.
    c. Wages Expense, debit $19,200, Cash, credit $19,200.
    d. Wages Payable, debit $14,400; Cash, credit $14,400.

13. On July 1 of the current year, Southeast Company purchased computer equipment for $15,000. The company got an unusual bargain, because the equipment normally sells for $20,000. The equipment has an estimated five-year useful life with no residual value. The amount of depreciation expense that should be recorded for the equipment in the current year is:
    a. $15,000.
    b. $1,500.
    c. $3,000.
    d. $2,000.

14. Which of the following entries is *not* an adjustment for a prepayment (deferral)?

   a. Supplies Expense $$
          Supplies $$

   b. Wages Expense $$
          Wages Payable $$

   c. Unearned Revenue $$
          Service Revenue $$

   d. Insurance Expense $$
          Prepaid Insurance $$

15. From the items listed below, indicate which activity must be done before the others:

   a. Prepare financial statements.

   b. Post adjusting entires.

   c. Journalize transactions during the period.

   d. Journalize adjusting entries.

16. The periodicity (time-period) assumption:

   a. ensures that accounting information is reported at regular intervals such as monthly, quarterly, or annually.

   b. means that net income may result from the use of estimates, such as for depreciation.

   c. creates the need for adjusting entries.

   d. all of the above.

17. On April 29, Miami–Dade partnership performed $1,000 of computer consulting for a client. The bill for services was sent to the client on May 5. The client paid the $1,000 on May 20. The partners are not sure if they should record the $1,000 of revenue in April or May. If GAAP is properly applied, the $1,000 of revenue should be recognized:

   a. in April, if cash basis accounting is used.

   b. in May, if cash basis accounting is used.

   c. in April, if accrual basis accounting is used.

   d. in May, if accrual basis accounting is used.

18. In the current period, Gulf Coast Company recorded a $5,000 payment for previously accrued advertising expense and also recorded $10,000 of prepaid advertising expense. What is the total effect of these two transactions on advertising expense in the current period?

   a. increase $15,000

   b. increase $5,000

   c. increase $10,000

   d. no effect

19. Broward, Broward, & Broward partnership charges $120 per hour for financial consulting services. On June 5, the company received an advance payment from a client for nine hours of service, which was correctly recorded. On June 30, four hours of time had been used. What adjusting entry is needed on June 30th?

   a. Cash   1,080
          Unearned Revenue   1,080

   b. Unearned Revenue   600
          Service Revenue   600

   c. Cash   480
          Unearned Revenue   480

   d. some other entry

CUMULATIVE TEST   Learning Goals 1–6, continued

20. Joliet Company purchased $4,800 of spare parts supplies on September 3 and properly recorded the purchase as the asset Spare Parts Supplies. At the end of the fiscal year, on October 31, an inventory of parts shows 15% of the parts purchased are still remaining. The adjusting entry on October 31 for the unrecorded expense is:

a. Supplies Expense   720
    Spare Parts Supplies   720
b. Spare Parts Supplies   4,080
    Supplies Expense   4,080
c. Supplies Expense   4,080
    Spare Parts Supplies   4,080
d. none of the above

21. On March 1, 2018, Oakton, Inc. sold a truck that had cost the company $22,000 and had an estimated $4,000 residual value. The truck had been purchased on January 2, 2017 and had an estimated five-year economic life. What was the balance in the Accumulated Depreciation account when the truck was sold?

a. $7,800
b. $10,800
c. $9,000
d. some other amount

22. Parkland Enterprises failed to prepare an adjusting entry for advertising expense that had been incurred but not yet paid. This will result in:

	Assets	Liabilities	Net Income
a.	no effect	overstated	understated
b.	overstated	no effect	overstated
c.	no effect	overstated	understated
d.	no effect	understated	overstated

23. On January 5, 2018, the Illinois Central Research Company recorded the following transaction:

Accounts Payable   4,000
Repairs Expense   1,500
    Cash   5,500

If there were no other accrued expenses in 2017, how much repairs expense did the company accrue at year end, December 31, 2017?

a. $4,000
b. $1,500
c. $5,500
d. some other amount

24. Southern Union Company made these adjustments at December 31, year end:

(A)
Repairs Expense   900
    Accounts Payable   900
(B)
Unearned Service Revenue   2,000
    Service Revenue   2,000

The entries above indicate what situations had created the need for adjustments?

a. *Entry A:* accrued expense; *entry B:* accrued revenue
b. *Entry A:* deferred (prepaid) expense; *entry B:* accrued revenue
c. *Entry A:* deferred (prepaid) expense; *entry B:* deferred revenue
d. *Entry A:* accrued expense; *entry B:* deferred revenue

25. What is the most important outcome of the accounting cycle?
    a. useful and reliable financial statements
    b. up-to-date journal entries and ledger postings
    c. an accurate adjusted trial balance
    d. all of the above

26. Which of the following is *not* a common quality of all adjusting entries?
    a. Adjusting entries are recorded at the end of an accounting period after all the other transactions are completed.
    b. Adjusting entries will often affect the cash account.
    c. Adjusting entries always affect at least one balance sheet account and one income statement account.
    d. The calculations for adjusting entries are done shortly after the accounting period to which the entries will apply.

27. Lansdale Company received a $12,000 advance payment from Jones Company on September 12 and a $5,000 advance payment from Smith Company on October 1. At December 31, year end, $2,700 of the amount from Jones Company would be earned in the next year whereas one-fourth of the amount from Smith Company had been earned in the current year. The December 31 adjusting entry for Lansdale should be:
    a. debit, Unearned Revenue $10,550; credit, Service Revenue $10,550.
    b. debit, Cash $14,700; credit, Service Revenue $14,700.
    c. debit, Service Revenue $14,300; credit, Unearned Revenue $14,300.
    d. some other entry.

28. Failure to record depreciation would result in:

	Assets	Liabilities	Net Income
a.	no effect	overstated	understated
b.	overstated	no effect	overstated
c.	no effect	overstated	understated
d.	no effect	understated	overstated

29. Which of the following transactions will *not* require an adjustment for an accrual?
    a. Pueblo Company was prepaid $1,200 by a customer. During the current period, the company earned $500 of the advance payment.
    b. Front Range Enterprises received the October telephone bill. At fiscal year end, on October 31, the bill is still unrecorded.
    c. Aims Technology Company performed $20,200 of safety design services in July but has not yet received payment from the customer as of July 31, fiscal year end.
    d. Arapahoe Company borrowed $50,000. Interest on the loan is payable semi-annually.

30. A time period that would *not* be called an interim period is:
    a. month.
    b. quarter.
    c. semi-annual.
    d. annual.

31. The January 1, 2018 balance of Prepaid Insurance was $1,500, from a one-year prepayment made on August 1, 2017. On June 2, 2018, the company made another prepayment in the amount of $1,800 for a one-year insurance policy. The adjusting journal entry on December 31, 2018 should be:
    a. debit, Prepaid Insurance $2,400; credit, Cash $2,400.
    b. debit, Insurance Expense $1,050; credit, Prepaid Insurance $1,050.
    c. debit, Prepaid Insurance $1,500; credit, Insurance Expense $1,500.
    d. debit, Insurance Expense $2,550; credit, Prepaid Insurance $2,550.

32. At year end, the accountant for Bismark Company forgot to make the adjusting entry for prepaid insurance that expired during the year. This error will result in:

	Assets	*Liabilities*	*Net Income*
a.	overstated	overstated	understated
b.	overstated	no effect	overstated
c.	no effect	overstated	understated
d.	no effect	understated	overstated

33. Oakland Enterprises rents computer equipment at a cost of $3,000 per month. The rental fee is paid on the 20th of each month. The year-end adjustment on June 30 is:
 a. debit, Rent Expense $3,000; credit, Cash $3,000.
 b. debit, Rent Expense $2,000; credit, Rent Payable $2,000.
 c. debit, Rent Expense $1,000; credit, Rent Payable $1,000.
 d. none of the above.

34. The Susan Lee law firm provided 30 hours of legal consultation services to Dave Philips at the rate of $175 per hour. As of June 30, fiscal year end, $2,500 had been billed to Mr. Philips and correctly recorded. What adjustment is required on June 30?
 a. Accounts Receivable   2,500
      Legal Fees Earned   2,500
 b. Accounts Receivable   5,200
      Legal Fees Earned   5,200
 c. Accounts Receivable   2,750
      Legal Fees Earned   2,750
 d. none of the above

35. Bristol Partnership shows the ledger account balances that you see below, on the dates indicated. No rent was prepaid in 2017.

Account Name	*December 31, 2016*	*December 31, 2017*
Prepaid Rent	$5,500	-0-
Rent Expense	$15,000	$17,000

The amount of cash paid for rent expense in 2017 is:
 a. The December 31, 2016 prepaid rent amount is used up in 2017 and becomes a non-cash expense in 2017. The cash paid for rent expense in 2017 is $17,000 − $5,500 = $11,500.
 b. $17,000.
 c. $20,000.
 d. none of the above.

36. On April 1, Otero Company loaned $10,000 to an important customer. Monthly interest payments from the borrower are $100 per month, payable on the first of each month. The adjusting entry on December 31, year end, is:
 a. debit, Interest Receivable $100; credit, Interest Earned $100.
 b. debit, Cash $100; credit, Interest Earned $100.
 c. debit, Interest Earned $100; credit, Interest Receivable $100.
 d. no adjusting entry is needed.

37. An adjusted trial balance should be prepared:
 a. before the adjusting entries and the financial statements are prepared.
 b. after the adjusting entries and the financial statements are prepared.
 c. after the adjusting entries and before the financial statements are prepared.
 d. may be prepared at any time.

38. Failure to record accrued revenue would have which effect?

	Assets	Liabilities	Net Income
a.	understated	no effect	understated
b.	overstated	understated	no effect
c.	overstated	no effect	understated
d.	understated	no effect	overstated

39. Which of the following is not true about an adjusted trial balance?
    a. It is prepared after the adjustments to the ending ledger account balances.
    b. The account balances on the adjusted trial balance are used on the financial statements.
    c. The balance of a prepaid expense would probably be higher on the adjusted trial balance than on the trial balance.
    d. The balance of a prepaid expense would probably be lower on the adjusted trial balance than on the trial balance.

40. An accrued revenue is a revenue that has been:
    a. earned and cash has been received.
    b. prepaid by the customer.
    c. earned and cash has not been received.
    d. none of the above.

CUMULATIVE TEST SOLUTIONS   Learning Goals 1–6

Multiple Choice

1. b

2. d *Note:* Adjusting entries are not needed in cash basis accounting because in cash basis accounting, revenues and expenses can only happen when cash is received or paid. There are no earned but unrecorded revenues or incurred but unrecorded expenses.

3. c because the liability Unearned Revenue should have been decreased and revenue should have been increased, but this did not happen. Remember, *you can visualize all changes*, either by drawing a picture or using the accounting equation. For example, suppose the entire $1,500 had been earned. To visualize the change:

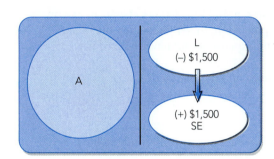

or you could use the accounting equation:

$$A = \quad L\downarrow \quad + \quad SE\uparrow$$
Unearned   Service
Revenue   Revenue
−$1,500   +$1,500

4. b Because the company should have debited Accounts Receivable and credited Revenue.

5. c

6. d Refer to the table of adjusting entry characteristics in Learning Goal 4.

7. c

8. c

9. d

10. c

11. a *Calculation:* $9,000/4 months = usage rate of $2,250 per month. $9,000 − $2,250 = $6,750 (one month of usage: December 1–December 31).

12. b *Calculation:* $24,000/5 = $4,800 per day. Monday–Thursday is four days. 4 × $4,800 = $19,200.

13. b *Calculation:* $15,000/5 = $3,000 per year. $3,000/2 = $1,500 for six months (owned for six months).
Note: The $20,000 "normal" selling price is irrelevant. Actual cost is what is depreciated.

14. b Refer to the table of adjusting entry characteristics in Learning Goal 4 and appendices.

15. c

16. d

17. c Cash basis accounting does not comply with GAAP.

18. d Paying the accrual from a previous period reduces a liability. Paying a future expense in the current period creates an asset called Prepaid Advertising. (*Remember:* Continue to visualize transactions if you feel the need!)

19. d *Calculation:* Rate of earning is $120/hour, so 4 hours × $120 = $480 earned. The correct entry is to debit Unearned Revenue, $480; credit Service Revenue, $480.

20. c *Calculation:* The actual ending balance of parts is 15% of $4,800, or $720. $4,800 − $720 = $4,080.

CUMULATIVE TEST SOLUTIONS   Learning Goals 1–6, continued

21. a *Calculation:* ($22,000 − $4,000)/60 months = $300 per month. Here, it is easier to calculate the rate of depreciation per month because we can just count the number of months from the time the asset was purchased until it was sold (rather than dealing with a fraction of a year). So, $300 × 26 months = $7,800.

22. d The entry should have debited an expense and credited a liability. The expense would reduce net income.

23. a In this case, the January 5 payment is for both the prior year accrual and a current year expense payable to the same party.

24. d

25. a

26. b

27. a

28. b The credit entry would have increased accumulated depreciation, thereby reducing the book value and reducing total assets. The debit to depreciation expense would have reduced net income.

29. a This is a deferral (prepaid). Cash has already been received and the transaction was recorded.

30. d

31. d $1,500 + ($1,800 × 7/12)

32. b The entry would have debited Insurance Expense, which reduces net income, and credited the asset Prepaid Insurance, which reduces total assets.

33. c The last third of the month must be accrued.

34. c The total revenue earned here is 30 × $175 = $5,250. So $5,250 − $2,500 = $2,750.

35. a This is a "related accounts" type of problem. The *decrease* in the Prepaid Rent (is a noncash rent expense that uses up non-cash assest of $5,500) is subtracted from Rent Expense. The balance of the Rent Expense must have been paid in cash.

36. a

37. c

38. a

39. c This is false because usually adjusting entries reduce the amount of prepaid expenses that were recorded as assets. Therefore, the asset balance on the adjusted trial balance would be lower.

40. c

HELP TABLE   Identify Your Strengths and Weaknesses

The questions in this test cover the 6 learning goals of Section I. After you have listed the number of each question that you missed, look at the table below.

Go to the first learning goal category in the table: Explain the Meaning of "Accounting Period." The second column in the table shows which questions on the test covered this learning goal. Look on the test to see if you listed numbers 8, 16, or 30. How many did you miss? Write this number in the "How Many Missed?" column. Repeat this process for each of the learning goal categories in the table.

If you *miss **two** or more questions* for any learning goal, you are too weak in that learning goal and you need to *review*. The last column shows you where to read and practice so you can improve your score.

Some learning goal categories have more questions because you need to be especially well prepared in these areas. More questions indicates where your performance must be better.

Learning Goal	Questions	How many missed?	Material begins on . . .
SECTION I			
1. Explain the Meaning of "Accounting Period"	8, 16, 30		page 7
2. Explain the Basic Principles for Recording Revenues and Expenses	1, 9, 17		page 16
3. Explain the Concept of Adjusting Entries	2, 10, 26		page 36
4. Analyze Accounts and Prepare Adjusting Entries	6, 14, 18, 24, 29, 35		page 43
4. Prepare Adjusting Entries for Prepaid Expenses (LG 4 appendix)	11, 20, 31, 32		page 71
4. Prepare Adjusting Entries for Unearned Revenues (LG 4 appendix)	3, 19, 27, 34		page 105
4. Depreciate Plant and Equipment Assets (LG 4 appendix)	5, 13, 21, 28		page 136
4. Prepare Adjusting Entries for Accrued Revenues (LG 4 appendix)	4, 36, 38, 40		page 151
4. Prepare Adjusting Entries for Accrued Expenses (LG 4 appendix)	12, 22, 23, 33		page 166
5. Prepare and Use an Adjusted Trial Balance	37, 39		page 186
6. Review the Accounting Cycle	7, 15, 25		page 191

Completing the Accounting Cycle

OVERVIEW

What this section does	This section focuses on the specialized activity that occurs at the end of an accounting period after finishing the adjusting entries.
Use this section if . . .	■ you want to learn how to complete the accounting cycle after you have finished the adjustments.

LEARNING GOALS

| LEARNING GOAL 7 | **Prepare and Use a Worksheet; Use a Classified Balance Sheet** |

Overview of Section II

Many Tasks at the End of a Period

The end of an accounting period involves several additional tasks, which together have the ultimate objectives of:

- providing timely and accurate financial statements, and
- making the accounting records correct and ready for the next period.

If you studied Section I, you are already familiar with one of the most important of these tasks, which is the preparation of adjusting entries. This section shows you the rest of the tasks that are involved.

In Learning Goal 7, you will find:

Step 2: Calculate the Adjustments and Enter Them in the Adjustments Column, *continued*

Worksheet Example and Adjustments Information

The worksheet on page 211 shows the adjusting entries entered into the adjustments columns. The adjustments information for this worksheet is:

(a) On May 31, an inventory of **office supplies** is taken. $520 of supplies remain. Therefore, $580 of office supplies must have been used up (1,100 – 520 = 580), so Office Supplies is credited and Office Supplies Expense is debited for $580.

(b) On May 31, an inventory of **modeling supplies** is taken. $600 of supplies remain. Therefore, $200 of modeling supplies must have been used up, so Modeling Supplies is credited and Modeling Supplies Expense is debited for $200. Notice that the Office Supplies Expense and Modeling Supplies Expense accounts apparently have not been used yet for the month, so we had to add them below the trial balance.

(c) The **office equipment** was purchased on November 1, 2016, and has a 60-month (five-year) life. It has a residual value of $100. Therefore, the monthly depreciation is ($9,700 – 100)/60 = $160. Depreciation Expense is debited for $160 and Accumulated Depreciation is credited for $160.

(d) Eight months of **prepaid fire insurance** was purchased on May 1, 2017 for $600 and recorded as the asset Prepaid Insurance. Therefore the monthly use of this insurance is $600/8 = $75. Insurance Expense is debited $75 and Prepaid Insurance is credited $75.

(e) The business recorded as the liability **Unearned Revenue** a fees prepayment of $3,000 it received in April. Some of this was earned in April, and $1,500 was earned in May. To record the May amount earned, debit Unearned Modeling Fees $1,500 and credit Fees Earned $1,500.

(f) On May 31, $900 of **employee salaries** had been earned by the employees but not yet paid to them. Debit Salaries Expense $900 and credit Salaries Payable $900 to accrue the salaries expense.

(g) The note payable is dated May 1, 2017, and has an interest rate of 8%. The principal and interest on the note are not payable until December 1, 2017. The monthly interest to accrue is $15,000 × .08 × 30/360 = $100. Debit Interest Expense $100 and credit Interest Payable $100.

(Use Principal × Interest Rate × (Days/360) as the simple interest calculation. If you need to review simple interest, see the math review in the disk at the back of the book.)

Step 2: Calculate the Adjustments and Enter Them in the Adjustments Column, *continued*

Applegate Modeling Agency, Inc.										
Worksheet										
For the Month Ended May 31, 2017										
	Trial Balance		Adjustments		Adjusted Trial Balance		Income Statement		Balance Sheet	
Account Titles	Dr.	Cr.	Dr.	Cr.	Dr.	Cr.	Dr.	Cr.	Dr.	Cr.
Cash	15,850									
Accounts Receivable	2,800									
Office Supplies	1,100			(a) 580						
Modeling Supplies	800			(b) 200						
Prepaid Insurance	600			(d) 75						
Office Equipment	9,700									
Accum. Dep'n.										
—Office Equipment		960		(c) 160						
Accounts Payable		1,400								
Unearned Fees		2,000	(e) 1,500							
Notes Payable		15,000								
Common Stock		2,000								
Retained Earnings		8,120								
Dividends	2,000									
Fees Earned		9,300		(e) 1,500						
Interest Earned		200								
Salaries Expense	4,100		(f) 900							
Rent Expense	1,450									
Income Tax Expense	300									
Utilities Expense	280									
Totals	38,980	38,980								
Office Supplies Expense			(a) 580							
Modeling Supplies										
Expense			(b) 200							
Depreciation Expense			(c) 160							
Insurance Expense			(d) 75							
Salaries Payable				(f) 900						
Interest Expense			(g) 100							
Interest Payable				(g) 100						
Totals			3,515	3,515						

Step 3: Enter Account Balances in the Adjusted Trial Balance Column

Procedure

1. On each line, to determine the amount that should go into the adjusted trial balance columns, combine the amount in the trial balance columns with the amount in the adjustments column.
2. When you are through, be sure that the total debits equal the total credits in the adjusted trial balance column.

Examples

In the continuation of the worksheet on page 213, note the following:

- **The Cash account:** In the trial balance columns, the Cash account has a debit balance of $15,850. There are no adjustments to Cash, so the amount extended into the adjusted trial balance column is a debit balance of $15,850.
- **The Modeling Supplies account:** In the trial balance columns, the Modeling Supplies account has a debit balance of $800. There is a credit (decrease) of $200 to Modeling Supplies in the adjustments columns. The adjusted balance of Modeling Supplies is $800 - 200 = $600 debit balance extended into the adjusted trial balance debit column.
- **The Fees Earned account:** In the trial balance columns, the Fees Earned account has a credit balance of $9,300. There is a credit (increase) of $1,500 to Fees Earned in the adjustments columns. The adjusted balance of Fees Earned is therefore $9,300 + 1,500 = $10,800 extended into the adjusted trial balance credit column.

Step 3: Enter Account Balances in the Adjusted Trial Balance Column, *continued*

Account Titles	Trial Balance Dr.	Trial Balance Cr.	Adjustments Dr.	Adjustments Cr.	Adjusted Trial Balance Dr.	Adjusted Trial Balance Cr.	Income Statement Dr.	Income Statement Cr.	Balance Sheet Dr.	Balance Sheet Cr.
Applegate Modeling Agency, Inc.										
Worksheet										
For the Month Ended May 31, 2017										
Cash	15,850				15,850					
Accounts Receivable	2,800				2,800					
Office Supplies	1,100			(a) 580	520					
Modeling Supplies	800			(b) 200	600					
Prepaid Insurance	600			(d) 75	525					
Office Equipment	9,700				9,700					
Accum. Dep'n.—										
Office Equipment		960		(c) 160		1,120				
Accounts Payable		1,400				1,400				
Unearned Fees		2,000	(e) 1,500			500				
Notes Payable		15,000				15,000				
Common Stock		2,000				2,000				
Retained Earnings		8,120				8,120				
Dividends	2,000				2,000					
Fees Earned		9,300		(e) 1,500		10,800				
Interest Earned		200				200				
Salaries Expense	4,100		(f) 900		5,000					
Rent Expense	1,450				1,450					
Income Tax Expense	300				300					
Utilities Expense	280				280					
Totals	38,980	38,980								
Office Supplies Expense			(a) 580		580					
Modeling Supplies Expense			(b) 200		200					
Depreciation Expense			(c) 160		160					
Insurance Expense			(d) 75		75					
Salaries Payable				(f) 900		900				
Interest Expense			(g) 100		100					
Interest Payable				(g) 100		100				
Totals			3,515	3,515	40,140	40,140				

continued on page 220.

Check Your Understanding

Practice 1

On a separate sheet of paper, write the correct Tamounts for the empty boxes. The answers are on page 217.

	Monticello Photographic Studio, Inc.						
	Worksheet						
	For the Month Ended March 31, 2017						
	Trial Balance		Adjustments		Adjusted Trial Balance		
Account Titles	Dr.	Cr.	Dr.	Cr.	Dr.	Cr.	
Cash	11,000				11,000		
Accounts Receivable	750		(g) 900		1,650		
Prepaid Insurance	2,400			(a)			
Office Supplies	955			(d) 90	865		
Photography Supplies	11,392			(b)	10,842		
Photography Equipment	84,500				84,500		
Accum. Dep'n.							
—Photography Equipment		71,300		(c) 825		72,125	
Office Equipment	5,590				5,590		
Accum. Dep'n.							
—Office Equipment		3,300		(c)		3,850	
Accounts Payable		4,341		(e) 214		4,555	
Unearned Revenue		1,500	(g) 1,000			500	
Common Stock		5,000				5,000	
Retained Earnings		38,000				38,000	
Dividends	2,500				2,500		
Fees Earned				(g)		13,900	
Wages Expense	2,500		(f)		3,005		
Rent Expense	3,000				3,000		
Insurance Expense	50		(a) 200		250		
Advertising Expense			(e) 214		3,214		
Office Supplies Expense	2,292		(d) 90		2,382		
Utilities Expense	5,512				5,512		
Totals	135,441	135,441					
Depreciation Expense			(c) 1,375		1,375		
Photography Supplies Expense			(b) 550		550		
Wages Payable				(f)			
Totals			4,834	4,834	138,435	138,435	

Practice 2

The accountant of the Winslow Tennis Club started on this worksheet but then had to fill in for a mixed-doubles finals tennis match. This leaves you, the assistant bookkeeper, to prepare the worksheet **up through the adjusted trial balance columns.** The accountant will finish the rest of the worksheet after the big match. She was able to assemble the adjustments information and has listed it below the worksheet. To complete this worksheet use a blank worksheet or the worksheet template for "worksheet practice 2" in the disk at the back of the book or at www.worthyjames.com (student info.) The answers are on page 218.

					Adjusted		Income		Balance	
	Trial Balance		Adjustments		Trial Balance		Statement		Sheet	
Account Titles	Dr.	Cr.	Dr.	Cr.	Dr.	Cr.	Dr.	Cr.	Dr.	Cr.
Cash	45,750									
Dues Receivable	2,800									
Office Supplies	1,100									
Tennis Supplies	2,002									
Notes Receivable	12,000									
Prepaid Insurance	600									
Office Equipment	14,520									
Accum. Dep'n.										
—Office Equipment		11,616								
Building	345,000									
Accum. Dep'n.										
—Building		19,500								
Accounts Payable		855								
Notes Payable		275,000								
Common Stock		5,000								
Retained Earnings		82,161								
Dividends	1,880									
Tennis Instruction										
Fees		9,500								
Dues Revenue		28,500								
Salaries Expense	4,100									
Equipment Rent										
Expense	1,750									
Utilities Expense	280									
Insurance Expense	100									
Maintenance Expense	250									
Totals	432,132	432,132								

Winslow Tennis Club, Inc.
Worksheet
For the Month Ended June 30, 2017

Check Your Understanding

Practice 2 (*continued*)
Adjustments Information

1. A physical inventory as of June 30 indicates $50 of office supplies and $215 of tennis supplies remaining.
2. The note receivable has an annual interest rate of 8%, and the note payable has an annual interest rate of 6%.
3. The office equipment was purchased four years ago. It has an estimated five-year life with no residual value.
4. The building cost of $345,000 includes $129,000 of land, which is not subject to depreciation. The building is being depreciated over a 30-year life with no residual value.
5. The prepaid insurance is for a six-month fire insurance policy.
6. $1,000 of July tennis lesson fees were paid in advance to the club and were included in Tennis Instruction Fees. Note: Because of the incorrect recording, Tennis Instruction Fees is overstated and Unearned Revenue is understated by $1,000.
7. $500 of maintenance wages are owed as of the end of June.

Answers

Practice 1

		Monticello Photographic Studio, Inc.					
		Worksheet					
		For the Month Ended March 31, 2017					
	Trial Balance		Adjustments		Adjusted Trial Balance		
Account Titles	Dr.	Cr.	Dr.	Cr.	Dr.	Cr.	
Cash	11,000				11,000		
Accounts Receivable	750		(g) 900		1,650		
Prepaid Insurance	2,400			(a) 200	2,200		
Office Supplies	955			(d) 90	865		
Photography Supplies	11,392			(b) 550	10,842		
Photography Equipment	84,500				84,500		
Accum. Dep'n.—							
Photography Equipment		71,300		(c) 825		72,125	
Office Equipment	5,590				5,590		
Accum. Dep'n.—							
Office Equipment		3,300		(c) 550		3,850	
Accounts Payable		4,341		(e) 214		4,555	
Unearned Revenue		1,500	(g) 1,000			500	
Common Stock		5,000				5,000	
Retained Earnings		38,000				38,000	
Dividends	2,500				2,500		
Fees Earned		12,000		(g) 1,900		13,900	
Wages Expense	2,500		(f) 505		3,005		
Rent Expense	3,000				3,000		
Insurance Expense	50		(a) 200		250		
Advertising Expense	3,000		(e) 214		3,214		
Office Supplies Expense	2,292		(d) 90		2,382		
Utilities Expense	5,512				5,512		
Totals	135,441	135,441					
Depreciation Expense			(c) 1,375		1,375		
Photography Supplies Expense			(b) 550		550		
Wages Payable				(f) 505		505	
Totals			4,834	4,834	138,435	138,435	

Commentary: Adjustment (a) to **Prepaid Insurance** is a $200 credit because adjustment (a) is also a debit to Insurance Expense. Adjustment (b) is similar. Adjustment (c) for **Accumulated Depreciation** relates to two assets: photography equipment and office equipment. The total depreciation expense is $1,375, and we see that the $825 of this was recorded as accumulated depreciation for photography equipment, so the balance of $550 must be for office equipment. The adjustment (f) for **Wages Expense** is $3,005 – $2,500. This is also recorded as a credit to Wages Payable. The $1,900 adjustment (g) to **Fees Earned** consists of two parts. First, $900 of revenue is accrued with the debit to Accounts Receivable. Secondly, $1,000 of Unearned Revenue is also earned.

Answers

Practice 2

Winslow Tennis Club, Inc.						
Worksheet						
For the Month Ended June 30, 2017						
	Trial Balance		Adjustments		Adjusted Trial Balance	
Account Titles	Dr.	Cr.	Dr.	Cr.	Dr.	Cr.
Cash	45,750				45,750	
Dues Receivable	2,800				2,800	
Office Supplies	1,100			(a) 1,050	50	
Tennis Supplies	2,002			(a) 1,787	215	
Notes Receivable	12,000				12,000	
Prepaid Insurance	600			(e) 100	500	
Office Equipment	14,520				14,520	
Accum. Dep'n.						
Office Equipment		11,616		(d) 242		11,858
Building	345,000				345,000	
Accum. Dep'n.						
—Building		19,500		(d) 600		20,100
Accounts Payable		855				855
Notes Payable		275,000				275,000
Common Stock		5,000				5,000
Retained Earnings		82,161				82,161
Dividends	1,880				1,880	
Tennis Instruction						
Fees		9,500	(f) 1,000			8,500
Dues Revenue		28,500				28,500
Salaries Expense	4,100				4,100	
Equipment Rent						
Expense	1,750				1,750	
Utilities Expense	280				280	
Insurance Expense	100		(e) 100		200	
Maintenance						
Expense	250		(g) 00		750	
Totals	<u>432,132</u>	<u>432,132</u>				

continued on next page

Answers

Practice 2, *continued*

Winslow Tennis Club, Inc.
Worksheet (*continued*)
For the Month Ended June 30, 2017

Account Titles	Trial Balance Dr.	Trial Balance Cr.	Adjustments Dr.	Adjustments Cr.	Adjusted Trial Balance Dr.	Adjusted Trial Balance Cr.
Unearned Tennis Fees				(f) 1,000		1,000
Office Supplies Expense			(a) 1,050		1,050	
Tennis Supplies Expense			(a) 1,787		1,787	
Depreciation Expense			(d) 842		842	
Salaries and Wages Payable				(g) 500		500
Interest Expense			(c) 1,375		1,375	
Interest Receivable			(b) 80		80	
Interest Earned				(b) 80		80
Interest Payable				(c) 1,375		1,375
Totals			6,734	6,734	434,929	434,929

*Interest: $12,000 × .08 × 1/12 = $80; $275,000 × .06 × 1/12 = $1,375

Step 4: Extend the Adjusted Trial Balance Amounts into the Financial Statement Columns

Procedure

In this step, you identify and then separate the income statement accounts from the balance sheet accounts. You place all the income statement accounts into the income statement columns and all the balance sheet accounts into the balance sheet columns.

If an item has a debit balance in the adjusted trial balance column, it is always extended to another debit column. If an item has a credit balance in the adjusted trial balance column, it is always extended to another credit column.

The worksheet on page 220 shows you the adjusted trial balance amounts extended into financial statement columns.

continued ▶

Step 4: Extend the Adjusted Trial Balance Amounts into the Financial Statement Columns, *continued*

Applegate Modeling Agency, Inc.									
Worksheet									
For the Month Ended May 31, 2017									
	Trial Balance		Adjustments		Adjusted Trial Balance		Income Statement		Balance Sheet	
Account Titles	Dr.	Cr.	Dr.	Cr.	Dr.	Cr.	Dr.	Cr.	Dr.	Cr.
Cash	15,850				15,850				15,850	
Accounts Receivable	2,800				2,800				2,800	
Office Supplies	1,100			(a) 580	520				520	
Modeling Supplies	800			(b) 200	600				600	
Prepaid Insurance	600			(d) 75	525				525	
Office Equipment	9,700				9,700				9,700	
Accum. Dep'n.—										
Office Equipment		960		(c) 160		1,120				1,120
Accounts Payable		1,400				1,400				1,400
Unearned Fees		2,000	(e) 1,500			500				500
Notes Payable		15,000				15,000				15,000
Common Stock		2,000				2,000				2,000
Retained Earnings		8,120				8,120				8,120
Dividends	2,000				2,000				2,000	
Fees Earned		9,300		(e) 1,500		10,800		10,800		
Interest Earned		200				200		200		
Salaries Expense	4,100		(f) 900		5,000		5,000			
Rent Expense	1,450				1,450		1,450			
Income Tax Expense	300				300		300			
Utilities Expense	280				280		280			
Totals	38,980	38,980								
Office Supplies Expense			(a) 580		580		580			
Modeling Supplies										
Expense			(b) 200		200		200			
Depreciation Expense			(c) 160		160		160			
Insurance Expense			(d) 75		75		75			
Salaries Payable				(f) 900		900				900
Interest Expense			(g) 100		100		100			
Interest Payable				(g) 100		100				100
Totals			3,515	3,515	40,140	40,140				

Step 5: Total the Financial Statement Columns and Compute the Net Income or Net Loss

Overview

In this step, you calculate the totals of the income statement columns and the balance sheet columns. You should see the same difference between the totals of each type of column. This difference is the net income or net loss.

Procedure

The table below shows you the procedure for completing the worksheet by adding the financial statement columns.

Step	Action		
1	Calculate the totals of the income statement debit and credit columns, and of the balance sheet debit and credit columns.		
	IF . . .	**THEN . . .**	**AND . . .**
	the income statement credit total is greater than the debit total . . .	enter the difference, which is the net *income*, on the next line under the debit column total,	enter the same number on the same line into the credit side of the balance sheet column.
	the income statement debit total is greater than the credit total . . .	enter the difference, which is the *net loss*, on the next line under the credit column total,	enter the same number on the same line into the debit side of the balance sheet column.
2	Calculate new totals for the income statement columns. The two columns for income statement must have the same total.		
3	Calculate new totals for the balance sheet columns. The two columns for the balance sheet must have the same total.		

Example

The completed worksheet on page 223 shows you the results of this procedure. The net income is $2,855 for the month of May.

continued ▶

Step 5: Total the Financial Statement Columns and Compute the Net Income or Net Loss, *continued*

Why the Difference Makes the Columns Balance

If you look at the Retained Earnings account in the balance sheet columns, you will see that it is $8,120. This is the prior retained earnings balance carried over from the *last* accounting period. The retained earnings account has not yet been updated by the amount of the net income from the current accounting period. *It is the only account in the balance sheet columns that does not yet show its current final balance as of May 31.*

The $2,855 net income entered into the credit side of the balance sheet column at the bottom of the worksheet is really the increase in retained earnings from the current period net income.

"Such a mystery! Why does the difference make the columns balance?"

Step 5: Total the Financial Statement Columns and Compute the Net Income or Net Loss, *continued*

Account Titles	Trial Balance Dr.	Trial Balance Cr.	Adjustments Dr.	Adjustments Cr.	Adjusted Trial Balance Dr.	Adjusted Trial Balance Cr.	Income Statement Dr.	Income Statement Cr.	Balance Sheet Dr.	Balance Sheet Cr.
\multicolumn{11}{c}{Applegate Modeling Agency, Inc.}										
\multicolumn{11}{c}{Worksheet}										
\multicolumn{11}{c}{For the Month Ended May 31, 2017}										
Cash	15,850				15,850				15,850	
Accounts Receivable	2,800				2,800				2,800	
Office Supplies	1,100			(a) 580	520				520	
Modeling Supplies	800			(b) 200	600				600	
Prepaid Insurance	600			(d) 75	525				525	
Office Equipment	9,700				9,700				9,700	
Accum. Dep'n.—										
Office Equipment		960		(c) 160		1,120				1,120
Accounts Payable		1,400				1,400				1,400
Unearned Fees		2,000	(e) 1,500			500				500
Notes Payable		15,000				15,000				15,000
Common Stock		2,000				2,000				2,000
Retained Earnings		8,120				8,120				8,120
Dividends	2,000				2,000				2,000	
Fees Earned		9,300		(e) 1,500		10,800		10,800		
Interest Earned		200				200		200		
Salaries Expense	4,100		(f) 900		5,000		5,000			
Rent Expense	1,450				1,450		1,450			
Income Tax Expense	300				300		300			
Utilities Expense	280				280		280			
Totals	38,980	38,980								
Office Supplies Expense			(a) 580		580		580			
Modeling Supplies										
Expense			(b) 200		200		200			
Depreciation Expense			(c) 160		160		160			
Insurance Expense			(d) 75		75		75			
Salaries Payable				(f) 900		900				900
Interest Expense			(g) 100		100		100			
Interest Payable				(g) 100		100				100
Totals			3,515	3,515	40,140	40,140	8,145	11,000	31,995	29,140
Net Income							2,855			2,855
Totals							11,000	11,000	31,995	31,995

Step 5: Total the Financial Statement Columns and Compute the Net Income or Net Loss, *continued*

Example of Net Loss

If there is a net loss, the total debits in the income statement column will be greater than the total credits in the income statement column.

Suppose that the company had paid an additional $4,000 in rent expense. If so, total expenses in the income statement debit column become $12,145 instead of $8,145. This will create a $1,145 loss. The debit total in the income statement column now exceeds the credit total. What you see below is how the totals of the financial statement columns will appear.

Income Statement		Balance Sheet	
Dr.	Cr.	Dr.	Cr.
12,145	11,000	27,875	29,020
	1,145	1,145	
12,145	12,145	29,020	29,020

Notice that a $1,145 debit is necessary to make the balance sheet columns balance. This represents the current period decrease in the retained earnings account as a result of the net loss.

The Three Results of Using a Worksheet

Overview

Three Results

At least three clear and useful results occur when period-end information is organized on a worksheet. When you use a worksheet like this, you get these three results:

- A source of the financial statements
- A source of the adjusting journal entries
- A source of the closing journal entries (discussed in Learning Goal 8)

Result 1: Financial Statements

How to Obtain Financial Statement Numbers

The formal financial statements are really the most important result of a period-end worksheet. After the worksheet is completed, financial statement preparation is easy. The final financial statement numbers are simply copied from the income statement and balance sheet columns of the worksheet.

TIP

The financial statements are the first items prepared from the worksheet. This is because financial statements have a time value.

Income Statement

To prepare the income statement, simply copy the numbers from the income statement columns in the worksheet onto a properly formatted and titled income statement. That's all there is to it!

Balance Sheet

For the balance sheet, copy the numbers from the balance columns onto a properly formatted and titled balance sheet. The only calculation you need to do is for the ending retained earnings balance. From the worksheet balance sheet column, combine the retained earnings balance, the dividends account balance, and the current period net income or net loss to get the final retained earnings balance for the balance sheet.

continued ▶

Result 1: Financial Statements, *continued*

Statement of Retained Earnings

Most worksheets have no separate set of columns for the statement of retained earnings, so you have to do this financial statement yourself. You can find the information for the statement of retained earnings like this:

Step	Item	Action
1	Beginning retained earnings balance	Available on the worksheet.
2	Net income or loss	This is easy. It is on the worksheet and on the income statement (Or use the ledger account).
3	Dividends	Another easy one. This is a separate account on the worksheet.

Caution

Be sure that the ending balance of the statement of retained earnings is the same number that shows as the retained earnings on the balance sheet.

Projection Tool

When a worksheet is used on a computer, the worksheet can also easily be adapted into a powerful device that quickly projects future financial statements, whenever estimated or projected financial data are entered.

Examples

The income statement, balance sheet, and statement of retained earnings prepared from the worksheet for the Applegate Modeling Agency are shown below (see also page 227).

Applegate Modeling Agency, Inc.
Income Statement
For the Month Ended May 31, 2017

Revenues		
Fees earned	$10,800	
Interest earned	200	
Total revenues		$11,000
Operating expenses		
Salaries expense	5,000	
Rent expense	1,450	
Office supplies expense	580	
Utilities expense	280	
Modeling supplies expense	200	
Depreciation expense	160	
Interest expense	100	
Insurance expense	75	
Total operating expenses		7,845
Income before tax		3,155
Income tax expense		300
Net income		$ 2,855

Result 1: Financial Statements, *continued*

Applegate Modeling Agency, Inc.
Statement of Retained Earnings
For the Month Ended May 31, 2017

Retained earnings, May 1, 2017	$8,120
Add: Net Income	2,855
Subtotal	10,975
Less: Dividends	2,000
Retained earnings, May 31, 2017	$8,975

Applegate Modeling Agency, Inc.
Balance Sheet
May 31, 2017

Assets			Liabilities		
Cash		$15,850	Accounts payable		$ 1,400
Accounts receivable		2,800	Unearned fees		500
Office supplies		520	Salaries payable		900
Modeling supplies		600	Interest payable		100
Prepaid insurance		525	Notes payable		15,000
Office equipment	$9,700		Total liabilities		17,900
Less: Accumulated					
depreciation	1,120		**Stockholders' Equity**		
		8,580	Paid-in capital		
			Common stock		2,000
			Retained earnings		8,975
			Total stockholders' equity		10,975
			Total liabilities and		
Total assets		$28,875	stockholders' equity		$28,875

- A quick review of corporation financial statements is available on pages 1–4.
- Keep in mind that a worksheet is a useful, but optional tool. Financial statements also can be prepared without a worksheet. For example, computer accounting systems can prepare financial statements on command. In a small business or a manual system, adjusted ledger account balances can be used for financial statement preparation.

TIP

Result 2: Adjusting Entries

How to Find the Journal Entries

The adjusting entries are simply copied from the adjustments column of the worksheet into the general journal. Then, as usual, these entries are posted into the ledger.

Result 3: A Source for the Closing Journal Entries

Closing Entries

Closing entries are discussed later as a separate learning goal (Learning Goal 8). However, at this point it is enough to know that the worksheet is the source of the numbers needed for the closing entries. These numbers are the account balances in the income statement columns plus the dividends account balance.

In a computerized system, a worksheet is not needed for the closing entries. The computer will identify the accounts to be closed and perform the closing procedure when the command is given.

The Concept and Example of Classification

Overview: The Concept of Classification

Definition: Classified

Classified means that the accounts on a financial statement are grouped into significant major categories.

It Is Better for the Users

Formatting financial statement accounts into significant categories makes the statements more useful to the users who want to analyze the business in greater detail. Exactly how the accounts are grouped depends upon what the accountant believes will be most useful to most users. However, there is a commonly accepted general format, which is what you see on the next page.

The Classified Balance Sheet

What It Is

A *classified balance sheet* is a balance sheet in which the assets and liabilities are subdivided into significant or meaningful categories. The categories are significant because they reveal certain important aspects of the condition of a business.

Example

As many as at least eight major classifications can appear on a balance sheet. Actually, most balance sheets use fewer categories because most companies do not have enough different kinds of accounts to use all the categories at the same time.

However, for your reference, here is a balance sheet (without numbers) showing the major types of classifications in their typical order:

The Vaporware Company, Inc.
Balance Sheet
June 30, 2017

Assets		Liabilities and Owner's Equity	
Current assets	$	Current liabilities	$
Long-term investments	$		
Property, plant, and equipment	$	Long-term liabilities	$
Intangible assets	$	Stockholders' (or owner's	$
Other assets	$	or partners') equity	
		Total liabilities and	
Total assets	$XXXX	stockholders' equity	$XXXX

Nonclassified Example

A nonclassified balance sheet simply lists all the assets and shows a total, and lists all the liabilities and stockholders equity and shows another total. An example of a nonclassified balance sheet is on page 227, for the Applegate Modeling Agency.

The Balance Sheet Classifications Explained

The Asset Classifications

Current Assets

Current assets are assets that will be turned into cash, or be used up instead of spending cash, within one year of the balance sheet date or the operating cycle of the business, whichever is longer, *as part of normal operations.*

For practical purposes, this usually means within one year from the balance sheet date.

The **operating cycle** of a business is the amount of time, on average, that it takes to turn cash spent on goods and services back into cash received from customers. Most businesses have an operating cycle that is much less than a year, but for a few (such as construction companies), it may be longer.

Synonym

Current assets are also called *liquid assets,* particularly cash and current receivables.

Order of Listing

Current assets are listed in order of liquidity. This means that the most liquid assets (closest to cash) are listed before less liquid assets. Some typical current assets are shown below, listed in the usual order.

Examples of Current Assets

- Cash
- Marketable securities (stocks, bonds, etc.) that will be held less than a year
- Accounts receivable
- Any part of a long-term note that will be collectible within one year
- Supplies
- Inventory (merchandise held for sale to customers)
- Prepaid expenses (such as prepaid insurance or prepaid rent)

NOT Current Assets

- Plant and equipment (not converted to cash as part of normal operations)
- Long-term investment (not converted to cash as part of normal operations)

Long-Term Investments

Long-term investments are investments that the business makes when it does not intend or expect to convert them into cash within a year of the balance sheet date, or its operating cycle, whichever is longer. For practical purposes, this usually means being held longer than one year. Examples are investments in long-term bonds or in stock acquired for the purpose of long-term ownership or control of another company.

The Asset Classifications, *continued*

Property, Plant, and Equipment	*Property, plant, and equipment* means long-term productive assets like building, equipment, automobiles, furniture and fixtures, and land. The business holds these assets with the intention of using them rather than selling them or holding them for investment. *Fixed assets* is another name for property, plant, and equipment.
Intangible Assets	*Intangible assets* usually refers to assets that have no physical substance and will last more than a year. Very often these assets are legal rights, such as patents, trademarks, copyrights, franchise rights, and lease rights. Although these assets have no physical substance, they still fulfill the definition of assets because the business owns them and they provide future benefits to the company. It costs money to buy or develop intangible assets.
Other Assets	This category is for any unusual or exotic assets that don't fit the other categories. It is not used very frequently.

The Liability Classifications

Current Liabilities	*Current liabilities* are liabilities that require payment within one year of the balance sheet date or the operating cycle of the business, whichever is longer. For practical purposes, this usually means within one year.
Examples of Current Liabilities	■ Wages payable ■ Short-term notes payable ■ Accounts payable ■ Any part of long-term debt that will be payable within one year ■ Taxes payable ■ Unearned revenues
Listing Order on the Balance Sheet	The customary listing arrangement of current liabilities is subject to variation. Often, wages payable or short-term notes payable are listed first, followed by accounts payable. After that, any order is acceptable.
Long-Term Liabilities	*Long-term liabilities* are debts of the business that require payment after one year from the balance sheet date or the operating cycle of the business, whichever is longer.

continued ▶

The Liability Classifications, *continued*

*Examples of
Long-Term
Liabilities*

- Long-term notes and mortgages
- Most bonds payable
- Pension plan obligations

Example for Applegate Modeling Agency

Overview

A classified balance sheet for the Applegate Modeling Agency (see page 233) demonstrates some of the categories that we presented above. Notice that there is a subtotal for each category.

This balance sheet is presented in report form. **Report form** means that the assets are shown on the top of a page and equities are beneath the assets.

Another balance sheet format that you have seen previously (page 227) is the account form. In the **account form**, the assets are presented on the left side, and the equities are presented on the right side.

Either form is perfectly acceptable, and the choice is usually made depending upon the size of the statement and the space available in the financial report.

*No Debits
or Credits*

Just a reminder: The columns you see on the balance sheet are only for the purpose of showing calculations for subtotals. Debits and credits never appear on financial statements.

Example for Applegate Modeling Agency, *continued*

Applegate Modeling Agency, Inc.
Balance Sheet
May 31, 2017

Assets

Current assets

Cash	$15,850	
Accounts receivable	2,800	
Office supplies	520	
Modeling supplies	600	
Prepaid insurance	525	
Total current assets		$20,295

Property, plant, and equipment

Office equipment	9,700	
Less: Accumulated depreciation	1,120	
Total property, plant, and equipment		8,580
Total assets		$28,875

Liabilities and Stockholders' Equity

Current liabilities

Salaries payable	$ 900	
Accounts payable	1,400	
Unearned modeling fees	500	
Interest payable	100	
Total current liabilities		$2,900

Long-term liabilities

Notes payable		15,000
Total liabilities		17,900

Stockholders' equity

Paid-in Capital		
Common stock	2,000	
Retained earnings	8,975	
Total stockholders' equity		10,975
Total liabilities and stockholder's equity		$28,875

QUICK REVIEW

- The five steps for completing the worksheet are:

  1. Prepare the trial balance on the worksheet
  2. Calculate and enter the adjustments
  3. Enter balances in adjusted trial balance columns
  4. Extend the adjusted trial balance amounts into the proper financial statement columns.
  5. Compute the net income or loss from the totals of the financial statement columns.

- As soon as a worksheet is completed, the financial statements are prepared. After that, journal entries for adjustments are prepared using the adjustments column information.

- A completed worksheet can be used to obtain:

  a) An income statement and balance sheet
  b) A source for formal adjusting entries
  c) A source for formal closing entries (Learning Goal 8).

If prepared on a computerized spreadsheet, the worksheet can easily be adapted as a tool that projects future financial statements.

- Financial statements are classified so that they are more useful to the users of the statements.

- A classified balance sheet can have up to eight to ten major categories, although it is unlikely that they would all be needed on a single balance sheet.

- The report form and account form are two acceptable formats for presenting balance sheet information. On a page, the report form presents assets above liabilities and equity. The account form presents assets on the left and liabilities and equity on the right.

Do You Want More Examples?

Most problems in this book have detailed solutions. To use them as additional examples, do this: 1) Select the type of problem you want 2) Open the solution on your computer or mobile device screen (from the disc or worthyjames.com) 3) Read one item at a time and look at its answer. Take notes if needed. 4) Close the solution and work as much of the problem as you can. 5) Repeat as needed.

VOCABULARY

Account form: a form of the balance sheet in which all the assets are placed on the left side of a page and the liability and the stockholders' equity claims are placed on the right side (page 232)

Classified balance sheet: a balance sheet in which the accounts are grouped into significant or meaningful categories (page 229)

Current assets: cash and other assets that can be expected to be turned into cash or used up instead of spending cash, all as part of normal operations, within one year of the balance sheet or the operating cycle of the business, whichever is longer (page 230)

Current liabilities: liabilities that require payment within one year of the balance sheet date or the operating cycle of the business, whichever is longer (page 231)

Fixed assets: another name for property, plant, and equipment (page 231)

General ledger packages: computerized accounting systems (page 206)

Intangible assets: assets without physical substance (page 231)

Liquid assets: another name for current assets (page 230)

Long-term liabilities: debts that require payment after one year from the balance sheet date or the operating cycle of the business, whichever is longer (page 231)

Operating cycle: the average amount of time required to turn cash spent on goods and services back into cash received from customers (page 230)

Property, plant, and equipment: long-term productive assets held with the intention of using them for operations, and not selling them (page 231)

Report form: a form of the balance sheet in which all the assets are placed above the equity claims (the liabilities and owner's equity) (page 232)

Working papers: the worksheet together with all other data and calculations used to prepare financial statements (page 206)

Working Trial balance: another name for the worksheet (page 206)

Worksheet: an informal document or computer file used to organize information from accounting records usually for the purpose of simplifying the preparation of financial statements or preparing financial statement projections. (page 206)

Learning Goal 7 is about completing a worksheet and preparing a classified balance sheet. Use these questions to practice what you have learned about completing a worksheet.

Multiple Choice
Select the best answer.

1. The Accounts Receivable balance should be extended from the adjusted trial balance column into:
   a. the income statement debit column.
   b. the balance sheet debit column.
   c. the balance sheet credit column.
   d. none of the above.
2. A worksheet is not a direct source of:
   a. the balance sheet.
   b. the income statement.
   c. the statement of statement of retained earnings.
   d. none of the above.
3. The Accumulated Depreciation balance should be extended from the adjusted trial balance column into:
   a. the income statement debit column.
   b. the balance sheet debit column.
   c. the balance sheet credit column.
   d. none of the above.
4. The journalizing of adjusting entries:
   a. is unnecessary if the worksheet is completed correctly.
   b. still must be done as usual after the worksheet is completed correctly.
   c. are unrelated to the completion of a worksheet.
   d. none of the above.
5. The retained earnings account balance in the balance sheet column of the worksheet:
   a. should be the correct final balance if the worksheet is completed correctly.
   b. is actually the ending balance from the prior accounting period.
   c. is actually the ending balance from the prior accounting period plus any owner's investments in the current accounting period.
   d. includes both owner's investments and dividends.
6. The net income on a worksheet is entered:
   a. in an income statement debit column and a balance sheet credit column.
   b. in an income statement credit column and a balance sheet debit column.
   c. in an income statement debit column and a balance sheet debit column.
   d. in an income statement credit column and a balance sheet credit column.
7. The net loss on a worksheet is entered:
   a. in an income statement debit column and a balance sheet credit column.
   b. in an income statement credit column and a balance sheet debit column.
   c. in an income statement debit column and a balance sheet debit column.
   d. in an income statement credit column and a balance sheet credit column.
8. During the accounting period, the purchase of insurance was debited to the Prepaid Insurance account. No adjustments were made to the account. This means that the amount of prepaid insurance showing in the unadjusted trial balance at the end of the period is:
   a. the cost of insurance still available and unused.
   b. the cost of insurance available at the beginning of the period.
   c. the cost of insurance used up during the period.
   d. the cost of insurance that was available during the period.

9. The point at which the worksheet is prepared is:
    a. at the end of the accounting period before adjusting entries are recorded in the journal.
    b. at the end of the accounting period after adjusting entries are recorded in the journal.
    c. after the financial statements are prepared.
    d. after the adjusted trial balance has been prepared.

10. On the worksheet, the reason that the balance sheet columns balance after the net income or net loss is added to the balance sheet column subtotals is because:
    a. the net income or net loss is really an adjustment to the retained earnings account that brings it up to date with the other balance sheet accounts as of the end of the current period.
    b. some of the other balance sheet account balances are probably incorrect.
    c. both a and b.
    d. none of the above.

11. Which of the following statements is not true about the worksheet?
    a. The total debits and credits are not equal in all the worksheet columns.
    b. The worksheet is not a permanent accounting record, like a journal or ledger.
    c. The main objective of a worksheet is to facilitate the preparation of financial statements.
    d. The worksheet is prepared after the adjustments are journalized.

12. In the worksheet for Waialae Avenue Company, the balance sheet column subtotal of debits is $125,000 and the balance sheet subtotal of credits is $147,000. This means that:
    a. the company has a net loss of $22,000.
    b. the total debits in the income statement column on the worksheet are more than the credits.
    c. net income or loss cannot be determined from this information.
    d. both a and b.

13. In the trial balance of Douglass Company, the account Supplies has a $500 debit balance, and a $100 credit entry to Supplies is made in the adjustments column of the worksheet. This means that:
    a. the amount of supplies showing on the balance sheet should not be $500.
    b. some supplies have been used up since the last time an entry was made in the Supplies account.
    c. none of the above.
    d. both a and b.

14. The worksheet adjusted trial balance of Tubman Company shows a credit balance of Unearned Revenue of $200. The trial balance column shows a credit balance of Unearned Revenue of $750. This means that:
    a. Unearned Revenue was increased by a $550 credit entry in the adjustments column.
    b. Unearned Revenue was decreased by a $550 credit entry in the adjustments column.
    c. Unearned Revenue was decreased by a $550 debit entry in the adjustments column.
    d. Unearned Revenue was increased by a $550 debit entry in the adjustments column.

15. In the trial balance of Bruce and Revels partnership, Wages Payable has a credit balance of $700. An entry is made in the adjustments column debiting Wages Expense and crediting Wages Payable for $100. The accountant enters the Wages Payable as an $800 debit balance in the adjusted trial balance column. This:
    a. will make the adjusted trial balance total credits $1,600 greater than total debits.
    b. will make the adjusted trial balance total debits $800 greater than total credits.
    c. will make the adjusted trial balance total credits $800 greater than total debits.
    d. will make the adjusted trial balance total debits $1,600 greater than total credits.

16. To prepare an income statement after completing the worksheet:
    a. simply copy the numbers from the income statement columns to an income statement.
    b. combine the adjusted trial balance columns with the income statement columns.
    c. do not use the numbers on the worksheet; use the ledger balances.
    d. none of the above.

17. To prepare a balance sheet after completing the worksheet:
    a. simply copy the numbers from the balance sheet column to a balance sheet.
    b. do not use the numbers on the worksheet; use the ledger balances.
    c. use all the numbers in the balance sheet columns except the retained earnings balance.
    d. none of the above.

18. When preparing a statement of retained earnings after completing the worksheet:
    a. use the retained earnings from the balance sheet column as the beginning amount.
    b. if the owner made investments during the period, the investments must be subtracted from the retained earnings in the balance sheet column.
    c. dividends must be added back to the retained earnings balance shown on the worksheet.
    d. none of the above

19. When preparing a balance sheet after completing the worksheet:
    a. the total assets on the balance sheet must equal the total debits in the balance sheet column.
    b. the total liabilities and stockholders' equity must equal the total credits in the balance sheet column.
    c. dividends must be added back to the common stock balance shown on the worksheet.
    d. none of the above.

20. When preparing an income statement after completing the worksheet:
    a. the net income on the income statement must be the same number as the difference between the total credits and the total debits on the income statement columns of the worksheet.
    b. the stockholders' equity must be the same amount as the number that accounts for the difference in the totals of the balance sheet columns
    c. a net loss would mean that the income statement columns on the worksheet show a smaller debit total than the credit total.
    d. you will use a date on the income statement that is after the date of the worksheet.

21. After completing a worksheet:
    a. recalculate the amounts for adjustments before entering the amounts in the journal.
    b. the adjusting entries are frequently different from what appears on the worksheet.
    c. the adjusting entries have already been entered in the journal.
    d. to enter the adjusting entries in the journal, simply copy the amounts from the adjustments columns on the worksheet as adjusting entries in the general journal.

22. The first thing to do after completing a correct worksheet is to:
    a. journalize the adjusting entries.
    b. journalize the closing entries.
    c. prepare the financial statements.
    d. prepare the post-closing trial balance.

23. Current assets are:
    a. any assets that can be converted to cash within one year of the balance sheet date.
    b. any assets that will be converted to cash as part of normal operations within one year of the balance sheet date or the operating cycle of the business.
    c. any assets that can be converted to cash within the normal operating cycle.
    d. usually intangible.

24. Which of the following is not a current asset?
    a. prepaid rent
    b. merchandise inventory
    c. equipment
    d. supplies

25. The time it takes to turn cash spent on goods and services into cash received from customers is the:
    a. operating cycle.
    b. accounting cycle.
    c. turnover ratio.
    d. conversion cycle.

26. Which of the following is (are) included as a long-term asset?
    a. supplies
    b. equipment
    c. prepaid rent
    d. both a and b

27. Which of the following is not a current liability?
    a. accounts payable
    b. a note payable due within 1 year
    c. the amount of a 5-year note payable that is due within 1 year
    d. a 5-year note payable

28. The account form balance sheet:
    a. is a left/right presentation of assets and claims on assets.
    b. is a top-of-page/bottom-of-page presentation of assets and claims on assets.
    c. is generally considered the least desirable presentation.
    d. is a two-page presentation of assets and claims on assets.

29. Current assets are usually listed in the order of:
    a. currency.
    b. their use in the operating cycle.
    c. liquidity.
    d. their appearance on either the report form or account form balance sheet.

30. Which of the following do you think is the most important resource for paying the current liabilities as they become due?
    a. property, plant, and equipment
    b. current assets
    c. intangible assets
    d. long-term investments

31. Use the following table for asset categories:

1	intangible assets
2	property, plant, and equipment
3	current assets
4	long-term investments
5	other assets

Which of the choices below shows the order sequence in which the assets above are normally presented on a classified balance sheet?
a. 1, 2, 3, 4, 5
b. 3, 1, 5, 4, 2
c. 2, 3, 5, 4, 1
d. 3, 4, 2, 1, 5

32. Use the following table for current asset types:

1	Accounts Receivable
2	Merchandise Inventory
3	Short-Term Investments (marketable securities)
4	Supplies
5	Cash
6	Prepaid Expenses

Which of the choices below shows the order sequence in which the current asset categories are normally presented on a classified balance sheet?
a. 5, 3, 1, 4, 2, 6
b. 1, 5, 3, 2, 6, 4
c. 5, 4, 1, 3, 2, 6
d. 3, 5, 1, 6, 2, 4

PRACTICE   Learning Goal 7, continued

Solutions are in the disk at the back of the book and at: www.worthyjames.com

Reinforcement Problems

LG 7-1. Complete the income statement and balance sheet columns. You remember the Winslow Tennis Club? That was the problem (on page 215) where the accountant had to leave suddenly to fill in for a mixed-doubles tennis match, leaving you, the assistant bookkeeper, to finish preparing the worksheet up to the adjusted trial balance. The accountant said that she would be back as soon as she finished the tennis match, but she has not returned for two weeks. Today you read in the newspaper that she has been discovered in a small town in the Loire Valley of France, where she is believed to be involved in a torrid love affair with her mixed doubles partner, a Spanish movie idol named Manuel Dexterity. Lawyers are filing lawsuits, psychiatrists are being consulted, and worst of all, now you have to finish the worksheet! Print out a copy of this worksheet from the disk at the back of the book and complete the worksheet.

	Trial Balance		Adjustments		Adjusted Trial Balance		Income Statement		Balance Sheet	
Account Titles	Dr.	Cr.	Dr.	Cr.	Dr.	Cr.	Dr.	Cr.	Dr.	Cr.
Cash	45,750				45,750					
Dues Receivable	2,800				2,800					
Office Supplies	1,100			(a) 1,050	50					
Tennis Supplies	2,002			(a) 1,787	215					
Notes Receivable	12,000				12,000					
Prepaid Insurance	600			(e) 100	500					
Office Equipment	14,520				14,520					
Accum. Dep'n.— Office Equipment		11,616		(d) 242		11,858				
Building	345,000				345,000					
Accum. Dep'n.— Building		19,500		(d) 600		20,100				
Accounts Payable		855				855				
Notes Payable		275,000				275,000				
Common Stock		5,000				5,000				
Retained Earnings		82,161				82,161				
Dividends	1,880				1,880					
Tennis Instruction Fees		9,500	(f) 1,000			8,500				
Dues Revenue		28,500				28,500				
Salaries Expense	4,100				4,100					
Equipment Rent Expense	1,750				1,750					
Utilities Expense	280				280					
Insurance Expense	100		(e) 100		200					
Maintenance Expense	250		(g) 500		750					
Totals	432,132	432,132								

Winslow Tennis Club, Inc.
Worksheet
For the Month Ended June 30, 2017

Solutions are in the disk at the back of the book and at: www.worthyjames.com

PRACTICE   Learning Goal 7, continued

LG 7-1, *continued*

	Trial Balance		Adjustments		Adjusted Trial Balance		Income Statement		Balance Sheet	
Account Titles	Dr.	Cr.	Dr.	Cr.	Dr.	Cr.	Dr.	Cr.	Dr.	Cr.
Unearned Tennis Fees				(f) 1,000		1,000				
Office Supplies Expense			(a) 1,050		1,050					
Tennis Supplies Expense			(a) 1,787		1,787					
Depreciation Expense			(d) 842		842					
Salaries/Wages Payable				(g) 500		500				
Interest Expense			(c) 1,375		1,375					
Interest Receivable			(b) 80		80					
Interest Earned				(b) 80		80				
Interest Payable				(c) 1,375		1,375				
Totals			6,734	6,734	434,929	434,929				

Winslow Tennis Club, Inc.
Worksheet (continued)
For the Month Ended June 30, 2017

LG 7-2. Complete an entire worksheet. *Instructions:* Complete the worksheet. Use a blank worksheet or the worksheet template for LG 7-2 in the disk at the back of the book or at www .worthyjames.com (student info.).

Leeward Swimming Pool Service, Inc.									
Worksheet									
For the Year Ended November 30, 2017									
	Trial Balance		Adjustments		Adjusted Trial Balance		Income Statement		Balance Sheet	
Account Titles	Dr.	Cr.	Dr.	Cr.	Dr.	Cr.	Dr.	Cr.	Dr.	Cr.
Cash	71,050									
Accounts Receivable	7,200									
Office Supplies	750									
Prepaid Insurance	4,200									
Tools and Equipment	244,500									
Accum. Dep'n.—										
—Tools and										
Equipment		12,500								
Office Equipment	15,000									
Accum. Dep'n.										
Office Equipment		3,700								
Common Stock		25,000								
Retained Earnings		287,500								
Dividends	50,000									
Fees Earned		205,000								
Salaries Expense	110,000									
Rentals Expense	26,200									
Income Tax Expense	2,000									
Utility Expense	2,800									
Totals	533,700	533,700								

Additional information:
1. A year-end count of office supplies shows a remaining balance of $200 on November 30.
2. On August 1, the company paid $4,200 for 12 months of insurance coverage.
3. Current year depreciation on the office equipment is $1,500 and $3,500 on the cleaning equipment.
4. Company employees had earned $1,100 of salaries in the last week of November. The wages will be paid in the first week of December.
5. During the last week of November, the company performed $750 of pool maintenance and heater installation for the Leeward Hotel, on account. This has not yet been recorded.

PRACTICE   Learning Goal 7, continued

LG 7-3. Complete the worksheet. *Instructions:* Complete the worksheet for Damon's Car Wash by printing a copy of this problem from the disk at the back of the book or www.worthyjames.com (student info.).

Damon's Car Wash, Inc.

Worksheet

For the Year Ended December 31, 2017

Account Titles	Trial Balance Dr.	Trial Balance Cr.	Adjustments Dr.	Adjustments Cr.	Adjusted Trial Balance Dr.	Adjusted Trial Balance Cr.	Income Statement Dr.	Income Statement Cr.	Balance Sheet Dr.	Balance Sheet Cr.
Cash	43,900									
Marketable Securities	101,250				101,250				101,250	
Accounts Receivable	1,200		(a)							
Office Supplies	520			(c)	110				110	
Cleaning/Washing Supplies	2,800			(f) 1,500	1,300				1,300	
Prepaid Insurance	4,600				4,600				4,600	
Prepaid Rent	1,200			(d)						
Office Equipment	15,000				15,000				15,000	
Accum. Dep'n—Off. Equip.		6,000		(h) 3,000		9,000				9,000
Wash Equipment	225,700				225,700				225,700	
Accum. Dep'n—Wash Equip.				(h) 25,000		63,500				63,500
Accounts Payable		3,700		(g) 750		4,450				4,450
Unearned Revenue		650	(b) 300			350				350
Notes Payable—Long Term		50,000				50,000				50,000
Common Stock		30,000				30,000				30,000
Retained Earnings		133,650				133,650				133,650
Dividends	3,500				3,500				3,500	
Services Revenue		305,200		(a) 150						
				(b)						
Wages Expense	114,500				114,500		114,500			
Washing Supplies Expense	7,630		(f) 1,500		9,130		9,130			
Advertising Expense			(g) 750		12,750					
Utilities Expense	28,500				28,500		28,500			
Dep'n. Expense—Off. Equip.			(h) 3,000		3,000		3,000			
Dep'n. Expense—Wash. Equip.			(h) 25,000		25,000		25,000			
Office Supplies Expense			(c)		410		410			
Rental Equipment Expense			(d) 900				900			
Insurance Expense	5,000				5,000		5,000			
Miscellaneous Expense	400				400		400			
Interest Expense			(e)		650					
Interest Payable				(e)						
Totals	567,700	567,700	32,660	32,660	597,250	597,250	200,240		397,010	291,600
Net Income										105,410

Reinforcement Problems

LG 7-4. **Complete a worksheet, prepare financial statements, prepare adjusting entries**

Instructions: Complete the worksheet, prepare an income statement, account form balance sheet, and statement of retained earnings, and then make adjusting entries, using the templates in the disk at the back of the book or at www.worthyjames.com (student info.).

	Maui Quick Print Services, Inc.									
	Worksheet									
	For the Year Ended December 31, 2017									
					Adjusted		Income		Balance	
	Trial Balance		Adjustments		Trial Balance		Statement		Sheet	
Account Titles	Dr.	Cr.	Dr.	Cr.	Dr.	Cr.	Dr.	Cr.	Dr.	Cr.
Cash	28,300									
Accounts Receivable	4,200									
Printing Supplies	800									
Prepaid Insurance	1,800									
Office Equipment	7,500									
Accum. Dep'n.—										
Office Equipment		1,000								
Printing/Copying Equipment	35,500									
Accum. Dep'n.— Printing/										
Copying Equipment		14,500								
Accounts Payable		1,400								
Unearned Revenue		3,500								
Notes Payable-Short term		36,000								
Common Stock		10,000								
Retained Earnings		25,550								
Dividends	12,000									
Services Revenue		108,700								
Salaries Expense	57,300									
Office Supplies Expense	1,300									
Rent Expense	36,000									
Travel Expense	3,250									
Printing Supplies Expense	4,200									
Interest Expense	3,300									
Utilities Expense	5,200									
Totals	200,650	200,650								

LG 7-4, *continued*

Supplementary information:

a. A year-end inventory shows $200 of printing supplies remaining.
b. The prepaid insurance is for a one-year policy purchased on April 1.
c. Depreciation for the year on the office equipment is $750 and for the printing/copying equipment is $7,000.
d. All of the unearned fees have been earned by year end.
e. The company owes $500 of unpaid salaries to employees at year end.
f. The interest expense on the note payable is $300 per month and is due on the first of each month.

LG 7-5. **Complete a worksheet, prepare financial statements.** Shown below is the trial balance portion of a worksheet for Anaheim Appraisal Services for the month ending November 30, 2017.

Instructions: a) Complete the worksheet b) Prepare an income statement, statement of retained earnings, and a report form classified balance sheet. Use either a blank worksheet or the worksheet template for LG7-5 from the disk at the back of the book or at www.worthyjames.com (student info.).

Other information:

a. At November 30, an antiques appraisal performed for a customer in the amount of $2,500 remained unpaid and unrecorded.
b. The amount of office supplies used during November was $220.
c. During the month, six airline tickets to New York were purchased for $3,750. Four of the tickets remain unused on November 30.
d. Monthly depreciation expense on the office equipment is $290 and is $415 for the automotive equipment. The business maintains individual depreciation expense accounts for depreciable assets.
e. $300 of prepaid insurance remains unexpired.
f. Unearned revenue deferred to the next month is $3,000.
g. Unpaid interest on the note payable is $330.

LG 7-5. *Continued*

Account Titles	Dr.	Cr.
Cash	61,350	
Short Term Investments	15,200	
Accounts Receivable	34,800	
Office Supplies	700	
Prepaid Insurance	900	
Prepaid Airline Tickets	3,750	
Office Equipment	18,400	
Accum. Dep'n.— Office Equip.		9,150
Automotive Equipment	28,000	
Accum. Dep'n.—Automotive		5,000
Accounts Payable		4,850
Unearned Revenue		6,280
Notes Payable (long-term)		41,000
Common Stock		30,000
Retained Earnings		52,280
Dividends	2,000	
Appraisal Revenue		39,300
Wages Expense	10,600	
Rent Expense	2,150	
Income Tax Expense	1,300	
Auto and Gas Expense	260	
Travel Expense	4,500	
Advertising Expense	3,600	
Utilities Expense	350	
Totals	187,860	187,860

Instructor-Assigned Problems

If you are using this book in a class, these review problems may be assigned by your instructor for homework, group assignments, class work, or other activities. Only your instructor has the solutions.

IA7-1. Complete a worksheet, prepare adjusting journal entries. Shown below is the trial balance portion of a worksheet for Merced Business Services, Inc. for the month ended November 30, 2017.

Instructions: a) Complete the worksheet b) Prepare adjusting journal entries using the completed worksheet as your source. Use either a blank worksheet or the worksheet template for IA7-1 from the disk at the back of the book or at www.worthyjames.com (student info.).

Account Titles	Dr.	Cr.
Cash	45,000	
Accounts Receivable	14,200	
Supplies	700	
Prepaid Insurance	1,800	
Office Equipment	20,000	
Accum. Dep'n. - Office Equip.		7,000
Accounts Payable		5,100
Unearned Revenue		1,000
Common Stock		10,000
Retained Earnings		30,500
Service Revenue		59,200
Salaries/Wages Expense	21,700	
Rent Expense	3,300	
Income Tax Expense	2,100	
Utilities Expense	1,500	
Insurance Expense	2,000	
Depreciation Expense		
Supplies Expense	500	
Total	112,800	112,800

Other information:

a. A physical count of supplies shows a month-end balance of $250.
b. The office equipment is depreciated using an estimated life of 5 years, with no residual value.
c. $500 of the unearned revenue was earned during the month.
d. A utilities bill for November was received in early December in the amount of $225.

IA7-2. Complete a worksheet, prepare financial statements. Shown below is the trial balance portion of a worksheet for the Lake Grove Consulting Company for the month ended August 31, 2017.

Instructions: a) Complete the worksheet b) Prepare an income statement, statement of retained earnings, and a report form classified balance sheet. Use either a blank worksheet or the worksheet template for IA7-2 from the disk at the back of the book or at www.worthyjames.com (student info.).

Account Titles	Dr.	Cr.
Cash	92,750	
Short-term Investments	15,830	
Accounts Receivable	41,320	
Supplies	1,440	
Prepaid Insurance	2,400	
Long-term Investments	14,100	
Office Equipment	26,400	
Accum. Dep'n. - Office Equip.		6,100
Accounts Payable		37,190
Notes Payable - Long Term		25,000
Common Stock		12,000
Retained Earnings		110,260
Dividends	15,000	
Service Revenue		104,880
Salaries/Wages Expense	40,700	
Rent Expense	16,500	
Utilities Expense	700	
Miscellaneous Expense	2,370	
Insurance Expense	1,800	
Travel Expense	12,500	
Depreciation Expense		
Supplies Expense		
Advertising Expense	10,220	
Interest Expense		
Interest Payable		
Salaries/Wages Payable		
Income Tax Expense	1,400	
Total	295,430	295,430

Other information:

a. A physical count of supplies shows a month-end balance of $690.
b. The balance of prepaid insurance is for a policy covering three months, beginning August 1.
c. The office equipment has an estimated useful life of 10 years, with no residual value.
d. At month end the company received a bill for $1,500 of advertising services, which remains unpaid.
e. Monthly interest due on the outstanding note payable is $190.
f. $1,000 of wages expense has been incurred but will not be paid until September 1.

IA7-3. Prepare classified balance sheets using both formats. Shown below are the December 31, 2017 adjusted ledger account balances for Manhattan Company presented in random order.

Instructions: Using the correct accounts:

a. Prepare a report form balance sheet
b. Prepare an account form balance sheet

Office Supplies	$ 2,900	Rent Expense	$48,000
Accounts Payable	53,100	Insurance Expense	2,500
Office Equipment	35,630	Accum. Dep'n—Office	
Interest Revenue	2,900	Equipment	21,220
Amortization Expense	21,00	Interest Expense	19,700
Computer System	325,900	Merchandise Inventory	12,000
Common Stock	72,000	Accounts Receivable	50,020
Patent	25,500	Short-Term Investments	25,000
Notes Receivable (due in 60 days)	15,000	Wages Expense	452,600
Prepaid Travel Expense	4,780	Depreciation Expense	42,400
Notes Payable (long-term)	125,200	Service Revenue	671,100
Trademark	10,500	Notes Payable (due in 90 days)	27,900
Cash	71,650	Long-Term Investments	35,800
Accumulated Depreciation—		Dividends	15,000
Computer System	35,000	Wages Payable	20,500
Retained Earnings	?	Unearned Revenue	42,000

Note: The current portion of long-term debt is $5,100.

IA7-4. Complete a worksheet, prepare financial statements. Shown below is the trial balance portion of a worksheet for Bellevue Advertising Services for the year ending December 31, 2017.

Instructions: a) Complete the worksheet b) Prepare an income statement, statement of retained earnings, and a report form classified balance sheet. Use either a blank worksheet or the worksheet for IA7-4 from the disk at the back of the book or at www.worthyjames.com (student info.).

Account Titles	Dr.	Cr.
Cash	75,620	
Short-term Investments	58,690	
Accounts Receivable	54,200	
Supplies	6,950	
Prepaid Travel	5,740	
Long-term Investments	75,210	
Office Equipment	67,900	
Accum. Dep'n.—Office Equip.		20,370
Trademark	35,100	
Accounts Payable		40,240
Unearned Revenue		7,500
Notes Payable - Long Term		92,330
Common Stock		25,000
Retained Earnings		171,270
Dividends	35,000	
Print Services Revenue		115,290
Internet Services Revenue		285,300
Salaries/Wages Expense	241,100	
Rent Expense	48,000	
Utilities Expense	8,850	
Miscellaneous Expense	4,510	
Insurance Expense	9,400	
Travel Expense	21,200	
Depreciation Expense		
Supplies Expense	4,830	
Income Tax Expense	5,000	
Total	757,300	757,300

Other information:

a. During December the company sent bills to clients totaling $14,500 for Internet advertising design. The amount is unpaid as of December 31.

b. The company performed $3,100 of additional Internet advertising services at year-end for clients who had paid in advance.

c. A physical count of supplies shows $2,840 on hand as of December 31.

d. During December three airline tickets totaling $3,600 purchased in November were used.

e. In early January a $450 December utilities bill was received.

f. The equipment is being depreciated over a 5-year life with no residual value.

g. Calculations show a total of $2,780 interest earned but not yet received.

h. $8,410 of unpaid interest on the note payable is due in January.

PRACTICE

Learning Goal 7, continued

Solutions are in the disk at the back of the book and at: www.worthyjames.com

INTERNET EXERCISES

Accounting careers (and a little fun). In this exercise, we will review the type of work done by people with an accounting background who work as employees in profit and non-profit enterprises. From a student point of view, this should give you an idea of the type of work, qualifications, and some salary information. From a business owner point of view, this should provide an idea of the type of accounting work that often needs to be done at different operational levels and what required qualifications should be—with some information about salaries and sources.

1. On the Internet, go to www.startheregoplaces.com, which is a link to an AICPA career site for students. (Use bookmark/favorites to save the location in an "Accounting References" folder.)

   a. Describe the main career options if you have an accounting background.
   b. What kind of salary can you expect for the different types? (Try the "futurizer" wheel.)
   c. After you finish this exercise, return to this site and try some of the games and tools.

2. On the Internet, do an accounting job search. *Suggestion:* You can do a general search for 'Accounting Jobs' and also try: jamyway.org/accounting and accounting.com.

   a. Prepare a table that lists at least fifteen different job titles in your state.
   b. For each job title, indicate:

   - What is the nature of the work and duties?
   - What education and background are required?
   - What salary and benefits are offered?

3. Did you notice that many positions do not indicate the salary and important benefits (such as medical insurance)? What research is absolutely essential before you begin to look for a position as an employee or to offer a position as an employer?

4. From a student point of view, federal, state, and local governmental accounting jobs also offer competitive salary and benefits, and they usually provide excellent training and experience. Example: Go to jobs.irs.gov. Identify at least five job descriptions and compare the requirements, salaries, and type of experience you will receive to those you listed above (Also use the "GS schedule" for salaries.)

Your Questions?

It is *very* important to be aware of what you need to understand better. What do you need to understand better about this learning goal? On a separate sheet of paper, write the questions that you want to discuss with your classmates, instructor, or supervisor. Try to be very specific about what is bothering you, such as explanations that you do not fully understand.

| LEARNING GOAL 8 | # Prepare Closing Entries |

In Learning Goal 8, you will find:

Review of Stockholders' Equity

Overview of Stockholders' Equity

Two Parts

The stockholders's equity in a corporation consists of two basic parts:

- Paid-in capital: This is a section that indicates the amount invested in a corporation. It shows what was received by the company from selling its stock to investors. This part always has at least one type of stock account called "common stock". See pages 2-4.
- Retained earnings: This is an account that contains the cumulative amount of all net income and net loss, minus any dividends that have been paid to stockholders. See pages 2-4.

Current Period Changes to Retained Earnings

Revenue, Expense, and Dividends

As indicated above, the retained earnings account is where all net income and net loss is accumulated. To determine income or loss each period, all revenue and expense transactions must have been recorded into revenue and expense accounts.

After all the *revenues* and *expenses* are recorded, at the end of the period we can then transfer the net result of the total revenues and the total expenses into retained earnings. This transfer updates retained earnings and is the main part of the closing process.

Dividend payments also affect retained earnings. Dividends are a distribution of profits to stockholders, usually by cash payment. When a dividend is paid, assets are reduced and the amount of the dividend is recorded in a dividends account. At the end of the period, the retained earnings is reduced by the amount of dividends recorded in the dividends account. This is the final step in the closing process.

Gains and Losses

- A *gain* is a current period incidental increase in net income. A gain is recorded in a gain account and has exactly the same effect as a revenue. Examples of gains: 1) Business equipment that cost $5,000 is sold for $8,000. The gain is $3,000. 2) A business wins a lawsuit.
- A *loss* is a current period incidental decrease in net income. A loss is recorded in a loss account and has exactly the same effect as an expense. Examples of losses: 1) Business equipment that cost $10,000 is sold for $3,000. The loss is $7,000. 2) Fire destroys a building, which is not fully insured.

Because gains and losses occur less frequently, and because we want to keep our examples as clear as possible, we do not include gains and losses in the examples below. However, gain and loss accounts have exactly the same effect as revenues and expenses in the closing process, and should be treated in the same manner.

Illustration

Even though they are separate accounts, you can think of revenues, expenses, and dividends as the current period changes in retained earnings. As illustrated below, the balance in retained earnings is $30,000 at the start of a period. During the period, net income (revenues minus expenses) is $5,000 and dividends are $2,000. Therefore the current period net change in retained earnings is a positive $3,000. After the closing, the retained earnings account increases to $33,000.

Current Period Changes to Retained Earnings, *continued*

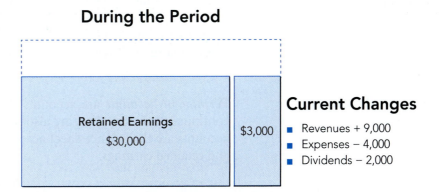

During the Period

Retained Earnings
$30,000

$3,000

Current Changes

- Revenues + 9,000
- Expenses − 4,000
- Dividends − 2,000

End of the Period After Closing

Retained Earnings
$33,000

The Concept of Closing

Overview

Effect of the Closing

The closing process formally separates the results of one accounting period from the next accounting period in the accounting records, and updates the balance of retained earnings. **Closing records the effect of a period's net income or net loss and dividends in stockholders equity, by means of the retained earnings account.**

- Net income: increases retained earnings (and stockholders' equity).
- Net loss: decreases retained earnings (and stockholders' equity).
- Dividends: decreases retained earnings (and stockholders' equity).

Temporary and Permanent Accounts

Temporary Accounts

By now, you have probably noticed that the current period accounts that are closed are the revenue, expense, and dividend accounts. These are called *temporary accounts* because they are closed at the end of each period into retained earnings. They are also sometimes referred to as "nominal accounts".

Permanent Accounts

Permanent accounts are accounts that are never closed. They maintain continuous balances. They are also sometimes called "real accounts". These accounts are the balance sheet accounts: assets, liabilities, common stock, and retained earnings.

Summary Table

The table below summarizes what accounts are affected by closing:

Type of Account	Accounts	Closed?	Permanent or Temporary?
Balance Sheet Accounts	Asset, Liability, Common Stock, Retained Earnings	Never Closed	Permanent Accounts
Income Statement Accounts	Revenue and Expense	Closed	Temporary Accounts
Other	Dividends Account	Closed	Temporary Account

When the Temporary Accounts Are Closed

As indicated above, closing occurs at the end of an accounting period. This can be at the end of any accounting period such as a month, a quarter, or a year, after all other transactions and adjusting entries for that period have been been recorded. This formally separates each reporting period from other reporting periods in the accounting records.

Three Specific Objectives of Closing

The Three Objectives

The closing process has these three specific objectives:

- Update retained earnings by transferring net income or net loss of the current period into retained earnings.
- Update retained earnings by reducing retained earnings for current period dividends.
- Ensure that all temporary accounts begin the next period with zero balances. This prevents temporary amounts of one period from being mixed with amounts of the next period.

Use the Accounting Equation to Understand Closing

Overview

As you know, the accounting equation describes the financial condition of a business at any point in time. For a corporation, this would be:

Assets = Liabilities + **Stockholders Equity**

Continuing further, we can identify the specific stockholders' equity accounts in bold type as you see below. The stockholder's equity consists of the common stock and retained earnings permanent accounts, plus the current period temporary accounts that change retained earnings.

Permanent Accounts	Temporary Accounts
Assets = Liabilities + **Common Stock** + **Retained Earnings** +	{ Revenue + Expense – Dividends –

The temporary accounts remain open during a period as revenues, expenses, and dividends are recorded. However, at the end of the period, we close the temporary accounts and update the balance in retained earnings. The accounting equation will show:

Permanent Accounts	Temporary Accounts
Assets = Liabilities + **Common Stock** + **Retained Earnings**	All closed – zero balances. Balances transferred into retained earnings

The temporary accounts now all have zero balances and are ready to begin the next accounting period. The retained earnings account now has a new updated balance, so the total of stockholders' equity is now also updated.

Example

Suppose that the Bevill Company, Inc. closes the books at the end of each month. At the start of business on June 1, the stockholders' equity is $7,000, which consists of $1,000 in common stock and $6,000 in retained earnings. As before, stockholders' equity accounts are shown in dark bold type. On June 1 all the account balances show the totals that you see below:

continued ▶

Use the Accounting Equation to Understand Closing, *continued*

Assets	=	Liabilities	+	**Stockholders Equity**
10,000	=	3,000	+	7,000

At the end of June, after all the June transactions are completed, the revenue accounts total $3,000, and the total of all expense accounts is $1,800, for a net income of $1,200. The dividends paid are $500.

	Permanent Accounts			Temporary Accounts
Assets = Liabilities +	**Common Stock** +	**Retained Earnings** +	**Revenue** 3,000 +	
10,700 3,000	1,000	6,000	**Expense** 1,800 −	
			Dividends 500 −	

The temporary accounts are all part of stockholders' equity, and when they are closed into retained earnings, the result is a $700 net change (increase) in retained earnings. After the closing is completed for the month of June, the equation will show:

	Permanent Accounts		Temporary Accounts
Assets = Liabilities +	**Common Stock** +	**Retained Earnings**	
10,700 = 3,000 +	1,000 +	6,700	–0–

As a result of the $1,200 net income minus the $500 of dividends paid out, the retained earnings have increased by $700, and the assets have increased by the same amount.

TIP

Keep in mind that only the accounts that involve net income or net loss and any distribution of profits to stockholders are the ones involved in the closing process.

Check Your Understanding

On a separate piece of paper, complete the sentences by filling in the blank spaces.

The account that shows the cumulative balance that has resulted from all prior net income, net loss, and dividends is called . . . . .The kinds of accounts that are closed into this account at the end of each period are called . . . . .accounts. Specifically, they are the . . . ., ..., and . . . . accounts. They are all part of . . . . .equity. Accounts that are not closed are called . . . . . . .accounts.

Answers

The account that shows the cumulative balance that has resulted from all prior net income, net loss, and dividends is called retained earnings. The kinds of accounts that are closed into this account at the end of each period are called temporary accounts. Specifically, they are the revenue, expense, and dividend accounts. They are all part of stockholders' equity. Accounts that are not closed are called permanent accounts.

The Closing Procedure

Overview

Summary of the Steps

The closing procedure can be completed in four steps:

Step 1: The balances of all the revenue accounts are totaled and entered into the credit side of an income summary account.
Step 2: The balances of all the expense accounts are totaled and entered into the debit side of an income summary account.
Step 3: The balance of the income summary account is transferred into the retained earnings account.
Step 4: The balance of the dividends account is transferred into the retained earnings account.

These entries are called *closing entries.*

The Income Summary Account

The *income summary account* is an account that is used only during the closing procedure. You could say that it is the "most temporary" of all the temporary accounts because it has a balance only during the brief period while the accounts are being closed. Sometimes it is called "income and expense summary".

continued ▶

Overview, *continued*

Reason for the Income Summary Account

The income summary account is used only to show the total of all revenues for the period on the right side of the account and to show the total of all expenses for the period on the left side of the account. By looking at both sides, it is then possible to easily determine the net income or loss for the period and easily transfer it to the retained earnings account.

Note: Computerized accounting systems can perform the closing with a single command and transfer net income or net loss and dividends directly into retained earnings without using an income summary account. An income summary account is used most often in manual systems, but can also be set up in some computerized systems.

"Now here comes the good part . . . the closing entries."

Overview of the Four Steps to Close the Accounts

Illustration   The imaginary ledger below shows the group of all expense accounts, all revenue accounts, and all other accounts (permanent accounts). The circled accounts are part of the closing process.

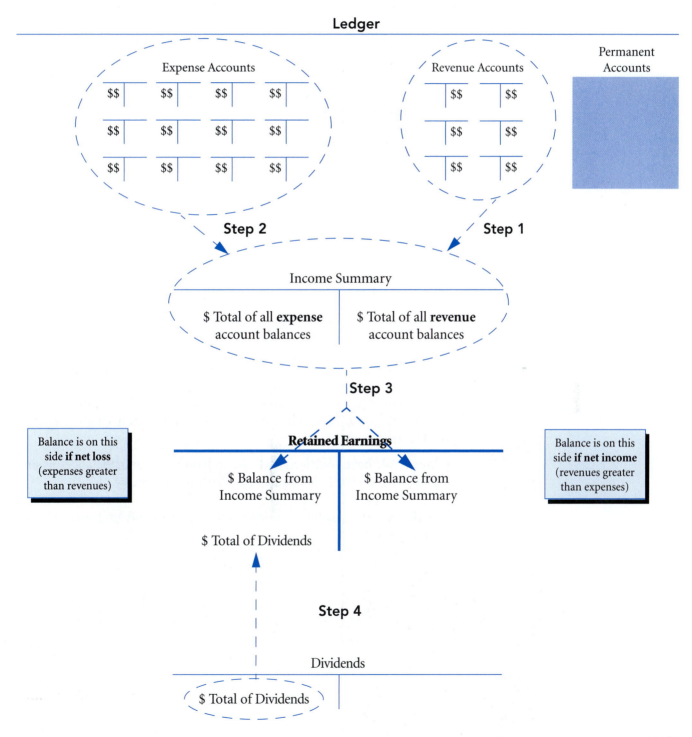

continued ▶

Simple T-Account Illustration of the Four Steps

Step 1 Illustrated (T-Account Analysis)

For simplicity, imagine that there are only two revenue accounts: Service Fees Earned and Interest Earned.

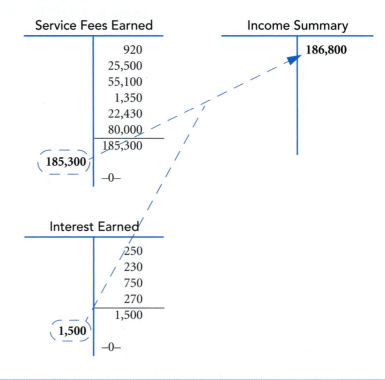

If a revenue account has a *credit* balance, what entry is needed to completely remove that balance? A *debit* entry of the same amount. Once the credit balance is removed with a debit, it is combined with other similar entries, and the total of all the entries is entered as a single credit to Income Summary.

> *Result:* We have transferred all the individual revenue balances as one total of $186,800 to the credit side of Income Summary.

Also, the revenue accounts now have zero balances and are ready to begin the new period.

Simple T-Account Illustration of the Four Steps, *continued*

Step 2 Illustrated (T-Account Analysis)

For simplicity, suppose that there are only three expense accounts to close: Rent Expense, Advertising, Expense, and Travel Expense.

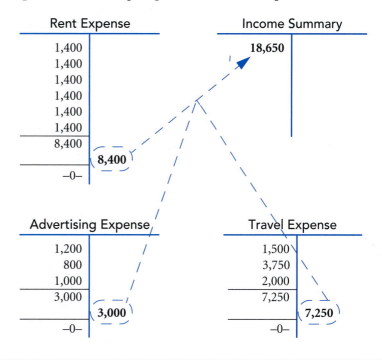

If an account has a *debit* balance, then a *credit* entry is needed to completely remove that balance. As shown above, Rent Expense has an $8,400 debit balance, so we remove it with an $8,400 credit entry. Likewise, the $3,000 debit balance in Advertising Expense is removed with a $3,000 credit entry. Travel Expense has a $7,250 debit balance so a $7,250 credit entry is needed to remove it. A debit *balance* is removed with a credit *entry*. The closing entries of $8,400, $3,000, and $7,250 are combined and entered as a single debit to Income Summary.

Result: We have transferred all the individual expense balances as one total to the debit side of Income Summary, and the expense accounts now have zero balances and are ready to begin the new period.

Simple T Account Illustration of the Four Steps, *continued*

**Step 3 Illustrated
(T Account Analysis)**

Let us assume that a company called J.M. Hass Corporation had a total of $153,000 of revenues and $141,000 of expenses for the current year. All the individual revenue and expense accounts have been closed and the totals posted into the income summary account you see below. The retained earnings account has a beginning balance of $25,000 from the start of the year.

Income Summary			Retained Earnings		
	153,000			25,000	Bal.
141,000					
	12,000	Bal.			

By looking at the income summary account, we can easily see that the $153,000 credit of revenues exceeds the $141,000 debit of expenses by $12,000, which results in a $12,000 credit balance, indicating net income. The next step is to close Income Summary and transfer the the $12,000 net income into Retained Earnings. This is illustrated by the arrow below.

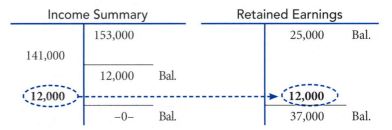

To close Income Summary, we ask: "What *entry* is needed to remove a $12,000 credit *balance*?" Answer: a $12,000 debit entry. The debit *entry* removes the credit *balance*. To keep the transaction in balance, we then make a $12,000 credit entry in Retained Earnings. Result: we have now transferred the $12,000 of net income into Retained Earnings. Also, Income Summary is reduced back to zero, ready for the next time we need to use it.

**Step 4 Illustrated
(T Account Analysis)**

Finally let us assume that there have been three dividend payments during the year in the amounts of $3,000, $2,000, and $4,000. These are recorded as debit entries in the dividends account you see below, resulting in a $9,000 debit balance. The arrow shows the closing of the dividends account into the retained earnings account.

continued ▶

Simple T Account Illustration of the Four Steps, *continued*

	Dividends			Retained Earnings	
	3,000			25,000	Bal.
	2,000				
	4,000			12,000	From Income Summary
Bal.	9,000			37,000	Bal.
Bal.	–0–	9,000 ----▶ 9,000	28,000	Bal.

To close Dividends, we ask: "What *entry* is needed to remove a $9,000 debit *balance*?" Answer: a $9,000 credit entry. The credit *entry* removes the debit *balance*. We then make a $9,000 debit entry in Retained Earnings. Result: we have now transferred the $9,000 Dividends debit balance as a reduction in Retained Earnings. The year-end balance of Retained Earnings is reduced to $28,000. Also, the dividends account is reduced back to zero, ready for the next period.

Illustration of a Net Loss

Step 3 Is
the Only Change

If a company incurs a net loss, the only step in the closing process that would be different is Step 3. This is because the income summary account will show a greater debit total (expenses) that the credit total (revenues), indicating a net loss. This changes the income summary closing entry. For example, look at the illustration below.

	Income Summary			Retained Earnings	
		153,000		25,000	Bal.
	160,000				
Bal.	7,000				

The income summary account has a $7,000 debit balance (net loss). To close this debit balance, a $7,000 credit to Income Summary is required, with a $7,000 debit to Retained Earnings, as illustrated below. Retained Earnings then decreases as a result of the loss.

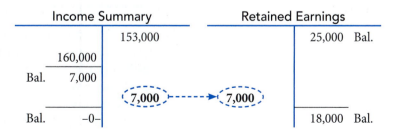

	Income Summary			Retained Earnings	
		153,000		25,000	Bal.
	160,000				
Bal.	7,000				
		7,000 ----▶ 7,000			
Bal.	–0–			18,000	Bal.

Where to Find the Balances for Closing

Three Good Sources

Three possible sources are available to find the closing balances.

- The revenue expense, and dividend account balances in the ledger after all the adjustments have been posted, OR
- The revenue, expense, and dividend account balances in the adjusted trial balance, OR
- The easiest location is the worksheet income statement account balances column, plus the balance of the dividends account in the balance sheet column.

Any temporary account with a credit balance is closed with a debit and any temporary account with a debit balance is closed with a credit.

Computerized Systems

If you use a computerized accounting system, the system will automatically do a closing procedure whenever you enter the necessary command. You do not need to look for any account balances. Nevertheless, you must still understand what the system is doing so that you can check the results.

TIP

Is it possible to prepare financial statements without actually making the formal closing entries in the journal and ledger to complete the process? Yes, it is. For example, financial statements are immediately prepared after a worksheet is completed, before adjusting and closing entries are recorded. As well, accounting software can prepare financial statements from adjusted account balances. However, frequent closing can make year end closing (which is necessary) quicker and easier because less data is involved at the end of the year. On the other hand, some companies wait until year-end to do a single journalizing and posting for closing all periods.

Journalizing the Closing Entries

Introduction

We have now seen an overview of the closing procedure by using an illustration of T accounts. However, just like any other transaction, the closing entries are always first recorded in a journal and then posted into ledger accounts. The following examples for Applegate Modeling Agency completes our discussion of that company and shows you how to make the general journal closing entries.

The four steps below are the same ones that you learned in the previous illustrations and discussion.

Step 1: Close the Revenue Accounts

Refer to the completed worksheet for Applegate Modeling Agency, Inc. on page 223. The worksheet is for the month of May, 2017, and this company closes its accounts monthly.

Refer to the income statement column and locate the revenue credit balances. You will see the account balances of two types of revenue: Fees Earned and Interest Earned. In the journal, debit each revenue account for the amount of its balance. Then credit income summary for the total of all the revenue.

GENERAL JOURNAL				J3
Date	**Account**	**Ref.**	**Dr.**	**Cr.**
June 30	Fees Earned		10,800	
	Interest Earned		200	
	Income Summary			11,000
	(To close revenue accounts)			

When the debit entries above are posted into the revenue ledger accounts, each of these accounts will have zero balances, which makes them closed for May.

Step 2: Close the Expense Accounts

Again refer to the income statement column and locate the expense debit balances. You will see a number of different expenses. In the journal, credit each expense account for the amount of its balance. Then debit income summary for the total of the expenses. (It is easiest to total expenses first and then debit income summary.)

continued ▶

Journalizing the Closing Entries, *continued*

GENERAL JOURNAL			J3
June 30	Income Summary	8,145	
	Salaries Expense		5,000
	Rent Expense		1,450
	Income Tax Expense		300
	Utilities Expense		280
	Office Supplies Expense		580
	Modeling Supplies Expense		200
	Depreciation Expense		160
	Insurance Expense		75
	Interest Expense		100
	(To close expense accounts)		

When the credit enries above are posted into the ledger expense accounts, each of these accounts will have a zero balance, which makes them closed for May.

Step 3: Close the Income Summary Account

The balance in the income summary account determines how it will be closed. If the account has a credit balance (net income) it is closed with a debit. If the account has a debit balance (net loss) it is closed with credit. The table below summarizes this.

IF...	THEN in the journal...
income summary has a credit balance (net income),	Income Summary $$$ Retained Earnings $$$
income summary has a debit balance (net loss),	Retained Earnings $$$ Income Summary... $$$

For the Applegate Modeling Agency, we can see from Step 1 that $11,000 will be posted as a credit to Income Summary. From Step 2 we can see that $8,145 will be posted as a debit. A T account for Income Summary would show a credit balance of $2,855 (net income):

```
           Income Summary
         8,145  |  11,000
   Bal.         |   2,855
```

Journalizing the Closing Entries, *continued*

Also, if you return to the worksheet for the company, you will see that the bottom of the income statement column shows $2,855 net income as the difference between the column totals with the same amounts.

After recording the $2,855 credit balance in income summary, we then make the following journal entry that will close the Income Summary account and transfer the credit balance into Retained Earnings:

June 30	Income Summary		2,855	
	Retained Earnings			2,855
	(To close income summary account)			

Step 4: Close the Dividends Account

The Dividends account shows the amount of distributions to stockholders, which is a reduction in a company's retained earnings. Returning to the worksheet, we see that the debit balance in Dividends is $2,000. Therefore, the Dividends account is closed with a credit and the debit balance is entered into Retained Earnings:

Date	Account	Ref.	Dr.	Cr.
June 30	Retained Earnings		2,000	
	Dividends			2,000
	(To close the dividends account)			

Notice that the dividends account is closed directly to Retained Earnings, **not Income Summary. Dividends are not an expense of operating a business.**

Summary of Retained Earnings

We can use a T account to see how the retained earnings account would appear after the closing journal entries from the Income Summary and Dividends accounts have been posted.

Retained Earnings

	Bal. 8,120
	2,855 (From Income Summary)
(From Dividends) 2,000	
	Bal. 8,975

The $8,975 is the same ending balance that you see in the statement of retained earnings on page 227.

continued ▶

Journalizing the Closing Entries, *continued*

The Post-Closing Trial Balance

After all the closing journal entries are posted into the ledger accounts, a third and final trial balance is prepared, called the *post-closing trial balance.* The post-closing trial balance is used to prove that the total of the debit account balances in the ledger still equals the total of the credit account balances after the closing is completed. This means that the accounting equation is still in balance. **There should be no temporary accounts in the post-closing trial balance because all these accounts will now have zero balances.**

Example

The Applegate Modeling Agency post-closing trial balance is shown below. These are the final ledger account balances after all transactions, adjusting entries, and closing entries have been completed and posted into the ledger for May. They are also the beginning balances for June.

<table>
<tr><td colspan="3" align="center">**Applegate Modeling Agency, Inc.**
Post-Closing Trial Balance
May 31, 2017</td></tr>
<tr><th>Account Titles</th><th>Dr.</th><th>Cr.</th></tr>
<tr><td>Cash</td><td>15,850</td><td></td></tr>
<tr><td>Accounts Receivable</td><td>2,800</td><td></td></tr>
<tr><td>Office Supplies</td><td>520</td><td></td></tr>
<tr><td>Modeling Supplies</td><td>600</td><td></td></tr>
<tr><td>Prepaid Insurance</td><td>525</td><td></td></tr>
<tr><td>Office Equipment</td><td>9,700</td><td></td></tr>
<tr><td>Accum. Dep'n.—Office Equip.</td><td></td><td>1,120</td></tr>
<tr><td>Salaries Payable</td><td></td><td>900</td></tr>
<tr><td>Accounts Payable</td><td></td><td>1,400</td></tr>
<tr><td>Interest Payable</td><td></td><td>100</td></tr>
<tr><td>Unearned Fees</td><td></td><td>500</td></tr>
<tr><td>Notes Payable</td><td></td><td>15,000</td></tr>
<tr><td>Common Stock</td><td></td><td>2,000</td></tr>
<tr><td>Retained Earnings</td><td></td><td>8,975</td></tr>
<tr><td>Totals</td><td>29,995</td><td>29,995</td></tr>
<tr><td></td><td></td><td></td></tr>
</table>

How Quickly Must I Do the Closing at Period End?

Process

A closing entry is dated as of the last day of an accounting period. However, this does not literally mean that an accountant has to work until late at night on the last day of the period to complete the closing before the next day begins.

The next day (June 1 in the example above), a new journal page will be started for the new accounting period. New ledger pages for the revenue, expense, and dividend accounts will be set up. This means that the actual closing entry and the posting for the period just ended can be done at a later date, even while the business continues to record transactions for the new period on the new pages.

As soon as it is convenient (or necessary), the journalizing and posting of the closing entries are completed on the journal and ledger pages for the old accounting period, but it's best not to wait too long.

Using Accounting Software

Sometimes accounting software for computerized systems may have initial settings that do not create a record of closing journal entries or closing posting amounts. The closing command simply updates the retained earnings account and records zero balances in temporary accounts. This setting should be changed to a default that always provides a complete record of every transaction item in both the journal and ledger – no exceptions.

TIP

You may encounter this closing terminology. Here is an explanation:

- A "soft close": This is a fast completion of the closing process by not fully completing all the necessary adjusting entries before closing, simply for the purpose of saving time. The idea is that a "soft close" provides results that can approximate correct balances; however, significant errors and inaccuracies can easily occur, and financial statements can be materially misstated. A "soft close" usually occurs in interim periods, and not at significant dates such as year end or quarter end.
- A "virtual close": This is a highly integrated and automated closing process performed by large companies. A "virtual close" typically allows very large companies to complete a closing within just 24-48 hours, rather than several weeks. The idea is that having very rapid access to performance results can provide a competitive advantage to management. However, this speed is achieved only by incurring very high costs to design and maintain a complex information system and ensuring that a large number of employees are coordinating and complying with the requirements of the process.

Appendix to Learning Goal 8

Closing Entries for Proprietorship

Overview

The closing procedure for a proprietorship is very similar to the closing procedure of a corporation. The only differences for a proprietorship are the following:

- Net income (or loss) in the income summary account is closed into the owner's capital account instead of a retained earnings account (which is not used in a proprietorship).
- A proprietorship uses an owner's drawing (withdrawals) account instead of a dividends account. The drawing account is closed into the capital account.

Example
(Net Income)

Date	Account	Ref.	Dr.	Cr.
xxx	Income Summary		10,000	
	Bill Smith, Capital			10,000
	Bill Smith, Capital		2,000	
	Bill Smith, Drawing			2,000

Closing Entries for a Partnership

Overview

The closing procedure for a partnership is very similar to the closing procedure of a corporation. The only differences for a partnership are the following:

- Net income (or loss) in the income summary account is closed into each partner's capital account based on the partnership allocation formula instead of into a retained earnings account (which is not used in a partnership).
- A partnership uses an owner's drawing (withdrawals) account for each partner instead of a dividends account. The balance of a partner's drawing account is closed into the capital account for that partner.

Closing Entries for a Partnership, *continued*

Baker and Cooper partnership allocates profit and loss 40% and 60%.

Example (Net Income)

Date	Account	Ref.	Dr.	Cr.
xxx	Income Summary		10,000	
	Baker, Capital (40%)			4,000
	Cooper Capital (60%)			6,000
	Baker, Capital		5,000	
	Cooper Capital		3,000	
	Baker, Drawing			5,000
	Cooper, Drawing			3,000

QUICK REVIEW

- In a corporation, the temporary accounts that require closing are revenues, expenses, gains, losses, and dividends. (Gains and losses occur less frequently than the other account types.)

- "Closing the accounts" refers to a procedure that formally separates the results of an accounting period from the next accounting period and updates the balance of retained earnings. Closing records the amount of a period's net income or net loss and dividends in stockholders equity, by means of the retained earnings account.

- Closing occurs at the end of an accounting period, after all transactions and adjustments have been recorded.

- The objectives of closing are to: 1) Transfer net income or net loss into retained earnings, 2) Transfer the amount of dividends into retained earnings, 3) Ensure that all temporary accounts begin the next period with zero balances.

- Credit balance temporary accounts are closed with debits. Debit balance temporary accounts are closed with credits.

- The four steps of journalizing a closing entry are: 1) Close revenue account balances into the credit side of the income summary account. 2) Close expense account balances into the debit side of the income summary account. 3) Close the income summary account into retained earnings. 4) Close the dividends account into the debit side retained earnings.

- After journal entries are posted, a post-closing trial balance is prepared. It should contain only permanent account balances.

VOCABULARY

Closing entries: journal entries that are part of the closing process (page 261)

Closing the accounts: transferring temporary account balances into permanent accounts (page 257)

Dividends: a decrease in stockholders' equity caused by distributing cash or other assets to stockholders (page 256)

Expense: a decrease in stockholders' equity that results from consuming resources in regular business operations (page 12)

Gain: an incidental increase in stockholders' equity not part of regular operations (page 256)

Income summary: an account used to summarize revenues and expenses during the closing process (page 261)

Loss: an incidental decrease in stockholders' equity not part of regular operations (page 256)

Permanent account: an account that is not closed; asset, liability, common stock, and retained earnings accounts (page 258).

Post-closing trial balance: a trial balance that is prepaid after closing entries have been posted (page 272)

Revenue: an increase in stockholders' equity that results from regular operations (sales of goods or services) (page 11)

Temporary account: (page 258) an account that is closed; revenue, expense, dividend (withdrawals in a proprietorship), and income summary accounts.

Do You Want More Examples?

Most problems in this book have detailed solutions. To use them as additional examples, do this: 1) Select the type of problem you want 2) Open the solution on your computer or mobile device screen (from the disc or worthyjames.com) 3) Read one item at a time and look at its answer. Take notes if needed. 4) Close the solution and work as much of the problem as you can. 5) Repeat as needed.

PRACTICE   **Learning Goal 8**

Learning Goal 8 is about the closing process. Use these questions to practice what you have learned about the closing process.

Multiple Choice
Select the best answer.

1. The purpose of closing entries is:
    a. to transfer the current net income or net loss into the retained earnings account.
    b. to prepare the temporary accounts for recording transactions in the next accounting period by reducing their balances to zero.
    c. to transfer the dividend account balance into the retained earnings account.
    d. all of the above.

2. A revenue account is closed:
    a. by debiting the balance of a revenue account and crediting income summary.
    b. by crediting the balance of a revenue account and debiting income summary.
    c. by crediting the balance of a revenue account and crediting income summary.
    d. by none of the above.

3. An expense account is closed:
    a. by debiting the expense and crediting income summary.
    b. by crediting the expense and debiting income summary.
    c. by crediting the expense and crediting income summary.
    d. by none of the above.

4. The dividends account is closed:
    a. by debiting the balance of the account and crediting income summary.
    b. by crediting the balance of the account and debiting income summary.
    c. by crediting the balance of the account and crediting income summary.
    d. by none of the above.

5. The income summary account:
    a. contains all revenue, expense, and drawing account totals for the current period.
    b. is not considered to be a temporary account.
    c. is closed into the retained earnings account.
    d. is described by none of the above.

6. Which one the following accounts would not be closed?
    a. Fees Revenue
    b. Accumulated Depreciation
    c. Income Summary
    d. Depreciation Expense

7. The closing entries:
    a. are most easily prepared using the worksheet as the source of the account balances.
    b. are most easily prepared using the ledger as a source of the account balances.
    c. are most easily prepared using the financial statements as the source of the account balances.
    d. are not required entries.

8. The closing entries:
    a. are the last entries done at the end of the accounting period.
    b. are done before the adjusting entries.
    c. are done after the post-closing trial balance.
    d. are done before the worksheet is prepared.

9. After the closing process is completed, the balance in the income summary account
   a. will be zero.
   b. will be a credit balance if the company had a net income.
   c. will be a debit balance if the company had a net loss.
   d. both b and c.
10. Which of the accounts would be debited in a closing entry?
   a. revenues, expenses, and dividends
   b. expenses and withdrawals
   c. revenues and gains
   d. revenues
11. Which of the accounts would be credited in a closing entry?
   a. revenues and gains
   b. expenses and dividends
   c. gains and losses
   d. expenses, losses, and dividends

Discussion Questions and Brief Exercises

1. Why are closing entries prepared?

2. When are closing entries prepared and recorded? Why?

3. Your friend Janet says to you: "I don't get it. If the account has a debit balance, why don't you close it with a debit? If it has a credit balance, why don't you close it with a credit?" Your answer? What four accounts did we emphasize in this learning goal?

4. What is the difference between a temporary account and a permanent account? Identify all the types of temporary and permanent accounts that we studied in this learning goal.

5. What is the difference between adjusting entries and closing entries?

6. Assume that an income summary account has a credit entry of $157,300 and a debit entry of $101,900. What is the correct entry to close income summary? Does this represent a net income or net loss?

7. What is the purpose of a post-closing trial balance?

8. Identify which of the following accounts would *not* appear in a post-closing trial balance: cash, accounts receivable, service revenue, notes receivable, merchandise inventory, depreciation expense, plant and equipment, accumulated depreciation.

9. Explain the relationship, if any, between the debit and credit totals of the income statement columns on a worksheet and the debit and credit entries to the income summary account.

10. Explain the four steps for closing the accounts.

11. Why do you think the dividends account balance is not closed into the income summary account?

PRACTICE   **Learning Goal 8, continued**   *Solutions are in the disk at the back of the book and at: www.worthyjames.com*

Reinforcement Problems

LG 8-1 Prepare closing journal entries. The Albany Company temporary account balances at the end of the period are shown below. *Instructions:* Prepare the closing journal entries.

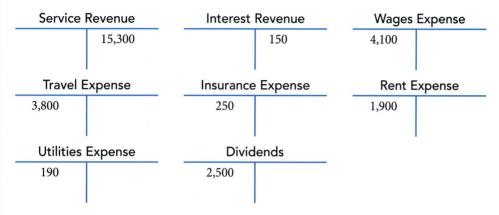

Service Revenue		Interest Revenue		Wages Expense	
	15,300		150	4,100	

Travel Expense		Insurance Expense		Rent Expense	
3,800		250		1,900	

Utilities Expense		Dividends	
190		2,500	

LG 8-2. Permanent and temporary account identification. Using a separate piece of paper, complete the table by placing a "✓" in the appropriate space. Use the first account as an example.

Account Name	Permanent	Temporary	Closed	Appears on the: Balance Sheet	Income Statement
Cash	✓			✓	
Unearned Revenue	(Reminder: Use a separate sheet of paper to complete the table.)				
Accumulated Depreciation					
Fees Earned					
Insurance Expense					
Prepaid Insurance					
Income Summary					
Supplies					
Supplies Expense					
Common Stock					
Rent Expense					
Depreciation Expense					
Interest Revenue					
Accounts Payable					
Office Equipment					
Dividends					

LG 8-3. Closing journal entries and T accounts. *Instructions:* Using the worksheet for Tallahassee Company that you see below.

a. Print out a copy of the worksheet template for LG 8-3 from the disk at the back of the book or at worthyjames.com (student info.). Then complete the worksheet.

b. Prepare the closing journal entries.

c. Draw T accounts for the accounts you see in the worksheet. In the T accounts, write the beginning balances. Write "bal." next to these balances. For any account that is adjusted, enter the adjusting entry in the account, and write the letter of the adjustment next to the adjustment. For each of these accounts, total the account and write the new account balance in the account.

d. Record the closing entries in the T accounts that are part of the closing process, and write the new account balances in these accounts.

Tallahassee Company, Inc.										
Worksheet										
(000's)	For the Year Ended June 30, 2017									
	Trial Balance		Adjustments		Adjusted Trial Balance		Income Statement		Balance Sheet	
Account Titles	Dr.	Cr.	Dr.	Cr.	Dr.	Cr.	Dr.	Cr.	Dr.	Cr.
Cash	200				200				200	
Accounts Receivable	30		(e) 8		38				38	
Office Supplies	15			(a) 3	12				12	
Prepaid Insurance	20			(b) 10	10				10	
Office Equipment	100				100				100	
Accum. Dep'n.—										
Office Equipment		20		(c) 2		22				22
Common Stock		30				30				30
Retained Earnings		302				302				302
Dividends	10				10				10	
Fees Earned		40		(e) 8		48				
Salaries Expense	5		(d) 5		10					
Rent Expense	11				11					
Income Tax Expense	1				1					
Totals	392	392								
Office Supplies										
Expense			(a) 3		3					
Depreciation Expense			(c) 2		2					
Insurance Expense			(b) 10		10					
Salaries Payable				(d) 5		5				5
Totals			28	28	407	407			370	359
Net Income										11
Totals									370	370

Solutions are in the disk at the back of the book and at: www.worthyjames.com

PRACTICE   Learning Goal 8, continued

LG 8-4. Closing entries, post-closing trial balance, retained earnings. Of course, you remember the famous Winslow Tennis Club (page 215). You are now the permanent, full-charge accountant (while you take tennis lessons to see if you can get into next year's tournament). In the meantime, your job is to do the following:

a. Prepare the closing entries from the adjusted trial balance. (For journal paper, use the template in the disk at the back of the book or at worthyjames.com (student info.))
b. Prepare the post-closing trial balance.
c. Explain the difference in Retained earnings that you see on the adjusted trial balance and what is on the post-closing trial balance.

Winslow Tennis Club
Adjusted Trial Balance
June 30, 2017

Account Title	Dr.	Cr.
Cash	$45,750	
Dues Receivable	2,800	
Office Supplies	50	
Tennis Supplies	215	
Notes Receivable	12,000	
Prepaid Insurance	500	
Office Equipment	14,520	
Accum. Dep'n.—Office Equipment		$11,858
Building	345,000	
Accum. Dep'n.—Building		20,100
Accounts Payable		855
Notes Payable		275,000
Common Stock		5,000
Retained Earnings		82,161
Dividends	1,880	
Tennis Instruction Fees		8,500
Dues Revenue		28,500
Salaries Expense	4,100	
Equipment Rent Expense	1,750	
Utilities Expense	280	
Insurance Expense	200	
Maintenance Expense	750	
Unearned Tennis Fees		1,000
Office Supplies Expense	1,050	
Tennis Supplies Expense	1,787	
Depreciation Expense	842	
Salaries and Wages Payable		500
Interest Expense	1,375	
Interest Receivable	80	
Interest Earned		80
Interest Payable		1,375
Total	$434,929	$434,929

   Solutions are in the disk at the back of the book and at: www.worthyjames.com

LG 8-5. Prepare closing entries, show T accounts. The table below shows selected adjusted account balances as of year end, December 31, 2018. However, the accounts are shown randomly.

Instructions:

a. Select the accounts that would be used in a closing entry and prepare the closing entries. (For journal paper, use the template in the disk at the back of the book.)
b. Draw T accounts for the accounts that are part of the closing procedure. Enter balances in the T accounts and then enter the closing entries from the journal into the T accounts. Enter the final account balances. (Use the T-account analysis paper from the template in the disk at the back of the book.)

Prepaid Insurance Expense	$4,800	Service Revenue	$248,100
Office Equipment	19,200	Wages Payable	14,500
Depreciation Expense—Office Equipment	2,500	Rent Expense	26,000
Unearned Revenue	22,150	Notes Payable, Short-Term	15,500
Advertising Expense	22,400	Automotive Equipment	30,000
Rental Revenue	20,000	Short-Term Investments	75,900
Accumulated Depreciation—Automotive Equipment	5,000	Cash	33,800
		Prepaid Rent Expense	3,750
Income Tax Expense	4,500	Wages Expense	115,300
Accounts Payable	12,600	Insurance Expense	9,900
Utilities Expense	5,700	Accumulated Depreciation—	
Accounts Receivable	7,250	Office Equipment	6,100
Dividends	35,000	Common Stock	10,000
Miscellaneous Expense	300	Retained Earnings	160,300
Interest Revenue	450	Merchandise Inventory	15,000
Patent	25,000	Depreciation Expense—Automotive	5,000
Interest Expense	7,500	Interest Payable	3,500
Office Supplies	1,250		

LG 8-6. Prepare closing entries for a corporation; compare to proprietorship closing. Pasadena Company has the accounts that you see on the next page and prepares monthly financial statements. At the end of August, each account shows an unadjusted balance, and some accounts show adjusting entries, indicated by letters. All necessary adjustments have been made (Taxes omitted).

Instructions:

a. Journalize the closing entries for the month. For journal paper, use the template for LG 8-6 in the disk at the back of the book or at worthyjames.com (student info.).
b. Enter the closing entries in the accounts and show all the final account balances.
c. Assume that this business is a proprietorship instead of a corporation, and that the owner is Mary Adams. Also assume that any dividends shown were withdrawals by Mary.

LG 8-6, *continued*

Cash	Accounts Receivable	Office Supplies	Prepaid Rent	Office Equipment
49,800	76,100 (a) 6,000	2,000 | (b) 500	11,100 | (c) 3,700	125,000

Accum. Dep'n—Office Equip.	Accounts Payable	Unearned Revenue	Common Stock	Retained Earnings
| 18,750 (d) 25,000	| 44,900 (f) 1,500	(e) 900 | 7,000	| 20,000	| 132,650

Dividends	Service Revenue	Wages Expense	Rent Expense	Office Supplies Expense
5,000	| 58,000 (a) 6,000 (e) 900	8,000	(c) 3,700	100 (b) 500

Depreciation Expense	Advertising Expense	Income and Expense Summary
(d) 25,000	4,200 (f) 1,500	

Instructor-Assigned Problems

If you are using this book in a class, these review problems may be assigned by your instructor for homework, group assignments, class work, or other activities. Only your instructor has the solutions.

IA 8-1. Prepare closing journal entries. The Redding Company temporary account balances at the end of the period are shown below.

Instructions: Prepare the closing journal entries.

Service Revenue		Interest Revenue		Wages Expense	
	21,600		370	12,100	

Travel Expense		Insurance Expense		Rent Expense	
7,800		390		4,800	

Utilities Expense		Dividends	
440		3,000	

IA 8-2. Prepare closing journal entries. Shown below are December 31 year-end adjusted ledger account balances for Maxwell Company, presented in random order, before closing entries are recorded.

Instructions: Using the correct accounts:
a) Prepare the year-end closing journal entries
b) Calculate the amount of net income or net loss.
c) Calculate the change in retained earnings in the current period.

Prepaid Rent Expense	$ 7,500	Wages Payable	$ 24,700
Trademark	15,800	Long-Term Investments	10,000
Notes Payable (long-term)	105,000	Rent Expense	56,000
Cash	76,250	Notes Payable (due in 60 days)	47,300
Machinery	91,600	Service Revenue	216,450
Accumulated Depreciation—Machinery	35,900	Dividends	10,000
Common Stock	50,000	Short-Term Investments	25,900
Automobiles	45,000	Unearned Revenue	22,150
Accumulated Depreciation—Auto	30,000	Accounts Payable	62,600
Accounts Receivable	67,850	Prepaid Insurance Expense	11,500
Office Supplies	1,350	Wages Expense	79,800
Notes Receivable (due in 120 days)	10,000	Retained Earnings	71,600
Miscellaneous Expense	300	Interest Expense	5,200
Interest Revenue	450	Merchandise Inventory	85,000
Patent	15,000	Depreciation Expense	22,500
Land	20,000	Income Tax Expense	9,600

IA 8-3. Complete a worksheet, prepare a statement of retained earnings, prepare closing entries.
Shown below is a partial worksheet for Decatur Consulting Services for the year ending December 31, 2017, with the adjusted trial balance columns completed.

Instructions:

a) Complete the worksheet
b) Prepare a statement of retained earnings.
c) Prepare closing entries from the worksheet below
d) Assume that this business is a proprietorship and the owner is Bill Smith. Assume that the dividends in the worksheet were withdrawals by Bill. Also assume that the Income Tax Expense was additional Travel Expense. Prepare the closing entries.

Use either a blank worksheet or the worksheet template for IA8-3 from the disk at the back of the book or at www.worthyjames.com (student info.).

Account Titles	Adjusted Trial Balance Dr.	Cr.	Income Statement Dr.	Cr.	Balance Sheet Dr.	Cr.
Cash	39,340					
Short-term Investments	34,770					
Accounts Receivable	23,190					
Supplies	1,800					
Prepaid Travel Expense	3,160					
Office Equipment	91,260					
Accum. Dep'n.—Office Equip.		24,300				
Accounts Payable		19,340				
Unearned Revenue		5,500				
Notes Payable—Long Term		25,000				
Common Stock		12,000				
Retained Earnings		67,930				
Dividends	6,500					
Consulting Revenue		286,900				
Interest Revenue		1,050				
Salaries/Wages Expense	172,100					
Rent Expense	52,000					
Utilities Expense	2,190					
Miscellaneous Expense	1,860					
Insurance Expense	2,400					
Travel Expense	1,730					
Depreciation Expense	4,120					
Income Tax Expense	4,700					
Supplies Expense	900					
Total	442,020	442,020				

LEARNING GOAL 9

Describe the Complete Accounting Cycle

In Learning Goal 9, you will find:

The Complete Accounting Cycle

Well Done . . .

. . . and congratulations! After much hard work, you have now reached a very important place in your study of accounting. This is the point where you have learned the complete accounting cycle.

Now you know all the basic accounting steps and the reasons for those steps. Naturally, there are further refinements (such as a payroll), but the important thing is that now you understand the process. Also, if you are interested in using computerized accounting systems, these same steps will apply in a computerized environment, except that the computer will do a lot of the repetitive and mechanical work for you.

"Congratulations! After much hard work, you have now reached a very important place in your study of accounting."

The Complete Accounting Cycle

Description

Description of the Cycle

The illustration on the next page shows how the accounting cycle is the sequence of all the steps necessary to record transaction information and prepare financial reports. These steps can be categorized into three major tasks: analyze, process, and communicate.

- **Analyze:** During a period, events are analyzed to determine if they should be recorded as transactions. Analysis is also done at the end of the period to determine how adjustments should be recorded.
- **Process:** Processing refers to recording, organizing, adjusting, and closing procedures. So far, you have learned the following processing procedures:
  - Recording (journalizing) recurring transactions (Volume 1)
  - Posting (Volume 1)
  - Preparing a trial balance (Volume 1)
  - Journalizing and posting the adjusting entries (Volume 2)
  - Preparing the adjusted trial balance (Volume 2)
  - Completing the worksheet (Volume 2)
  - Journalizing and posting the closing entries (Volume 2)
  - Preparing the post-closing trial balance (Volume 2)
- **Communicate:** Communication refers to the preparation of financial reports, and disclosures and interpretations of the reports.

Use of a Worksheet

The steps affected by the use of a worksheet are contained within the dotted lines. Often, if a manual worksheet is used, the journalizing and posting part of Step 5 is skipped and the financial reports (Step 7) are prepared immediately from the worksheet. This is because these reports are always needed quickly. *After* the reports are finished, when the accountant has more time, he or she then journalizes and posts the adjusting entries (finishing Step 5), *using the same* worksheet information.

Computerized Compared to Manual

In a computerized accounting system, with or without a built-in worksheet, the computer does Steps 5–9 with a single command, after the accountant has calculated the adjustments and entered them into the computer. The computer also does Steps 3 and 4 with separate commands.

Illustration—The Accounting Cycle

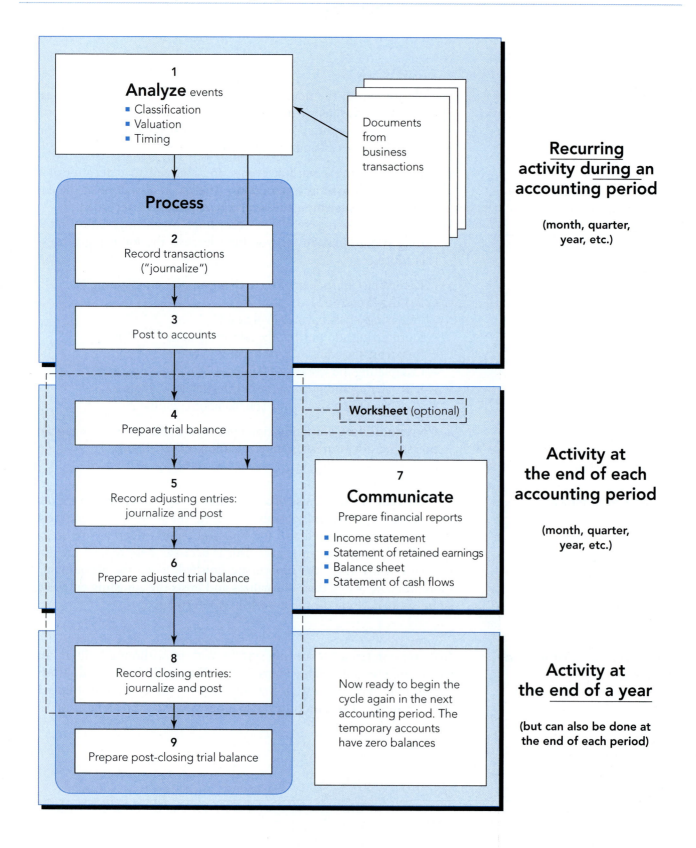

PRACTICE   Learning Goal 9

Solutions are in the disk at the back of the book and at: www.worthyjames.com

LG 9-1. **Comprehensive problem: Worksheet, adjusting entries, closing entries, financial statements, classified balance sheet analysis.**

Instructions:

a. Complete the worksheet for Johnson's Cleaning Service for the month of December. (Use the worksheet for this problem that is available in the accounting paper file in the disk at the back of the book.)

b. Prepare an income statement, statement of retained earnings, and a report form classified balance sheet.

c. Journalize the adjusting entries. For journal paper, use the template in the disk at the back of the book.

d. Journalize the closing entries.

e. Using the classified balance sheet, compare the current assets to the current liabilities. Look at the individual components of these classifications. How are current assets likely to be affected in January by this situation?

	Johnson's Cleaning Service, Inc.									
	Worksheet									
	For the Month Ended December 31, 2017									
	Trial Balance		Adjustments		Adjusted Trial Balance		Income Statement		Balance Sheet	
Account Titles	Dr.	Cr.	Dr.	Cr.	Dr.	Cr.	Dr.	Cr.	Dr.	Cr.
Cash	17,800									
Short-Term Investments	10,200									
Accounts Receivable	9,620									
Cleaning Supplies	5,700									
Prepaid Insurance	4,600									
Office Equipment	18,400									
Accum. Dep'n—Off. Equip.		9,150								
Cleaning Equipment	58,000									
Accum. Dep'n—Clean. Equip.		5,000								
Vans	123,500									
Accum. Dep'n—Vans		28,980								
Accounts Payable		25,850								
Unearned Revenue		7,500								
Note Payable		40,100								
Common Stock		25,000								
Retained Earnings		93,940								
Dividends	5,000									
Cleaning Service Revenue		68,100								
Wages Expense	39,800									
Rent Expense	4,500									
Auto & Gas Expense	550									
Advertising Expense	2,900									
Utilities Expense	450									
Repairs Expense	1,100									
Income Tax Expense	1,500									
Totals	303,620	303,620								

continued ▶

LG 9-1, *continued*

Other Information:

a. Prepaid insurance in the amount of $6,900 was paid on August 1 for a one-year insurance policy.
b. The amount of cleaning supplies still on hand on December 31 is $1,850.
c. Monthly depreciation for the office equipment is $150, for the cleaning equipment is $500, and for the vans is $2,500. One depreciation expense account is used for all depreciation.
d. Revenue unearned on December 31 is $2,000.
e. Unrecorded and unpaid interest expense on the note payable for December is $270.
f. Unrecorded and unpaid monthly gasoline bills total $310.
g. The note payable is due in 5 years, with no principal payable in the next year.

PRACTICE   Learning Goal 9, continued

IA 9-1. Comprehensive problem: prepare a worksheet, prepare financial statements, record adjusting and closing entries. Shown below is the trial balance for Boulder Internet Consulting Services for the year ending December 31, 2017.

Instructions:

a. Complete the worksheet
b. Prepare an income statement, statement of retained earnings, and a report form balance sheet.
c. Record the adjusting entries
d. Record the closing entries

Use either a blank worksheet or the worksheet template for IA9-1 from the disk at the back of the book or at www.worthyjames.com (student info.).

Account Titles	Dr.	Cr.
Cash	107,620	
Short-term Investments	120,640	
Accounts Receivable	61,900	
Supplies	3,150	
Prepaid Travel	4,400	
Long-term Investments	75,930	
Office Equipment	41,300	
Accum. Dep'n. - Office Equip.		22,120
Patent	55,700	
Accounts Payable		66,740
Unearned Revenue		2,900
Notes Payable - Long Term		45,000
Common Stock		15,000
Retained Earnings		288,990
Dividends	10,000	
Consulting Services		45,420
Internet Design Services		381,450
Salaries/Wages Expense	267,510	
Rent Expense	93,000	
Utilities Expense	8,720	
Miscellaneous Expense	1,120	
Insurance Expense	3,680	
Travel Expense	8,850	
Income Tax Expense	4,100	
Total	867,620	867,620

Other information:

a. Invoices totaling $3,790 for consulting work performed at year-end was sent to clients in December.
b. $1,500 of unearned revenue for design services was earned in December.
c. A physical count of supplies indicates $900 remain unused at year-end.
d. $2,100 of airline tickets paid in advance remain unused at year-end.
e. Interest earned but not received on investments is $1,480.
f. The office equipment is being depreciated over seven years, with no residual value.
g. Unrecorded interest owing on the notes payable is $225.
h. The current portion of long-term debt is $8,200

PRACTICE   Learning Goal 9, continued

IA 9-2. Comprehensive problem: prepare a worksheet, prepare financial statements, record adjusting and closing entries. Record closing entries Shown below is the trial balance for Santa Clara Moving Services for the year ending December 31, 2017.

Instructions:

a. Complete the worksheet
b. Prepare an income statement, statement of retained earnings, and a report form balance sheet.
c. Record the adjusting entries
d. Record the closing entries

Use either a blank worksheet or the worksheet template for IA9-2 from the disk at the back of the book or at www.worthyjames.com (student info.).

Account Titles	Dr.	Cr.
Cash	57,100	
Short-term Investments	5,650	
Accounts Receivable	67,320	
Supplies	4,200	
Prepaid Insurance	10,500	
Long-term Investments	42,000	
Office Equipment	34,500	
Accum. Dep'n.—Office Equip.		24,150
Trucks	375,900	
Accum. Dep'n.—Trucks		206,740
Trademark	7,500	
Accounts Payable		71,070
Unearned Revenue		7,900
Notes Payable - Long Term		185,200
Common Stock		18,000
Retained Earnings		86,300
Dividends	5,000	
Commercial Move Revenue		381,400
Residential Move Revenue		249,120
Salaries/Wages Expense	529,250	
Office Rental Expense	25,800	
Equipment Rental Expense	16,410	
Utilities Expense	3,100	
Advertising Expense	25,600	
Interest Expense	14,600	
Miscellaneous Expense	1,950	
Insurance Expense	3,500	
Total	1,229,880	1,229,880

PRACTICE   Learning Goal 9, continued

IA 9-2, *continued*

Other information:

a. Unpaid and unrecorded invoices sent to commercial customers at year-end total $6,500
b. The year-end balance of unearned revenue, which is from residential customers, is $4,000.
c. A physical count of supplies at year end indicates a balance of $2,600
d. $3,000 of prepaid insurance expired during December.
e. Office equipment is being depreciated over a life of 10 years with no residual value and trucks are being depreciated over a life of 5 years, with no residual value. Only one depreciation expense account is used.
f. Advertising bills were received in January for December advertising in the amount of $3,100.
g. Interest earned but unrecorded is $2,700.
h. The current portion of long-term debt is $5,500

IA 9-3. Prepare financial statements The accountant for Mountain View Enterprises prepared the following adjusted account balances that you see below for the quarter ending June 30, 2018.

Instructions: For the current quarter:

a. Prepare an income statement
b. Prepare a statement of retained earnings.
c. Prepare a report form balance sheet.

Office Equipment	$115,600	Service Revenue	$186,850
Utilities Expense	8,500	Wages Payable	14,500
Trademark	4,800	Advertising Expensee	20,000
Taxes Payable	75,000	Rent Expense	16,000
Cash	66,250	Long-term Notes Payable	47,300
Accumulated Depreciation-Office Equip	35,500	Dividends	50,000
Common Stock	50,000	Short-Term Investments	25,900
Automobiles	145,000	Unearned Revenue	22,150
Accounts Payable	32,600	Prepaid Insurance Expense	11,500
Long-term Investments	112,500	Wages Expense	83,900
Notes Receivable (due in 6 months)	10,000	Accumulated Depreciation – Auto	101,000
Miscellaneous Expense	300	Interest Expense	5,200
Interest Revenue	450	Supplies Inventory	35,000
Patent	35,000	Depreciation Expense	22,500
Retained Earnings	241,350	Accounts Receivable	57,850
		Depreciation Expense	22,500

Income tax: 20% of income before tax.
* $5,000 of the note payable is due
December 31 of the current year.

PRACTICE SET
Cumulative Problem

Service business complete accounting cycle. *Instructions:* Journalize recurring transactions, post to ledger, prepare a worksheet, prepare financial statements, journalize and post adjusting entries, journalize and post closing entries, prepare a post-closing trial balance.

Information:

Keisha's Catering Service Inc. is a successful business that provides catering services to both business and private clients by selecting, delivering, and arranging food and drink for meetings, parties, and special occasions. All stock is owned by Keisha Ames. The business prepares monthly financial statements. Using the information on pages 295–296 for the business:

1. Record the recurring transactions for October 2017 in a general journal. Explanations are not required. (For journal paper, make copies from the general journal templates from the disk at the back of this book.)
2. Post the October journal information into the ledger. Before you begin the posting, create the necessary ledger accounts by entering account names and numbers on the ledger accounts. Use the chart of accounts that you see on page 295. Use the account balances from September 30 as the October 1 beginning balances: Cash, $143,800; Accounts Receivable, $22,700; Office Supplies, $150; Prepaid Rent, $8,250; Office Equipment, $27,500; Accumulated Depreciation—Office Equipment, $13,750; Accounts Payable, $4,300; Common Stock, $10,000, Retained Earnings, $174,350. (For ledger paper, make copies from the ledger templates from the disk at the back of this book.)
3. Prepare a worksheet. Carefully *analyze each transaction plus the additional information* to make sure that you have identified all the adjustments that are needed.
4. Upon completion of the worksheet prepare an income statement and statement of retained earnings for the month ending October 31, 2017, and prepare a classified report-form balance sheet as of October 31, 2017.
5. Using the worksheet information, journalize the adjusting entries.
6. Post the adjusting entries.
7. Using the worksheet information, journalize the closing entries.
8. Post the closing entries.
9. Prepare a post-closing trial balance.

PRACTICE SET

Keisha's Catering Services Chart of Accounts			
Assets:		*Stockholders' Equity*	
Cash	101	Common Stock	301
Short-Term Investments	105	Retained Earnings	302
Accounts Receivable	115	Dividends	305
Office Supplies	125	Income and Expense Summary	340
Prepaid Insurance	135		
Prepaid Rent	140	*Revenues:*	
Office Equipment	180	Business Client Revenue	405
Accum. Dep'n—Office Equip	181	Private Client Revenue	410
Automotive Equipment	185		
Accum. Dep'n—Auto. Equip	186	*Expenses:*	
		Rent Expense	505
Liabilities:		Wages Expense	510
Wages Payable	205	Food/Beverage Expense	512
Accounts Payable	210	Auto Expense	515
Unearned Revenue	215	Insurance Expense	520
Interest Payable	220	Advertising Expense	525
Notes Payable, Current	225	Utilities Expense	530
Notes Payable, Long-Term	280	Office Supplies Expense	535
		Dep'n. Expense—Office Equip.	581
		Dep'n. Expense—Auto. Equip.	586
		Interest Expense	590

October Events:

October 1: (Begin on journal page 10.) The business paid one year of liability insurance in advance, $1,800.

October 2: Keisha Ames contributed some personal office supplies to the business. The supplies were valued at $500.

October 2: The business collected $1,400 from a customer who paid an amount owing for prior services.

October 2: The business purchased a van that cost $36,250 by paying $10,000 cash and signing a 5-year note payable for the balance. The note has an annual interest rate of 8%, and payments are due on the first of each month.

October 3: The business opened a short-term investment account and transferred $75,000 into the account.

October 3: Received a $5,000 advance payment from Ann Arbor Enterprises to cater a board of directors meeting later in the month.

October 4: Catered a wedding party at a private home. Billed the client $15,000.

October 5: Paid the amount owing for the September utilities services, $200.

October 6: Paid $500 for advertising in the October local newspaper Sunday supplement.

October 8: Received a telephone call from a corporation that indicated that it would be interested in catering services for the annual employee party. Ms. Ames quoted a price of $18,000.

October 10: Purchased office supplies on account, $300.

October 12: Provided catering services to Spruce Knob Enterprises for a retirement party. The company paid cash of $2,500.

PRACTICE SET

October 14: (Begin journal page 11.) Received a $5,000 advance payment from Flint Company.

October 16: Received a bill for the food and beverage cost for the Spruce Knob company party, $1,500, and paid the bill in full.

October 16: Paid several vendors for amounts owing on account for a total of $1,100.

October 18: Paid bi-weekly (every two weeks) wages of $4,500 the day following the end of the two-week payroll period.

October 18: Collected $6,500 cash on account.

October 20: Provided the catering services for Ann Arbor Enterprises (Oct. 3 above) and billed the client $17,000. The client paid the amount owing in full.

October 21: Provided catering services for a private anniversary party and received $5,000 cash.

October 23: Received a bill for the food and beverage cost for the October 4 wedding party, $8,300, and received a bill for gasoline expense in the amount of $180.

October 24: Received cash in advance from Saginaw Company in the amount of $8,000 for payment in full for two retirement parties. The client was billed $4,000 for each party.

October 27: Paid $4,000 dividends to K. Ames.

October 30: Received a bill for the food and beverage cost for the Ann Arbor Enterprises party, $10,500.

October 31: (Begin journal page 12.) Paid several vendors for amounts owing on account for a total of $15,375.

October 31: Received the current month's utility bill of $175.

Additional Information:

a. On October 31, one of the Saginaw Company's (see October 24) retirement parties was catered. The bill to Keisha's Catering service for the food and beverages cost for this party was $2,500. Nothing has been recorded yet concerning the party.

b. The office equipment was purchased 2-1/2 years ago. The equipment has an estimated useful life of 8 years with no residual value. The van has an estimated useful life of 5 years with $3,250 of estimated residual value. (Depreciation calculations can be rounded to the nearest $10.)

c. A count of office supplies on October 31 shows $150 worth of supplies still on hand.

d. Of the balance showing in the Prepaid Rent account, $5,500 is for November and December rent.

e. A small private Halloween party was catered on October 30 for $750. The bill to the client had been overlooked and is still unrecorded.

f. The current portion of the long-term note payable is $5,000.

CUMULATIVE VOCABULARY REVIEW

This is a vocabulary review for Learning Goals 7 through 9. On a separate piece of paper, match each description with the term that it describes. The answer for each term is in the right column. (Suggestion: Cover the answers in the right column as you test your vocabulary.)

Term	Description	Answers
1. Worksheet	a. Another name for current assets.	1j
2. Working papers	b. A balance sheet format in which assets are placed on the left and equities on the right.	2l
3. Account form	c. An account used only during the closing process.	3b
4. Liquid assets	d. Assets that do not have physical substance.	4a
5. Operating cycle	e. Revenue, expense, dividend, and income summary accounts.	5m
6. Report form	f. The last step in the accounting cycle.	6k
7. Classified balance sheet	g. A journal entry that transfers the total of all the revenues and all the expenses into income summary, and the net income from income summary into the permanent retained earnings account.	7h
8. Marketable securities	h. A balance sheet in which all the accounts are grouped into standardized significant categories.	8o
9. Inventory	i. The regular sequence of steps for recording transactions in the accounting records and preparing financial statements.	9n
10. Closing entry	j. An accounting device used at the end of a period to organize accounting data and to prepare financial statements.	10g
11. Temporary accounts	k. A balance sheet format in which assets are placed at the top of a page and equities are placed below the assets at the bottom of the page.	11e
12. Permanent accounts	l. The worksheet and all other documents and calculations used to prepare financial statements.	12r
13. Post-closing trial balance	m. The time it takes, on average, between spending cash on goods or services and when cash is received from customers.	13f
14. Income summary	n. Merchandise that a business sells to customers.	14c
15. Accounting cycle	o. Short-term investments in stocks and bonds that are actively traded.	15i
16. Intangible assets	p. Assets that become cash or used instead of cash within a year, or the operating cycle, if longer.	16d
17. Current assets	q. Debts that need to be paid within a year.	17p
18. Current liabilities	r. Assets, liabilities, and stockholder equity.	18q

CUMULATIVE TEST   Learning Goals 7–9

Time Limit: 45 minutes

Instructions

*On a separate sheet of paper, enter the best answer to each question. Do **not** look back in the book when taking the test. (If you need to do this, you are not ready.) After you finish the test, refer to the answers and circle the number of each question that you missed. Then go to the **Help Table** (on page 304) to identify your strong and weak knowledge areas by individual learning goal.*

Multiple Choice
On the line provided, enter the letter of the best answer for each question.

1. The preparation of the worksheet is done
   a. after closing entries have been journalized at the end of the period.
   b. at any time during the accounting period.
   c. before financial statements are prepared but after adjustments have been journalized.
   d. before financial statements are prepared and before adjustments have been journalized.

2. Which of the following is not true of the worksheet?
   a. The primary purpose is to facilitate the preparation of financial statements.
   b. It shows the debits and credits to be entered in the general journal for adjusting entries.
   c. It is a permanent accounting record, like a journal or ledger.
   d. It provides the information necessary for the closing entries.

3. Which of the following account groups are all temporary accounts?
   a. revenues, expenses, and dividends
   b. revenues expenses, and retained earnings
   c. assets, liabilities, and dividends
   d. assets, liabilities, and retained earnings

4. If Accounts Receivable has a normal $5,000 balance in the adjusted trial balance column of the worksheet and a $500 debit has been made to Accounts Receivable in the adjustments column, then the balance of Accounts Receivable in the trial balance column must have been
   a. $4,500 credit balance.
   b. $4,500 debit balance.
   c. $5,500 credit balance.
   d. $5,500 debit balance.

5. The sequence of recurring steps that are performed during an accounting period is called the
   a. operating cycle.
   b. accounting cycle.
   c. closing process.
   d. business cycle.

6. Which of the following is *not* true of the worksheet?
   a. It shows the total revenues and expenses.
   b. It shows the ending balance of the retained earnings account.
   c. It shows the net income or net loss.
   d. It shows the required adjustments to the ledger accounts.

7. Which of the following is the correct sequence for preparing the closing entries for a corporation?
   a. Close the total of revenue and expense accounts into the income summary account, close the dividends account into income summary, then close the income summary into the retained earnings account.
   b. Close the revenue and expense accounts into the retained earnings account, and then close the dividends account into the retained earnings account.
   c. Close the revenue and expense accounts into the income summary account, close income summary into the retained earnings account, and then close the dividends account into the retained earnings account.
   d. None of the above.

CUMULATIVE TEST   Learning Goals 7–9, continued

8. The Riverwalk Touring Company shows the following totals in the income statement and balance sheet columns in the worksheet:

	Income Statement		Balance Sheet	
	Dr.	Cr.	Dr.	Cr.
Totals	57,300	49,500	52,400	60,200

The net income or loss for the period is:
a. $7,800 net income.
b. $49,500 net income.
c. $7,800 net loss.
d. $2,900 net loss.

9. On the year-end worksheet for the Ludlow Street Drugstore, a number is entered under and added to the subtotal of credits in the balance sheet column. When the total of credits in the balance sheet column is then compared to the total debits in the balance sheet column, the two numbers are not equal. Therefore, it is likely that:
a. there is an error that was caused by entering an asset as a credit in the balance sheet column.
b. there is an error that was caused by entering an expense as a debit in the balance sheet column.
c. there is an error that was caused by entering a revenue as a credit in the balance sheet credit column.
d. this does not indicate an error.

10. Which accounts should *not* appear in the post-closing trial balance but *do* appear on the adjusted trial balance?
a. assets, liabilities, and retained earnings
b. revenues, expenses, and dividends
c. assets, revenues, and retained earnings
d. expenses, dividends, and liabilities

11. Which financial statements are prepared directly from the worksheet?
a. the balance sheet and income statement
b. the balance sheet, income statement, and statement of retained earnings
c. the balance sheet, income statement, statement of retained earnings, and statement of cash flows
d. the balance sheet, income statement, and statement of cash flows

12. Which of the following is the final step in the accounting cycle?
a. preparing the trial balance
b. preparing the worksheet
c. making the closing entries
d. preparing the post-closing trial balance

13. The Lee Electrical Contracting Company has the following adjusted ledger accounts at the end of November:

Income Summary		Dividends		Retained Earnings	
11/30 12,000	11/30 17,000	11/15 2,000	11/30 4,000	11/30 4,000	11/1 125,000
11/30 5,000		11/30 2,000			11/30 5,000

What is the amount of net income or net loss for November?

14. If the Unearned Revenue account of the Provo Company has a $3,200 normal balance in the trial balance column of the worksheet and a $400 debit adjustment is made to Unearned Revenue in the adjustments column:
a. the balance sheet column will show a $3,600 credit balance for Unearned Revenue.
b. the income statement column will show a $2,800 debit balance for Unearned Revenue.
c. the balance sheet column will show a $2,800 credit balance for Unearned Revenue.
d. none of the above.

15. The most important document(s) resulting from the accounting cycle is (are):
    a. the worksheet.
    b. the adjusted ledger accounts.
    c. the financial statements.
    d. the post-closing trial balance.

16. The Depreciation Expense and Accumulated Depreciation accounts appear on the trial balance in the worksheet of the Vancouver Company. Which of the following is true?
    a. The Depreciation Expense amount should be extended to the debit side of the balance sheet column, and the Accumulated Depreciation amount should be extended to the credit side of the balance sheet column.
    b. The Depreciation Expense amount should be extended to the debit side of the income statement column, and the Accumulated Depreciation amount should be extended to the credit side of the income statement column.
    c. The Depreciation Expense amount should be extended to the debit side of the income statement column, and the Accumulated Depreciation amount should be extended to the credit side of the balance sheet column.
    d. The Depreciation Expense amount should be extended to the debit side of the balance sheet column, and the Accumulated Depreciation amount should be extended to the credit side of the income statement column.

17. Which one of the following is *not* correct?
    a. Revenues are always closed by debiting all revenue accounts and crediting the income summary account.
    b. Expenses are always closed by crediting all expenses and debiting the income summary account.
    c. The dividends account is always closed by crediting the dividends account and debiting the retained earnings account.
    d. The income summary account is always closed by debiting income summary and crediting the retained earnings account.

18. Which of the accounting cycle steps listed below comes before all the other steps listed?
    a. journalize the closing entries
    b. prepare the worksheet
    c. journalize the adjusting entries
    d. prepare the financial statements

19. To identify the *beginning* balance of the retained earnings for the statement of retained earnings, you must:
    a. use the retained earnings balance in the balance sheet column of the worksheet.
    b. subtract the balance of the dividends account in the balance sheet column of the worksheet from the retained earnings balance in the balance sheet column of the worksheet.
    c. subtract the net income from the retained earnings balance in the balance sheet column of the worksheet.
    d. Either "a" or look at ledger account.

Selected account information from the worksheet financial statement columns of the Santa Clara Company appears below. Use this information for Questions 20–24:

Cash	$20,000	Marketable Securities	$12,000	Wages Payable	$5,700
Accounts Receivable	2,500	Land Held for Future Use	50,000	Notes Payable (due in 5 years)	15,000
Computer Equipment	81,000	Office Supplies	200	Total Revenues	350,000
Accounts Payable	1,900	Trademark	15,000	Total Expenses	310,000
Prepaid Insurance	1,500	Office Furniture	7,500	Common Stock	100,000

20. What is the amount of total current assets?
21. What is the amount of total current liabilities?
22. What is the amount of total property, plant, and equipment?
23. What is the amount of total intangible assets?
24. What is the total of all long-term assets?
25. Which of the following is a correct description of a worksheet?
    a. Practically all companies use a worksheet to prepare financial statements.
    b. Worksheet are not well adapted for use on computers.
    c. Worksheets should never be used as tools for making projections.
    d. Some companies use worksheets as an optional tool to facilitate financial statement preparation.
26. The adjustments column of a worksheet:
    a. eliminates the need to record adjustments in the journal because the adjustments are already recorded on the worksheet.
    b. makes it easy to record adjustments in the journal because the debits and credits can be copied directly from the adjustments column into the journal.
    c. should have no effect on the financial statements when they are prepared.
    d. both b and c.
27. If a company uses a worksheet:
    a. the closing journal entries can easily be made by referring to the adjusted trial balance columns in the worksheet and by debiting all credit balance accounts and crediting all debit balance accounts.
    b. the closing journal entries can easily be made by referring to the income statement columns in the worksheet and by debiting all credit balance accounts and crediting all debit balance accounts.
    c. the closing journal entries can easily be made by referring to the balance sheet columns in the worksheet and by debiting all credit balance accounts and crediting all debit balance accounts.
    d. none of the above are correct.
28. Which of the following is *not* a correct closing journal entry? (The choices are not related.)
    a. Income Summary   950
          Fees Earned   900
          Interest Earned   50
    b. Income Summary   800
          Rent Expense   400
          Utility Expense   300
          Supplies Expense   100
    c. Income Summary   500
          Retained Earnings   500
    d. Retained Earnings   1,000
          Dividends   1,000
29. Which item below shows the correct sequence of assets and liabilities on a classified balance sheet?

Assets	Liabilities
a. Current assets; property, plant, and equipment; and intangible assets	Long-term liabilities, current liabilities
b. Property, plant, and equipment; current assets; and intangible assets	Current liabilities, long-term liabilities
c. Property, plant, and equipment; intangible assets; and current assets	Long-term liabilities, current liabilities
d. Current assets; property, plant, and equipment; and intangible assets	Current liabilities, long-term liabilities

CUMULATIVE TEST SOLUTIONS Learning Goals 7–9, continued

Multiple Choice

1. d

2. c

3. a Assets, liabilities, and stockholders' equity are permanent accounts. Also, the income summary account is a temporary account.

4. b If you're not sure, it would probably help you to draw the accounts receivable line on the worksheet and enter question marks, like this:

	Dr.	Cr.	Dr.	Cr.	Dr.	Cr.
Accounts Receivable	?	?	500		5,000	

Answer:

	Dr.	Cr.	Dr.	Cr.	Dr.	Cr.
Accounts Receivable	**4,500**		500		5,000	

5. b

6. b The ending balance of the retained earnings account has to be calculated. The statement of retained earnings shows the calculation.

7. c Notice that the dividends account is not closed into income summary because dividends is not an expense.

8. c This is the excess of debits over credits in the income statement column (or credits over debits in the balance sheet column).

9. a Items b and c are also errors, but in these cases the total of debits and credits in the balance sheet column will still balance when the net income is plugged into the balance sheet column! However, the net income will be wrong, so the balance sheet column will balance at the incorrect amount. The best way to remember this is to play with a worksheet for a few minutes, and you will see it happen. By the way, "error"-type questions are favorites with many instructors because they like to see if you can figure out what effect the error has.

10. b They do not appear in the post-closing trial balance because they have been closed and therefore have zero balances.

11. a The statement of retained earnings has to be calculated, and the statement of cash flows uses a different worksheet.

12. d

13. $5,000 net income. The income summary shows more credits than debits, so the difference must be net income, which is then closed into retained earnings with a $5,000 credit entry.

14. c $3,200 – 400 = $2,800. Unearned revenue is a liability, so it will appear on the credit side of the balance sheet column.

15. c

16. c

17. d This is how income summary would be closed only if there were net *income*. With a net *loss*, it would be the opposite.

18. b

19. d The best way is to look at the ledger account.

20. $36,200 (Cash $20,000) + (Accounts Receivable $2,500) + (Prepaid Insurance $1,500) + (Marketable Securities $12,000) + (Office Supplies $200) = $36,200.

CUMULATIVE TEST SOLUTIONS Learning Goals 7–9, continued

21. $7,600 (Accounts Payable $1,900) + (Wages Payable $5,700) = $7,600.
22. $88,500 (Computer Equipment $81,000) + (Office Furniture $7,500) = $88,500. (Land held for future use is a long-term investment.)
23. $15,000 (trademark).
24. $153,500. (Computer equipment $81,000) + (Land held for future use $50,000) + (Trademark $15,000) + (Office Furniture $7,500). All of the assets have a useful life of more than a year.
25. d
26. b
27. b
28. a The debits and credits are reversed.
29. d Be sure that you can identify what *kinds of items* go into each category!

HELP TABLE   Identify Your Strengths and Weaknesses

The questions in this test cover the three learning goals of Section II. After you have listed the number of each question that you missed, look at the table below.

Go to the first learning goal category in the table: "Explain What a Worksheet Is and What It Does." The second column in the table shows which questions on the test covered this learning goal. Look on the test to see if you missed numbers 2 or 25. How many did you miss? Write this number in the "How Many Missed?" column. Repeat this process for each of the learning goal categories in the table.

If you *miss two or more questions* for any learning goal, you are too weak in that learning goal and you need to *review*. The last column shows you where to read and practice so you can improve your score.

Some learning goal categories have more questions because you need to be especially well prepared in these areas. More questions indicates where your performance must be better.

Learning Goal	Questions	How many missed?	Material begins on . . .
SECTION II			
7. Explain What a Worksheet Is and What It Does	2, 25		page 206
7. Prepare a Worksheet	1, 4, 8, 9, 14, 16		page 208
7. Use the Completed Worksheet	6, 11, 19, 26, 27		page 225
7. Prepare a Classified Balance Sheet	20, 21, 22, 23, 24, 29		page 228
8. Prepare Closing Entries	3, 7, 10, 13, 17, 28		page 255
9. Describe the Complete Accounting Cycle	5, 12, 15, 18		page 287

Note: In addition to these items, you should also practice preparing financial statements from a worksheet. **Be sure the balance sheet is classified correctly!**

Merchandising Operations

OVERVIEW

What this section does	This section explains what a merchandising business is, and the accounting procedures that are used for merchandising businesses.
Use this section if . . .	■ you want to know how to apply specific accounting procedures to merchandising operations.
Do not use this section if . . .	■ you do not need to learn about merchandising operations.

LEARNING GOALS

LEARNING GOALS

| **LEARNING GOAL 10** | # Distinguish Service Operations from Merchandising Operations |

In Learning Goal 10, you will find:

Compare Service and Merchandising

Service and Merchandising Operations Defined

Introduction

Only two possible economic resources can be created and sold: goods and services. *Goods* means property—things that can be owned. *Services* means the use of someone's labor or property. Services cannot be owned because they are consumed as they are provided.

Merchandise

Merchandise is a term for goods that are offered for sale to customers.

Service Operations

Service operations are business operations that create and sell services.

Examples:

- An advertising company
- A doctor
- An automobile rental company
- An accountant

continued ▶

Service and Merchandising Operations Defined, *continued*

Merchandising Operations	Merchandising operations are business operations that purchase goods from suppliers and resell the goods to customers. A merchandising operation adds value by offering selection and convenience to customers.

Examples:
- A grocery store
- A jewelry store
- An automobile dealer

Nonexamples: |

Not merchandising	because . . .
An athletic health club	it sells the **services** of membership and use of facilities.
A computer repair service	it sells the **services** of repairs.
An automobile manufacturer	it makes the final product rather than buying it from a supplier.

Combination Operations	Some businesses combine service and merchandising operations. A business may have operations that are predominately one kind of operation, with a little of the other, or a business may have significant emphasis on both types.

Example:
Some jewelry stores may offer significant repair and maintenance services in addition to their merchandising operations. |
| *Retail and Wholesale* | A *retail* merchandising business sells to customers who are the final users of a product. They will use it and not resell it. A *wholesale* merchandising business sells to customers who are other merchants or manufacturers. |

The Operating Cycles Compared

Definition	Have you ever heard this expression, "You have to spend money to make money!"? The *operating cycle* of a business refers to the process by which the cash that a business spends for operations eventually causes the business to receive cash from customers.

The Operating Cycles Compared, *continued*

Operating Cycle: Service Operations

The illustration below shows you how an operating cycle is typically viewed for service operations. Money is spent for salaries. In turn, employees perform services for customers. If a customer pays immediately, cash is received as soon as the services are performed. If services are performed on account, the business must wait until it can collect the account receivable.

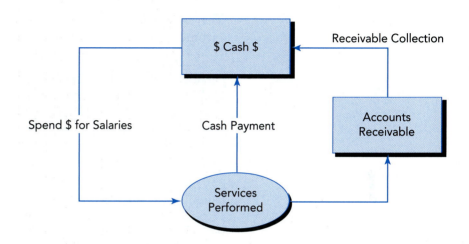

Operating Cycle: Merchandising Business

The illustration below shows you how an operating cycle is typically viewed for merchandising operations. Money is spent for merchandise inventory. In turn, the inventory is sold to customers. If a customer pays immediately, cash is received as soon as the inventory is sold. If the inventory is sold on account, the business must wait until it can collect the account receivable.

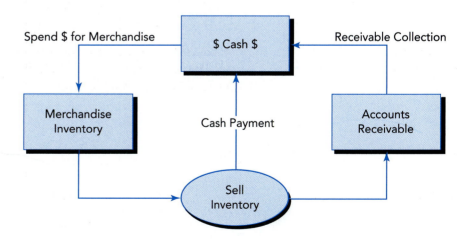

Note: For a merchandising business, up to three current asset accounts are significant in the operating cycle: Cash, Merchandise Inventory, and Accounts Receivable.

Terminology of Income Calculations

Introduction

Both service operations and merchandising operations make sales and incur expenses in order to operate. Thus, the basic concept of income calculation is the same for both types of operations. However, some of the terminology used in each procedure is different. Additionally, some terms are used in a merchandising business that do not apply to a service business.

Terminology Comparison

The table below compares the terminology used in the calculation of income for a service business and a merchandising business.

Item	in a service business is called . . .	and in a merchandising business is called . . .
A sale to a customer	Fees Earned, Service Revenue	Sales, Sales Revenue
The cost of merchandise sold	*	Cost of Goods Sold, Cost of Merchandise Sold, Cost of Sales
The excess of revenue over cost of merchandise sold		Gross Profit, Gross Profit on Sales, Gross Margin
The expenses of operating the business	Operating Expenses	Operating Expenses

* Some service companies show "cost of service revenue" for costs that are directly incurred in order to create the revenue; this is subtracted from service revenue, resulting in gross profit, etc.

Check Your Understanding

Write the completed sentences on a separate sheet of paper. The answers are below.

A service operation sells the · · · · · · · · of someone's · · · · · · · · or · · · · · · · · · .
A merchandising operation sells · · · · · · · · , which are property.

The operating cycle of a business refers to the process in which the · · · · · · · · that is spent eventually causes the business to receive · · · · · · · · back from · · · · · · · · · ·

For a merchandising business, up to (how many?) · · · · · · · · current asset accounts are significant in the operating cycle.

Answers

A service operation sells the use of someone's labor or property. A merchandising operation sells goods, which are property.

The operating cycle of a business refers to the process in which the cash that is spent eventually causes the business to receive cash back from customers.

For a merchandising business, up to three current asset accounts are significant in the operating cycle. (Note: They are cash, merchandise inventory, and accounts receivable.)

Income Calculation and Reporting

Key Difference

The key difference between the financial reporting for a service operation and a merchandising operation is the way that net income is calculated and reported. This difference shows up on the income statement.

Key Difference Illustrated

The diagram below illustrates the income calculation differences. Net sales and cost of goods sold calculations are the major differences.

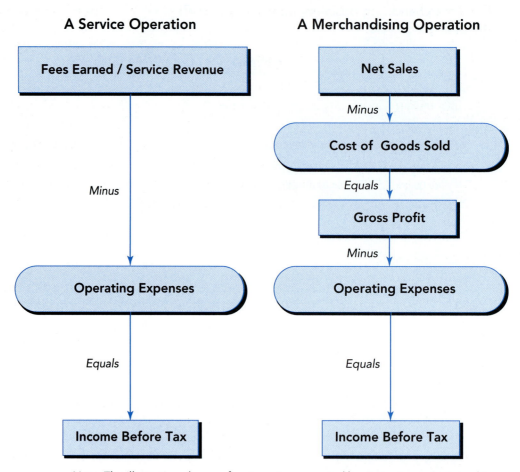

A Service Operation

Fees Earned / Service Revenue

Minus

Operating Expenses

Equals

Income Before Tax

A Merchandising Operation

Net Sales

Minus

Cost of Goods Sold

Equals

Gross Profit

Minus

Operating Expenses

Equals

Income Before Tax

Note: The illustration above refers to an incorporated business. In a proprietorship or partnership, "Income Before Tax" in the illustration would become "Net Income", because there would not be income tax expense.

Net Sales

In a merchandising operation, frequently there are items that reduce the amount of sales revenue that is earned. The two most common items are sales discounts and sales returns and allowances. These items are subtracted from gross sales to obtain *net sales*. These topics are discussed in Learning Goals 11 and 13.

Cost of Goods Sold

Overview

Cost of goods sold is an expense. It is the cost of the merchandise sold.

The two methods for calculating the cost of goods sold (C of GS) are the *periodic inventory method* and the *perpetual inventory method*, which are discussed in detail in Learning Goal 11 and Learning Goal 13. They are alternate methods—a business uses either one method or the other for each type of item.

The two methods are actually based on the same simple formula. If the formula is used one way, then it becomes the "periodic" method. If the formula is applied in a slightly different way, then it becomes the "perpetual" method.

Cost of Goods Sold Formula

The formula for calculating the cost of goods sold is:

$$BI + P - EI = C\ of\ GS$$

- **BI** means the cost of the beginning inventory at the start of the period
- **P** means the net cost of the purchases during the period
- **EI** means the cost of the ending inventory remaining at the end of the period
- **C of GS** means the cost of goods sold

Periodic Method: Quick Overview

The periodic method applies this formula **only at the end of the period**. At the end of each accounting period, ending inventory is counted to determine what is left over, and its cost is determined. This is the only time the current amount of inventory is known. Then the formula is applied.

Example:
Atlantic City Company had $50,000 of beginning inventory on January 1. During the year, the business purchased $200,000 of inventory. So, a total cost of $250,000 was available during the year. At year end, a count shows that ending inventory of $30,000 is still unsold. Therefore, cost of goods sold is: $50,000 + $200,000 − $30,000 = $220,00.

Cost of Goods Sold, *continued*

Perpetual Method: ***Quick Overview***	The perpetual method slightly rearranges the elements in the formula and continuously applies the formula *with every sale that is made.*

The formula is slightly changed to look like this:

BI + P – C of GS = EI, which is calculated with each sale.

Here, the business uses the cost of each sale (C of GS), which is subtracted to determine the ending inventory that is left over after the sale.

When this is done for each sale, the ending inventory after one sale becomes the beginning inventory before the next sale. This is done continuously in the accounting records, so the total cost of goods sold is known each day during a period. The ending inventory at the end of each day is also known. The details of how this is done are presented in Learning Goal 13.

Example

On Monday morning, a business has $100,000 of merchandise inventory. Later in the day, it purchases $3,000 of inventory. The cost of inventory sold during the day was $5,000. Ending inventory on Monday evening is:

$$\$100,000 + \$3,000 - \$5,000 = \$98,000$$

Beginning and ***Ending Inventories***

For both methods, each ending inventory becomes the next beginning inventory. For the periodic method, the ending inventory at the end of one period becomes the beginning inventory at the start of the next period. For the perpetual method, inventory is continuously updated, so the ending inventory after one sale becomes the beginning inventory before the next sale or purchase.

TIP

Even when the perpetual method is used inventory is counted at the end of a period to verify the correctness of the records.

Quick Comparison of Periodic and Perpetual

Overview

The periodic method is simpler and much cheaper. The perpetual method provides much faster and more detailed information, but it is more expensive.

Comparison

The table below compares the essential features of the two methods. The illustration compares how the formula is applied.

Perpetual	Periodic
Keeps a continuous daily record of *both* the merchandise purchased and sold.	Keeps a continuous daily record of *only* the merchandise purchased.
A new inventory balance is calculated after each sale.	A new inventory balance is determined by physical count only at the end of the period.
Cumulative C of GS is known continuously.	Cumulative C of GS is known only at the end of the period.
Keeps close control over inventory.	Does not closely control inventory.
Can be time consuming and expensive.	Is not so time consuming or expensive.
Tends to be used for low-volume or expensive goods, unless computer systems are extensively utilized.	Tends to be used for high-volume, inexpensive goods, although can be used for any type.

	During Current Period	At End of the Period
Perpetual:	BI + P − C of GS = **EI** (with each sale)	
Periodic:	BI + P	− EI = **C of GS** (for all items sold)

Summary

The perpetual method records the cost of goods sold with each sale, so we know the cumulative total cost of goods sold at all times. We also know the inventory on hand at all times. With the periodic method, we only know cost of goods sold at the end of a period, when we count the ending inventory and subtract it from the cost of the goods available for sale.

How Do I Know Which Kind of Problem It Is?

Introduction

When working homework, quizzes, and exam problems, how can you tell if you are being asked to solve a periodic inventory problem or a perpetual inventory problem?

Identification Procedure

The table below shows you how to easily identify which method is required.

IF . . .	THEN . . .
the problem identifies units that were purchased but not units that were sold,	you can only use the periodic method.
the problem identifies *both* units that were purchased *and* units that were sold,	you can use either the perpetual method or the periodic method.

*"Perpetual, periodic . . .
I can do them all, mon cherie!"*

QUICK REVIEW

- A service operation sells the use of someone's labor or property. A merchandising operation buys and resells goods, which are property.

- The operating cycle for a service business is different, and usually faster, than for a merchandising business.

- The most important accounting difference between a service business and a merchandising business is the way that net income is calculated and reported. In a merchandising business, it is necessary to calculate net sales and cost of goods sold when calculating net income.

- Cost of goods sold and inventory can be calculated using either the periodic method or the perpetual method.

- When the perpetual method is used, cost of goods sold and inventory are calculated continuously. Use:
  $BI + P - C \text{ of } GS = EI$

- When the periodic method is used, cost of goods sold and inventory are calculated only at the end of a period. Use:
  $BI + P - EI = C \text{ of } GS$

VOCABULARY

Cost of goods sold: an expense that is the cost of the merchandise that was sold (page 310)

Cost of sales: another term for cost of goods sold (page 310)

Gross margin: another term for gross profit (page 310)

Gross profit: the excess of sales revenue over cost of the merchandise sold (page 310)

Merchandise: the goods that a merchandising business sells to customers (page 307)

Net sales: gross sales less sales discounts and sales returns and allowances (page 312)

Operating cycle: the process by which cash that is spent for operations eventually causes the business to receive cash from customers (page 308)

Periodic inventory method: a method of determining ending inventory by periodically counting it, and then calculating cost of goods sold by using the formula $BI + P - EI = C \text{ of } GS$ (page 313)

Perpetual inventory method: a method of determining ending inventory by continuously updating the inventory balance by subtracting the cost of all goods sold, as well as adding the cost of goods purchased (page 313)

Retail: a business that sells goods to customers who are the final users of the goods (page 308)

Wholesale: a business that sells goods to customers who are other merchants or manufacturers (page 308)

PRACTICE Learning Goal 10

Solutions are in the disk at the back of the book and at: www.worthyjames.com

Learning Goal 10 is about distinguishing service business operations from merchandising business operations. Use these questions and problems to practice what you have learned about these two types of operations.

Multiple Choice
Select the best answer.

1. When cost of goods sold is subtracted from net sales, the result is called:
   a. net income.
   b. gross profit.
   c. gross margin.
   d. either b or c.

2. For a merchandising company to have a net income:
   a. gross profit must be less than net sales.
   b. gross profit must be more than operating expenses.
   c. net sales must be more than operating expenses.
   d. cost of goods sold must be more than net sales.

3. For a service company to have a net income:
   a. operating expenses must be less than the fees earned.
   b. operating expenses must be less than the net sales.
   c. cost of goods sold must be more than operating expenses.
   d. cost of goods sold must be less than net sales.

4. Which of the following is *not* primarily a service business?
   a. an apartment management company
   b. an apartment owner
   c. an accountant
   d. a clothing store

5. Which type of business probably has the shortest operating cycle?
   a. a dry-cleaning business
   b. a home builder
   c. a wholesale furniture store
   d. a grocery store

6. Which company probably has the longest operating cycle?
   a. an accounting business
   b. a movie theatre
   c. a hardware store
   d. a car wash

7. The income statement of a service business would *not* have:
   a. operating expenses.
   b. gross profit.
   c. net income.
   d. fees earned.

8. Which of the following is correct?
   a. The perpetual method calculates the cost of goods sold with each sale.
   b. The periodic method calculates cost of goods sold only at the end of a period.
   c. The perpetual method subtracts ending inventory to determine cost of good sold.
   d. Both a and b are correct.

9. The periodic inventory method has which characteristic?
   a. It is more expensive to install and operate.
   b. It provides the most current information.
   c. It maintains a record of only the units purchased.
   d. It maintains a record of both the units purchased and the units sold.
10. Which of the following would be seen on the income statement of a merchandising business?
    a. cost of goods sold
    b. net income
    c. gross profit
    d. all the above
11. Which of the following is correct?
    a. Both the periodic and perpetual methods record purchases continuously every day, but the periodic method does not record daily cost of sales.
    b. Both the periodic and perpetual methods record purchases and sales continuously each day.
    c. BI + P − C of GS = EI is the formula applied to the periodic method.
    d. BI + P − EI = C of GS is the formula applied to the perpetual method.
12. The formula that best describes the application of the periodic inventory method is:
    a. BI + P − EI = C of GS, calculated daily.
    b. BI + P − EI = C of GS, calculated only at the end of a period.
    c. BI + P − C of GS = EI, calculated daily.
    d. BI + P − C of GS = EI, calculated only at the end of a period.
13. The formula that best describes the application of the perpetual inventory method is:
    a. BI + P − EI = C of GS, calculated daily.
    b. BI + P − EI = C of GS, calculated only at the end of a period.
    c. BI + P − C of GS = EI, calculated daily.
    d. BI + P − C of GS = EI, calculated only at the end of a period.

Reinforcement Problems

LG 10-1. Understanding the elements of net income for a merchandising business.

Instructions: Calculate the amount of the missing item for each business.

Business	Net Sales	Cost of Goods Sold	Gross Profit	Operating Expenses	Net Income (Loss)
Belleville Company	$52,000	$29,000	(a)	$12,000	(b)
Blackhawk Corp.	(c)	$125,000	$72,000	$22,000	(d)
Danville Enterprises	$210,000	(e)	(f)	$45,000	$15,000
Elgin Partnership	(g)	$84,000	(h)	$99,000	($15,000)
Sandberg Company	$35,000	(i)	$21,000	(j)	$5,000
Truman Company	(k)	$210,000	$180,000	(l)	($12,000)
Wright Corp.	$97,000	$56,000	(m)	(n)	$22,000

PRACTICE   Learning Goal 10, continued

Solutions are in the disk at the back of the book and at: www.worthyjames.com

LG 10-2.   Evaluating the periodic and perpetual methods for business situations. Explain which method—periodic or perpetual—would be most appropriate for each of the following business situations:

a. You are just beginning a small discount cleaning supplies business. You do not have much cash, and the cost and profit margin on the supplies are low. You are hoping that you will have high volume.

b. Your business sells disk drives for computers. They are expensive and easy to steal.

c. At year end, you were shocked at how low the gross profit of your business was. You need better and more timely information to manage your operations.

d. Your operations are very predictable. Calculating gross profit only at the end of each fiscal year would be acceptable.

INTERNET EXERCISES

A closer look at annual reports. Search the Internet to locate the annual reports of three large companies suggested by your instructor or selected by you. For each company:

a. Identify the financial statements in the annual report.

b. Does the company use the cash or accrual method of accounting? How can you tell?

c. What is the fiscal year of the company?

d. Does the company use the names "income statement" and "balance sheet," or are different names used to refer to these financial statements?

e. What are the trends in total revenues, operating income, and net income?

f. Locate the cash account in the balance sheet. Calculate the change in the cash balance from the end of the previous year to the end of the current year. Use the statement of cash flows to verify this difference.

g. Read the MD&A (management discussion and analysis). Do you detect some favorable bias?

h. Scan the entire annual report. Does it appear to be a promotional tool as well as a source of financial information? Give some examples of promotional-type commentary in the report.

Your Questions?

It is *very* important to be aware of what you need to understand better. What do you need to understand better about this learning goal? On a separate sheet of paper, write the questions that you want to discuss with your classmates, instructor, or supervisor. Try to be very specific about what is bothering you, such as explanations that you do not fully understand.

| LEARNING GOAL 11 | # Explain and Use the Periodic Inventory Method |

Overview

Introduction

Learning Goal 11 introduces you to the periodic inventory method in greater detail. You will learn how each element of net income is calculated and recorded with this method.

Concept

The *periodic inventory method* is a procedure for determining cost of goods sold and ending inventory only periodically—at the end of each accounting period—by counting the ending inventory.

After the counting is done, the cost of the inventory on hand is determined and a formula is applied to calculate cost of goods sold.

Check with Your Instructor

If you are using this book for a class, before you read this learning goal, be sure that your instructor wants you to learn the periodic inventory method. Some instructors prefer that you learn the perpetual method instead of the periodic method. The perpetual method is in Learning Goal 13 starting on page 437.

"So, did you check with your instructor?"

In Learning Goal 11, you will find:

Part I

Net Sales

Shipping Charges and Sales Tax

Part II

The Cost of Goods Sold Formula

Cost of Goods Available for Sale

Ending Inventory

Net Sales

When to Record Revenue

Overview

The same revenue recognition principle applies to the sale of merchandise as to a service company. That is, revenue is *recognized* (recorded) only after the revenue has been *earned*. Generally, this is at the point of sale, when the seller provides what was agreed upon and the buyer accepts it. Receipt of cash is not required.

Goods That Are Shipped

For merchandising operations, a *sale* means that *ownership of the goods passes to the buyer.*

If the goods are shipped to the buyer, the point at which ownership transfers to the buyer is frequently the **FOB point**. FOB means *free on board*. This is specified as part of the shipping terms.

Example:

The seller is in Los Angeles and sells goods to a merchant in Dallas. The sale requires shipping terms that are "FOB destination." This means that title (ownership) of the goods does not transfer to the buyer until they are offloaded at the point of destination (Dallas). If the terms had been "FOB shipping point," title would have passed to the buyer at the shipping point (Los Angeles) when the transport company picked up the goods from the seller.

When FOB didn't matter . . .

Overview of Net Sales

Introduction

As you may recall from the comparison diagram on page 312, net sales is the starting point in the calculation of net income for a merchandising company. The merchandising diagram is illustrated again below, this time with dollar amounts.

To show you a consistent example, these dollar amounts are part of a continuing example that you can follow through this learning goal and Learning Goal 12, for a business called the "Queensborough Patio Mart."

Illustration

The diagram below illustrates the process of net income calculation for a merchandising business. On the right, the net sales portion of the illustration is expanded to show you the elements that make up a net sales calculation.

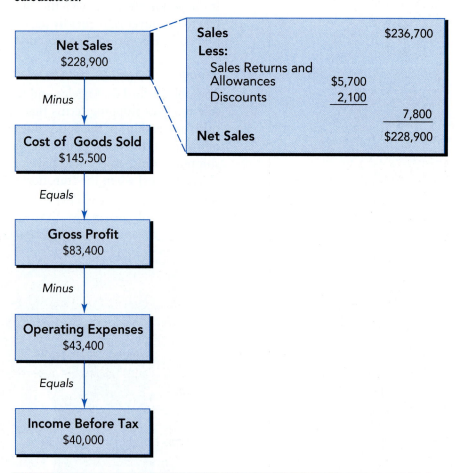

Gross Sales

The gross amount of sales, which in the expanded diagram is $236,700, is simply the total amount of recorded sales before any returns, allowances, discounts, or other changes.

Overview of Net Sales, *continued*

Sales Invoice ("Invoice")

A *sales invoice* is a bill that identifies the type and quantity of merchandise that was sold, the total amount due, and how payment is to be made. The seller sends the sales invoice document to the buyer. A sales invoice provides the information for recording a sale on account.

Journal Entry for a Sale on Account

The example below shows a general journal entry for sales on account.

June 9	Accounts Receivable	900	
	Sales		900
	Sales Invoices #2207 and #2208		

Journal Entry for a Cash Sale

The example below shows a general journal entry that records cash sales.

June 9	Cash	2,500	
	Sales		2,500
	Daily sales per cash register tapes total		

Sales Discounts

Definition

A *sales discount* is an incentive from a seller to a buyer to encourage quick payment for sales on account. If the buyer pays within a specified time period, a reduced amount will be accepted by the seller. Sales discounts only apply to credit sales.

Based Only on Invoice Price

A sales discount calculation is based only on the invoice price. Any returns, allowances, shipping cost, or sales tax are not discounted.

Synonym "Cash Discount"

A sales discount given because of early payment is also called a *cash discount*.

Industry—Specific

Each type of business or industry has its own conventions and rules for whether or not sales discounts are offered and how they are offered.

Credit Terms

Credit Terms

Credit terms means the manner of payment that is agreed upon between buyer and seller. This includes the discount calculation. Credit terms are often written in a specific, abbreviated manner on the sales invoice.

Examples of Credit Terms

The table below shows three common credit terms and the meaning of each abbreviated expression. Different businesses offer different credit terms.

Expression	Interpretation
2/10, n/30	This is read as "two ten, net thirty." ■ The "2" is the percent discount allowed. ■ The "10" is the maximum number of days allowable before payment must be made in order to get the discount. This is known as the **discount period**. ■ The "n" means the balance still owed. ■ "30" is the maximum number of days allowed for full payment of any balance still owed.
1/5 EOM, n/30	This is read as "one five EOM, net thirty." ■ The "1" is the percent discount allowed. ■ The "5 EOM" means that the discount period ends 5 days following the end of the month in which the sale was made. After that, any balance is due in full.
n/30	This is read as "net thirty." ■ No discount. Full amount is due in 30 days.

How to Count Discount Time

Normally you begin counting the days of the discount period on the day following the day of sale. For example, if a sale is made on October 9, count October 10 as the first day in the discount period.

Calculating Discounts

Overview of Calculation

A discount is recorded at the time the customer pays within the discount period. The method used to calculate the correct cash payment and discount is the same for both the seller and purchaser. Although the seller and purchaser make different journal entries to record the transaction, the calculated amounts are exactly the same for both parties.

Payment Patterns

There are three possible payment patterns, two of which involve recording a discount:

1. A full payment is made within the discount period (full discount).
2. A full payment is made after the discount period (no discount).
3. A partial payment is made within the discount period (partial discount), and the balance owing is paid after the discount period (no discount).

Procedure Summary

The table below shows how to calculate the correct cash payment and discount for each payment pattern. As an example, assume that on June 12, a sale of $1,500 is made with terms of 2/10, n/30.

IF the payment pattern is . . .	THEN to calculate the cash payment . . .	AND the discount calculation is . . .	Example
1. full payment within the discount period	multiply the full amount due by (1 − discount %)	full invoice amount − cash payment	■ Cash payment: $1,500 × .98 = $1,470 ■ Discount: $1,500 − $1,470 = $30
2. full payment after the discount period	no calculation; full amount is due	none	$1,500 is due
3. partial cash payment within the discount period	no calculation; the customer has already made a cash payment	partial invoice amount − cash payment	■ Cash payment: (customer pays $490 cash) ■ Discount: ($490/.98) = $500 $500 − $490 = $10 discount

TIP

Partial payments are also known as short payments.

continued ▶

Calculating Discounts, *continued*

***Reasons for
the Calculations***

Pattern 1. Because the customer pays the amount due within the discount period, the discount applies against the full amount of the sale. If the discount percent is 2%, then the cash payment will be 98% of the entire sale amount.

Pattern 2. The full invoice amount is due because the discount was missed.

Pattern 3. Any cash received from a customer within the discount period is *already the net amount*—the amount remaining *after* a discount has been applied. This means, in this example, that whatever is received must be 98% of some larger (partial invoice) amount. The objective is to figure out what that larger amount is, that is some part of the total sale. The result here is $500.

> *Note:* This usually happens when a customer cannot afford to make a full payment but uses whatever cash is available to obtain some discount.

***Partial Payment
Information***

Partial payments can be a little tricky. Frequently, as just illustrated in pattern 3, the cash payment is given and the invoice portion must be calculated. However, sometimes the invoice portion is the information given and the cash payment must be calculated.

IF you are given . . .	THEN . . .
the amount of **cash** payment,	you determine how much of **the invoice** is being paid: Example: $490 cash /.98 = $500
how much of the **invoice** is being paid*	you determine the **cash payment** needed: Example: $500 of invoice x .98 = $490

*Excluding freight, insurance, and other items to which a discount does not apply.

Calculating Discounts, *continued*

Examples

- **Invoice amount given.** Cuyahoga Company sold $8,000 of merchandise on terms of 2/10, n/30 and received $4,900 *of the invoice amount* within the discount period: $4,900 × .98 = $4,802 actual cash received. (Discount is $4,900 − $4,802 = $98.)

- **Amount of cash payment given.** Cuyahoga Company sold $8,000 of merchandise on terms of 2/10, n/30 and received $4,900 *cash* within the discount period: $4,900 / .98 = $5,000 of invoice amount was paid. (Discount is $5,000 − $4,900 = $100.)

Journal Entries for Above Examples

#1	Cash		4,802	
	Sales Discounts		98	
	Accounts Receivable			4,900
	$4,900 invoice amount × .98 = $4,802 cash			

#2	Cash		4,900	
	Sales Discounts		100	
	Accounts Receivable			5,000
	$4,900 cash/.98 = $5,000 invoice amount.			

Summary

When you know the invoice amount, you calculate the cash payment. When you know the cash payment, you calculate the invoice amount for that payment.

Recording Payments from Customers

Overview

The journal entries below show the three customer payment possibilities for a $1,500 sale, terms 2/10, n/30 on June 12. The amounts come from the three examples in the table on page 327.

1. *Full payment received within the discount period:*

June 18	Cash	1,470	
	Sales Discounts	30	
	Accounts Receivable		1,500
	Collection within discount period—		
	Sales Invoice #2209		

Credit the full amount!

2. *Full payment received after the discount period:*

July 7	Cash	1,500	
	Accounts Receivable		1,500
	Collection of Sales Invoice #2209		

3. *Partial $490 cash payment received within the discount period:*

June 19	Cash	490	
	Sales Discounts	10	
	Accounts Receivable		500
	Partial collection within discount		
	period Invoice #2209		

Sales Discounts Is a Contra Account

The Sales Discounts account has a debit balance, but it is not an expense. However, it has the same effect as an expense. This is because it is a *contra Sales account*, which means that it is a direct offset against Sales and thus reduces net income.

Recording Payments from Customers, *continued*

T Accounts for Example 1

The example below shows how the sale and June 18 full customer payment would be recorded in accounts.

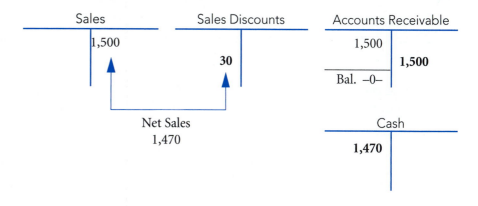

T Accounts for Example 2

The example below shows how the sale and July 7 customer payment after the discount period would be recorded in accounts.

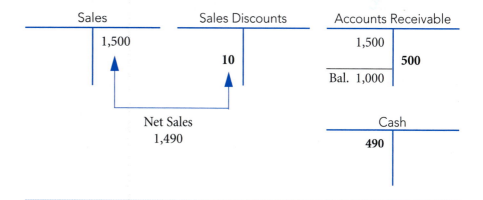

T Accounts for Example 3

The example below shows how the sale and June 19 partial customer payment would be recorded in accounts.

A practical problem for sellers in many businesses is the customer who pays late but still takes the discount. This is called an ***unearned discount***. It is most common when a small seller is selling to a large buyer.

continued ▶

Check Your Understanding

Write the completed sentences on a separate sheet of paper. Answers are on page 333.

A · · · · · · · · is an incentive given by the seller to encourage quick payment by the buyer. In the ledger, it is a · · · · · · · · Sales account, so it offsets Sales. An example of credit terms is: 2/10, n/30, which mean that a · · · · · · · · % discount is allowed if the buyer pays within · · · · · · · · days, and any balance is due within · · · · · · · · days.

The table below contains the three common payment patterns for sales on account. For each independent situation, calculate the amount of cash received and the amount of the discount.

Situation	Cash Received	Discount Amount
1. On May 12, a $1,000 sale is made with terms of 1/10, n/30. The customer pays in full on May 19.	(Reminder: Use a separate sheet of paper to complete the table.)	
2. On November 30, a $3,500 sale is made with terms of 1/5, n/30. The customer pays $2,000 cash on December 3.		
3. On September 25, a $4,500 sale is made with terms of 2/10, n/45. The customer pays in full on November 15.		
4. On February 9, a $2,700 purchase is made with terms of 2/10, n/30. The customer pays $1,500 of the invoice amount on February 12.		
5. On February 9, a $2,700 purchase is made with terms 2/10, n/30. The customer paid $1,500 cash on February 12.		
6. On August 11, a $5,000 purchase is made with terms 2/10, n/30. On August 19, the customer pays $500 cash and on August 21 also pays $750.		

Answers

A <u>sales discount</u> is an incentive given by the seller to encourage quick payment by the buyer. In the ledger, it is a <u>contra</u> Sales account, so it offsets Sales. An example of credit terms is: 2/10, n/30, which mean that a <u>2</u>% discount is allowed if the buyer pays within <u>10</u> days, and any balance is due within <u>30</u> days.

Situation	Cash Received	Discount Amount
1. On May 12, a $1,000 sale is made with terms of 1/10, n/30. The customer pays in full on May 19. *Calculation:* $1,000 × .99 = $990 $1,000 − $990 = $10	$990	$10
2. On November 30, a $3,500 sale is made with terms of 1/5, n/30. The customer pays $2,000 cash on December 3. *Calculation:* $2,000/.99 = $2,020.20 $2,020.20 − $2,000 = $20.20	$2,000	$20.20
3. On September 25, a $4,500 sale is made with terms of 2/10, n/45. The customer pays in full on November 15. *Calculation:* Paid after discount period—full amount is due.	$4,500	$-0-
4. On February 9, a $2,700 purchase is made with terms of 2/10, n/30. The customer pays $1,500 of the invoice amount on February 12. *Calculation:* $1,500 × .98 = $1,470 $1,500 − $1,470 = 30	$1,470	$30
5. On February 9, a $2,700 purchase is made with terms 2/10, n/30. The customer paid $1,500 cash on February 12. *Calculation:* $1,500/.98 = $1,530.61 $1,530.61 − $1,500 = $30.61	$1,500	$30.61
6. On August 11, a $5,000 purchase is made with terms 2/10, n/30. On August 19, the customer pays $500 cash and on August 21 also pays $750. *Calculation:* $1,250/.98 = $1,275.51 $1,275.51 − $1,250 = $25.51	$1,250	$25.51

Recording Payments from Customers, *continued*

Trade Discount Compared to Cash Discount

A type of discount that is not usually entered in accounting records is called a *trade discount*. Trade discounts are a percentage reduction in the list price of merchandise. *List price* is the price at which merchandise is normally listed. After the trade discount is subtracted from the list price, the remaining amount is the *invoice price*.

Trade discounts are given for various reasons, such as large order quantities, special promotions, or just simply to avoid frequent reprinting of listed prices. For example, if the listed price of merchandise is $3,000 and a trade discount of 20% is given, the invoice price to the buyer becomes: $3,000 – ($3,000 × .2) = $2,400 (or, more quickly: $3,000 × .8 = $2,400).

A trade discount generally is not recorded. Here in our example, it is just a calculation used to arrive at the invoice price of $2,400 on the invoice sent to the buyer. If a cash discount for early payment is later taken, it is then calculated on the $2,400. The trade discount is calculated first because it is always possible that the early payment discount might not be taken later.

Chain Discount

Sometimes a series of trade discounts are offered on the same sale. This is called a *chain discount*. Example: A seller offers a 20% discount plus a 10% discount if the sale exceeds a certain number of units. Assume a $10,000 list price: $10,000 × .8 × .9 = $7,200 invoice price.

"Stop arguing with me, Doris! A trade discount is ALWAYS calculated before a cash discount."

Calculating and Recording Sales Returns and Allowances

Definition

Sales Returns and Allowances refers to the decrease in total sales caused by shipping unsatisfactory merchandise to the buyer. A "sales return" means that the customer returned the merchandise and the seller reduced the amount of the account receivable. An ***allowance*** means that the customer received a price reduction from the seller without returning the merchandise.

Example of Return

Suppose that Queensborough Patio Mart agrees to sell $1,000 of unusual white patio fixtures on account to David Green, who specializes in selling rare patio accessories. When the boxes are opened by David, $200 of the shipment is the wrong type. This is returned, and the transactions are recorded by the seller as follows:

Sale

June 11	Accounts Receivable	1,000	
	Sales		1,000
	Sales Invoice #2210		

Return

June 14	Sales Returns and Allowances	200	
	Accounts Receivable		200
	Return of unsatisfactory		
	merchandise CM 443		

Example of Using T Accounts

The example below shows how the June 11 and June 14 entries would appear when recorded into T accounts. Net sales is $800.

Recording an Allowance

An allowance occurs when a seller reduces the amount owing from the customer to avoid the inconvenience and expense of receiving and restocking returned merchandise. An allowance is recorded in exactly the same manner as a return, as shown in the $200 example above. Allowances are usually a percentage of the merchandise price, not the full value.

continued ▶

Calculating and Recording Sales Returns and Allowances, *continued*

Example of Allowance

Instead of returning the merchandise, David Green keeps the merchandise, and Queensborough Patio Mart agrees to give him a $250 allowance.

June 14	Sales Retuns and Allowances		250	
	Accounts Receivable			250

Estimating Returns and Allowances

In all the examples and problems in this book, sales returns and allowances are simply recorded as they occur. This is acceptable when amounts are small or very consistent. However, when returns and allowances are significant and potentially unpredictable, an estimate should be recorded in advance. A period-end adjusting entry is recorded that debits Sales Returns and Allowances and also reduces the net accounts receivable. (See Learning Goal 17 for further accounts receivable discussion.)

Sales Returns and Allowances: a Contra Account

The Sales Returns and Allowances account has a debit balance, but it is not an expense. However, it has the same effect, because it is a *contra Sales account*, which means that is an offset, and is subtracted from Sales. Sales Returns and Allowances reduces net sales just like sales discounts.

Credit Memorandum (Credit Memo)

When an account receivable is reduced (credited) by a seller, because of a return or allowance, the seller usually sends the buyer a document called a **credit memorandum** that shows the amount of the credit to accounts receivable with an explanation and reference to the invoice number.

Shipping Charges and Sales Tax

Shipping Charges Paid by the Seller

Definition

An account name frequently used for shipping charges paid by the seller is called ***Freight-out***. Freight-out is usually considered to be a selling expense and is not part of cost of goods sold.

When Seller Pays the Freight Company

The two common payment patterns for when the seller pays the freight company are:

1. the seller pays the shipping charges and is not reimbursed by the buyer
2. the seller prepays the shipping charges and will be reimbursed by the buyer

Examples

On June 23, Queensborough Patio Mart shipped patio furniture to the La Belle restaurant in Rochester, New York. Shipping charges from Queens to Rochester are $170.

1. *Seller pays—buyer will not reimburse seller*

June 23	Freight-out		170	
	Cash			170
	Shipping charges: Novotna Motor			
	Freight			

2. *Seller prepays shipping charges—buyer agrees to reimburse seller*

June 23	Accounts Receivable—La Belle		170	
	Cash			170
	Shipping charges: Novotna Motor			
	Freight			

Note: The $170 is added to the Accounts Receivable because the buyer has agreed to pay the shipping charges in addition to the cost of the merchandise.

Sales Tax

Definition

A *sales tax* is a tax levied by a state or local government entity as a percentage of *retail* sales of many kinds of merchandise. These sales are called *taxable sales*. The buyer pays the sales tax, which is added to the price of the merchandise. The merchant is simply a collector of the tax from the buyer at the point of sale and is obligated to send the tax proceeds collected to the taxing authority in a timely manner.

Caution

The sales tax collected is neither a revenue nor an expense. It is a liability to send the cash that is collected to a local taxing authority.

Example

For example, Queensborough Patio Mart made $2,500 of cash sales on June 9. Assume these were taxable sales to retail customers and the sales tax rate was 8%. The sales tax calculation and journal entry would be:

Sales tax collection: $2,500 \times .08 = 200$

June 9	Cash		2,700	
	Sales			2,500
	Sales Tax Payable			200
	Daily retail sales plus sales tax per			
	cash register tape			

Later, when Queensborough Patio Mart pays the state taxing authority for the month of June, this collection will be part of the total larger payment (assume sales tax total for the month is $5,250), and the journal entry is:

July 10	Sales Tax Payable		5,250	
	Cash			5,250
	Paid sales tax liability for month			
	of June			

Alternate Calculation Method

Some merchants consider it too troublesome to record the sales tax liability with each individual transaction. Instead, they prefer to calculate the entire sales tax for the period with one calculation. To do this, they *include the sales tax collection as part of Sales* and then adjust the account later, when they need to know the correct amount of sales tax.

Sales Tax, *continued*

Example of Alternate Method	On June 9, Queensborough Patio Mart had $2,500 of taxable retail sales. 8% tax was included as part of Sales. Clearly, this overstates the Sales account and understates the Sales Tax Payable. This must be corrected later, when the calculation for the full monthly sales tax is made.	

June 9	Cash	2,700	
	Sales		2,700
	Daily retail sales collection		

Adjustment Calculation

The Sales account now includes *both* the sales *and* the sales tax collections. So, if the sales tax rate is 8%, then the Sales account must be 108% of the actual sales revenue. Assume the Sales account for the entire month of June shows $70,875, which now includes both sales and sales tax collections:

- **Step 1: Calculate actual sales revenue:** $70,875/1.08 = $65,625
- **Step 2: Calculate the sales tax:** $70,875 − $65,625 = $5,250

Note: You cannot multiply $70,875 by .08 to calculate the sales tax. This is because the $70,875 *already includes the sales tax.* You would be calculating sales tax on sales tax!

Journal Entry

The following adjustment is made to the accounts at the end of June, and reduces the overstated Sales and increases the understated Sales Tax Payable:

June 30	Sales	5,250	
	Sales Tax Payable		5,250
	To record correct amount of		
	sales tax liability		

Sales Tax and Discounts

Sales tax does not usually apply to sales between merchants. (These are *non-taxable* sales.) However, in any situation where sales tax is calculated and a discount is involved, the sales tax should be calculated only on the net amount of the sale, after any discounts are taken.

Sales Tax and Merchandise Returns

If a customer returns taxable merchandise, the cash returned to the customer must include both the sales price of the merchandise and the sales tax. For example, if a customer had returned $100 of taxable merchandise and sales tax paid was 8%, then the journal entry would be:

June 18	Sales Returns and Allowances	100	
	Sales Tax Payable	8	
	Cash		108
	(Taxable merchandise returned)		

Note: If the sales tax had been included in the Sales account, only Sales Returns and Allowances would be debited in the amount of $108.

The Cost of Goods Sold Formula

Overview of Income Calculation

Introduction

When you first study a merchandising business, one of the most important topics for you to understand is how a merchandising business calculates net income. This section discusses the cost of goods sold part of net income.

Illustration

The diagram below illustrates the process of net income calculation for a merchandising business. On the right, the cost of goods sold portion of the illustration is expanded to show the main elements that make up a cost of goods sold calculation.

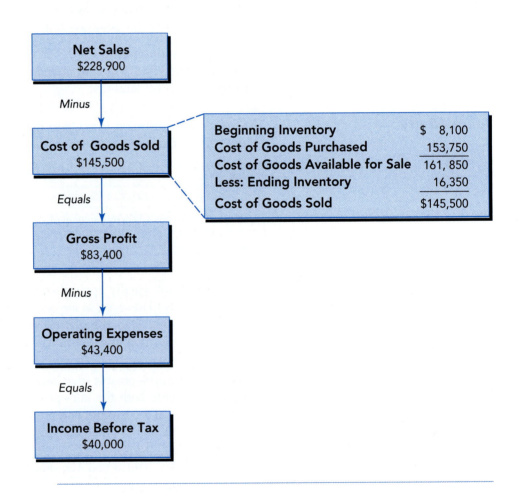

Net Sales $228,900	
Minus	
Cost of Goods Sold $145,500	Beginning Inventory $ 8,100
	Cost of Goods Purchased 153,750
	Cost of Goods Available for Sale 161,850
	Less: Ending Inventory 16,350
	Cost of Goods Sold $145,500
Equals	
Gross Profit $83,400	
Minus	
Operating Expenses $43,400	
Equals	
Income Before Tax $40,000	

Formula for Cost of Goods Sold Calculation

Definition	*Cost of goods sold* is an expense that is the seller's cost of the merchandise that was sold.

Cost of Goods Sold Formula	Cost of goods sold can be expressed as a formula:

$$BI + P - EI = C \text{ of } GS$$

- **BI** means the cost of the beginning inventory at the start of the period
- **P** means the net cost of the goods purchased, including freight costs
- **EI** means the cost of the ending inventory remaining at the end of the period
- **C of GS** means the cost of goods sold

Example	Queensborough Furniture Mart has a December 31, 2016, ending inventory of $8,100 and a December 31, 2017, ending inventory of $16,350. During the year 2017, net purchases and freight-in totaled $153,750. Applying the formula, what is the cost of goods sold for 2017?

BI		P		EI		C of GS
8,100	+	153,750	–	16,350	=	145,500

Cost of Goods Available for Sale	If you add the beginning inventory to the net cost of goods purchased, you get the total cost of all the merchandise inventory that was available to be sold to customers during the period. This is called *cost of goods available for sale*. The cost of the goods available for sale is important because this is the total cost of all merchandise available during the period, and it will end up in one of two places, either as:

- goods that were sold, which is cost of goods sold, or
- goods that are unsold, which is ending inventory.

Example	In the formula above, cost of goods available for sale is $161,850. Of this amount, $145,500 is the cost of the merchandise sold to customers. $16,350 is the cost of the remaining unsold inventory.

continued ▶

Formula for Cost of Goods Sold Calculation, *continued*

Illustration

The illustration below shows the cost of goods available for sale and what has happened to it.

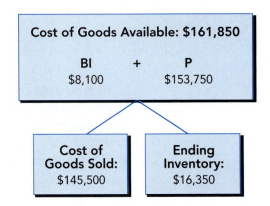

Test the Illustration

Put your finger over the "Ending Inventory" box above. You can subtract cost of goods sold from cost of goods available to get ending inventory. Then put your finger over the "Cost of Goods Sold" box. Subtract ending inventory from cost of goods available to get the cost of goods sold. This shows you what happens to cost of goods available for sale: It becomes either ending inventory or cost of goods sold. It also shows that if one outcome gets larger, the other one must get smaller.

"He just realized how to use the formula."

Check Your Understanding

Write the completed sentences on a separate piece of paper. Answers are on page 344.

When the periodic inventory method is used, cost of goods sold is calculated at the · · · · · · · · of an accounting period. In the periodic formula of BI + P − EI = C of GS, the letters BI refer to · · · · · · · · · · · · · · · ·, the letter P refers to the cost of the goods · · · · · · · · (including freight cost), and the letters EI refer to · · · · · · · · · · · · · · · · ·.

Instructions: On a separate sheet of paper, calculate the missing amounts as indicated by a "?".

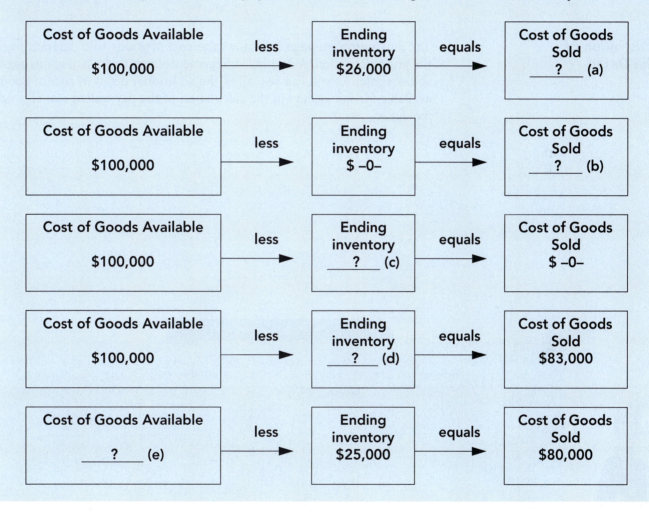

Cost of Goods Available for Sale

Overview

Introduction

We will now focus on an important part of cost of goods sold—the detailed elements cost of goods available for sale. Cost of goods available for sale consists of two basic parts: "beginning inventory" and "cost of goods purchased." This discussion explains the details of these two parts.

Illustration of the Detail

The illustration on page 345 shows the cost of goods sold diagram from the prior discussion. A detailed enlargement shows the cost of goods available for sale. As you can see, all of the additional detail in cost of goods available for sale occurs in the calculation of the part called *cost of goods purchased*.

Answers

When the periodic inventory method is used, cost of goods sold is calculated at the <u>end</u> of an accounting period. In the periodic formula of BI + P − EI = C of GS, the letters BI refer to <u>beginning inventory</u>, the letter P refers to the cost of the goods <u>purchased</u> (including freight cost), and the letters EI refer to <u>ending inventory</u>.

a. $74,000
b. $100,000
c. $100,000
d. $17,000
e. 105,000

Overview, *continued*

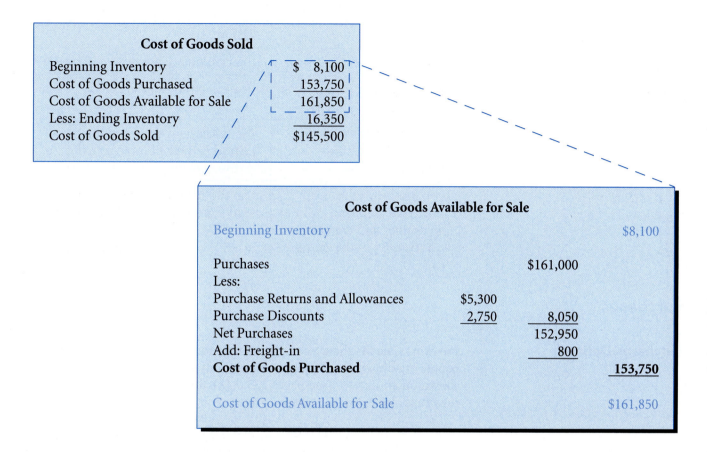

Beginning Inventory

Definition	*Beginning inventory* is the cost of the inventory that is on hand as of the start of the first day of a new accounting period.
How to Determine	The table on page 346 shows the different ways that you can determine the beginning inventory of a current accounting period.

continued ▶

Beginning Inventory, *continued*

IF . . .	THEN . . .
it is a brand-new business,	the beginning inventory will be –0–.
the beginning inventory is given to you,	use the amount given.
you are given the ending inventory of the prior period,	the ending inventory of the prior period is the beginning inventory of the current period.
you are given the purchases, ending inventory, and cost of goods sold of the current period,	use the formula BI + P – EI = C of GS to solve for the BI.

Purchases

Purchases Defined

Purchases means the cost of the merchandise purchased, before any discounts or adjustments. A purchases amount is the total amount due that is shown on an invoice (see pages 325, 348). Sometimes this amount on the invoice is also called the *invoice price*.

Account Used

When recording purchases using the periodic method, the cost of purchases is debited to the account Purchases. This account is used only with the periodic method.

What Kind of Account Is It?

Purchases is a temporary account that accumulates the total cost of merchandise purchased during a period. Purchases always has a debit balance. The easiest way to think of Purchases is as an expense account that later becomes part of the cost of goods sold expense.

Caution . . .

The Purchases account is used *only* for purchasing merchandise that will be sold to customers. It is not used for supplies, plant and equipment, or any other type of purchase.

Purchases, *continued*

Example of Journal Entry

The general journal entry below shows that Queensborough Patio Mart purchased $1,500 of merchandise on account.

Nov. 8	Purchases		1,500	
	Accounts Payable			1,500
	App. purchase Invoice #99–45			
	Lafayette Supply Co.			

Check Your Understanding

Write the completed sentences on a separate piece of paper. Answers are below.

Cost of goods available for sale consists of two basic parts, which are · · · · · · · · · · · · · · and cost of · · · · · · · · · · · · · ·. For a new business, the beginning inventory would be $· · · · · · · ·. For an ongoing business, beginning inventory would be the · · · · · · · · · · · · · of the prior period.

X Corporation receives Invoice #138 from Y, Inc., showing the merchandise cost as $5,000 for a purchase made on December 3. Record the purchase in the journal shown below, assuming the manager approves the invoice.

Answers

Dec. 3	Purchases		5,000	
	Accounts Payable			5,000

Cost of goods available for sale consists of two basic parts, which are beginning inventory and cost of goods purchased. For a new business, the beginning inventory would be $–0–. For an ongoing business, beginning inventory would be the ending inventory of the prior period.

How Purchases Are Made

The Request

When a business identifies the need to purchase inventory or other items, the department making the request completes a form called a **purchase requisition**. This form identifies the type and quantity of the items needed. The form is sent to the purchasing department.

The Order

The purchasing department reviews the request and (if approved) makes the purchase. The responsibility of the purchasing department is to locate a vendor (seller) that will sell the required items at the best price, consistent with the quality needed. To place the order, the purchasing department sends a form called the **purchase order** to the vendor. The purchase order identifies the items, the quantities, prices, and payment terms.

> *Note:* In a small business, the owner or manager completes the purchase orders. Purchase requisitions are often not needed.

The Invoice

When the items are shipped from the vendor to the buyer, the vendor sends an **invoice** to the buyer. The invoice is a request for payment (a bill). The invoice confirms items, quantities, prices, and the terms of payment. A vendor often refers to an invoice as a *sales invoice*, whereas a buyer often refers to an invoice as a *purchase invoice*.

Purchase Discounts

Definition

A **purchase discount** is a discount received by the buyer for early payment within a specified discount period.

Other Key Features

A purchase discount:

- is recorded only in the books of a *buyer* at the time of payment.
- reduces the net cost of the merchandise purchased.
- applies only to purchases made on account.

Purchase Discounts, *continued*

Be Careful . . .	Do not confuse a purchase discount with a *sales* discount, which is the same discount amount, but is recorded on the books of the seller.
Synonym "Cash Discount"	A purchase discount is also called a ***cash discount***.
Credit Terms	***Credit terms*** means the manner of payment that is agreed upon between buyer and seller. This includes the discount calculation. Credit terms are often written in a specific, abbreviated manner on the sales invoice.
Examples of Credit Terms	For examples of credit terms, see the table on page 326.

Calculating Purchase Discounts

How to Calculate a Purchase Discount	For an explanation of how to calculate a discount, see pages 327 through 329, which discuss calculating a sales discount. The exact same calculation applies for the buyer. However, the buyer will call it a *purchase discount*.
Trade Discounts	Another kind of discount, called a *trade discount*, is not the same as a purchase (cash) discount. For an explanation of trade discounts, see page 334.

TIP

Is it worth it to pay early and take a discount? Most of the time, yes, if the cash is not needed for other reasons. Example: 2/10, n/30 terms on a $1,000 invoice amount. In effect, the 2% discount means that you earn $20 (because by waiting 20 more days you have to pay $20 more) on a net out-of-pocket investment of $980.

We evaluate financial transactions such as loans or investments on an annual percentage basis ("annualizing"). The number of 20-day periods in one year: 365/20 = 18.25. Result: 18.25 × 20/980 = 37.24% annualized return on the $980.

Recording Payments to the Sellers

Recording the Cash Payment

The journal entries below show you how to record each of the possible payment patterns.

Example: a November 18 $1,500 purchase with credit terms of 2/10, n/30.

1. Full payment made within the discount period

Nov. 28	Accounts Payable		1,500	
	Purchase Discounts			30
	Cash			1,470
	Payment within discount			
	period—Invoice #2209			

> **Debit the full amount!**

2. Full payment made after the discount period

Nov. 30	Accounts Payable		1,500	
	Cash			1,500
	Payment of Invoice #2209			

3. Partial payment of $490 cash is made within the discount period

Nov. 28	Accounts Payable		500	
	Purchases Discounts			10
	Cash			490
	Partial payment within discount			
	period Invoice #2209			

Note: Any amount paid within a discount period is considered to be the net amount after a discount has been subtracted. The amount of cash paid is usually whatever the buyer thinks he or she can afford to pay.

Normal Balance

The Purchase Discounts account has a normal credit balance. It reduces the net cost of goods purchased.

Purchase Discounts: A Contra Account

The Purchase Discounts account has a credit balance because it is a *contra Purchases account*, which means that it is an offset against the debit balance of Purchases. The two accounts are "companion" accounts in the ledger.

Recording Payments to the Sellers, *continued*

T Accounts for Example 1

The example below shows how the $1,500 purchase on November 18 and a November 28 full payment would be recorded in accounts.

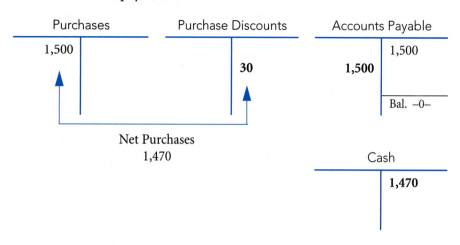

T Accounts for Example 2

The example below shows how the $1,500 purchase on November 18 and the November 30 payment after the discount period would be recorded in accounts.

Purchases	Accounts Payable	Cash
1,500	1,500	1,500
	1,500	
	Bal. –0–	

T Accounts for Example 3

The example below shows how the $1,500 purchase on November 18 and a November 28 partial payment of $490 would be recorded in accounts.

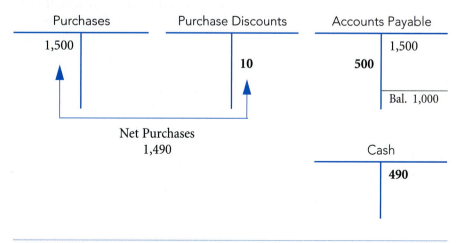

Purchase Returns and Allowances

Definition

Purchase returns and allowances is an account on the books of the buyer that refers to a decrease in total purchase cost because of having received unsatisfactory merchandise. A *purchase return* means that the buyer returned merchandise and reduced the account payable. An *allowance* means that the buyer and seller agreed that the buyer could reduce the account payable without returning the merchandise.

Example of Return

Suppose that Queensborough Patio Mart discovered that $400 of merchandise that it purchased is defective. On November 13, the company calls the seller, and returns the merchandise. At the same time, it issues a debit memorandum to the seller indicating that Accounts Payable will be debited $400 because of the returned merchandise and referencing the seller's invoice number.

Nov. 13	Accounts Payable	400	
	Purchase Returns and		
	Allowances		400
	Returned defective items to seller		
	(See debit memo #231, Invoice #2209)		

Example of Allowance

In the situation above, the seller tells Queensborough that it prefers not to have the expense and disruption of dealing with defective returned merchandise. The seller offers Queensborough a $200 reduction in the amount payable, if Queensborough will keep the defective items. This is an allowance.

Nov. 13	Accounts Payable	200	
	Purchase Returns and		
	Allowances		200
	(Allowance: see debit memo #231,		
	Invioce #2209)		

Purchase Returns and Allowances, *continued*

Another Contra Account	Purchase Returns and Allowances, like Purchase Discounts, is a contra Purchases account, which means that it is an offset against the debit balance of Purchases. Purchase Returns and Allowances has a credit balance and reduces the net cost of goods purchased just like Purchase Discounts.
Debit Memorandum (Debit Memo)	When an account payable is reduced (debited) by a buyer because of a return or allowance, the buyer usually sends the seller a *debit memorandum* that shows the amount of the debit with an explanation and reference to the sales invoice.
Discounts and Returns	Occasionally, a discount has been taken and merchandise is later returned. The cash returned should be for the actual net amount paid, after discounts. For a buyer this means a debit to cash (or accounts payable), a debit to purchase discounts, and a credit to purchases returns and allowances for the amount of the purchase. For a seller, debit sales returns and allowances for the amount of the sale, credit sales discounts, and credit cash (or accounts receivable).

Check Your Understanding

Write the completed sentences on a separate piece of paper. Answers are on page 354.

A · · · · · · · · discount is a discount received by the · · · · · · · · for an early payment made to the seller within a specified discount period. A Purchase · · · · · · · · and · · · · · · · · is a reduction in the amount owing to the seller because of unsatisfactory merchandise received. Both items have normal · · · · · · · · account balances.

On August 15, Catawba Partnership purchased $10,000 of merchandise with terms of 4/15, n/30. On a separate page, journalize payment under each of the following independent situations:

a. Assume that Catawba pays in full on August 30.
b. Assume that Catawba pays in full on September 12.
c. Assume that Catawba pays $2,500 of the invoice amount on August 20.
d. Assume that Catawba makes a cash payment of $4,800 on August 20.

A <u>purchase</u> discount is a discount received by the <u>buyer</u> for an early payment made to the seller within a specified discount period. A Purchase <u>return</u> and <u>allowance</u> is a reduction in the amount owing to the seller because of unsatisfactory merchandise received. Both items have normal <u>credit</u> account balances.

(a)	Accounts Payable		10,000	
	Purchase Discounts			400
	Cash			9,600

(b)	Accounts Payable		10,000	
	Cash			10,000

(c)	Accounts Payable		2,500	
	Purchase Discounts			100
	Cash			2,400

(d)	Accounts Payable		5,000	
	Purchase Discounts			200
	Cash			4,800

Freight-in

Definition

Freight-in is a buyer's expense account for the shipping cost incurred in order to obtain delivery of merchandise purchases. Freight-in is also sometimes called *transportation-in*.

What Kind of Account?

Freight-in is a separate account that adds to the cost of the purchase. On the income statement, freight-in becomes part of the calculation of cost of goods sold.

Freight-In, *continued*

Normal Balance	Freight-in has a normal debit balance.

Be Careful . . .

Do not confuse freight-in with freight-out. The table below shows you the differences.

Freight-in is . . .	Freight-out is . . .
the shipping cost paid when merchandise is purchased	the shipping cost paid when merchandise is sold
part of cost of goods sold	part of operating expenses—specifically, selling expenses.

Not Part of Discount Calculation

A purchase discount *cannot* be calculated on freight-in costs. The discount is only applied to the invoice price of the *merchandise.*

Journal Entry Example: Seller Pays Shipping Company

On October 5, Edgecombe Corporation purchased merchandise with terms of 2/10, n/30. The seller paid $300 of shipping charges and billed Edgecombe $5,300, of which $300 is for shipping costs paid by the seller. Edgecombe paid on October 15.

Oct. 5	Purchases		5,000	
	Freight-in		300	
	Accounts Payable			5,300

Oct. 15	Accounts Payable		5,300	
	Purchase Discounts			100
	Cash			5,200

continued ▶

Freight-In, *continued*

Journal Entry Example: Buyer Pays Shipping Company

In the example above, if Edgecombe had paid the shipping costs directly to the freight company, the journal entry would appear as you see below.

Oct. 5	Purchases		5,000	
	Accounts Payable			5,000

Oct. 15	Accounts Payable		5,000	
	Purchase Discounts			100
	Cash			4,900
	Freight-in		300	
	Cash			300

Shipping Documents

The shipping documents from a shipping company—such as a trucking, airline, or train company—show the shipping costs and the freight terms. A shipping document is frequently called a *freight bill* or *bill of lading*.

Freight Terms

Freight terms—agreed upon by the seller and purchaser and shown on the sales invoice—are also shown on the freight bill. One commonly used freight term is FOB. *FOB* means *free on board* and refers to the point at which ownership title of the merchandise and the shipping costs are transferred to the purchaser.

Examples

- Dallas Corporation buys merchandise from Los Angeles Corporation. The shipping term is *FOB shipping point*. This means that Dallas Corporation owns the merchandise as soon as the goods are loaded onto the carrier in Los Angeles. Dallas Corporation must also pay shipping costs from Los Angeles.

- If the shipping term above had been *FOB destination*, then Los Angeles Corporation would own the merchandise until it was offloaded in Dallas. Los Angeles Corporation would have incurred the shipping costs as well.

Summary Illustration: Cost of Goods Available and Cost of Goods Purchased

Illustration   The illustration below shows all the elements of cost of goods available for sale and cost of goods purchased in a picture format. The T accounts at the bottom of the illustration show account balances that correspond to the elements in the illustration. All the dollar amounts are for the Queensborough Patio Mart.

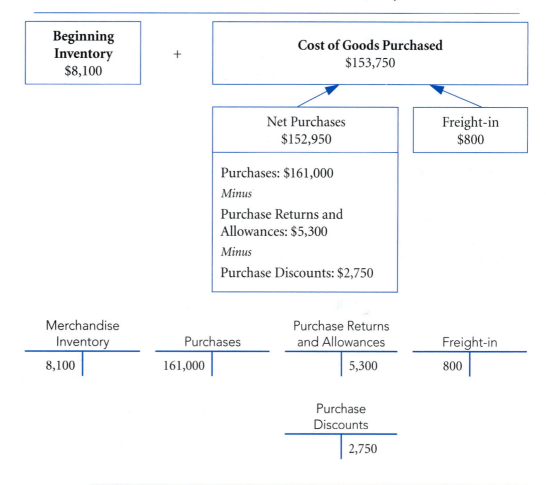

 The most common method is to record purchases using the **gross method,** at the invoice amount, as shown above ($161,000). An alternate method is to record purchases net of discounts ($161,000 − $2,750 = $158,250). This approach shows discounts *lost* when payment is made, if the credit to cash is greater than the debit to accounts payable because the discount was missed.

Comparison Table—Seller and Buyer Journal Entries

Comparison

The table below helps you to remember some frequently occurring journal entries made on the books of the seller and the buyer when both use the periodic method.

Transaction	Seller Journal Entries	Buyer Journal Entries

$2,000 sale of merchandise on account, terms 2/10, n/30.	Accounts Receivable 2,000
	    Sales 2,000
		Purchases 2,000
		    Accounts Payable 2,000

$500 of merchandise is returned by the buyer.	Sales Returns/
	Allowances 500
	    Accounts Receivable 500
		Accounts Payable 500
		    Purchase Returns/
		    Allowance 500

Buyer pays the full amount within the discount period.	Cash 1,470
	Sales Discounts 30
	    Accounts Receivable 1,500
		Accounts Payable 1,500
		    Purchase Discounts 30
		    Cash 1,470

Buyer pays the full amount, but missed the discount.	Cash 1,500
	    Accounts Receivable 1,500
		Accounts Payable 1,500
		    Cash 1,500

$3,000 sale on account. Seller pays shipping cost but buyer will not reimburse.	Accounts Receivable 3,000
	    Sales 3,000
	Freight-out 100
	    Cash 100
		Purchases 3,000
		    Accounts Payable 3,000

$3,000 sale on account. Seller pays shipping cost, buyer will reimburse the seller.	Accounts Receivable 3,100
	    Sales 3,000
	    Cash 100
		Purchases 3,000
		Freight-in 100
		    Accounts Payable 3,100

Buyer makes full payment within the discount period, including reimbursement of freight cost. Terms were 1/10, n/30.	Cash 3,070
	Sales Discounts 30
	    Accounts Receivable 3,100
		Accounts Payable 3,100
		    Purchase Discounts 30
		    Cash 3,070

Buyer pays $200 directly to shipping company.	No entry	Freight-in 200 Cash 200

Ending Inventory

Description

Definition

Ending inventory is the cost of the merchandise inventory remaining at the end of the accounting period after all transactions for the period are completed.

Relationship to Cost of Goods Available

As you recall, the cost of goods available for sale will end up in one of two places—either as cost of goods sold or as ending inventory. You can also look at ending inventory as the part of cost of goods available for sale that has not yet been sold. Ending inventory also completes the cost of goods sold calculation: BI + P – EI = C of CS.

How to Calculate Ending Inventory

Overview

To be sure of the correct amount of ending inventory, it must be counted. This counting is called a *physical inventory*. Then, to determine the total cost of the ending inventory, the units of each type are multiplied by their unit cost.

Example

The table below shows you an example of determining ending inventory for Queensborough Patio Mart:

- All the inventory is counted to determine the number of units of each item.
- The number of units of each item are multiplied by the unit cost of the item.
- The total item costs are added to obtain a final total of $16,350.

Item	Units	$ Unit Cost	$ Total
Patio tables, wood	15	$250	$3,750
Patio tables, iron	15	195	2,925
Chairs, wood	50	75	3,750
Chairs, iron	48	40	1,920
Swings	8	110	880
Umbrellas	25	45	1,125
Barbecues	15	50	750
Accessories	50	25	1,250
Total			**$16,350**

continued ▶

How to Calculate Ending Inventory, *continued*

When to Do It

Ending inventory is counted at the end of the accounting period but before the period-end procedures such as adjusting, closing, and financial statement preparation are done.

Determining Unit Cost

There are many ways to determine the unit cost of ending inventory—it is a big topic; we return to this topic in Learning Goal 18. However, for now we will assume that Queensborough Patio Mart has kept a computer file of all purchases and that the cost of each particular type of item on hand is readily available and identifiable.

Inventory Shrinkage

Inventory shrinkage means an unidentified loss of inventory. The usual reasons are theft, accidents, and spoilage. If something has been stolen, broken, or is otherwise unusable, it cannot be counted as part of ending inventory. In a periodic inventory system shrinkage automatically becomes part of cost of goods sold because ending inventory is lower (BI + P − EI = C of GS).

How to Report Ending Inventory

Overview

Ending inventory is part of the cost of goods sold calculation that appears on the income statement. Ending inventory is also shown as a current asset on the balance sheet.

Effect on Cost of Goods Sold

Because ending inventory is subtracted from cost of goods available for sale to determine cost of goods sold, the size of the ending inventory has a direct effect on cost of goods sold. The larger the ending inventory is, the smaller the cost of goods sold will be. The reverse is also true. The smaller the ending inventory is, the larger the cost of goods sold will be. Review the illustration on page 342 to see this effect.

How to Report Ending Inventory, *continued*

*Merchandise
in Transit*

When merchandise is being shipped from seller to buyer, who owns the inventory? Who reports this inventory as an asset on the balance sheet?

The answer depends on when the buyer and seller agreed that the title (ownership) of the goods would transfer from seller to buyer. Frequently, this can be determined by examining the FOB shipping terms as follows:

If the terms are . . .	then . . .
FOB shipping point,	title is transferred when the goods are loaded on the carrier, so the buyer owns the goods while in transit.
FOB destination,	title is transferred when the goods are unloaded at destination, so the seller owns the goods while in transit.
FOB any interim point,	title transfers at the designated interim point.

Consigned Merchandise

When merchandise is shipped but ownership does not transfer to the receiving company, the merchandise is ***consigned***. Usually the receiving company displays the merchandise for sale. Consigned merchandise should be included in the ending inventory of the company that owns it.

*Merchandise on the
Financial Statements*

- *Balance sheet:* Merchandise inventory is a current asset.
- *Income statement:* If a multiple-step statement is used, showing a detailed calculation of cost of goods sold, the ending inventory will appear as part of this calculation.

*It Becomes Beginning
Inventory*

The ending inventory of one accounting period is also the beginning inventory of the next accounting period.

*Gross Profit and
Gross Profit %*

On the income statement, cost of goods sold is subtracted from net sales. The result is ***gross profit***. (See illustration on page 340.) Gross profit is the remaining sales dollars available to cover operating expenses and provide a net income. The gross profit percentage is an important measuring device to compare merchandising businesses. Gross profit percentage is: gross profit/net sales. From the illustration on page 340, the gross profit percentage is $83,400/228,900 = .364 = 36.4\%$, which means 36.4% of sales is left to cover expenses and provide net income.

Check Your Understanding

Write the completed sentences on a separate piece of paper. The answers are below.

Freight-in is the shipping cost paid when merchandise is ·······, and freight-out is the shipping cost paid when merchandise is ·······. Both freight-in and freight-out accounts have normal ······· balances. Only the freight-······· is part of the cost of goods sold calculation. The freight term FOB stands for ······· ········ ·······.

To calculate the cost of the ending inventory, all the items must first be ·······. As ending inventory becomes larger, cost of goods sold will become ·······.

Answers

Freight-in is the shipping cost paid when merchandise is purchased, and freight-out is the shipping cost paid when merchandise is sold. Both freight-in and freight-out accounts have normal debit balances. Only the freight-in is part of the cost of goods sold calculation. The freight term FOB stands for free on board. To calculate the cost of the ending inventory, all the items must first be counted. As ending inventory becomes larger, cost of goods sold will become smaller.

QUICK REVIEW

- Revenue is recorded in the period in which it is earned; for goods that are shipped, this generally happens after the goods have passed the FOB point.

- The starting point for the net income calculation is net sales, which is gross sales reduced by sales discounts and sales returns and allowances.

- Sales discounts give the buyer an incentive to pay quickly but also reduces net sales.

- Three common payment patterns are associated with sales on account that offer discounts:
  - Payment in full within the discount period.
  - Payment in full after the discount period.
  - Partial payment within the discount period.

- Partial payments can be stated in terms of either invoice amounts or cash amounts.

- Shipping charges and sales tax are also associated with merchandise sales, but they do not affect the amount of revenue that should be reported.

- Sales tax creates a liability called Sales Tax Payable. Sales tax is not a revenue or an expense.

- Sales tax can be calculated as a percentage of sales or included with sales and adjusted later.

- Sales tax should be calculated only on net sales and should be reduced when there are returns and allowances.

- The cost of goods sold formula for the periodic method is: BI + P − EI = C of GS.

- Cost of goods available for sale is the BI + P part of the formula.

- Purchase discounts for early payment, and purchase returns and allowances, for unsatisfactory merchandise, reduce the cost of merchandise inventory.

QUICK REVIEW   continued

- There are three common payment patterns associated with purchase discounts:

  - Payment in full within the discount period
  - Payment in full after the discount period
  - Partial payment within the discount period

- Freight-in adds to the cost of merchandise inventory. It is not part of the discount calculation.

- Ending inventory must be counted at the end of the period in order to calculate the cost of goods sold.

- The gross profit percentage is an important calculation that shows what percent of each sales remains after subtracting cost of goods sold.

VOCABULARY

Allowance: a reduction in the amount owed to the seller, without returning the merchandise (page 335)

Beginning inventory: the cost of the inventory that is on hand as of the start of the first day of a new accounting period (page 345)

Bill of lading: another term for freight bill (page 356)

Cash discount: another term for sales discount (page 325) or a sales discount.

Cash discount: another name for a purchase discount (page 349)

Chain discount: multiple trade discounts on the same sale (page 334)

Consignment: merchandise that is held by a business that does not own it (page 361)

Cost of goods available for sale: cost of beginning merchandise inventory plus net merchandise purchases and freight-in (page 341)

Cost of goods sold: A seller's expense that is the cost of the merchandise that was sold (page 341).

Credit memorandum: a document that indicates a credit to an account—most often issued by a seller to a buyer, when the seller has credited the account receivable owing from the buyer due to unsatisfactory merchandise (page 336)

Credit terms: the manner of payment that is agreed upon between buyer and seller (page 326)

Debit memorandum: a document issued by a buyer to inform the seller of a debit to accounts payable (page 353)

Discount period: the days allowed in which a buyer can pay and receive a discount (page 326)

Ending inventory: the merchandise inventory remaining at the end of an accounting period, after all transactions for the period are completed (page 359)

FOB ("free on board") point: the point in the shipping process at which title of the goods transfers to the buyer and beyond which the buyer usually pays shipping costs (page 323)

Freight bill: a shipping document from a shipping company (page 356)

Freight-in: a buyer's payment the shipping cost incurred in order to obtain delivery of merchandise purchases (page 354)

Freight-out: an expense account used by a seller who incurs the shipping charges (page 337)

Gross method: the method of recording the account payable at the gross purchase amount before any discounts (page 357)

VOCABULARY   continued

Gross profit: the amount of sales dollars that remain after subtracting cost of goods sold (page 361)

Inventory shrinkage: an unidentified loss of inventory (page 360)

Invoice: a bill from a vendor (page 348)

Invoice price: the cost of a purchase, as shown on an invoice (page 334)

Invoice price: the gross amount owed by the buyer of merchandise (page 334)

List price: the price at which merchandise is currently being offered for sale (page 334)

Periodic inventory method: a procedure for determining cost of goods sold and ending inventory only periodically—at the end of a period—by counting the ending inventory (page 321)

Physical inventory: counting inventory by physical inspection (page 359)

Purchase discount: a discount received by the buyer for early payment within a specified discount period (page 348)

Purchase order: an order form sent to a vendor (page 348)

Purchase requisition: an internal form sent to the purchasing department to request a purchase (page 348)

Purchase returns and allowances: an account on the books of the buyer that refers to a decrease in the total cost of purchases because of having received unsatisfactory merchandise (page 352)

Purchases: the cost of merchandise purchased excluding discounts or adjustments (page 346)

Sales discount: an incentive from a seller to a buyer to encourage quick payment (page 325)

Sales invoice: a bill sent to a buyer from the seller of merchandise (page 325)

Sales Returns and Allowances: a contra account that records a decrease in total sales caused by shipping unsatisfactory merchandise, which the buyer does not pay for (page 335)

Sales tax: a tax levied by a state or local government and calculated as percentage of retail sales that are designated by law to be subject to sales tax (page 338)

Trade discount: a percentage reduction in list price (page 334)

Transportation-in: another term for freight-in (page 354)

Unearned discount: a discount taken by a customer that pays after the discount period (page 331)

Do You Want More Examples?

Most problems in this book have detailed solutions. To use them as additional examples, do this: 1) Select the type of problem you want 2) Open the solution on your computer or mobile device screen (from the disc or worthyjames.com) 3) Read one item at a time and look at its answer. Take notes if needed. 4) Close the solution and work as much of the problem as you can. 5) Repeat as needed.

PRACTICE Learning Goal 11

Learning Goal 11 is about the periodic inventory method.

Multiple Choice
Select the best answer.

1. When a customer pays in full within the discount period, then:
   a. Accounts Receivable is credited for the full sales price.
   b. Accounts Receivable is credited for the sales price minus whatever discount is taken.
   c. Cash is debited for the full sales price.
   d. none of the above.

2. A cash discount taken by a customer for early payment would be described for the seller as a:
   a. trade discount.
   b. purchase discount.
   c. sales discount.
   d. sales allowance.

3. A description of the amount and timing of payments agreed upon between seller and buyer is called:
   a. cash discount.
   b. sales discount.
   c. credit sales.
   d. credit terms.

4. Who pays sales tax?
   a. the seller of retail merchandise
   b. buyer of wholesale merchandise
   c. both seller and buyer of any merchandise
   d. buyer of retail merchandise

5. The term that describes the point at which ownership of goods passes to the buyer is:
   a. FOB.
   b. EOM.
   c. COD.
   d. DOA.

6. Dayton Company recorded sales of $110,500, of which credit sales were $81,000. During the period, Sales Returns and Allowances were $3,700 and Sales Discounts were $1,800. Dayton Company's net sales were:
   a. $110,500.
   b. $75,500.
   c. $105,000.
   d. $108,700.

7. Hamilton Company sold some merchandise with terms of 2/10, n/30. The customer paid $12,250 cash within the discount period, which was payment in full. What amount should the Sales account have been credited by Hamilton Company?
   a. $12,250
   b. $12,500
   c. $12,005
   d. $11,025

Solutions are in the disk at the back of the book and at: www.worthyjames.com

PRACTICE   Learning Goal 11, continued

8. Nelsonville Company had total Sales of $108,000, of which $14,000 were not retail sales, and so not subject to sales tax. If the sales tax rate is 7%, what amount should Nelsonville Company record as the debit to cash?
   a. $100,580
   b. $114,580
   c. $94,000
   d. none of the above

9. Marion Company collected $20,580 from a customer account receivable. The credit terms were 2/10, n/45 and the customer paid in full within the discount period. As a courtesy to the buyer, Marion Company paid shipping charges of $1,960, which the buyer had agreed to reimburse. What amount should Marion Company have credited the Sales account?
   a. $19,000
   b. $18,620
   c. $18,247.60
   d. $21,000

10. Seller Company sold $10,000 of merchandise to Buyer Company, terms 2/10, n/30. Buyer Company returned $2,000 of defective items and then paid the amount due within the discount period. When the merchandise was returned, the seller company should have sent:
    a. a new invoice.
    b. a credit memo.
    c. a debit memo.
    d. an allowance.

11. Which of the following is true?
    a. Shipping charges paid by the seller affect net sales.
    b. Sales returns and allowances affect net sales.
    c. Sales taxes affect net sales.
    d. All of the above are true.

12. Which of the following is true if the credit terms are 2/10, n/30?
    a. $1,000 cash received within 10 days of the sale results in a $20 discount.
    b. $1,000 cash received within 30 days of the sale results in a $20 discount.
    c. $1,000 of the invoice amount paid within 10 days of the sale results in a $20 discount.
    d. None of the above is true.

13. Seller Company sold $10,000 of merchandise to Buyer Company, terms 2/10, n/30. Buyer Company returned $2,000 of defective items and then paid the amount due within the discount period. Seller Company should send a:
    a. $1,960 credit memo.
    b. $1,960 debit memo.
    c. $2,000 credit memo.
    d. $2,000 debit memo.

14. Seller Company offered a 25%, 15% chain discount from list price to Buyer Company and payment terms of 2/10, n/30. Buyer Company purchased $8,000 list price of merchandise and paid in full within the discount period. What was the amount of payment?
    a. $4,998
    b. $5,100
    c. $4,704
    d. $4,800

15. In the periodic inventory system:
   a. merchandise inventory is debited whenever merchandise is purchased.
   b. a physical inventory, although usually done, is not required.
   c. cost of goods sold is calculated as cost of goods available for sale plus beginning inventory.
   d. none of the above.

16. A discount from the list price of merchandise is called a:
   a. cash discount.
   b. purchase discount.
   c. trade discount.
   d. none of the above.

17. Which of the following is *not* part of the cost of goods purchased calculation?
   a. beginning inventory
   b. purchase discounts
   c. purchase returns and allowances
   d. freight-in

18. The terms 1/10, n/45:
   a. are credit terms, which mean to take a 1% discount if payment is made within 45 days.
   b. are shipping terms, which mean to take a 1% discount if payment is made within 45 days.
   c. are credit terms, which mean to take a 1% discount if payment is made within 10 days.
   d. none of the above.

Exhibit I, for Questions 19–22

Wake Forest Company, which records purchases using the invoice price, needs to record the following events:

- On September 15, purchased $8,000 of inventory, terms 2/10, n/30.
- On September 20, returned $1,000 of the purchase.
- On September 24, paid the amount owing in full.

19. The entry to record the purchase should include a:
   a. debit to Purchases of $8,000 on September 15.
   b. debit to Purchases of $7,000 on September 20.
   c. debit to Purchases of $7,000 on September 24.
   d. none of the above.

20. The entry to record the return should include a:
   a. debit to Purchase Returns and Allowances of $1,000.
   b. debit to Purchase Returns and Allowances of $980.
   c. credit to Purchase Discounts of $980.
   d. credit to Purchase Returns and Allowances of $1,000.

21. The entry to record the payment on September 24 should include a:
   a. debit to Accounts Payable of $7,000 and a credit to Cash of $7,000.
   b. debit to Accounts Payable of $7,000 and a credit to Cash of $6,840.
   c. debit to Accounts Payable of $7,000 and a credit to Cash of $6,860.
   d. debit to Accounts Payable of $6,860 and a credit to Cash of $6,860.

22. If the freight cost had been $200 and shipping terms were FOB destination, then:
    a. Wake Forest would not pay any freight cost.
    b. Wake Forest would pay $200 of freight cost to the shipping company.
    c. Wake Forest would pay $196 of freight cost to the shipping company.
    d. Wake Forest would pay $200 of freight cost to reimburse the seller.

23. If Baylor Company always records purchases using the net amount rather than the invoice (gross) amount, and returns $100 of merchandise that was purchased at 2/10, n/30:
    a. the return should always be recorded at invoice amount: $100.
    b. the return should always be recorded at net amount: $98.
    c. the return should always be recorded at invoice amount: $98.
    d. the return should always be recorded at net amount: $100.

24. If beginning inventory is $8,100, ending inventory is $5,000, and the cost of goods available for sale is $161,850, then the cost of goods purchased must be:
    a. $153,750.
    b. $169,950.
    c. $158,750.
    d. none of the above.

25. The normal account balances for Purchases and Purchase Discounts, respectively, are:
    a. debit; debit.
    b. credit; credit.
    c. debit; credit.
    d. credit; debit.

26. Which of the following is *not* part of cost of goods available for sale calculation?
    a. beginning inventory
    b. purchases
    c. purchase returns
    d. ending inventory

27. San Marcos Company credited cash $582 and credited purchase discounts $18 within 10 days of the date the merchandise was ordered, the last day of the discount period. The seller requires that all payments be made within 30 days of the order. What were the discount terms offered by the seller?
    a. 1/10, n/30
    b. 2/10, n/30
    c. 3/10, n/30
    d. 2/10, n/40

28. If a buyer pays $3,300 cash within the discount period and the terms are 3/10, n/30, what is the invoice amount (the debit to Accounts Payable) that is being paid?
    a. $3,402.06
    b. $3,300.00
    c. $3,201.00
    d. none of the above

PRACTICE

Learning Goal 11, continued

Solutions are in the disk at the back of the book and at: www.worthyjames.com

Reinforcement Problems

LG 11-1. Describe the journal entry. For each journal entry, write a one-sentence explanation that clearly and completely describes the entry. All sales on account offer early payment discounts.

a.

March 1	Cash		3,500	
	Accounts Receivable			3,500

b.

March 3	Cash		3,430	
	Sales Discounts		70	
	Accounts Receivable			3,500

c.

March 4	Sales Returns and Allowances		250	
	Accounts Receivable			250

d.

March 5	Accounts Receivable		500	
	Freight-out Expense		50	
	Sales			500
	Cash			50

LG 11-2. Make the journal entry.

Instructions: For each of the transactions listed below, prepare the proper journal entry. You may omit explanations. For journal paper, use the template in the disk at the back of the book or worthyjames.com (student info.).

June 8 Sold $5,800 merchandise on account, terms 1/15, n/30 to Hurst Company.

11 Sold $750 merchandise on account, terms 2/10, n/30 to Fort Worth Company and paid $100 transportation cost, which the buyer will not reimburse.

14 Sold $3,750 merchandise on account, terms 2/10, n/30 to Dallas Company and paid $200 transportation cost, which the buyer agreed to reimburse.

19 Hurst Company returned $700 of merchandise.

20 Fort Worth Company paid in full.

21 Hurst Company paid in full.

23 Dallas Company paid in full.

LG 11-3. Merchandise sales general journal entries—wholesale and retail sales; two sales tax methods.

Instructions: For each of the transactions below, prepare the proper journal entry for Decatur Company. You may omit explanations. For journal paper, use the templates in the disk at the back of the book or at worthyjames.com (student info.).

Decatur Company sells office furniture and office supplies to both wholesale and retail customers. The company is located in a county that collects 8% sales tax on retail sales. For retail office furniture sales, the company records sales tax with each sale. For retail office supplies sales, the sales tax is recorded as part of the sales revenue, then the sales tax is calculated at the end of the month. All sales are FOB shipping point.

Nov. 3 Sold office furniture priced at $5,000 to a retail customer and collected the full amount.

7 Sold furniture for $2,000 to Augusta Co. a wholesale customer, terms 2/10, n/30.

8 Collected $840 from a retail customer for a sale of office supplies.

10 Received a debit memo from Augusta Company, which returned $650 of furniture because the wrong type was shipped.

13 Sold $10,000 of office furniture to Atlanta Company, a wholesale customer, terms 2/10, n/30. Decatur Company paid $400 of shipping charges and will be

14 reimbursed by Atlanta Company.

15 Collected $1,900 from a retail customer for a sale of office supplies.

16 Sold office furniture priced at $2,700 to a retail customer and collected the full amount.

17 Received payment in full from Augusta Company.

20 Collected $500 from a retail customer for a sale of office supplies.

22 Offered the following discount to Columbus Company, a wholesale customer: If Columbus Company purchased up to $15,000 of furniture, a 10% discount would apply to the total purchase; for a purchase above $15,000, an additional 20% discount would apply to the total after the first discount is calculated. Columbus Company purchased furniture with a total list price of $27,000. The terms were 2/10, n/30.

26 Received payment in full from Atlanta Company.

29 Sold office furniture priced at $2,500 to a retail customer and collected the full amount.

30 Recorded the sales tax liability for office supplies sales to retail customers.

PRACTICE   Learning Goal 11, continued

LG 11-4. Journalize sales, returns, and payments transactions, no sales tax.

Instructions: Record each of the transactions below in a general journal for the Lawn Guiland Garden Company. Because all of the sales are to companies that will resell the merchandise, no sales are subject to sales tax. All sales are on account. For journal paper, use the template in the disk at the back of the book or at worthyjames.com (student info.).

March 2 Sold $5,200 of gardening merchandise to Brooklyn Enterprises, terms 2/10, n/30, FOB shipping point.

    5 Sold $7,000 of plumbing merchandise to Knickerbocker Company, terms 2/10, n/30, FOB shipping point.

    8 Brooklyn Company sent a debit memo and returned $900 of merchandise.

  11 Sold $4,000 of gardening merchandise to Nassau Landscape, terms 2/10, n/30, FOB shipping point, and paid $150 shipping charges, which were added to the invoice because the buyer agreed to reimburse the shipping charges.

  12 Received payment in full from Brooklyn Enterprises.

  15 Received a cash payment of $5,880 from Knickerbocker Company.

  17 Sold $15,000 of patio furniture to East Hampton Boutique, terms 2/10, n/30, FOB shipping point. Paid $350 shipping charges that the buyer will not reimburse.

  21 Received payment in full from Nassau Landscape.

  22 Sold $3,000 of gardening merchandise to Moriches Company, terms 2/10, n/30, FOB destination.

  24 Sold $5,000 of plumbing merchandise to Yonkers Supply Emporium.

  30 Received balance due from East Hampton Boutique.

  31 Received balance due from Knickerbocker Company.

  31 Received $1,000 of the invoice amount from Yonkers Supply Emporium.

LG 11-5. Merchandise sales journal entries—wholesale and retail sales, sales tax, various payment patterns, two sales tax methods.

Instructions: For each of the transactions below, prepare the proper journal entry for Hartford Enterprises. Round all amounts to the nearest dollar. You may omit explanations. For journal paper, use the template in the disk at the back of the book or at worthyjames.com (student info.).

Hartford Enterprises sells computer equipment and computer supplies. The company is located in a county that collects 6% sales tax on retail sales. For retail computer equipment sales, the company records sales tax with each sale. For retail computer supplies sales, the sales tax is recorded as part of the sales revenue, then the sales tax is calculated at the end of the month for all supplies sales. All sales are FOB shipping point.

March 1 Sold computer equipment with a list price of $3,700 to a retail customer and collected the full amount.

    3 Collected $600 from a retail customer for a sale of computer supplies.

    4 Sold $7,500 of computer equipment to Bridgeport Company, a wholesale customer, terms 2/10, n/30.

    7 Sold $11,800 of computer equipment to Norwalk Company, a wholesale customer, terms 2/10, n/30. Hartford Enterprises paid $620 of freight charges, which the customer will not reimburse.

    8 Sold computer equipment with a list price of $6,300 to a retail customer and collected the full amount.

  10 Collected $2,650 from a retail customer for a sale of computer supplies.

  12 Received $5,000 cash from Bridgeport Company.

LG 11-5, *continued*

March 13   Sold $10,000 of computer equipment to Waterbury Corporation, a wholesale customer, terms 2/10, n/30. Hartford Enterprises paid $240 of freight charges, which the customer will reimburse.

14   Received a debit memo from Norwalk Company, which returned $1,000 of equipment.

14   Collected $725 from a retail customer for a sale of computer supplies.

15   Sold $3,800 of computer equipment to Pomfret Partnership, a wholesale customer, terms 2/10, n/30.

17   Received $7,500, from Norwalk Company.

24   Offered the following discount to Groton Enterprises, a wholesale customer: For purchases up to $20,000, the discount is 5% for the total purchase. For purchases exceeding $20,000, an additional 10% discount is applied to the total after the first discount is calculated. Groton purchased $40,000 of computer equipment. The terms were 2/10, n/30.

24   Received the balance due from Bridgeport Company.

29   Received payment in full from Waterbury Corporation.

30   Received payment in full from Groton Enterprises.

31   Received payment in full from Norwalk Enterprises.

31   Recorded the sales tax liability for computer supplies sales to retail customers.

LG 11-6. **Journalize purchase-related transactions.** *Instructions*: Record each of the transactions in the general journal below for Grambling Company. You may omit descriptions. For journal paper, use the templates in the disk at the back of the book or at worthyjames.com (student info.).

June 11:   Purchased $15,000 of merchandise on account from St. John's Company, terms 2/10, n/30. The company records purchases of the gross amount.

12:   Purchased $9,000 of merchandise on account from Montclair Company, terms 1/10, n/30, FOB shipping point, with $200 prepaid transportation charges paid by Montclair added to the invoice.

15:   Returned $1,000 of the merchandise purchased from St. John's Company on June 11.

15:   Purchased $2,000 of office supplies on account.

17:   Purchased $5,000 of merchandise from Savannah Enterprises, terms 2/10, n/30, FOB shipping point.

20:   Paid the balance owing to St. John's Company.

22:   Paid the amount owing to Montclair Company.

27:   Paid $3,920 to Savannah Enterprises.

29:   Paid a $150 freight bill for the merchandise purchased from Savannah Company.

LG 11-7. **Journalize purchase-related transactions: various purchase terms and payment patterns.**

a.   Record each of the transactions in a general journal for the Santa Cruz Company. Round amounts to the nearest dollar. You may omit explanations. This problem has many different purchase and payment terms, so read carefully! For journal paper, use the template in the disk at the back of the book or at worthyjames.com (student info.).

b.   Using a T account, show the activity and the October 31 balance in the Accounts Receivable account for Boulder Creek Company.

October 3   Santa Cruz Company purchased $11,000 of merchandise on account from Boulder Creek Enterprises, terms 3/10, n/20. The company records purchases at the gross amount.

5   Purchased $2,700 of merchandise on account from Carmel Company, terms 2/10, n/20, FOB shipping point.

LG 11-7, *continued*

October 9	Purchased $6,500 of merchandise on account from Corralitos Company, terms 1/10, n/30, FOB shipping point, with $220 of prepaid transportation charges paid by Corralitos Company and added to the invoice.
10	Issued a credit memo and returned $2,000 of the merchandise to Boulder Creek Enterprises.
12	Purchased $15,000 of merchandise from Morgan Hill Corporation, terms 2/10, n/30, FOB shipping point. Santa Cruz company paid $125 to the shipping company directly.
13	Made a cash payment to Boulder Creek Enterprises of $3,500.
18	Purchased $7,500 of merchandise on account from Monterey Company, terms 2/10, n/30, FOB destination.
19	Paid the amount owing to Corralitos Company.
20	Purchased $10,000 of merchandise from Brookdale Company, terms 2/10, n/30, FOB shipping point. Santa Cruz Company will be billed by the shipping company.
22	Paid $7,500 of the invoice amount to Morgan Hill Corporation.
23	Paid the balance due to Boulder Creek Enterprises.
25	Purchased $12,500 of merchandise from Watsonville Partnership, terms 2/10, n/30, FOB shipping point.
29	Paid Brookdale Company in full. The bill from the shipping company was $125 and this was also paid.
31	Paid Carmel Company in full.

LG 11-8. Calculate various steps in determining gross profit.

Instructions: For each letter (a–o) shown below, calculate the missing amount.

Sales	Sales Discounts	Net Sales	Cost of Goods Sold	Gross Profit	Gross Profit%
a	$3,000	$125,400	b	$50,160	k
$212,500	c	201,600	$128,700	d	l
e	7,500	f	330,700	99,200	m
117,350	2,500	g	71,000	h	n
320,500	i	314,850	j	103,900	o

LG 11-9. Calculate cost of goods available and cost of goods sold.

Instructions: Using the relevant information in the T accounts shown below:

a. Calculate cost of goods available for sale. Show cost of goods available for sale using the format illustrated in this learning goal on page 341.

b. Calculate cost of goods sold. When calculating cost of goods sold use the formula shown in this learning goal on page 341. Ending inventory is $3,750.

PRACTICE   Learning Goal 11, continued

Solutions are in the disk at the back of the book and at: www.worthyjames.com

LG 11-9, *continued*

Cash		Accounts Receivable		Office Supplies		Merchandise Inventory		Accounts Payable	
3,000		1,600		400		4,000			5,650
18,000			900		120				700
	2,700		150					4,800	
	3,800	2,100							
14,500		2,650		280		4,000			1,550

Purchases		Purchase Returns and Allowances		Purchase Discounts		Freight in		G. Jurickovich, Capital	
2,600			200		50	25			44,900
7,150			1,250		120	260			
3,900					80	115			
13,650			1,450		250	400			44,900

LG 11-10. Combined Sales and Purchase transactions. Journalize transactions for buyer and seller—wholesale and retail sales and sales tax.

Instructions:

a. Record each of the transactions below in a general journal for the Buyer Company.

b. After you record the transactions for the Buyer Company, record the transactions again in another general journal for the Seller Company, which sells merchandise, equipment, and supplies to both wholesale and retail buyers. Assume a 5% sales tax, when applicable. You may omit explanations in this problem. For journal paper, use the template in the disk at the back of the book or at worthyjames.com (student info.).

April 1   Buyer purchased $15,000 of merchandise inventory on account from Seller Company, terms 2/10, n/30, FOB shipping point. The company records purchases at the gross amount.

3   Buyer purchased $9,000 of merchandise inventory on account from Seller Company, terms 1/10, n/30, FOB shipping point, with $200 prepaid transportation charges paid by Seller added to the invoice.

4   Buyer sent a credit memo and returned $5,000 of the merchandise purchased on April 1.

5   Buyer purchased $5,000 of merchandise inventory from Seller Company, terms 2/10, n/30, FOB shipping point.

6   Buyer Company purchased $3,500 of equipment from Seller Company on account. The equipment is for Buyer Company's own use as a retail customer and will not be resold to customers.

11   Buyer Company paid the balance owing for the April 1 purchase.

13   Buyer paid the amount owing for the April 3 purchase.

15   Buyer purchased merchandise inventory on account from Seller Company, terms 2/10, n/30, FOB shipping point. Seller Company applied the following chain discount to the $20,000 purchase price: 5% discount in total for purchases up to $10,000. For purchases above $10,000 an additional 10% discount applies to the total after the first discount is applied.

15   Buyer paid $3,920 cash for the merchandise purchased on April 5.

LG 11-10, *continued*

April 19   Buyer Company paid $500 cash to Seller Company for supplies. The supplies are for Buyer Company's own use.

      20   Buyer purchased $11,000 of merchandise inventory on account from Seller Company, terms 2/10, n/30, FOB shipping point.

      23   Buyer purchased $3,000 of merchandise inventory on account from Seller Company, terms 2/10, n/30, FOB destination.

      30   Buyer paid $5,500 of the invoice price for the merchandise purchased on April 20.

      31   Buyer paid the balance owing for the April 5 purchase.

LG 11-11.   Various invoice and discount situations.

Instructions: Complete the calculations for each of the independent situations below. All purchases are recorded at gross amounts. (Thanks to Karen Gobright at One Work Place for suggesting some of these problems.)

1. Baychester Company received an invoice for an $18,000 purchase made on May 10. The invoice shows terms of 2/10, n/30. Baychester makes a partial payment of $10,000 of the invoice amount on May 15. What is the discount?

2. Morrisania Company received an invoice for an $18,000 purchase made on May 10. The invoice shows terms of 2/10, n/30. Morrisania pays $10,000 cash on May 15. What is the discount?

3. Kingsbridge Company purchased $20,000 of merchandise on November 20. The seller offered a chain discount of 15% and 5% and terms of 2/10, n/30. Kingsbridge paid in full on November 30. What is the invoice price? What is the discount?

4. Tremont Company purchased $50,000 of merchandise on July 12, terms 2/10, n/30. Tremont paid in full on July 19. On August 3, $20,000 of the merchandise was discovered to be defective and was returned. What is the amount of credit Tremont should receive? The seller sent a credit memo for use against the next purchase. How much should it show?

5. Fordham Company sold $10,000 of merchandise to Westchester Company. Fordham Company also purchased $15,000 of merchandise from Westchester. Fordham sells at terms of 1/10, n/30. Westchester's terms are 2/10, n/30. Fordham offsets its account payable to Westchester against the account receivable owing from Westchester. If Fordham pays in full within the discount period, how much should it pay?

6. Mott Haven Company purchased merchandise on June 3 with terms of 2/10, n/30. When checking the invoice, which showed an invoice price of $12,000, Mott Haven believed that the correct amount on the invoice should be $9,000 and made payment on June 12, taking the discount. On June 15, the seller corrected Mott Haven's calculation; both companies now agree that the correct amount is $12,000. How much discount should Mott Haven take on the invoice? What is the balance in Accounts Payable?

Instructor-Assigned Problem

If you are using this book in a class, these review problems may be assigned by your instructor for homework, group assignments, class work, or other activities. Only your instructor has the solutions.

IA 11-1.   Net sales and cost of goods available for sale calculations. *Instructions:* a) Calculate the missing items in the illustration below. b) Calculate ending inventory if the gross profit percentage is 40%

Sales.....................................			?
Less:			
Sales returns and allowances		?	
Sales discounts............................		14,100	24,600
Net Sales			127,300

Beginning inventory			?
Purchases		?	
Less:			
Purchase returns and allowances	9,050		
Purchase discounts	45,300	?	
Net purchases...........................		340,650	
Add: Freight-in		3,860	
Cost of goods purchased			?
Cost of goods available for sale			394,140

IA 11-2.   Journalize sales transactions—wholesale and retail operations, sales tax. Tulsa Enterprises sells clothing and accessories to wholesale and retail customers. The local sales tax rate is 5%, and Tulsa Enterprises uses a Sales Tax Payable account for retail sales. All retail sales are for cash and all sales to wholesale customers are on terms of 2/10, n/30, FOB shipping point.

Instructions:

a. Record each of the transactions below in a general journal. You may omit explanations in this exercise. For journal paper, use the template in the disk at the back of the book or at www.worthyjames.com (student info.).
b. Suppose that Tulsa Enterprises combined all sales and sales tax collections together in one account called "Sales" and did not use a separate liability account for Sales Tax Payable. Show the calculation to determine the sales tax liability at the end of the month.

January 3	Sold $10,000 of merchandise wholesale to Oklahoma City Company.
5	Sold $5,800 of merchandise to retail customers.
6	Sold $8,600 of merchandise wholesale to Dallas Supply Company.
9	Received a debit memo from Oklahoma City Company, which returned $2,000 of merchandise.
11	Received $4,000 of the invoice amount from Oklahoma City Company.
12	Sold $5,000 of merchandise to retail customers.
13	Received $5,390 cash from Dallas Supply Company
14	Sold $3,700 of merchandise to retail customers.
16	A retail customer returned $1,600 of merchandise for a cash refund.
19	Received the balance due from Oklahoma City Company.
20	Sold $15,000 of merchandise wholesale to Plano Partnership.

IA 11-2, *continued*

January 24   Sold $2,500 of merchandise to retail customers.
28   Received payment in full from Plano Partnership.
31   Paid the amount of the sales tax collected during the month to the local tax authority.

IA 11-3 Record buyer and seller transactions with various discount situations, no sales tax. For each of the independent situations below, record the transactions for the buyer and for the seller company, using separate general journal pages for buyer and seller. Both companies use the periodic inventory method. Calculate payment amounts to the nearest dollar for this problem.

1. On May 12, merchandise is sold to Buyer Company for $15,000, terms 2/10, n/30. On May 21 Buyer pays in full.
2. On September 9, merchandise is sold to Buyer Company for $9,000, terms 2/10, n/30. On October 1 Buyer pays in full.
3. On February 5, merchandise is sold to Buyer Company for $12,000, terms 2/10, n/30. On February 15 Buyer pays $8,000 cash and pays the balance due on March 15.
4. On August 23, Buyer Company purchases $20,000 of merchandise, terms 2/15, n/45. On September 4 Buyer discovers that 30% of the merchandise is incorrect and returns this to the Seller, sending a debit memo to Seller, receiving a credit memo in return. On September 5, Buyer pays the balance due.
5. On November 17, merchandise is sold to Buyer Company for $6,000, terms 1/10, n/30. The seller offers trade chain discounts of 10% and 5% if certain types of merchandise are purchased. Buyer purchased this kind of merchandise. On November 25 Buyer pays $3,000 cash and pays the balance due on December 15.

IA 11-4 Record various transactions with and without sales tax Marin Home Design., Inc. has both wholesale and retail sales and purchases. Sales tax is 7%, only on retail transactions. The company uses a Sales Tax Payable account. Discount terms are offered on wholesale sales. All merchandise transactions are FOB shipping point.

Instructions:

a. Record each of the October transactions below in a general journal for Marin Design Company. Simplify calculations by rounding to the nearest dollar. You may omit explanations.
b. Assume that the company does not use a separate Sales Tax Payable account. How would the transactions on October 5, 20, 29, and 31 be recorded? Show calculation and journal entry.

2   Sold $15,000 of merchandise inventory to Alameda Co., terms 2/10, n/30.
5   Sold $1,900 of merchandise inventory for cash to retail customers.
11 Received payment in full from Alameda Co.
14 Purchased $20,000 inventory from Porterville Co., with a 15%, 8% chain discount, terms 1/10, n/30.
15 Purchased $500 of office supplies from Los Medanos Company on account.
18 Alameda Co. returned all merchandise for cash because of incorrect color.
20 Sold $2,950 of merchandise to retail customers for cash.
21 Purchased $12,000 of inventory from Las Positas Co., terms 2/10, n/30, plus $500 freight charges.
24 Paid Portville Co. in full.
28 Returned $10,000 invoice price of merchandise to Porterville Co., due to incorrect model number.

IA 11-4, *continued*

29   A retail customer returned $200 of merchandise.
30   Paid Las Positas Co. invoice in full.
31   Paid state taxing authority for October sales tax collections.

IA 11-5. Combined Purchase and Sales transactions. Journalize transactions, no sales tax.

Instructions: Record each of the transactions below in a general journal for the Miami Merchandise Company. All of the sales are to companies that will resell the merchandise, so no sales are subject to sales tax. All sales are on account and FOB shipping point. You may omit explanations in this exercise. For journal paper, use the template in the disk at the back of the book.

August 1   Miami Company purchased $10,000 of merchandise inventory on account from Pensacola Enterprises, terms 2/10, n/30, FOB shipping point. The company records purchases at the gross amount.

2   Miami Company purchased $4,000 of merchandise inventory on account from Tallahassee Company, terms 1/10, n/30, FOB shipping point, with $100 prepaid transportation charges paid by Seller added to the invoice.

7   Made $8,000 sale of merchandise to Baton Rouge Corporation, terms 3/10, n/30.

9   Made $4,000 sale of merchandise to Jacksonville Company, terms 3/10, n/30.

10   Returned $2,000 of merchandise and sent a debit memo to Pensacola Enterprises.

11   Paid the balance due on the August 1 invoice from Pensacola Enterprises. Also paid $150 shipping charges.

12   Paid the balance due on the August 2 invoice from Tallahassee Company.

15   Baton Rouge Corporation returned $500 of merchandise.

16   Made $10,000 sale of merchandise to St. Petersburg Company, terms 3/10, n/30.

17   Received a payment of $2,500 of the invoice amount from Baton Rouge Corporation.

18   Received payment in full from Jacksonville Company.

24   Purchased $25,000 of merchandise from Tampa Company, 2/10, n/30, FOB shipping point.

25   Received $2,910 cash from St. Petersburg Company as a partial payment.

27   Purchased $6,000 of merchandise from Orlando Company, 2/10, n/30, FOB destination. The merchandise has not arrived.

31   Borrowed cash from 4th National Bank by signing a note payable. Used the loan proceeds to pay Tampa Company in order to take advantage of the discount terms.

IA 11-6. Should a discount be taken? The Kitchen Store is a retail merchant that specializes in selling kitchen appliances, kitchen interior decorating supplies, and cooking utensils. The partners who own the store cannot agree on whether or not it would be a good policy to pay early to take advantage of discounts regularly offered by their suppliers. The current discussion concerns a $10,000 order of kitchen utensils on which the vendor is offering credit terms of 2/10, n/30. Today is January 5, the last day of the 10-day period in which payment can be made to take advantage of the discount. The business would have to borrow the cash from its bank credit line to pay for the purchase until it collects a large payment from a major customer on January 26, when it would pay off the loan from the bank. The annual interest rate on the credit line is 12%. Janet Chen, one of the partners, wants to take the discount "because it is always a good idea to save money." Dave Harris, another partner, says, "It is going to cost interest on the line of credit from the bank. We would be wasting the money!"

a.   Should the company pay early to take the discount?
b.   A different vendor offers the terms 1/10, n/45. What is your advice for paying this vendor?

INTERNET EXERCISES

Merchant credit card processing service. Suppose that you are beginning a new business and will soon open a specialty cell phone store in a local mall. You want to be able to make credit card sales to walk-in customers and to customers who purchase merchandise from your store's website. Therefore, you need to obtain a credit card sales system.

1. Do an Internet search for "merchant credit card services," "merchant bank account," and "Internet credit card services." How many responses did you get?
2. Review at least 15 links from your search results. What are the necessary equipment and important features of a merchant credit card system for *walk-in* customers?
3. What are the costs of setting up the system? What are the costs involved in using the system?
4. What are the steps to set up an online system to process credit card sales?
5. What are the costs for setting up and for using an *online* system?
6. Do you think that the expenditures for using a credit card system should be classified as part of cost of goods sold or as operating expenses?

Your Questions?

It is *very* important to be aware of what you need to understand better. What do you need to understand better about this learning goal? On a separate piece of paper, write the questions that you want to discuss with your classmates, instructor, or supervisor. Try to be very specific about what is bothering you, such as explanations that you do not fully understand.

LEARNING GOAL 12

Complete the Period-End Procedures—Periodic Method

Overview

Four Procedures

The period-end procedures for a merchandising business are the same basic procedures as for a service business, which are:

1. adjusting entries
2. closing entries
3. financial statement preparation
4. post-closing trial balance

Because you already know how to prepare a post-closing trial balance, we will not repeat the procedure in this learning goal. The post-closing trial balance is discussed on page 272.

Coming Up . . .

In the next sections, you will see how to complete the first three procedures shown above.

To organize the overall process, we will use a worksheet. As you may recall, a worksheet is often prepared on a computer and can also be prepared using paper format. A worksheet is not a required device, but many accountants find it to be a helpful tool. Therefore, we include the use of a worksheet in our discussion.

Period-End Procedures: Closing System

Completing the Worksheet: Closing System

Caution! . . .
Select the System
You Need

Two worksheet and journal entry methods are commonly taught for merchandising businesses. *Check with your instructor* to determine which one you need to learn. They are:

- **The Closing System:** In the closing system, beginning and ending inventory balances are in the worksheet income statement column, and they are part of the closing entries. We study the closing system in this section.
- **The Adjusting System:** In the adjusting system, beginning and ending inventory balances are in the adjustments column, and they are part of the adjusting entries. (This method is used most often in accounting software.) The discussion of the adjusting system begins on page 399.

continued ▶

Completing the Worksheet: Closing System, *continued*

	Trial Balance		Adjustments		Adjusted Trial Balance		Income Statement		Balance Sheet	
Account Titles	Dr.	Cr.	Dr.	Cr.	Dr.	Cr.	Dr.	Cr.	Dr.	Cr.
Cash	$$$				$$$					
Accounts Receivable	$$$				$$$					
Merchandise										
Inventory	**8,100**				**8,100**					
Store Supplies	$$$			(b) $$$	$$$					
Prepaid Insurance	$$$			(c) $$$	$$$					
Office Equipment	$$$				$$$					
Accum. Dep'n—										
Office Equipment		$$$		(a) $$$		$$$				
Store Equipment	$$$				$$$					
Accum. Dep'n—										
Store Equipment		$$$		(a) $$$		$$$				
Accounts Payable		$$$		(d) $$$		$$$				
Sales Tax Payable		$$$				$$$				
Common Stock		$$$				$$$				
Retained Earnings		$$$				$$$				
Dividends	$$$				$$$					
Sales		**236,700**				**236,700**				
Sales Returns and										
Allowances	**5,700**				**5,700**					
Sales Discounts	**2,100**				**2,100**					
Purchases	**161,000**				**161,000**					
Purchase Returns and										
Allowances		**5,300**				**5,300**				
Purchase Discounts		**2,750**				**2,750**				
Freight-in	**800**				**800**					
Freight-out	$$$				$$$					
Advertising Expense	$$$				$$$					
Insurance Expense	$$$		(c) $$$		$$$					
Salaries and Wages										
Expense	$$$				$$$					
Rent Expense	$$$				$$$					
Income Tax Expense	$$$				$$$					
Utilities Expense	$$$		(d) $$$		$$$					
Totals	$$$	$$$								
Supplies Expense			(b) $$$		$$$					
Depreciation Expense			(a) $$$		$$$					
Totals			$$$	$$$	$$$	$$$				

Completing the Worksheet: Closing System, *continued*

*Overview of
the Worksheet
Procedure*

To complete the worksheet after you have finished the adjusting entries and the adjusted trial balance columns, use this procedure:

Step	Action
1	Enter all the net sales accounts in the income statement columns.
2	Enter all the cost of goods available for sale accounts in the income statement columns.
3	Enter the ending inventory as a credit in the income statement columns and a debit in the balance sheet columns. (This completes cost of goods sold.)
4	Enter all the other income statement accounts in the income statement columns.
5	Enter all the other balance sheet accounts in the balance sheet columns.
6	Total the income statement and balance sheet columns and compute net income or net loss.

*Step 1:
Net Sales*

In the income statement columns, enter the account balances that together make up net sales on the income statement. These are:

- Sales
- Sales Returns and Allowances
- Sales Discounts

The circular dashed line on the worksheet contains the accounts that comprise net sales.

continued ▶

Completing the Worksheet: Closing System, *continued*

Account Titles	Trial Balance Dr.	Trial Balance Cr.	Adjustments Dr.	Adjustments Cr.	Adjusted Trial Balance Dr.	Adjusted Trial Balance Cr.	Income Statement Dr.	Income Statement Cr.	Balance Sheet Dr.	Balance Sheet Cr.

Queensborough Patio Mart, Inc.
Worksheet
For the Year Ended December 31, 2017

Account Titles	Dr.	Cr.	Dr.	Cr.	Dr.	Cr.	Dr.	Cr.	Dr.	Cr.
Cash	$$$				$$$					
Accounts Receivable	$$$				$$$					
Merchandise Inventory	8,100				8,100					
Store Supplies	$$$			(b) $$$	$$$					
Prepaid Insurance	$$$			(c) $$$	$$$					
Office Equipment	$$$				$$$					
Accum. Dep'n—										
Office Equipment		$$$		(a) $$$		$$$				
Store Equipment	$$$				$$$					
Accum. Dep'n—										
Store Equipment		$$$		(a) $$$		$$$				
Accounts Payable		$$$		(d) $$$		$$$				
Sales Tax Payable		$$$				$$$				
Common Stock		$$$				$$$				
Retained Earnings		$$$				$$$				
Dividends	$$$				$$$					
Sales		236,700				236,700		236,700		
Sales Returns and										
Allowances	5,700				5,700		5,700			
Sales Discounts	2,100				2,100		2,100			
Purchases	161,000				161,000					
Purchase Returns and										
Allowances		5,300				5,300				
Purchase Discounts		2,750				2,750				
Freight-in	800				800					
Freight-out	$$$				$$$					
Advertising Expense	$$$				$$$					
Insurance Expense	$$$		(c) $$$		$$$					
Salaries and Wages										
Expense	$$$				$$$					
Rent Expense	$$$				$$$					
Income Tax Expense	$$$				$$$					
Utilities Expense	$$$		(d) $$$		$$$					
Totals	$$$	$$$	$$$	$$$	$$$	$$$				

Completing the Worksheet: Closing System, *continued*

Location on the Income Statement

The example below shows where the net sales accounts appear on the income statement, after the worksheet is completed. The net sales amounts are highlighted for emphasis in the example.

Queensborough Patio Mart, Inc.		
Income Statement		
For the Year Ended December 31, 2017		
Sales revenue		$236,700
Less: Sales returns and allowances	$5,700	
Sales discounts	2,100	7,800
Net sales revenue		$228,900
Cost of goods sold	$$$	
	$$$	
	$$$	$$$
Gross profit		$$$
Operating expenses	$$$	
	$$$	
	$$$	
	$$$	
	$$$	
	$$$	$$$
Income before tax		$$$
Income tax expense		$$
Net income		$$$

Step 2: Cost of Goods Available for Sale

In the worksheet income statement columns, enter the account balances that together make up cost of goods available for sale. These are:

- Beginning Inventory (debit balance)
- Purchases
- Purchase Returns and Allowances
- Purchase Discounts
- Freight-in

The worksheet example is on page 386.

continued ▶

Completing the Worksheet: Closing System, *continued*

Account Titles	Trial Balance Dr.	Trial Balance Cr.	Adjustments Dr.	Adjustments Cr.	Adjusted Trial Balance Dr.	Adjusted Trial Balance Cr.	Income Statement Dr.	Income Statement Cr.	Balance Sheet Dr.	Balance Sheet Cr.
Cash	$$$				$$$					
Accounts Receivable	$$$				$$$					
Merchandise										
Inventory	8,100				8,100		8,100			
Store Supplies	$$$			(b) $$$	$$$					
Prepaid Insurance	$$$			(c) $$$	$$$					
Office Equipment	$$$				$$$					
Accum. Dep'n—										
Office Equipment		$$$	(a) $$$			$$$				
Store Equipment	$$$				$$$					
Accum. Dep'n—										
Store Equipment		$$$	(a) $$$			$$$				
Accounts Payable		$$$	(d) $$$			$$$				
Sales Tax Payable		$$$				$$$				
Common Stock		$$$				$$$				
Retained Earnings		$$$				$$$				
Dividends	$$$				$$$					
Sales		236,700				236,700		236,700		
Sales Returns and										
Allowances	5,700				5,700		5,700			
Sales Discounts	2,100				2,100		2,100			
Purchases	161,000				161,000		161,000			
Purchase Returns and										
Allowances		5,300				5,300		5,300		
Purchase Discounts		2,750				2,750		2,750		
Freight-in	800				800		800			
Freight-out	$$$				$$$					
Advertising Expense	$$$				$$$					
Insurance Expense	$$$		(c) $$$		$$$					
Salaries and Wages										
Expense	$$$				$$$					
Rent Expense	$$$				$$$					
Income Tax Expense	$$$				$$$					
Utilities Expense	$$$		(d) $$$		$$$					
Totals	$$$	$$$								
Supplies Expense			(b) $$$		$$$					
Depreciation Expense			(a) $$$		$$$					
Totals			$$$	$$$	$$$	$$$				

Queensborough Patio Mart, Inc.
Worksheet
For the Year Ended December 31, 2017

cost of goods available for sale

Completing the Worksheet: Closing System, *continued*

Location on the Income Statement

The example below shows (in bold type) where accounts that are part of cost of goods available for sale appear on the income statement, after it is prepared from the completed worksheet. On the worksheet, the cost of goods available amounts are highlighted for emphasis.

Queensborough Patio Mart, Inc.
Income Statement
For the Year Ended December 31, 2017

Sales revenue				$236,700
Less: Sales returns and allowances			$5,700	
Sales discounts			2,100	7,800
Net sales revenue				228,900
Cost of goods sold				
Inventory, January 1			**8,100**	
Purchases		**$161,000**		
Less: Purchase returns and allowances	$5,300			
Purchase discounts	2,750	8,050		
Net purchases		152,950		
Add: Freight-in		**800**		
Cost of goods purchased			153,750	
Cost of goods available for sale			161,850	
Inventory, December 31			Step 3	
Cost of goods sold				Step 3
Gross profit				Step 3
Operating expenses			$$$	
			$$$	
			$$$	
			$$$	
			$$$	
			$$$	$$$
Income before tax				$$$
Income tax expense				$$
Net income				$$$

---

continued ▶

Completing the Worksheet: Closing System, *continued*

Step 3: Ending Inventory and Cost of Goods Sold

Ending inventory is the part of cost of goods available for sale that is still unsold. Ending inventory is an asset and is not part of the cost of goods sold expense in the current period. Therefore we need to reduce cost of goods sold by a credit to inventory in the income statement column and show it as an asset in the balance sheet debit column. When this is done, all the items that comprise cost of goods sold are in the income statement columns.

On the line for inventory in the income statement column, enter a credit for the amount of ending inventory. Then, on the same line in the balance sheet column, enter a debit for the same amount.

TIP

Remember that cost of goods sold is an expense that is calculated as the combination of beginning inventory, net purchases (purchases, purchase discounts, purchase returns and allowances, freight-in) minus ending inventory.

*"Well, sport, did you find cost of goods
sold in the worksheet?"*

Completing the Worksheet: Closing System, *continued*

<table>
<tr><td colspan="11" align="center">Queensborough Patio Mart, Inc.</td></tr>
<tr><td colspan="11" align="center">Worksheet</td></tr>
<tr><td colspan="11" align="center">For the Year Ended December 31, 2017</td></tr>
<tr>
<td rowspan="3">Account Titles</td>
<td colspan="2">Trial Balance</td>
<td colspan="2">Adjustments</td>
<td colspan="2">Adjusted
Trial Balance</td>
<td colspan="2">Income
Statement</td>
<td colspan="2">Balance
Sheet</td>
</tr>
<tr>
<td>Dr.</td><td>Cr.</td>
<td>Dr.</td><td>Cr.</td>
<td>Dr.</td><td>Cr.</td>
<td>Dr.</td><td>Cr.</td>
<td>Dr.</td><td>Cr.</td>
</tr>
<tr>
<td></td><td></td><td></td><td></td><td></td><td></td><td></td><td></td><td></td><td></td>
</tr>
<tr><td>Cash</td><td>$$$</td><td></td><td></td><td></td><td>$$$</td><td></td><td></td><td></td><td>$$$</td><td></td></tr>
<tr><td>Accounts Receivable</td><td>$$$</td><td></td><td></td><td></td><td>$$$</td><td></td><td></td><td></td><td>$$$</td><td></td></tr>
<tr><td>**Merchandise**</td><td></td><td></td><td></td><td></td><td></td><td></td><td></td><td></td><td></td><td></td></tr>
<tr><td> **Inventory**</td><td>8,100</td><td></td><td></td><td></td><td>8,100</td><td></td><td>8,100</td><td>16,350</td><td>16,350</td><td></td></tr>
<tr><td>Store Supplies</td><td>$$$</td><td></td><td></td><td>(b) $$$</td><td>$$$</td><td></td><td></td><td></td><td>$$$</td><td></td></tr>
<tr><td>Prepaid Insurance</td><td>$$$</td><td></td><td></td><td>(c) $$$</td><td>$$$</td><td></td><td></td><td></td><td>$$$</td><td></td></tr>
<tr><td>Office Equipment</td><td>$$$</td><td></td><td></td><td></td><td>$$$</td><td></td><td></td><td></td><td>$$$</td><td></td></tr>
<tr><td>Accum. Dep'n—</td><td></td><td></td><td></td><td></td><td></td><td></td><td></td><td></td><td></td><td></td></tr>
<tr><td> Office Equipment</td><td></td><td>$$$</td><td></td><td>(a) $$$</td><td></td><td>$$$</td><td></td><td></td><td></td><td></td></tr>
<tr><td>Store Equipment</td><td>$$$</td><td></td><td></td><td></td><td>$$$</td><td></td><td></td><td></td><td>$$$</td><td></td></tr>
<tr><td>Accum. Dep'n—</td><td></td><td></td><td></td><td></td><td></td><td></td><td></td><td></td><td></td><td></td></tr>
<tr><td> Store Equipment</td><td></td><td>$$$</td><td></td><td>(a) $$$</td><td></td><td>$$$</td><td></td><td></td><td></td><td>$$$</td></tr>
<tr><td>Accounts Payable</td><td></td><td>$$$</td><td></td><td>(d) $$$</td><td></td><td>$$$</td><td></td><td></td><td></td><td>$$$</td></tr>
<tr><td>Sales Tax Payable</td><td></td><td>$$$</td><td></td><td></td><td></td><td>$$$</td><td></td><td></td><td></td><td>$$$</td></tr>
<tr><td>Common Stock</td><td></td><td>$$$</td><td></td><td></td><td></td><td>$$$</td><td></td><td></td><td></td><td>$$$</td></tr>
<tr><td>Retained Earnings</td><td></td><td>$$$</td><td></td><td></td><td></td><td>$$$</td><td></td><td></td><td></td><td>$$$</td></tr>
<tr><td>Dividends</td><td>$$$</td><td></td><td></td><td></td><td>$$$</td><td></td><td></td><td></td><td>$$$</td><td></td></tr>
<tr><td>Sales</td><td></td><td>236,700</td><td></td><td></td><td></td><td>236,700</td><td></td><td>236,700</td><td></td><td></td></tr>
<tr><td>Sales Returns and</td><td></td><td></td><td></td><td></td><td></td><td></td><td></td><td></td><td></td><td></td></tr>
<tr><td> Allowances</td><td>5,700</td><td></td><td></td><td></td><td>5,700</td><td></td><td>5,700</td><td></td><td></td><td></td></tr>
<tr><td>Sales Discounts</td><td>2,100</td><td></td><td></td><td></td><td>2,100</td><td></td><td>2,100</td><td></td><td></td><td></td></tr>
<tr><td>Purchases</td><td>161,000</td><td></td><td></td><td></td><td>161,000</td><td></td><td>161,000</td><td></td><td></td><td></td></tr>
<tr><td>Purchase Returns and</td><td></td><td></td><td></td><td></td><td></td><td></td><td></td><td></td><td></td><td></td></tr>
<tr><td> Allowances</td><td></td><td>5,300</td><td></td><td></td><td></td><td>5,300</td><td></td><td>5,300</td><td></td><td></td></tr>
<tr><td>Purchase Discounts</td><td></td><td>2,750</td><td></td><td></td><td></td><td>2,750</td><td></td><td>2,750</td><td></td><td></td></tr>
<tr><td>Freight-in</td><td>800</td><td></td><td></td><td></td><td>800</td><td></td><td>800</td><td></td><td></td><td></td></tr>
<tr><td>Freight-out</td><td>$$$</td><td></td><td></td><td></td><td>$$$</td><td></td><td></td><td></td><td></td><td></td></tr>
<tr><td>Advertising Expense</td><td>$$$</td><td></td><td></td><td></td><td>$$$</td><td></td><td></td><td></td><td></td><td></td></tr>
<tr><td>Insurance Expense</td><td>$$$</td><td></td><td>(c) $$$</td><td></td><td>$$$</td><td></td><td></td><td></td><td></td><td></td></tr>
<tr><td>Salaries and Wages</td><td></td><td></td><td></td><td></td><td></td><td></td><td></td><td></td><td></td><td></td></tr>
<tr><td> Expense</td><td>$$$</td><td></td><td></td><td></td><td>$$$</td><td></td><td></td><td></td><td></td><td></td></tr>
<tr><td>Rent Expense</td><td>$$$</td><td></td><td></td><td></td><td>$$$</td><td></td><td></td><td></td><td></td><td></td></tr>
<tr><td>Income Tax Expense</td><td>$$$</td><td></td><td></td><td></td><td>$$$</td><td></td><td></td><td></td><td></td><td></td></tr>
<tr><td>Utilities Expense</td><td>$$$</td><td></td><td>(d) $$$</td><td></td><td>$$$</td><td></td><td></td><td></td><td></td><td></td></tr>
<tr><td> Totals</td><td>$$$</td><td>$$$</td><td></td><td></td><td></td><td></td><td></td><td></td><td></td><td></td></tr>
<tr><td></td><td></td><td></td><td></td><td></td><td></td><td></td><td></td><td></td><td></td><td></td></tr>
<tr><td>Supplies Expense</td><td></td><td></td><td>(b) $$$</td><td></td><td>$$$</td><td></td><td></td><td></td><td></td><td></td></tr>
<tr><td>Depreciation Expense</td><td></td><td></td><td>(a) $$$</td><td></td><td>$$$</td><td></td><td></td><td></td><td></td><td></td></tr>
<tr><td> Totals</td><td></td><td></td><td>$$$</td><td>$$$</td><td>$$$</td><td>$$$</td><td></td><td></td><td></td><td></td></tr>
<tr><td></td><td></td><td></td><td></td><td></td><td></td><td></td><td></td><td></td><td></td><td></td></tr>
</table>

continued ▶

Completing the Worksheet: Closing System, *continued*

Queensborough Patio Mart, Inc.
Income Statement
For the Year Ended December 31, 2017

Sales revenue			$236,700
Less: Sales returns and allowances		$5,700	
Sales discounts		2,100	7,800
Net sales revenue			228,900
Cost of goods sold			
Inventory, January 1		8,100	
Purchases	$161,000		
Less: Purchase returns and allowances	$5,300		
Purchase discounts	2,750	8,050	
Net purchases		152,950	
Add: Freight-in		800	
Cost of goods purchased		153,750	
Cost of goods available for sale		161,850	
Inventory, December 31		16,350	
Cost of goods sold			145,500
Gross profit			83,400
Operating expenses		$$$	
		$$$	
		$$$	
		$$$	
		$$$	
		$$$	$$$
Income before tax			$$$
Income tax expense			$$
Net income			$$$

Step 4: Finish Income Statement Columns

To complete the income statement columns, we can now enter all the other revenue and expense accounts into the income statement columns. This is normally all the operating expenses plus any miscellaneous revenues and expenses.

Step 5: Finish Balance Sheet Columns

To complete the balance sheet columns, enter the balance sheet account balances in the balance sheet columns.

Step 6: Net Income or Loss

The last step for the completion of the worksheet is to total the income statement and balance sheet columns to determine net income or net loss.

Completing the Worksheet: Closing System, *continued*

Account Titles	Trial Balance Dr.	Trial Balance Cr.	Adjustments Dr.	Adjustments Cr.	Adjusted Trial Balance Dr.	Adjusted Trial Balance Cr.	Income Statement Dr.	Income Statement Cr.	Balance Sheet Dr.	Balance Sheet Cr.
Cash	37,950				37,950				37,950	
Accounts Receivable	5,500				5,500				5,500	
Merchandise Inventory	8,100				8,100		8,100	16,350	16,350	
Store Supplies	4,335			(b) 250	4,085				4,085	
Prepaid Insurance	1,800			(c) 385	1,415				1,415	
Office Equipment	12,750				12,750				12,750	
Accum. Dep'n— Office Equip.		3,200		(a) 150		3,350				3,350
Store Equipment	44,880				44,880				44,880	
Accum. Dep'n— Store Equipment		15,650		(a) 350		16,000				16,000
Accounts Payable		12,800		(d) 100		12,900				12,900
Sales Tax Payable		2,100				2,100				2,100
Common Stock		10,000				10,000				10,000
Retained Earnings		57,380				57,380				57,380
Dividends	16,300				16,300				16,300	
Sales		236,700				236,700		236,700		
Sales Returns and Allowances	5,700				5,700		5,700			
Sales Discounts	2,100				2,100		2,100			
Purchases	161,000				161,000		161,000			
Purchase Returns and Allowances		5,300				5,300		5,300		
Purchase Discounts		2,750				2,750		2,750		
Freight-in	800				800		800			
Freight-out	880				880		880			
Advertising Expense	2,800				2,800		2,800			
Insurance Expense	715		(c) 385		1,100		1,100			
Salaries and Wages Expense	19,200				19,200		19,200			
Rent Expense	16,100				16,100		16,100			
Income Tax Expense	2,500				2,500		2,500			
Utilities Expense	2,470		(d) 100		2,570		2,570			
Totals	345,880	345,880								
Supplies Expense			(b) 250		250		250			
Depreciation Expense			(a) 500		500		500			
Totals			1,235	1,235	346,480	346,480	223,600	261,100	139,230	101,730
Net Income							37,500			37,500
Totals							261,100	261,100	139,230	139,230

Queensborough Patio Mart, Inc.
Worksheet
For the Year Ended December 31, 2017

Financial Statements

Income Statement from Worksheet

The income statement that you see below is called a ***multiple-step income statement***. It shows the individual calculation steps, including cost of goods sold and operating expenses, needed to determine net income. It is also called a *classified* income statement, because the operating expenses are classified using the convenient categories *selling* and *administrative*

Queensborough Patio Mart, Inc.
Income Statement
For the Year Ended December 31, 2017

Sales revenue				$236,700
Less: Sales returns and allowances			$5,700	
Sales discounts			2,100	7,800
Net sales revenue				228,900
Cost of goods sold				
Inventory, January 1			8,100	
Purchases		$161,000		
Less: Purchase returns and allowances	$5,300			
Purchase discounts	2,750	8,050		
Net purchases		152,950		
Add: Freight-in		800		
Cost of goods purchased			153,750	
Cost of goods available for sale			161,850	
Inventory, December 31			16,350	
Cost of goods sold				145,500
Gross profit				83,400
Operating expenses				
Selling expenses				
Salaries and wages expense		5,000		
Advertising expense		2,800		
Freight-out		880		
Supplies expense		50		
Total selling expenses			8,730	
Administrative expenses				
Rent expense		16,100		
Salaries and wages expense		14,200		
Utilities expense		2,570		
Insurance expense		1,100		
Depreciation expense		500		
Supplies expense		200		
Total administrative expenses			34,670	
Total operating expenses				43,400
Income before income tax				40,000
Income tax expense				2,500
Net income				$37,500

Financial Statements, *continued*

Statement of Retained Earnings and Balance Sheet

The statement of retained earnings is unchanged from that of a service business. The balance sheet has only two significant changes: a new current asset *called merchandise inventory, and a liability called sales tax payable.*

Queensborough Patio Mart, Inc.
Statement of Retained Earnings
For the Year Ended December 31, 2017

Retained Earnings, January 1, 2017	$ 57,380
Add: Net income	37,500
Subtotal	94,880
Less: Dividends	16,300
Retained Earnings, December 31, 2017	$ 78,580

Queensborough Patio Mart, Inc.
Balance Sheet
December 31, 2017

Assets

Current assets			
Cash		$37,950	
Accounts receivable		5,500	
Merchandise inventory		16,350	
Store supplies		4,085	
Prepaid insurance		1,415	
Total current assets			$65,300
Property, plant, and equipment			
Office equipment	$12,750		
Less: Accumulated depreciation	3,350	9,400	
Store equipment	44,880		
Less: Accumulated depreciation	16,000	28,880	
Total property, plant, and equipment			38,280
Total assets			$103,580

Liabilities and Stockholders' Equity

Current liabilities			
Accounts payable		$12,900	
Sales tax payable		2,100	
Total current liabilities			$15,000
Stockholders' equity			
Paid-in Capital			
Common Stock		10,000	
Retained Earnings		78,580	
Total Stockholders' Equity			88,580
Total liabilities and stockholders' equity			$103,580

Financial Statements, *continued*

Other Revenues and Expenses	Sometimes a business has other revenues and gains and other expenses and losses that are not part of the operating activities needed to produce a service or product. These "other" or ***nonoperating*** items would not be expected to be part of normal operations, but rather are incidental to being in business.
	If they are material, "other" items must be shown separately on the income statement, and never hidden inside of the operating expense numbers.

Examples

There is no single list of items—judgment is required to decide if an item should be classified as "other." However, here are some typical examples:

Other revenues and gains:

- Interest earned
- Rental revenue (main business not rental)
- Gain on sale of equipment

Other expenses and losses:

- Interest expense
- Lawsuit losses
- Loss on sale of equipment

How to Show

If there are "other" nonoperating items, do this:

- Calculate ***operating income***, which is gross profit minus operating expenses, before nonoperating items.
- Show the "other" items under operating income.
- After the total of the "other" items, calculate the income before income tax. Then subtract income tax expense to obtain net income.

Example

Here is how the affected part of the Queensborough Patio Mart income statement would appear if there were "other" items. We are using assumed numbers for the "other" items:

Supplies expense	200		
Total administrative expenses		37,170	
Total operating expenses			43,400
Operating income			**40,000**
Other revenue and gains			
Interest revenue	**500**		
Gain on sale of land	**2,500**	**3,000**	
Other expenses and losses			
Interest expense	**3,200**		
Loss on sale of equipment	**5,000**	**(8,200)**	**(5,200)**
Income before income tax			**34,800**
Income tax expense			**2,500**
Net income			**$32,300**

Financial Statements, *continued*

Example (continued)

Note: The $5,200 for the "other" items is a net amount, the difference between $8,200 and $3,000. Because other expenses exceed other income, the $5,200 net amount is subtracted.

Single-Step Income Statement Format

The ***single-step income statement*** is an income statement format in which the net income is calculated in a single step, by subtracting the total of all expenses from the total of all revenues.

Example

Here is how the Queensborough Patio Mart income statement, including the additional "other" items on the preceding page, would appear as a single-step statement. Usually, the statement is condensed, as you see below, with the line items representing final totals of the calculation steps.

Queensborough Patio Mart, Inc.
Income Statement
For the Year Ended December 31, 2017

Revenues		
Net sales		$228,900
Interest earned		500
Gain on sale of land		2,500
Total revenues		231,900
Expenses		
Cost of goods sold	$145,500	
Selling expenses	8,730	
Administrative expenses	34,670	
Interest expense	3,200	
Equipment sale loss	5,000	
Income tax expense	2,500	
Total expenses		199,600
Net income		$ 32,300

Essential Features

- All revenue items, including "other" revenues, are grouped together.
- All expense items, including "other" expenses, are grouped together.
- Net income can always be calculated in a single step, by subtracting total expenses from total revenues.

TIP

Sometimes cost of goods sold will also be condensed to a single amount on a multiple-step income statement. For example, on page 392, cost of goods sold could be shown as a single line item of $145,500.

continued ▶

Recording Adjusting and Closing Entries: Closing System

Adjusting Entries Procedure

The adjusting entries are simply copied from the worksheet adjusting entries columns and recorded into the general journal. The example below shows the entries that come from the Queensborough Patio Mart worksheet.

GENERAL JOURNAL				J43
Date	Account Titles and Explanation	Post. Ref.	Debit	Credit
2017				
Dec.	ADJUSTING ENTRIES			
	(A)			
31	Depreciation Expense		500	
	Accumulated Depreciation—Office Equipment			150
	Accumulated Depreciation—Store Equipment			350
	To record one year of depreciation expense			
	(B)			
31	Supplies Expense		250	
	Store Supplies			250
	To adjust the supplies on hand to actual balance			
	(C)			
31	Insurance Expense		385	
	Prepaid Insurance			385
	To record the expiration of Prepaid Insurance			
	(D)			
31	Utilities Expense		100	
	Accounts Payable			100
	To accrue utilities expense			

Closing Entries Source

In the worksheet, the income statement columns and the balance in drawing account are the sources for the closing entries.

Closing Entries Procedure

The table on page 397 shows the steps in the closing entries procedure.

Recording Adjusting and Closing Entries: Closing System, *continued*

Step	Action
1	Close accounts that increase net income. In the income statement columns of the worksheet, all accounts with credit balances are closed by debiting them in the general journal. The total of all the debits is recorded as a credit to Income Summary.
2	Close accounts that decrease net income. In the income statement columns of the worksheet, all accounts with debit balances are closed by crediting them in the general journal. The total of all the credits is recorded as a debit to Income Summary.
3	Calculate the balance of the Income Summary account and close this into the retained earnings account. A credit balance in Income Summary is closed by debiting Income Summary and crediting retained earnings. A debit balance in Income Summary is closed with the opposite entry.
4	Close the dividends account into the retained earnings account. Credit the dividends account and debit the retained earnings account.

Example of Step 1

The general journal entry below illustrates Step 1. Notice that the ending inventory balance is part of this entry. By debiting the Merchandise Inventory account, the ending inventory is properly recorded as an asset.

GENERAL JOURNAL				J44
Date	Account Titles and Explanation	Post. Ref.	Debit	Credit
2017				
Dec. 31	CLOSING ENTRIES			
	Merchandise Inventory, December 31		**16,350**	
	Sales		236,700	
	Purchase Returns and Allowances		5,300	
	Purchase Discounts		2,750	
	Income Summary			261,100
	To record ending inventory and to close credit balance			
	temporary accounts			

This must be the same as the credit total in the worksheet income statement column.

continued ▶

Recording Adjusting and Closing Entries: Closing System, *continued*

Example of Step 2

The general journal entry below illustrates Step 2. Notice that the beginning inventory balance is part of this entry. The credit to the Merchandise Inventory account removes the beginning inventory from the account because this inventory has been used up and is part of cost of goods sold.

31	Income Summary			223,600	
	Merchandise Inventory, January 1				**8,100**
	Sales Returns and Allowances				5,700
	Sales Discounts				2,100
	Purchases				161,000
	Freight-in				800
	Freight-out				880
	Advertising Expense				2,800
	Insurance Expense				1,100
	Salaries and Wages Expense				19,200
	Rent Expense				16,100
	Income Tax Expense				2,500
	Utilities Expense				2,570
	Supplies Expense				250
	Depreciation Expense				500
	Income Tax Expense				2,500
	To record the use of beginning inventory and to close				
	debit balance temporary accounts				

This must be the same as the debit total in the worksheet income statement column.

Example of Step 3

The general journal entry below shows the credit balance of $37,500 in Income Summary closed by a debit to Income Summary and a credit to retained earnings. This represents the net income from the current period operations.

Note: The $37,500 is the difference between the $261,100 credit to Income Summary in Step 1 and the $223,600 debit to Income Summary in Step 2.

This must be the same as the net income on the worksheet.

31	Income Summary			37,500	
	Retained Earnings				37,500
	To transfer net income to retained earnings				

Recording Adjusting and Closing Entries: Closing System, *continued*

Example of Step 4

The general journal entry below closes the dividends account into the retained earnings account. This is the decrease in retained earnings resulting from distribution of assets—usually cash—for stockholders' personal use.

31	Retained Earnings		16,300	
	Dividends			16,300
	To close the dividends into the capital account			

Period-End Procedures: Adjusting System

Overview

Four Procedures

The period-end procedures for a merchandising business are the same basic procedures as for a service business:

1. Adjusting entries
2. Closing entries
3. Financial statement preparation
4. Post-closing trial balance

Coming Up . . .

In the next sections, you will see how to complete the four procedures listed above. To organize the overall process, we will use a worksheet. A worksheet is not a required device, but many accountants find it to be a helpful tool in completing the four procedures. Thus, we will use a work- sheet here.

Completing the Worksheet: Adjusting System

**Caution!
Two Different
Systems**

Two worksheet methods are commonly used for merchandising businesses. You probably do not need to know both of the them. *Check with your instructor* to determine which method you need to learn. They are:

- **The adjusting system:** Beginning and ending inventory balances are both in the adjustments column and are part of the adjusting entries. (This is the method used most often in computerized accounting systems.) We study the adjusting system in this section.
- **The closing system:** Beginning and ending inventory balances are both in the income statement column and are part of the closing entries. The discussion of the closing system begins on page 381.

continued ▶

Completing the Worksheet: Adjusting System, *continued*

Procedure

The table below shows the procedure for completing the worksheet.

Step	Action
1	**Adjustments columns** ▪ Eliminate the beginning inventory and record the ending inventory. ▪ Record the rest of the adjustments and total the columns.
2	**Adjusted trial balance columns** ▪ Enter the amounts and total the columns.
3	**Income statement columns** ▪ Enter the amounts for the accounts that make up net sales. ▪ Enter the amounts for the accounts that make up cost of goods sold. ▪ Enter the rest of the income statement accounts and total the columns.
4	**Balance sheet columns** ▪ Enter the amounts for the balance sheet accounts and total the columns.
5	Determine the final net income or loss.

Step 1:
Adjustments

▪ **Beginning inventory—adjustment (a):** The beginning inventory has been sold and is gone. Therefore, it is part of the cost of goods sold expense. When beginning inventory is used up and becomes an expense, it is credited, and then recorded as a debit to Income Summary, where total expenses are recorded. Although it would be possible to use a Cost of Goods Sold Expense account to record the using up of the beginning inventory, it is faster to simply debit the amount directly into Income Summary. Inventory is the only asset treated in this way.

▪ **Ending inventory—adjustment (b):** After the beginning inventory is gone, we must then record the new amount of inventory that remains at the end of the period. This is the ending inventory. To record the new amount of inventory, debit Merchandise Inventory. Income Summary is credited because ending inventory reduces cost of goods sold and therefore increases net income.

Starting Point

An example of the worksheet for the Queensborough Patio Mart is shown on page 401. Our starting point is to assume that we have completed the trial balance columns.

The important accounts that are specific to merchandising operations are highlighted in bold type. For the moment, we will use "$$" to indicate the balances in the other accounts, so we can focus attention on the new merchandising accounts. You can see adjustments (a) and (b) in the adjustments columns.

Completing the Worksheet: Adjusting System, *continued*

Account Titles	Trial Balance Dr.	Trial Balance Cr.	Adjustments Dr.	Adjustments Cr.	Adjusted Trial Balance Dr.	Adjusted Trial Balance Cr.	Income Statement Dr.	Income Statement Cr.	Balance Sheet Dr.	Balance Sheet Cr.
Cash	$$$									
Accounts Receivable	$$$									
Merchandise Inventory	8,100		(b) 16,350	(a) 8,100						
Store Supplies	$$$									
Prepaid Insurance	$$$									
Office Equipment	$$$									
Accum. Dep'n—										
Office Equipment		$$$								
Store Equipment	$$$									
Accum. Dep'n—										
Store Equipment		$$$								
Accounts Payable		$$$								
Sales Tax Payable		$$$								
Common Stock		$$$								
Retained Earnings		$$$								
Dividends	$$$									
Sales		236,700								
Sales Returns and										
Allowances	5,700									
Sales Discounts	2,100									
Purchases	161,000									
Purchase Returns and										
Allowances		5,300								
Purchase Discounts		2,750								
Freight-in	800									
Freight-out	$$$									
Advertising Expense	$$$									
Insurance Expense	$$$									
Salaries and Wages										
Expense	$$$									
Rent Expense	$$$					$$$				
Income Tax Expense	$$$					$$$				
Utilities Expense	$$$		$$$			$$$				
Totals	$$$	$$$								
Income Summary			(a) 8,100	(b) 16,350						
Supplies Expense										
Depreciation Expense										
Totals										

Queensborough Patio Mart, Inc.
Worksheet
For the Year Ended December 31, 2017

Beginning inventory (increases cost of goods sold)

Ending inventory (decreases cost of goods sold)

continued ▶

Completing the Worksheet: Adjusting System, *continued*

Step 1, continued

The final part of Step 1 is to record the rest of the adjustments and total the adjustments column.

Adjustments Information

The rest of the adjustments (see next page) are based on the following:

- **Adjustment (c):** $385 of Prepaid Insurance has expired since the insurance was purchased.
- **Adjustment (d):** a physical count reveals that $250 of Store Supplies has been used up.
- **Adjustment (e):** $500 of depreciation expense must be recorded, which is $150 for Office Equipment and $350 for Store Equipment.
- **Adjustment (f):** $100 of unpaid utility expenses are accrued

Completing the Worksheet: Adjusting System, *continued*

Step 2   The following worksheet shows the adjustments and the adjusted trial balance columns completed. The "$$$" have been replaced by actual numbers.

Queensborough Patio Mart, Inc.
Worksheet
For the Year Ended December 31, 2017

Account Titles	Trial Balance Dr.	Trial Balance Cr.	Adjustments Dr.	Adjustments Cr.	Adjusted Trial Balance Dr.	Adjusted Trial Balance Cr.	Income Statement Dr.	Income Statement Cr.	Balance Sheet Dr.	Balance Sheet Cr.
Cash	37,950				37,950					
Accounts Receivable	5,500				5,500					
Merchandise										
Inventory	8,100		(b) 16,350	(a) 8,100	16,350					
Store Supplies	4,335			(d) 250	4,085					
Prepaid Insurance	1,800			(c) 385	1,415					
Office Equipment	12,750				12,750					
Accum. Dep'n—										
Office Equipment		3,200		(e) 150		3,350				
Store Equipment	44,880				44,880					
Accum. Dep'n—										
Store Equipment		15,650		(e) 350		16,000				
Accounts Payable		12,800		(f) 100		12,900				
Sales Tax Payable		2,100				2,100				
Common Stock		10,000				10,000				
Retained Earnings		57,380				57,380				
Dividends	16,300				16,300					
Sales		236,700				236,700				
Sales Returns and										
Allowances	5,700				5,700					
Sales Discounts	2,100				2,100					
Purchases	161,000				161,000					
Purchase Returns and										
Allowances		5,300				5,300				
Purchase Discounts		2,750				2,750				
Freight-in	800				800					
Freight-out	880				880					
Advertising Expense	2,800				2,800					
Insurance Expense	715		(c) 385		1,100					
Salaries and Wages										
Expense	19,200				19,200					
Rent Expense	16,100				16,100					
Income Tax Expense	2,500				2,500					
Utilities Expense	2,470		(f) 100		2,570					
Totals	345,880	345,880								
Income Summary			(a) 8,100	(b) 16,350	8,100	16,350				
Supplies Expense			(d) 250		250					
Depreciation Expense			(e) 500		500					
Totals			25,685	25,685	362,830	362,830				

continued ▶

Completing the Worksheet: Adjusting System, *continued*

Step 3: Income statement Columns

■ **Net sales**

This consists of the accounts:
- Sales
- Sales Returns and Allowances
- Sales Discounts

Notice that Sales Returns and Allowances and Sales Discounts have debit balances because they are contra Sales accounts that offset Sales.

■ **Cost of goods sold**

This consists of the accounts:
- Purchases
- Purchase Returns and Allowances
- Purchased Discounts
- Freight-in
- The beginning and ending inventory balances in Income Summary

Notice that Purchase Returns and Allowances and Purchase Discounts have credit balances because they are contra Purchases accounts that offset Purchases.

Completing the Worksheet: Adjusting System, *continued*

Account Titles	Trial Balance Dr.	Trial Balance Cr.	Adjustments Dr.	Adjustments Cr.	Adjusted Trial Balance Dr.	Adjusted Trial Balance Cr.	Income Statement Dr.	Income Statement Cr.	Balance Sheet Dr.	Balance Sheet Cr.
Cash	37,950				37,950					
Accounts Receivable	5,500				5,500					
Merchandise Inventory	8,100		(b) 16,350	(a) 8,100	16,350					
Store Supplies	4,335			(d) 250	4,085					
Prepaid Insurance	1,800			(c) 385	1,415					
Office Equipment	12,750				12,750					
Accum. Dep'n—Office Equipment		3,200		(e) 150		3,350				
Store Equipment	44,880				44,880					
Accum. Dep'n—Store Equipment		15,650		(e) 350		16,000				
Accounts Payable		12,800		(f) 100		12,900				
Sales Tax Payable		2,100				2,100				
Common Stock		10,000				10,000				
Retained Earnings		57,380				57,380				
Dividends	16,300				16,300					
Sales		236,700				236,700		236,700		
Sales Returns and Allowances	5,700				5,700		5,700			
Sales Discounts	2,100				2,100		2,100			
Purchases	161,000				161,000		161,000			
Purchase Returns and Allowances		5,300				5,300		5,300		
Purchase Discounts		2,750				2,750		2,750		
Freight-in	800				800		800			
Freight-out	880				880					
Advertising Expense	2,800				2,800					
Insurance Expense	715		(c) 385		1,100					
Salaries and Wages Expense	19,200				19,200					
Rent Expense	16,100				16,100					
Income Tax Expense	2,500				2,500					
Utilities Expense	2,470		(f) 100		2,570					
Totals	345,880	345,880								
Income Summary			(a) 8,100	(a) 16,350	8,100	16,350	8,100	16,350		
Supplies Expense			(d) 250		250					
Depreciation Expense			(e) 500		500					
Totals			25,685	25,685	362,830	362,830				

continued ▶

Completing the Worksheet: Adjusting System, *continued*

*Location on the
Income Statement*

The example below shows where net sales and cost of goods sold accounts appear on the income statement, after it is prepared from the completed worksheet. On the worksheet, the net sales and cost of goods sold amounts are shown within dashed lines.

Queensborough Patio Mart, Inc.
Income Statement
For the Year Ended December 31, 2017

Sales revenue			$236,700
Less: Sales returns and allowances		$5,700	
Sales discounts		2,100	7,800
Net sales revenue			228,900
Cost of goods sold			
Inventory, January 1		8,100	
Purchases	$161,000		
Less: Purchase returns and allowances	$5,300		
Purchase discounts	2,750	8,050	
Net purchases		152,950	
Add: Freight-in		800	
Cost of goods purchased		153,750	
Cost of goods available for sale		161,850	
Inventory, December 31		16,350	
Cost of goods sold			145,500
Gross profit			83,400
Operating expenses		$$$	
		$$$	
		$$$	
		$$$	
		$$$	
		$$$	$$$
Income before tax			$$$
Income tax expense			$$
Net income			$$$

 TIP Remember that there are no debits or credits on financial statements. The columns are only for totals and sub-totals.

Completing the Worksheet: Adjusting System, *continued*

Queensborough Patio Mart, Inc.
Worksheet
For the Year Ended December 31, 2017

Account Titles	Trial Balance Dr.	Trial Balance Cr.	Adjustments Dr.	Adjustments Cr.	Adjusted Trial Balance Dr.	Adjusted Trial Balance Cr.	Income Statement Dr.	Income Statement Cr.	Balance Sheet Dr.	Balance Sheet Cr.
Cash	37,950				37,950				37,950	
Accounts Receivable	5,500				5,500				5,500	
Merchandise Inventory	8,100		(b) 16,350	(a) 8,100	16,350				16,350	
Store Supplies	4,335			(d) 250	4,085				4,085	
Prepaid Insurance	1,800			(c) 385	1,415				1,415	
Office Equipment	12,750				12,750				12,750	
Accum. Dep'n.—Office Equip.		3,200		(e) 150		3,350				3,350
Store Equipment	44,880				44,880				44,880	
Accum. Dep'n.—Store Equipment		15,650		(e) 350		16,000				16,000
Accounts Payable		12,800		(f) 100		12,900				12,900
Sales Tax Payable		2,100				2,100				2,100
Common Stock		10,000				10,000				10,000
Retained Earnings		57,380				57,380				57,380
Dividends	16,300				16,300				16,300	
Sales		236,700				236,700		236,700		
Sales Returns and Allowances	5,700				5,700		5,700			
Sales Discounts	2,100				2,100		2,100			
Purchases	161,000				161,000		161,000			
Purchase Returns and Allowances		5,300				5,300		5,300		
Purchase Discounts		2,750				2,750		2,750		
Freight-in	800				800		800			
Freight-out	880				880		880			
Advertising Expense	2,800				2,800		2,800			
Insurance Expense	715		(c) 385		1,100		1,100			
Salaries and Wages Expense	19,200				19,200		19,200			
Rent Expense	16,100				16,100		16,100			
Income Tax Expense	2,500				2,500		2,500			
Utilities Expense	2,470		(f) 100		2,570		2,570			
Income Summary			(a) 8,100	(a) 16,350	8,100	16,350	8,100	16,350		
Supplies Expense			(d) 250		250		250			
Depreciation Expense			(e) 500		500		500			
Totals	345,880	345,880	25,685	25,685	362,830	362,830	223,600	261,100	139,230	101,730
Net Income							37,500			37,500
Totals							261,100	261,100	139,230	139,230

Financial Statements

Overview

The financial statements are prepared from the completed worksheet. The completed worksheet is shown on page 407. Financial statements are on pages 392–393. (If you also reviewed the closing method, you will see that both methods, result in exactly the same financial statements.)

Other Revenues and Expenses

Sometimes a business has other revenues and gains and other expenses and losses that are not part of the operating activities needed to produce a service or product. These "other" or nonoperating items would not be expected to be part of normal operations, but rather are incidental to being in business.

If they are material, "other" items must be shown separately on the income statement, and never "buried" inside of the operating expense numbers.

Examples

There is no single list of items—judgment is required to decide if an item should be classified as "other." However, here are some typical examples:

Other revenues and gains
- Interest revenue
- Rental revenue (main business not rental)
- Gain on sale of equipment

Other expenses and losses
- Interest expense
- Lawsuit losses
- Loss on sale of equipment

How to Show

For an example of how to show these "other" items on the income statement, refer to the example on page 394.

Single-Step Income Statement

An alternative to the multiple-step income statement is the single-step income statement. For an example of the single-step statement, turn to page 395.

Recording Adjusting and Closing Entries: Adjusting System

Adjusting Entries Procedure

The adjusting entries are simply copied from the worksheet adjusting entries columns and recorded into the general journal. The example on page 409 shows the entries that come from the Queensborough Patio Mart worksheet.

Recording Adjusting and Closing Entries: Adjusting System, *continued*

GENERAL JOURNAL				J43
Date	Account Titles and Explanation	Post. Ref.	Debit	Credit
2017				
Dec.	ADJUSTING ENTRIES			
	(A)			
31	Income Summary		8,100	
	Merchandise Inventory			8,100
	(B)			
31	Merchandise Inventory		16,350	
	Income Summary			16,350
	(C)			
31	Depreciation Expense		500	
	Accumulated Depreciation—Office Equipment			150
	Accumulated Depreciation—Store Equipment			350
	To record one year of depreciation expense			
	(D)			
31	Supplies Expense		250	
	Store Supplies			250
	To adjust to actual balance			
	(E)			
31	Insurance Expense		385	
	Prepaid Insurance			385
	To record the expiration of Prepaid Insurance			
	(F)			
31	Utilities Expense		100	
	Accounts Payable			100
	To accrue utilities expense			

Closing Entries Source

In the worksheet, the income statement columns and the balance in drawing account are the sources for the closing entries.

Closing Entries Procedure

The table on page 410 shows you the steps in the closing entries procedure.

continued ▶

Recording Adjusting and Closing Entries: Adjusting System, *continued*

Step	Action
1	Close accounts that increase net income.
	In the income statement columns of the worksheet, all accounts (except Income Summary) with credit balances are closed by debiting them in the general journal. The total of all the debits is recorded as a credit to Income Summary.
2	Close accounts that decrease net income.
	In the income statement columns of the worksheet, all accounts (except Income Summary) with debit balances are closed by crediting them in the general journal. The total of all the credits is recorded as a debit to Income Summary.
3	Calculate the balance of the Income Summary account and close this into the Retained Earnings account.
	A credit balance in Income Summary is closed by debit- ing Income Summary and crediting Retained Earnings. A debit balance in Income Summary is closed with the opposite entry.
4	Close the dividends account into the Retained Earnings account. Credit the dividends account and debit the Retained Earnings account.

Example of Step 1

The general journal entry below illustrates Step 1.

GENERAL JOURNAL					J44
Date	Account Titles and Explanation	Post. Ref.	Debit		Credit
2017					
Dec. 31	CLOSING ENTRIES				
	Sales		236,700		
	Purchase Returns and Allowances		5,300		
	Purchase Discounts		2,750		
	Income Summary				244,750
	To close credit balance temporary accounts				

Do not include the credit to Income Summary that was recorded as an adjusting entry.

Recording Adjusting and Closing Entries: Adjusting System, *continued*

Example of Step 2

The general journal entry below illustrates Step 2.

31	Income Summary		215,500		
	Sales Returns and Allowances				5,700
	Sales Discounts				2,100
	Purchases				161,000
	Freight-in				800
	Freight-out				880
	Advertising Expense				2,800
	Insurance Expense				1,100
	Salaries and Wages Expense				19,200
	Rent Expense				16,100
	Income Tax Expense				2,500
	Utilities Expense				2,570
	Supplies Expense				250
	Depreciation Expense				500
	To close debit balance temporary accounts				

> Do not include the debit to Income Summary that was recorded as an adjusting entry.

Example of Step 3

The general journal entry below shows the credit balance of $37,500 in Income Summary closed by a debit to Income Summary and a credit to owner's capital. This represents the net income from the current period operations.

Note: The $37,500 is the difference between the two credits of $16,350 and $244,750 to Income Summary and the two debits of $8,100 and $215,500 to Income Summary.

> This must be the same as the net income on the worksheet.

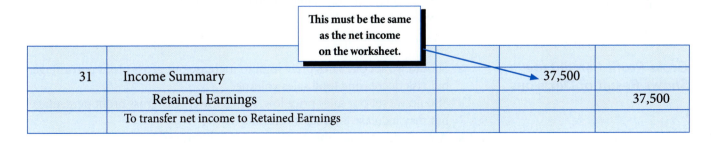

31	Income Summary			37,500	
	Retained Earnings				37,500
	To transfer net income to Retained Earnings				

continued ▶

Recording Adjusting and Closing Entries: Adjusting System, *continued*

Example of Step 4

The general journal entry below closes the drawing account into the owner's capital account. This is the decrease in Retained Earnings resulting from distribution of assets—usually cash—for stockholders' personal use.

31	Retained Earnings		16,300	
	Dividends			16,300
	To close the drwaing into the capital account			

The Gross Profit Percentage

Overview

For all merchants, gross profit as a percentage of net sales is an extremely important number. This calculation shows what portion of every sales dollar is left over to cover expenses and provide a profit after the cost of the merchandise is paid.

Definition

Gross profit percentage is gross profit divided by net sales.

Example

Refer to the Queensboro Patio Mart multiple-step income statement. The gross profit percentage is $83,400/$228,900 = 36.4\%$. This means that 36.4% of net sales revenue, or about 36.4 cents of every net sales dollar, is left over after subtracting the cost of goods sold expense.

Why It Is So Important

Several key factors make the gross profit percentage very important.

- The gross profit percentage is a number that shows the result of making several very important business decisions.
- The gross profit percentage has a major effect on net income.
- The gross percentage makes it possible to fairly compare different businesses of different sizes.

Gross Profit Percentage Shows Result of Decisions

- Should we set our sales price high to increase our gross profit percentage, but risk decreasing total sales volume?
- Should we set our sales price low, which lowers the gross profit percentage but may increase total sales volume?
- Are we minimizing the cost of our merchandise?
- If merchandise is too cheap, will we lose customers and reduce net sales?

The Gross Profit Percentage, *continued*

Comparison of Businesses

Suppose we want to compare the efficiency of operations of Big Company and Small Company. Here is the information for each company:

- Net sales: Big Company, $4,880,500; Small Company, $375,000
- Gross profit: Big Company, $1,952,200; Small Company, $168,750

Although the dollar amounts are very different:

- The gross profit efficiency of Big Company is less than Small Company. Big Company's gross profit is 40%, Small Company's gross profit is 45%. Small Company has more gross profit per dollar of sales.
- Big Company may have more total sales and total gross profit because it has set lower sales prices.

QUICK REVIEW

To complete the period-end procedures:

- If a worksheet is used, prepare it using either the closing or adjusting method.

- The major difference in financial statements for a merchandising company and that of a service company is the merchandising company income statement, which includes cost of goods sold. The balance sheet also shows Merchandise Inventory as a current asset.

- The basic procedure for adjusting and closing entries remains the same as for a service company, except that there are more accounts. Merchandise Inventory is always part of either adjusting or closing, depending on the method used.

- The gross profit percentage is a key measurement of profitability.

VOCABULARY

Gross profit percentage: gross profit divided by net sales (page 412)

Multiple-step income statement: a detailed income statement format that shows the several steps used to calculate net income (page 392)

Nonoperating: a phrase that refers to revenues and gains or expenses and losses that do not occur as part of normal businesses operations to create and sell goods and services (page 394)

Operating income: when there are nonoperating items, this is the gross profit minus operating expenses (page 394)

Single-step income statement: an income statement format in which net income can always be calculated in one step (page 395)

Solutions are in the disk at the back of the book and at: www.worthyjames.com

PRACTICE
Learning Goal 12

Learning Goal 12 is about the period-end procedures of the periodic inventory method. Use these questions and problems to practice what you have learned about these period-end procedures.

Multiple Choice
Select the best answer.

1. In the worksheet, the correct balance of Purchases should appear as:
    a. a debit balance in the income statement column.
    b. a credit balance in the income statement column.
    c. a debit balance in the balance sheet column.
    d. a credit balance in the balance sheet column.

2. In the worksheet, the correct balance of Purchases discounts should appear as:
    a. a debit balance in the income statement column.
    b. a credit balance in the income statement column.
    c. a debit balance in the balance sheet column.
    d. a credit balance in the balance sheet column.

3. In the worksheet, the correct balance of Sales Returns and Allowances should appear as:
    a. a debit balance in the income statement column.
    b. a credit balance in the income statement column.
    c. a debit balance in the balance sheet column.
    d. a credit balance in the balance sheet column.

4. (If you studied the adjusting system) The beginning and ending inventory will appear in the worksheet in the:
    a. income statement column showing as a debit to Inventory for the beginning inventory and a credit to Inventory for the ending inventory.
    b. balance sheet column showing as a debit to Inventory for the beginning inventory and a credit to Inventory for the ending inventory.
    c. income statement column showing as a debit to Inventory for the ending inventory and a credit to Inventory for the beginning inventory.
    d. balance sheet column showing as a debit to Inventory for the ending inventory and a credit to Inventory for the beginning inventory.

5. (If you studied the closing system) The merchandise inventory appears in the worksheet in the:
    a. income statement column showing as a debit to Inventory for the beginning inventory and the balance sheet column as a credit to Inventory for the ending inventory.
    b. income statement column showing as a credit to Inventory for the ending inventory and the balance sheet column as a debit to Inventory for the ending inventory.
    c. income statement column showing as a debit to Inventory for the ending inventory and a credit to Inventory for the beginning inventory.
    d. balance sheet column showing as a debit to Inventory for the ending inventory and a credit to Inventory for the beginning inventory.

6. On a single-step income statement:
    a. interest expense is "other" expense, and cost of goods sold is an operating expense.
    b. interest expense is an operating expense, and cost of goods sold is an operating expense.
    c. interest expense is an "other" expense, and cost of goods sold is calculated in several steps.
    d. none of the above.

7. Which of the following would *not* be debited in a closing entry using the closing system?
   a. Sales Returns and Allowances
   b. Purchase Returns and Allowances
   c. Ending Inventory
   d. Purchase Discounts

8. On a multiple-step income statement:
   a. columns to the left are for debits, and columns to the right are for credits.
   b. only the far left and far right columns are for debits and credits.
   c. columns are used only to calculate totals and subtotals; debits and credits should never appear.
   d. any column can be designated as a debit or credit.

9. On a worksheet for a company using the periodic method:
   a. cost of goods sold appears as a single amount in the income statement column.
   b. cost of goods sold appears as a single amount in the balance sheet column.
   c. cost of goods sold cannot be identified.
   d. cost of goods sold can be identified using individual accounts in the income statement column.

10. If beginning inventory was $3,000 less than ending inventory and net purchases (including freight costs) are $25,000, then cost of goods sold is:
    a. $22,000.
    b. $25,000.
    c. $28,000.
    d. $31,000.

11. If cost of goods sold is $50,000 and ending inventory is $5,000 less than beginning inventory, then net purchases must have been:
    a. $60,000.
    b. $55,000.
    c. $50,000.
    d. $45,000.

12. In the Income Summary account the difference between total debits and total credits should be:
    a. the same number that on the worksheet makes the income statement columns balance.
    b. the same number that on the worksheet makes balance sheet columns balance.
    c. should be the same number as the net income on the income statement.
    d. all of the above.

13. The following information is presented on the Rockland Corporation multiple-step income statement: Net sales, $539,600; Cost of goods sold, $297,475; Net income, $48,650. The gross profit percentage is:
    a. 44.9%.
    b. 9%.
    c. 18.9%.
    d. 20%.

14. An income statement shows the following: Sales $310,000; selling expenses $24,000; cost of goods sold $200,000; interest expense $10,000; sales returns and allowances, $5,000; and general expenses $30,000. How much is operating income?

PRACTICE   Learning Goal 12, continued

Solutions are in the disk at the back of the book and at: www.worthyjames.com

Discussion Questions and Brief Exercises

1. Describe how the balance of net sales is calculated.

2. Use the following amounts to prepare a cost of goods sold section of a multiple-step income statement:

Purchases	$27,000	Purchase returns & allowances	$ 500
Beginning inventory	4,500	Ending inventory	6,100
Purchases discounts	1,800	Freight-in	1,200

3. Explain the meaning of the following terms: a) gross profit, b) operating income, c) net income

4. If a company sold supplies, would this be sales revenue or part of "other revenues and gains"?

5. Beginning merchandise inventory is $15,000 and ending inventory is $12,000.
   a) If you studied the adjustments method, describe how these would appear in a worksheet.
   b) If you studied the closing method, describe how these would appear in a worksheet.

6. Suppose that the net sales account balance is $450,000 and cost of goods sold balance is $288,000. How is the gross profit percentage calculated? Explain two important ways that it is used.

7. Explain the difference between a single-step and a multiple-step income statement.

8. If beginning inventory was $175,000, ending inventory was $186,000, and cost of goods sold was $950,000, what was the net amount of purchases during the year?

9. Indicate which account balances below would be closed with a debit entry or a credit entry:

Sales	Freight-in	Purchases Discounts	Sales Discounts
Purchases	Beginning Inventory	Ending Inventory	Purchase Returns/Allowances

10. How could a merchant increase the gross profit percentage? When would this be a good idea? When would this not be a good idea?

Reinforcement Problems

LG 12-1. Prepare income statements and closing entries. The table below presents final account balance information of Kutztown, Inc. for the year ended December 31, 2017.

Instructions: On separate pages, prepare the items for a, b, and c below. The corporation tax rate is 30% of income before tax.

a. A multiple-step income statement, grouping operating expenses into the categories of either selling expenses or administrative expenses. The corporation tax rate is 30% of income before tax.
b. A single-step income statement, grouping operating expenses into the categories of either selling expenses or administrative expenses. The corporation tax rate is 30% of income before tax.
c. The closing entries. You can use either the closing system on the adjusting system.

Beginning Inventory	$15,350	Rent Expense	$26,000	Merchandise Purchases	$109,900
Ending Inventory	$9,500	Utilities Expense	$4,850	Purchase Discounts	$3,100
Purchase Returns and Allowances	$700	Sales Salaries Expense	$55,500	Sales Returns and Allowances	$2,550
Sales	$294,000	Freight-in	$920	Sales Discounts	$3,900
Interest Earned	$300	Freight-out	$370	Interest Expense	$1,700
Insurance Expense	$5,000	Advertising	$3,500	Depreciation Expense	$7,500

LG 12-2. **Complete worksheet, prepare multi-step and single-step income statements, prepare closing entry.**

Instructions:

a. Complete the worksheet below using the closing system if you studied the closing system. Complete the worksheet using the adjusting system if you studied the adjusting system. Use a formatted worksheet available in the disk at the back of the book, or at worthyjames.com (student info.).

b. Prepare a multiple-step income statement and a single-step income statement.

c. Briefly describe the purpose and effect of each adjusting entry on the worksheet.

d. Prepare closing entries. The December 31 merchandise inventory is $11,500.

Northern Colorado Company, Inc.											
Worksheet											
For the Year Ended December 31, 2017											
	Trial Balance		Adjustments		Adjusted Trial Balance		Income Statement		Balance Sheet		
Account Titles	Dr.	Cr.	Dr.	Cr.	Dr.	Cr.	Dr.	Cr.	Dr.	Cr.	
Cash	95,160										
Accounts Receivable	15,200										
Merchandise Inventory	22,100										
Store Supplies	1,100			(b) 700							
Prepaid Insurance	2,950			(c) 2,000							
Office Equipment	15,500										
Accum. Dep'n—Office Equipment		10,250		(a) 500							
Store Equipment	127,800										
Accum. Dep'n—Store Equipment		127,800									
Accounts Payable		51,300									
Sales Tax Payable		750									
Common Stock		10,000									
Retained Earnings		57,900									
Dividends	25,000										
Sales		510,500									
Sales Returns and Allowances	2,500										
Sales Discounts	3,250										
Merchandise Purchases	345,000										
Purchase Discounts		800									
Purchase Returns and Allowances		900									
Freight-in	1,100										
Insurance Expense	1,590		(c) 2,000								
Admin. Salaries and Wages	85,500										
Rent Expense	18,500										
Income Tax Expense	5,500										
Utilities Expense	2,450										
Supplies Expense			(b) 700								
Depreciation Expense			(a) 500								
Totals	770,200	770,200									

(Reminder: Print a copy of this worksheet from the disk at the back of the book to complete the problem.)

LG 12-3. Complete the worksheet, prepare financial statements, analyze adjustments, prepare closing entry.

Instructions:

a. Complete the worksheet on page 419 using either the closing procedure for inventory or the adjusting procedure, depending on which procedure you studied. Use the formatted worksheet template that is available for this problem in the Accounting Paper section in the disk at the back of the book, or at worthyjames.com (student info.).

b. Prepare a multiple-step and a single-step income statement, a statement of retained earnings, and a report form classified balance sheet.

c. Briefly describe the purpose and the effect of each adjusting entry. Then prepare the closing entries for either the closing or adjusting method. For journal paper, use the template in the disk at the back of the book.

d. Using the classified balance sheet, compare the current assets to the current liabilities. Look at the components of these classifications. How are the most liquid current assets likely to be affected in July?

LG 12-3, *continued*

Account Titles	Trial Balance		Adjustments		Adjusted Trial Balance		Income Statement		Balance Sheet	
	Dr.	Cr.	Dr.	Cr.	Dr.	Cr.	Dr.	Cr.	Dr.	Cr.
Cash	11,300									
Short-Term Investments	28,250									
Accounts Receivable	26,700		(a) 2,750							
Merchandise Inventory	34,020									
Office Supplies	920									
Office Equipment	25,800									
Accum. Dep'n—										
Office Equipment		6,700		(b) 150						
Store Equipment	314,500									
Accum. Dep'n.—										
Store Equipment		91,500		(b) 1,400						
Wages Payable				(d) 3,200						
Accounts Payable		34,200								
Notes Payable (10 year)		135,000								
Common Stock		15,000								
Retained Earnings		105,260								
Dividends	4,500									
Sales		378,500		(a) 2,750						
Sales Returns and Allow.	8,150									
Sales Discounts	4,200									
Purchases	258,000									
Purchase Discounts		5,720								
Purchase Ret. & Allow.		2,500								
Freight-in	1,850									
Admin. Wages Expense	21,500		(d) 2,000							
Sales Wages Expense	17,000		(d) 1,200							
Income Tax Expense	3,500									
Insurance Expense	2,150									
Rent Expense	4,000									
Advertising Expense	3,880									
Freight-out	2,960									
Utilities Expense	3,200									
Depreciation Expense—										
Office Equipment			(b) 150							
Depreciation Expense—										
Store Equipment			(b) 1,400							
Interest Expense			(c) 1,450							
Interest Payable				(c) 1,450						
Rental income		2,000								
Totals	776,380	776,380								

Sioux City Enterprises — Worksheet — For the Month Ended June 30, 2017

PRACTICE   Learning Goal 12, continued

LG 12-3, *continued*

Other information:

a. There were no investments during the period.

b. The amount of the long-term note payable that is payable within the year is $3,200.

c. The ending merchandise inventory balance is $19,650.

LG 12-4. Journalize adjusting and closing entries. The information below shows unadjusted account balances and the adjustments information needed to adjust the accounts

Instructions: Journalize the adjusting and closing entries for the month ended June 30. Use either the adjusting system or the closing system. Explanations are not required. For journal paper, use the template in the disk at the back of the book.

Merchandise Inventory, June 1	$25,420	Store Equipment	$115,000
Rent Expense	4,500	Sales Revenue	204,200
Prepaid Insurance Expense	3,600	Sales Discounts	3,500
Wages Expense	12,100	Freight-out Expense	700
Sales Returns and Allowances	1,700	Cash	43,500
Accumulated Depreciation—Store		Utilities Expense	1,600
Equipment	36,500	Unearned Revenue	4,500
Purchase Discounts	2,950	Purchases	114,700
Accounts Payable	21,390	Purchase Returns and Allowances	3,400
Office Supplies	1,100	Advertising Expense	1,900
Merchandise Inventory, June 30	17,800	Dividends	5,000
Interest Revenue	300	Prepaid Travel Expense	580
Freight-in Expense	560	Accounts Receivable	36,200
Retained Earnings	197,300	Notes Receivable	45,000
Common Stock	15,000		

Adjustments Information:

a. A count of office shows $500 of supplies still on hand at June 30.

b. Employee wages earned but not paid at June 30 are $2,600.

c. Depreciation expense for the month is $650.

LG 12-5. Identify cost of goods sold in the worksheet.

a) Look at the cartoon on page 388. Now look at the worksheet for Queensborough Patio Mart on the next page. Can you answer the man's question by identifying where cost of goods sold is on the worksheet?

b) Explain in what part of the accounting equation the following items should be included: sales discounts, sales returns and allowances, freight-in, freight-out, purchases, purchase discounts and purchase returns and allowances.

Solutions are in the disk at the back of the book and at: www.worthyjames.com

PRACTICE   **Learning Goal 12, continued**

LG 12-6. Analyze adjustments, prepare closing entries. The T accounts that you see below show account balances after all necessary adjusting entries have been posted into the accounts at December 31 year end. All account balances before the adjustments were recorded into the accounts and are shown as normal beginning balances. All adjusting entries are identified with letters. Using the T accounts:

a. Identify the purpose and the effect of each adjusting entry.
b. Prepare the closing general journal entries, using the closing method. The ending merchandise inventory balance is $64,000. For journal paper, use the template in the disk at the back of the book, or worthyjames.com (student info.).
c. Does the business have net income or net loss? How do you know?

Cash		Accounts Receivable		Merchandise Inventory		Prepaid Rent		Office Supplies	
...	...	...	...	...	...	...	...	...	...
90,200		12,500		59,800		3,500		750	
		(b) 1,500					(a) 2,500		(d) 350
		14,000				1,000		400	

Accounts Payable		Unearned Revenue		Common Stock		Retained Earnings		Dividends	
...	...	...	...	...	...	...	...	...	...
	14,900		7,700		16,000		71,300	4,700	
	(e) 550	(c) 6,400							
	15,450		1,300						

Sales		Sales Returns and Allowances		Sales Discounts		Purchases		Purchase Returns and Allowances	
...	...	...	...	...	...	...	...	...	...
	260,500	1,500		1,200		188,900			4,100
	(b) 1,500								
	(c) 6,400								
	268,400								

Purchase Discounts		Freight-in Expense		Rent Expense		Wages Expense		Supplies Expense	
...	...	...	...	...	...	...	...	...	...
	3,600	1,400				13,200		450	
		(e) 550		(a) 2,500				(d) 350	
		1,950						800	

PRACTICE Learning Goal 12, continued

Solutions are in the disk at the back of the book and at: www.worthyjames.com

LG 12-7. Fill in missing amounts, prepare income statement.

Instructions:

a. For each letter shown below, calculate the missing amount.
b. Prepare a multiple-step corporate income statement for Company #3. Assume that operating expenses were $38,500 and the statement is for the year ended June 30, 2017. Show the steps of the cost of goods sold calculation on the income statement. Omit taxes.
c. Compare the profitability of each company.

Company	Net Sales	Beginning Inventory	Net Purchases	Ending Inventory	Cost of Goods Sold	Gross Profit	Gross Profit%
#1	$215,300	$25,700	a	$31,280	b	$63,450	i
#2	c	50,410	$281,200	15,300	d	51,540	j
#3	150,500	e	98,320	17,600	$100,330	f	k
#4	g	22,150	125,800	h	135,150	57,900	l

Instructor-Assigned Problems

If you are using this book in a class, these review problems may be assigned by your instructor for homework, group assignments, class work, or other activities. Only your instructor has the solutions.

IA 12-1. Prepare Closing Entries. Accounts and their June 30 year-end adjusted balances are listed below in random order.

Instructions: Prepare the closing entry using either the adjusting or closing method. Does the business have a net income or net loss? How much?

Inventory, June 30	$64,800	Retained Earnings	$112,940
Sales Returns and Allowances	1,100	Purchase Discounts	2,410
Accounts Payable	39,420	Sales	364,240
Rent Expense	31,000	Sales Tax Payable	6,640
Wages Expense	59,300	Interest Revenue	210
Equipment	146,250	Inventory, July 1	66,500
Accumulated Depreciation-Equi.	38,100	Advertising Expense	37,280
Accounts Receivable	41,220	Sales Discounts	2,790
Depreciation Expense	14,600	Freight-in	4,730
Prepaid Travel Expense	5,500	Supplies Expense	540
Freight-out	2,700	Wages Expense	61,370
Dividends	10,000	Purchases	139,450
		Income Tax Expense	2,000

Solutions are in the disk at the back of the book and at: www.worthyjames.com

PRACTICE   **Learning Goal 12, continued**

IA 12-2. Prepare financial statements and closing entries. The December 31, 2017 adjusted account balances of Tappan Company are shown below (in random order). The inventory balance is the correct year-end balance. The retained earnings account balance is the January 1 balance before completing the closing entries.

a. Prepare multiple-step and single-step income statements for the year ended December 31, 2017.
b. Prepare the December 31, 2017 classified balance sheet.
c. Prepare the closing entries for the year ended December 31, 2017 using either the adjusting or closing method.

Office Supplies	$1,800	Sales Discounts	$6,400
Purchase Discounts	6,950	Accounts Receivable	19,300
Accounts Payable	27,390	Notes Payable (5 years)	117,000
Gain on Sale of Equipment	25,200	Unearned Revenue	3,000
Insurance Expense	2,910	Dividends	52,500
Cash	57,240	Purchases	321,500
Accum. Dep'n—Office Equipment	10,500	Short-Term Investments	25,750
Sales Revenue	567,200	Sales Returns and Allow.	9,870
Accum. Dep'n.—Store Equipment	84,500	Merchandise Inventory	52,600
Freight-out	4,950	Rent Expense	18,500
Office Equipment	35,500	Retained Earnings	165,590
Interest Expense	12,580	Advertising Expense	7,950
Supplies Expense	3,100	Store Equipment	295,550
Salaries and Wages Expense	45,700	Freight-in	1,150
Utilities Expense	5,200	Depreciation Expense	5,670
Purchase Returns and Allowances	5,880	Rental Revenue	3,600
Income Tax Expense	52,390	Common Stock	10,000

Other information

- The January 1 merchandise inventory balance was $41,300.
- 30% of wages are for sales employees.
- 20% of supplies used are for sales department activities.
- A small amount of extra office space is rented to another company.

IA 12-3. Complete a worksheet; prepare financial statements and adjusting entries and closing entries
Shown below is the trial balance for Palomar Enterprises, Inc. for the year ending December 31, 2017.

Instructions:

a. Complete the worksheet, using either the closing or adjusting method.
b. Prepare a multiple-step income statement, statement of retained earnings, and a report form classified balance sheet.
c. Record the adjusting entries.
d. Record the closing entries.
e. Describe the purpose of each adjusting entry.

Solutions are in the disk at the back of the book and at: www.worthyjames.com

PRACTICE   Learning Goal 12, continued

IA 12-3. *continued*

Use either a blank worksheet or the worksheet template for IA12-3 from the disk at the back of the book or at www.worthyjames.com (student info.).

Account Titles	Trial Balance Dr.	Trial Balance Cr.	Adjustments Dr.	Adjustments Cr.
Cash	56,750			
Short-term Investments	10,500			
Accounts Receivable	21,320			
Merchandise Inventory	57,790			
Supplies	1,940			d) 550
Prepaid Travel	1,500			
Long-term Investments	20,100			
Office Equipment	19,300			
Accum. Dep'n.—Office Equip.		9,650		c) 3,860
Trademark	10,000			
Wages Payable		4,500		
Accounts Payable		29,680		a) 550
Unearned Revenue		3,500	b) 700	
Notes Payable (3 years)		17,000		
Common Stock		14,000		
Retained Earnings		119,150		
Dividends	7,500			
Sales		580,200		b) 700
Sales Returns and Allow.	4,500			
Sales Discounts	8,800			
Purchases	367,090			
Purchase Returns and Allow.		3,800		
Purchase Discounts		7,100		
Freight-Out	7,580		a) 550	
Advertising Expense	40,750			
Insurance Expense	11,200			
Salaries/Wages Expense	99,700			
Utilities Expense	14,360			
Rent Expense	37,200			
Interest Expense	1,700			
Gain on Sale: Equipment		11,000		
Total	799,580	799,580		
Depreciation Expense			c) 3,860	
Supplies Expense			d) 550	
Totals			5,660	5,660

PRACTICE Learning Goal 12, continued

Solutions are in the disk at the back of the book and at: www.worthyjames.com

Other information:

a. $3,400 of the long-term debt principal is due within the next year.
b. Supplies expense is equally allocated between selling and administrative activities.
c. January 1, 2017 merchandise inventory balance is $57,790.
d. December 31, 2017 merchandise inventory balance is $46,990.

IA12-4 Fill in missing amounts; prepare income statement

Instructions:

a. For each letter shown below, calculate the missing amount.
b. Prepare a multiple-step income statement for company #2 for year ended December 31, 2017. Assume operating expenses are $120,700 and assume a 20% tax rate. Show the steps for cost of goods sold.
c. Compare the profitability of each company.

Company	Net Sales	Beginning Inventory	Net Purchases	Ending Inventory	Cost of Goods Sold	Gross Profit	Gross Profit %
#1	$308,000	$61,500	a	$416,900	b	$142,200	j
#2	605,000	c	299,200	171,100	d	e	48%
#3	f	158,300	199,400	46,900	g	170,900	k
#4	h	71,400	157,900	i	80,900	126,300	60%

INTERNET EXERCISES

Ethics—analyze cases. Go to the Carnegie Mellon University Business Ethics site at ba.tepper .cmu.edu/ethics/AA/acctmini.htm to locate the case study page, and select three mini-cases (any type) that interest you or that are suggested by your instructor. For each case:

a. Write down the case name. Read the case and do the following:
  - Identify the essential facts and identify the parties involved.
  - Identify the moral issue of a potentially wrongful act(s) that can result in a loss, injury, or damage.
  - Make a list of alternative decisions.
b. What decision would you make? Why?
c. *After* you complete part b, look at the teaching notes for the case. Do you agree or disagree with the teaching notes? After reading the notes, what would you do differently?
d. What would be the ethical meaning and practical results for you if you had looked at the teaching notes before you completed part b of this exercise?

CUMULATIVE VOCABULARY REVIEW   Part I

This is a vocabulary review for Learning Goals 10 through 12. On a separate piece of paper, match each description with the term that it describes. The answer for each term is in the right column. (Suggestion: Cover the answers in the right column as you test your vocabulary.)

Term	Description	Answers
1. Invoice price	a. Counting inventory by physical inspection	1m
2. FOB	b. The cost of merchandise that is sold	2i
3. Purchase discount	c. A reduction in the invoice amount owed to the seller without the merchandise being returned	3p
4. Merchandise	d. Another term for gross profit	4j
5. Operating cycle	e. A bill sent from the seller of merchandise to the buyer	5u
6. Beginning inventory	f. Determining the cost of ending inventory and the cost of goods sold at intervals by counting the inventory	6r
7. Operating income	g. An income statement format in which net income can always be calcu- lated in one step	7o
8. Cost of goods sold	h. The manner of payment agreed upon between buyer and seller	8b
9. Gross method	i. The point at which ownership often transfers from seller to buyer; "free on board" point	9w
10. Physical inventory	j. Goods that a merchandising business sells to customers	10a
11. Cash discount	k. Revenues and gains or expenses and losses that are not considered to be part of business operations	11x
12. Sales invoice	l. The gross cost of merchandise to the buyer	12e
13. Trade discount	m. The gross amount owed by a buyer (before discounts.	13s
14. Allowance	n. Another term for freight-in	14c
15. Gross margin	o. When there are nonoperating items, gross profit minus operating expenses	15d
16. Retail	p. A discount received by buyer who makes a payment to the seller within a specified time period	16y
17. Periodic method	q. A document indicating a debit to an account—usually sent from buyer to seller to show a debit by buyer to Accounts Payable due to the seller	17f
18. Sales tax	r. Cost of inventory on hand at the start of an accounting period	18z
19. Single-step income statement	s. A percentage reduction in the list price of merchandise	19g
20. Nonoperating	t. Shipping cost paid by buyer for merchandise delivery to buyer	20k
21. Invoice price	u. The process by which the cash that is spent on operations is returned to a business as collections from customers	21l
22. Transportation-in	v. Another term for a freight bill	22n
23. Debit memo	w. Recording accounts payable at the invoice price	23q
24. Freight-in	x. Another name for purchase discount	24t
25. Credit terms	y. Income Statement and Period-End Procedures: Closing System:	25h
26. Bill of lading	z. Income Statement and Period-End Procedures: Adjusting System:	26v

CUMULATIVE VOCABULARY REVIEW   Part II

Term	Description	Answers
1. Net sales	a. Another term for cost of goods sold	1g
2. Shipping charges	b. A business that sells goods to customers who are other merchants or manufacturers	2r
3. Inventory shrinkage	c. A means of determining ending inventory and cost of goods sold by continuously recording merchandise purchases and sales	3n
4. Multiple-step	d. The excess of net sales revenue over cost of goods sold	4l
5. Cost of goods available for sale	e. A document indicating a credit to an account—usually sent from seller to buyer to show a credit by seller to Accounts Receivable due from the buyer	5q
6. Discount period	f. A series of trade discounts calculated on the same sales price	6s
7. List price	g. Gross sales less sales discounts and sales returns and allowances	7t
8. Wholesale	h. The cost of merchandise on hand at the end of a period	8b
9. Cost of sales	i. Formula used for the periodic inventory method	9a
10. Perpetual inventory method	j. A contra account that records a decrease in total sales as a result of unsatisfactory merchandise sold to customers	10c
11. Gross profit	k. The cost of merchandise purchased excluding discounts or adjustments	11d
12. Credit memo	l. An income statement with a detailed format that shows the several steps used to calculate net income	12e
13. Freight-out	m. Happens when a customer pays late but also takes a discount	13p
14. Chain discount	n. A unidentified loss of inventory	14f
15. Sales returns and allowances	o. A contra account that records a decrease in purchases cost as a result of unsatisfactory merchandise purchased	15j
16. Ending inventory	p. A seller's operating expense account	16h
17. Purchase returns and allowances	q. The cost of beginning inventory plus net purchases and freight-in	17o
18. Purchases	r. The cost of shipping merchandise from seller to buyer	18k
19. BI + P − EI = C of GS	s. The days allowed by the seller for the buyer pay for merchandise and receive a discount	19i
20. Unearned discount	t. The price at which merchandise is currently offered for sale	20m

CUMULATIVE TEST   Learning Goals 10–12

Time Limit: 55 minutes

Instructions

*Select the best answer to each question. Do **not** look back in the book when taking the test. (If you need to do this, you are not ready.) After you finish the test, refer to the answers and circle the number of each question that you missed. Then go to the **Help Table** (on page 436) to identify your strong and weak knowledge areas by individual learning goal.*

Multiple Choice

1. Which of the following would be classified primarily as a merchandising operation?

	Tennis Instructor	Sporting Goods Store	Tennis Ball Manufacturer
a.	yes	no	yes
b.	yes	yes	no
c.	no	yes	no
d.	yes	no	no

2. Net sales is calculated as:
   a. sales discounts minus sales returns and allowances.
   b. sales revenue minus sales discounts.
   c. sales revenue minus sales discounts and sales returns and allowances.
   d. sales revenue minus sales discounts plus sales returns and allowances.

3. The sales tax that is added to the list price on the invoice by the seller on the seller's records will be:
   a. debited to sales tax expense.
   b. credited to sales tax payable.
   c. debited to sales discounts.
   d. credited to sales tax income.

4. On January 1, 2017, Butler Company records indicated merchandise inventory of $12,500. On December 31, 2017, the records showed merchandise inventory of $15,200. During the year, net purchases and freight-in costs totaled $285,000. The cost of goods sold during the year was:
   a. $269,800.
   b. $285,000.
   c. $287,700.
   d. $282,300.

Use the information in the table below to answer the next two questions.

Sales: $52,000	Sales returns and allowances: $4,500
Purchase discounts: $3,500	Purchase returns and allowances: $5,200
Beginning inventory: $1,000	Purchases: $31,000
Transportation-in: $700	Ending inventory: $3,000

5. Net purchases is:
   a. $24,000.
   b. $22,300.
   c. $27,500.
   d. $23,000.
6. Cost of goods available for sale is:
   a. $24,000.
   b. $22,300.
   c. $27,500.
   d. $23,000.
7. A method of accounting that records all the costs of merchandise as it is acquired but does not keep a continuous record of the merchandise as it is sold or of ending inventory, is called a:
   a. periodic inventory system.
   b. net method inventory system.
   c. perpetual inventory system.
   d. gross method inventory system.
8. The multiple-step income statement of Monaca Company contains the following:

Beginning inventory: $11,250	Total selling expense: $41,250	Purchase returns: $3,500
Purchases: $284,300	Interest expense: $1,940	Total (gross) sales: $381,200
Sales discounts: $4,150	Total administrative expense: $30,500	Ending inventory: $17,050
Purchase discounts: $1,550	Gain on sale of equipment: $1,000	Sales returns and allowances: $1,900

   The multiple-step income statement will show:
   a. operating income of $101,700.
   b. net income of $29,950.
   c. operating income of $71,750.
   d. net income of $29,010.
9. Gross profit (also called gross margin) would appear on the income statement of which business?
   a. furniture moving company
   b. furniture store
   c. law offices
   d. both a and b
10. If a seller in Chicago ships goods by truck to a buyer in Las Vegas and the shipping terms are "FOB destination," then the seller is allowed to record revenue when:
   a. the goods are loaded on the truck in Chicago.
   b. the order is received from the buyer.
   c. the goods are off-loaded from the truck in Las Vegas.
   d. any of the above, provided that the company policy is consistent and reasonable.

11. If a seller pays $250 of shipping charges and seller and buyer agree that buyer will not reimburse the seller for the cost of shipping, then the seller will:
    a. debit freight-out expense $250.
    b. debit accounts receivable $250.
    c. debit cost of goods sold $250.
    d. none of the above.

12. During the year 2017, Youngwood Enterprises recorded a cost of goods sold of $255,000. The accounting records also show that by December 31, the Merchandise Inventory account balance decreased by $19,000 from the January 1 balance. What was the net cost of merchandise purchases during the year?
    a. $236,000
    b. $274,000
    c. $255,000
    d. more information is needed

13. A bookkeeper incorrectly recorded a purchase return to a seller by debiting Purchase Returns and Allowances and crediting Accounts Payable. This would cause:
    a. purchase returns and allowances to be overstated.
    b. cost of goods available to be overstated.
    c. accounts payable to be understated.
    d. purchases to be overstated.

14. Merchandise that has been shipped "FOB shipping point" and is still in transit (not delivered to buyer) on the last day of the current accounting period should be included as part of the ending inventory of:
    a. the buyer.
    b. the seller.
    c. the freight company.
    d. the buyer or seller, based upon mutual agreement.

15. For a merchandising company, the main source of revenue is called · · · · ·, whereas the biggest expense is called:
    a. sales/cost of goods sold.
    b. fees earned/operating expense.
    c. gross profit/cost of goods sold.
    d. sales/operating expense.

16. On June 7, North Platte Company sold $7,500 list price of merchandise on terms of 2/10, n/30 to Scottsbluff Company. If Scottsbluff Company paid in full on June 15, the amount of net sales that North Platte Company should report is:
    a. $7,350.
    b. $7,500.
    c. $6,750.
    d. some other amount.

17. Seller Company sold $5,000 list price of merchandise on account to Buyer Company, terms 1/10, n/30. If the buyer pays for all the merchandise, regardless of whether or not payment is within the discount period or after the discount period, in both cases Seller Company will:
    a. debit Cash $5,000.
    b. debit Sales Discounts $50.
    c. credit Accounts Receivable $5,000.
    d. credit Sales $4,950.

18. If a seller collects $43,200 from accounts receivable and the amount includes sales tax, how much of the collection was for the sales tax if the sales tax rate was 8%?
    a. $3,456
    b. $1,600
    c. $3,200
    d. some other amount
19. On May 12, Hagerstown Company sold $10,000 list price of merchandise to Wor Wic Company, terms 4/10, n/30. Wor Wic made a payment of $6,000 cash on May 17 and paid the balance owing on May 28. What amount of net sales should Hagerstown Company report?
    a. $10,000
    b. $9,600
    c. $9,760
    d. some other amount
20. If cost of goods available for sale is $147,300, cost of goods sold is $101,200, and beginning inventory is $21,500, what is the amount of ending inventory?
    a. $79,700
    b. $67,600
    c. $46,100
    d. $24,600
21. On August 9, Buyer Company purchased $50,000 list price of merchandise from Seller Company, terms 1/10, n/20. Buyer Company's journal entry on August 18 to record full payment would be:

a. Accounts Payable	50,000		c. Accounts Payable	50,000	
Cash		50,000	Purchase Discounts		500
			Cash		49,500
b. Purchases	49,500		d. Accounts Payable	49,500	
Purchase Discounts	500		Purchase Discounts	500	
Cash		50,000	Cash		50,000

22. The ending inventory that is determined by physical count at the end of an accounting period appears on the balance sheet:
    a. as a current asset.
    b. with the plant and equipment assets.
    c. as a current liability.
    d. does not appear on the balance sheet.
23. If merchandise that was sold on account is later returned to the seller, the journal entry by the seller would include a
    a. credit to Sales Revenue.
    b. debit to Accounts Receivable.
    c. redit to Sales Returns and Allowances.
    d. debit to Sales Returns and Allowances.
24. The cost of goods sold is $145,000, net purchases is $153,750, and ending inventory is $16,350. Beginning inventory must have been:
    a. $88,100.
    b. $7,600.
    c. $25,100.
    d. $8,750.

25. Muncie Company purchased $20,000 list price of merchandise from Bloomington Company on September 15, with terms of 2/10, n/30. The seller prepaid the freight cost of $200 and added that amount to the invoice price. The seller also gave a 10% trade discount. On September 28, Muncie Company paid the balance due in full. What was the amount of the payment?
    a. $19,600
    b. $18,200
    c. $17,640
    d. $17,840

26. On June 10, Des Moines Company purchased $7,800 list price of merchandise from Kirkwood Company, terms 2/10, n/30, and paid the balance in full on June 19. The Des Moines journal entry to record the purchase would be:

a. Accounts Payable	7,800		c. Purchases	7,648	
Cash		7,800	Purchase Discounts		152
			Cash		7,800
b. Accounts Payable	7,800		d. Purchases	7,800	
Purchase Discounts		152	Accounts Payable		7,800
Accounts Payable		7,648			

27. Which of the following selections is *not* true when comparing a multiple-step income statement with a single-step income statement?

	Multiple-Step	Single-Step
a.	Calculates net income in several substeps.	Calculates net income in one step.
b.	Net sales is shown with "other" revenues in the same section.	Cost of goods sold is shown with operating expenses in the same section.
c.	Shows three or more subtotals.	Usually shows only two subtotals.
d.	Shows "other" (nonoperating) revenues and expenses in a separate section.	Combines "other" (nonoperating) revenues and expenses as one number.

Note: **If you studied the closing method, answer questions 28, 29, and 30. If you studied the adjusting method, answer questions 31, 32, and 33.**

28. The proper closing entries to the Income Summary account require what kind of entries to the accounts shown below?

	Inventory (for beginning)	Purchases	Inventory (for ending)
a.	Debit	Credit	Credit
b.	Credit	Credit	Debit
c.	Credit	Debit	Credit
d.	Debit	Debit	Credit

29. Which of the following shows correct closing entries?

a. Income Summary	xxx		c. Income Summary	xxx	
Purchases		xxx	Purchases		xxx
Sales Returns		xxx	Purchase Returns		xxx
Inventory (beginning)		xxx	Inventory (beginning)		xxx
Rent Expense		xxx	Rent Expense		xxx
Inventory (ending)	xxx		Inventory (ending)	xxx	
Sales	xxx		Sales	xxx	
Income Summary		xxx	Income Summary		xxx
b. Income Summary	xxx		d. Purchases	xxx	
Purchases		xxx	Inventory (beginning)	xxx	
Sales Returns		xxx	Sales	xxx	
Inventory (ending)		xxx	Sales Returns	xxx	
Rent Expense		xxx	Income Summary		xxx
Inventory (beginning)	xxx		Inventory (ending)	xxx	
Sales	xxx		Purchases	xxx	
Income Summary		xxx	Income Summary		xxx

30. In the worksheet, if beginning inventory is $3,000 and ending inventory is $5,000, which of the following worksheet column entries for the Merchandise Inventory account is correct?

	Income Statement		Balance Sheet	
a.	5,000	3,000		
b.	5,000	3,000	3,000	
c.	3,000	5,000	5,000	
d.		3,000	5,000	

31. If the beginning inventory is $3,000 and the ending inventory is $5,000, which of the following would be the correct adjusting entry?

a. Income Summary	5,000		c. Income Summary	3,000	
Inventory		5,000	Inventory		3,000
Income Summary	3,000		Inventory	5,000	
Inventory		3,000	Income Summary		5,000
b. Inventory	3,000		d. Inventory	3,000	
Income Summary		3,000	Income Summary		3,000
Income Summary	5,000		Inventory	5,000	
Inventory		5,000	Income Summary		5,000

32. Which of the following shows correct closing entries?

a. Income Summary	xxx	
Purchases		xxx
Inventory		xxx
Rent Expense		xxx
Sales	xxx	
Income Summary		xxx

c. Income Summary	xxx	
Purchases		xxx
Purchase Returns		xxx
Rent Expense		xxx
Sales	xxx	
Income Summary		xxx

b. Income Summary	xxx	
Purchases		xxx
Sales Returns		xxx
Rent Expense		xxx
Sales	xxx	
Income Summary		xxx

d. Purchases	xxx	
Sales	xxx	
Sales Returns	xxx	
Income Summary		xxx
Purchases	xxx	
Income Summary		xxx

33. When using the adjusting method to close beginning and ending inventory balances, the Income Summary account will have amounts entered that:
a. only come from the closing entries.
b. only come from the adjusting entries.
c. come from both closing entries and adjusting entries.
d. come from either the closing entries or the adjusting entries, depending on the situation.

CUMULATIVE TEST SOLUTIONS   Learning Goals 10–12

Multiple Choice

1. c

2. c

3. b

4. d Substitute in **BI** + (net **P** + **frt-in**) – **EI** = **C of GS**. Therefore, $12,500 + $285,000 – $15,200 = $282,300.

5. d Net purchases is purchases – purchase returns and allowances – purchases discounts + freight-in. Therefore, net purchases is $31,000 – $5,200 – $3,500 + $700 = $23,000.

6. a Cost of goods available for sale is net purchases + beginning inventory: $23,000 + $1,000 = $24,000.

7. a

8. d The best method is to prepare a quick, informal, multiple-step statement so you can see the amounts.

9. b Because the furniture store is the only merchandising business listed here (the others are services).

10. c Ownership title passes to the buyer at the destination, so that is when the sale can be recorded.

11. a

12. a The decrease in inventory means that purchases were not enough to satisfy the total cost of goods sold, and so they must have been less than cost of goods sold by $19,000. So $255,000 – $19,000 = $236,000. You can also visualize the formula BI + net P – EI = C of GS and visualize the EI being less than the BI.

13. b Purchase Returns and Allowances should have been credited, so it is understated. Because it is a contra (offset) account, understating purchase returns and allowances overstates net purchases and so overstates cost of goods available for sale.

14. a "FOB shipping point" means that ownership of the goods is transferred to the buyer at the shipping point, and the buyer owns the goods while they are being shipped.

15. a

16. a $7,500 × .98 = $7,350

17. c The full amount of the receivable must be removed if the merchandise is fully paid for.

18. c which is $43,200 – ($43,200/1.08) = $3,200.

19. d The correct amount is $9,750. First, the $6,000 is the discounted amount paid within the discount period. The remaining undiscounted amount of sales is $10,000 – ($6,000/.96) = $3,750. Therefore, $6,000 + $3,750 is the total net amount of the sale, which is $9,750. In effect, a $250 discount on the total sale was taken because of the early $6,000 payment, which is a net amount because it was paid within the discount period. The $6,000 is the net amount of $6,250 part of the sales price: $6,000/.96 = $6,250.

20. c This is $147,300 – $101,200.

21. c

22. a

23. d

24. b Substitute in **BI** + (net **P** + **frt-in**) – **EI** = **C of GS**. Therefore, x + $153,750 – $16,350 = $145,000.

25. b which is ($20,000 × .9) + $200 = $18,200. The discount period expired before payment.

26. d Notice that the question asks about recording the purchase, not the payment.

27. d

28. b

29. a

30. c

31. c

32. b

33. c

HELP TABLE

Identify Your Strengths and Weaknesses

The questions in this test cover the main subparts of Learning Goal 10, Learning Goal 11 and, Learning Goal 12. After you have circled the number of each question that you missed, look at the table below.

Go to the first subpart category in the table, "Compare Service and Merchandising." The second column in the table shows which questions on the test covered this topic. Look on the test to see if you circled question numbers 1, 9, or 15. How many of these did you miss? Write the number you missed in the "How Many Missed?" column. Repeat this process for each of the remaining subpart categories in the table.

If you miss *two or more questions* for any subpart category, you are too weak in that topic and you need to review. The last column shows you where to read and practice so you can improve your score in that topic.

Some subpart categories have more questions because you need to be especially well prepared in these areas. More questions means your performance must be better.

Subpart	Questions	How many missed?	Material begins on . . .
SECTION III			
Compare Service and Merchandising	1, 9, 15		page 307
Net Sales	2, 10, 16, 17, 19, 23		page 323
Shipping Charges and Sales Tax	3, 11, 18		page 337
The Cost of Goods Sold Formula	4, 12, 20, 24		page 341
Cost of Goods Available for Sale	5, 6, 13, 21, 25, 26		page 344
Ending Inventory	7, 14, 22		page 359
Period-End Procedures: Closing System	8, 27, 28, 29, 30		page 381
Period-End Procedures: Adjusting System	8, 27, 31, 32, 33		page 399

Note: In addition to the questions above, you should also practice the following:

- Prepare complete multiple-step and single-step income statements.
- Prepare complete closing entries.

Use separate sheets of paper and work problems from any text in which answers are also available to you

| LEARNING GOAL 13 | # Explain and Use the Perpetual Inventory Method |

Overview

Introduction

Learning Goal 13 continues the analysis of merchandising operations by focusing on the calculation, recording, and reporting of all the elements of cost of goods sold. The method used in this learning goal is known as the *perpetual inventory method*.

Concept

The ***perpetual inventory method*** is a procedure for determining cost of goods sold and inventory continuously. The inventory balance is updated after every purchase and every sale.

Check with Your Instructor

If you are using this book for a class, check with your instructor.

Some instructors prefer that you learn the periodic method instead of the perpetual method. The periodic method begins in Learning Goal 11 on page 321. Check with your instructor.

"So, did you check with your instructor?"

The Cost of Goods Sold Calculation

Overview

Introduction

Cost of goods sold is an expense. It is the cost of the merchandise sold. Cost of goods sold is an essential part of the net income calculation.

In the perpetual inventory method, the calculation of cost of goods sold depends upon keeping a continuous daily record of the merchandise inventory balance. The calculation of cost of goods sold and of the balance of inventory both happen together as part of a continuous cycle.

Illustration

The left side of the diagram below shows the process of net income calculation for a merchandising business. The illustration below shows the daily inventory cycle in which purchases and sales transactions require the merchandise inventory balance to be updated. When there is a sale, it increases cost of goods sold as it reduces the inventory. A purchase increases the inventory balance.

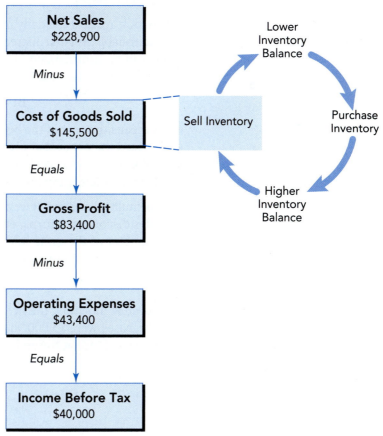

continued ▶

Overview, *continued*

Determining Cost of Goods Sold

- **For each sale:** To record the cost of goods sold for each sale, detailed record-keeping will maintain a careful record of the individual inventory costs and quantities. For each sale, the cost of an item is multiplied by the number of units sold to determine the cost of the goods sold for that sale. (The exact methods by which the record-keeping is done and how the unit costs are determined are not necessary to study at this point. However, you will see this topic later in your study of accounting.)
- **For the period:** The cost of goods sold for the entire period is simply the cumulative total cost for all the individual sales. This is recorded in the ledger account for cost of goods sold.

Optional Formula

Introduction

Some people prefer to use formulas whenever possible to precisely describe events. It is not absolutely necessary to do so here, but some may find it helpful. The discussion below shows a formula for the continuous balance of inventory.

Formula for Inventory Balance

If you look again at the daily inventory cycle diagram on page 439, you can see identifiable, regular increases and decreases in the inventory balance. These can be summarized in the following formula to calculate the inventory balance at any time:

$$BI + P - C \text{ of } GS = EI$$

- **BI** means the cost of the beginning inventory units
- **P** means the net cost of the new units purchased
- **C of GS** means the cost of goods sold
- **EI** means the ending inventory, which is the new inventory balance

The formula tells us that if we add the net cost of the units purchased (which includes discounts, returns, etc.) to the beginning inventory balance, then subtract cost of the units sold, we will have the cost of the new inventory balance (ending inventory).

Example

On Tuesday morning, the inventory balance was $35,000. During the day, net purchases were $3,000, and the cost of units sold was $7,200. The new inventory balance at the end of the day on Tuesday evening was $30,800.

Transactions That Involve Buying Merchandise

Purchases

Overview

Whenever merchandise inventory is purchased, the cost of the inventory is added to the Merchandise Inventory account.

Example of Journal Entry

The general journal entry below shows that Queensborough Patio Mart purchased $1,500 of merchandise on account.

June 9	Merchandise Inventory	1,500	
	Accounts Payable		1,500
	Purchase Invoice #99–45		
	Lafayette Supply Co.		

The method you see above, which is the most common way of recording purchases, is called the **gross method** because it uses the total invoice cost. This is based on the **invoice price,** which is the cost shown on the invoice.

An alternative is the "net method" that initially records a purchase net of a discount, and a late payment results in a debit to Discounts Lost expense.

Source Document: Invoice

The invoice is a document prepared by the seller and sent to the buyer. An invoice describes the merchandise sold, the total amount due, and how payment is to be made. An invoice is the source document for recording both sales on the seller's books and purchases on the buyer's books.

Purchase Discounts

Definition

A **purchase discount** is a discount received by the buyer for early payment within a specified discount period.

Other Key Features

A purchase discount:

- is recorded only on the books of a *buyer* at the time of payment.
- reduces the cost of the merchandise.
- applies only to purchases made on account.
- usually occurs between merchants or manufacturers.

Be Careful . . .

Do not confuse a purchase discount with a sales discount, which is the same discount amount but is recorded on the books of the seller.

continued ▶

Purchase Discounts, *continued*

Synonym   A purchase discount is frequently called a ***vendor*** or ***cash discount.***

Credit Terms

Credit Terms   ***Credit terms*** means the manner of payment that is agreed upon between
                                buyer and seller. This includes the discount calculation. Credit terms are
                                often written in a specific, abbreviated manner on the sales invoice.

**Examples of
Credit Terms**   The table below shows three common credit terms and the meaning of
                                each abbreviated expression. Different businesses offer different credit
                                terms.

Expression	Interpretation
2/10, n/30	This is read as "two ten, net thirty." ■ The "2" is the percent discount allowed. ■ The "10" is the maximum number of days allowable before payment must be made in order to get the discount. This is known as the ***discount period***. ■ The "n" means the balance still owed. ■ "30" is the maximum number of days allowed for full payment of any balance still owed.
1/5 EOM, n/30	This is read as "one five EOM, net thirty." ■ The "1" is the percent discount allowed. ■ The "5 EOM" means that the discount period ends 5 days following the end of the month in which the sale was made. After that, any balance is due in full.
n/30	This is read as "net thirty." ■ No discount. Full amount is due in 30 days.

Credit Terms, *continued*

How to Count Discount Time	Normally you begin counting the days of the discount period on the day following the day of sale. For example, if a sale is made on October 9, count October 10 as the first day in the discount period.

Calculating Discounts

Overview of Calculation	A discount is recorded at the time the customer pays within the discount period. The method used to calculate the correct cash payment and discount is the same for both the seller and purchaser. Although the seller and purchaser make different journal entries to record the transaction, the calculated amounts are exactly the same for both parties.
Payment Patterns	There are three possible payment patterns, two of which involve recording a discount: 1. A full payment is made within the discount period (full discount). 2. A full payment is made after the discount period (no discount). 3. A partial payment is made within the discount period (partial discount), and the balance owing is paid after the discount period (no discount).
Procedure Summary	The table below shows how to calculate the correct cash payment and discount for each payment pattern. As an example, assume that on June 12, a sale of $1,500 is made with terms of 2/10, n/30.

IF the payment pattern is . . .	THEN to calculate the cash payment . . .	AND the discount calculation is . . .	Example
1. full payment within the discount period	multiply the full amount due by (1 − discount %)	full invoice amount − cash payment	■ Cash payment: $1,500 × .98 = $1,470 ■ Discount: $1,500 − $1,470 = $30
2. full payment after the discount period	no calculation; full amount is due	none	$1,500 is due
3. partial cash payment within the discount period	no calculation; the customer has already made a cash payment	partial invoice amount − cash payment	■ Cash payment: (customer pays $490 cash) ■ Discount: ($490/.98) = $500 $500 − $490 = $10 discount

TIP   Partial payments are also known as short payments.

continued ▶

Calculating Discounts, *continued*

Reasons for the Calculations

Pattern 1. Because the customer pays the amount due within the discount period, the discount applies against the full amount of the sale. If the discount percent is 2%, then the cash payment will be 98% of the entire sale amount.

Pattern 2. The full invoice amount is due because the discount was missed.

Pattern 3. Any cash received from a customer within the discount period is *already the net amount*—the amount remaining *after* a discount has been applied. This means, in this example, that whatever is received must be 98% of some larger (partial invoice) amount. The objective is to figure out what that larger amount is, that is some part of the total sale. The result here is $500.

> *Note:* This usually happens when a customer cannot afford to make a full payment but uses whatever cash is available to obtain some discount.

Partial Payment Information

Partial payments can be a little tricky. Frequently, as just illustrated in pattern 3, the cash payment is given and the invoice portion must be calculated. However, sometimes the invoice portion is the information given and the cash payment must be calculated.

IF you are given . . .	THEN . . .
the amount of **cash** payment,	you determine how much of **the invoice** is being paid: Example: $490 cash /.98 = $500
the amount of **invoice** that is being paid,	you determine the **cash payment** needed: Example: $500 of invoice x .98 = $490

Check Your Understanding

Situation	Cash Paid	Discount Amount
1. On May 12, a $1,000 purchase is made with terms of 1/10, n/30. The customer pays in full on May 19.	(Reminder: Use a separate sheet of paper to complete the table.)	
2. On November 30, a $3,500 purchase is made with terms of 1/5, n/30. The customer pays $2,000 cash on December 3.		
3. On September 25, a $4,500 purchase is made with terms of 2/10, n/45. The customer pays in full on November 15.		
4. On February 9, a $2,700 purchase is made with terms of 2/10, n/30. The customer pays $1,500 of the invoice amount on February 12.		
5. On February 9, a $2,700 purchase is made with terms 2/10, n/30. The customer paid $1,500 cash on February 12.		
6. On August 11, a $5,000 purchase is made with terms 2/10, n/30. On August 19, the customer pays $500 cash and on August 21 also pays $750.		

Answers

Situation	Cash Paid	Discount Amount
1. On May 12, a $1,000 purchase is made with terms of 1/10, n/30. The customer pays in full on May 19. *Calculation*: $1,000 × .99 = $990 $1,000 − $990 = $10	$990	$10
2. On November 30, a $3,500 purchase is made with terms of 1/5, n/30. The customer pays $2,000 cash on December 3. *Calculation*: $2,000/.99 = $2,020.20 $2,020.20 − $2,000 = $20.20	$2,000	$20.20
3. On September 25, a $4,500 purchase is made with terms of 2/10, n/45. The customer pays in full on November 15. *Calculation*: Paid after discount period—full amount is due.	$4,500	$−0−
4. On February 9, a $2,700 purchase is made with terms of 2/10, n/30. The customer pays $1,500 of the invoice amount on February 12. *Calculation*: $1,500 × .98 = $1,470 $1,500 − $1,470 = 30	$1,470	$30
5. On February 9, a $2,700 purchase is made with terms 2/10, n/30. The customer paid $1,500 cash on February 12. *Calculation*: $1,500/.98 = $1,530.61 $1,530.61 − $1,500 = $30.61	$1,500	$30.61
6. On August 11, a $5,000 purchase is made with terms 2/10, n/30. On August 19, the customer pays $500 cash and on August 21 also pays $750. *Calculation*: $1,250/.98 = $1,275.51 $1,275.51 − $1,250 = $25.51	$1,250	$25.51

TIP

A practical problem for sellers in many businesses is the customer who pays late but still takes the discount. This is called an ***unearned discount***. It is most common when a small seller is selling to a large buyer.

Recording Payments for Purchases and Discounts

Overview

Purchase discounts reduce the cost of merchandise. The discount amount will appear as a credit to Merchandise Inventory at the time of payment (if within the discount period).

Recording the Cash Payment

The journal entries below show you how to record each of the possible payment patterns.

Example: A $1,500 purchase on June 9 with credit terms of 2/10, n/30.

1. Full payment made within the discount period

June 18	Accounts Payable	1,500	
	Merchandise Inventory		30
	Cash		1,470
	Payment within discount		
	period—Invoice #2209		

Debit the full amount!

2. Full payment made after the discount period

July 7	Accounts Payable	1,500	
	Cash		1,500
	Payment of Invoice #2209		

3. Partial payment of $490 is made within the discount period

June 18	Accounts Payable	500	
	Merchandise Inventory		10
	Cash		490
	Partial payment within discount		
	period, Invoice #2209		

TIP

Is it worth it to pay early and take a discount? Most of the time, yes, if the cash is not needed for other reasons. Example: 2/10, n/30 terms on a $1,000 invoice amount. In effect, the 2% discount means that you earn $20 (because by waiting 20 more days you have to pay $20 more) on a net out-of-pocket investment of $980.

We evaluate financial transactions such as loans or investments on an annual percentage basis ("annualizing"). The number of 20-day periods in one year: $365/20 = 18.25$. Result: $18.25 \times 20/980 = 37.24\%$ annualized return on the $980.

Recording Payments for Purchases and Discounts, *continued*

Note: Any amount paid within a discount period is considered to be the net amount after a discount has been subtracted. The amount of cash paid is usually whatever the buyer thinks he or she can afford to pay.

The discount is calculated as ($490/.98 = $500) – $490 = $10.

Recording Purchase Returns and Allowances

Definition

Purchase returns and allowances are transactions that decrease the amount owing because of having received unsatisfactory merchandise. A purchase return means that the buyer returned merchandise and reduced the account payable. An allowance means that the buyer can reduce the account payable without returning the merchandise.

Example of Return

Queensborough Patio Mart discovers that $400 of merchandise is defective. On July 9, the company calls the seller and returns the merchandise. At the same time, it issues a debit memorandum to the seller, indicating that Accounts Payable will be debited $400 because of the returned merchandise and referencing the seller's invoice number.

July 9	Accounts Payable	400	
	Merchandise Inventory		400
	Returned defective items to seller;		
	see debit memo #231		

Example of Allowance

Suppose that in the situation above, the seller instead tells Queensborough Patio Mart that it prefers not to have the expense and disruption of dealing with defective returned merchandise. The seller offers Queensborough Patio Mart a $200 reduction in the amount payable, if Queensborough will keep the defective items. This is an allowance. Notice that this reduces the cost of the merchandise even though nothing was returned.

July 9	Accounts Payable	200	
	Merchandise Inventory		200
	Allowance for defective items;		
	see debit memo #231		

Unpaid invoices should be filed by discount expiration date, so that discounts will not be missed.

continued ▶

Check Your Understanding

Write the completed sentences on a separate piece of paper. Answers are below.

A · · · · · · · · discount is a discount received by the · · · · · · · for an early payment made to the seller within a specified discount period. A purchase · · · · · · · · or · · · · · · · · is a reduction in the amount owing to the seller because of unsatisfactory merchandise received. All of these items are recorded by a (debit/credit) · · · · · · · · to the Merchandise Inventory account.

On August 15, Catawba Partnership purchased $10,000 of merchandise with terms of 4/15, n/30. Print journal paper from the disk in the back of the book or at worthyjames.com (student info.) and journalize payment under each the following independent situations:

a. Assume that Catawba pays in full on August 30.
b. Assume that Catawba pays in full on September 12.
c. Assume that Catawba pays $2,500 of the invoice amount on August 20.
d. Assume that Catawba makes a cash payment of $2,500 on August 20.

Answers

A purchase discount is a discount received by the buyer for an early payment made to the seller within a specified discount period. A purchase return or allowance is a reduction in the amount owing to the seller because of unsatisfactory merchandise received. All of these items are recorded by a credit to the Merchandise Inventory account.

c: $2,500 × .96 = $2,400   d: $2,500/.96 = $2,604.17

(a)	Accounts Payable	10,000	
	Merchandise Inventory		400
	Cash		9,600

| (b) | Accounts Payable | 10,000 | |
| | Cash | | 10,000 |

(c)	Accounts Payable	2,500	
	Merchandise Inventory		100
	Cash		2,400

(d)	Accounts Payable	$2,604.17	
	Merchandise Inventory		104.17
	Cash		2,500.00

Recording Purchase Returns and Allowances, *continued*

Debit Memorandum (Debit Memo)

When an account payable is reduced (debited) by a buyer because of a return or allowance, the buyer usually sends the seller a *debit memorandum* that shows the amount of the debit to the account payable, with an explanation and reference to the sales invoice.

Discounts and Returns

When a discount has been taken and merchandise is later returned, the cash returned should be for the actual net amount paid, after discounts. For a buyer this means a debit to cash (or accounts payable), a debit to purchase discounts, and a credit to purchases returns and allowances for the amount of the purchase. For a seller, debit sales returns and allowances for the amount of the sale, credit sales discounts, and credit cash (or accounts receivable).

TIP

Some businesses record purchases by using what is called the "net method." For example, if the invoice price of a purchase is $1,500 with terms of 2/10, n/30, the debit to Inventory and credit to Accounts Payable would be recorded as $1,470. This method assumes that the true cost of merchandise should be the net amount. When a discount is missed, a debit to "Discounts Lost" is recorded (here, $30) when cash is paid ($1,500) and Accounts Payable debited ($1,470).

Recording Freight Costs

Overview

Freight costs that are paid by the buyer increase the net cost of the merchandise. These costs are called *freight-in* costs, and they are added to the Merchandise Inventory account. Freight costs are also sometimes called *transportation-in* costs.

Be Careful . . .

Freight-in costs paid by the buyer should not be confused with freight-out. The table below shows the differences.

Freight-in paid by buyer is . . .	Freight-out is . . .
▪ the shipping cost paid when merchandise is purchased.	▪ the shipping cost paid by the seller when merchandise is sold.
▪ added to the cost of merchandise.	▪ part of operating expenses—specifically, selling expenses.

Not Part of Discount Calculation

A purchase discount *cannot* be calculated on freight costs. The discount is only applied to the invoice price of the *merchandise*.

continued ▶

Recording Freight Costs, *continued*

Journal Entry Example

On October 5, Edgecombe Corporation purchased merchandise with terms of 2/10, n/30. The seller billed Edgecombe $5,300, of which $300 is for shipping costs paid by the seller.

Oct. 5	Merchandise Inventory	5,300	
	Accounts Payable		5,300
	Purchased inventory @ 2/10, n/30		
	plus $300 freight cost, Invoice #4435		

Oct. 15	Accounts Payable	5,300	
	Merchandise Inventory		100
	Cash		5,200
	Paid amount owing on invoice		
	#4435, less 2% discount; total		
	includes $300 freight cost		

If Buyer Pays the Freight-In

In the example above, if Edgecombe had separately paid the shipping costs directly, the journal entries would appear as you see below.

Oct. 5	Merchandise Inventory	5,000	
	Accounts Payable		5,000
	Purchased inventory @ 2/10, n/30		
	Invoice #4435		

Oct. 15	Accounts Payable	5,000	
	Merchandise Inventory		100
	Cash		4,900
	Paid invoice #4435		
	Merchandise Inventory	300	
	Cash		300
	Paid freight cost for purchase		
	on invoice #4435		

Shipping Documents

The shipping documents from a shipping company—such as a trucking, airline, or train company—show the shipping costs and the freight terms. A shipping document is frequently called a ***freight bill*** or ***bill of lading***.

Recording Freight Costs, *continued*

Freight Terms	Freight terms that were agreed upon by the seller and purchaser and shown on the sales invoice are also shown on the freight bill. One commonly used freight term is FOB. **FOB** means *free on board* and refers to the point at which ownership title of the merchandise and the shipping costs are transferred to the purchaser.
Examples	■ Dallas Corporation buys merchandise from Los Angeles Corporation. The shipping terms are "FOB shipping point." This means that Dallas Corporation owns the merchandise as soon as the goods are loaded onto the carrier in Los Angeles. Dallas Corporation must also pay shipping costs from Los Angeles.
	■ If the shipping terms above had been "FOB destination," then Los Angeles Corporation would own the merchandise until it was offloaded in Dallas. Los Angeles Corporation would have incurred the shipping costs as well.

Summary of the Merchandise Inventory Account

Items in the Account	We have used a merchandise inventory account to record the cost of purchases and freight-in and the cost of discounts and returns and allowances. For example, assume that our business made a purchase of $100,000 of merchandise. (No beginning inventory) Shipping costs to our location were $2,000, purchase discounts were $1,500, and purchase returns and allowances were $3,200. Also assume that $85,000 of the merchandise was sold. The T accounts below summarize how these items would be entered into the accounts.

Item/(balance)	Merchandise Inventory		Item	Cost of Goods Sold
Purchases	100,000	3,200	Returns and allow.	
Freight-in	2,000	1,500	Purchase discounts	
(Cost of goods available)	97,300			
(Ending inventory)	12,300	85,000	Cost of goods sold	85,000

Alternative Method for Discounts, Returns, Allowances, and Freight

Method	If a business wishes to keep any type of item under especially close observation, the accountant sets up an individual account just for that item. Some companies do this for discounts, returns, allowances, and freight costs. Each item is a separate account.

continued ▶

Alternative Method for Discounts, Returns, Allowances, and Freight, *continued*

Examples

- If managers believe that too much unsatisfactory merchandise is being purchased, they use separate accounts to follow the total amounts of returns and allowances.
- Management may want to know the amount of discounts being taken relative to the amount of merchandise being purchased. To do this, a separate account that tracks purchase discounts must be used.

Account Balances

The table below shows how to record the items if individual accounts are maintained.

This item . . .	is recorded with a . . .
Purchase discounts of $1,500	Credit to Purchase Discounts
Purchase returns of $3,000	Credit to Purchase Returns
Purchase allowances of $200	Credit to Purchase Allowances
Freight-in costs of $2,000	Debit to Freight-in

Total Merchandise Inventory Cost

At any time, the total cost of the merchandise inventory can be determined by combining the merchandise inventory balance with the account balances above as follows:

Merchandise inventory		$100,000
Less:		
Purchase discounts	$1,500	
Purchase returns	3,000	
Purchase allowances	200	4,700
Add:		
Freight-in cost		2,000
Total cost of merchandise inventory		$ 97,300

TIP

The illustration that you see on the previous page shows cost of goods sold that contains total transaction amounts. While the account totals are correct, a practical issue is determining a unit cost for each individual inventory item that includes freight-in, discounts, and returns and allowances at an item level. How this is be done depends on the accounting software used and inventory method used.

Merchants track individual items using either a "UPC" (universal product code) or an "SKU" (stock keeping unit) number. A UPC is a unique identifier regardless of where the product is sold. It is created by a central authority. An SKU is created for use by a particular company.

Transactions That Involve Selling Merchandise

Recording Sales Transactions

Rule for Sale

To record a sale when using the perpetual inventory method, you must always make this *pair* of entries to record:

- The amount of revenue
- The cost of the merchandise given up

Notice that this requires you to record the cost of the inventory sold in addition to recording the amount of the sale.

Example

On June 29, Queensborough Patio Mart sells $2,000 of patio furniture on account. The inventory records show the cost of this merchandise as $1,200.

June 29	Accounts Receivable	2,000	
	Sales		2,000
	Cost of Goods Sold	1,200	
	Merchandise Inventory		1,200
	Sales Invoice #721 CD		

Note that the credit to merchandise inventory updates the Merchandise Inventory account by reducing the inventory balance after the sale is made.

Recording Sales Discounts

Procedure

A sales discount is a discount offered by the seller to encourage fast payment. It is recorded when the buyer makes a payment.

Do not confuse the journal entries for *sales* discounts, which are recorded on the books of the seller, with the journal entries for *purchase* discounts, which are recorded on the books of the buyer. Journal entries for purchase discounts are discussed on pages 446–447. A sales discount is calculated in exactly the same way as the purchase discount illustrated on pages 443–444.

Example

Assume that the sale above included discount terms of 2/10, n/30 and the customer paid on July 7, within the 10-day discount period.

continued ▶

Recording Sales Discounts, *continued*

GENERAL JOURNAL				J3
Date	Account	Ref.	Dr.	Cr.
July 7	Cash		1,960	
	Sales Discounts		40	
	Accounts Receivable			2,000

The Sales Discounts account is a *contra Sales account*, which means that it has a debit balance that offsets Sales and so reduces net sales.

Recording Sales Returns and Allowances

Rules for Sales Returns

To record a return of merchandise from a buyer when using the perpetual inventory method, you must always make this *pair* of entries to record:

- The amount of decrease in the account receivable
- The cost of the merchandise that is returned

Example

On July 8, a customer returns merchandise that was sold for $500. Records indicate the cost of merchandise as $350.

July 8	Sales Return and Allowances		500	
	Accounts Receivable			500
	Merchandise Inventory		350	
	Cost of Goods Sold			350
	Merchandise return re Sales			
	Invoice #883 AX			

Notice that the debit to merchandise inventory updates the Merchandise Inventory account by increasing the inventory because the goods were returned from the buyer.

Sales Returns and Allowances Account

The *Sales Returns and Allowances* account is a *contra Sales account*, which means that it offsets sales and reduces net sales, as does sales discounts.

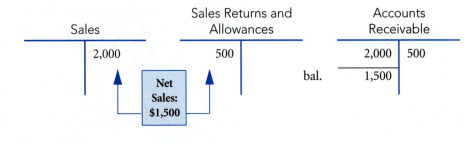

Recording Sales Returns and Allowances, *continued*

Rule for Sales Allowances	An allowance to a customer means a reduction in the amount owed by the customer, but the merchandise is not returned. Therefore, only a single journal entry is required that shows the decrease in the receivable.

Example

On July 9, an allowance of $100 was granted to a customer.

July 9	Sales Returns and Allowances	100	
	Accounts Receivable		100
	Allowance re Sales Invoice #915 CD		

Caution!

Do not confuse the journal entries for sales returns and allowances, which are recorded on the books of the seller, with the journal entries for *purchase* returns and allowances, which are recorded on the books of the buyer. Purchase returns and allowances are discussed on page 447.

Credit Memorandum (Credit Memo)

When an account receivable is reduced (credited) by a seller because of a return or allowance, the seller usually sends the buyer a document called a ***credit memorandum*** that shows the amount of the credit to the account receivable with an explanation and reference to the sales invoice.

TIP

Some merchants use a separate "Defective Inventory" account for defective merchandise that is returned.

"Sales returns and allowances?
Purchase returns and allowances?"

Shipping Charges and Sales Tax

Shipping Charges Paid by the Seller

Definition

An account name that is frequently used for shipping charges paid by the seller is *freight-out*. Freight-out is usually recorded as a selling expense and is not part of cost of goods sold.

Payment Patterns

Two common payment patterns are used when shipping charges are paid by the seller:

- The seller pays the shipping charges and is not reimbursed by the buyer.
- The seller prepays the shipping charges and will be reimbursed by the buyer.

Example

Suppose that on June 23, Queensborough Patio Mart shipped patio furniture to the La Belle restaurant in Rochester, New York. Shipping charges from Queens to Rochester are $170.

Seller prepays shipping charges, buyer will not reimburse seller:

June 23	Freight-out	170	
	Cash		170
	(Shipping charges: Novotna		
	Motor Freight)		

Seller prepays shipping charges, buyer agrees to reimburse seller:

June 23	Accounts Receivable—La Balle	170	
	Cash		170
	(Shipping charges: Novotna		
	Motor Freight)		

Note: The $170 is added to the Accounts Receivable because the buyer has agreed to pay the shipping charges in addition to the cost of the merchandise.

Sales Tax

Definition

A **sales tax** is a tax levied by a state or local government entity as a percentage of *retail* sales of many kinds of merchandise. These are called *taxable sales*. The buyer pays the sales tax, which is added to the cost of the merchandise. The merchant is simply a collector of the tax from the buyer at the point of sale and is obligated to send the collected taxes to the taxing authority in a timely manner.

Caution

Sales tax is neither a revenue nor an expense. It is a liability for the additional cash that is collected on behalf of a taxing authority.

Example

For example, the Queensborough Patio Mart made $2,500 of cash sales on June 9. Assume these were taxable sales to retail customers and the sales tax rate was 8%. Cost of goods sold is $1,500. The sales tax calculation and journal entry would be:

- Sales tax collection: $2,500 \times .08 = 200$

June 9	Cash		2,700	
	Sales			2,500
	Sales Tax Payable			200
	Cost of Goods Sold		1,500	
	Merchandise Inventory			1,500

Later, when Queensborough Patio Mart pays the state taxing authority for the month of June, this collection will be part of the total larger payment (assume that the total monthly sales tax was $5,250), and the journal entry will be:

July 10	Sales Tax Payable		5,250	
	Cash			5,250
	(Paid sales tax liability for			
	month of June)			

continued ▶

Sales Tax, *continued*

| Alternate Calculation Method | Some merchants consider it too troublesome to record the sales tax liability with each individual transaction. Instead, they prefer to calculate the entire sales tax for the period with one calculation. To do this, they *include the sales tax collection as part of Sales* and adjust the account later, when they need to know the correct amount of sales tax. |

| Example of Alternate Method | On June 9, Queensborough Patio Mart had $2,500 of taxable retail sales. This was all recorded as Sales. Clearly, this overstates the Sales account and understates the Sales Tax Payable, so this must be corrected later. |

June 9	Cash	2,700	
	Sales		2,700
	(Daily retail sales collection)		

Adjustment Calculation

The Sales account includes *both* the sales *and* the sales tax collections. So, if the sales tax rate is 8%, then the Sales account must be 108% of the actual sales revenue. Assume the Sales account for the month of June shows $70,875, which includes both sales and sales tax collections:

- **Step 1: Calculate actual sales revenue** $70,875/1.08 = $65,625
- **Step 2: Calculate the sales tax** $70,875 − $65,625 = $5,250

Note: You cannot multiply $70,875 by .08 to calculate the sales tax. This is because the $70,875 *already includes the sales tax*. You would be calculating sales tax on sales tax!

Journal Entry

The following adjustment is made to the accounts at the end of June. It reduces the overstated Sales and increases the understated Sales Tax Payable:

June 30	Sales	5,250	
	Sales Tax Payable		5,250
	(To record correct amount of sales		
	tax liability)		

Sales Tax, *continued*

Sales Tax and Discounts

Sales tax does not usually apply to sales between merchants (non-taxable sales). However, in any situation where sales tax is calculated and a discount is involved, the sales tax should be calculated only on the net amount paid by the customer, after any discounts are taken.

Sales Tax and Merchandise Returns

If a customer returns taxable merchandise, the cash returned to the customer must include both the sales price of the merchandise and the sales tax. For example, if a customer had returned $100 of taxable merchandise and sales tax paid was 8%, then the journal entry would be:

June 18	Sales Return and Allowances	100	
	Sales Tax Payable	8	
	Cash		108
	Merchandise Inventory	70	
	Cost of Goods Sold		70

Note: If the sales tax had been included in the Sales account, only Sales Returns and Allowances would be debited in the amount of $108. In either case, Merchandise Inventory is debited to record the merchandise returned.

Comparing Journal Entries

Comparison Table: Seller and Buyer Journal Entries

Comparison

The table below helps you to remember some frequently occurring journal entries made on the books of the seller and the buyer—if both are using the perpetual method. The entries are compared side by side.

Transaction	Seller Journal Entries	Buyer Journal Entries

$2,000 sale of merchandise on account, terms 2/10, n/30. Cost is $1,200.	Accounts Receivable 2,000
	     Sales 2,000
	Cost of Goods Sold 1,200
	     Merchandise Inventory 1,200
		Merchandise Inventory 2,000
		     Accounts Payable 2,000

$500 of merchandise is returned by the buyer. Seller's cost is $350.	Sales Returns/Allowances 500
	     Accounts Receivable 500
	Merchandise Inventory 350
	     Cost of Goods Sold 350
		Accounts Payable 500
		     Merchandise Inventory 500

Buyer pays the full amount within the discount period.	Cash 1,470
	Sales Discounts 30
	     Accounts Receivable 1,500
		Accounts Payable 1,500
		     Merchandise Inventory 30
		     Cash 1,470

Buyer pays the full amount, but missed the discount.	Cash 1,500
	     Accounts Receivable 1,500
		Accounts Payable 1,500
		     Cash 1,500

$3,000 sale on account. Cost is $2,300. Seller pays $100 shipping cost but buyer will not reimburse.	Accounts Receivable 3,000
	     Sales 3,000
	Cost of Goods Sold 2,300
	     Merchandise Inventory 2,300
	Freight-out 100
	     Cash 100
		Merchandise Inventory 3,000
		     Accounts Payable 3,000

$3,000 sale on account. Cost is $2,300. Seller pays $100 shipping cost; buyer agrees to reimburse the seller.	Accounts Receivable 3,100
	     Sales 3,000
	     Cash 100
	Cost of Goods Sold 2,300
	     Merchandise Inventory 2,300
		Merchandise Inventory 3,100
		     Accounts Payable 3,100

Buyer makes full payment within the discount period, including reimbursement of freight cost. Terms: 1/10, n/30.	Cash 3,070
	Sales Discounts 30
	     Accounts Receivable 3,100
		Accounts Payable 3,100
		     Merchandise Inventory 30
		     Cash 3,070

Buyer directly pays $100 to the shipping company instead of the seller.	No entry	Merchandise Inventory 100 Cash 100

Ending Inventory

Recording Ending Inventory Adjustments

Overview

Even though the perpetual method maintains a continuous record of the inventory balance, after a period of time the balance showing on the record may not be the same as the actual balance. This can happen for various reasons, such as errors in record-keeping, theft, and vandalism.

Definition

Ending inventory means the amount of merchandise inventory remaining at the end of an accounting period, after all transactions for the period are completed.

Procedure

To verify the correct ending inventory balance, the inventory is counted. This counting is called a *physical inventory*. Then, to determine the total cost of the inventory, the units of each type are multiplied by their unit cost.

Inventory Shrinkage

Inventory shrinkage means an unidentified loss of inventory. The usual reasons are theft, accidents, and spoilage. If something has been stolen, broken, or is otherwise unusable, it cannot be counted as part of ending inventory. Usually, this loss becomes part of cost of goods sold.

Adjustment Example

The perpetual inventory records of Mansfield Company show a year-end balance of $251,300. A physical inventory results in a value of $247,800. The records are always adjusted to the actual count.

Dec. 31	Cost of Goods Sold		3,500	
	Merchandise Inventory			3,500
	Shrinkage adjustment			

Adjustment Example

What if the situation is the opposite? Suppose that the perpetual inventory records of Nelsonville Company show a year-end balance of $110,500. A physical inventory results in a value of $115,100.

	Merchandise Inventory		4,600	
	Cost of Goods Sold			4,600
	Inventory increase adjustment			

continued ▶

Recording Ending Inventory Adjustments, *continued*

Merchandise in Transit

When merchandise is being shipped from seller to buyer, who owns the inventory? Who reports this inventory as an asset on the balance sheet?

The answer depends on when the buyer and seller agreed that the title (ownership) of the goods would transfer from seller to buyer. Frequently, this can be decided by examining the FOB shipping terms as follows:

If the terms are . . .	then . . .
FOB shipping point,	title is transferred when the goods are loaded on the carrier, so the buyer owns the goods while in transit.
FOB destination,	title is transferred when the goods are unloaded at destination, so the seller owns the goods while in transit.
FOB any interim point,	title transfers at the designated interim point.

Merchandise on the Financial Statements

- *Balance sheet*: Merchandise inventory is a current asset.
- *Income statement*: If a multiple-step statement is used, showing a detailed calculation of cost of goods sold, the ending inventory will appear as part of this calculation.

Consignment Inventory

When merchandise is shipped but ownership does not transfer to the receiving company, the merchandise is **consigned.** It remains part of the ending inventory of the shipper.

QUICK REVIEW

- The cost of goods sold is determined with each sale, as part of a continuous daily cycle of inventory decreases and increases.
- Purchases, discounts, returns, allowances, and freight cost payments are all recorded by debiting or crediting Merchandise Inventory. However, some companies prefer to keep separate accounts for each of these items, to provide more detailed information.
- Whenever a sale is made, a pair of entries is required: one to record the sale and the other to record the cost of goods sold and decrease in inventory.
- Sales returns always increase the Merchandise Inventory account, but sales allowances do not.
- Ending inventory must be counted at the end of the period, even though a perpetual record is maintained.
- Sales tax creates a liability called *Sales Tax Payable.*

VOCABULARY

Bill of lading: another term for freight bill (page 450)

Cash discount: another name for a purchase discount (page 442)

Consignment: merchandise held, but not owned, by another party (page 462).

Credit memorandum: a document issued by a seller to inform the buyer of a credit to accounts receivable (page 455)

Credit terms: the manner of payment that is agreed upon between buyer and seller (page 442)

Debit Memorandum: a document issued by a buyer to inform the seller of a debit to accounts payable (page 449)

Ending inventory: the merchandise inventory remaining at the end of an accounting period, after all transactions for the period are completed (page 461)

FOB ("free on board") **location:** the location up to which the buyer is not responsible for shipping costs; the point at which ownership and risk of loss often transfer from seller to buyer (page 451)

Freight bill: a shipping document from a shipping company (page 450)

Freight-in: a buyer's payment for the shipping cost incurred to obtain delivery of merchandise purchases (page 449)

Freight-out: Shipping charges paid by the seller (page 456)

Gross method: the method of recording the account payable at the gross amount before any discounts (page 441)

Inventory shrinkage: an unidentified loss of inventory (page 461)

Invoice price: the cost of a purchase, as shown on an invoice (page 441)

Perpetual inventory method: a procedure for determining cost of goods sold and ending inventory by maintaining a constant record of the inventory balance and its changes (page 437)

Physical inventory: counting inventory by inspection (page 461)

Purchase discount: a discount received by the buyer for early payment within a specified discount period (page 441)

Purchase returns and allowances: an account on the books of the buyer that refers to a decrease in the amount owing because of having received unsatisfactory merchandise (page 447)

Sales returns and allowances: a contra account that records a decrease in total sales caused by shipping unsatisfactory merchandise, which the buyer does not pay for (page 454)

Sales tax: a tax collected by sellers and levied by a state or local government and calculated as a percentage of retail sales that are designated by law as subject to sales tax (page 457)

Vendor discount: another term for an early payment discount (page 442)

Do You Want More Examples?

Most problems in this book have detailed solutions. To use them as additional examples, do this: 1) Select the type of problem you want 2) Open the solution on your computer or mobile device screen (from the disc or worthyjames.com) 3) Read one item at a time and look at its answer. Take notes if needed. 4) Close the solution and work as much of the problem as you can. 5) Repeat as needed.

PRACTICE   **Learning Goal 13**

Solutions are in the disk at the back of the book and at: www.worthyjames.com

Learning Goal 13 explains the purchase and sales merchandise transactions using the perpetual inventory method. Use these questions to practice what you have just read.

Multiple Choice
Select the best answer.

1. In the perpetual inventory method, a purchase of merchandise inventory requires a:
    a. debit to Purchases.
    b. debit to Merchandise Inventory.
    c. debit to Cost of Goods Sold.
    d. credit to Sales.
2. Which of the following is *false*? A purchase discount:
    a. is recorded on the books of the buyer.
    b. applies only to purchases on account.
    c. is given for payment made within a designated time period.
    d. is recorded at the time of the purchase.
3. For a $5,000 purchase made on June 3, terms 2/10, n/30, a payment on June 13 of the full amount due results in:
    a. a $100 discount.
    b. a $500 discount.
    c. a $30 discount.
    d. no discount.
4. For a $5,000 purchase made on June 3, terms 2/10, n/30, a $1,000 cash payment on June 13 results in:
    a. a discount less than $20 but more than $10.
    b. a discount more than $20 but less than $30.
    c. a $30 discount.
    d. a $10 discount.
5. For a $2,500 purchase made on June 3, terms 1/15, n/30, to which the seller added $150 of shipping costs to the invoice, a full payment on June 13 results in:
    a. a discount of $26.50.
    b. a debit to Accounts Payable of $2,475.
    c. a debit to Accounts Payable of $2,500.
    d. a cash payment of $2,625
6. When goods are shipped FOB destination:
    a. the buyer would normally debit delivery expense for the cost of the shipping.
    b. the seller should record the sale as soon as the goods are shipped.
    c. the buyer would normally not incur shipping charges.
    d. the buyer should debit inventory for the cost of the shipping.
7. In the perpetual inventory system, a return of merchandise sold on account for $2,500 with a cost of $1,800 is recorded by the seller with an entry that includes a:
    a. debit to Sales Returns and Allowances for $1,800.
    b. credit to Sales Returns and Allowances for $1,800.
    c. debit to Sales for $2,500.
    d. credit to Cost of Goods Sold for $1,800.
8. Using the perpetual inventory system, the entry to record inventory shrinkage includes a:
    a. credit to Purchases.
    b. credit to Cost of Goods Sold.
    c. credit to Merchandise Inventory.
    d. credit to Sales.

Solutions are in the disk at the back of the book and at: www.worthyjames.com

PRACTICE   **Learning Goal 13, continued**

9. In a perpetual inventory system, a return of merchandise purchased on account for $3,800 is recorded by the buyer with an entry that includes a:
   a. credit to Merchandise Inventory for $3,800.
   b. credit to Purchase Returns and Allowances for $3,800.
   c. credit to Sales Returns and Allowances for $3,800.
   d. debit to Cost of Goods Sold for $3,800.

10. The account for sales tax on the books of the seller is:
   a. an expense.
   b. a liability.
   c. a revenue.
   d. a receivable.

11. If the shipping terms are FOB destination, the merchandise being shipped:
   a. is an asset of the seller.
   b. should be recorded as a sale by seller.
   c. is an asset of the buyer.
   d. none of the above.

12. Smith Company consigned $2,000 of inventory to Jones Company:
   a. Smith Company should show a sale.
   b. The inventory should appear as an asset on the balance sheet of Smith Company.
   c. The inventory should appear as an asset on the balance sheet of Jones Company.
   d. Jones Company should record a liability when the goods arrive.

13. A seller sold $2,000 of merchandise inventory on account, terms 2/10, n/30, FOB destination, and the goods were delivered. Freight charges were $100. The journal entry to record the sale would include a:
   a. credit to Accounts Receivable for $1,600.
   b. credit to Sales for $2,100.
   c. debit to Accounts Receivable for $1,960.
   d. credit to Sales for $2,000.

Reinforcement Problems

LG 13-1. Write a concise, accurate answer to each of the following questions.

a. What new contra accounts were discussed in this learning goal? What effect do they have?

b. What does "FOB" mean? Why is it important?

c. Explain where the following items should go in the accounting equation: sales discounts sales returns and allowances, freight-in, freight-out, and cost of goods sold.

d. If a seller lists merchandise inventory at $1,000 but also offers a 20% trade discount and credit terms of 2/10, n/30, what will the buyer pay if all discounts are taken? What is the difference between the two discounts offered?

e. What is the difference between a purchase return and allowance and a sales return and allowance?

f. What is the difference between a $500 cash payment and a $500 payment of the invoice amount?

LG 13-6. Journalize sales, returns, and payments transactions, no sales tax.

Instructions.

a. Record each of the transactions below in a general journal for the Lawn Gyland Garden Company, which uses the perpetual inventory method. Because all of the sales are to companies that will resell the merchandise, sales are not subject to sales tax. All sales are on account. Cost of goods sold is maintained at 65% of sales price. For journal paper, use the template in the disk at the back of the book or at worthyjames.com.

b. Using a T account, show the activity and the July 31 balance in the Accounts Payable account of Brooklyn Enterprises. There was no beginning balance in the account.

March 2 Sold $5,200 of gardening merchandise to Brooklyn Enterprises, terms 2/10, n/30, FOB shipping point.

5 Sold $7,000 of plumbing merchandise to Knickerbocker Company, terms 2/10, n/30, FOB shipping point.

8 Brooklyn Enterprises returned merchandise priced at $900.

11 Sold $4,000 of gardening merchandise to Nassau Landscape, terms 2/10, n/30, FOB shipping point, and paid $150 shipping charges, which were added to the invoice because the buyer agreed to reimburse the shipping charges.

12 Received a short payment of $2,940 cash from Brooklyn Enterprises.

15 Received a short payment of $5,880 cash from Knickerbocker Company.

17 Sold $15,000 of patio furniture to East Hampton Boutique, terms 2/10, n/30, FOB shipping point. Paid $350 shipping charges that the buyer will not reimburse.

21 Received payment in full from Nassau Landscape.

24 Sold $3,000 of gardening merchandise to Moriches Company, terms 2/10, n/30, FOB destination.

26 Granted a $1,000 allowance to East Hampton Boutique.

31 Received payment in full from East Hampton Boutique.

31 Received balance due from Knickerbocker Company.

LG 13-7. Journalize merchandise transactions, no sales tax.

Instructions: Record each of the transactions below in a general journal for the Miami Merchandise Company. Because all of the sales are to companies that will resell the merchandise, sales are not subject to sales tax. All sales are on account and FOB shipping point except as indicated. You may omit explanations in this exercise. For journal paper, you can use the template in the disk at the back of the book or at worthyjames.com.

August 1 Miami Company purchased $12,000 of merchandise inventory on account from Pensacola Enterprises, terms 2/10, n/30, FOB shipping point.

2 Miami Company purchased $4,000 of merchandise inventory on account from Tallahassee Company, terms 1/10, n/30, FOB shipping point, with $100 prepaid transportation charges paid by Seller added to the invoice.

7 Made an $8,000 sale of merchandise to Baton Rouge Corporation, terms 3/10, n/30. Cost of merchandise is $4,500.

9 Made a $4,000 sale of merchandise to Jacksonville Company, terms 3/10, n/30. Cost of merchandise is $2,100.

10 Returned $2,000 of merchandise to Pensacola Enterprises.

11 Paid the balance due on the August 1 invoice from Pensacola Enterprises. Also paid $150 shipping charges.

12 Paid the balance due on the August 2 invoice from Tallahassee Company.

15 Baton Rouge Corporation returned $500 of merchandise. Cost of merchandise is $275.

16 Sold $10,000 of merchandise to St. Petersburg Company, terms 3/10, n/30. Cost of merchandise is $6,500.

LG 13-7, *continued*

August 17 Received a payment on $2,500 of the invoice amount from Baton Rouge Corporation.

18 Received payment in full from Jacksonville Company.

24 Purchased $25,000 of merchandise from Tampa Company, 2/10, n/30, FOB shipping point.

25 Received $2,910 cash from St. Petersburg Company as a partial payment.

27 Purchased $6,000 of merchandise from Orlando Company, 2/10, n/30, FOB destination.

31 Borrowed $24,500 from 4th National Bank by signing a note payable. The loan proceeds were used to pay Tampa Company in order to take advantage of the discount terms.

31 A physical count of merchandise shows that the actual merchandise inventory on hand is $1,800 less than the perpetual inventory records.

Instructor-Assigned Problems

If you are using this book in a class, these review problems may be assigned by your instructor for homework, group assignments, class work, or other activities. Only your instructor has the solutions.

IA 13-1. Record buyer and seller transactions with various discount situations, no sales tax.
For each of the independent situations below, record the transactions for the buyer and for the seller company, using separate general journal pages for buyer and seller. Both companies use the perpetual inventory method. Calculate payment amounts to the nearest dollar.

1. On May 12, merchandise is sold to Buyer Company for $15,000, terms 2/10, n/30, cost $9,000. On May 21 Buyer pays in full.

2. On September 9, merchandise is sold to Buyer Company for $9,000, terms 2/10, n/30, cost $4,500. On October 1 Buyer pays in full.

3. On February 5, merchandise is sold to Buyer Company for $12,000, terms 2/10, n/30, cost $7,200. On February 15 Buyer pays $8,000 cash and pays the balance due on March 15.

4. On August 23, Buyer Company purchases $20,000, terms 2/15, n/45, cost $12,000. On September 4 Buyer discovers that 30% of the merchandise is incorrect and returns this to the Seller, sending a debit memo to Seller, receiving a credit memo in return. On September 5, Buyer pays the balance due.

5. On November 17, merchandise is sold to Buyer Company for $6,000, terms 1/10, n/30, cost $3,600. The seller offers trade chain discounts of 10% and 5% if certain types of merchandise are purchased. Buyer purchased these kinds of merchandise. On November 25 Buyer pays $3,000 cash and pays the balance due on December 15.

IA 13-2. Record various transactions and discount situations, two sales tax methods. Marin Home Design., Inc. has both wholesale and retail sales and purchases. Sales tax is 7%, only on retail transactions. The company uses a Sales Tax Payable account. Discount terms are offered on wholesale sales. All merchandise transactions are FOB shipping point.

Instructions.

a. Record each of the October transactions below in a general journal for Marin Design Company. Simplify calculations by rounding to the nearest dollar. You may omit explanations.

b. Assume that the company does not use a separate Sales Tax Payable account. How would the transactions on October 5, 20, 29, and 31 be recorded? Show the journal entries.

IA 13-2, *continued*

   2 Sold $15,000 of merchandise inventory to Alameda Co., terms 2/10, n/30. Cost: $9,000.

   5 Sold $1,900 of merchandise inventory for cash to retail customers. Cost: $800.

  11 Received payment in full from Alameda Co.

  14 Purchased $20,000 inventory from Porterville Co., with a 15%, 8% chain discount, terms 1/10, n/30.

  15 Purchased $500 of office supplies from Los Medanos Company on account.

  18 Alameda Co. returned all merchandise for cash because of incorrect color.

  20 Sold $2,950 of merchandise to retail customers for cash. Cost: $1,400.

  21 Purchased $12,000 of inventory from Las Positas Co., terms 2/10, n/30, plus $500 freight charges.

  24 Paid Portville Co. in full.

  28 Returned $10,000 invoice price of merchandise to Porterville Co., due to incorrect model number.

  29 A retail customer returned $200 of merchandise, cost $100.

  30 Paid Las Positas Co. invoice in full.

  31 Paid state taxing authority for October sales tax collections.

IA 13-3. **Journalize merchandise transactions—retail operations, sales tax.** North Devon Company sells clothing and accessories to retail customers. The local sales tax rate is 8%, and North Devon Company uses a Sales Tax Payable account. All sales are for cash, and the company uses the perpetual inventory method.

Instructions:

a. Record each of the transactions below in a general journal. For journal paper, you can use the template in the disk at the back of the book or at worthyjames.com (student info.)

b. Suppose that North Devon Company combined all sales and sales tax collections together in one account called Sales and did not use a separate liability account for Sales Tax Payable. Show the calculation you would use to determine the amount of the sales tax liability at the end of the month.

October 1 North Devon Company purchased $12,500 of merchandise inventory on account from Aurora Company, terms 2/10, n/30, FOB shipping point.

   2 Purchased $10,000 of merchandise inventory from Evanston Enterprises on account, terms 1/10, n/30, FOB shipping point, with $350 prepaid transportation charges paid by the Seller added to the invoice.

   5 Issued a debit memo and returned $1,500 of the merchandise purchased on October 1 from Aurora Company.

   6 Sold $5,800 of merchandise. Cost is $3,800.

   8 Purchased $15,000 of merchandise inventory from Urbana Suppliers, terms 2/15, n/30, FOB shipping point. North Devon Company will pay shipping costs separately.

   9 Sold $4,000 of merchandise. Cost is $2,500.

  11 Paid the balance owing for the October 1 purchase.

  12 Paid the balance owing for the October 2 purchase.

  15 Purchased $11,000 of merchandise from Springfield Corporation, terms 2/10, n/30, FOB shipping point.

  17 Sold $5,000 of merchandise. Cost $3,250

  18 A buyer who made a purchase on October 9 returned $300 of unsatisfactory merchandise. The cost was $170.

  19 Made a $3,430 payment to Urbana Suppliers. Also paid $150 of shipping costs.

IA 13-3, *continued*

October 21 Sold $10,000 of merchandise. Cost $6,500.

23 Paid $7,000 of the invoice amount owing to Springfield Corporation.

29 Purchased $11,000 of merchandise from Belleville Enterprises, terms 2/10, n/30, FOB destination. The merchandise has not arrived.

30 Paid the balance owing for the October 15 purchase from Springfield Corporation.

30 Paid the balance owing for the October 8 purchase from Urbana Suppliers.

31 Paid the amount of the sales tax collected during the month to the local tax authority.

IA 13-4. Journalize merchandise transactions, retail and wholesale, various discounts, sales tax.

Instructions:

a. Record each of the transactions below in a general journal for the *Buyer* Company.

b. Record each of the transactions below in a general journal for the *Seller* Company. Seller Company sells wholesale merchandise and retail equipment and supplies. For simplicity, Seller Company uses a single Cost of Goods Sold account for all sales. Assume a 5% sales tax, when applicable. The cost to the seller for wholesale merchandise inventory is 60% of the sales price before any discounts. You may omit explanations in this exercise. For journal paper, use the template in the disk at the back of the book or at worthyjames.com.

April 1 Buyer purchased $15,000 of merchandise inventory on account from Seller Company, terms 2/10, n/30, FOB shipping point.

3 Buyer purchased $9,000 of merchandise inventory on account from Seller Company, terms 1/10, n/30, FOB shipping point, with $200 prepaid transportation charges paid by Seller added to the invoice.

4 Buyer returned $5,000 of the merchandise purchased on April 1.

5 Buyer purchased $5,000 of merchandise inventory from Seller Company, terms 2/10, n/30, FOB shipping point.

6 Buyer Company purchased $3,500 of equipment from Seller Company on account. The equipment is for Buyer Company's own use as a retail customer and will not be resold to customers. Cost to Seller is $2,100.

11 Buyer Company paid the balance owing for the April 1 purchase.

13 Buyer paid the amount owing for the April 3 purchase.

15 Buyer purchased merchandise inventory on account from Seller Company, terms 2/10, n/30, FOB shipping point. Seller Company applied the following chain discount to the $20,000 purchase price: 5% on total amount for purchases up to $10,000. For purchases above $10,000, an additional 10% discount applies to the total after the first discount is applied to the total sale.

15 Buyer paid $3,920 cash for the merchandise purchased on April 5.

19 Buyer Company paid $500 cash to Seller Company for supplies. The supplies are for Buyer Company's own use. Cost to Seller is $200.

20 Buyer purchased $11,000 of merchandise inventory on account from Seller Company, terms 2/10, n/30, FOB shipping point.

23 Buyer purchased $3,000 of merchandise inventory on account from Seller Company, terms 2/10, n/30, FOB destination. The merchandise has not arrived.

30 Buyer paid $5,500 of the invoice price for the merchandise purchased on April 20.

31 Buyer paid the balance owing for the April 5 purchase.

31 Buyer returned $120 of defective supplies from the April 19 purchase for a cash refund of $120.

IA 13-5. Should a discount be taken? The Kitchen Store is a retail merchant that specializes in selling kitchen appliances, kitchen interior decorating supplies, and cooking utensils. The partners who own the store cannot agree on whether or not it would be a good policy to pay early to take advantage of discounts regularly offered by their suppliers. The current discussion concerns a $10,000 order of kitchen utensils on which the vendor is offering credit terms of 2/10, n/30. Today is January 5, the last day of the 10-day period in which payment can be made to take advantage of the discount. The business would have to borrow the cash from its bank credit line to pay for the purchase until it collects a large payment from a major customer on January 26, when it would pay off the loan from the bank. The annual interest rate on the credit line is 12%. Janet Chen, one of the partners, wants to take the discount "because it is always a good idea to save money." Dave Harris, another partner, says, "It is going to cost interest on the line of credit from the bank. We would be wasting the money!"

a. Should the company pay early to take the discount?
b. A different vendor offers the terms 1/10, n/45. What is your advice for paying this vendor?

IA 13-6. Journalize sales, returns, payment transactions, with and without sales tax.

Instructions:

a. Record each of the transactions below in a general journal for the Portsmouth Merchandise Company, Inc., which uses a perpetual inventory system. Cost of goods sold is maintained at 65% of wholesale sales and 50% of retail sales, which are all for cash. Sales tax on retail sales is 5%. (Use the journal paper in the disk at the back of this book or at www.worthyjames.com, student info. link.)
b. Create an Accounts Receivable T account just for Roanoke Enterprises transactions. Record all relevant activity in that account for the month of June and show the ending balance. Do exactly the same for an Accounts Payable account for the Roanoke Company. The beginning balances in both accounts are zero.

June 3 Sold $1,700 of merchandise to a retail customer.
6 Made a $10,580 sale to Roanoke Enterprises, terms 2/10, n/30 FOB shipping point.
9 Received a short payment from Charleston Company in the amount of $4,900 on a $10,000 sale made on May 31, terms 2/10, n/30 FOB shipping point.
12 Made a $500 sale to a retail customer.
14 Roanoke Company returned $900 of merchandise.
16 Received a short payment from Roanoke Company in the amount of $5,880.
20 Sold $6,000 of merchandise to Pasadena Enterprises, terms 2/10, n/30 FOB shipping point. Paid $450 of shipping costs, which were added to the customer invoice.
23 The retail customer on June 12 returned $300 of the merchandise.
28 Received payment in full from Pasadena Enterprises for the balance due.
30 Received the balance due from Roanoke Enterprises.
30 Sold $4,400 of merchandise to Little Rock, Inc., terms 2/10, n/30 destination.

Solutions are in the disk at the back of the book and at: www.worthyjames.com

PRACTICE   Learning Goal 13, continued

IA 13-7 Comprehensive review of different merchandising transactions.

Instructions:

The problem below contains various merchandising transactions. Each transaction is an independent event unless otherwise stated. Create a table similar to the one below, and for each transaction, record the proper entry, as it would appear in a general journal for the seller and for the buyer. Leave enough space for compound entries. Both buyers and sellers use a perpetual inventory system.

Event	Seller Journal Entry	Buyer Journal Entry

Events:

1. $1,000 sale with 6% sales tax. Cost of sale is $425.
2. $5,000 sale on account, terms 2/10, n/30. Cost of goods is $3,000.
3. $3,000 sale, terms 3/15, n/30, cost $1,500. Seller pays $650 shipping, buyer will not reimburse.
4. $3,000 sale, terms 3/15, n/30, cost $1,500. Seller pays $650 shipping, buyer will reimburse.
5. $3,000 sale, terms 3/15, n/30, cost $1,500. Buyer will pay $650 shipping cost to shipper.
6. Buyer in "1" returns $400 of merchandise.
7. Full payment is received from buyer in "3" within the discount period.
8. A short payment of $700 is received from buyer in "3" within the discount period.
9. Full payment is received from buyer in "3" after the discount period.
10. Full payment is received from buyer in "4" within the discount period.
11. Buyer in "5" pays the shipping cost.
12. Buyer in "8" pays the remaining full amount due after the discount period.
13. Merchandise is returned to a seller. Purchase was $5,000 terms 2/10, n/30 and was paid in full within the discount period. Cost is $3,000.
14. Merchant records sales tax liability, then pays sales tax to taxing authorities. Sales tax rate is 6.5%. Merchant included sales tax with sales in the sales account. The account balance is $293,514.

Your Questions?

It is *very* important to be aware of what you need to understand better. What do you need to understand better about this learning goal? On a separate piece of paper, write the questions that you want to discuss with your classmates, instructor, or supervisor. Try to be very specific about what is bothering you, such as explanations that you do not fully understand.

Completing the Worksheet, *continued*

Queensborough Patio Mart, Inc.
Worksheet
For the Year Ended December 31, 2017

Account Titles	Trial Balance Dr.	Trial Balance Cr.	Adjustments Dr.	Adjustments Cr.	Adjusted Trial Balance Dr.	Adjusted Trial Balance Cr.	Income Statement Dr.	Income Statement Cr.	Balance Sheet Dr.	Balance Sheet Cr.
Cash	37,950				37,950				37,950	
Accounts					5,500				5,500	
Receivable	5,500									
Merchandise										
Inventory	16,850			(d) 500	16,350				16,350	
Store Supplies	4,335			(b) 250	4,085				4,085	
Prepaid Insurance	1,800			(c) 385	1,415				1,415	
Office Equipment	12,750				12,750				12,750	
Accum. Dep'n.—										
Office Equip.		3,200		(a) 150		3,350				3,350
Store Equipment	44,880				44,880				44,880	
Accum. Dep'n.—										
Store Equipment		15,650		(a) 350		16,000				16,000
Accounts Payable		12,800		(e) 100		12,900				12,900
Sales Tax Payable		2,100				2,100				2,100
Common Stock		10,000				10,000				10,000
Retained Earnings		57,380				57,380				57,380
Dividends	16,300				16,300				16,300	
Sales		236,700				236,700		236,700		
Sales Returns and										
Allowances	5,700				5,700		5,700			
Sales Discounts	2,100				2,100		2,100			
Cost of Goods										
Sold	145,000		(d) 500		145,500		145,500			
Freight-out	880				880		880			
Advertising										
Expense	2,800				2,800		2,800			
Insurance Expense	715		(c) 385		1,100		1,100			
Salaries and Wages										
Expense	19,200				19,200		19,200			
Rent Expense	16,100				16,100		16,100			
Income Tax Expense	2,500				2,500		2,500			
Utilities Expense	2,470		(e) 100		2,570		2,570			
Totals	337,830	337,830								
Supplies Expense			(b) 250		250		250			
Depreciation										
Expense			(a) 500		500		500			
Totals			1,735	1,735	338,430	338,430	199,200	236,700	139,230	101,730
Net Income							37,500			37,500
Totals							236,700	236,700	139,230	139,230

Financial Statements

Income Statement

The income statement below is a ***multiple-step income statement***. It shows the individual calculation steps, including cost of goods sold and operating expenses, that are needed to determine net income. A multiple-step statement discloses detailed information about net income or loss. It is also called a classified income statement because it classifies operating expenses into the convenient categories *selling* and *administrative*.

Queensborough Patio Mart, Inc. Income Statement For the Year Ended December 31, 2017			
Sales revenue			$236,700
Less: Sales returns and allowances		$5,700	
Sales discounts		2,100	7,800
Net sales revenue			228,900
Cost of goods sold			145,500
Gross profit			83,400
Operating expenses			
Selling expenses			
Salaries and wages expense	$5,000		
Advertising expense	2,800		
Freight-out	880		
Supplies expense	50		
Total selling expenses		8,730	
Administrative expenses			
Rent expense	16,100		
Salaries and wages expense	14,200		
Utilities expense	2,570		
Insurance expense	1,100		
Depreciation expense	500		
Supplies expense	200		
Total administrative expenses		34,670	
Total operating expenses			43,400
Income before income tax			40,000
Income tax expense			2,500
Net income			$37,500

Memory Aid

To help you remember the parts of the multiple-step income statement, think of it as three pieces:

- The part to calculate gross profit
- The part for operating expenses, selling and administrative
- The part that has net income

The dashed lines across the statement will help you visualize these parts.

continued ▶

Financial Statements, *continued*

Statement of Retained Earnings and Balance Sheet

The statement of retained earnings is unchanged from that of a service business. The balance sheet has only two significant changes: a new current asset called *merchandise inventory,* and a liability *sales tax payable.*

Queensborough Patio Mart, Inc.
Statement of Retained Earnings
For the Year Ended December 31, 2017

Retained earnings, January 1, 2017	$ 57,380
Add: Net income	37,500
Subtotal	94,880
Less: Dividends	16,300
Retained earnings, December 31, 2017	$ 78,580

Queensborough Patio Mart, Inc.
Balance Sheet
December 31, 2017

Assets

Current assets			
Cash		$37,950	
Accounts receivable		5,500	
Merchandise inventory		16,350	
Store supplies		4,085	
Prepaid insurance		1,415	
Total current assets			$65,300
Property, plant, and equipment			
Office equipment	$12,750		
Less: Accumulated depreciation	3,350	9,400	
Store equipment	44,880		
Less: Accumulated depreciation	16,000	28,880	
Total property, plant, and equipment			38,280
Total assets			$103,580

Liabilities and Stockholders' Equity

Current liabilities			
Accounts payable		$12,900	
Sales tax payable		2,100	
Total current liabilities			$15,000
Stockholders' equity			
Paid-in capital			
Common stock		10,000	
Retained earnings		78,580	
Total stockholders' equity			88,580
Total liabilities and stockholders' equity			$103,580

Financial Statements, *continued*

Other Revenues and Expenses

Sometimes a business has other revenues and gains and other expenses and losses that are not part of the operating activities needed to produce a service or product. These "other" or ***nonoperating*** items would not be expected to be part of normal operations, but rather are incidental to being in business. If they are material, "other" items must be shown separately on the income statement, and never "buried" inside of the operating expense numbers.

Examples

There is no single list of items—judgment is required to decide if an item should be classified as "other." However, here are some typical examples:

Other revenues and gains:
- Interest earned
- Rental revenue (not a rental business)
- Gain on sale of equipment

Other expenses and losses:
- Interest expense
- Lawsuit losses
- Loss on sale of equipment

How to Show

If there are "other" nonoperating items, then do this:
- Calculate ***operating income***, which is gross profit minus operating expenses, before nonoperating items.
- Show the "other" items under operating income.
- Calculate net income, which is operating income plus/minus net "other" items.

Example

Here is how the affected part of the Queensborough Patio Mart income statement would appear if there were "other" items. We are using assumed numbers for the "other" items:

Supplies expense	200		
Total administrative expenses		37,170	
Total operating expenses			43,400
Operating income			**40,000**
Other revenue and gains			
Interest revenue	500		
Gain on sale of land	2,500	3,000	
Other expenses and losses			
Interest expense	3,200		
Loss on sale of equipment	5,000	(8,200)	(5,200)
Income before income tax			34,800
Income tax expense			2,500
Net income			$32,300

Note: The $5,200 for the "other" items is a net amount, the difference between $8,200 and $3,000. Because other expenses exceed other income, the $5,200 net amount is subtracted.

continued ▶

Financial Statements, *continued*

Single-Step Income Statement Format

The *single-step income statement* is a format in which the net income is calculated in a single step, by subtracting the total of all expenses from the total of all revenues.

Example

Here is how the Queensborough Patio Mart income statement, including the additional "other" items on page 479, would appear as a single-step statement. Usually, but not always, the statement is condensed as you see below, with the line items representing final totals.

Queensborough Patio Mart, Inc. Income Statement For the Year Ended December 31, 2017		
Revenues		
Net sales		$228,900
Interest earned		500
Gain on sale of land		2,500
Total revenues		231,900
Expenses		
Cost of goods sold	$145,500	
Selling expenses	8,730	
Administrative expenses	34,670	
Interest expense	3,200	
Equipment sale loss	5,000	
Income tax expense	2,500	
Total expenses		199,600
Net income		$ 32,300

Essential Features

- All revenue items, including "other" revenues, are grouped together.
- All expense items, including "other" expenses, are grouped together.
- Net income can always be calculated in a single step, by subtracting total expenses from total revenues.

Recording Adjusting Entries

Adjusting Entries Procedure

The adjusting entries are simply copied from the worksheet adjusting entries columns and recorded into the general journal. The following example shows the entries that come from the Queensborough Patio Mart worksheet.

Recording Closing Entries

Closing Entries Source

In the worksheet, the income statement columns and the balance in the dividends account are the sources for the closing entries.

Closing Entries Procedure

The table below shows the steps in the closing entries procedure.

Step	Action
1	Close accounts that increase net income. In the income statement columns of the worksheet, all accounts with credit balances are closed by debiting them in the general journal. The total of all the debits is recorded as a credit to Income Summary.
2	Close accounts that decrease net income. In the income statement columns of the worksheet, all accounts with debit balances are closed by crediting them in the general journal. The total of all the credits is recorded as a debit to Income Summary.
3	Calculate the balance of the Income Summary account and close this into the retained earnings account. A credit balance in Income Summary is closed by debiting Income Summary and crediting retained earnings. A debit balance in Income Summary is closed with the opposite entry.
4	Close the dividends account into the retained earnings account. Credit the dividends account and debit the retained earnings account.

continued ▶

Recording Closing Entries, *continued*

Example of Step 1

GENERAL JOURNAL				J44
Date	**Account Titles and Explanation**	**Post. Ref.**	**Debit**	**Credit**
2017				
Dec. 31	CLOSING ENTRIES			
	Sales		236,700	
	Income Summary			236,700
	To close credit balance temporary accounts			

Example of Step 2

31	Income Summary		199,200	
	Sales Returns and Allowances			5,700
	Sales Discounts			2,100
	Cost of Goods Sold			145,500
	Freight-out			880
	Advertising Expense			2,800
	Insurance Expense			1,100
	Salaries and Wages Expense			19,200
	Rent Expense			16,100
	Utilities Expense			2,570
	Supplies Expense			250
	Depreciation Expense			500
	Income Tax Expense			2,500
	To close debit balance temporary accounts			

This must be the same as the debit total in the worksheet income statement column.

Example of Steps 3 and 4

31	Income Summary		37,500	
	Retained Earnings			37,500
	Retained Earnings		16,300	
	Dividends			16,300

The Gross Profit Percentage

Overview

For all merchants, gross profit as a percentage of net sales is an extremely important number. This calculation shows what portion of every sales dollar is left over to cover expenses and provide a profit, after the cost of the merchandise is paid for.

Definition

Gross profit percentage is gross profit divided by net sales.

Example

Refer to the Queensboro Patio Mart multiple-step income statement. The gross profit percentage is $83,400/$228,900 = 36.4%. This means that 36.4% of net sales revenue, or about 36.4 cents of every net sales dollar, is left over after subtracting the cost of goods sold expense.

Why It Is So Important

Several key factors make the gross profit percentage so important.

- The gross profit percentage is a number that shows the result of making several very important business decisions.
- The gross profit percentage has a major effect on net income.
- The gross percentage makes it possible to fairly compare different businesses of different sizes.

Gross Profit Percentage Shows Result of Decisions

- Should we set our sales price high to increase our gross profit percentage (but risk losing customers)?
- Should we set our sales price low, which lowers the gross profit percentage but may increase total sales volume?
- Are we minimizing the cost of our merchandise purchases?
- If merchandise is too cheap, will we lose customers and reduce net sales?

Comparison of Businesses

Suppose we want to compare the efficiency of operations of Big Company and Small Company. Here is the information for each company:

- Net sales: Big Company $4,880,500; Small Company $375,000
- Gross profit: Big Company $1,952,200; Small Company $168,750

Although the dollar amounts are very different:

- The gross profit efficiency of Big Company is less than Small Company. Big Company's gross profit is 40%; Small Company's gross profit is 45%. Small Company has more gross profit per dollar of sales.
- Big Company may have more total sales and total gross profit because it has set lower sales prices.

27. The sales tax that is added to the list price on the invoice by the seller will be:
    a. debited to sales tax expense.
    b. credited to sales tax payable.
    c. debited to sales discounts.
    d. credited to sales tax income.

28. On May 12, Hagerstown Company sold $10,000 list price of merchandise to Wor Wic Company, terms 4/10, n/30. Wor Wic made a payment of $6,000 cash on May 17 and paid the balance owing on May 28. What is the cost of merchandise to Wor Wic Company?
    a. $10,000
    b. $9,600
    c. $9,760
    d. some other amount

CUMULATIVE TEST SOLUTIONS   Learning Goals 13 and 14

Multiple Choice

1. c
2. c
3. c
4. c
5. c
6. d The best method is to prepare a quick, informal, multiple-step statement so you can see the amounts.
7. b The other two companies are service companies.
8. a Substitute in: **BI** + (net **P** + **frt-in**) − **C of GS** = **EI**. Therefore, $11,500 + $2,850 − x = $8,200.
9. b which is ($20,000 × .9) + $200 = $18,200. The discount period has passed.
10. a
11. c
12. d The single-step statement does not combine "other" items into one number.
13. a
14. a If inventory decreases, it means that the purchases of merchandise inventory were not enough to meet the demand of the product sales, so goods had to be taken out of inventory. The decrease in inventory of $19,000 is the amount by which purchases were less than the cost of goods sold. Therefore, purchases were $255,000 − $19,000 = $236,000.
15. c
16. d
17. a Title (ownership) transferred to the buyer at the shipping point.
18. c Visualize an income statement, then substitute the numbers that you know. Working backwards (bottom to top), net income + other expenses + operating expenses = gross profit. Net sales − gross profit = cost of goods sold.
19. b Substitute in: **BI** + (net **P** + **frt-in**) − **C of GS** = **EI**. Therefore, x + $153,750 − $16,350 = $145,000.
20. d The error overstated cost of goods sold, which understates net income. Because the inventory was never recorded as an asset, total assets are also understated.
21. d
22. a
23. a
24. d
25. d No payment has been made yet, so 2% discount cannot be included, but freight is added.
26. d Shrinkage is recorded by crediting Merchandise Inventory. Usually cost of goods sold is debited unless the shrinkage amount is large, in which case a separate account should be used.
27. b
28. d The key to this problem is remembering that any partial cash payment within the discount period is a net amount. So, the portion of the gross sales price that the payment relates to is some larger number. In this case, the $6,000 is 96% of some larger amount: $6,000/.96 = $6,250. The remaining (undiscounted) part of the sale is: $10,000 − $6,250 = $3,750. Therefore, $6,000 + $3,750 is the final net amount of the purchase, which is $9,750.

HELP TABLE   Identify Your Strengths and Weaknesses

The questions in this test cover the main parts of Learning Goal 13 and Learning Goal 14. After you have listed the number of each question that you missed, look at the table below.

Go to the first subpart category in the table: Compare Service and Merchandising. The second column in the table shows which questions on the test covered this topic. Look on the test to see if you circled question numbers 1, 7, or 13. How many of these did you miss? Write the number you missed in the "How Many Missed?" column. Repeat this process for each of the subpart categories in the table.

If you miss *two or more questions* for any subpart category, you are too weak in that topic and you need to *review*. The last column shows you where to read and practice so you can improve your score in that topic.

Some subpart categories have more questions because you need to be especially well prepared in these areas. More questions indicates where your performance must be better.

Subpart	Questions	How many missed?	Material begins on . . .
Compare Service and Merchandising	1, 7, 13		page 307
The Cost of Goods Sold Calculation	8, 14, 19		page 439
Transactions That Involve Buying Merchandise	3, 9, 15, 20, 25, 28		page 441
Transactions That Involve Selling Merchandise	2, 4, 10, 16, 21, 27		page 453
Ending Inventory	5, 11, 17, 22		page 461
Complete the Period-End Procedures—Perpetual Method	6, 12, 18, 23, 24, 26		page 474

Note: In addition to the questions above, you should also practice the following:

- Prepare complete multiple-step and single-step income statements.
- Prepare complete closing entries.

Use separate sheets of paper and work problems from any text in which answers are also available to you.

Accounting Systems

In Learning Goal 15, you will find:

Definition and Main Features of Accounting Systems

Subsidiary Ledgers

Special Journals

Other Journal Types

Computerized Accounting Systems Overview

LEARNING GOAL 15	# Identify an Accounting System; Explain and Use Its Features

Overview

In This Learning Goal . . .

The purpose of this learning goal is to make you aware of what an accounting system is and what its most important features are. Then you will have the opportunity to practice with the commonly used elements of most accounting systems. The subject of accounting systems is a large one: many books are devoted entirely to this subject. Here, our goal is to acquire a general overview and understanding and basic skills.

A Closer Look

When you began your study of accounting, you probably read that "accounting" is defined as a financial information system. Until now, you have been studying the basics of that information system. This has included all the steps in the accounting cycle, which eventually resulted in financial statements used by decision makers.

Now, you will begin to learn more details about how accounting information is processed. The basic elements that you have studied so far may be enough for a very small business, but they will not be sufficient for larger businesses. Accounting as an information system meets information needs of a more complex business by:

- developing specialized subsystems that process only certain types of transactions, and
- using computer applications to process greater amounts of data and perform more complex analyses.

The discussion that follows introduces you to these ideas.

Definition and Main Features of Accounting Systems

Accounting System Defined

Definition	The term ***accounting system*** means a system that combines people, physical records, and procedures to process financial information for the purpose of creating useful reports.
Synonym	An accounting system is also called an ***accounting information system***.

The Essential Elements

Overview	The essential elements of an accounting system are: ■ Usefulness ■ Cost-benefit ■ Internal control ■ Adaptability
Usefulness	To be "useful," an accounting system must meet the information needs of the business or organization that is using it. This information may be critical in determining the very survival of a business. An accounting system "goes wrong" when it does not provide critical financial information in a timely way. Here are some examples of questions that ask for critical financial information: ■ Who owes us money, how much, and for how long? ■ To whom do we owe money, how much, and when must we pay it? ■ How much of each kind of inventory do we have? ■ Do we have the information that we need for the tax returns? ■ How much does each of our services or products contribute to the total profit?
Cost-benefit	*Cost-benefit* refers to the cost effectiveness of the information being provided. Even if the information is useful, is it worth what we are paying to obtain it? Does the value of the information exceed the cost of the information?
Internal Control	*Internal control* means the procedures and records in the system that ensure assets are safeguarded. Internal control in an accounting system reduces the possibility that assets will be stolen or otherwise lost by error and oversight. Maintaining adequate internal control requires a regular assessment of the business operations to understand the exposure to theft and error and what can be done to minimize them.

The Essential Elements, *continued*

Adaptability

Adaptability addresses the information needs of a business that are constantly evolving and growing. If a business is to grow, *the information system must grow with it*. Information needs that were nonessential for a small business can become critical for a larger or changed business. An accounting system should be designed in such a way that it can accommodate greater or different information requirements.

Growing Importance of Information Systems

The Revolution Has Arrived!

At this time, amazing changes are happening in the development of information systems and the accessibility of information. These changes are causing a major impact on all areas of life, business, and, of course, they also affect accounting.

How Accounting Systems Will Affect You

Traditionally, only those individuals entering the fields of accounting or management information systems needed a working understanding of accounting systems. This was because the daily interaction with accounting systems was generally limited to these people.

Two events that have changed this are: (1) the development of inexpensive and powerful computers, and (2) the Internet. Here are just a few examples of changes that are coming:

■ New accounting systems are being designed as "intranet" systems within a company that will have the power to combine accounting information with information from any other business activity, such as production, marketing, and human resources. Large, fully integrated systems are called *ERP (Enterprise Resource Planning) systems*. All this means that many more employees will be expected to use the system and to have some understanding of what it does and how it works—including the ability to locate and use accounting data.

"Traditionally, only those individuals entering the fields of accounting or management information systems needed a working understanding of accounting systems."

continued ▶

Growing Importance of Information Systems, *continued*

- Businesses are beginning to share accounting information with each other on the Internet. This is called **electronic data integration,** or "EDI." One example is the supplier/buyer relationship. Some companies allow suppliers to have Internet access to production information so supplies can be automatically ordered at specific prices and quantities as needed. Managers who can understand an EDI accounting system and can use its data or help develop new systems will have an advantage.

- Manual data entry for larger companies will eventually disappear with the advent of machine-readable documents because journal entries will automatically be created from the documents. However, there will be a demand for individuals who can modify and improve an accounting information system to design useful reports and who understand the meaning of accounting transactions.

- *Cloud computing* means using the Internet to access a service provider that specializes in electronically storing data and providing services over the Internet. (The word "cloud" is just a reference to the Internet.) Services can include automated accounting and ERP functions at all levels of complexity. This means that a business can have many of its accounting functions performed in a simultaneous and coordinated way using input from different locations. As well, documents and files can be stored and accessed from different locations. A key benefit of cloud computing is its low cost, compared to what a business would have to spend to obtain these same resources. For that reason, the greatest initial interest was primarily from small and moderate-size businesses; however, this is now expanding with significant transition into the cloud by large businesses. The greatest risks with cloud computing are data security, reliability, and ownership of data.

- *XBRL* means "Extensible Business Reporting Language". This is a digital financial reporting method based on a widely used computer language. The advantage of XBRL is that once it is set-up, it is very efficient to share, search, extract, and analyze practically any kind of financial statement information, eliminating much manual work. XBRL does not change GAAP or the meaning of accounting information, but improves accessibility. The Securities and Exchange Commission and regulators in various major countries require that most public companies include XBRL reporting.

Subsidiary Ledgers

What Are Subsidiary Ledgers?

Overview

Earlier we said that one way accounting systems meet the needs of more complex operations is by the development of specialized subsystems. One relatively common type of subsystem is the subsidiary ledger.

The reason for this development is that some general ledger accounts can accumulate enormous amounts of detailed information. This detail is very important, but because of the great amount of it, the information must be carefully organized or it will quickly become unmanageable and useless.

Examples of Potential Problems

- Some businesses that sell on account can have hundreds or even thousands of customers, each of whom owes varying amounts of money and makes varying amounts of payments. It would be impossible for a single large account to determine each customer's correct balance.
- Some businesses, such as large retail stores, can have hundreds or thousands of different inventory items. The units, unit cost, and total cost of each of these items will be lost unless properly accounted for by using some type of subsidiary ledger, with each item tracked individually.

Solution

General ledger accounts that have balances representing many items need individual sub-accounts to track the changes and balance of each item.

Definition

A *subsidiary ledger* is a separate ledger that contains only accounts showing the detail of a single general ledger account.

Examples of Subsidiary Ledgers

- An Accounts Receivable subsidiary ledger would contain only accounts for each of the individual customers, with one account per customer.
- An Accounts Payable subsidiary ledger would contain only accounts for amounts owing to individual creditors, with one account per creditor.
- A Merchandise Inventory subsidiary ledger would contain only accounts of Merchandise Inventory, with one account per inventory item.

Controlling Account

Any account in the general ledger that has a subsidiary ledger is called a *controlling account*.

continued ▶

What Are Subsidiary Ledgers? *continued*

Features of a Subsidiary Ledger

■ A subsidiary ledger is a *completely separate* ledger. Therefore, entering a debit or credit in a subsidiary ledger account does not cause total debits and credits to be out of balance in the general ledger. (There is no "double-counting" in the general ledger.)

Example:

A merchandise return is received from Mr. Jones, a customer. The general journal entry records a debit to Sales Returns and Allowances and a credit to Accounts Receivable for $100. The $100 credit is posted to the controlling account, Accounts Receivable, in the general ledger. A $100 credit is also posted to the subsidiary account for Mr. Jones in the subsidiary ledger.

■ Postings to the subsidiary ledger should be done daily. In this way, up-to-date balances for any customer, creditor, or other subsidiary account are immediately available.

■ Because the subsidiary ledger is simply a breakdown of the controlling account, the total of all the accounts in a subsidiary ledger must equal the balance in its controlling account.

Example:

At June 30, the controlling Accounts Receivable account balance is $251,300. The Accounts Receivable subsidiary ledger has 145 individual accounts, one for each customer. The individual debit balances of these 145 accounts must add up to $251,300 on June 30.

■ Any general ledger account can have a subsidiary ledger.

Subsidiary Ledgers That Most Businesses Need

■ Practically every business must have an Accounts Payable subsidiary ledger.
■ Any business that makes sales on account must have an Accounts Receivable subsidiary ledger.
■ A business that has inventory items needs an Inventory subsidiary ledger.

Customer Statements

For any business that makes credit sales, the subsidiary Accounts Receivable ledger accounts are the sources of the information that go on the statements (the billings) sent to the customers.

Illustrations of Subsidiary Ledgers

Illustration

The illustration below shows the relationship of subsidiary ledgers to the controlling accounts. The general ledger accounts are on the left. The Accounts Receivable and Accounts Payable accounts are highlighted. The subsidiary ledger accounts for Accounts Receivable and Accounts Payable, which have one account for each customer or creditor, are on the right. The total of the individual accounts in each subsidiary ledger is the same as the total in its controlling account.

General Ledger Accounts

Subsidiary Ledger Accounts

Accounts Payable Subsidiary Ledger (creditors)

Accounts Receivable Subsidiary Ledger (customers)

Numerical Example

The illustration on the next page shows you the controlling account for Accounts Receivable and a subsidiary ledger that has six subsidiary accounts, one for each customer who has made a purchase on account. The controlling account shows a debit balance of $8,000. To simplify the illustration, the debit and credit entries in the controlling account are replaced by "$" signs. Notice that the total of all the six subsidiary account balances is $8,000, the same as the controlling balance.

continued ▶   **515**

Illustrations of Subsidiary Ledgers, *continued*

Controlling

Accounts Receivable

bal. 7,100	
$ ⋮	$ ⋮
bal. 8,000	

Subsidiary

Ames

bal. 900	
	900
2,100	
	1,400
700	

Brown

| bal. 2,000 | |
| 2,000 | |

Carswell

bal. 4,200	
	2,000
	2,200
–0–	

Garcia

4,150	
	1,150
3,000	

Simons

700	
	100
	100
	100
400	

Yuen

| 1,900 | |
| 1,900 | |

Solving Problems Using Subsidiary Account Information

Overview

Subsidiary accounts contain much detailed information. If you are taking an accounting class or are working with accounts receivable, it is likely that you will be required to prove you know how to use this information. Some common examples are described below.

Total Sales on Account

In the numerical example above, what are the current period sales on account? No information is given to you about the total debits or credits in the controlling account. But if you total all the current period debits in the subsidiary accounts, that will be the total credit sales: $2,100 + $4,150 + $700 + $1,900 = $8,850.

Reconstruct Controlling Account Totals

You can reconstruct the total of the current period debits and the total of the credits in the controlling account. The debit total entered in the controlling account is the same total amount as the sum of the individual subsidiary accounts: $8,850. Likewise, the credit total in the controlling account is the same total amount as the sum of subsidiary credits: $7,950.

Caution: The $8,850 and $7,950 are single total entries in the controlling account. The entire subsidiary account detail is *not* repeated in the controlling account.

Solving Problems Using Subsidiary Account Information, *continued*

Cash Collections	It is tempting to think that the total credits in the subsidiary Accounts Receivable must be the amount of cash collected from the customers. But remember that Accounts Receivable is credited for the full amount when a discount is taken, so less cash may be received than the full amount. Also remember that Accounts Receivable is credited for Sales Returns and Allowances. So, you must first know the amount of discounts allowed and the returns and allowances allowed and then subtract these from the total credits to know the amount of cash collected. This is also true for bad receivables (see Learning Goal 17).
General Rule	To use subsidiary account information to help solve problems, always visualize the journal entry that created the debit or credit in the subsidiary account. This will indicate the cause of the debit or credit.
Examples	The table below shows you some examples of transactions for applying the rule.

Subsidiary Account Type	Transactions That Make a Debit	Transactions That Make a Credit
Accounts Receivable	▪ Sales on account	▪ Cash collections: (collection amount may be less than the credit) ▪ Sales return or allowance
Accounts Payable	▪ Cash payment: (payment amount may be less than debit because of discount) ▪ Purchase return or allowance	▪ Purchase of asset on account ▪ Incurring an expense on account

Special Journals

Overview

Introduction

Until this point in your accounting study, you have probably used only the general journal to record transactions. However, over many years, accountants discovered that it is more efficient to record similar types of frequently recurring transactions in special journals that are designed just for those types of transactions. Any type of business can use special journals.

For Manual Systems

Special journals are primarily intended for use in **manual accounting systems**. These are accounting systems in which all the steps in the accounting cycle are done by hand, without the use of computers. This includes journalizing, posting, totaling accounts, and so on.

Adaptability to Computers

Special journals are very adaptable to computerized accounting systems. The concept of recording similar types of transactions together is still used, but instead of using pens and pencils, special screens are designed for entering transaction data. We discuss computerized systems later in this learning goal.

Learn a Manual System First

This book discusses special journals as they are used in manual systems. There are several reasons for this:

- Practice with manual special journals will help familiarize you with report formats used in both computerized and manual systems.
- An understanding of manual system use transfers easily to a computerized system, but not the reverse.
- You may actually need to use a manual system.

What Is a Special Journal?

Definition

A *special journal* is a journal that records only specified types of similar transactions.

Examples

- Use one journal to record *only* sales on account.
- Use one journal to record *only* receipts of cash.

Nonexample

The general journal. (It can be used to record any kind of transaction.)

Why Are Special Journals More Efficient?

Division of Labor

There is only one general journal, so only one person can use it at a time. However, there can be several special journals, and each one can be used separately.

Error Reduction

When similar types of transactions are being recorded, the transaction patterns become familiar, and errors are reduced.

Faster Recording and Posting

Special journals are designed in columnar form, often with one column assigned to a set of accounts. This reduces the amount of entries required. Also, the column totals can be posted into the ledger accounts, which is much faster than posting each entry one at a time into the ledger. (We will see samples of this coming up.)

The Most Common Special Journals

Overview

A special journal is designed to record only a specified type of transaction. So, a special journal could be designed for any kind of transaction: sales returns and allowances, owner withdrawals, merchandise purchases—anything you want. However, there is a practical limit to this. Special journals only increase efficiency if they are used for *frequently recurring* types of transactions.

The Four Most Frequently Recurring Transactions

Over years of practice, accountants have discovered that most merchandising businesses (and, in fact, most businesses of all types) encounter four kinds of transactions the most frequently:

- Purchases on account
- Sales on account
- Cash payments
- Cash receipts

Therefore, most businesses have a special journal for each of these kinds of transactions.

Still Keep the General Journal

Don't throw out the general journal! It is still used to record any transactions that cannot be entered in the special journals. Therefore, most businesses have five journals: four special journals and the general journal.

continued ▶

The Most Common Special Journals, *continued*

Purchases Journal

The ***purchases journal*** is used for purchases on account. This may be only merchandise purchases; however, most companies expand the purchases journal and use it for the purchase of any assets if the items are "on account." That is how we will use the journal.

Sales Journal

The ***sales journal*** is used for all transactions that are for sales on account, and *only* sales on account. This means that any transaction that is a *sale on account* must be recorded in the sales journal, but a cash sale is never recorded here. Also, the sales journal is only for merchandise or service sales, and not for incidental sales of other assets.

Cash Payments Journal

The ***cash payments journal*** is used for *all* transactions that involve *payments of cash*. This means that any transaction that involves a payment of cash—even one cent—*must* be recorded in the cash payments journal.

Cash Receipts Journal

The ***cash receipts journal*** is used for *all* transactions that involve *receipts of cash*. This means that *any* transaction that involves a receipt of cash—even one cent—*must* be recorded in the cash receipts journal.

TIP

When using special journals, remember: A transaction is *never* double-recorded. A transaction is recorded in only *one* journal—either a special journal or the general journal.

Custom Design

A business is not limited to the above types. Special journals can be custom-designed to meet the particular information needs of any business.

The Most Common Special Journals, *continued*

Examples

Transaction	Record it in the . . .	because . . .
A sale on account is made to Mr. Jefferson.	sales journal	it is a sale *and* it is on account.
A cash sale is made to Mrs. Nguyen.	cash receipts journal	it involves a receipt of cash.
We collect $500 from a customer's account receivable.	cash receipts journal	it involves a receipt of cash.
$200 of merchandise is purchased on credit.	purchases journal	it is a purchase *and* it is on account.
$200 of merchandise is purchased for cash.	cash payments journal	it involves a payment of cash.
We pay $300 owing on account, and take a discount.	cash payments journal	it involves a payment of cash.
We purchase $800 of merchandise and pay $100 cash. The balance is on account.	cash payments journal	(The entire transaction is recorded here because it involves a cash payment.)
Merchandise is returned from a customer.	general journal	it will not "fit" in any special journal.
We record adjusting and closing entries.	general journal	they will not "fit" in any special journal.

Features

Common Features

Special journals are designed with certain common features, including:

- The journal is designed with columns for whatever accounts that are needed, and the debit and credit amounts are entered in the columns.
- The amounts in the columns are totaled.
- Total debits must equal total credits, just as with a general journal.
- Posting must be done, just as with a general journal.

Coming Up

We will now look at each journal in detail.

The Design and Use of a Purchases Journal

Purpose

The purchases journal (example on the opposite page for Sept. 2017) is for any kind of purchase that is "on account." *All purchases on account are entered here.* Some businesses also use this journal for recording accrued expenses.

Column Titles

The *right half* of this journal has the debit and credit dollar amounts. The *left half* of the journal has columns for recording transaction date, name of subsidiary account, terms, and posting reference.

- **Debits:** Debits to Inventory occur frequently in these transactions, so a column is dedicated just to the Inventory account. Debits to accounts other than Inventory are recorded in the "other accounts" section.
- **Credits:** Because every purchase is on account, Accounts Payable is credited with every entry; therefore, a dedicated column is provided for this purpose.

Examples of Entries

From data on a supplier's invoice, a transaction is entered on a line:

- On September 3, inventory is purchased from Ramos Corporation. So, "Sept. 3" is entered in the date column, the name of the creditor "Ramos Corp." is entered in the Account Credited column, and the terms of the purchase (2/10, n/30) is entered in the terms column. Then the purchase amount of $1,500 is entered as a credit to Accounts Payable and a debit to Inventory.
- On September 4, supplies are purchased from Angstrom Company. Because there is no column just for supplies, the $400 debit to Supplies is entered in the "other" accounts section in the Amount column, and the account name "Supplies" is entered in the Name column in the same section.
- On September 5, furniture is purchased from Winthrop Partners for $5,000. The amount is entered in the "other" accounts section because there is no dedicated column for the Furniture account. Payment terms are "net 30."

Posting

- **Dedicated columns:** At the end of the period, post the column total into its general ledger account, with the journal reference ("P") and the journal page number (here P9). Then write the account number under the column total in the journal. Example: $7,080 Inventory total is posted as a debit to account #125.
- **"Other" accounts column:** This total cannot be posted as one amount because it consists of more than one type of item. Example: The $400 and $5,000 in the "other" column are posted individually, and the account numbers 123 and 150 are entered in the journal "Ref." column after each amount is posted into its ledger account.
- **Subsidiary accounts:** These are posted daily, and a check mark is placed in the "Post. Ref." column (left section) *after* each subsidiary item is posted.

  Note: always check in the journal to make sure that total debits ($7,080 + $5,400) equal total credits ($12,480) *before* you do the posting.

The Design and Use of a Purchases Journal, *continued*

Purchases Journal   page 9

				Credit		Debits		
						Other Accounts		
Date	Account Credited	Terms	Post. Ref.	Accounts Payable	Inventory	Name	Ref.	Amount
2017								
Sept. 3	Ramos Corp.	2/10 n/30	✓	1,500	1,500			
4	Angstrom Company	n/30	✓	400		Supplies	123	400
5	Patel Company	2/10 n/30	✓	1,180	1,180			
5	Winthrop Partners	n/30	✓	5,000		Furniture	150	5,000
12	Wong Imports	1/10 n/30	✓	2,500	2,500			
18	Bergman's	1/10 n/30	✓	1,500	1,500			
25	Wong Imports	1/10 n/30	✓	400	400			
30	Totals			12,480	7,080			5,400
				(205)	(125)			(x)

A/P Subsidiary Ledger

Angstrom Co.

Date	Ref.	Debit	Credit	Balance
Sept 4	P9		400	400

Bergman's

Date	Ref.	Debit	Credit	Balance
Sept 18	P9		1,500	1,500

Patel Co.

Date	Ref.	Debit	Credit	Balance
Sept 1	Bal.			250
5	P9		1,180	1,430

Ramos Corp.

Date	Ref.	Debit	Credit	Balance
Sept 3	P9		1,500	1,500

Winthrop Partners

Date	Ref.	Debit	Credit	Balance
Sept 1	Bal.			3,800
5	P9		5,000	8,800

Wong Imports

Date	Ref.	Debit	Credit	Balance
Sept 12	P9		2,500	2,500
25	P9		400	2,900

General Ledger (partial)

Supplies   123

Date	Ref.	Debit	Credit	Balance
Sept 1	Bal.			250
4	P9	400		650

Inventory   125

Date	Ref.	Debit	Credit	Balance
Sept 1	Bal.			11,920
30	P9	7,080		19,000

Furniture   150

Date	Ref.	Debit	Credit	Balance
Sept 1	Bal.			250
5	P9	5,000		5,250

Accounts Payable   205

Date	Ref.	Debit	Credit	Balance
Sept 1	Bal.			4,050
30	P9		12,480	16,530

Periodic System: If this journal were used with a periodic inventory system, the only difference you would see in the journal is that the "Inventory" column would be replaced by a "Purchases" column for a purchases account.

Record these October 2017 purchases, total the journal, and complete the necessary posting to the accounts. Use the September 30 account balances from the previous example as beginning permanent account balances. (For paper, use the blank journal and ledger accounts from the disk at the back of the book.)

October 2:   Purchased $1,700 of inventory from Bergman's, terms 2/10, n/30.
October 8:   Purchased $520 of supplies from Angstrom Company on account, terms net 30.
October 17: Purchased $3,100 of inventory from Patel Company, terms 1/15, n/30.
October 17: Purchased $5,000 of computer equipment from Ramos Corp., terms 2/10, n/45.
October 25: Purchased $4,750 of inventory from Wong Imports, terms 2/10, n/30.

Purchases Journal page 10

| | | | | Credit | | Debits | | |
| | | | | | | | Other Accounts | |
Date	Account Credited	Terms	Post. Ref.	Accounts Payable	Inventory	Name	Ref.	Amount
2017								

A/P Subsidiary Ledger (partial)

Angstrom Co.

Date	Ref.	Debit	Credit	Balance

Bergman's

Date	Ref.	Debit	Credit	Balance

Patel Co.

Date	Ref.	Debit	Credit	Balance

Ramos Corp.

Date	Ref.	Debit	Credit	Balance

Winthrop Partners

Date	Ref.	Debit	Credit	Balance

Wong Imports

Date	Ref.	Debit	Credit	Balance

General Ledger (partial)

Supplies 123

Date	Ref.	Debit	Credit	Balance

Inventory 125

Date	Ref.	Debit	Credit	Balance

Computer Equip. 155

Date	Ref.	Debit	Credit	Balance

Accounts Payable 205

Date	Ref.	Debit	Credit	Balance

Answers

Purchases Journal page 10

Date	Account Credited	Terms	Post. Ref.	Credit Accounts Payable	Inventory	Other Accounts Name	Ref.	Amount
2017								
Oct. 2	Bergman's	2/10, n/30	✓	1,700	1,700			
8	Angstrom Company	n 30	✓	520		Supplies	123	520
17	Patel Company	1/15, n/30	✓	3,100	3,100			
17	Ramos Corp.	2/10, n/45	✓	5,000		Comp. Eqp.	155	5,000
25	Wong Imports	2/10, n/45	✓	4,750	4,750			
31	Totals			15,070	9,550			5,520
				(205)	(125)			(X)

A/P Subsidiary Ledger

Angstrom Co.
Date	Ref.	Debit	Credit	Balance
Sept. 30	Bal.			400
Oct. 8	P10		520	920

Bergman's
Date	Ref.	Debit	Credit	Balance
Sept. 30	Bal.			1,500
Oct. 2	P10		1,700	3,200

Patel Co.
Date	Ref.	Debit	Credit	Balance
Sept. 30	Bal.			1,430
Oct. 17	P10		3,100	4,530

Ramos Corp.
Date	Ref.	Debit	Credit	Balance
Sept. 30	Bal.			1,500
Oct. 17	P10		5,000	6,500

Winthrop Partners
Date	Ref.	Debit	Credit	Balance
Sept. 30	Bal.			8,800

Wong Imports
Date	Ref.	Debit	Credit	Balance
Sept. 30	Bal.			2,900
Oct. 25	P10		4,750	7,650

General Ledger (partial)

Supplies 123
Date	Ref.	Debit	Credit	Balance
Sept. 30	Bal.			650
Oct. 8	P10	520		1,170

Inventory 125
Date	Ref.	Debit	Credit	Balance
Sept. 30	Bal.			19,000
Oct. 31	P10	9,550		28,550

Computer Equip. 155
Date	Ref.	Debit	Credit	Balance
Oct. 17	P10	5,000		5,000

Accounts Payable 205
Date	Ref.	Debit	Credit	Balance
Sept. 30	Bal.			16,530
Oct. 31	P10		15,070	31,600

Check: Did you record all of the posting references in the subsidiary and general ledger accounts and in the purchases journal? Verify that the totals of the beginning and ending balances of all subsidiary Accounts Payable equal the beginning and ending balances in the controlling account Accounts Payable ($16,530 and $31,600).

The Design and Use of a Sales Journal

Purpose	The sales journal (example on opposite page) records sales of merchandise on account. All merchandise sales on account are entered here. Sales of other business assets sold on credit do not occur often and are recorded in the general journal. The sales journal of a service company records all service revenue on account. (No inventory involved.)

Column Titles

Debits and credits appear on the right half of the journal.

- Every revenue entry always is both a debit to Accounts Receivable and a credit to Sales. So a single number placed in one column applies to both the debit to Accounts Receivable and the credit to Sales.
- This is a sales journal for a perpetual inventory system so every sale also requires a cost of goods sold entry. Because this entry is always a debit to Cost of Goods Sold and a credit to Inventory, a single number placed in one column applies to both the debit and credit.

  Note: If this were a periodic inventory system, the Cost of Goods Sold/Inventory column would not be required.

The left part of the journal shows the columns used to record transaction date, name of subsidiary account, invoice number, and posting reference.

Example of Entry

From data on a sales invoice, a transaction is entered on a line. Example:

On September 6, a sale on account was made to Maples Company for $500. The cost of the inventory sold was $300. So "Sept. 6" is entered in the date column, the name of the customer "Maples Co." is entered in the Customer Account column, and our invoice number is entered in the Invoice Number column. After that, the amount of the revenue ($500) is entered in the Accounts Receivable/Sales column, and the cost of the inventory ($300) is entered in the Cost of Goods Sold/Inventory column.

Posting

- **Column totals:** At the end of the period, post the journal column totals into the general ledger accounts using "S" as reference for "sales journal." The account numbers under the column totals are written left/right to show what account was debited and what account was credited. (Example: 120/401 means that the column total of $16,750 was posted as a debit to account 120 and a credit to account 401).
- **Subsidiary accounts:** These are posted daily, and a check mark is placed in the journal "Post Ref." column *after* each subsidiary item is posted. (Example: The $500 and $1,100 sales to Maples Company are posted as debits in the "Maples Co." subsidiary ledger account.)

The Design and Use of a Sales Journal, *continued*

Sales Journal					page 4
Date	Customer Account	Invoice Number	Post. Ref.	Dr. Accounts Receivable Cr. Sales	Dr. Cost of Goods Sold Cr. Inventory
2017					
Sept. 6	Maples Co.	3444	✓	500	300
8	Maples Co.	3445	✓	1,100	900
15	Kleinman's	3446	✓	3,100	1,860
19	Corrigan Co.	3447	✓	8,000	6,430
25	Vaidya Corp.	3448	✓	4,050	1,890
	Totals			16,750	11,380
				(120/401)	(510/125)

A/R Subsidiary Ledger

Corrigan Co.

Date	Ref.	Debit	Credit	Balance
Sept. 19	S4	8,000		8,000

Kleinman's

Date	Ref.	Debit	Credit	Balance
Sept. 1	Bal.			2,500
15	S4	3,100		5,600

Maples Co.

Date	Ref.	Debit	Credit	Balance
Sept. 1	Bal.			10,700
6	S4	500		11,200
8	S4	1,100		12,300

Vaidya Corp.

Date	Ref.	Debit	Credit	Balance
Sept. 1	Bal.			1,750
25	S4	4,050		5,800

General Ledger (partial)

Accounts Receivable   120

Date	Ref.	Debit	Credit	Balance
Sept. 1	Bal.			14,950
30	S4	16,750		31,700

Inventory   125

Date	Ref.	Debit	Credit	Balance
Sept. 1	Bal.			11,920
30	P9	7,080		19,000
30	S4		11,380	7,620

Sales   401

Date	Ref.	Debit	Credit	Balance
Sept. 30	S4		16,750	16,750

Cost of Goods Sold   510

Date	Ref.	Debit	Credit	Balance
Sept. 30	S4	11,380		11,380

Periodic System: If this journal were used with a periodic inventory system, the only difference you would see in the journal is that the far right journal column would be removed because the business would not record the cost of goods sold with each sale. Also, the cost of goods sold account would not be used.

This is also true for the cash receipts journal.

Review: Posting Procedure for a Special Journal

Procedure

You have probably noticed that two kinds of posting must be done: *Posting to the general ledger* and *posting to the subsidiary ledger*. The two tables below show you the steps using the sales journal on the previous page as an example.

Posting to the General Ledger		
Step	**Action**	**Example**
1	Select any journal column total that has not been posted.	We begin with Accounts Receivable and Sales column in the sales journal.
2	Look at the title at the top of the column to determine the account name(s) and whether it is to be debited or credited.	In this case, the same amount is posted as both a debit and credit: ■ Debit to Accounts Receivable ■ Credit to Sales
3	Locate the account in the general ledger and enter the debit or credit.	Accounts Receivable in the general ledger is debited for $16,750.
4	Cross reference: Enter the page number of the journal into the reference column of the ledger account. Use the date on which all the column totals are being posted.	S4 (S means "sales journal," 4 is for page 4) is entered in the reference column of the Accounts Receivable ledger account. The posting date for column totals is Sept. 30.
5	Cross reference: Return to the journal and locate the amount just posted. Write the account number under that amount.	Because this column total is both a debit and credit to different accounts, we write the account number 120 to the left of a "/" under the column total of $16,750. This shows that the amount has been posted as a debit in account 120. (For credits, enter account number to right of "/".)
6	Repeat steps 1–5 until all column totals have been properly posted.	We return to the same column because we know we have to post the $16,750 again, this time as a credit to Sales. (For a column that is posted to only one account, we would write only one ledger account number and then go to the next column.)

Note: In special journals, the "Other" accounts not part of column totals are posted individually into ledger accounts, using the transaction date. An account number is entered next to the amount in the journal.

Rule for Posting References

Do not write a cross-reference unless you have actually done the posting. The cross-references (in this example, "S4" and "120") are very important. They show where the amounts were posted in the general ledger and which journal they came from. They are part of what is called the "audit trail."

Review: Posting Procedure for a Special Journal, *continued*

	Posting to the Subsidiary Ledger **(Done Daily on the Transaction Date)**	
Step	**Action**	**Example**
1	In the journal, select a subsidiary account name not yet posted.	Assume no subsidiary accounts have been posted, so begin with Maples Co. on Sept. 6.
2	On the same line, find the dollar amount for that account.	$500
3	Look at the top of the column for that amount to determine what kind of account it is. Verify this by finding it in the subsidiary ledger.	The names at the top of the amount column are both a debit to Accounts Receivable and a credit to Sales. However, only Accounts Receivable is in the subsidiary ledger.
4	Locate the subsidiary ledger and make the appropriate entries in the subsidiary accounts receivable account.	■ Date of Sept. 6: the transaction date ■ S4 in the ref. column (Maples Co.) ■ $500 entered as a debit ■ Balance updated to $11,200
5	Return to the journal. Enter a check ✓ mark in the reference column to show that the amount was posted.	See ✓ mark in the Post. Ref. Column to the left of the $500. *Note:* If subsidiary accounts are numbered, enter the account number.
6	Repeat steps 1–5 until all subsidiary accounts are properly posted.	The rest of the accounts have been posted.

When to Post Amounts from the Journal

Column totals are posted at the end of a designated period. This can be weekly, monthly, and for some companies, even daily. Individual "other" account amounts and subsidiary amounts should be dated as of the day the transaction happened, but actual posting can be any time up to the date the column totals are posted.

Use the end of the period date as the transaction date to post the column totals in the general ledger. Use the actual transaction dates for the "other" individual amounts and the subsidiary ledger amounts.

Reconciling the Ledgers

You must verify that the total of all the account balances in the subsidiary ledger equals the total in the controlling account. *Example:* In the sales journal illustration, the individual subsidiary balances (Corrigan, Kleinman's, Maples, Vaidya) together add to $31,700, which equals the balance in Accounts Receivable in the general ledger. If the total of the subsidiary balances do not equal the balance of the controlling account, you must find the error.

Check Your Understanding

Record the October 2017 sales on account, total the journal, and complete the necessary posting to the accounts. Assume that the books were closed on September 30. Use the September 30 account balances in the example on page 527 as the beginning Accounts Receivable balance and Inventory balance. (Use the blank journal and ledger accounts from the disk at the back of the book.)

October 4: Invoice 3449, sold $700 of merchandise to Maples Co., cost $420
October 9: Invoice 3450, sold $4,600 of merchandise Etheridge Corp., cost $2,700
October 21: Invoice 3451, sold $1,900 of merchandise to Kleinman's, cost $1,350
October 29: Invoice 3452, sold $2,500 of merchandise to Corrigan Co., cost $1,500

Sales Journal
page 5

Date	Customer Account	Invoice Number	Post. Ref.	Dr. Accounts Receivable / Cr. Sales	Dr. Cost of Goods Sold / Cr. Inventory
				(Reminder: Print out a copy of the sales journal from the disk at the back of the book.)	

A/R Subsidiary Ledger

Corrigan Co.

Date	Ref.	Debit	Credit	Balance

Etheridge Corp.

Date	Ref.	Debit	Credit	Balance

Kleinman's

Date	Ref.	Debit	Credit	Balance

Maples Co.

Date	Ref.	Debit	Credit	Balance

Vaidya Corp.

Date	Ref.	Debit	Credit	Balance

General Ledger (partial)

Accounts Receivable 120

Date	Ref.	Debit	Credit	Balance

Inventory 125

Date	Ref.	Debit	Credit	Balance

Sales 401

Date	Ref.	Debit	Credit	Balance

Cost of Goods Sold 510

Date	Ref.	Debit	Credit	Balance

Answers

Sales Journal   page 5

Date	Customer Account	Invoice Number	Post. Ref.	Dr. Accounts Receivable Cr. Sales	Dr. Cost of Goods Sold Cr. Inventory
2017					
Oct. 4	Maples Co.	3449	✓	700	420
9	Etheridge Corp	3450	✓	4,600	2,700
21	Kleinman's	3451	✓	1,900	1,350
29	Corrigan Co.	3452	✓	2,500	1,500
31	Totals			9,700	5,970
				(120/401)	(510/125)

A/R Subsidiary Ledger

Corrigan Co.

Date	Ref.	Debit	Credit	Balance
Sept. 30	Bal.			8,000
Oct. 29	S5	2,500		10,500

Etheridge Corp.

Date	Ref.	Debit	Credit	Balance
Oct. 9	S5	4,600		4,600

Kleinman's

Date	Ref.	Debit	Credit	Balance
Sept. 30	Bal.			5,600
Oct. 21	S5	1,900		7,500

Maples Co.

Date	Ref.	Debit	Credit	Balance
Sept. 30	Bal.			12,300
Oct. 4	S5	700		13,000

Vaidya Corp.

Date	Ref.	Debit	Credit	Balance
Sept. 30	Bal.			5,800

General Ledger (partial)

Accounts Receivable   120

Date	Ref.	Debit	Credit	Balance
Sept. 30	Bal.			31,700
Oct. 31	S5	9,700		41,400

Inventory   125

Date	Ref.	Debit	Credit	Balance
Sept. 30	Bal.			7,620
Oct. 31	S5		5,970	1,650

Sales   401

Date	Ref.	Debit	Credit	Balance
Oct. 31	S5		9,700	9,700

Cost of Goods Sold   510

Date	Ref.	Debit	Credit	Balance
Oct. 31	S5	5,970		5,970

Check: Did you record all of the posting references in the subsidiary and general ledger accounts? Do the totals of the beginning and ending balances of all subsidiary Accounts Receivable equal the beginning and ending balances in the controlling account Accounts Receivable ($31,700 and $41,400)? The Sales and Cost of Goods Sold accounts have no beginning balances because they are temporary accounts that were closed out on September 30.

The Design and Use of a Cash Receipts Journal

Purpose	It is most efficient to record all receipts of cash in one place. The cash receipts journal (example on opposite page) records *all* receipts of cash. If any transaction involves *any* cash receipt, *the entire transaction* is recorded here.
Column Titles	■ **Debits:** Because cash is received with every transaction, there is a dedicated column for Cash. Because there are frequent receipts on account within the discount period, there is a dedicated column for debits to Sales Discounts. ■ **Credits:** Because there are frequent transactions that record credits to Accounts Receivable, Sales, and Sales Tax, there are columns for these accounts. ■ **Other Accounts:** The "other accounts" section on the left side of the journal performs a double duty: it is used to record the account names and posting references for *both* subsidiary accounts *and* for amounts entered in either the debits or credits "other accounts" columns.
Examples of Entries	■ On September 8, a customer paid a $5,000 amount owing within the discount period. This is recorded as a credit to Accounts Receivable for $5,000 and debits to Cash for $4,900 and Sales Discounts for $100. The customer's name "Maples Co." (subsidiary account) is entered in the Account Name column. ■ On September 9, an $800 cash sale is made on which $56 of sales tax is added for a total cash collection of $856. Cost of goods sold is $525. ■ On September 12, a $1,300 bank card (such as Mastercard or Visa) sale is made and $91 of sales tax is added. The bank charges the seller a $52 fee and electronically records the $1,339 as a deposit into the seller's bank account, so cash is debited. The $52 fee goes into the "other" debit column and the account title of "Bank Card Fees" is entered in the Account Name column. Cost of goods sold is $620. ■ On September 17, the business borrowed $25,000. In addition to the Cash debit, $25,000 is also entered in the Other Accounts credit column. The account name "Notes Payable" is entered in the Account Name column.
Posting	The posting reference for this journal is "CR7" (page 7). *Before* you begin posting, verify that debit column totals ($42,535 + $310 + $52) equal the credit column totals ($15,500 + $2,100 + $147 + $25,150).
Reconcile Subsidiary Accounts	After you finish the posting, verify that the total of the subsidiary account balances is the same as the controlling general ledger account balance. Here, the totals are: Corrigan $0; Kleinman's $3,100; Maples Co. $7,300; Vaidya Corp. $5,800; for a total of $16,200. This equals the balance of Accounts Receivable.

The Design and Use of a Cash Receipts Journal, *continued*

Cash Receipts Journal
page 7

Date	Account Name	Post. Ref.	Cash	Sales Discount	Other Accounts	Accounts Receivable	Sales	Sales Tax Payable	Other Accounts	Dr. Cost of Goods Sold Cr. Inventory
			Debits			**Credits**				
2017										
Sept. 8	Maples Co.	✓	4,900	100		5,000				
9			856				800	56		525
12	Bank Card Fee	585	1,339		52		1,300	91		620
16	Kleinman's	✓	2,450	50		2,500				
17	Supplies	123	150						150	
17	Notes Payable	240	25,000						25,000	
28	Corrigan Co.	✓	7,840	160		8,000				
30	Totals		42,535	310	52	15,500	2,100	147	25,150	1,145
			(101)	(405)	(X)	(120)	(401)	(212)	(X)	(510/125)

A/R Subsidiary Ledger

Corrigan Co.

Date	Ref.	Debit	Credit	Balance
Sept. 19	S4	8,000		8,000
28	CR7		8,000	–0–

Kleinman's

Date	Ref.	Debit	Credit	Balance
Sept. 1	Bal.			2,500
15	S4	3,100		5,600
16	CR7		2,500	3,100

Maples Co.

Date	Ref.	Debit	Credit	Balance
Sept. 1	Bal.			10,700
6	S4	500		11,200
8	S4	1,100		12,300
8	CR7		5,000	7,300

Vaidya Corp.

Date	Ref.	Debit	Credit	Balance
Sept. 1	Bal.			1,750
25	S4	4,050		5,800

General Ledger (partial)

Cash 101

Date	Ref.	Debit	Credit	Balance
Sept. 1	Bal.			11,850
30	CR7	42,535		54,385

Accounts Receivable 120

Date	Ref.	Debit	Credit	Balance
Sept. 1	Bal.			14,950
30	S4	16,750		31,700
30	CR7		15,500	16,200

General Ledger (partial, continued)

Supplies 123

Date	Ref.	Debit	Credit	Balance
Sept. 1	Bal.			250
4	P9	400		650
17	CR7		150	500

Inventory 125

Date	Ref.	Debit	Credit	Balance
Sept. 1	Bal.			11,920
30	P9	7,080		19,000
30	S4		11,380	7,620
30	CR7		1,145	6,475

Sales Tax Payable 212

Date	Ref.	Debit	Credit	Balance
Sept. 30	CR7		147	147

Notes Payable 240

Date	Ref.	Debit	Credit	Balance
Sept. 17	CR7		25,000	25,000

Sales 401

Date	Ref.	Debit	Credit	Balance
Sept. 30	S4		16,750	16,750
30	CR7		2,100	18,850

Sales Discounts 405

Date	Ref.	Debit	Credit	Balance
Sept. 30	CR7	310		310

Cost of Goods Sold 510

Date	Ref.	Debit	Credit	Balance
Sept. 30	S4	11,380		11,380
30	CR7	1,145		12,525

Bank Card Fees 585

Date	Ref.	Debit	Credit	Balance
Sept. 30	CR7	52		52

The Design and Use of a Cash Payments Journal

Purpose

It is most efficient to record all cash payments in one place. The cash payments journal (example on opposite page) records all payments of cash. (Also called "disbursements journal"—"disbursement" means payment.) If a transaction involves *any* payment of cash, *the entire transaction* is recorded here. Every cash payment is recorded in this journal.

Column Titles

Debits and Credits: Similar to the cash receipts journal, all debits and credits are in columns under the headings for Debits and Credits. This journal has "Other Accounts" columns for both the Debits and Credits sections. Dedicated account columns are for frequently-used accounts.

The column titles on the left of the journal are used to record transaction date, check number, name of subsidiary account, and posting reference.

Examples of Entries

- On September 2, the business wrote check 488 to pay the monthly rent. $2,200 is entered in the Other Accounts debit column and $2,200 is entered in the Cash credit column.
- On September 9 the business wrote check 489 to pay $900 of the amount owing to Ramos Company. The payment was made within the discount period, so Accounts Payable is debited $900 and Inventory is credited $18 for the discount and Cash is credited $882. (As another example, notice that the discount was missed on the September 20 payment to Patel Company.)
- The second transaction recorded on September 29 shows that the business purchased $15,000 of equipment by signing a $12,000 note payable and making a $3,000 cash down payment. Notice that two lines are required to make all the entries for this transaction. On one line, the account name "Notes Payable" is entered in the Account Name column, and on the next line the account name "Equipment" is entered; however, total debits still equals credits.

Posting

The posting reference is "CP8" (page 8). Notice that the amounts in the Other Accounts columns must be posted individually and the ledger account number is entered in the Post. Ref. column when each amount is posted. *Note:* Always check that debit column totals ($17,200 + $3,450) equal the credit column totals ($12,000 + $33 + $8,617) before you do the period-end posting.

Reconcile

Make sure that the total of all the subsidiary account payable balances equals the balance in the Accounts Payable controlling account ($13,080).

The Design and Use of a Cash Payments Journal, *continued*

Cash Payments Journal
page 8

Date	Ck. No.	Account Name	Post. Ref.	Other Accounts (Debits)	Accounts Payable (Debits)	Other Accounts (Credits)	Inventory (Credits)	Cash (Credits)
2017								
Sept. 2	488	Rent Expense	550	2,200				2,200
9	489	Ramos Corp.	✓		900		18	882
20	491	Patel Company	✓		250			250
29	492	Bergman's	✓		1,500		15	1,485
29	493	Notes Payable	240			12,000		3,000
		Equipment	185	15,000				
30	494	Wong Imports	✓		800			800
30		Totals		17,200	3,450	12,000	33	8,617
				(x)	(205)	(x)	(125)	(101)

A/P Subsidiary Ledger

Angstrom Co.

Date	Ref.	Debit	Credit	Balance
Sept. 4	P9		400	400

Bergman's

Date	Ref.	Debit	Credit	Balance
Sept. 18	P9		1,500	1,500
29	CP8	1,500		–0–

Patel Co.

Date	Ref.	Debit	Credit	Balance
Sept. 1	Bal.			250
5	P9		1,180	1,430
20	CP8	250		1,180

Ramos Corp.

Date	Ref.	Debit	Credit	Balance
Sept. 3	P9		1,500	1,500
9	CP8	900		600

Winthrop Partners

Date	Ref.	Debit	Credit	Balance
Sept. 1	Bal.			3,800
5	P9		5,000	8,800

Wong Imports

Date	Ref.	Debit	Credit	Balance
Sept. 12	P9		2,500	2,500
25	P9		400	2,900
30	CP8	800		2,100

General Ledger (partial)

Cash 101

Date	Ref.	Debit	Credit	Balance
Sept. 1	Bal.			11,850
30	CR7	42,535		54,385
30	CP8		8,617	45,768

Inventory 125

Date	Ref.	Debit	Credit	Balance
Sept. 1	Bal.			11,920
30	P9	7,080		19,000
30	S4		11,380	7,620
30	CR7		1,145	6,475
30	CP8		33	6,442

Equipment 185

Date	Ref.	Debit	Credit	Balance
Sept. 1	Bal.			25,100
29	CP8	15,000		40,100

Accounts Payable 205

Date	Ref.	Debit	Credit	Balance
Sept. 1	Bal.			4,050
30	P9		12,480	16,530
30	CP8	3,450		13,080

Notes Payable 240

Date	Ref.	Debit	Credit	Balance
Sept. 17	CR7		25,000	25,000
29	CP8		12,000	37,000

Rent Expense 550

Date	Ref.	Debit	Credit	Balance
Sept. 1	Bal.			17,600
2	CP8	2,200		19,800

Periodic System: If this journal were used with a periodic inventory system, the only difference you would see is that the Inventory column is replaced by a Purchase Discounts column for a Purchase Discounts account.

a. Print a blank cash receipts journal from the disk at the back of the book, then enter the cash receipt transactions below for Fort Wayne Company for the month of July. Use the journal below as your model. Show how the journal would look if it had been posted to appropriate accounts. (Cash: 102, Accounts Receivable: 115, Inventory: 125, Sales Tax: 215, Notes Payable: 244, Sales: 400, Sales Discounts: 405, Cost of Goods Sold: 510)

July 1: Vetter Co. paid the amount due on a $3,100 account balance in the discount period, terms 2/10, n/30.

July 7: Made a cash sale for $900. Sales tax is 6%. Cost of inventory is $600.

July 14: Collected $5,000 from Singh Corp. after the discount period expired.

July 20: Borrowed $18,000 from National Bank.

July 28: Collected $6,500 from Hopkins Co., the discount to record is $130.

Cash Receipts Journal — page 8

| | Other Accounts | | | Debits | | | Credits | | | | | Dr. Cost of Goods Sold |
	Account Name	Post. Ref.	Cash	Sales Discount	Other Accounts	Accounts Receivable	Sales	Sales Tax Payable	Other Accounts		Cr. Inventory
Date											
2017	(Reminder: Use a blank cash receipts journal from the disk at the back of the book.)										

b. Print a blank cash payments journal from the disk at the back of the book, then enter the cash payments for Duluth Company for August. Show how the journal would look if it had been posted to appropriate accounts. (Cash: 103, Inventory: 123, Computer Equipment: 150, Accounts Payable: 211, Notes Payable: 220, Rent Expense 305)

Aug. 1: Paid the August rent, $3,400, check 512.

Aug. 5: Paid Concordia Co. amount due on $3,000 in the discount period, terms 2/10, n/30, check 513.

Aug. 11: Paid $10,000 for computer equipment, check 514.

Aug. 18: Paid $5,000 owing on loan principal for note payable, check 515.

Aug. 25: Paid Mankato Co. $2,100 on account; check 516. The discount to record is $50.

Cash Payments Journal — page 9

| | | | | Debits | | Credits | | |
Date	Ck. No.	Account Name	Post. Ref.	Other Accounts	Accounts Payable	Other Accounts	Inventory	Cash
2017	(Reminder: Use a blank cash payments journal from the disk at the back of the book.)							

Answers

Cash Receipts Journal   page 8

Date	Account Name	Post. Ref.	Cash	Sales Discount	Other Accounts	Accounts Receivable	Sales	Sales Tax Payable	Other Accounts	Dr. Cost of Goods Sold Cr. Inventory
	Other Accounts		**Debits**			**Credits**				
2017										
July 1	Vetter Co.	✓	3,038	62		3,100				
7			954				900	54		600
14	Singh Corp.	✓	5,000			5,000				
20	Notes Payable	244	18,000						18,000	
28	Hopkins Co.	✓	6,500	130		6,630				
31	Total		33,492	192		14,730	900	54	18,000	600
			(102)	(405)		(115)	(400)	(215)	(X)	(510/125)

Cash Payments Journal   page 9

Date	Ck. No.	Account Name	Post. Ref.	Other Accounts	Accounts Payable	Other Accounts	Inventory	Cash
				Debits		**Credits**		
2017								
Aug. 1	512	Rent Expense	305	3,400				3,400
5	513	Concordia Co.	✓		3,000		60	2,940
11	514	Computer Equip.	150	10,000				10,000
18	515	Notes Payable	220	5,000				5,000
25	516	Mankato Company	✓		2,150		50	2,100
31		Totals		18,400	5,150		110	23,440
				(X)	(211)		(123)	(103)

Comments:

- Notice that in the cash receipts journal there is debit to cash for every transaction, and in the cash payments journal there is a credit to cash for every transaction.
- The total debits in a journal are equal to the total credits.
- Posting references are account numbers that identify the account to which an amount was posted. ✓ marks are used to indicate posting to subsidiary accounts. (However, many businesses assign account numbers to subsidiary accounts.)
- Each business will have its own unique group of account numbers.

Using the General Journal with Special Journals

Procedure

Using special journals does not mean that the general journal is eliminated. The general journal continues to be used for any transaction that should not or cannot be entered into a special journal. Typically, the general journal continues to be used to record items such as sales returns and allowances, purchase returns and allowances, adjustments, reversing, and closing entries.

Example

Assume that a purchase return occurred on September 18 and is entered in page 3 of the general journal. The example below shows the general journal entry and the posted subsidiary and controlling ledger accounts. In the posting reference column in the journal the Accounts Payable must be posted twice—to the controlling account and to the subsidiary account. The posting reference in the Ledger is GJ3.

Sept. 18	Accounts Payable, Patel Co.	205/✓	150	
	Inventory	125		150
	Returned defective merchandise to Patel Company			

General Ledger

Accounts Payable   205

Date	Ref.	Debit	Credit	Balance
Sept. 1	Bal.			4,050
18	GJ3	150		3,900
30	P9		12,480	16,380
30	CP8	3,450		12,930

Inventory   125

Date	Ref.	Debit	Credit	Balance
Sept. 1	Bal.			11,920
18	GJ3		150	11,770
30	P9	7,080		18,850
30	S4		11,380	7,470
30	CR7		1,145	6,325
30	CP8		33	6,292

Subsidiary Ledger

Patel Company

Date	Ref.	Debit	Credit	Balance
Sept. 1	Bal.			250
5	P9		1,180	1,430
18	GJ3	150		1,280
20	CP8	250		1,030

Using the General Journal with Special Journals, *continued*

Account Analysis: "Posting Ref." Tells a Story	It is a good habit to take a close look at the posting references—they will tell you a story about what has happened to an account. Then you may want to investigate more closely by going back to the referenced journal. For example, assume that you are looking at the Inventory ledger account above and you see the following. Should you take a closer look at the journals?

- GJ3 *credit* during the month: Something from the general journal reduced the inventory (purchase returns?).
- P9 *debit* at month end: September total inventory purchases on credit?
- S4 *credit* at month end: September total cost of goods sold for credit sales?
- CR7 *credit* at month end: September total cost of goods sold for cash sales?
- CP8 *credit* at month end: Small credit—early payment discounts?

Accrued Expenses: Two Methods for Recording	There are two common methods for recording accrued expenses:

- Often a business uses the general journal to accrue unpaid expenses *only at the end of an accounting period* as an adjusting entry. During a period, unpaid bills are simply paid as they become due and are recorded as expenses at the time they are paid. The idea is that an unpaid expense only needs to be accrued when a period comes to an end and the financial statements are prepared. This saves time during the period.
- A second method for accrued expenses is to use the purchases journal to continuously record accrued expenses as they occur during a period. The liabilities resulting from the accruals are paid as they become due. A business with a computerized accounting system using a purchases/accounts payable module (see next section) generally uses this method. This is done because an automated system can process data quickly and can create a useful "cash requirements" report that details the total amount of unpaid liabilities at any point in time.

In this book, we use the general journal to record accrued expenses as part of the adjusting entries at the end of a period.

Accrued Revenue	If a company uses a sales journal, all accrued revenues are recorded as sales on account during a period. The only adjusting entry required for accrued revenues is for revenues that for some reason have not been recorded into the sales journal.

Overview of the Special Journals

Illustration

The diagram below identifies the type of transaction data that flow from the journals to the ledgers when special journals are used to record transactions.

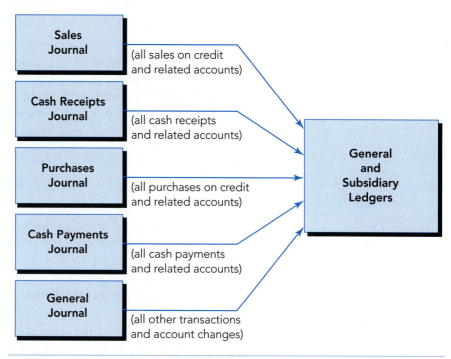

Special Journals for Service Businesses

Overview

So far in this learning goal all the examples of special journals have involved merchandising companies. This does not mean that only companies with merchandise use special journals.

Service businesses also use special journals. The sales, cash receipts, purchases, and cash payments journals, as well as the general journal, are all used regularly by many types of service businesses.

Other Journal Types

The Combination Journal

Overview

The combination journal is normally used in small service companies that do not have a high volume of transactions and do not want to use multiple journals. These companies want to have only one journal—one that uses some of the time-saving features of special journals, especially the use of dedicated columns for frequently used accounts. The result is a compromise: A single journal that is flexible enough to record any transaction but still has some of the time-saving features of a special journal. For example, a combination journal can record any type of sale. However, in a full special-journal system, a sales journal is used to record a sale on account and a cash receipts journal is used to record a cash sale.

Column Titles

- You can visualize the combination journal in three basic sections. The middle section (General Accounts) is basically a general journal and has the same column titles: Account, Post. Ref., Dr., and Cr.
- The left section (after the date column) is dedicated strictly to the Cash account. One column is for increases (Dr.) and the other for decreases (Cr.).
- The right section (Other Accounts) is used for frequently recurring entries to specific other accounts. The account titles and debit/credit entry types that are selected depends on the specific business and its experience with which entries seem to occur the most frequently.

	Cash		General Accounts				Other Accounts		
Date	Dr.	Cr.	Account	Post. Ref.	Dr.	Cr.	Service Revenue Cr.	Travel Expense Dr.	Supplies Expense Dr.
2017									
Mar. 3	15,000		James Rialto, Capital	350		15,000			
4		1,200	Rent Expense	525	1,200				
5			Supplies	125	250				
			Accts. Pay.—Chen	302/✔		250			
7	2,750						2,750		
9		135						135	
10			Supplies	125		40			40
15		90						90	
19			Accts. Rec.—Jones	110/✔	950		950		
27			Telephone Expense	530	215				
			Accts. Pay.—Acme	302/✔		215			
	17,750	1,425			2,615	15,505	3,700	225	40
	(105)	(105)			(X)	(X)	(401)	(505)	(503)

Combination Journal — page 4

Total Debits: $20,630   Total Credits: $20,630

continued ▶

The Combination Journal, *continued*

Entries

- Any kind of entry can be recorded in a combination journal.
- With each transaction, debits must equal credits.
- The dollar amounts for a transaction can be entered in any of the three sections, provided that the debits equal the credits.

Transaction Examples:

- On March 3, the owner invested $15,000 cash. Because there is a dedicated Cash debit column, the cash debit is entered here. There is no special column for "James Rialto, Capital," so the $15,000 credit is entered in the middle general journal section. (March 4 also uses the left section and center section.)

- On March 5, $250 of supplies are purchased on credit. There are no dedicated columns for Supplies or Accounts Payable, so the entire transaction is recorded in the center section, just like a general journal entry. (March 27 is similar: it also uses only the center section.)

- On March 7, the business received $2,750 of cash for services performed. Because there is a dedicated cash debit column, the cash debit is entered here. Because there is a dedicated Service Revenue credit column, the credit to the revenue is entered here. (March 9 and 15 also use the left and right sections.)

Posting

Posting is done in exactly the same manner as with special journals. This includes posting to any subsidiary ledgers. (The posting is indicated in the example with check marks, ✓.)

Note: Just as with special journals, the Account column in the center section can be used for the names of subsidiary accounts.

See Special Journals As Reports

Overview

We have spent a lot of time looking at special journals as a way of entering transaction data into a manual accounting system. Because this is probably new to you, it is likely that so far the focus of your effort has been trying to understand how the journals are designed and how to enter the transaction data.

However, in a manual accounting system, a special journal is used for more than just data entry. A special journal is also used as an internal report that summarizes transactions by type and that can quickly provide information to help managers analyze operations. For some types of data this is especially useful when financial statements have not yet been prepared.

See Special Journals As Reports, *continued*

The Purchases Journal as a Report	Refer to the example of the purchases journal on page 523. The journal is a quick single reference that makes it easy to:

- see the various types of purchases on account (most purchases are on account),
- review the terms offered by various vendors, and
- check a purchase date to determine a discount deadline for payment.

The Sales Journal as a Report	Refer to the example of the sales journal on page 527. The journal is a quick single reference that makes it easy to:

- see total credit sales revenues for the period and how the sales revenues are distributed among the various customers,
- calculate the percentage of sales to each customer,
- quickly see the approximate cost of goods sold for the period (not including purchase returns and discounts) for all credit sales,
- quickly estimate the average cost of goods sold and gross profit as a percentage of sales for the period (not including returns and discounts) for all credit sales, and
- see a sales date for purposes of checking a discount taken by a customer.

The Cash Receipts Journal as a Report	Refer to the example of the cash receipts journal on page 533. The journal is a quick single reference that makes it easy to:

- see total cash receipts for the period and the sources of those cash receipts,
- verify the cash receipts against those shown on a bank statement,
- see the total sales discounts taken by customers,
- check the date payments are received to determine if customers are actually paying within the discount period,
- quickly see the approximate cost of goods sold for the period (not including returns and discounts) for all cash sales,
- quickly estimate the average cost of goods sold and gross profit as a percentage of sales for the period (not including returns and discounts) for all cash sales, and
- compare total cash sales, cost of goods sold, and gross profit to the same information from the sales journal for sales on account.

The Cash Payments Journal as a Report	Refer to the example of the cash payments journal on page 535. The journal is a quick single reference that makes it easy to:

- see total cash payments for the period and to whom the payments were made,
- verify the cash payments against those shown on a bank statement,
- see the total discounts taken, and
- calculate the discounts taken as a percentage of total purchases made (purchases journal).

Invoices As Journals

Overview

In a very small business, it is sometimes more efficient to simply keep a binder of invoices by date, which can function as both source documentation and a kind of special journal. For example, sales invoices can be kept in a binder by date. The information in the sales invoices is then posted directly to the ledger accounts. This system can also be used with various types of vendor invoices for goods and services by placing them into other separate binders. In both cases, care must be taken to retain and post all relevant financial information. Checkmarks or other indicators are entered on the invoices to verify recording.

Variations in Journals

Overview

The essential functions and basic formats of the special journals presented in this learning goal apply to all special journals. The journals that you have seen presented here are examples of what you would see in the real world of manual special journals.

However, special journals do have many variations. For example, you might encounter other cash payments journals that have a different number of columns, columns in a different sequence, or with different column titles. Nevertheless, the essential purpose is still the same, and if you understand how to use the journals in this learning goal, you will be able to quickly adapt to any of the variations.

Computerized Accounting Systems Overview

Features Compared to a Manual System

Which Is Best?

Computerized accounting systems can quickly process huge amounts of data and save a tremendous amount of time when doing repetitive calculations. Computerized accounting systems can perform functions that are difficult to do in a manual system. For all but the smallest businesses, using some level of computerized accounting is probably the right decision.

Features Compared to a Manual System, *continued*

Hidden Costs

There is a natural tendency to be impressed by what a computerized accounting system can potentially do without understanding the necessary costs involved. Here is a quick summary of some potential hidden costs and other bad things:

- **Selecting the wrong system:** This is a big potential cost. Paying for an unnecessarily large system that you will not need is like throwing $100 bills into the street. On the other hand, buying a system that lacks the functions you really require (or will require in the near future) will make you feel as though you are wearing handcuffs whenever you use it. The future hours of manual time will add a lot to the original cost. It is extremely important to carefully analyze the requirements of your present and future operations. (See following section and Appendix III for a checklist of accounting software features and functions.)
- **Training time:** This is another big cost. Considerable training time is usually required to use a computerized accounting system effectively. If you cannot afford sufficient training time, you will have to pay someone to operate the system and/or fix mistakes.
- **Customer support:** For an extended period of time you will probably need help to properly use the software. The company that created the software will charge a fee for this service or you can pay a consultant to help you.
- **Maintenance:** Every system requires maintenance; this is particularly true of internet servers and computer networks.
- **Updates:** Periodic software updates will be necessary, particularly for payroll software. This may also be true for sales and property tax calculations.
- **Internal control issues:** If someone else operates your computerized accounting system, that person can potentially gain access to all accounting records with the ability to cover up numerous kinds of thefts and frauds. Safeguards must be in place and be constantly monitored.
- **Database maintenance:** You must always be sure that data for customers (also for vendors, prices, employee information, etc.) is correct and current. This ongoing time requirement can be substantial, and it will increase as operations expand.

The Parts of the System

Overview and Comparison to Manual System

Computerized and manual systems involve the same three elements of entering input, processing data, and creating output. What you learn when practicing with a manual system will definitely help you to understand a computerized system. The main differences with a computerized system are:

Input:
- Data are entered in a somewhat different way than a manual system.
- Much of the data entry requires little or no accounting knowledge.

Processing: Processing and updating is instantaneous and more reliable.

Output: A much larger selection of reports can be immediately created.

continued ▶

The Parts of the System, *continued*

Modules

Except for the smallest systems, most accounting software systems are composed of modules. A **module** refers to a distinct, identifiable part of the accounting software that performs a specific group of related functions.

- Modules are usually sold separately and added as needed.
- In well-designed systems, all modules are designed to automatically work together. (They are **integrated.**) This is an important feature.
- The basic module that every business must have is called the **general ledger module,** which contains the general journal and general ledger accounts and produces basic financial statements. In this module, debits and credits are entered in a general journal, which can handle any transaction but is not as efficient. Also, it does not have all the features and functionality of specialized modules (see below).

What the Specialized Modules Do

Here are typical module functions in a small/moderate computerized system:

- **Sales/accounts receivable module:** Enters sales on account and cash receipts, updates data in Accounts Receivable controlling and subsidiary accounts, prints the sales and cash receipts journals, sales invoices, and numerous reports. (Larger systems have a separate "order entry" module.)
- **Purchases/accounts payable module:** Enters purchases on account and cash payments transactions, updates data in Accounts Payable controlling and subsidiary accounts, prints the purchases and cash payments journals, checks, and numerous reports.
- **Payroll module:** Records payroll transactions, updates general ledger accounts related to payroll, prints payroll checks, the payroll journal, and numerous payroll reports.
- **Inventory module:** Receives input from purchases and sales and tracks inventory balances, calculates unit costs, and creates numerous reports.

Synonyms

Sometimes a module is also called a "program," a "package," or a "system."

Illustration

The illustration below shows a computerized accounting system for a company that has merchandise sales. This example illustrates a general ledger module and four specialized modules. Because this is a fully integrated system, the lines indicate that related information is automatically shared between the connected modules.

The Parts of the System, *continued*

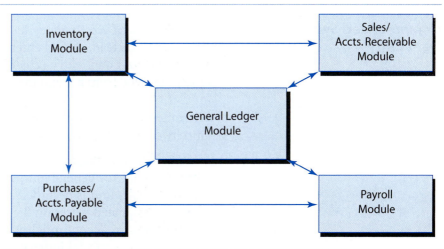

Examples

- **To record and write payroll checks** to the employees, the bookkeeper selects the Payroll module from a screen menu of transaction types. The payroll module contains all wage rates and payroll tax information. When the employee hours are entered, the payroll module automatically calculates the amounts for all accounts affected. The module then shares the transaction data with the General Ledger module so that the debits and credits can be recorded in the general ledger accounts. The same transaction data will also be recorded in the cash payments journal (part of the Purchases/Accts. Payable module), which will record and print the checks.

- **To record a sale on account**, the bookkeeper selects the Sales/Accts. Receivable module. When the data is entered here, the module records the transaction in a sales journal and automatically shares transaction information with the General Ledger module. The debit to Accounts Receivable and credit to Sales (and possibly Sales Tax Payable) is then recorded in the ledger. If the company is using a perpetual inventory system, the Sales module also shares the information with the Inventory module. The Inventory module records the decrease in the specific inventory and then tells the general ledger and sales modules to debit Cost of Goods of Sold and credit Inventory in the ledger accounts and sales journal.

Entering Data

Overview

From a bookkeeping point of view, the most noticeable difference between a manual accounting system and a computerized accounting system is how data is entered.

Manual System Data Entry

In a manual accounting system with special journals, transaction data is entered directly into a selected journal. The journal is selected based on the type of transaction involved. To use this system, knowledge of double-entry, debit/credit accounting is required because the transaction data must be analyzed and then recorded with debits and credits.

continued ▶

Entering Data, *continued*

Computerized System Data Entry

In a computerized accounting system transaction data is not entered into special journals. Instead, data is entered into modules, each of which has its own customized data entry screen. A module is chosen by selecting the transaction type from a menu that initially appears on the screen.

When the module is selected and the data entry screen appears, you will notice two key differences in a computerized system:

- The transaction data does not need to be entered using debits and credits (except for the general journal). A module records debits and credits automatically and is designed so that the user simply enters specific data in designated places on the screen.
- A module can accept much more transaction information than is entered into a special journal in a manual system. This is because a computerized system can use the data to perform many calculations and prepare many reports.

More advanced systems use bar code scanners to enter data directly into modules from bar codes on merchandise and documents.

What Happened to the Special Journals?

In a computerized accounting system, all special journals still exist and are still important. However, they are created as reports rather than places to enter data. For example, a computerized accounting system still produces a cash receipts journal. Similar to a manual system, this journal shows all the individual cash receipts, by date, with columns for the various accounts. But it would be a report only—the result of entering transaction data into the module data entry screen or a scanner.

Two Data Entry Similarities

- Both manual and computerized systems have general journals, which require a knowledge of debits and credits and transaction analysis to enter data.
- Both manual systems and computerized systems are subject to data entry errors. If the input contains errors, the results will also contain errors.

Example of a Data Entry Screen

Suppose that you are using a computerized accounting system and want to record the sale of some merchandise on account. The computer screen will show you a list (called a *menu*) of various functions and transaction types. Computer software that allows you to select from a menu of choices is called *menu-driven* software. In this example, you would select "sales on account" from the list of choices.

The sales/accounts receivable module will automatically open and show a sales data entry screen designed for recording this type of transaction. The illustration below shows a sales data entry screen with some typical features.

Entering Data, *continued*

Features Described

In the data entry screen above, data has been entered in the screen. Here we assume a fully integrated module and a perpetual inventory system.

- Either type the name and address of the customer into the **"invoice to"** box—or for a previous customer the name and address will automatically appear by typing the purchase order number into the **"P.O. no."** box and typing the customer name. An invoice will automatically be created, ready for printing.

- Select the **terms** (here, 2/10, n/30). The system will show the terms on the invoice and calculate any applicable discount when payment is received.

- Multiple items can be entered on the **invoice detail** part of the screen. By entering an item number or name, the system automatically shows the current sales price and totals the current sales amount. For example, by entering "482A," the correct price of $400 is shown, and by entering 3 units, the total of $1,200 is automatically calculated. Notice that labor hours can also be entered.

- From the address information, sales tax is automatically calculated, and the state and city are shown in the **tax area** part of the screen. This part of the screen can also be used to override sales tax calculations.

continued ▶

Entering Data, *continued*

- The **balance due** is automatically shared with the general ledger module, and the system will debit Accounts Receivable for $5,046.50 and credit Sales Revenue for $4,200, Service Revenue for $500, and Sales Tax Payable for $346.50. The revenue items will also be recorded in a sales journal.

- The items sold data is shared with the inventory module, which records a decrease in the stock and cost of hard drives and color monitors and sends this information to the general ledger module. Here Cost of Goods Sold is debited and Inventory is credited. The sales and cost of goods sold will also appear on the sales journal.

- Any special information (such as delivery/shipping instructions) can be entered into the **memo** space.

Compared to a Special Journal

Compare this sales data entry screen to the sales journal shown on page 527. You can see that much more information is entered on this screen than just the accounting transaction data you see on the sales journal. This is done because the computerized system can perform many more functions with the information. Also, the person entering data in the computerized system does not require knowledge of debits and credits.

Faster Data Entry

Data entry is the slowest part of a computerized system. Data entry speed can be improved in the following ways:

1. Use bar code tags on merchandise or documents that are read by a scanner. The scanner reads bar code information and automatically identifies the merchandise, the cost, and the price.
2. Create customer accounts in which only an account number needs to be entered after the merchandise is scanned.
3. Electronically integrate the accounting systems of suppliers and buyers over the Internet so transactions are automatically recorded on both systems. This new technology is being developed for large companies.

Different System Sizes

Overview

The examples we have discussed so far are most relevant to active small businesses and moderate-sized businesses.

Very Big Systems

Large businesses with many employees, many products, manufacturing operations, international operations, and so on use large computerized accounting systems that are custom or semi-custom designed. These systems are called *enterprise systems.* Very large systems can cost tens of millions of dollars and require a large well-trained staff to operate and maintain.

Different System Sizes, *continued*

The larger the system, the more modules that are used. For example, a large system removes the cash receipts function from the sales/accounts receivable module and also removes the cash payments function from the purchases/accounts payable module. A large system uses a separate cash module, or even separate modules, for cash receipts and cash disbursements.

Very Small Systems

Very small systems are non-modular accounting systems. These systems are limited, and their functions are fixed and cannot be expanded as with a modular system. Many of them are simply electronic checkbooks that do not maintain a ledger. They are primarily designed to write checks, keep a record of receipts and expenditures, show totals by category, and compare budgeted amounts to actuals. They do not contain a general journal and have no capability of entering debits and credits. They cannot produce GAAP-compliant financial statements. This type of system is appropriate for a very small one-person, cash-basis service business.

"Running Parallel"

"Running parallel" means that when any new system is started (large or small), the old system should be maintained, and the same data should be entered in both systems for a period of time—at least several months. Although this procedure takes more time, it identifies errors in the new system and avoids costly and very time-consuming mistakes.

Checklist for Computerized Accounting System Features

See the Appendix

The appendix to this volume contains a detailed checklist for accounting software evaluation. The checklist contains features to consider before acquiring a computerized accounting system.

TIP

A computerized accounting system should never allow deletion of posted entries. A computerized accounting system should never allow entries to be unrecorded.

Do You Want More Examples?

Most problems in this book have detailed solutions. To use them as additional examples, do this: 1) Select the type of problem you want 2) Open the solution on your computer or mobile device screen (from the disc or worthyjames.com) 3) Read one item at a time and look at its answer. Take notes if needed. 4) Close the solution and work as much of the problem as you can. 5) Repeat as needed.

QUICK REVIEW

- An accounting system is a system that processes financial information. It should contain the following essential elements: Usefulness, cost-benefit, internal control, and adaptability.

- A subsidiary ledger is an example of a specialized subsystem. Most businesses have subsidiary ledgers for accounts payable and accounts receivable.

- A subsidiary ledger must reconcile to its controlling account.

- Special journals record transactions in groups, by specified type.

- Special journals were created to increase efficiency in manual systems, but they have also been adapted to computerized systems.

- A special journal may be designed for any transaction type, but they only increase efficiency if there is a relatively high number of those transactions.

- There are four commonly-used special journals: Purchases journal, sales journal, cash payments journal, and cash receipts journal. The general journal continues to be used with the special journals.

- Computerized accounting systems involve the same three elements as manual systems: entering input, processing data, and creating output. However, computerized systems are different in the following ways:

  - Data are entered on a data entry screen, often without debits or credits. The amount of data is usually greater.
  - Processing is instantaneous and reliable.
  - A wide variety of reports can be created.

- Computerized accounting systems can have substantial hidden costs.

- Computerized systems are usually modular.

VOCABULARY

Accounting system: a system that combines people, physical records, and procedures, and that processes financial information for the purpose of creating useful reports (page 510)

Accounting information system: another term for accounting system (page 510)

Cash payments journal: a journal used to record only transactions that involve the payment of cash (page 520)

Cash receipts journal: a journal used to record only transactions that involve the receipt of cash (page 520)

Cloud computing : using Internet service providers for data storage and retreival and specialized service applications (page 512)

Controlling account: any account that has a subsidiary ledger (page 513)

Electronic data integration: sharing accounting information on the Internet (page 512)

Manual accounting systems: accounting systems in which all the steps in the accounting cycle are done by hand, without the use of computers (page 518)

Purchases journal: a journal used to record only transactions that involve purchases on account (page 520)

Sales journal: a journal used to record only transactions that involve sales of merchandise on account (page 520)

Special journal: a journal that records only specified types of similar transactions (page 518)

Subsidiary ledger: a separate ledger that only contains accounts that show the detail of a single general ledger account (page 513)

XBRL: Extensible Business reporting language (page 512)

Learning Goal 15 is about understanding the meaning of accounting information systems. Use these questions and problems to practice what you have learned about accounting information systems.

Multiple Choice

Select the best answer.

1. The ledger that contains the accounts used in the financial statements of a business is:
   a. the general ledger.
   b. the subsidiary ledger.
   c. both (a) and (b).
   d. none of the above.

2. Posting an amount in both a general ledger account and a subsidiary ledger account:
   a. would create an out-of-balance condition because of the double posting.
   b. will never create an out-of-balance condition in the general ledger.
   c. is done only in manual accounting systems.
   d. is usually done only for asset accounts.

3. A permanent record that is designed and used for the purpose of recording only a particular kind of transaction is called a:
   a. general ledger.
   b. subsidiary ledger.
   c. general journal.
   d. special journal.

4. The important relationship between a controlling account and a subsidiary ledger is that:
   a. the account balances must be posted from a journal.
   b. all general ledger asset accounts will have subsidiary ledgers.
   c. the total of account balances in the subsidiary ledger must equal the controlling account balance.
   d. the exact same entries must be made in both accounts.

5. If a business uses the typical number of special journals and the general journal, it is using:
   a. five journals.
   b. three journals.
   c. two journals.
   d. none of the above.

6. An inexperienced bookkeeper used the general journal to record a sale on account instead of correctly using the sales journal. The amounts and accounts are correct. As a result:
   a. the trial balance does not balance.
   b. the subsidiary ledger account totals do not equal the controlling account total.
   c. sales revenue and accounts receivable balances are be understated.
   d. none of the above.

7. When special journals are used, the correct place to record a payment on account from a customer is:
   a. the general journal.
   b. the sales journal.
   c. the cash receipts journal.
   d. the cash payments journal.

8. When special journals are used, the correct place to record a $10,000 purchase of equipment by paying $1,000 cash and signing a promissory note for the balance is:
   a. the general journal.
   b. the purchases journal.
   c. combination of general journal and cash payments journal.
   d. the cash payments journal.

PRACTICE   **Learning Goal 15, continued**   *Solutions are in the disk at the back of the book and at: www.worthyjames.com*

9. When special journals are used:
   a. all transactions must be recorded in the correct special journals and also recorded in the general journal.
   b. all purchases must be recorded in the purchases journal.
   c. all sales must be recorded in the sales journal.
   d. none of the above.

10. Internal control in an accounting system:
    a. is desirable, but because of the cost involved, it is optional.
    b. will practically always prevent fraud.
    c. means the procedures and records used to safeguard assets.
    d. once established, is not necessary to frequently re-evaluate.

11. An inexperienced bookkeeper made the following error: In the sales journal a $50 sale was recorded as a $500 sale. This error will most probably be discovered when:
    a. the trial balance is prepared.
    b. the subsidiary Accounts Receivable ledger is reconciled to the controlling account.
    c. the customer receives the current month statement.
    d. the debit and credit totals of the sales journal are checked.

12. An inexperienced bookkeeper made the following error: In the sales journal a $500 sale was correctly recorded but was posted to the customer's subsidiary account as $50. This error will most probably be discovered when:
    a. the trial balance is prepared.
    b. the subsidiary Accounts Receivable ledger is reconciled to the controlling account.
    c. the customer receives the current month statement.
    d. the debit and credit totals of the sales journal are checked.

13. In a computerized accounting system, special journals:
    a. do not exist.
    b. are not used for input as in a manual system but are used as transaction reports, which is similar to a manual system.
    c. are used in essentially the same way as in manual accounting systems.
    d. require the user to be proficient with debits and credits.

14. Assume that an integrated modular computerized accounting system is used for a business that uses the perpetual method. Recording a sale on account will automatically record the transaction data into the:
    a. sales journal.
    b. sales journal, Sales ledger account and Accounts Receivable ledger account.
    c. sales journal, Sales ledger account and Accounts Receivable ledger account and all affected subsidiary accounts.
    d. sales journal, Inventory ledger account, Cost of Goods Sold ledger account, Accounts Receivable ledger account, and all affected subsidiary accounts.

15. Two key similarities of manual and computerized accounting systems are:
    a. both use a general journal, and both are vulnerable to data entry errors.
    b. both use a general journal, and both require a knowledge of debits and credits for all journals.
    c. both require that data be entered directly into all journals.
    d. both are sometimes designed as enterprise systems.

16. The cash receipts journal of Topeka Enterprises shows a debit to cash of $1,683 and a debit to Sales Discounts of $17. What should be the amount of the credit to the customer's account in the subsidiary ledger?
    a. $1,683
    b. $1,700
    c. $1,717
    d. some other amount

17. Waterloo Company sold some equipment that cost $7,000 for $9,000 cash. The transaction would be recorded in which journal and include which account entry?
   a. in the cash receipts journal, with a debit to Gain on Sale for $2,000
   b. in the sales journal, with a credit to Gain on Sale for $2,000
   c. in the cash receipts journal, with a credit to Gain on Sale for $2,000
   d. in the sales journal, with a debit to Gain on Sale for $2,000

18. Which of the following selections would probably be the most expensive hidden cost when using a computerized accounting system?
   a. software updates
   b. software support
   c. internal control safeguards
   d. employee training

Reinforcement Problems

LG 15-1. Select the correct journal. Milpitas Company uses the following journals:

- Sales journal (S)
- Purchases journal (used for all purchases on account) (P)
- Cash receipts journal (CR)
- Cash payments journal (CP)
- General journal (J)

Instructions: In the table below, for each separate transaction, identify which type of journal should be used to record the transaction. Use the abbreviations S, P, CR, CP, and J to indicate the journal.

Transaction	Journal
1. Owner invested $5,000 in her business.	(Reminder: Use a Separate piece of paper to complete the table.)
2. Sold $1,000 of merchandise on account.	
3. Sold $300 of excess office supplies on account.	
4. Paid $2,000 cash to pay accounts payable.	
5. Bought $3,000 of merchandise on account.	
6. Made a $500 cash sale of merchandise.	
7. Customer returned $100 of defective merchandise.	
8. Purchased computer for $4,000; paid $500 cash and signed a note payable for the balance.	
9. Sold the company van; received $7,000 cash and a $7,000 note receivable for the balance.	
10. Bought $5,000 of merchandise, terms 2/10, n/30.	
11. Bought $250 of office supplies on account.	
12. Sold $275 of merchandise, terms 2/10, n/30.	
13. Returned the merchandise purchased in transaction #12, above.	
14. A business paid $4,000 in dividends.	
15. Received $650 payment from customer for amount owing from previous month's sale.	
16. Bought $100 of supplies for cash.	
17. Made adjusting and closing entries.	

LG 15-2. Draw journals and record transactions. Writing and drawing are excellent ways to help you remember details. We apply these techniques in the following problem. Jackson Company uses special journals. The March 2017 transactions below for Jackson Company involve the use of the sales journal and the cash receipts journal.

Instructions:

a. Draw a sales journal and draw a cash receipts journal. (If you wish to complete the problem without drawing, you can print a blank journal from the disk or at worthyjames.com/student info.)

b. Record the Jackson Company transactions in the appropriate journals and total the journals.

Note: Solutions are available for both perpetual and periodic systems.

March Transactions

3   Jackson Company uses terms of 2/15, n/30 for all sales on account. Jackson Company sold $2,400 of merchandise on account to Tupelo Partnership, invoice #152. No sales tax is required. The cost of the merchandise is $1,800.

8   The owner of the company, John Madison, invested an additional $10,000 in the business.

11 The company made a cash sale of $900 of merchandise to a retail customer. The sales tax rate is 5%. The cost of the merchandise is $600.

14 Collected payment in full from Tupelo Partnership.

15 Sold merchandise on account to Magnolia Enterprises, $3,800, invoice #153. The cost of the merchandise is $2,500.

21 Sold merchandise on account to Oxford Company, $5,500, invoice #154. The cost of the merchandise is $3,600.

27 Collected payment in full from Magnolia Enterprises.

28 Made a cash sale of $500 of merchandise to a retail customer. The cost of the merchandise is $250. Sales tax is 5%.

31 Received an advance payment from Meridian, Inc. in the amount of $4,200. Merchandise will be shipped next week.

LG 15-3. Draw journals and record transactions. Writing and drawing are excellent ways to help you remember details. We apply these techniques in the following problem. Cheyenne Company uses special journals. The October 2017 transactions below for Cheyenne Company involve the use of the purchases journal and the cash payments journal.

Instructions:

a. Draw a purchases journal and draw a cash payments journal. (If you wish to complete the problem without drawing, you can print a blank journal from the disk or at worthyjames. com/student info.)

b. Record the Cheyenne Company transactions in the appropriate journals and total the journals.

Note: Solutions are available for both perpetual and periodic systems.

October Transactions

4   Cheyenne Company purchased $3,900 of merchandise inventory on account from Rock Springs Corporation, terms 2/10, n/30.

6   Purchased equipment from Torrington Supplies for $10,000. Paid $3,000 cash with check #455 and signed a note payable for the balance.

11 Purchased $5,000 of merchandise on account from Laramie Corporation, terms 1/10, n/30.

14 Paid Rock Springs Corporation in full, check #456.

17 Paid employee wages in the amount of $4,000, check #457.

Solutions are in the disk at the back of the book and at: www.worthyjames.com

PRACTICE   Learning Goal 15, continued

LG 15-3, *continued*

19 Purchased $11,000 of merchandise on account from Riverton Enterprises, terms 2/10, n/30.
21 Paid Laramie Corporation in full, check #458.
27 Purchased $900 of supplies from Torrington Supplies, terms 1/15, n/30.
30 Paid $520 to Casper Shipping for freight charges on merchandise purchases, check #459.

LG 15-4. Complete the journal entries and enter posting references; use either perpetual or periodic inventory method. The partially completed cash receipts journal for Amherst Enterprises is presented below. Amherst Enterprises uses the perpetual inventory system.

Instructions:

a. For each transaction, record the missing entry into the journal.
b. Enter the totals into the journal.
c. Record all the necessary posting references in the journal as if all posting had been completed.

Other information: Amherst Enterprises makes sales on account with terms of 2/10, n/30. The sales tax on cash sales is 6%. J. Akers paid after the discount period.

If you want to use the periodic inventory method instead of the perpetual method, ignore the far right column—you will not record cost of goods sold with each sale.

Make a copy of this page to use to complete the problem. (You can also print out a cash receipts journal from the disk at the back of the book or at worthyjames.com (student info.))

Cash Receipts Journal

	Other Accounts		Debits			Credits				Dr. Cost of Goods Sold Cr. Inventory
Date	Account Name	Post Ref.	Cash	Sales Discount	Other Accounts	Accounts Receivable	Sales	Sales Tax Payable	Other Accounts	
May 1			530					30		350
4	R. Donlevy			16		800				
8	J. Akers		900							
13	Notes Payable		10,000							
17	C. Tran		1,960			2,000				
22	Notes Receivable		7,500						7,000	
	Interest Revenue									
30							900	54		600
	Totals									

The chart of accounts includes the following selected general ledger accounts, with account numbers:

Cash	102	Notes Payable	250
Accounts Receivable	125	Sales	410
Inventory	135	Sales Discounts	415
Notes Receivable	150	Cost of Goods Sold	520
Sales Tax Payable	210	Interest Revenue	605

PRACTICE   Learning Goal 15, continued

Solutions are in the disk at the back of the book and at: www.worthyjames.com

LG 15-5. **Complete the journal entries and enter posting references; use either perpetual or periodic inventory method.** The partially completed cash payments journal for Fayetteville Company is presented below. Fayetteville Company uses the perpetual inventory method.

Instructions:

a. For each transaction, record the missing entry into the journal.
b. Enter the totals into the journal.
c. Record all the necessary posting references in the journal as if all posting had been completed.

Other information: Both Hammond Company and Moreno Wholesale, Inc. offer 2% discount terms, and Fayetteville Company paid within the discount period. Fayetteville Company uses the perpetual inventory method and credits all discounts taken to the Inventory account.

If you want to use the periodic method instead of the perpetual method: (i) Change the "Inventory" credit column title to "Purchase Discounts" and use account number 612. (ii) Record the freight-in cost in an account called "Freight-in" with account number 650. The October 31 transaction with Ace Transport is for freight-in cost related to a merchandise purchase.

Make a copy of this page to use to complete the problem. (You can also print out a cash payments journal from the disk in the back of the book.) In this way, you can use the problem again without seeing previous answers.

				Debits		Credits		
Date	Ck. No.	Account Name	Post. Ref.	Other Accounts	Accounts Payable	Other Accounts	Inventory	Cash
Oct. 2	1184	Office Supplies		1,100				
5	1185	Rent Expense						4,500
9	1186	Hammond Company			900			
15	1187	Notes Payable		10,000				
		Interest Expense		500				
21	1188	Moreno Wholesale, Inc.					50	
25	1189	Pine Bluff Supply Company						2,700
31	1190	**Inventory**						750
		Totals						

Cash Payments Journal

The chart of accounts includes the following selected general ledger accounts, with account numbers:

Cash	101	Accounts Payable	210
Office Supplies	120	Notes Payable	250
Inventory	145	Rent Expense	615
Equipment	170	Interest Expense	710

LG 15-6. Complete the journal entries and enter posting references; use either perpetual or periodic inventory method. The partially completed purchases journal for Lansing Company, which uses the perpetual inventory method, is presented below.

Instructions:

a. For each transaction, record the missing entry into the journal.
b. Enter the totals into the journal.
c. Record all the necessary posting references in the journal as if all of the posting had been completed.

Other information: All purchases are for inventory except those shown. The cash payments journal of Lansing Company shows a January 5 credit to Cash in the amount of $2,450 for a payment to O'Keefe Company and a discount credit in the amount of $50. O'Keefe requires full payment within 30 days and offers a discount for payment within 10 days.

If you want to use the periodic method, change the "Inventory" column title to "Purchases" and use account number 610.

Make a copy of this page to complete the problem. (You can also print out a purchases journal from the disk in the back of the book.) In this way, you can use the problem again without seeing previous answers.

				Credit		Debits			
			Post.	Accounts			Other Accounts		
Date	Account Credited	Terms	Ref.	Payable	Inventory	Name	Ref.	Amount	
Dec. 1	Bizzell Supply Company	1/10, n/30		3,100					
4	Coast Corporation	2/10, n/30			2,650				
12	East Asia Imports	3/10, n/30		15,200		Furniture			
19	Weintraub Supply, Inc.	2/10, n/30			900				
22	Gupta Enterprises	3/10, n/30		1,750		Supplies		480	
28	O'Keefe Company								
	Totals								

Purchases Journal

The chart of accounts includes the following selected general ledger accounts, with account numbers:

Cash	101	Furniture	175
Supplies	124	Accounts Payable	215
Inventory	155		

LG 15-7. Journalizing and entering posting references; use either perpetual or periodic inventory method. Tonopah Company makes all merchant sales on terms of 1/15, n/30 and uses a perpetual inventory system. The sales tax rate is 6% for retail cash sales. Sales invoice numbers begin at #125.

Instructions:

a. Record the transactions shown below into the appropriate journals. (If you wish to do the problem using a periodic system, do not use the far right column in each journal.)

For journal paper, make copies from the special journal forms in the disk at the back of this book. Use the journals below as your models for column headings.

Sales Journal

Date	Customer Account	Invoice Number	Post. Ref.	Dr. Accounts Receivable Cr. Sales	Dr. Cost of Goods Sold Cr. Inventory
2017					

Cash Receipts Journal

	Other Accounts		Debits			Credits				Dr. Cost of Goods Sold Cr. Inventory
Date	Account Name	Post. Ref.	Cash	Sales Discount	Other Accounts	Accounts Receivable	Sales	Sales Tax Payable	Other Accounts	
2017										

Jan. 3	Sold merchandise on account to Carson City Company, $3,500. Inventory cost: $2,750.
4	Received cash on account from Elko Enterprises in full settlement of a December 20 sale of $9,500.
5	Made retail cash sale in the amount of $750. Inventory cost: $460.
11	Sold merchandise on account to Las Vegas, Inc., $20,000. Inventory cost: $15,000.
11	Received payment in full from Carson City Company.
19	Received cash on account from Reno Company in full settlement of a December 15 sale of $4,750.
23	Sold merchandise on account to Ely Co., $2,800. Inventory cost: $1,900.
25	Received a $300 cash refund from a vendor of defective supplies that are being returned.
26	Received payment in full from Las Vegas, Inc.
29	Sold merchandise on account to Virginia City Company, $880. Inventory cost: $610.
30	Made a retail cash sale in the amount of $400. Inventory cost: $275.

Solutions are in the disk at the back of the book and at: www.worthyjames.com

PRACTICE Learning Goal 15, continued

LG 15-7, *continued*

b. The general ledger of this company includes the account numbers that you see in the table below. Now assume that the journals above have been posted. Enter the appropriate posting references into the journals.

Cash	105	Inventory	115	Sales	410
Accounts Receivable	110	Land	125	Sales Discounts	411
Supplies	112	Sales Tax Payable	220	Cost of Goods Sold	505

LG 15-8. Journalizing and entering posting references; use either perpetual or periodic inventory method. Owings Mills Company uses a perpetual inventory system and completed the 2017 transactions you see listed below.

Instructions:

a. Record the transactions shown below into the appropriate journals. (If you wish to complete the problem using the periodic method, change the "Inventory" column title to "Purchases" in the purchases journal; in the cash payments journal, change "Inventory" column to a "Purchase Discounts" column. Also, use "Freight-in" for freight charges.)

For journal paper, make copies from the special journal forms in the disk at the back of this book. Use the journals below as your models for column headings.

Purchases Journal

Date	Account Credited	Terms	Post. Ref.	Credit Accounts Payable	Inventory	Other Accounts Name	Ref.	Amount

Cash Payments Journal

Date	Ck. No.	Account Name	Post. Ref.	Debits Other Accounts	Accounts Payable	Credits Other Accounts	Inventory	Cash

LG 15-8, *continued*

Nov. 3   Purchased merchandise on account from Baltimore Enterprises, $2,750. Terms 2/10, n/30.

5   Wrote check #521 for $495 to Annapolis Co. in full settlement of an October 31 purchase, terms 1/5 eom.

7   Purchased supplies on account from Rockville Co., $275. Terms net 30 days (no discount).

12   Purchased merchandise on account from Silver Spring, Inc., $4,800. Terms 2/15, n/30.

13   Wrote check #522 for full payment to Baltimore Enterprises.

19   Wrote check #523 for $2,200 to fully pay an October 15 purchase from Abell Company, terms 2/10, n/30.

22   Purchased merchandise on account from Largo Company, $7,500. Terms 2/10, n/30.

27   Wrote check #524 in the amount of $2,330 for 1-year fire insurance coverage.

27   Wrote check #525 in full settlement of Silver Spring, Inc. purchase.

29   Received bill for advertising services for November, $500 from Cumberland Agency. Due in 30 days. Accrued the amount in the purchases journal.

30   Wrote check #526 to pay sales tax liability, $1,210.

30   Wrote Check #527 to pay freight-in charges of $500 for merchandise purchases.

b. The general ledger of this company includes the account numbers that you see in the table below. Now assume that the journals above have been posted. Enter the appropriate posting references into the journals.

| Cash | 103 | Inventory | 110 | Accounts Payable | 205 | Cost of Goods Sold | 520 |
| Supplies | 108 | Prepaid Insurance | 120 | Sales Tax Payable | 208 | Advertising Expense | 580 |

If you are using the periodic method, use account #508 for Purchases, #510 for Purchase Discounts, and #512 for Freight-in.

LG 15-9. **Create journals from related ledger accounts.** Shown below are some 2017 ledger accounts in the general ledger and Accounts Payable subsidiary ledger of Okalahoma Merchandise Company. All vendors use terms of 2/10, n/30, except Enid Wholesale, which uses 1/15, n/30. The journals are not shown to you.

Instructions: Using the information in the ledger accounts, create the following items.

a. Purchases journal
b. General journal

You can print blank copies of purchase and general journals from the disk at the back of the book.

LG 15-9, *continued*

General Ledger

Store Supplies					132
Date	Explanation	Ref.	Debit	Credit	Balance
May 3		P5	1,700		1,700

Merchandise Inventory					145
Date	Explanation	Ref.	Debit	Credit	Balance
May 11		GJ3		250	
20		GJ3	400		
29		GJ3		1,700	
31		P5	43,000		

Office Equipment					170
Date	Explanation	Ref.	Debit	Credit	Balance
May 1	Bal. Fwd.				10,000
17		P5	9,100		19,100

Accounts Payable					210
Date	Explanation	Ref.	Debit	Credit	Balance
May 1	Bal. Fwd.				2,500
11		GJ3	250		2,250
20		GJ3		400	2,650
29		GJ3	1,700		950
31		P5		43,000	43,950

Subsidiary Accounts Payable Ledger

Enid Wholesale, Inc.					
Date	Explanation	Ref.	Debit	Credit	Balance
May 1	Bal. Fwd.				2,500
2		P5		3,200	5,700
15		P5		4,700	10,400

Norman Resources					
Date	Explanation	Ref.	Debit	Credit	Balance
May 8		P5		5,600	5,600
11		GJ3	250		5,350
25		P5		7,200	12,550

OK City Enterprises					
Date	Explanation	Ref.	Debit	Credit	Balance
May 10		P5		4,900	4,900
16		P5		5,200	10,100
28		P5		1,400	11,500

Stillwater Supply					
Date	Explanation	Ref.	Debit	Credit	Balance
May 3		P5		1,700	1,700
17		P5		9,100	10,800
29		GJ3	1,700		9,100

Tulsa Freight Company					
Date	Explanation	Ref.	Debit	Credit	Balance
May 20		GJ3		400	400

Note: For a periodic system solution, assume that Okalahoma Merchandise Company uses the Purchases Account #500 to record merchandise purchases instead of the Merchandise Inventory account, Purchase Returns and Allowances Account #510, and Freight-in Account # 511.

LG 15-10. Use special journals as reports to help analyze operations. The sales journal, purchases journal, cash receipts journal, and cash payments journal for Myers Company for the month of November are shown below. Myers Company uses terms of 2/10, n/30 for all credit sales and has a perpetual inventory system.

Instructions: Use the journals to do an analysis that will answer the following questions from the owner.

a. What are total sales for the period, and who are the three biggest customers as a percentage of total sales? (There were no returns for the month.)

LG 15-10, *continued*

b. Can you provide a quick estimate of the gross profit as a percentage of credit sales, excluding returns and discounts? Do the same for cash sales.

c. Have all November customers who have taken discounts actually paid within the discount period?

d. What are the discount deadline dates for payment of the currently unpaid November purchases?

e. Who are the three biggest inventory suppliers as a percentage of total inventory purchases?

f. What are the top three sources of cash receipts for the period as a percentage of total cash received? Is it likely these sources will be recurring in December?

g. Are discounts important to our customers? What percent of November credit sales resulted in customers taking discounts?

h. What effective percentage of discounts are we taking on our outstanding accounts payable?

i. Excluding cash receipt and payment items that are probably one-time events, use the November cash receipts and cash payments to make a quick estimate of our November "recurring items" cash flow.

Sales Journal

Date	Customer Account	Invoice Number	Post. Ref.	Dr. Accounts Receivable Cr. Sales	Dr. Cost of Goods Sold Cr. Merchandise Inventory
2017					
Nov. 5	Nguyen Co.	8146	✓	5,500	2,255
10	Scott Co.	8147	✓	2,500	1,025
12	Cabot Co.	8148	✓	4,300	1,760
18	Gethin Partners	8149	✓	1,900	780
23	Rodriguez, Inc.	8150	✓	3,700	1,520
27	Anwen Enterprises	8151	✓	5,250	2,100
29	Scott Co.	8152	✓	4,500	1,800
	Totals			27,650	11,240
				(115/405)	(520/125)

Purchases Journal

Date	Account Credited	Terms	Post. Ref.	Credit Accounts Payable	Debits Inventory	Other Accounts Name	Other Accounts Ref.	Other Accounts Amount
2017								
Nov. 1	Ontario Enterprises	2/10, n/30	✓	5,100	5,100			
4	Greenspan Company	2/10, n/30	✓	3,650	3,650			
7	Office Suppliers	—	✓	5,500		Furniture	175	5,500
13	Bernanke Company	2/10, n/30	✓	4,800	4,800			
18	Computer Supply Co.	1/15, n/30	✓	9,570		Computers	170	9,570
22	Greenspan Company	2/10, n/30	✓	4,360	4,360			
27	Canyon Wholesale	1/10, n/30	✓	1,500	1,500			
	Totals			34,480	19,410			15,070
				(115/405)	(125)			(X)

Note: For a periodic system, you can assume that cost of goods sold is the same and use a Purchases account in the purchases journal instead of an Inventory account.

LG 15-10, *continued*

Cash Receipts Journal

	Other Accounts		Debits			Credits				Dr. Cost of Goods Sold Cr. Inventory
Date	Account Name	Post. Ref.	Cash	Sales Discount	Other Accounts	Accounts Receivable	Sales	Sales Tax Payable	Other Accounts	
2017										
Nov. 1	Notes Payable	260	15,000						15,000	
4	Eccles Corp.	✓	3,675	75		3,750				
4	Volker Corp.	✓	2,744	56		2,800				
9			1,029				980	49		500
12	Common Stock	305	12,000						12,000	
14	Nguyen Co.	✓	5,390	110		5,500				
17			1,575				1,500	75		775
27	Equipment	170	4,500						9,000	
	Notes Receivable	145			4,500					
28	Scott Co.	✓	2,500			2,500				
30	Cabot Co.	✓	4,214	86		4,300				
	Totals		52,627	327	4,500	18,850	2,480	124	36,000	1,275
			(105)	(415)	(X)	(115)	(405)	(225)	(X)	(520/125)

Cash Payments Journal

				Debits		Credits		
Date	Ck. No.	Account Name	Post. Ref.	Other Accounts	Accounts Payable	Other Accounts	Inventory	Cash
2017								
Nov. 1	1190	Rent Expense	550	3,100				3,100
1	1191	Sales Tax Payable	225	850				850
3	1192	Roosevelt Corporation	✓		1,200		36	1,164
6	1193	Inventory	125	120				120
7	1194	Land	190	17,000				7,000
		Notes Payable	260			10,000		
14	1195	Ontario Enterprises	✓		5,100			5,100
15	1196	Prepaid Insurance	145	1,800				1,800
15	1197	Greenspan Company	✓		3,650		73	3,577
24	1198	Bernanke Company	✓		4,800		50	4,750
28	1199	Inventory	125	1,220				1,220
29	1200	Dividends	310	1,000				1,000
30	1201	Washington Company	✓		800			800
		Totals		25,090	15,550	10,000	159	30,481
				(X)	(220)	(X)	(125)	(105)

Note: For a periodic system, you can assume that cost of goods sold is the same and use a Purchases account instead of an Inventory account in the cash payments journal.

LG 15-11. Comprehensive proprietorship problem using all journals, use either perpetual or periodic system, proprietorship review. During January Newark Company, which sells wholesale and retail home decorating supplies, completed the transactions that you see listed below. Newark Co. is a proprietorship. For sales on account the company uses terms of 2/10, n/30 and all sales on account are to merchants and are exempt from sales tax. The tax rate on retail sales is 6%. Purchases are either not taxable or include tax. For ledger and journal paper, make copies of the ledger and journal paper from the disk at the back of this book.

Instructions:

a. Use either the perpetual or the periodic inventory system. Write the headings and column titles in the blank journals using the examples from this learning goal. Scan the transactions to see the kind of transactions you will be recording.

b. Using the blank journal paper, record the January transactions in the appropriate journals. Begin the general journal on page 5, the sales journal on page 11, the purchases journal on page 14, the cash receipts journal on page 18, and the cash payments journal on page 20.

c. Using the blank ledger paper, open any needed ledger accounts by writing their names and account numbers onto the accounts. Use separate pages for the subsidiary ledgers. Shown below is a December 31 post-closing trial balance that includes zero-balance accounts. Use this to enter beginning account balances.

d. Post from all journals into the appropriate ledger accounts.

e. For Accounts Receivable and Accounts Payable, verify that the total of the final balances of the subsidiary accounts equals the final balance of the general ledger controlling account.

January Transactions

2017

Jan. 2 Purchased $3,500 of inventory, terms 2/10, n/30, from Plainfield Supply Company.

4 Issued invoice #844 for $800 sale on account to Trenton Company. Cost of merchandise is $320.

5 Made a $400 cash sale to a retail customer. Cost of merchandise is $160.

6 Purchased $8,000 of inventory, terms 1/10, n/15, from Diamond Resources.

8 Issued check #301 for January rent, $4,800.

9 Received payment from New Brunswick, Inc. for the balance due.

10 Issued check #302 to pay Orange Office Supply balance due.

10 Issued invoice #845 for $2,750 sale on account to Elizabeth, Inc. Cost of merchandise is $1,100.

11 Issued invoice #846 for $5,900 sale on account to New Brunswick, Inc. Cost of merchandise is $2,360.

12 Purchased $12,000 of equipment by paying $2,400 cash and signing a note payable for the balance.

12 Issued check #304 to pay Plainfield Supply Company in full for January 2 purchase.

13 Received payment in full from Trenton Company for January 4 sale.

14 Received a debit memo from Elizabeth, Inc., which returned merchandise with a sale price of $1,000. Cost of the merchandise is $400.

14 Issued invoice #847 for $3,250 sale on account to Camden Company. Merchandise cost is $1,300.

16 Issued check #305 to pay Diamond Resources in full for January 6 purchase.

17 Purchased $1,620 of supplies on account from Orange Office Supply. No discount terms.

18 Purchased $2,800 of inventory, terms 2/10, n/30, from Plainfield Supply Company.

19 Sold some extra supplies for $1,500 cash. The supplies had cost $1,170 (nontaxable sale).

20 Received a $1,715 payment from Elizabeth, Inc. for the January 10 sale.

21 Received a $2,450 payment from New Brunswick, Inc. for the January 11 sale.

22 Issued a debit memo and returned $650 of damaged merchandise to Plainfield Supply.

LG 15-11, *continued*

24 Issued invoice #848 for $7,180 sale on account to Trenton Company. Merchandise cost is $2,870.
27 Received payment in full from Camden Company for January 14 sale.
27 Made a cash sale to a retail customer in the amount $1,700. Cost of inventory is $735.
28 A fire in the warehouse destroyed $1,500 of inventory. Insurance does not cover this amount.
30 Purchased $5,000 of equipment on account from Patterson Equipment. No discount terms.
31 Issued check #306 to pay the monthly wages, $10,500.
31 Issued check #307 to pay monthly Internet website services, $830.
31 Issued check #308 to owner for $1,000.
31 Received a $700 freight bill from Superior Freight Company for merchandise purchased.

Newark Company Post-Closing Trial Balance December 31, 2016			
Name	Acct. #	Dr.	Cr.
Cash	103	36,200	
Accounts Receivable	115	1,500	
Supplies	122	250	
Merchandise Inventory	126	15,650	
Equipment	140	8,600	
Accounts Payable	215		5,000
Sales Tax Payable	220		445
Notes Payable	280		
A. Torelli, Capital	301		56,755
A. Torelli, Drawing	302		
Sales Revenue	410		
Sales Returns & Allow.	412		
Sales Discounts	415		
Interest Earned	480		
Cost of Goods Sold	512		
Wages Expense	525		
Rent Expense	550		
Internet Expenses	570		
Loss on Sale	610		
Casualty Loss	650		
Gain on Sale	710		
Total		62,200	62,200

Note: The December 31 balance of Accounts Receivable is from a December 30 sale made to New Brunswick, Inc. The December 31 balance of Accounts Payable is for an amount owing to Orange Office Supply, no discount.

Note: For the periodic system use the following accounts: Purchases, #508; Purchase Discounts, #510; Purchase Returns and Allowances, #511; Freight-in, #512. (You will not need the Cost of Goods Sold account.)

Instructor-Assigned Problems

If you are using this book in a class, these review problems may be assigned by your instructor for homework, group assignments, class work, or other activities. Only your instructor has the solutions.

IA 15-1. **Journalize sales and cash receipts transactions and enter posting references; use either perpetual or periodic inventory method.** Sioux City Company makes all merchant sales on terms of 2/10, n/30 and uses a perpetual inventory system. The sales tax rate is 7% for retail sales which are cash or bank card sales. Sales invoice numbers begin at 300, sales journal is page 15, and cash receipts is page 30.

Instructions:

a. Print out the necessary journals from the disk at the back of this book or go to the 'student info.' link at www.worthyjames.com and print from the selection of accounting journals, or create your own blank journals.
b. Enter the appropriate column titles and record the transactions below using a perpetual inventory system. (If you wish to use a periodic system you would not require columns for recording cost of goods sold.)
c. Total the columns and enter posting references as if you had completed the posting.

Mar. 5 Sold merchandise on account to Waterloo Enterprises, $7,100. Inventory cost: $4,250.
    6 Made a cash retail sale in the amount of $1,000. Inventory cost: $500.
    9 Received a cash advance payment of $2,500 from Omaha Inc.
  12 Sold merchandise on account to Lewiston, Inc., $5,700. Inventory cost: $3,420.
  14 Received cash on account from West Yellowstone Company in full settlement of a February 23 sale of $12,000.
  17 Sold merchandise on account to Springfield, Inc., $8,900. Inventory cost: $5,340.
  17 Received cash from Waterloo Enterprises in full settlement of the March 5 sale.
  22 Received a $4,900 cash payment from Lewiston Company.
  26 Made a retail credit card sale in the amount of $1,200. Inventory cost: $570. Bank fee was $21.
  27 Sold merchandise on account to Bismarck Inc. for $11,750. Inventory cost: $7,050.
  30 Delivered the full amount of merchandise ordered to Omaha Inc.
  31 Borrowed $25,000 from National Bank.

The chart of accounts includes the following selected accounts and account numbers:

Cash	104	Sales	401
Sales Tax Payable	225	Cost of Goods Sold	501
Unearned Revenue	210	Inventory	118
Bank Card Fees	610	Sales Discounts	405
Accounts Receivable	115	Notes Payable	250

IA 15-2. **Journalize purchases and cash payments transactions and enter posting references; use either perpetual or periodic inventory method.** Madison Company uses a perpetual inventory system.

Instructions:

a. Print out the necessary journals from the disk at the back of this book or go to the 'student info.' link at www.worthyjames.com and print from the selection of accounting journals, or create your own blank journals.

IA 15-2, *continued*

b. Enter the appropriate column titles and record the transactions below using a perpetual inventory system. (If you wish to use a periodic system you would replace the "inventory" name with "purchases".) Begin the purchases journal at page 18 and cash payments journal at page 32.

c. Total the columns and enter posting references as if you had completed the posting.

July	2	Purchased merchandise on account from Cincinnati Co., $4,200. Terms 1/10, n/30.
	6	Purchased $740 of supplies on account from Racine Company. No discounts.
	11	Wrote check #356 to Macon Enterprises in full settlement of $500 June 15 invoice, terms 2/10, n/30.
	12	Wrote check #357 to Cincinnati Co. in full settlement of invoice.
	12	Purchased merchandise on account from New Castle, Inc., $6,950. Terms 2/10, n/30.
	19	Wrote check #358 for 6 months of prepaid fire insurance, $2,880.
	21	Purchased merchandise on account from Dallas, Co., $4,300. Terms 2/10, n/30.
	22	Wrote check #359 to New Castle, Inc. in full settlement of invoice.
	28	Wrote check #360 to pay freight charges on New Castle purchase, $380.
	30	Wrote check #361 for $950 to make a loan payment: $750 interest expense, $200 note principal.
	31	Wrote check #362 to Dallas Co., $1,960.
	31	Purchased $10,000 of equipment from Eau Claire Co. Paid $5,000 at purchase date.

The chart of accounts includes the following selected accounts and account numbers:

Cash	102	Interest Expense	605
Prepaid Insurance	130	Sales Tax Payable	220
Notes Payable	215	Inventory	112
Freight-in (periodic)	114	Cost of Goods Sold	505
Supplies	111	Equipment	150
Accounts Payable	210		

IA 15-3. Journalize all transaction types and enter posting references; use either perpetual or periodic inventory method. Denver Ventures, Inc. makes all merchant sales on terms of 2/10, n/30 and uses a perpetual inventory system. The sales tax rate is 3.8% for retail sales which are cash or bank card sales. Sales invoice numbers begin at #520, sales journal is page 25, cash receipts is page 40, purchases journal 29, cash payments journal at 51, and general journal at 12.

Instructions:

a. Print out the necessary journals from the disk at the back of this book or go to the 'student info.' link at www.worthyjames.com and print from the selection of accounting journals, or create your own blank journals.

b. Enter the appropriate column titles and record the transactions below using a perpetual inventory system. (If you wish to use a periodic system you would not require columns for recording cost of goods sold and you would replace the name "inventory" with "purchases".)

c. Total the columns and enter posting references as if you had actually completed the posting.

Oct.	2	Sold merchandise on account to Quail Creek Co., $9,500. Inventory cost: $6,080.
	6	Purchased merchandise on account from Reno Corp. , $14,600. Terms 1/15, n/45.
	8	Sold merchandise on account to Santa Fe, Inc., $3,900. Inventory cost: $2,496. Received a check in the amount of $1,960 as immediate payment.
	9	Received a cash advance payment from Truckee Co., $7,000.
	10	Wrote check #707 for 5 airline tickets, $2,500.

Reporting Cash

Cash Defined

Overview

The following discussion identifies items that are included in the definition of "Cash" and explains how and where cash appears on the financial statements.

Currency and Coin

Most of us are familiar with the money we carry in our wallets and the coins in our pockets. We refer to this paper and metal money as *currency and coin*. Usually, most businesses keep a relatively small amount of this on hand—only as much as is needed to make change or pay for small expenditures.

Dollar-Labeled Items

Checks, money orders, stamps, and travelers' checks are examples of items labeled in dollar amounts. Are they cash?

Rule: Include as cash any dollar-labeled item that a bank will accept as a deposit.

Examples of Cash: Checks, money orders, travelers checks
Not Cash: Stamps (a prepaid expense) and coupons.

Bank Account Balances

Checking and savings account balances are also included in the definition of cash because these accounts must be paid to the depositor in the form of currency, on demand.

Cash Defined, *continued*

Cash Equivalents

A few limited types of very short-term and very safe ("liquid") investments are considered to be the equivalent of cash. The most common examples are money market funds and short-term bank certificates of deposit and U.S. treasury securities with original maturities of not more than three months.

Not Cash Equivalents:

- Corporate stocks and bonds
- Any government securities with an original maturity longer than 3 months

How Cash Is Reported on the Balance Sheet

Typical Reporting

Normally cash is a current asset. Because assets on a balance sheet are usually presented in order of liquidity, cash should be the first asset shown—the most liquid of the current assets.

The total cash shown on a balance sheet includes all the items included in our definition of cash. This is often reported as "Cash and Cash Equivalents."

Restricted Cash

A cash balance is **restricted** when the cash can only be used for a specific purpose. For example, some cash may be designated exclusively for an asset purchase or for a loan repayment. Restricted cash is reported as a separate cash balance.

A restricted cash balance should be classified as either a short-term or long-term investment asset depending on when the cash is likely to be used.

Compensating Balances

A **compensating balance** is a minimum cash balance that a business is required to maintain in an account. Such a requirement usually occurs as part of a bank loan agreement. The part of the total cash that is a compensating balance must be disclosed in the notes to the financial statements.

Cash Reported on the Statement of Cash Flows

Same Definition

The statement of cash flows explains the change in the cash account balance between two balance sheet dates. Therefore, the definition of cash (including cash equivalents) is exactly the same on the statement of cash flows as it is on the balance sheet.

The format of the statement of cash flows classifies the causes of change in the cash balance into three activities: operating, investing, and financing. The net result of these three activities during the latest period, combined with the cash balance at the beginning of the period, equals the ending cash balance that is shown on the current balance sheet at the end of the period.

The statement of cash flows is reviewed in Volume 1 of this set and discussed in detail in Learning Goal 21 in this book.

Controlling Cash

Internal Control

Definition

Internal control means the policies, procedures, and organizational design that a company uses for the purpose of:

- safeguarding assets,
- recording accurate and reliable accounting information, and
- encouraging operating efficiency.

Internal Control for Cash

Internal control is a big topic with many applications. In this learning goal, however, we are primarily concerned with using internal control to safeguard cash. Cash is the easiest asset to steal and the most desirable asset. Cash thefts are often the most difficult to identify, and loss of cash can be extremely damaging to a business. For these reasons, it is essential to establish adequate internal control for cash. In the following sections, we will discuss the following widely used and important cash controls:

- Use of a checking or savings account
- The bank reconciliation
- The imprest petty cash system
- Use of credit cards
- The voucher system
- Cash receipts procedures
- Basic internal control principles that apply to all assets
- Internet and e-commerce requirements

Internal Control, *continued*

Limitations	Internal control is not a guarantee against theft; it is intended to be a barrier to theft and to reduce the probability of asset loss. Human error and fraud are potentially serious weaknesses of internal control.
	For example, several employees acting together to steal cash, called ***collusion***, can defeat an internal control system. Also, simple carelessness, neglect, or fatigue can weaken internal control. Finally, good internal control costs money. The cost required to maintain an internal control system should not exceed the losses that it prevents.

Using a Checking Account

Overview	A checking account is an important internal control device. It allows a business to minimize the use of currency and keep funds safe and helps control payments and receipts. A bank checking account also serves as an independent detailed record of cash received and paid. To properly use a checking account, you should understand the use of the following five items:
	■ Signature card ■ Check ■ Deposit form ■ Bank statement ■ Bank reconciliation
The Signature Card	A signature card is a bank document that is required to open a checking account. The card contains the signatures of people who are authorized to sign checks. A check is not valid without an authorized signature, and a bank will not process a check unless it has a signature that corresponds to a signature on the card.
The Check	A ***check*** is a document given by a maker to a payee that directs the maker's bank to pay a specified amount to the payee, on demand. The check is a "three-party document": the maker, the payee, and the bank.

continued

Using a Checking Account, *continued*

Check Features

The example of a check below identifies the following features.

A check involves these three parties:

1. The **maker** (sometimes called **drawer** or **payor**) is the party who is making the payment and whose account is being reduced—here, the Paia company.
2. The **payee** is the party named on the check to receive the cash payment. Here, the payee is Lee Office Supplies.
3. The bank—here, Metro—makes payment and reduces the maker's account. (Sometimes called "payer")

Other features of the check are:

4. Check number: As an internal control device, checks are sequentially numbered so all checks are accounted for.
5. ABA (American Bankers' Association) transit number. This is a unique number that serves as back-up to the routing number (item 7) if there is an electronic routing problem. This number is also used to identify each check listed on a deposit slip.
6. Cleared check amount. When a bank pays a check, the verified amount of actual payment is recorded in special magnetic ink characters on the lower right part of the check.

7. Routing number (for clearing checks and electronic transfers)
8. Account number

Note: banks provide photocopies of paid checks as part of bank statements.

Using a Checking Account, *continued*

How Does a Check Get Paid?

At one time, checks were physically processed. Most checks now are electronically scanned and processed digitally. When you write a check, the payee deposits the check in a bank account; this can be done either physically or by a mobile device camera or a scanner with Internet service. If, by chance, the payee's bank happens to be the same as your bank, the bank simply transfers funds out of your account into the payee's account.

If the payee deposits the check in an account at a different bank, there are several possibilities. 1) The payee's bank has a direct relationship with your bank: This means that each bank has an account with the other bank. In this situation, the payee's bank sends an electronic copy to your bank, which credits the payee bank's account and reduces your balance. At the same time the payee's bank increases the payee's individual account. 2) There is no direct relationship between the banks: In this case, the payee's bank sends an electronic copy to an intermediary. An intermediary can be a large bank, a commercial clearinghouse, or a federal reserve bank. A key factor is that each bank maintains an account with the intermediary. When the intermediary receives the electronic copy, it increases the balance of the payee bank and reduces the balance of your bank. In turn, the payee's bank increases the payee's account balance and your bank decreases your account balance.

The back of a check is marked to indicate payment; a paid check is called a ***cleared check*** or a ***canceled check***. With electronic processing most checks clear within a few days or less.

The Deposit Form

A deposit form is used to identify the amount of the total deposit and the amount of cash and checks that are in a deposit. Deposit forms, like checks, are standard printed forms that show account number and customer and bank information.

A completed deposit form should show:

1. The total amount of currency
2. The total amount of coins
3. The total amount of checks. List each check individually and show:

- The part of the ABA number of each check deposited (item 5 in check example above) before the diagonal line (95-3164 in the example) followed by
- The amount of the check

Hidden feature: If you look carefully at the signature line of a check, you will see that it is not a solid line, but very small print. This is a security feature called "microprint" (MP), making checks difficult to accurately copy.

continued ▶

Using a Checking Account, *continued*

Example

The example below shows a typical deposit form.

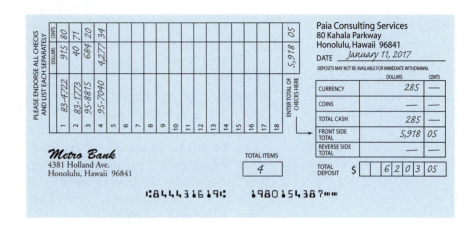

Endorsed Checks

A check must be endorsed before it can be deposited. A *check endorsement* is a legal transfer by the payee to another party (in this case, a bank) of ownership of a check, and therefore the right to receive payment from the maker. There are two types of endorsements:

- *Blank endorsement:* The payee simply signs the back of the check. This makes the check payable to anyone who physically possesses it.
- *Restrictive endorsement:* The payee signs the back of the check but adds a restriction, such as "for deposit only" (or "pay Jane Doe only" if transferred to another individual). It is safer to use restrictive endorsements.

Automated Payments

Most banks offer a no-cost automatic payment feature for checking accounts. This is accomplished by: 1) designating a recurring payee that can receive direct electronic payments, such as a utility company, or 2) Entering payee names and amounts in an online account using a bank website, which can make direct electronic payments or create checks for payees unable to receive electronic payments.

The Bank Statement

The *bank statement* is a report from a bank to the customer that shows in detail the bank's record of the account activity and balances for a specified period of time, generally monthly. An example of a bank statement is presented in the next section on page 594.

Coming Up . . .

The overview to this section indicated that an essential procedure used with a checking account is the bank reconciliation. The next section explains what a bank reconciliation is and the procedure for preparing one.

Check Your Understanding

Write the completed sentences on a separate sheet of paper.

Any item that a bank accepts as a · · · · · · · · can be considered to be cash. A few limited types of very short-term items that are very safe and are very liquid investments such as short-term bank certificate of deposits and money market funds are called · · · · · · · · · · · · · · · and are treated as cash. Cash that can only be used for a specific purpose is called · · · · · · · · cash, and if not available to pay current liabilities is shown on the balance sheet as either a short- or long-term · · · · · · · ·, depending on the type of · · · · · · · · · . A minimum balance of cash that is required to maintained at all times is called a · · · · · · · · · · · · · · · · ·, and this part of the cash balance must be disclosed in the · · · · · · · · .

The essential means of protecting cash and other assets is called · · · · · · · · · · · · · · · · · ·, and a checking account is an important way of applying this protection to cash. The party who writes a check is called the · · · · · · · · and the party who will receive payment is called the · · · · · · · · .

A check · · · · · · · · is a legal transfer of funds by the payee to another party of the right to receive payment from the maker. A · · · · · · · · · · · · · · · transfers the right to receive payment to any party who physically holds a check. A · · · · · · · · · · · · · · · · · transfers the right to receive payment to a specific party.

Answers

Any item that a bank accepts as a deposit can be considered to be cash. A few limited types of very short-term items that are very safe and are very liquid investments such as short-term bank certificate of deposits and money market funds are called cash equivalents and are treated as cash. Cash that can only be used for a specific purpose is called restricted cash, and if not available to pay current liabilities is shown on the balance sheet as either a short- or long-term investment, depending on the type of restriction. A minimum balance of cash that is required to maintained at all times is called a compensating balance, and this part of the cash balance must be disclosed in the footnotes.

The essential means of protecting cash and other assets is called internal control, and a checking account is an important way of applying this protection to cash. The party who writes a check is called the maker and the party who will receive payment is called the payee.

A check endorsement is a legal transfer of funds by the payee to another party of the right to receive payment from the maker. A blank endorsement transfers the right to receive payment to any party who physically holds a check. A restrictive endorsement transfers the right to receive payment to a specific party.

The Bank Reconciliation

Overview

What Is It?

A *bank reconciliation* is an analysis prepared by a depositor (a bank customer) that compares the cash balance in the depositor's books to the cash balance that shows on the bank statement.

There are really two records of cash. First, the depositor maintains accounting records that show receipts, payments, and cash balance. Second, the bank keeps its own record of receipts, payments, and cash balance, which it presents to the customer in the form of a bank statement. These two records seldom show the same cash balance.

What Does It Do?

The reconciliation: (1) corrects the bank statement balance for missing items located in the depositor's records and (2) corrects the depositor's book balance for missing items that are shown on the bank statement. The result is the same number for both records called the *adjusted cash balance*, or the *true cash balance* or the *reconciled cash balance*.

What Does It Look Like?

A bank reconciliation is divided into two sections: one section shows adjustments to the bank balance and the other section shows adjustments to the book balance. When the reconciliation is complete, the totals of both sections must agree. This is the reconciled cash balance. An example is shown on the next page.

Frequency

Bank reconciliations are prepared at regular intervals, such as monthly for smaller businesses and weekly for larger businesses (which require weekly bank statements).

Internal Control Rule

You may recall from our discussions on pages 580 and 581 that internal control refers to the methods used to safeguard assets. The bank reconciliation is a very important internal control device for safeguarding cash.

Rule: For a bank reconciliation to function properly, *when an employee prepares a bank reconciliation, that employee must never be involved in receiving cash, paying cash, or have any other access to cash.*

If this rule is violated, the employee will be able to steal cash in various ways and hide the theft by falsifying the bank reconciliation.

Overview, *continued*

Example

The example below shows a completed bank reconciliation.

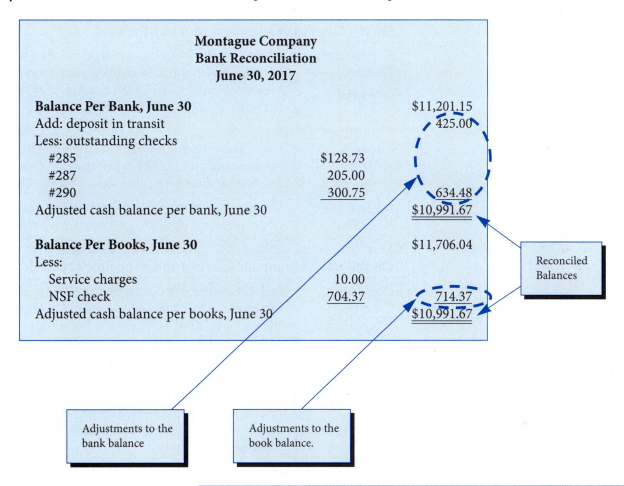

Montague Company
Bank Reconciliation
June 30, 2017

Balance Per Bank, June 30		$11,201.15
Add: deposit in transit		425.00
Less: outstanding checks		
#285	$128.73	
#287	205.00	
#290	300.75	
Adjusted cash balance per bank, June 30		634.48
		$10,991.67
Balance Per Books, June 30		$11,706.04
Less:		
Service charges	10.00	
NSF check	704.37	
Adjusted cash balance per books, June 30		714.37
		$10,991.67

Reconciled Balances

Adjustments to the bank balance

Adjustments to the book balance.

Reconciling Items

Overview

The reason that the cash balance on the depositor's (bank customer's) books and the cash balance on the bank statement seldom agree is that some items are included on one set of records but not on the other. These items are called *reconciling items*. They have two causes: timing differences and errors.

continued ▶

Reconciling Items, *continued*

Common Types of Reconciling Items

The table below identifies common types of reconciling items.

On the Depositor's Records (but not the bank's):	
Outstanding Checks (time delay)	Checks written that have not yet cleared the bank for payment. The checks have been recorded in the depositor's books but do not yet appear on the bank statement.
Deposits in Transit (time delay)	Deposits recorded in the depositor's books but not appearing on the bank statement. Caused by deposits that do not reach the bank before the bank statement is printed.
Depositor's Book Errors	Usually the result of mis-recording the amount of a check or a deposit, or math errors in journals or ledgers.
On the Bank Statement (but not the depositor's records):	
Debit and Credit Memoranda (time delay)	A debit memo is a notice by the bank of a reduction in the account balance. It is often shown by a "DM" followed by the amount of reduction. A credit memo is a notice by the bank of an increase in the account balance. It is often shown by a "CM" followed by the amount of increase. *The bank customer may not be aware of debit and credit memo items until the bank statement is received,* so will not have recorded them.
Bank Errors	Usually an error in recording the amount or source of a deposit or a check.

Debits and Credits on the Bank Statement

From a bank's viewpoint, a bank account is a liability because the bank has an obligation to pay out funds from the account at any time the depositor wants to withdraw them. Thus, decreases in the account, such as by paying checks, reduce the bank's liability, and the bank reports this to the depositor as a "debit." When an account increases, such as by a deposit, the bank's liability increases and the bank reports this as a "credit." Notice that these debits and credits are the opposite of the depositor's own cash records.

In addition to checks and deposits, there can be many other bank statement debit (liability decrease) and credit (liability increase) items. These items are usually reported on the bank statement as specific kinds of debit and credit memoranda. The following table shows you some common items.

Reconciling Items, *continued*

Specific Debit Memo Items	Description of Decrease
Service Charges and Fees	SC means charges for maintaining the account or other bank activities, such as printing checks.
NSF Checks	NSF stands for "non-sufficient funds." After a check is deposited and the bank discovers that the check is not good, the bank reduces the depositor's account by the amount of the bad deposit—the worthless check. Often the bank also charges the depositor an additional fee.
EFT Transactions	EFT stands for "electronic funds transfer." With this system, banks transfer funds out of and into accounts electronically using little or no paper. Transfers out, such as for paying debts or expenses or making purchases, are account decreases.
Specific Credit Memo Items	**Description of Increase**
Collections	CM or other symbol. A bank often accepts payment for a note receivable and interest on behalf of a depositor. Credit card sales are also credited directly to an account.
Interest Earned	IN or CM or other symbol. Some checking accounts—usually personal, not business—pay interest.
EFT Transactions	EFT stands for "electronic funds transfer." Transfers into an account, such as for various types of collections or borrowing, are account increases.

TIP

An NSF check is any check for which the maker's account does not have sufficient funds in the account to pay the amount of the check.

It is easy to confuse "NSF" with "RTM." RTM means **"return to maker,"** which is a more general term indicating that the check is not good for a variety of other possible reasons.

Any check that is deposited and later turns out not to have sufficient funds is then subtracted from the depositor's account by the bank. Such a check is often jokingly referred to as a **"bounced" check**. An intentionally fraudulent check is sometimes called a **"hot" check**.

Check Your Understanding

Write the completed sentences on a separate sheet of paper.

A bank reconciliation is a document prepared by the · · · · · · · (depositor/bank) because the cash balances shown by the bank and the depositor's records usually · · · · · · · (are/are not) the same on any given date. The reason for this is that certain items are included on one set of records but not the other. These are called · · · · · · · items.

A common type of this item that is in the depositor's records but not in the bank statement are checks written by the depositor that have not yet cleared the bank for payment. These are called · · · · · · · · · · · · · · · ·. Another common item that is in the depositor's records but not on the bank statement is a · which is a cash receipt recorded by the depositor but not by the bank statement.

Items that have been recorded by the bank that *reduce* the depositor's balance are shown by the bank as · · · · · · · (debit/credit) memoranda. Examples of these items are service charges, electronic withdrawals, and bad checks in a deposit, which are called · · · · · · · · checks. Items recorded by the bank that *increase* the depositor's balance are shown by the bank as · · · · · · · · (debit/credit) memoranda. An example is an electronic deposit from a customer's account. Electronic transactions are called · · · · · · · transactions.

Answers

A bank reconciliation is a document prepared by the <u>depositor</u> (depositor/bank) because the cash balances shown by the bank and the depositor's records usually <u>are not</u> (are/are not) the same on any given date. The reason for this is that certain items are included on one set of records but not the other. These are called <u>reconciling</u> items.

A common type of this item that is in the depositor's records but not in the bank statement are checks written by the depositor that have not yet cleared the bank for payment. These are called <u>outstanding checks</u>. Another common item that is in the depositor's records but not on the bank statement is a <u>deposit in transit</u> which is a cash receipt recorded by the depositor but not by the bank statement.

Items that have been recorded by the bank that *reduce* the depositor's balance are shown by the bank as <u>debit</u> (debit/credit) memoranda. Examples of these items are service charges, electronic withdrawals, and bad checks in a deposit, which are called <u>NSF</u> checks. Items recorded by the bank that *increase* the depositor's balance are shown by the bank as <u>credit</u> (debit/credit) memoranda. An example is an electronic deposit from a customer's account. Electronic transactions are called <u>EFT</u> transactions.

Frank and Ernest

BANK

MORE BOUNCED CHECKS! LET'S SWITCH OUR ACCOUNT TO A BANK THAT DOES HAVE SUFFICIENT FUNDS!

THAVES

The Bank Reconciliation Procedure

Procedure   The following table shows all the steps to prepare a bank reconciliation.

Getting Started	
Step	**Action**
1	*Title:* On three lines at the top of the page, write: ■ The company name ■ The document identification as "Bank Reconciliation" ■ The date (the end of some period) as of which you want to reconcile the cash balance in the accounting records (balance per books) to the ending balance on a bank statement (balance per bank).
2	On the same page, begin two separate sections by writing the: ■ *Ending cash balance from the bank statement* for the period that ends on or before the date selected in Step 1. ■ *Ending cash balance per books* on the date selected in Step 1.

Deposits and Other Receipts	
3	*Compare each deposit* on the bank statement to each deposit shown in the cash receipts journal (or other record of receipts) for the same period:

	IF a deposit . . .	AND the deposit . . .	THEN
A	in the accounting records is *not on the bank statement,*	is verified as authentic and valid	add the deposit ("deposits in transit" or bank error) to the balance per bank.
		is *not* authentic or valid	subtract the deposit from the balance per books (book errors).
B	on the bank statement is *not in the accounting records,*	is ours, authentic and valid	add the deposit to the balance per books (unrecorded deposits)
		is *not* ours, authentic or valid	subtract the deposit from the balance per bank and inform the bank (bank error).
C	matches on the books and bank statement by date, but the amounts differ,		analyze the difference, which will result in adding or subtracting for either a bank or book error.

4	*Credit memoranda* from bank statement: Identify and add any unrecorded amounts to the balance per books (bank collections, EFT receipts, credit card sales, etc.).
5	*Undeposited cash* on hand: Add to the balance per bank. (This should be very temporary.)

continued ▶

The Bank Reconciliation Procedure, *continued*

Checks and Other Payments	
6	In the accounting records, locate the individual check amounts (cash payments journal or checkbook.)
7	*Compare each check amount:* If canceled checks (or paper copies) are: ■ Returned by the bank, sort the canceled checks into check number sequence, examine each check, and then compare the amount on each check to the amount shown in the cash payments journal or checkbook. ■ Not returned by the bank, compare each check amount printed on the bank statement to each check amount recorded in the cash payments journal or checkbook.

	IF a check . . .	AND the check is . . .	THEN
A	is on the accounting records but *not on the bank statement,*	verified as approved	list and subtract the check ("outstanding checks") from balance per bank.
		not approved	add the check amount to the cash balance per books and possibly stop payment (book errors).
B	is on the bank statement but *not on the accounting records,*	verified as ours, authentic and valid	subtract the check from the cash balance per books (book errors). (Also consider employee fraud.)
		not ours, authentic and valid	add the check to the balance per bank and inform the bank (bank errors).
C	matches on the books and the bank statement by check number, but the amounts are different		analyze the difference, which may result in adding or subtracting for either a bank or book error.

8	*Debit memoranda* from bank statement: Identify and subtract any unrecorded amounts from the balance per books (bank fees, NSF checks, EFT payments, etc.).
9	*Prior outstanding checks:* List and subtract all checks still outstanding from prior period reconciliations from the balance per bank. (Include them sequentially with 7A above.)

TIP

For an easy way to analyze book errors, use the table below. Subtract the book amount from the actual (cleared) amount. The difference is the adjustment amount. Notice that for negative items the adjustment is the opposite of a positive or negative difference. Examples are in the table.

	Deposit (+)	Check (−)
Cleared amount	$100	$1,000
Recorded in books	1,000	100
Difference	(900)	900
Adjustment to cash	(900)	(900)

Some Explanations and Practical Suggestions

The following explanations and suggestions will clarify the process, reduce errors, and help safeguard cash. (The step numbers refer to the steps in the procedure tables on the previous pages.)

Step 2	The reason we prefer not to use a bank statement that has a balance after the selected reconciliation date is that the statement might contain some checks and deposits that occurred after the reconciliation date. This complicates the procedure because these items must be removed from the bank balance (deposits subtracted, checks added).

The ending balance per books is usually available in the Cash ledger account or the checkbook record. But, if not, you might have to begin with the prior reconciled cash balance and then add the current period's receipts (cash receipts journal) and subtract the current period's checks (cash payments journal) to get the ending balance per books. |
| **Step 3A** | Every deposit in transit should appear as a cleared deposit on the very next bank statement. If this does not happen, check your records immediately and call the bank. |
| **Step 7A** | *How do I Examine Checks?* When you examine canceled checks and compare them to check amounts in the accounting records, do not refer to the amount written on the check by the maker. Instead, refer to the amount printed by the bank in magnetic ink characters on the bottom right part of the check. This is the amount that the check actually cleared for, and sometimes this is different than the amount written on the check by the maker.

Investigate any checks that (1) are outstanding for more than a month (2) have a number not in sequence with the rest of the checks (3) have a questionable signature, or (4) have a questionable payee. |
| **Other issues** | *What if the Cash account has never been reconciled?* If the bank account is relatively new—say, several months—begin reconciling the first period and work your way to the current period. (Do not try to do all the periods together.) However, if the bank account is not new and has had substantial activity, it is best to open another bank account. Use only the new account while you let all the items clear out through the old account. In the meantime, you can reconcile the new account. Close the old account when all the checks and deposits have cleared.

What if we want to maintain more than one bank account? Keep a separate account in the ledger for each bank account and reconcile each account separately. |

Example Coming Up . . .

An example of a bank reconciliation, including needed adjustments to the accounting records, appears on the following pages. The example is for Paia Consulting Services company, which opened a new checking account in early November.

Bank Reconciliation Example

Bank Statement

The bank statement below is for the Paia Company as of November 30.

Metro Bank
4381 Holland Ave
Honolulu, Hawaii 96839

Account Number 1980154387

Paia Consulting Services
80 Kahala Parkway
Honolulu, HI 96841

Period of: November 2 to
November 30, 2017

Prior Balance	Total Deposits	Total Withdrawals	Ending Balance
$00.00	$12,225.00	$3,683.07	$8,541.93

Checks and Other Debits			Deposits and Other Credits		Daily Balance	
Date	Number	Amount	Date	Amount	Date	Amount
11/05	101	40.29	11/2	10,000.00	11/02	10,000.00
11/06	103	1,200.00	11/14	500.00	11/05	9,959.71
11/08	104	379.21	11/22	CM 1,725.00	11/06	8,759.71
11/09		SC 7.50			11/08	8,380.50
11/14	105	585.00			11/09	8,373.00
11/16	106	488.33			11/14	8,288.00
11/20		DM 14.50			11/16	7,799.67
11/24	110	717.99			11/20	7,785.17
11/29		NSF 250.25			11/22	9,510.17
					11/24	8,792.18
					11/29	8,541.93

Note: The "total deposits" of $12,225.00 includes all credit items, and the "total withdrawals" of $3,683.07 includes all debit items

Symbols:	**CM** Credit Memo	**DM** Debit Memo	**SC** Service Charge	**ATM** Automatic Teller
	NSF Not Sufficient Funds	**EC** Error Correction	**INT** Interest Earned	**OD** Overdraft

Procedure Illustrated

Following each step in the procedure table, we can prepare the bank reconciliation illustrated below. Highlighted numbers in boxes identify the steps in the previous procedure table that correspond to specific items.

This bank reconciliation is for a new business called Paia Consulting Services, which began business by opening a bank account at Metro Bank on November 2. The company reconciles its cash balance as of the last day of each month. This is the first bank reconciliation for the company.

Bank Reconciliation Example, *continued*

Check No.	Account Name		Cash	
101	Supplies	. . . .	✓	40.29
102	Utility Deposits	. . . .		50.00
103	Rent Expense	. . . .	✓	1,200.00
104	Supplies	. . . .	✓	390.21
105	Advertising Expense	. . . .	✓	585.00
106	Travel Expense	. . . .	✓	488.33
107	Postage Expense	. . . .		87.14
108	Accounts Payable	. . . .		421.00
109	Equipment	. . . .		3,900.00
110	Computer Software	. . . .	✓	717.99
111	Utility Expense	. . . .		196.81
	Total	. . . .		8,076.77

Additional Information

- The November cash payments journal (some columns deleted) is shown above.
- The cash receipts journal shows the following deposits during November: Nov. 2, $10,200; Nov. 14, $500; Nov. 29, $1,500. Total: $12,200.
- The cash ledger account shows an ending balance on November 30 of $4,123.23.

The numbers in the boxes below refer to the steps in the procedure.

1 Date: The reconciled cash balance is prepared as of November 30, 2017.

2 The unadjusted ending bank and book cash balances are written down.

3a Compare the book deposits to the deposits per bank. The November 29 deposit did not appear on the bank statement.

3c The accountant notices that the bank understated the November 2 deposit by $200. The correct amount of the deposit is $10,200.

4 A credit memo on the bank statement indicates a $1,725 cash increase from a November 22 electronic transfer of funds from a customer's bank into Paia Company's bank account.

7a Outstanding checks: compare each check in the accounting records to each check returned by the bank. Enter a mark next to each check amount that appears both on the bank statement and in the accounting records. When we do this, we see in the cash payments journal that checks #102, #107, #108, #109, and #111 are not on the bank statement.

7c When comparing each check on the bank statement to the cash payments journal record of checks, we find that check #104 was recorded for $11 more than it actually cleared for.

8 Three unrecorded bank debits will reduce the book balance by $272.25.

continued ▶

Bank Reconciliation Example, *continued*

Paia Consulting Services
Bank Reconciliation
1 **November 30, 2017**

Balance Per Bank, November 30.................................... 2		$ 8,541.93
Add: 3a		
Deposit in transit, November 29......................	1,500.00	
Bank error, November 2 deposit..................... 3c	200.00	1,700.00
Less:		
Outstanding Checks 7a		
#102.......................	$ 50.00	
#107.......................	87.14	
#108.......................	421.00	
#109.......................	3,900.00	
#111.......................	196.81	4,654.95
Adjusted Cash Balance Per Bank, November 30		**$5,586.98**
Balance Per Books, November 30....................... 2		$ 4,123.23
Add:		
Bank collection—EFT from customer's bank 4	$1,725.00	
Book error, check #104 overstated 7c	11.00	1,736.00
Less:		
Bank service charge	7.50	
Check printing charge 8	14.50	
NSF customer check	250.25	272.25
Adjusted Cash Balance Per Books, November 30		**$5,586.98**

**Adjusting Journal
Entry Required**

Rule: Every reconciliation adjustment that affects *the balance per BOOKS* must be recorded in an adjusting entry (an exception to the rule that adjusting entries do not affect cash).

Reason: The bank reconciliation itself does not directly affect the accounting records. The reconciliation is an analysis tool separate from the journals and ledgers. However, if the adjusted book balance on the reconciliation is different than the unadjusted book balance in the ledger, it means that the balance in the accounting records and must be corrected.

Example: The unadjusted book balance for the Paia company is $4,123.23. The adjusted book balance in the reconciliation is $5,586.98. Therefore, adjusting entries are required that will result in a net increase to the Cash account in the amount of the difference: $1,463.75. This amount consists of a total of $1,736.00 of increase items and a total of $272.25 of decrease items.

Bank Reconciliation Example, *continued*

Adjustment for Items That Increase Cash	A single compound entry can be made to increase cash with a debit, with credits to the various items that cause an increase in cash:

- The EFT increased cash because of a revenue transaction.
- Check #104 for supplies was overstated. The actual payment was $11 less.

Nov. 30	Cash	1,736.00	
	Service Revenue		1,725.00
	Supplies		11.00

Adjustment for Items That Decrease Cash	A single compound entry can be made to decrease cash with a credit, with debits to the various items that cause a decrease in cash:

- The bank service charge for $7.50 and the check printing charge for $14.50 decreased the Cash account by $22. Because these are small related items, we can group them together as a miscellaneous expense. They could also be recorded as a bank charge expense.
- Because of the NSF check, the bank reduced the cash balance by $250.25. The business will try again to collect this amount from the 607.eps customer, so it is recorded as an account receivable.

Nov. 30	Miscellaneous Expense	22.00	
	Accounts Receivable—Ames	250.25	
	Cash		272.25

Bank Adjustments	Paia Company does not have to adjust its books for adjustments to the bank balance—the outstanding checks and deposits in transit will eventually appear on future bank statements, and any bank errors are the bank's responsibility to correct in its own records.

Continuing Example	A second example of a bank reconciliation for Paia Consulting Services for December is in the appendix to this learning goal.

Check Your Understanding

Part I: For each reconciling item in the table, place a check mark in the correct box to identify the item as an increase or decrease to the bank balance or an increase or decrease to the book cash balance when doing a bank reconciliation.

Item	Bank Balance Adjustment		Book Balance Adjustment	
	Increase	Decrease	Increase	Decrease
Deposit in transit				
Bank debit memo	(Reminder: Use a separate sheet of paper to complete the table.)			
NSF check				
Outstanding checks				
Bank statement shows another company's check				
Bank credit memo				
Understating a deposit in the cash receipts journal				
Overstating a check in the cash payments journal				
Bank statement shows another company's deposit				
EFT item for an expense paid				
EFT item for a revenue collected				

Answers

Item	Bank Balance Adjustment		Book Balance Adjustment	
	Increase	Decrease	Increase	Decrease
Deposit in transit	✓			
Bank debit memo				✓
NSF check				✓
Outstanding checks		✓		
Bank statement shows another company's check		✓		
Bank credit memo			✓	
Understating a deposit in the cash receipts journal			✓	
Overstating a check in the cash payments journal			✓	
Bank statement shows another company's deposit		✓		
EFT item for an expense paid				✓
EFT item for a revenue collected			✓	

Check Your Understanding

Part II: Using the information below, prepare a bank reconciliation for Feather River Company as of May 31.

- Balance per bank statement, May 31: $14,473.39
- Balance per books (Cash ledger account), May 31: $13,110.65
- One deposit is in transit in the amount of $770.00
- There are two outstanding checks: #302 for $712.44 and #305 for $88.50
- Other items:

  - Debit memo: Bank service charges $15.00
  - NSF check $275.50
  - Book error: May 12 deposit understated by $122.30
  - EFT collection from customer $1,500

Answer

Feather River Company
Bank Reconciliation
May 31, 20XX

Balance Per Bank, May 31		$14,473.39
Add: Deposit in transit		770.00
Less: Outstanding checks:		
#302	$712.44	
#305	88.50	800.94
Adjusted Bank Balance, May 31		$14,442.45
Balance Per Books, May 31		$13,110.65
Add: Book error May 12 understated deposit	$122.30	
EFT collection	1,500.00	1,622.30
Less: Bank service charges	15.00	
NSF check	275.50	290.50
Adjusted Book Balance, May 31		$14,442.45

A Tip and a Caution

TIP

Avoid This Shortcut: You may occasionally encounter someone who does a "quickie" bank reconciliation by using only the balance per bank and subtracting the outstanding checks and adding the deposits in transit. The result is then considered to be the reconciled balance, and the book cash balance is adjusted to this amount by using some kind of "miscellaneous" account for the difference.

The problems with this are: (1) Bank errors are not identified. (2) Book adjustment items are not classified into the correct accounts—you don't know which accounts are affected or by how much. (3) Cash data in the books are not examined and compared to the bank statement, greatly increasing possibilities for fraud.

Software Caution: Some commercial accounting and personal financial software programs do "bank reconciliations" by simply adjusting the checkbook record so that it includes all items shown on the bank statement. Items appearing on the bank statement are entered into the checkbook record as either "cleared" (deposits and checks) or "recorded" (other bank statement debit and credit items). The result is that adjustments are made only to the checkbook record for differences that are caused by items that appear on the bank statement. No adjustments are made to the bank statement balance.

The dangers in this system are: (1) It leads the user to think that the bank statement is always right. (2) The method assumes everything else in the checkbook is correct. This minimizes the analysis of cash payments and cash receipts records, which creates the potential for dangerous results. (3) The reconciliation can be completed without a separate listing of outstanding checks and deposits in transit to review, which is important for internal control.

The Petty Cash Fund

Overview

What Is It?

A *petty cash fund* is a fund of currency and coin kept on the business premises and used to pay for small cash expenditures.

Why Is It Needed?

The time, effort, and cost required to write checks for small amounts is often inefficient and impractical. Also, some small payments require cash, such as paying taxi fare or buying snacks for the office staff. Therefore, a business is required to maintain some small amount of cash on hand. A petty cash fund is an internal control device that controls these types of expenditures.

Using the Fund: Three Elements

Three elements of a petty cash fund are: (1) establishing the fund, (2) disbursing cash from the fund, and (3) replenishing the fund.

Establishing the Fund

Appoint the Custodian

The person who is responsible for the petty cash fund is called the *petty cash custodian*. This person controls the cash in a locked box or safe and accounts for the disbursements and replenishment of the fund. However, management usually prohibits certain types of disbursements, such as for personal loans, and makes unannounced examinations of the petty cash box.

Create the Fund

The amount of the fund created should be a fixed amount large enough only for regular small expenditures during a period of no more than a few weeks. When the amount has been decided, a check payable to the petty cash custodian is written and cashed by the custodian, and the money is placed in the petty cash box. A journal entry records the transaction:

| Sept. 1 | Petty Cash | 200 | |
| | Cash | | 200 |

Notice that there are now two cash accounts: Petty Cash and Cash.

Petty Cash Payments

Petty Cash Vouchers

The word *voucher* refers to a document that authorizes a cash payment by providing assurance of a transaction's authenticity. A *petty cash voucher* is a voucher that authorizes a petty cash payment. Petty cash vouchers (like checks) are sequentially prenumbered tickets that must be filled in before the petty cash custodian can disburse cash from the box.

Procedure

The table below shows the procedure for petty cash disbursements.

Step	Action
1	An employee makes a request for cash.
2	The petty cash custodian gives the employee the next blank numbered voucher.
3	The employee fills in the name, date, amount, and expenditure description and signs the voucher.
4	The custodian gives the requested amount to the employee, co-signs the voucher, and notes the account classification on the voucher. The voucher is placed in the box.
5	For an expenditure of more than a minimum amount, such as $5, the employee must return with a receipt, which the custodian attaches to the petty cash voucher. (Any unspent money is returned and the voucher amount is adjusted.)

Imprest System

The system described above in the procedure table is called an *imprest* petty cash system. This means that the remaining amount of cash plus the total of the filled-in vouchers must always equal the fixed total amount of the fund.

Example: A petty cash fund is established for $100, and the four filled-in vouchers in the petty cash box total $37.12. Therefore, the remaining amount of cash in the box must be $62.88.

Payment Record

The petty cash custodian maintains a *petty cash payment record.* This is simply a classification of the total of all the individual petty cash disbursements by account, such as for travel, postage, entertainment, repairs, and so on. The payment record acts as a summary showing the total spent for each account classification. It is also used when the fund is replenished, as discussed next.

Replenishing the Fund

Two Purposes

Periodically, the petty cash payments will have reduced the amount of cash in the fund to a minimum level, and the fund needs to be replenished. Replenishing the fund serves two purposes:

1. The amount of cash used is replaced.
2. A journal entry records the accounts affected by the payments.

Cash Replaced

The petty cash custodian makes a request to a manager or the treasurer to replenish the fund, submitting a copy of the petty cash record and all receipts, which are now marked "paid." When the request is approved, a check made payable to the petty cash custodian is written for the amount needed to restore the fund to its approved total. The custodian cashes the check, places the currency in the petty cash box, and the fund is replenished.

Journal Entry

A journal records the amount taken from the Cash account to replace the petty cash funds spent. Using the petty cash record as a reference, the journal entry debits the various accounts affected by the petty cash disbursements.

Example: Suppose the petty cash record shows that $144 has been spent from the $200 petty cash fund previously established. The record shows the various accounts affected by these disbursements:

- Travel: $79 ■ Postage: $12 ■ Entertainment: $53

The journal entry is:

Sept. 22	Travel Expense	79	
	Postage Expense	12	
	Entertainment Expense	53	
	Cash		144

Notice that the Petty Cash account is not involved. On the books, it simply remains at its $200 balance because we know that we always restore it to that amount periodically.

continued ▶

Replenishing the Fund, *continued*

Over and Short Account

Sometimes, when the custodian makes a request to replenish the fund, the amount of remaining cash plus the total of the petty cash vouchers do not equal the approved fund total. This difference should be a small amount and is usually the result of mistakes in making change. When this happens an account called ***Cash Over and Short*** is used. It is debited for the amount of a shortage and credited for the amount of an overage—a tiny "mini-expense" or a "mini-revenue," depending on whether it has a debit balance or credit balance.

Example: In the previous example the vouchers totaled $144, so there should have been $56 remaining in the petty cash box. Suppose a petty cash count shows $54 remaining (which is $2 short) and requires an extra $2 replenishment:

Sept. 22	Travel Expense	79	
	Postage Expense	12	
	Entertainment Expense	53	
	Cash Over and Short	2	
	Cash		146

Conversely, if there had been $58 in the petty cash box, only $142 would be needed, and Cash Over and Short would be credited for $2.

TIP

The petty cash fund is replenished at two different times: (1) Whenever the cash in the fund becomes low, and (2) at the end of an accounting period before the financial statements are prepared, so that all expense and cash accounts are accurate on the financial statement.

Changing the Balance

Occasionally, it may be necessary to change the Petty Cash account balance. The petty cash balance can be increased by replacing more than the amount used or decreased by replacing less than the amount used. The examples below repeat the journal entry above but either increase or decrease the fund balance by $50. Changing the fund balance is the only time Petty Cash is debited or credited.

Increase Balance by $50				Decrease Balance by $50		
Petty Cash	**50**			Travel Expense	79	
Travel Expense	79			Postage Expense	12	
Postage Expense	12			Entertainment Expense	53	
Entertainment Expense	53			Cash Over and Short	2	
Cash Over and Short	2			**Petty Cash**		**50**
Cash		196		Cash		96

Other Cash Payment Controls

The Change Fund

Change Fund Overview

Businesses that make regular cash sales, such as retailers, need to make change frequently. They use change funds, which are similar to petty cash funds because they are established at a fixed amount.

Example

Suppose a retail store has two cash registers. The owner wants each register to begin every day with a $50 change fund. A check is cashed and the $50 cash amounts are placed in each register. This journal entry is made:

May 1	Change Fund	100	
	Cash		100

At the end of the day, the two cash register tapes together show $1,830 of sales made, and the total cash in the registers is $1,930. The cash journal entry is:

May 1	Cash	1,830	
	Sales		1,830

The amount of the bank deposit will also be $1,830; the change fund account and cash for the registers remain at $100 for the start of the next day.

Over and Short

The Cash Over and Short account is also used when the amount of the cash in the registers does not equal the total of sales shown on the tapes plus the change fund. In the example above suppose the amount of cash in the registers is $1,912 (the total should be $1,930):

May 1	Cash	1,812	
	Cash Over and Short	18	
	Sales		1,830

Caution: Continuous or growing debits to Cash Over and Short may indicate theft. Overages and shortages should be accounted for at each register at the end of each shift.

Credit Cards

Overview

Many businesses, particularly larger ones, permit the use of company credit cards by authorized employees. This minimizes the use of cash and provides a clear record of expenditures.

Example

Assume that at the end of the month that the treasurer's office receives the credit card statement from the issuing bank. The statement is reviewed by the treasurer and shows the following expenditure totals:

- Supplies: $121   ■ Entertainment: $105   ■ Travel: $490

If the statement is approved, the journal entry is:

Aug. 30	Supplies	121	
	Entertainment Expense	105	
	Travel Expense	490	
	Credit Card Payable		716

The liability is later paid within the required time period.

Debit Cards:
Use With Caution

When you use a credit card, a liability is created. In effect, the bank that issues you the credit card is making you a short-term loan at no interest for the amount of the purchase, provided the payment is timely made.

However, a debit card permits the bank to immediately withdraw and pay out funds from a designated checking or savings account. For a business or an individual, debit cards have serious disadvantages when compared to credit cards:

1. When you use a debit card, your account balance is immediately reduced, limiting your use of cash.
2. When you use a debit card, the bank can temporarily freeze your account for more than the purchase amount.
3. If a debit card is ever lost or stolen and is accessed by an unauthorized person, the entire cash balance in an account can be taken. Restitution of the stolen funds is not required if the card loss is not reported within 60 days of the bank statement date. To make matters worse, if your account has an overdraft line of credit, this can also be accessed by the debit card. If the report of the loss is within 60 days but after 2 days, maximum loss is $500. How these rules are enforced often depends on the individual bank.
4. Returning defective merchandise or not paying for bad service can be much more difficult with a debit card than with a credit card because the merchant or service provider has already received the payment. However, with timely notice the law limits a *credit card* loss to only $50 in many situations.

Cash Payment Controls for Large Businesses

Voucher System Overview

What Is It?

A voucher system is a means of controlling cash payments. A voucher system is used in medium to large companies. Because a voucher system involves extensive controls and procedures that require the cooperation of numerous people, only a larger company can use it efficiently.

Why Is It Necessary?

Have you ever wondered just how a large corporation makes cash payments? Think of all the different requests for payment coming from the diverse divisions and departments of the company: payroll, materials, supplies, contract payments, debt payments, tax payments, and many, many more cash payment requests. The department writing the checks has no idea if the requests are authentic and honest unless some system of verification is used.

How Does It Work?

In a voucher system no cash payment can be made without documented approval. Every potential payment must first be authorized by a voucher document and, second, recorded as a liability. Only then can a payment be made.

Five Functions of the Voucher System Process

The voucher system can be viewed as five basic functions in a process. These five functions and the related actions are presented in the illustration on page 611. The five functions are: Validation, verification, authorization, recording, and payment. The arrows in the illustration represent the flow of physical documents. Notice how the process applies internal control by separating the duties and that no one person can control the process or a significant part of it.

Validation and Verification in a Voucher System

Overview

Validation means demonstrating a valid or genuine purpose. *Verification* means obtaining proof of accuracy or evidence of an event.

continued ▶

Validation and Verification in a Voucher System, *continued*

Validation Example

Suppose that an employee needs a new tool. The employee prepares a form called a *purchase requisition* (an authenticating document) and sends it to a supervisor for approval. A purchase requisition is a formal request describing the item and why it is needed. The requisition slip and its approval by a supervisor validate the need. A requisition can also be made for a service or to pay other items.

The supervisor then sends the requisition to the purchasing department, which identifies where to obtain the item at the best price, and then sends a *purchase order* to the supplier. A purchase order is a document sent to a vendor that identifies the item to be purchased and the specific price and terms of the purchase.

Verification Example

When the item arrives, the receiving department verifies what was received and completes a *receiving report*, which verifies type of item and its quantity and condition. Also, the vendor sends an invoice to the company. An *invoice* is a bill that identifies the item, quantity, amount owed, and payment terms. The invoice verifies the amount owed and the terms of payment. The requesting department compares the item to the purchase requisition.

Authorization and Recording in a Voucher System

Overview

The second part of the process completes the functions of authorization and recording. *Authorization* means giving final approval for preparing a voucher. *Recording* means recording all the parts of the transaction in the accounting records.

Authorization

Continuing with the example, copies of all the validation & verification documents from various departments are sent to the voucher section of the accounting department. Here the documents are placed in a file and reviewed. If everything is in order, a supervisor approves the completion of a voucher. A *voucher* is a document that authorizes a cash payment. The voucher document has spaces for approval signatures, item identification, amount, due date, payment terms, and accounts to be debited. Vouchers, like checks, are prenumbered. Some companies use the name *check authorization* or *approval form*. When the voucher is completed, it is placed in a file with the supporting documents.

Authorization and Recording in a Voucher System, *continued*

Recording Step 1: Voucher Register Journal	A completed and signed voucher permits an item to be recorded in a journal called the **voucher register**. The voucher register is like an expanded purchases journal with many more debit columns. An entry in the Voucher Register credits the liability account Vouchers Payable for the amount authorized and debits whatever account (Wages Expense, Notes Payable, Accounts Payable, Equipment, Merchandise Purchases, etc.) the payment is for.
	Remember: In a voucher system *every* payment item must *first* be recorded in the voucher register as a credit to Vouchers Payable before payment can be made.
	The purchases journal is eliminated because the voucher register journalizes *every potential payment* item as a liability by crediting Vouchers Payable and debiting the related account.

Payment in a Voucher System

Recording Step 2: Check Register Journal	After an item is recorded as a Vouchers Payable liability, it is paid within a few days. This payment is recorded in a journal called the **check register**. The check register is like a cash payments journal, although it is much simpler because it has fewer debit columns—the various debits for the Vouchers Payable liabilities have already been recorded in the voucher register as each liability was recorded.
	Each entry in the check register is simply a credit to Cash and a debit to Vouchers Payable, with a credit to Purchase Discounts, if applicable. The check register eliminates the cash payments journal because *all* the credits to Cash are recorded in the check register.
Voucher Files	The accounting department maintains a file of paid and unpaid vouchers. In this way, all vouchers (by number) are accounted for, and unpaid vouchers are available by due date as a reminder and verification for payment, the next function described.

continued ▶

Payment in a Voucher System, *continued*

Example

Payment takes place outside of the accounting department, in a treasurer or cashier's office. Before the check is written, the voucher and its supporting documents are reviewed, and the voucher is checked for authorizing signatures. *No check can be written without a fully completed voucher supported by validation and verification documents.*

After the check is written, the voucher and the documents are stamped "canceled" or "paid" so they cannot be used again. The voucher and documents are then placed in the paid vouchers file.

> *Note:* Some companies do not require vouchers for payments below a minimum amount, such as $100.

Variety of Voucher Systems

Variations and Limitations

In practice, there are numerous variations on the basic example presented here. The names and procedures may vary. For example, a company might circulate a "voucher" as a manila envelope for supporting documents with signatures placed in designated spaces on the outside of the envelope. Also, it is important to remember that no system is perfect. Employee collusion can defeat even a good internal control system, although it may be more difficult than with weaker systems. However, the essential idea of all voucher systems is the same: apply verifying, validating, and authorizing internal control requirements before any cash is paid.

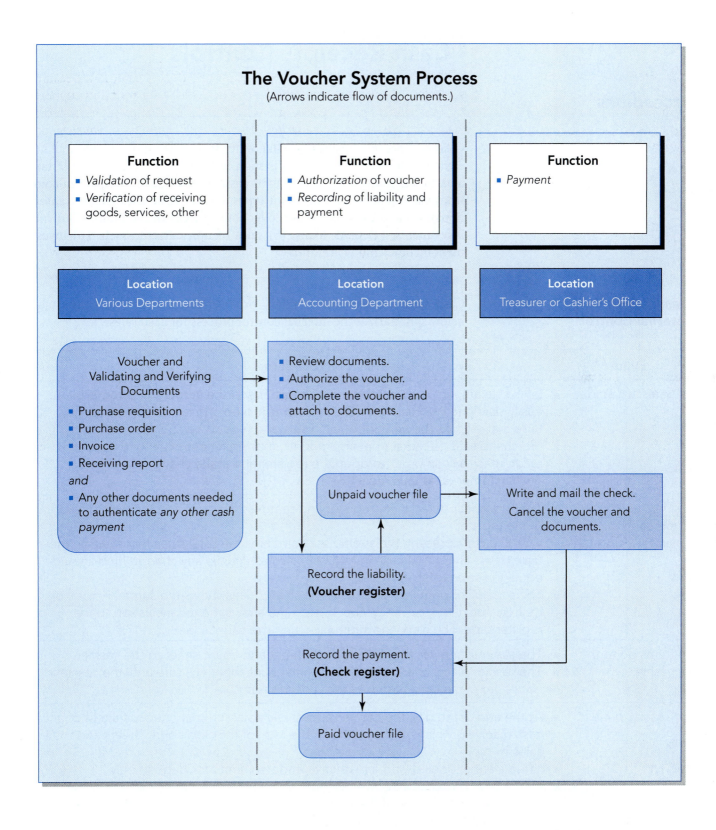

The Voucher System Process
(Arrows indicate flow of documents.)

Function
- *Validation* of request
- *Verification* of receiving goods, services, other

Function
- *Authorization* of voucher
- *Recording* of liability and payment

Function
- *Payment*

Location
Various Departments

Location
Accounting Department

Location
Treasurer or Cashier's Office

Voucher and Validating and Verifying Documents
- Purchase requisition
- Purchase order
- Invoice
- Receiving report
and
- Any other documents needed to authenticate *any other cash payment*

- Review documents.
- Authorize the voucher.
- Complete the voucher and attach to documents.

Unpaid voucher file

Write and mail the check.
Cancel the voucher and documents.

Record the liability.
(Voucher register)

Record the payment.
(Check register)

Paid voucher file

Cash Receipts Controls

Procedures

Overview

Cash receipts to a business are like water to a growing plant—without adequate cash receipts a business is soon in trouble. A business should take a particular interest in protecting its cash receipts. Cash receipts can come from various sources. Important types are: (1) cash sales (retail transactions), (2) accounts receivable collections (checks in the mail), (3) owner investments, (4) bank loans, (5) sales of non-current assets, (6) investment income, and (7) refunds.

Cash Sales Internal Control

Cash sales are also called "retail" or "over-the-counter" sales. The table below summarizes the internal control process for cash sales.

Event	Procedure
Sales are made.	■ Each sale amount is entered in a cash register and the amount entered is made easily visible to the customer. The register is locked and has an internal paper tape that records the amount of each sale and type of item. ■ Merchandise is priced at uneven amounts, making it necessary for the clerks to record each sale in order to open the register and make change. ■ The customer receives a receipt.
The sales person's shift ends.	■ The supervisor unlocks the register and removes the tape and the cash drawer of the register. ■ With the clerk present, the supervisor compares the total sales recorded on the tape to the amount of cash in register. The cash minus any change fund should equal the sales total. ■ The supervisor prepares a "cash count sheet." This shows the summary total of cash by item (coin, currency, check, etc.) and shows the reconciliation to the register tape. The clerk and supervisor sign the count sheet.
Items go to the cashier.	■ The supervisor gives the cash, register tape, and count sheet to the cashier. ■ The cashier places the cash with tape and count sheet in a safe until the cashier's duties are completed and the cash is deposited.
Cashier duties	■ At the end of the day, the cashier prepares a daily summary deposit sheet of all cash received, which must agree with the total of the cash count sheets and total sales by type. ■ Checks are endorsed with a restrictive endorsement "for deposit only." ■ The cashier prepares a deposit slip in duplicate, makes a daily deposit at the bank, and sends copies of the cash count sheet daily summary, and stamped deposit slip to the accounting department.
Accounting department duties	■ The accounting department compares the cash count sheet and deposit summary sheet to the stamped bank deposit slip. ■ The department records the sales for the day.

Procedures, *continued*

Accounts Receivable Collections Internal Control

Many companies make sales on credit and, therefore, frequently receive checks in the mail as customer's payments for amounts owing on the accounts receivable. The table below summarizes the internal control process for accounts receivable mail collections.

Event	Procedure
Checks arrive in the mail.	■ A bonded mailroom employee opens the mail. (In a small business, the owner can open all the mail.) All checks are immediately restrictively endorsed using a "deposit only" stamp. ■ An employee who opens envelopes also prepares a list of checks received showing the amount, customer name, and purpose of each payment (as usually indicated by a remittance slip enclosed with the check). The employee who prepares the list also signs it. *Note:* a **remittance slip** is the part of the bill that is torn off and returned with a payment. The remittance slip shows the amount due, and the customer enters the amount paid on the slip.
Items go to the cashier and accounting department.	■ The mailroom employee gives the original copy of the list and the checks to the cashier (or treasurer). ■ The employee sends a second copy of the list, with the remittance slips, to the accounting department.
Cashier duties	■ The cashier totals the checks and verifies that the total equals the total of the mailroom list. Then the cashier records the checks in the daily cash summary. ■ The cashier makes the daily deposit and sends the stamped deposit slip to the controller (chief accountant) in the accounting department.
Accounting department duties	■ Using the remittance slips and list of checks, the accounting department records the accounts receivable collections for the day. The remittance slips and list of checks are then sent to the controller's office. ■ The controller compares the bank deposit slip to the list of checks and remittance slips.

continued

Procedures, *continued*

Other Procedures

- *Bank reconciliation:* As we saw in our discussion of the bank reconciliation, it is an analysis of both cash payments as well as cash receipts.

- *Bank card sales:* For a bank card (credit card) sale, cash is electronically credited directly into a seller's bank account at the time of sale. This creates strong internal control and reduces operating costs by eliminating accounts receivable and reducing internal control procedures.

  Note: A bank card is usually refered to as a "credit card." However, a true credit card is simply for a sale on account that creates an account receivable. *Examples:* Discover card, store credit cards.

- *Lock box:* A lock box is a collection procedure in which a seller instructs a buyer to send payments directly to a bank that collects and records the buyer's payments, and then immediately credits the seller's bank account for the amount received. This avoids all cash receipt handling by the seller for accounts receivable collections.

- *EFT (electronic funds transfer) system:* An electronic variation of the lock box idea is to have the buyer's payments electronically transferred from the buyer's bank account to the seller's bank account. No checks are written. Many customers also like to have payments automatically deducted from their checking accounts because it saves time and avoids late payment charges.

Comparison: Review of Internal Control for Cash Payments

Overview

In this learning goal, we have discussed several important internal control methods for both cash payments and cash receipts. As a review, the cash payment internal control methods are summarized for you here:

Summary of Cash Payment Controls

- Use of checks and a checking account
- Performing regular and frequent bank reconciliations
- A voucher system or other authorization procedure
- Using authorized and controlled credit cards instead of cash
- An electronic funds transfer system (EFT)
- A petty cash system for small disbursements
- Change funds

Internet and E-Commerce Requirements

Key Points

Overview

For Internet business transactions (*e-commerce*), the primary internal control requirements are the protection of sensitive information and protection from computer viruses. These are very big topics that are growing in importance as the volume of Internet transactions increase. Here, we provide a quick internal control summary.

Sensitive Information

Stolen credit card numbers and theft of personal or company information is a constant threat. This theft is accomplished by unauthorized parties retrieving and reading the data used in Internet transactions and communication, or by using the Internet to gain access to a computer system for the purpose of retrieving and reading information within the system. Internal control requires the use of high-level *encryption*. This is a mathematical means of arranging the transmitted data so that the data can only be read by the parties with a decoding formula built into their software.

Computer Viruses

Computer viruses are destructive software programs that can invade a computer system, destroy critical data, damage application software, and often reproduce to spread throughout connected systems. Although viruses can be manually entered into computer systems, the primary means of access is via the Internet. Internal control requires the use a *firewall* to prevent access. A firewall consists of several mechanisms at different levels of a system. Basic examples are passwords and personal identification numbers. Electronic firewalls that consist of special software coding that limits access, identifies viruses, and destroys viruses are also needed.

Updates are Essential

To maintain proper encryption, and especially to maintain a proper firewall, *constant updates are essential*. This is because technology always evolves and new viruses are constantly developed. New versions of protective software are also always being developed and updated. Any company involved in e-commerce should consider these updates to be a high-priority internal control requirement.

Additionally, identification codes and access procedures should be regularly changed to prevent any type of unauthorized access.

Automatic Updates

Many types of virus-protection software will automatically update your system with the latest protection available from the company that provides the software. Whenever you are connected to the Internet your system will be automatically connected to the provider's website that updates your software.

Summary of Internal Control Principles

Overview

Eight Basic Principles

On page 580, we defined and described internal control. We have studied specific internal control procedures for cash payments and receipts. The table below summarizes eight basic internal control principles with examples related to cash. However, the principles apply to the protection of all assets.

Principle	Cash Procedure Examples
1. *Separation of critical duties:* Properly done, this requires separation at several levels: ■ The accounting function is always separated from access to assets. ■ Other departmental authority is always separated from accounting functions. ■ Related duties are always separated.	■ Employees performing accounting duties never have any kind of access to cash or other assets. *Example:* The bookkeeper never writes checks or makes deposits. ■ Only the accounting department has authority to record transactions. ■ The person who authorizes payment is never the person who makes the payment; the person who prepares the billing never collects payments.
2. *Assignment of responsibilities:* Each employee's responsibilities must be specific, clear, and limited.	■ Only the cashier or owner makes the bank deposits. ■ Only the treasurer distributes payroll checks.
3. *Asset control:* Assets are separated, and access is limited and controlled physically and/or electronically.	■ Cash receipts are kept in a safe until deposited. ■ A bank checking account is used. ■ Computer passwords are controlled and changed. ■ Equipment is marked and identified in a master file.
4. *Independent verification:* Assets and liabilities are verified at regular and frequent intervals by individuals who are not involved in record-keeping tasks. Transactions are verified.	■ Bank reconciliations are prepared at least monthly. ■ A manager counts the cash in the register and compares it to the amount recorded on the tape. ■ Discount calculations are checked. ■ Receiving reports matched against orders before payment.
5. *Authorization/Validation:* Designated transaction types require approval by designated individuals.	■ NO check is written without completed purchase order and request (validation). ■ NO refunds given without approval (authorization).
6. *Documentation:* All transactions must be supported by timely documentation. Document standards are established. Document controls are established.	■ NO check is written unless documents show that the transaction is authentic (valid). ■ Certain documents must have specific information. ■ Prenumbered checks and invoices account for all these documents so all transactions are recorded.
7. *Recording:* All transactions must be recorded—no exceptions.	■ All cash receipts and payments are timely recorded.
8. *Human Resources policy:* Only competent and ethical employees are hired, and they are properly compensated.	■ Employees have adequate experience and training. ■ Employees receive adequate wages and benefits. ■ Management promotes an ethical environment.

Overview, *continued*

Note: an employee **bond** is an insurance policy for employee theft. Bonding employees improves internal control because: (1) The insurance company will do a background check on the employee, and (2) bonded employees know that if they commit a theft, the insurance company has a powerful incentive to find them, ensure that they are prosecuted, and try to recover stolen property.

Business Size

Needs and Resources

As a business changes, its internal control needs will also change. The volume and complexity of transactions, the number of employees, and the diversity of uses of assets determine how internal control is applied.

Large Companies

Large companies are complex, having many transactions and a variety of assets. This complexity requires numerous procedures and the interaction and oversight of many people. However, large companies also have more resources and are able to employ a large staff that divides the internal control responsibilities among many people. This can prevent the concentration of too much authority and influence and greatly improves internal control.

Small Companies

Can a small company that employs just a few people have adequate internal control? How can the duties be divided? The answer is that in a small company most of the internal control reposes with the owner. In addition to all other responsibilities, *the owner must also be able to understand and perform internal control* on a daily basis and, at intervals, be willing to pay for an independent expert to check the results of operations.

Unfortunately, many small business owners are frequently so busy with other duties that seem more urgent or more interesting that they overlook the importance of internal control. This explains the frequent small business vulnerability to surprising and often crippling theft losses.

Do You Want More Examples?

Most problems in this book have detailed solutions. To use them as additional examples, do this: 1) Select the type of problem you want 2) Open the solution on your computer or mobile device screen (from the disc or worthyjames.com) 3) Read one item at a time and look at its answer. Take notes if needed. 4) Close the solution and work as much of the problem as you can. 5) Repeat as needed.

Solutions are in the disk at the back of the book and at: www.worthyjames.com

Learning Goal 16 is about cash and internal control principles. Use these questions and problems to practice what you have learned about applying these principles.

Multiple Choice

1. When preparing a bank reconciliation, you must be especially careful about where to add or subtract a bank error. For example, a *bank* error that on the bank statement shows:
   a. another company's check—may be either added to the balance per bank or subtracted from the balance per books, and in both cases the reconciliation totals will agree.
   b. an overstated deposit—may be either subtracted from the balance per bank or added to the balance per books, and in both cases the reconciliation totals will agree.
   c. an understated deposit—may be either added to the balance per bank or subtracted from the balance per books, and in both cases the reconciliation totals will agree.
   d. none of the above.

2. When preparing a bank reconciliation, certain adjustment items are always added or subtracted the same way every time. For example, outstanding checks are always:
   a. added to the balance per books.
   b. subtracted from the balance per bank.
   c. added to the balance per bank.
   d. subtracted from the balance per books.

3. When preparing a bank reconciliation, certain adjustment items are always added or subtracted the same way every time. For example, debit memos such as for NSF checks are always:
   a. added to the balance per books.
   b. subtracted from the balance per bank.
   c. added to the balance per bank.
   d. subtracted from the balance per books.

4. When preparing a bank reconciliation, certain adjustment items are always added or subtracted the same way every time. For example, deposits in transit are always:
   a. added to the balance per books.
   b. subtracted from the balance per bank.
   c. added to the balance per bank.
   d. subtracted from the balance per books.

5. If an outstanding check on the June 30 bank reconciliation is still outstanding when the July 31 reconciliation is being prepared, then that outstanding check should be:
   a. added back to the balance per books on the July 31 reconciliation.
   b. subtracted from the balance per bank on the July 31 reconciliation.
   c. subtracted from the balance per books on the July 31 reconciliation.
   d. added to balance per bank on the June 30 reconciliation.

6. Money market funds and 3-month U.S. treasury bills are:
   a. cash.
   b. cash equivalents and not included as part of the balance sheet cash balance.
   c. cash equivalents and included as part of the balance sheet cash balance.
   d. cash, but only disclosed in the financial statement footnotes.

7. On the balance sheet restricted cash should be:
   a. shown as part of either the short or long term investments balance.
   b. disclosed only in the footnotes to the financial statements.
   c. included in the total cash balance.
   d. subtracted from the total in the cash account.

8. On the balance sheet, a compensating cash balance should be:
   a. shown as part of the total of the investments balance.
   b. disclosed only in the footnotes to the financial statements.
   c. included in the total cash balance and disclosed in the footnotes to financial statements.
   d. subtracted from the total in the cash account.

9. In a small business with just a few employees:
   a. the owner provides most of the internal control.
   b. internal control is not possible.
   c. internal control is not necessary.
   d. the cash, inventory, and other assets are not usually vulnerable to theft.

10. Bank reconciliations, surprise petty cash counts, and managers comparing cash in the register to the cash count are all examples of which internal control principle?
    a. separation of critical duties
    b. assignment of responsibilities
    c. documentation
    d. independent verification

11. Making sure that the person doing the bookkeeping never writes checks or receives checks or makes deposits is an example of which internal control principle?
    a. separation of critical duties
    b. assignment of responsibilities
    c. authorization
    d. independent verification

12. Defining the exact duties of merchandise purchasing and who will perform them is an example of which internal control principle?
    a. asset control
    b. assignment of responsibilities
    c. authorization
    d. independent verification

13. Which of the following is an example of internal control for only cash receipts?
    a. a voucher system
    b. bank reconciliations
    c. using cash count sheets and duplicate deposit slips
    d. using company credit cards

14. The three basic events occurring with the use of a petty cash fund are:
    a. establishing the fund, writing checks from the fund, replenishing the fund.
    b. establishing the fund, making journal entries, replenishing the fund.
    c. establishing the fund, increasing the fund, decreasing the fund.
    d. establishing the fund, disbursing cash from the fund, replenishing the fund.

15. The journalizing of the expenses resulting from petty cash expenditures:
    a. will occur when the fund is established.
    b. will occur when the fund is replenished.
    c. should be done as the petty cash expenditures are made.
    d. should be done only by the petty cash custodian when the fund is replenished.

16. When a petty cash fund is replenished, a $200 check is written to the petty cash custodian. The petty cash box contains $187 of completed petty cash vouchers and $9 cash. The journal entry to record the replenishment will include:
  a. a credit to Cash Over and Short for $4.
  b. a debit to Petty Cash for $187 and a credit to Cash Over and Short for $4.
  c. a debit to Cash Over and Short for $4.
  d. a credit to Petty Cash for $187 and a debit to Cash Over and Short for $4.

17. After a bank reconciliation is completed, which of these reconciling items will require an adjusting entry in the accounting records of the bank customer?
  a. deposits in transit
  b. outstanding checks
  c. bank error
  d. bank service charges

18. The primary purpose of internal control is to:
  a. prevent fraud.
  b. ensure employee efficiency and honesty.
  c. ensure accurate financial statements.
  d. provide reasonable assurance that assets are safeguarded.

19. In a voucher system:
  a. every cash disbursement must first be validated, verified, and authorized with documentation.
  b. vouchers control all cash receipts and require full receipt documentation.
  c. the voucher is a document that validates and verifies a potential cash payment.
  d. all of the above.

20. A voucher is:
  a. a document that validates and verifies the authenticity of a cash payment.
  b. an authorization to make a cash payment.
  c. an expanded purchases journal.
  d. a type of cash payments journal.

21. In a voucher system:
  a. when the voucher is completed, the cash payment can be made.
  b. when the voucher is completed, a liability must be recorded before payment is made.
  c. cash payments must be made by the accounting department.
  d. internal control is made unnecessary by the use of vouchers.

Discussion Questions and Brief Exercises

1. What are cash equivalents? How are cash and cash equivalents reported on a balance sheet? How are restricted cash and compensating balances reported?

2. What is the meaning and purpose of internal control? Identify five kinds of internal control procedures for cash, and descibe how they help safeguard cash. Do these procedures have any limitations?

PRACTICE   Learning Goal 16, continued

Discussion Questions and Brief Exercises, *continued*

3. Whenever a check is written, at least three parties are involved. Who are the three parties?

4. What is a check endorsement? What are two types of endorsements?

5. What is the meaning of debits and credits on a bank statement? Are they the same as the debits and credits to cash in a company's accounting records?

6. The bank statement balance of Empire Company is $15,200 before the bank reconciliation is completed. The following items were part of the bank reconciliation: (a) bank service charges, $15; (b) outstanding checks, $750; (c) NSF check, $157; (d) deposits in transit, $200. What is the adjusted bank balance on the bank reconciliation?

7. Explain the purpose of a voucher system. What type of internal control does it provide—for cash receipts or cash payments? Describe the five basic functions that comprise a voucher system.

8. This learning goal describes eight basic internal control principles. Identify and briefly describe each principle.

9. The following cash receipts internal control procedures were described for cash sales: (1) use a cash register when a sale is made, (2) a cash count is made at the end of shift, (3) both the sales clerk and supervisor perform the cash count and complete a cash count sheet, (4) the cash, the cash register tape, and the cash count sheet are sent to the cashier, (5) the cashier makes the deposit and sends copies of the deposit slip and cash summary to the accounting department. What internal control principles are being applied by each of these five procedures?

10. Companies make sure that petty cash is always replenished at the end of an accounting period, before financial statements are prepared. What is the purpose of this procedure?

11. Separation of duties is often considered one of the most important elements of internal control. Why might this be true?

12. Can a small business with only one owner and just a few employees have adequate internal control? If you think this is possible, how would it be accomplished?

Solutions are in the disk at the back of the book and at: www.worthyjames.com

PRACTICE   Learning Goal 16, continued

Discussion Questions and Brief Exercises, *continued*

13. Record general journal entries for the following:

- Established a petty cash fund in the amount of $300 on October 5.
- Replenished the petty cash fund on October 31. The petty cash box contained the following petty cash vouchers (petty cash tickets): taxi, $34; entertainment, $88.50; office supplies, $31.27.

14. When you purchase a movie ticket using cash, you pay a person in a booth who takes your cash and gives you a ticket for the movie. Then, when you enter the theater, another person tears off part of the ticket and gives you the remaining half. What internal control features are being applied in this situation? How might dishonest employees attempt to steal cash in this situation?

15. Why are documents such as checks, receipts, and vouchers printed with identifying sequential numbers?

16. Lake Worth Enterprises is a small but rapidly growing retail clothing store. The owner has been so busy with company operations that she has not had time to consider internal control issues. The following procedures are part of company operations. Evaluate the procedures from an internal control point of view and identify any risks that you think are significant.

- The company bookkeeper is responsible for making daily cash deposits. After each deposit the deposit slip is given to the owner at the end of the day.
- When the owner is very busy, merchandise purchases are made by a store manager who also is responsible for verifying the receipt of all merchandise when it is delivered.
- When the owner is busy, the bookkeeper has the responsibility of opening the mail and making a list of checks received. This list of checks together with the customer remittance slip is then given to the owner, who can compare it with the bank deposit slips.
- The store manager approves invoices for payment. The invoices are sent to the owner who writes a check and then returns the invoice to the store manager who places all invoices in a single file called "paid invoices."
- Customers take returned merchandise to cash register clerks who examine the merchandise and pay the customer for the amount of the purchase.
- The manager of the sales department records all sales on account.

17. Suppose that a bookkeeper is permitted to write checks and make deposits. If the bookkeeper is dishonest and steals money by writing checks to himself, what options are available to him to cover the theft?

PRACTICE   **Learning Goal 16, continued**

Solutions are in the disk at the back of the book and at: www.worthyjames.com

Reinforcement Problems

LG 16-1. Make the correct calculation for reconciling items. The table below shows a list of items that need to be added to or subtracted from either the balance per bank or the balance per books.

Instructions: Enter each item as either an addition to or subtraction from the balance per bank or the balance per books, as if you were doing a bank reconciliation. The column totals should reconcile to the same amount.

	Bank	Book
Unadjusted Balances Per Bank and Per Books to Reconcile	$9,810	$3,293
Item	**Bank Adjustments**	**Book Adjustments**
1. NSF check: $500		
2. Outstanding checks from this month: $7,200.		
3. Bank service charges: $25		
4. Bank error: Charging account for check of another company: $310.		
5. Deposits in transit: $4,500.		
6. $450 check recorded as $504 in cash payments journal		
7. $820 check recorded as $208 in cash payments journal		
8. Outstanding checks from prior periods that are still outstanding: $400 . . .		
9. Unrecorded EFT payment to a supplier on account: $2,500		
10. Credit memo regarding note transaction: $5,000 principal, $200 interest. .		
11. Debit memo for ATM transaction by owner: $100		
12. $3,000 deposit recorded as $300 in the cash receipts journal.		
13. Bank error: Understating amount of deposit: $500		
14. $10 interest earned on checking account.		
Total Adjustments		
Reconciled Balance		

Solutions are in the disk at the back of the book and at: www.worthyjames.com

LG 16-2. Prepare a bank reconciliation. Don Williamson, the owner of Sunol Enterprises, is preparing financial statements for his business and needs a bank reconciliation as of June 30.

Instructions:

a. Prepare the June 30 bank reconciliation.
b. What is the amount of cash that should appear on the June 30 balance sheet?

Information:

Sunol Company Bank Statement for Month of June 2017			
Beginning Balance	Total Deposits	Total Withdrawals	Ending Balance
$9,808.51	$6,971.05	$4,374.07	$12,405.49

Checks and Other Debits			**Deposits and Other Credits**	
Date	*Number*	*Amount*	*Date*	*Amount*
6/05	252	122.75	6/09	2,700.00
6/07		NSF 204.37	6/15	950.00
6/07	254	38.62	6/25	3,321.05
6/09	255	3,500.00		
6/12	256	33.79		
6/14	257	241.54		
6/23	258	75.00		
6/27	260	148.00		
6/30		SC 10.00		

1. The Cash ledger account shows a June 30 balance of $12,521.46.
2. On June 30, the following checks are outstanding: #259 for $328.65, #261 for $95.00, and #262 for $500.25.
3. On June 30, one deposit is in transit for the amount of $825.50.
4. The June NSF check and bank service charge amounts are $204.37 and $10.00

LG 16-3. Preparing a bank reconciliation and adjusting entries.

Instructions: Based on the information below, complete the following:

1. Prepare a bank reconciliation as of February 28, 2017.
2. Prepare the related journal entries.

On February 28, 2017, American River Company had an unadjusted Cash ledger balance of $2,568.27. The February 28 bank statement showed an ending cash balance of $8,472.21. The following information concerning the cash account and the bank statement is available:

a. The current month bank service charge is $8.00.
b. The bank collected a note receivable for American River Company on February 12 in the amount of $5,000 plus $127 interest. No accrued interest has been recorded for the note.

LG 16-3, *continued*

c. On the afternoon of February 28, the company made a cash deposit of $1,250.88. This deposit did not appear on the bank statement because the bank was in the process of preparing the statement for the month.

d. February check #490 in the amount of $352 to pay for current month newspaper advertising was recorded in the cash payments journal as $325.

e. February 28 outstanding checks total $2,293.15.

f. The bank returned an NSF check in the amount of $220.33 on February 11. This has not yet been recorded. The bank charged a $10 fee for the returned check

LG 16-4. **Fixing an incorrect reconciliation; making journal entries.** The owner of a business prepared this bank reconciliation, but could not finish it.

Instructions: On a separate sheet of paper:

1. Prepare a corrected bank reconciliation. If needed, use an analysis of increase and decrease items to help you.
2. Prepare the necessary adjusting entries.

Barlowe's Automotive Service
Bank Reconciliation
July 31, 2017

Balance Per Bank, July 31		$5,500.39
Add: Deposit in transit	$975.00	
NSF check	387.00	1,362.00
Less: Service charge		25.00
Adjusted Bank Balance, July 31		$6,887.39
Balance Per Books, July 31		$6,559.39
Add: Outstanding checks: #390	$495.00	
#395	266.00	
#396	317.00	1,098.00
Less: Account debited by bank for Beasley Company check		750.00
Adjusted Book Balance, July 31		$6,907.39

LG 16-5. **Internal control: Cash receipts.** The table on page 612 shows the flow of events involved in cash sales receipts. With each event, specific procedures are identified.

Instructions: Starting with the first event (sales are made) identify which basic internal control principle is being applied for each procedure. Do this for all the procedures for each event.

LG 16-6. Internal control applications: Various situations. In the independent situations below, identify how a potential loss could happen and which internal control procedure(s) is (are) needed:

a. Bill, the bookkeeper, writes and signs the checks and handles the monthly bank reconciliation.

b. To save time, the owner of a small liquor store keeps daily cash receipts in his briefcase, in his office, and he makes deposits every Friday.

c. In a small clothing store, several sales employees use the same cash register during the same hours. Also, to improve customer relations, the owner allows each clerk to accept returned merchandise even if the customer does not have a sales receipt from the store, provided that the store actually carries the returned item.

d. In the recreation department at the city offices of Jonesville, the director of recreation authorizes and makes all recreation equipment purchases using the required purchase order forms. The city prints its own purchase order forms, but it does not sequentially prenumber the forms. Instead, a blank space on the form is used for numbering, which the director does by hand before using the forms.

e. The chief executive officer of a charitable organization requires that she alone prepares all purchase orders and approves all vendor invoices for payment.

f. Donna works in the corporate office of a chain of furniture stores. Donna's job is to review and approve all invoices (for payment), which she then sends to the cashier who writes the checks, with document copies going to the accounting department. Donna's responsibilities also include receiving and processing any invoice overpayment checks that are received in the mail.

g. Paul is a busy physician with a small medical practice. Doris, his bookkeeper, also does the bank reconciliations, all the billing, and opens all the mail.

h. Seymour, the bookkeeper of a small company, prepares the calculations for gross pay and withholding used on the payroll checks, which are signed and distributed by the owner. Seymour overstates his own gross pay and that of another employee, Jane, who is his friend.

i. The owner of Swifty's Sporting Goods noticed that although net sales have stayed fairly constant, the business is beginning to experience cash flow difficulties. She also noticed that the cost of goods sold as a percentage of net sales is growing—even though the markup percentage on all merchandise has remained the same. Business is good, with lots of customers. The owner makes all daily bank deposits, which always match the amount of net sales recorded on the cash register tapes. The owner also carefully supervises the inventory on hand and is confident that nothing is being stolen and that all sales are properly recorded. Two employees are responsible for all cash register duties, which include entering sales, returns, and discount allowances. Randy, one of these employees, has recently started coming to work in an expensive new car.

j. Greg, the author of this textbook, once worked as an independent CPA in offices that were subleased by several small CPA firms from a larger firm. The larger firm provided secretarial services to each of the smaller firms. At the end of each month, the secretary reviewed her timesheet and billed her time to each small firm. Each firm, being busy, usually paid the relatively modest amount without further inspection of the packet of time slips that were stapled to the bill as documentation. Over a period of many months, the amount billed continually increased, and the time slips became so heavily stapled together that the packet was practically bulletproof.

k. To save money on slow days during the week, the management of Main Street Movie Theater assigns one employee to sell tickets and also to tear the tickets in half to show that they were used for admission. The employee retains one half of the ticket and places it in a box. The tickets in the box are counted later by the manager and compared to the cash receipts.

l. Master's Wholesale Golf Equipment assigns the bookkeeper the task of opening and sorting all incoming mail. Most of the company sales are made on account to numerous small clients. The bookkeeper makes all necessary journal entries and forwards all customer payments

LG 16-6, *continued*

to the manager. The bookkeeper also performs all monthly customer billing duties. Lately, the manager has become concerned because the amount of old accounts receivable has been growing while cash flow has been declining. The manager received a memo from the bookkeeper notifying her that $10,000 of old accounts receivable will be written off as uncollectible.

LG 16-7. Petty cash procedures

Instructions: Record general journal entries for the following petty cash transactions:

September 1: Established a petty cash fund in the amount of $150.

September 30: Replenished the petty cash fund. The petty cash record shows the following totals: Travel, $55; supplies, $12.50; meals and entertainment, $47.25; postage $18.45. The remaining cash in the petty cash box is $11.30.

October 31: Replenished the petty cash fund. The petty cash record shows the following totals: Travel, $38; supplies, $17.80; meals and entertainment, $91.20. The remaining cash in the petty cash box is $10. The petty cash account is also increased to a balance of $200.

Solutions are in the disk at the back of the book and at: www.worthyjames.com

PRACTICE   Learning Goal 16, continued

Instructor-Assigned Problems

If you are using this book in a class, these review problems may be assigned by your instructor for homework, group assignments, class work, or other activities. Only your instructor has the solutions.

IA 16-1. Identify Adjustments, Reconcile Balances

Item:	Bank Adjustments	Book Adjustments
Ending Balances Per Bank and Per Book to Reconcile	$21,926	$15,166
1. Unrecorded EFT credit card sales $3,225		
2. Outstanding checks from prior periods that are still outstanding: $872.....		
3. $29 interest earned on checking account...............................		
4. $250 check recorded as $502 in cash payments journal		
5. NSF check: $750		
6. Debit memo for ATM withdrawals by owner: $250......................		
7. Deposits in transit: $2,885		
8. Bank error: Charging account for check of another company: $544........		
9. Outstanding checks from this month: $4,780...........................		
10. $4,200 deposit recorded as $2,400 in the cash receipts journal		
11. Bank error: Overstated amount of deposit: $395.......................		
12. $750 check recorded as $50 in cash payments journal		
13. Bank service charges: $34		
14. Unrecorded EFT for deposit paid to supplier: $2,000		
15. Credit memo regarding note transaction: $2,500 principal, $70 interest ...		
Total Adjustments		
Reconciled Balance		

IA 16-2. Prepare a bank reconciliation and adjusting entries.

Instructions: based on the information below, complete the following:

1. Prepare a bank reconciliation as of August 31, 2017.
2. Prepare the related journal entries. Make one entry for cash increase items and one entry for cash decrease items.

On August 31, 2017 Kelseyville Company had an unadjusted Cash ledger balance of $5,372.71. The August 31 bank statement showed an ending cash balance of $9,737.53. The following information concerning the cash account and the bank statement is available:

a. The current month bank service charge is $17.00.
b. The bank statement included an EFT credit item in the amount of $2,923 for credit card sales.
c. On August 30, the company made a cash deposit of $1,386.55. This deposit did not appear on the August 31 bank statement.
d. An August check in the amount of $712 to pay for current month utilities was recorded in the cash payments journal as $271.
e. August 31 outstanding checks total $4,005.99.

IA 16-2, *continued*

   f. The bank returned an NSF check in the amount of $448.50 on August 20. The NSF check has not yet been recorded in the books. The check was written by John Miller.

   g. The bank charged the account of Kelseyville Company $271.12 for a check written by Kelso Company.

IA 16-3. **Internal Control Issues**

Instructions: In each independent situation below, identify the internal control weakness and how a loss could occur. Then, recommend an internal control procedure that should be used. Suggestion: refer to the table of the eight basic internal control principles to assist your analysis.

   a. Jim and Jane's Kitchen Store is a small retail store that sells gourmet kitchen products. On most days, the owners employ Cecil to handle retail customer sales in the store, using a cash register. At the end of the day, Cecil delivers the proceeds from the cash register to one of the owners, who counts the cash, makes a deposit, and files the deposit slip.

   b. Bates Motel is experiencing a decline in reservations and cash flow. Therefore, in order to save cash, the owner is allowing the manager to reduce printing costs by not requiring pre-numbered checks and pre-numbered receipts.

   c. In Acme Company, Jane is responsible for verifying the authenticity of customer refund requests and authorizing the refund amounts, which are submitted to the cashier. The cashier prepares the refund checks and mails them.

   d. Snidely, the long-time, reliable cashier in a small company, never takes a vacation. His associates marvel at his dedication to the company. He is admired by everyone for his long hours, work ethic, and willingness to help others with their duties in all situations.

   e. Local Appliance Company sells and services household appliances. The owner is extremely busy and works with three technicians to service appliances and to run the store. Because of his heavy workload, the owner allows Max, the bookkeeper, to write checks, open the mail, make deposits, prepare reconciliations, and prepare monthly financial reports, which the owner reviews.

   f. Mega Company has been growing rapidly. Because of this, engineers in the company frequently require tools, software, and equipment. To obtain what is needed, an engineer or other employee is required to fill out a purchase requisition form, which is then sent to the purchasing department, which then orders the item and receives an invoice. The item arrives directly from seller to the department from which it was ordered.

   g. A manufacturing company with large accounting and sales departments routinely allows its employees to work from home two days per week; as well, accounting and sales staff usually work while traveling. For this reason the company provides many employees with laptop computers. It is not unusual for an employee to report a laptop missing or stolen. As well recently the company, which uses many Internet functions to control its manufacturing processes, experienced severe damage to a manufacturing process. This was caused by Internet criminals who had gained access to the Internet control systems.

   h. Mary Anne is just starting a small business. She is asking you for the best way to protect her business cash from fraud and theft.

IA 16-3. *continued*

i. In Jones Company, three people work in the payroll department. Based on workload, they rotate the responsibility of receiving employee wage and employment information from the human resources department and entering employee wage data into a payroll computer program that calculates wages and withholding and prints checks. Checks are then mailed to employees or electronically credited to their bank accounts based on direct deposit information provided by the employee. The company has recently discovered names of several part-time employees who never worked for the company and were paid wages, and two full-time salary employees who used to work for the company that are still on the payroll.

j. In a large software company with various sales programs and products, the supervisors of the accounting department and sales department work together to determine the correct amount of revenue to recognize each month, based on facts and circumstances.

IA 16-4. **Prepare bank reconciliation and record journal entries.** The June bank statement for Comet Commodities Company, Inc. is presented below.

Instructions:

a. Use the bank statement and summaries of the cash payments and cash receipts journals, and additional information, to prepare the June 30, 2017 bank reconciliation.

b. Prepare the necessary journal entries related to the bank reconciliation.

c. What internal control procedure would you suggest for check #404? Which of the eight basic internal control procedures would your suggested procedure relate to?

IA 16-4, *continued*

San Jose Bank

3442 Border Avenue
San Jose, California 95035

Account 1200165348

Comet Commodities Company, Inc.
385 Enterprise Avenue
Cupertino, CA. 94085

Period from June 1
to June 30, 2017

Prior Balance	Total Deposits	Total Withdrawals	Ending Balance
$77,232.51	$44,622.05	$48,100.25	$73,754.31

Checks and Other Debits			Deposits and Other Credits		Daily Balance	
Date	*Number*	*Amount*	*Date*	*Amount*	*Date*	*Amount*
6/01	361	310.44	6/01	1,005.00	6/01	80,527.07
6/02	387	186.05	6/01	2,600.00	6/02	79,601.02
6/02	393	740.00	6/04	184.20	6/04	91,785.22
6/07	390	88.09	6/04	12,000.00	6/06	98,285.22
6/11	381	7,500.00	6/06	6,500.00	6/07	90,697.13
6/12	395	3,001.53	6/15	500.00	6/11	87,659.13
6/12	EC	36.15	6/21	11,081.12	6/12	87,659.45
6/14	399	601.39	6/23	9,051.48	6/14	87,058.06
6/17	406	12,550.25	EFT 6/29	1,700.25	6/15	87,558.06
6/17	NSF	50.00			6/17	62,407.56
6/17	400	12,550.25			6/18	62,308.24
6/18	SC	12.00			6/21	73,389.36
6/18	401	87.32			6/23	82,340.84
6/23	397	100.00			6/27	81,849.04
6/27	389	491.80			6/29	78,423.11
6/29	391	5,126.18			6/30	73,754.31
6/30	394	3,985.64				
6/30	396	283.16				
6/30	EFT	400.00				

Symbols: **CM** Credit Memo   **DM** Debit Memo   **SC** Service Charge   **ATM** Automatic Teller
NSF Not Sufficient Funds   **EC** Error Correction   **OD** Overdraft   **INT** Interest
EFT Electronic Funds Transfer

IA 16-4, *continued*

June Cash Receipts Summary

Date	Account	Cash (Debits)
6/01	Sales Revenue	$1,005.00
6/01	Accounts Receivable	2,600.00
6/04	Sales Revenue	148.20
6/04	Notes Payable	12,000.00
6/06	Accounts Receivable	6,500.00
6/15	Sales Revenue	500.00
6/21	Unearned Revenue	11,081.12
6/23	Accounts Receivable	9,051.48
6/29	Accounts Receivable	5,185.00
	Total	$48,070.80

June Cash Payments Summary

Check Number	Account	Cash (Credits)
389	Supplies	$491.80
390	Freight-in	88.09
391	Wages Expense	5,126.18
392	Rent Expense	2,750.00
393	Advertising Expense	740.00
394	Merchandise Inventory	3,985.64
395	Office Equipment	3,037.68
396	Utilities Expense	283.16
397	Utilities Expense	100.00
398	Sales Tax Payable	486.40
399	Merchandise Inventory	601.39
400	Accounts payable	12,550.25
401	Advertising Expense	87.32
402	Prepaid Travel	849.50
403	Accounts Payable	2,500.00
404	Void	--------
405	Miscellaneous Expense	21.03
406	Merchandise Inventory	12,550.25
	Total	46,248.69

IA 16-4, *continued*

Other Information:

- As of the beginning of June, the following checks were still outstanding from prior months' bank reconciliation as follows: From April: #361; From May: #381, #387.
- An electronic funds transfer was received on June 29 for an outstanding account receivable and a second transfer was made on June 30 for an insurance prepayment.
- A customer's check for a freight charge reimbursement was returned.
- It was verified with the bank that a single bank error was made during the month, related to check number 395, and was corrected by the bank.
- Reconciled cash balance as of May 31: $69,236.02

IA 16-5. Record petty cash transactions. Record the following petty cash transactions:

May 7:   Established a petty cash fund in the amount of $400.
May 26:   The petty cash fund was replenished based on the following petty cash vouchers: Supplies, $46.21; Postage, $55.11; Transportation, $21.86; Donations, $20.00. The remaining cash in the petty cash box was $258.50. All items are expensed.
June 30:   The petty cash fund was replenished based on the following petty cash vouchers: Supplies, $26.21; Postage, $105.28; Transportation, $19.44. Meals and Entertainment. $215.74. The remaining cash in the petty cash box was $24.18. The petty cash fund was also allowed to decrease to a balance of $300.00.

IA 16-6. Bank reconciliation, analysis of differences, adjusting entries, internal control weaknesses. Fayetteville, Inc. is a small corporation that for many years has operated a successful college bookstore supply business, creating customized imprints on binders, shirts, pens, and other college items. The two owners of the business, Alan and Denise Patton, are always very busy operating the business. For a long time, Mr. and Mrs. Patton have relied on Arthur Chadwick, the bookkeeper, to maintain the records, make deposits, and pay the bills.

The information below shows the company records for May cash receipts and cash payments and the Cash ledger account, all maintained by Mr. Chadwick. Also shown below is the bank statement for May. Mr. Chadwick has been stealing from the company. In April, he omitted an outstanding check on the bank reconciliation to cover up a $1,250 theft of cash by writing a check to himself that he did not record on the cash payments journal. In May, he stole money from undeposited cash on hand and covered the theft by overstating the May 30 cash receipt from customer payments on account. Mr. Chadwick suddenly resigned from his job in early June, and Mr. and Mrs. Patton have hired you to maintain the books and prepare a bank reconciliation.

Instructions:

a. Prepare the May bank reconciliation, including an analysis that identifies the book and bank differences.
b. Prepare the May adjusting entries from the bank reconciliation.
c. Prepare a short memo to Mr. and Mrs. Patton identifying internal control weaknesses concerning cash.

IA 16-6, *continued*

Cash Receipts	
Date	**Cash (debits)**
May 1	$4,125
4	822
8	344
12	2,440
18	1,780
24	476
30	2,311
Total	$12,298

Cash Payments	
Check #	**Cash (credits)**
750	$ 277
751	1,264
752	481
753	75
754	283
755	412
756	5,280
757	1,750
758	880
759	343
Total	$11,045

Cash Ledger Account

Cash					110
Date	**Explanation**	**Ref.**	**Debit**	**Credit**	**Balance**
May 1	Bal.				22,385
31		CR8	12,298		34,683
31		CP12		11,045	23,638

Fayetteville, Inc. Bank Statement for Month of May 2017			
Beginning Balance	Total Withdrawals	Total Deposits	Ending Balance
$21,960	$11,509	$15,288	$25,739

Checks and Other Debits				Deposits and Other Credits	
Date	*Number*	*Amount*		*Date*	*Amount*
5/01	742	190		5/01	1,000
5/01	748	1,250		5/02	4,125
5/03	749	385		5/04	822
5/04	750	277		5/08	344
5/09		NSF 822		5/12	2,440
5/11	751	1,264		5/18	1,780
5/12	752	481		5/24	476
5/18	753	75		5/30	1,311
5/21	756	5,280		5/31	Note Coll. 2,990
5/22	1590	500			
5/24	758	880			
5/30		SC 25			
		Box Rent 80			

PRACTICE   Learning Goal 16, continued

Solutions are in the disk at the back of the book and at: www.worthyjames.com

IA 16-6, *continued*

- The collection of a note receivable included $90 of interest earned on the note.
- Check #1590 belongs to Fulton Company.
- All prior outstanding checks have cleared on the May statement.

IA16-7 Bank reconciliation and internal control analysis

Carefree Merchandise Co., Inc. has hired you as a consultant to prepare their September 30 bank reconciliation, which they are unable to complete, and to advise them on internal control. The bookkeeper excluded an August outstanding check #480 of $600.27. Check #505 for utilities was written for $128 but recorded for $182.

Instructions: Prepare a new reconciliation and journal entries. Advise the client on internal control.

Balance Per Bank, September 30		$85,663.85
Add: EFT for note receivable collection		15,000.00
Less: Outstanding and NSF Checks		
NSF	220.00	
No. 502	3,108.32	
No. 507	92.75	
No. 571	4,451.00	(7,872.07)
Adjusted Bank Balance, September 30		$92,791.78
Balance Per Books, September 30		**68,997.26**
Bank service charges	19.00	
Check error, #505	54.00	
EFT for payroll taxes	2,500.25	(2,564.25)
Adjusted Book Balance, September 30		$66,433.01

Your analysis shows: The owner, who is very busy, has authorized the bookkeeper to write checks, while the owner makes deposits. The bookkeeper prepares the billing, opens mail and summarizes accounts receivable receipts, then gives the checks to the owner. Cash register clerks prepare a cash count and deliver cash receipts to the owner. They also process merchandise refunds. All purchase requests are sent to a supervisor, who makes purchases and reviews deliveries.

INTERNET EXERCISES

Ethics—analyze cases. Go to the Santa Clara University Markkula Center for Applied Ethics (at https://www.scu.edu/markkula). Select Ethics Resources and three cases that interest you. (Use bookmark/favorites to save the location in an Accounting References folder.)

a. Read each case, then write down the name of the case. If you are using Volume 1 in this set, apply the ethics discussion and guidelines in Learning Goal 10 to analyze the case. If you are not using Volume 1, do the following: 1) Identify the facts and the parties involved. 2) Determine if there a moral issue of a possibly wrongful act.

b. Make a decision or take a position. Write a paragraph to explain how you reached your decision or position.

Appendix to Learning Goal 16

What to Do When The Reconciliation Does Not Reconcile

Overview

Additional Procedures

Regardless of how carefully you follow the reconciliation procedure, it is still very easy to overlook something or to make a mistake. The following additional procedures will help you to find the amounts that you need to complete a bank reconciliation. To complete the procedures: (1) make sure that you understand the reconciling items and (2) analyze the three parts of a reconciliation.

Understand the Reconciling Items

The reconciling items are the items that you add or subtract to either the balance per bank or balance per books. Understanding these items means knowing what they are, which balance they affect, and whether to add or subtract. These are items such as NSF checks, outstanding checks, deposits in transit, service charges, and book errors and bank errors. Be sure that these items are in the right place and correctly added or subtracted.

For a review of these items, see the list of reconciling items on page 588 and 589, the previous bank reconciliation examples, and work the first problem at the end of this learning goal.

Analyze the Three Parts

A bank reconciliation can be analyzed as three separate parts:

- Entering beginning balances
- Reconciling the increase items per bank to the increase items per books
- Reconciling the decrease items per bank to the decrease items per books

If the adjusted totals in your reconciliation do not reconcile to the same amount and there are no math or copying errors, then *the total of the unidentified difference will be in these three parts.* The procedure tables below show how to do the analysis of each part.

Overview, *continued*

Beginning Balances

The table below shows how to check beginning balances.

Step	Action
1	Check the date of the bank statement. Have you used the statement that ends closest to, but not after, the date in the title of the reconciliation?
2	Examine the balance per bank that you started with on the reconciliation. Is the amount the same as the ending balance on the bank statement?
3	a) Does the current period's beginning cash balance match the ending balance of the prior period? b) Does the current book ending cash balance match the unreconciled balance used in the reconciliation?

Reconcile the Increase Items

Example

The table below shows how to separately reconcile the increases on the bank statement (deposits and credits) to the increases in the accounting records (the "books"). The example column amounts are from the November 30, Paia Company bank reconciliation. *Before you begin, be sure that you have checked each step in your work for math and copying errors.*

Step	Action	Example
1	Enter the total increases (deposits and credits) shown on the bank statement.	$12,225.00
2	Subtract: Deposits in transit on the previous bank reconciliation.	–0–
3	Add: Deposits in transit for this bank reconciliation.	$1,500.00
4	Current period increases per bank: Prior deposits are removed and all current deposits are included, so increases per bank should match current period increases per books.	$13,725.00
5	Enter total current period increases per books.	$12,200.00
6	Compare bank increases in Step 4 to the book increases in Step 5. If the balances are the same, there is no difference to identify. If there is a difference, go to the next step.	$1,525.00 difference
7	Look for differences that affect total increases on the *bank* statement. Add or subtract these differences to/from the total bank increases in Step 4. ■ Bank deposit error. (Bank increases should be greater.)	$13,725.00 200.00 $13,925.00
8	Look for differences that affect the increases on the *books*. Add or subtract differences to/from the total book increases in Step 5. ■ Unrecorded deposit. (Book increases should be greater.)	$12,200.00 1,725.00 $13,925.00
	When Steps 7 and 8 show the same totals, you have identified all the increase differences. You can enter these as bank or book balance adjustments on the bank reconciliation (see next table).	

continued ▶

Reconcile the Increase Items, *continued*

Use the Differences

The differences in the increase items that you identified in Steps 7 and 8 are adjustments that you use on the bank reconciliation. Use the following procedure:

Step	Action	Example
1	Bank balance adjustments (Step 7): ■ Add positive differences to the bank balance. ■ Subtract negative differences from the bank balance.	$200.00 none
2	Book balance adjustments (Step 8): ■ Add positive differences to the book balance. ■ Subtract negative differences from the book balance.	$1,725.00 none

Note: The difference between the adjustment totals is the difference between the bank and book balances in Step 6: $1,725 – $200 = $1,525.

Reconcile the Decrease Items

Example

The table below shows how to separately reconcile the checks and debits on the bank statement to the decreases in the accounting records (the "books"). The example column amounts are from the November 30, Paia Company bank reconciliation. *Before you begin, be sure that you have checked each step in your work for math and copying errors.*

Step	Action	Example
1	Enter the total decreases (checks and debits) shown on the bank statement.	$3,683.07
2	Subtract: Outstanding checks on the previous bank reconciliation.	–0–
3	Add: Outstanding checks from the current period cash payments.	4,654.95
4	Current period decreases per bank: Prior outstanding checks are removed and all the current period outstanding checks are included, so decreases per bank should match current period decreases per books.	8,338.02
5	Enter total current period decreases per books.	8,076.77
6	Compare bank decreases in Step 4 to the book decreases in Step 5. If the balances are the same, there is no difference to identify. If there is a difference, go to the next step.	$261.25 difference
7	Look for differences that affect total decreases on the *bank* statement. Add or subtract these differences to/from the total bank decreases in Step 4. ■ No difference items that affect bank decreases	$8,338.02 –0– $8,338.02
8	Look for differences that affect the total decreases on the *books*. Add or subtract differences to/from the total book decreases in Step 5. ■ Service charges. (Book decreases should be greater.) ■ Check printing charge. (Book decreases should be greater.) ■ NSF check. (Book decreases should be greater.) ■ Book error check #104. (Book decreases should be less.)	$8,076.77 7.50 14.50 250.25 (11.00) $8,338.02
	When Steps 7 and 8 show the same totals, you have identified all the decrease differences. You can enter these as bank or book balance adjustments on the bank reconciliation (see next table).	

continued ▶

Reconcile the Decrease Items, *continued*

Use the Differences

The differences in the decrease items that you identified in Steps 7 and 8 are adjustments that you use on the bank reconciliation. Use the following procedure:

Step	Action	Example
1	Bank balance adjustments (Step 7): ■ Multiply each item by negative one. This is necessary because decrease items are subtractions on the bank reconciliation.	No bank adjustment items
2	■ Add positive results to the bank balance. ■ Subtract negative results from the bank balance.	−0−
3	Book balance adjustments (Step 8): ■ Multiply each item by negative one. This is necessary because decrease items are subtractions on the bank reconciliation. • $7.50 \times (1) =$ • $14.50 \times (1) =$ • $250.25 \times (1) =$ • $(11.00) \times (1) =$	(7.50) (14.50) (250.25) 11.00
4	■ Add positive results to the book balance. ■ Subtract negative results from the book balance.	$11.00 (7.50) (14.50) (250.25)

Note: The difference between the adjustment totals is the difference between the bank and book balances in Step 6: $0 - \$261.25 = -\$261.25$.

Another Reconciliation Example

Overview

This example shows an unfinished bank reconciliation for Paia company as of December 31, the second month of operations, using the bank statement that you see below. The reconciliation is unfinished because it does not balance yet. Following the unfinished reconciliation, the differences are identifed using the procedures presented above. The completed reconciliation follows.

Metro Bank

4381 Holland Ave
Honolulu, Hawaii 96839

Account Number 1980154387

Paia Consulting Services
80 Kahala Parkway
Honolulu, HI 96841

Period of: November 30 to
December 31, 2017

Prior Balance	Total Deposits	Total Withdrawals	Ending Balance
$8,541.93	$6,625.35	$7,944.97	$7,222.31

Checks and Other Debits			Deposits and Other Credits		Daily Balance	
Date	Number	Amount	Date	Amount	Date	Amount
12/01	102	50.00	12/01	1,500.00	12/01	10,241.93
12/02	107	87.14	12/01	250.00	12/02	10,154.79
12/07	108	401.00	12/08	4,125.35	12/05	5,054.79
12/05	109	3,900.00	12/17	755.50	12/07	4,653.79
12/05	112	1,200.00	12/17	EC (5.50)	12/08	8,779.14
12/10	113	888.00			12/10	7,891.14
12/22	114	44.96			12/14	7,495.93
12/14	117	395.21			12/17	8,245.93
12/23		SC 7.50			12/22	8,200.97
12/30	118	141.84			12/23	8,193.47
12/29	119	125.95			12/29	8,067.52
12/30	2273	118.37			12/30	7,807.31
12/31	120	585.00			12/31	7,222.31

Symbols: **CM** Credit Memo   **DM** Debit Memo   **SC** Service Charge   **ATM** Automatic Teller
NSF Not Sufficient Funds   **EC** Error Correction   **INT** Interest Earned   **OD** Overdraft

continued ▶

Another Reconciliation Example, *continued*

Other Information

- The Cash ledger account shows an ending balance at December 31 of $6,945.70.
- The December cash receipts journal shows the following deposits: 12/08, $4,125.35; 12/17, $755.50; 12/29, $1,375. Total: $6,255.85.
- The December cash payments journal (some columns deleted) is shown below:

Check No.	Account Name		Cash
112	Rent Expense	....	1,200.00
113	Travel Expense	....	838.33
114	Supplies	....	44.96
115	Equipment	....	395.44
116	Prepaid Insurance	....	752.00
117	Accounts Payable	....	395.21
118	Utility Expense	....	141.84
119	Accounts Payable	....	125.95
120	Advertising Expense	....	585.00
121	Telephone Expense	....	218.40
	Total	....	4,697.13

Here is the unfinished bank reconciliation:

Paia Consulting Services
Bank Reconciliation
December 31, 2017

Balance Per Bank, December 31		$7,222.31
Add: Deposit in transit, December 29...............................		1,375.00
		8,597.31
Less:		
Outstanding Checks #115.......................................	$395.44	
# 116...	752.00	
# 121...	218.40	1,365.84
Adjusted Cash Balance Per Bank, December 31		**$7,231.47**
Balance Per Books, December 31		$6,945.70
Less:		
Bank service charge		7.50
Adjusted Cash Balance Per Books, December 31		**$6,938.20**

?

Another Reconciliation Example, *continued*

Additional Information

A closer review of the records and reconciliation steps highlights more facts:

- The company failed to record a $250 November 30 sales revenue deposit that is on the December bank statement.
- An examination of returned checks revealed that on December 30, a Peters Company check was incorrectly charged to the Paia account by the bank.
- By comparing returned checks to the cash payments journal, two book recording errors were discovered for checks #108 (outstanding from the November reconciliation) and #113 (current month travel expense check).
- There was a bank debit for a deposit error correction of $5.50. The deposit had come from an accounts receivable collection from Janet Smith.
- Finally, check #111, still outstanding from November, was omitted from the current period reconciliation.

continued

Another Reconciliation Example, *continued*

Reconcile the Increase Items   First, follow the procedure for checking the beginning balances. After you have followed the procedure for checking the beginning balances, you are ready to use the procedure table below to identify the differences in increase items.

Step	Action	Example
1	Enter the total increases (deposits and credits) shown on the bank statement.	$6,625.35
2	Subtract: Deposits in transit on the previous bank reconciliation.	(1,500.00)
3	Add: Deposits in transit for this bank reconciliation.	1,375.00
4	Current period increases per bank: Prior deposits are removed and all current deposits are included, so increases per bank should match current period increases per books.	6,500.35
5	Enter total current period increases per books.	6,255.85
6	Compare bank increases in Step 4 to the book increases in Step 5. If the balances are the same, there is no difference to identify. If there is a difference, go to the next step.	244.50 difference
7	Look for differences that affect total increases for the *bank*. Add or subtract these differences to/from the total bank increases in Step 4. ■ No difference items that affect bank increases.	$6,500.35 –0– $6,500.35
8	Look for differences that affect the increases for the *books*. Add or subtract differences to/from the total book increases in Step 5. ■ Unrecorded deposit. (Book increases should be greater.) ■ Overstated deposit. (Book increases should be less.)	$6,255.85 250.00 (5.50) $6,500.35
	When Steps 7 and 8 show the same totals, you have identified all the increase differences. You can enter these as bank or book balance adjustments on the bank reconciliation (see next table).	

Another Reconciliation Example, *continued*

Use the Differences

The differences in the increase items that you identified in Steps 7 and 8 are adjustments that you use on the bank reconciliation. Use the following procedure:

Step	Action	Example
1	Bank balance adjustments (Step 7): ■ Add positive differences to the bank balance. ■ Subtract negative differences from the bank balance.	none none
2	Book balance adjustments (Step 8): ■ Add positive differences to the book balance. ■ Subtract negative differences from the book balance.	$250.00 (5.50)

(The completed reconciliation is on page 650. $250 has been added to the book balance for the unrecorded November 30 deposit. $5.50 has been subtracted from the book balance for the overstated December 17 deposit.)

continued

Another Reconciliation Example, *continued*

Reconcile the Decrease Items   Use the procedure table below to identify the differences in decrease items.

Step	Action	Example
1	Enter the total decreases (checks and debits) shown on the bank statement.	$7,944.97
2	Subtract: Outstanding checks on the previous bank reconciliation.	(4,654.95)
3	Add: Outstanding checks from the current period cash payments.	1,365.84
4	Current period decreases per bank: Prior outstanding checks are removed and all the current period outstanding checks are included, so decreases per bank should match current period decreases per books.	4,655.86
5	Enter total current period decreases per books.	4,697.13
6	Compare bank decreases in Step 4 to the book decreases in Step 5. If the balances are the same, there is no difference to identify. If there is a difference, go to the next step.	(41.27) difference
7	Look for differences that affect total decreases for the *bank*. Add or subtract these differences to/from the total decreases per bank in Step 4. ■ Omitted November check #111 that is still outstanding. (Bank decreases should be greater in the reconciliation.) ■ Bank error: Peters Company check. (Bank decreases should be less.)	$4,655.86 196.81 (118.37) $4,734.30
8	Look for differences that affect the total decreases for the *books*. Add or subtract differences to/from the total decreases per books in Step 5. ■ Service charges. (Book decreases should be greater.) ■ Book error check #108. (Book decreases should be less.) ■ Book error check #113. (Book decreases should be greater.)	$4,697.13 7.50 (20.00) 49.67 $4,734.30
	When Steps 7 and 8 show the same totals, you have identified all the decrease differences. You can enter these as bank or book balance adjustments on the bank reconciliation (see next table).	

Another Reconciliation Example, *continued*

Use the Differences

The differences in the decrease items that you identified in Steps 7 and 8 are adjustments that you use on the bank reconciliation. Use the following procedure:

Step	Action	Example
1	Bank balance adjustments (Step 7): ■ Multiply each item by *negative* one. This is necessary because decrease items are subtractions on the bank reconciliation. • 196.81 × (1) = • (118.37) × (1) =	 (196.81) 118.37
2	■ Add positive results to the bank balance. ■ Subtract negative results from the bank balance	118.37 (196.81)
3	Book balance adjustments (Step 8): ■ Multiply each item by negative one. This is necessary because decrease items are subtractions on the bank reconciliation. • 7.50 × (1) = • (20.00) × (1) = • 49.67 × (1) =	 (7.50) 20.00 (49.67)
4	■ Add positive results to the book balance. ■ Subtract negative results from the book balance.	$20.00 (7.50) (49.67)

Note: Total adjustments to the bank balance are (78.44), and total adjustments to the book balance are (37.17). The difference is the same (41.27) from Step 6.

The completed bank reconciliation is on the next page.

continued ▶

LG A16-2, *continued*

Information: During the period, the bank received an EFT deposit from a company in Hong Kong in the amount of $7,500.00 in payment of an outstanding account receivable. Bank fees for the period were $27.00. Interest earned on the account was $2.57, and an NSF check was returned with the statement in the amount of $650.28. These items were unrecorded by Lomas. The accountant noted that a May 12 deposit for a sales collection in the amount of $4,450.00 was recorded by Lomas Company as $6,900.80. The accountant identified two other errors: (1) In the checkbook, check #1301 was overstated by $3,324.00, and (2) on the bank statement a check from Landreau company was charged against the Lomas Company account in the amount of $349.08.

Analysis of Increase Items	
Item	Amount
Total increases per bank	$15,982.02
Less: Prior deposits in transit	4,950.00
Add: Current deposits in transit	7,005.25
Total current increases per bank	18,037.27
Total current increases per books	12,985.50
Difference (bank exceeds books)	5,051.77

Analysis of Decrease Items	
Item	Amount
Total decreases per bank	$15,356.18
Less: Prior outstanding checks	9,398.65
Add: Current outstanding checks	7,725.33
Total current decreases per bank	13,682.86
Total current decreases per books	15,980.50
Difference (bank less than books)	(2,297.64)

PRACTICE

LG A16-3. Bank reconciliation, adjustments analysis, journal entries.

Instructions: Using the information you see below for Merced Company for the month of June: (1) Prepare the June 30 bank reconciliation, (2) prepare an analysis of the increase items and of the decrease items for the reconciliation, and (3) prepare the adjusting journal entries after you have finished the bank reconciliation.

Cash Receipts Journal (some columns deleted)		
Date		**Cash (Dr.)**
June		
1	. . . . . .	1,354.13
5	. . . . . .	750.00
11	. . . . . .	2,185.50
12	. . . . . .	552.00
19	. . . . . .	5,825.00
23	. . . . . .	2,461.98
29	. . . . . .	1,005.44
Total	. . . . . .	14,134.05

Cash Payments Journal (some columns deleted)			
Check #	**Account**		**Cash (Cr.)**
449	Utilities Expense		199.22
450	Prepaid Rent	. . . . . .	3,850.00
451	Supplies	. . . . . .	876.65
452	Training Expense	. . . . . .	1,424.92
453	Accounts Payable	. . . . . .	700.50
454	Misc. Expense	. . . . . .	47.99
455	Taxes Payable	. . . . . .	646.11
456	Travel Expense	. . . . . .	122.78
457	Utilities Expense	. . . . . .	391.45
458	Equipment	. . . . . .	4,755.00
459	Wages Expense	. . . . . .	1,031.24
460	Ad. Expense	. . . . . .	541.17
Total		. . . . . .	14,587.03

LG A16-3, *continued*

Merced Company Bank Statement for Month of June 2017			
Beginning Balance	Total Deposits	Total Withdrawals	Ending Balance
$11,404.75	$14,128.61	$9,397.77	$16,135.59

Checks and Other Debits			Deposits and Other Credits	
Date	Number	Amount	Date	Amount
6/01	436	301.88	6/01	EFT 1,000.00
6/01		NSF 204.37	6/01	1,354.13
6/01	448	87.50	6/05	750.00
6/03	449	199.22	6/12	2,737.50
6/04	1201	688.50	6/19	5,825.00
6/07	450	3,850.00	6/23	2,461.98
6/12	451	876.65		
6/15	452	1,424.92		
6/21	453	700.50		
6/22	456	122.78		
6/23	457	931.45		
6/30		SC 10.00		

Additional Information:

a. Checks still outstanding from May: #431 for $705.33; #444 for $181.00
b. The bank erroneously charged the Merced Company account for a check from another company. There were no other bank errors.
c. The bank collected a note receivable for Merced Company in the amount of $900 plus $100 interest that had not been recorded by Merced Company.
d. The Cash ledger account shows a June 30 unadjusted balance of $9,676.06.
e. On May 31, there were no deposits in transit, and the outstanding checks were $1,275.71.

LG A16-4. Bank reconciliation, adjustments analysis, journal entries. By now, you have had enough practice to try this: (1) Return to the information about the December cash activity for the Paia Company in this learning goal. Using the information, but *not looking at the solution in the learning goal,* prepare the complete December 31 bank reconciliation for the Paia Company. As part of the exercise, also prepare the adjustments analysis of the reconciling increase and decrease items. (2) Prepare the adjusting journal entries.

LEARNING GOAL 17

Record, Report, and Control Receivables

In this Learning Goal, you will find:

Receivables

Valuation of Accounts Receivable

Disposing of Receivables

Notes Receivable

Financial Statement Presentation of Accounts and Notes Receivable

GAAP Weakness

Receivables

Overview of Receivables

Accounts Receivable

An *account receivable* is the legal right to collect money from customers as the result of sales of services or merchandise not already paid for. A sales invoice amount, less discounts taken and less returns and allowances, determines the amount of an account receivable. Accounts receivable are generally due in 30 to 90 days and do not charge interest during this period, although the time period varies by industry.

- Accounts receivable usually arise from services and products sold to customers.
- Accounts receivable are usually classified as current assets on the balance sheet.
- Many retail businesses give installment credit to customers, and this results in *installment receivables*, which are accounts receivable that are paid off in monthly payments. Installment receivables frequently charge interest. (Installment receivables due in more than one year are classified as long-term assets.)

Notes Receivable

A *note receivable* is the legal right to collect money as the result of a borrower or customer signing a promissory note. A *promissory note* is a written unconditional promise to pay a sum of money, called the *principal*, plus interest, either on demand or at a certain date. The due date of a note is called the *maturity date*. The borrower or customer who is obligated to make the payment is called the *maker*, and the recipient of the money is called the *payee*. A note receivable results from making a sale to a customer or from loaning money. On the balance sheet, if a note receivable is due within a year, it is a current asset. Otherwise, it is a long-term asset.

Interest Receivable

Interest receivable is the payee's legal right to collect any unpaid interest that has accrued from a note receivable. This current asset is a separate account.

Trade and Non-Trade Receivables

A *trade receivable* is any receivable that is owed by a customer. These are usually accounts and notes receivable. Non-trade receivables can be of many types: accounts and notes receivable due from employees, tax refunds due, deposits, interest and dividends receivable, insurance claims, and others.

Valuation of Accounts Receivable

Overview of the Process

Introduction

As we have discussed in previous learning goals, an asset is initially recorded at its original transaction value. Later, it may become necessary to revalue an asset. Up to this point in our study of accounting, we have assumed that all accounts receivable are collectible. In practice, however, this assumption is not realistic because some customers do not pay what they owe. This overview summarizes the process for recognizing the potential loss of value in accounts receivable. Following the overview, we look at the specific procedures in more detail.

GAAP Rule

GAAP requires that accounts receivable be shown on the balance sheet at the estimated cash collectible value—called *net realizable value*. Net realizable value is the amount that is likely to actually be collected.

Effect of the Rule

The effect of the GAAP rule is that the accounts receivable balance must be reduced by the amount of the receivables that are estimated to be uncollectible. The reduction is done by estimating the uncollectible amount and then making an adjusting entry. The estimate and the adjusting entry are done at the end of each accounting period, before the financial statements are prepared. The adjustment is a valuation-type adjustment that reduces the value of the asset. (We will study the details of how to do the estimate a little later.)

Example

Suppose that on December 31 year end, the ledger balance of Accounts Receivable is what you see in the T account below:

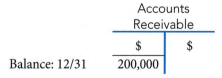

	Accounts Receivable	
	$	$
Balance: 12/31	200,000	

Based on past experience, we estimate that 2.5% ($5,000) of the accounts receivable balance will become uncollectible. Therefore, we need to reduce the total value of the accounts receivable to a net realizable value of $195,000. We also need to record a debit to Uncollectible Accounts Expense to record the decrease in the stockholders' equity caused by the reduction in the asset.

continued ▶

Overview of the Process, *continued*

The Problem

Our first (incorrect) reaction probably would be to credit Accounts Receivable and debit expense:

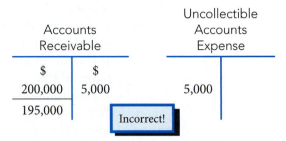

Unfortunately, it is not possible to credit Accounts Receivable at this point. Why? Because Accounts Receivable is a controlling account. It has subsidiary accounts receivable for each customer, and the total of these subsidiary accounts must equal the balance of the controlling account. The problem is that we do not yet know which particular customer subsidiary account will become uncollectible. The estimate is only for a total, based on past experience.

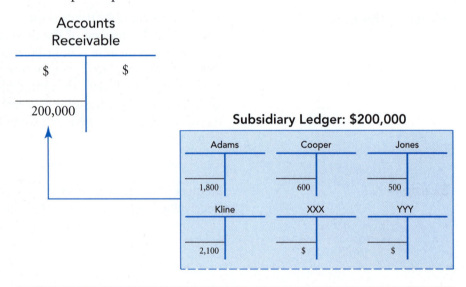

The Solution

Instead of recording the credit directly into Accounts Receivable, we create an account that acts as an offset to Accounts Receivable. This is a contra account called *Allowance for Uncollectible Accounts*. We then record our credit entry into this account. Think of this allowance account as a temporary "holding tank" for the total of unidentified bad receivables.

continued ▶

Overview of the Process, *continued*

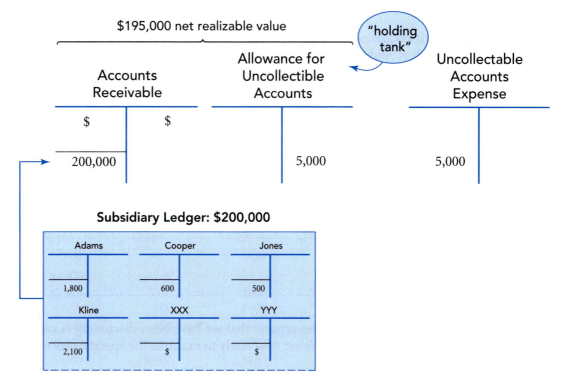

When we can identify a particular receivable as uncollectible, we simply remove the bad amount from the holding tank (debit) and use that same amount as a credit to Accounts Receivable. For example, if on March 8, we determine that the Jones receivable for $500 has become uncollectible, we can now do this:

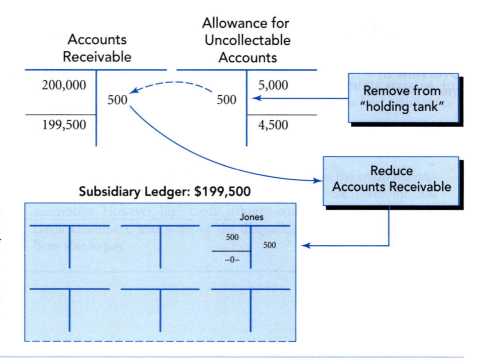

Result: the Accounts Receivable controlling account has been reduced by $500, and the total of all the subsidiary accounts (in their separate ledger) is reduced by $500 because we know that we can now reduce the Jones account by $500.

continued ▶

Aging of Accounts Receivable, *continued*

Journal Entry Example

Assume that this aging schedule is prepared at year end. As of December 31, the account balances are shown below, before the adjustment. The required December 31 ending balance of $2,872 in the Allowance for Uncollectible Accounts is also shown.

	Accounts Receivable		Allowance for Uncollectible Accounts
12/31 Balance:	32,850		450 (unadjusted balance)
			?
12/31 Required balance:			**2,872**

The amount of the adjusting journal entry will be whatever is necessary to bring the December 31 unadjusted balance in the Allowance for Uncollectible Accounts to the required balance of $2,872. This is a credit entry for the difference between $2,872 and $450, or $2,422.

Adjustment

12/31	Uncollectible Accounts Expense	2,422	
	Allowance for Uncollectible Accounts		2,422

$$A \downarrow = L + \downarrow SE$$
$$2,422 \qquad 2,422$$

Analysis

After journalizing the adjustment, the **net accounts receivable** decreases to $29,978 ($32,850 − $2,872 = $29,978). The balance in the Allowance for Uncollectible Accounts will be the required amount of $2,872, which is the estimate of the actual bad receivables. For Newcastle Company in our example, the receivables portion on the balance sheet would appear as:

Accounts Receivable	$32,850	
Less: Allowance for Uncollectible Accounts	2,872	
Net Realizable Accounts Receivable		$29,978

Debit Balance in Allowance Account

In the prior example, the Allowance for Uncollectible Accounts account had a credit balance of $450 before the adjusting entry was made. Sometimes, as the result of the actual bad receivables exceeding the previous estimate, the allowance account will show a debit balance. For example, if the $450 above had been a debit balance, then the required adjustment (to go from a $450 *debit* balance to a $2,872 *credit* balance) would have been $450 + $2,872 = $3,322.

Aging of Accounts Receivable, *continued*

Debit Balance Example

Here we can see that the Allowance for Uncollectible Accounts has an unadjusted debit balance of $450. The required December 31 ending balance of $2,872 in the Allowance for Uncollectible Accounts is also shown.

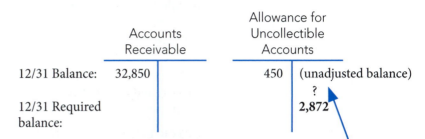

	Accounts Receivable	Allowance for Uncollectible Accounts
12/31 Balance:	32,850	450 (unadjusted balance)
		?
12/31 Required balance:		**2,872**

The amount of the adjusting journal entry will be whatever is necessary to bring the December 31 unadjusted balance in the Allowance for Uncollectible Accounts to the required balance of $2,872. This is a credit entry for the sum of $2,872 plus $450, or $3,322.

Adjustment

12/31	Uncollectible Accounts Expense	3,322	
	Allowance for Uncollectible Accounts		3,322

$$A \downarrow = L + \downarrow SE$$
$$3,322 \quad\quad 3,322$$

Review

Notice that the $2,872 balance in the allowance accounts acts as offset against the $32,850 total balance in Accounts Receivable. We are not able to credit Accounts Receivable directly because at this point the $2,872 estimate is just a total. We do not know which particular Accounts Receivable customer accounts will become uncollectible. This prevents us from crediting Accounts Receivable because we would not know which Accounts Receivable subsidiary accounts to credit.

Percentage of Net Sales

Overview of the Procedure

The percentage of net sales method uses a percent of the net credit sales of the current accounting period to estimate the amount of uncollectible accounts expense. The current period estimate is usually based on whatever percentage of the prior periods' credit sales revenue could not be collected. The percentage can be adjusted as business conditions change. To estimate the current uncollectible accounts expense, multiply the percentage times the current period's net credit sales.

continued ▶

Percentage of Net Sales, *continued*

Calculation Example

Suppose that Newcastle Company uses the percentage of net sales approach to estimate uncollectible accounts expense. The current period's net credit sales are $215,000. (Remember that *net sales* means that sales returns and allowances and sales discounts have been subtracted from gross sales.) Based on past experience, the company estimates that 1.5% of these sales will become uncollectible.

This period's net credit sales	$215,000
Estimated % uncollectible	× .015
This period's estimated uncollectible accounts expense	$ 3,225

Note: There is some variation in the application of this method. Some companies use total sales instead of net credit sales. If cash sales remain a relatively constant percentage of total sales, then total sales can be used. However, if cash sales are known, they should be subtracted from total sales because cash sales do not become uncollectible.

Analysis

This method estimates the amount of uncollectible accounts *expense*. It is justified on the basis of best matching of revenue and expense. Because it includes no examination or analysis of the accounts receivable as with an aging schedule, there is no targeted balance in the Allowance for Uncollectible Accounts account. Unlike the aging method, **the final balance in the allowance account is not a specified amount**. (*Note:* The final balance in the allowance is not the objective, but if it continues to grow larger or grow smaller every period, then the percentage of sales estimate can be modified.)

Adjustment

12/31	Uncollectible Accounts Expense	3,225	
	Allowance for Uncollectible Accounts		3,225

$$A \downarrow = L + \downarrow SE$$
$$3,225 \qquad 3,225$$

Accounts

	Uncollectible Accounts Expense		Allowance for Uncollectible Accounts	
12/31 Balance:				450
	3,225			3,225
Adjusted Balance:	3,225			3,675

Writing Off an Account

Procedure

In the period after the adjusting entry has been recorded, some receivables will become uncollectible. *Writing off* means that a company decides to record an asset as worthless. The procedure for Accounts Receivable is to debit Allowance for Uncollectible Accounts and credit Accounts Receivable. **No expense is recorded**—an expense was already recorded *in the adjusting entry* in the previous period.

The Holding Tank

Think of the allowance account as a temporary holding tank for an amount of potentially bad receivables. When a particular customer's bad receivable is identified, the write-off removes it from the allowance holding tank and then directly reduces the Accounts Receivable account (and the subsidiary account of that customer). The write-off is an identification procedure, nothing more.

Example

Suppose that on February 11 in the next period, the $245 account receivable for P. Jones is determined to be uncollectible. Here is the journal entry:

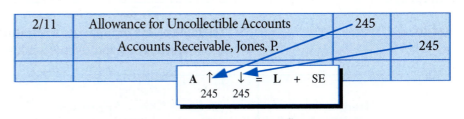

| 2/11 | Allowance for Uncollectible Accounts | 245 | |
| | Accounts Receivable, Jones, P. | | 245 |

A ↑ ↓ = L + SE
245 245

No Change in Net Accounts Receivable

The T accounts below illustrate what you see in the accounting equation above. There is no change in total assets because there is *no change in the net accounts receivable*. The asset and the contra asset accounts both decrease by $245.

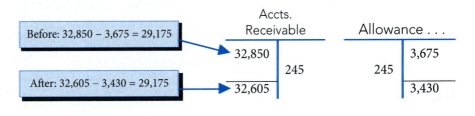

Before: 32,850 − 3,675 = 29,175

After: 32,605 − 3,430 = 29,175

Accts. Receivable		Allowance . . .	
32,850			3,675
	245	245	
32,605			3,430

continued ▶

Writing Off an Account, *continued*

| *Recovery of an Account Written Off* | Occasionally an account will be written off and later determined, in part or in whole, to be collectible. The procedure is: (1) reverse the write-off for the amount collectible and (2) record the cash collection in the usual way. |

Example

Suppose that on May 5, P. Jones from the previous example decides to pay $100 of the written-off receivable. The journal entries to record this are:

5/5	Accounts Receivable, Jones, P.	100	
	Allowance for Uncollectible Accounts		100

	Cash	100	
	Accounts Receivable, Jones, P.		100

Summary

Table

The table below summarizes the features and procedures of aging (percentage of receivables) and the percentage of sales methods.

Item	Aging (Balance Sheet Approach)	Percentage of Sales (Income Statement Approach)
What is being estimated?	The uncollectible amount (value) of the accounts receivable	The uncollectible accounts expense
Where does this estimate appear in the accounts or financial statements?	The adjusted balance of the Allowance for Uncollectible Accounts account	The adjusted balance of the Uncollectible Accounts Expense account
What is the estimate based on?	A % of Accounts Receivable by age category	A % of net credit sales
Does the allowance account have a specified balance?	Yes—the amount of the receivables estimated to be uncollectible	No
How does the unadjusted allowance account balance affect the journal entry?	The unadjusted allowance account balance is added if a debit balance or subtracted if a credit balance.	Allowance balance does not affect the journal entry. Simply record the estimated amount.
What is the meaning of the debit or credit balance in the allowance account before the adjustment?	This represents the error in the previous estimate: overestimated, credit balance; underestimated, debit balance.	This is the cumulative error of all prior adjustments: overestimated, credit balance; underestimated, debit balance.

Summary, *continued*

Valuation Adjustment

- The adjustment that results from the allowance method, and particularly the aging procedure, is a valuation adjustment. Earlier in this book, we concentrated on adjustments as a means of ensuring proper timing of revenue and expenses and proper account classification. But we also noted that adjusting entries are used for the purpose of adjusting asset value.
- If an asset is adjusted for the purpose of a value change, its historical cost is eliminated. The historical cost (original transaction value) no longer applies to that asset. GAAP permits or requires an exception to historical cost in numerous situations. This is your first example.

Check Your Understanding

Write the completed sentences on a separate piece of paper. The answers are below.

There are two acceptable methods used for recording uncollectible receivables. When these methods are used, an adjusting entry (is/is not) · · · · · · · required at the end of an accounting period to record an estimated amount. The first method is the · · · · · · · · method, in which receivables are analyzed by age category, to determine the probable amount of uncollectible receivables. This method (does/does not) · · · · · · · require a specific balance in the allowance account after the adjustment is made. The second method is the · · · · · · · of · · · · · · · · method, which uses an income statement amount in the calculation. This method (does/does not) · · · · · · · require a specific balance in the allowance account after the adjustment is made.

The journal entry to record the adjustment at the end of a period is a debit to · · · · · · · · and credit · · · · · · · ·. This entry (does/does not) · · · · · · · · cause the net amount of accounts receivable to decrease. The journal entry to record the write-off of a particular account receivable is a debit to · · · · · · · · and a credit to · · · · · · · ·. This entry (does/does not) · · · · · · · cause the net amount of accounts receivable to decrease.

Answers

There are two acceptable methods used for recording uncollectible receivables. When these methods are used, an adjusting entry (is/is not) <u>is</u> required at the end of an accounting period to record an estimated amount. The first method is the <u>aging</u> method, in which receivables are analyzed by age category, to determine the probable amount of uncollectible receivables. This method (does/does not) <u>does</u> require a specific balance in the allowance account after the adjustment is made. The second method is the <u>percentage</u> of <u>sales</u> method, which uses an income statement amount in the calculation. This method (does/does not) <u>does not</u> require a specific balance in the allowance account after the adjustment is made.

The journal entry to record the adjustment at the end of a period is a debit to Uncollectible Accounts Expense and credit Allowance for Uncollectible Accounts. This entry (does/does not) <u>does</u> cause the net amount of accounts receivable to decrease. The journal entry to record the write-off of a particular account receivable is a debit to Allowance for Uncollectible Accounts and a credit to Accounts Receivable. This entry (does/does not) <u>does not</u> cause the net amount of accounts receivable to decrease.

Direct Write-Off Method

The Method

The *direct write-off method* is a different and simple method that does not require any estimates or the use of an allowance account. Whenever a receivable is believed to be uncollectible, an entry is made to write off the account by debiting Uncollectible Accounts Expense and crediting Accounts Receivable (and a subsidiary account). Companies that do not require GAAP-approved financial statements often use this method.

Not Acceptable by GAAP

The direct write-off method is not acceptable by GAAP. This is because:

1. Significant time may elapse before management decides that a receivable is actually uncollectible. In the meantime, the balance sheet has been showing the receivables at an amount that overstates the actual collectible value. This is a violation of the GAAP requirement for valuation at *net realizable value.*

2. Due to the passage of time before a bad receivable is eliminated, Uncollectible Accounts Expense is not recorded in the same period as the sales transaction that created the receivable. This means that revenue from a sale is recorded in one period, but the expense of the bad receivable created by the sale is recorded in a later period. This violates the GAAP matching principle.

Income Tax Rules

Although income taxes are not a central topic of this book, you should be aware that for federal income tax purposes, the direct write-off method is *required*, and estimates of bad receivables are not permitted.

Adjustment for Sales Returns and Allowances

When we discussed sales returns and allowances in previous learning goals, we simply recorded the returns and allowances *as they occurred.* This is perfectly acceptable, provided that the amount of sales returns and allowances is relatively stable each period and there are no large questionable sales.

However, when these conditions do not exist, GAAP requires that the amount of sales returns and allowances be *estimated* and recorded as an adjusting entry in the same manner as the adjusting entry for estimated uncollectible accounts. The journal entry looks like this:

Sales Returns and Allowances	$$$	
Allowance for Uncollectible Accounts		$$$

 Should an account receivable be recognized (recorded) even if no bill has been sent to the customer? Yes, this is done by accruing a revenue (Learning Goal 4). If a sale has been made, a right to collect exists.

TIP

Disposing of Receivables

Selling Receivables

Overview

So far in our discussion of receivables, we have seen that one of two things eventually happens to an account receivable: either the receivable is collected or it is written off as uncollectible. However, a third possibility exists for disposing of a receivable. Accounts receivable can be sold.

Why Receivables Are Sold

When a business needs cash and cannot or does not want to obtain the cash by borrowing or by obtaining money from new investors, then the business has no other choice except to sell some of its assets. A type of asset that is frequently selected for sale is accounts receivable. Another reason that receivables are sold is that a business may not want to be involved in the expensive and time-consuming process of collection.

Factoring

A *factor* is a finance company that specializes in buying accounts receivable. The factor charges the seller a fee when the factor buys the receivables. The fee is often quite substantial: 1–5% on the total amount plus interest on any receivables the factor is unable to collect, up to some maximum percentage of the total amount. In addition, the factor may be able to return some or all of the receivables that are uncollectible. When receivables are purchased by a factor, the customers are notified that payments are to be made to the factor, and the factor keeps the payments.

Example

Suppose that on June 3 Bluechip Company sells $50,000 of accounts receivable to Ace Factoring Services. Ace charges a 4% fee. Bluechip would record the following journal entry:

6/3	Cash	48,000	
	Factoring Charges Expense	2,000	
	Accounts Receivable		50,000

Factoring charges are generally recorded as a selling expense on the income statement. If the charges are small, it is acceptable to show them in the Other Expenses and Losses section.

Selling Notes Receivable

Notes receivable can be sold just as Accounts Receivable can be sold. (See the notes receivable discussion that follows.) The principle is the same that you see above; that is, the buyer charges a fee or a discount based on the value of the note. However, the value of the note includes both principle and future interest, so the calculation is somewhat more complicated.

Internal Control for Accounts Receivable

Overview

In addition to the accounting issues related to accounts and notes receivable that are discussed above, a second issue is controlling receivables so that the cash flow is not diverted by dishonest employees. Receivables, particularly accounts receivable, are "sensitive" assets from an internal control viewpoint because they are a regular source of cash.

Separation of Duties

The duties that are most closely related to accounts receivable are credit-authorization/billing, mail opening, cash deposits, refunds, and write-offs.

- Whenever duties are related, they should be performed by different people.
- The person with access to accounting records should never be involved in any of the duties listed above.

Credit Authorization

To ensure that a prospective business customer has the ability to pay, many companies do a business credit check. It can be performed by a business that specializes in these services. For internal control purposes, the person who reviews and approves credit should not perform billing, collections, or accounting. If this occurs, several kinds of receivable frauds are possible. These include stealing a customer check and then crediting the account and debiting a fake or old receivable, or reporting a write-off, or continually crediting accounts of the wrong customers, or recording fake discounts or expenses. (The stolen check is then deposited by means of a fake company endorsement stamp.)

Opening Mail

All mail should be opened by two employees with no other related duties, or for a small business, by the owner. To reduce the chance of fraud, one employee opens mail while the other observes and stamps a "for deposit only" endorsement on each check, lists the names and amounts of payments received, and totals the amounts. Copies are sent to the accounting department and to the cashier with the checks. Mailroom duties should be rotated regularly.

Deposits

Checks received in the mail should be deposited only by the cashier or the owner and deposit amounts should exactly conform to the checks received list.

Refunds and Write-Offs

Refunds and write-offs must be approved by the sales manager and billing manager, or owner. All collection efforts should be reviewed before a write-off.

Accounting Activities

Employees performing accounting and bookkeeping duties should never perform the other duties listed above. The accounts receivable subsidiary ledger balances should be regularly reconciled with the balance in the controlling account.

Internal Control for Accounts Receivable, *continued*

Lock Box	A *lock box* is a bank collection service. A seller instructs customers to send payments directly to a bank that collects and records the payments and credits the payments into the seller's bank account. The collections can be for customer checks or electronic transfers from a customer's bank to the seller's bank.

Credit Card Sales

Substituting credit card sales for sales on account has many advantages.

- A credit card sale with a card such as VISA or Master Card (technically called *bank cards*) creates a cash deposit into the seller's bank account shortly after time of sale. This greatly speeds up the cash flow, reduces the *cash cycle gap* (see below), and eliminates any cash handling.
- All other internal control issues associated with managing accounts receivable are eliminated because the seller's bank account is directly credited for each sale.
- The time and the expense of managing an accounts receivable operation, which can be quite substantial, is eliminated. Most banks charge merchants a transaction fee of 2–6% with each credit card transaction. This fee may well be worth eliminating or greatly reducing accounts receivable operations.

Example: Bank Card Journal Entry

A merchant makes a $500 sale to a customer who pays with a bank credit card.

Cash	485	
Credit Card Fees	15	
Sales		500

Credit Card Sales and the Cash Cycle Gap

A business that sells merchandise on account must be particularly vigilant about cash flow. A business must promptly pay its accounts payable. Generally, a business has to make payment within 30–90 days to avoid penalties and within 5–15 days to obtain discounts. However, a business must also wait to receive cash back from merchandise that it has purchased. There are two waiting periods to receive cash back from merchandise:

- The merchant must wait for the merchandise to be sold.
- Then the merchant must wait to collect the account receivable.

Example

Suppose that it takes 50 days to sell the merchandise plus another 45 days to collect the receivable. The merchant pays for the merchandise in 10 days to take advantage of a vendor's discount. This results in a *cash cycle gap* (also called a *financing period*) of 85 days, during which the merchant must have sufficient cash reserves or must obtain a short-term loan. Credit card sales eliminate 45 days of the cash cycle gap because of the immediate collection.

Notes Receivable

Calculating Simple Interest

Overview

Notes receivable usually occur as the result of loaning money, making a sale, or a customer agreeing to sign a note because an account receivable has not been paid. Notes receivable earn interest revenue. The interest can be calculated as either simple interest or compound interest. We use simple interest calculations in our discussion. Compound interest is also an important topic; however, it is an extensive topic that is not necessary at this point in our study.

Simple Interest Formula

Simple interest is interest that is earned only on the principal, not on principal *plus* previously earned interest. The interest is calculated as a percentage rate of the principal. Generally the interest rate is an annual rate, so the time is expressed in years or parts of a year. This is the formula for simple interest:

$$\text{Principal} \times \text{Interest Rate} \times \text{Time}$$

Think of the formula like this:

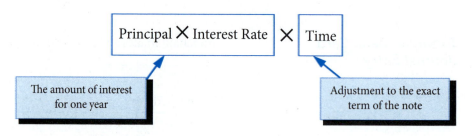

Examples

Example 1: Blinn Company loaned $10,000 to Powers Company for one year. The interest rate on the note is 9%. The total interest is:

$$\$10,000 \times .09 = \$900$$

Example 2: Blinn Company loaned $10,000 to Powers Company for two years. The interest rate on the note is 9%. The total interest is:

$$\$10,000 \times .09 \times 2 = \$1,800$$

Example

Example 3: Sometimes the term of a note is calculated in whole months. Suppose that on August 2, Blinn Company loaned $10,000 to Powers Company for 5 months and required Powers Company to sign a 5-month note with a 9% rate of interest. How much interest will Blinn earn when the note is due?

$$\$10,000 \times .09 \times \left(\frac{5 \text{ months}}{12 \text{ months}}\right) = \$375.00$$

Calculating Simple Interest, *continued*

Example

Example 4: Sometimes the term of a note is expressed in days. If the time factor is days, it is frequently calculated as the number of days elapsed divided by 360. Assuming a 360-day year simplifies calculations (but it also slightly raises the amount of interest). Some notes use 365 days instead.

For the Powers Company note above, assume that the note is a 141-day note due on December 21.

$$\$10{,}000 \times .09 \times \left(\frac{141 \text{ days}}{360 \text{ days}}\right) = \$352.50$$

Calculating Days

To calculate the number of days elapsed or the number of days to maturity, do not count the date the note was issued, but do count the last day or the maturity day. Using the example above, follow the procedure table below:

Step	Procedure	Example
1	Subtract the date the note is issued from the number of days in the month in which the note was issued.	For August: 31 – 2 = 29 days
2	Beginning with the next month, add the number of days elapsed until you reach the total days of the note or the maturity date. The last day is included.	Aug. 29 days Sept. 30 days 59 Oct. 31 days 90 Nov. 30 days 120 Dec. 21 days **141** Total 141 days

For *short-term notes*, GAAP requires valuation at net collectible value, like accounts receivable. If evidence exists as to possible uncollectibility an allowance for uncollectible accounts may be created for notes receivable just as with accounts receivable. Valuing *long-term* notes can be more subjective and require a different process, and is not within the scope of our discussion.

Note Transaction Examples

Example of Typical Note Transactions

On May 14, 2017, Olaf Company accepted a $15,000 note receivable from Norbert Company in settlement of an account receivable. The note bears interest at 10%, calculated in days, and is due on November 10, 2017. Olaf Company has a June 30 year end. The journal entries by Olaf show: (1) recording the note, (2) the year-end interest accrual, and (3) collection of the note, accrued interest, and current period interest revenue.

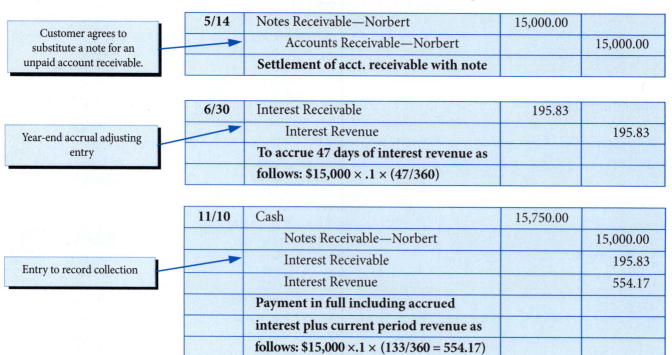

5/14	Notes Receivable—Norbert	15,000.00	
	Accounts Receivable—Norbert		15,000.00
	Settlement of acct. receivable with note		

Customer agrees to substitute a note for an unpaid account receivable.

6/30	Interest Receivable	195.83	
	Interest Revenue		195.83
	To accrue 47 days of interest revenue as		
	follows: $15,000 × .1 × (47/360)		

Year-end accrual adjusting entry

11/10	Cash	15,750.00	
	Notes Receivable—Norbert		15,000.00
	Interest Receivable		195.83
	Interest Revenue		554.17
	Payment in full including accrued		
	interest plus current period revenue as		
	follows: $15,000 ×.1 × (133/360 = 554.17)		

Entry to record collection

Dishonored Note

When a note is not paid as required, it is called a **dishonored note**. If the note above is dishonored on November 10, and there remains a possibility of collection: 1) Debit Accounts Receivable—Norbert, instead of Cash. 2) Continue accruing interest on the principal in future periods, increasing the account receivable. If the note becomes uncollectible, debit Allowance for Uncollectible Accounts and credit the receivable. If uncollectible at time of default, debit a loss and credit the note, then reverse any interest accruals.

Renewed Note

Assume that Norbert could only pay $5,000 at maturity, so Olaf agreed to accept a new 90-day note for the amount still due:

11/10	Notes Receivable (new)—Norbert	10,750.00	
	Cash	5,000.00	
	Notes Receivable (old)—Norbert		15,000.00
	Interest Receivable		195.83
	Interest Revenue		554.17

Financial Statement Presentation of Accounts and Notes Receivable

Examples

Balance Sheet

Accounts receivable and short-term notes receivable (due within one year) are reported in the current assets category of a balance sheet. They are listed after the Short-Term Investments category or, if there are no short-term investments, then after Cash. Here are three typical examples:

Accounts receivable	$50,000	
Less: Allowance for uncollectible accounts	3,000	
Net realizable accounts receivable		47,000
Notes receivable, short-term		100,000

Accounts receivable, net of allowance for uncollectible accounts of $3,000:	47,000
Notes receivable, short-term	100,000

Accounts and short-term notes receivable	$150,000	
Less: Allowance for uncollectible accounts	3,000	
Net realizable accounts and notes receivable		147,000

Long-term notes receivable are reported in a separate asset category as long-term receivables or as part of long-term investments. However, the total of any principal installment payments to be received within one year is reported as part of current receivables. (The treatment is similar for notes payable on the liability side of the balance sheet, in which the current portion of long-term notes are reported as current liabilities.)

Income Statement

- Uncollectible Accounts Expense is an operating expense on the income statement. It is normally shown as part of selling expenses.

- Interest revenue and interest expense are reported in the "Other" section of the income statement and are not operating revenues or expenses.

IFRS and GAAP

The IFRS (International Financial Reporting Standards) and GAAP accounting procedures for receivables are basically the same. There are some differences in receivables valuation procedures.

GAAP Weakness

Comparability and Reliability

Overview

As you studied the procedures acceptable by GAAP, you may have wondered why two procedures are allowed and why the estimated amounts and journal entries were different. Even for the same company, the two procedures result in different adjustment amounts! The specific GAAP rule for accounts receivable is a valuation rule: receivables should be shown at their net collectible value. However, the percent of sales method focuses more on the broad GAAP rule of matching expenses to revenues. The result is that because one adjustment method (aging) focuses on valuation and the other method (percent of sales) focuses more on timing (matching), the results are different.

*Financial Statements
Not Comparable*

One unfortunate result of this situation is that when different companies use different methods, their financial statements are not comparable because net receivables and bad debt expense result from rules that measure different things and give different answers. Investors and other stakeholders are unable to clearly compare financial condition and operating results. The difficulty that results from the application of different methods is a recurring problem with GAAP in various areas. To date the issue remains unresolved.

*Manipulating Financial
Statements*

An even more serious problem is that unethical management can select a method from GAAP choices not for the purpose of accurate reporting, but rather for the purpose of manipulating the financial statements to make them appear more favorable. The problem is made worse by the necessary use of estimates. For example, an unethical manager could change percentages for the purpose of manipulating the amount of uncollectible receivables or the uncollectible accounts expense.

QUICK REVIEW

- Common types of receivables are accounts receivable, installments receivable, notes receivable, and interest receivable.

- Accounts receivable are determined by the invoice price of a sale. Returns and allowances and discounts reduce both net sales and accounts receivable.

- Some accounts receivable will become uncollectible. Accounts receivable (and other receivables) must be shown at their net realizable value. This is done by use of the allowance method, which is required by GAAP.

- The allowance method involves the use of an estimate and a period-end adjusting entry. The allowance method can be applied in two ways:

  - Accounts receivable aging, which estimates actual bad receivables.
  - Percentage of sales, which estimates the uncollectible accounts expense.

- Regardless of which procedure is used to apply the allowance method, the adjusting entry for the allowance method is always: debit to an expense for uncollectible accounts and credit to an allowance for uncollectible accounts.

- The direct write-off method is not acceptable for GAAP accounting.

- Notes receivable require interest revenue to be calculated, recorded, and sometimes allocated between accounting periods (as an accrual adjustment).

- Simple interest is calculated as principle × interest × time, where interest means annual rate and time can be expressed in years, months, or days.

- Internal control for receivables is essential. Key elements of control include separation of duties, credit authorization and billing, opening mail, accounting, cash deposits, and refunds/write-offs. Substituting credit card sales for accounts receivable can eleminate internal control issues and reduce the cash cycle gap.

- The financial statement presentation of receivables requires that each major type of receivable be classified separately as part of current assets or long-term assets. The receivables are shown on the balance sheet at their net amount.

- Uncollectible accounts expense is an operating expense, usually classified as part of selling expense.

VOCABULARY

Account receivable: the right to collect money, usually as the result of a sale to a customer; payment usually within 30 to 60 days (page 656)

Aging schedule: a classification of receivables by age (page 661)

Direct write-off method: a procedure that records uncollectible accounts receivable without the use of an estimate and period-end adjustment (page 668)

Dishonored note: a note that is not paid when due (page 674)

Factor: a company that specializes in buying accounts receivable (page 669)

Installment receivable: an account receivable paid in regular payments (page 656)

Interest receivable: a payee's right to collect unpaid interest (page 656)

Lock box: a bank collection service (page 671)

Maker: the borrower or customer obligated to make payment (page 656)

Maturity date: the due date for payment of a promissory note (page 656)

Net accounts receivable: the balance in Accounts Receivable minus the balance in the Allowance for Uncollectible Accounts (page 662)

Note receivable: the right to collect money resulting from a promissory note (page 656)

Net realizable value: the estimated collectible amount of accounts receivable (page 657)

Payee: the party named on a promissory note who will receive payment (page 656)

Principal: the amount of money owed as stated on a promissory note (page 656)

Promissory note: a written unconditional promise to pay a sum of money (page 656)

Simple interest: interest calculated only on the principal (page 672)

Trade receivable: another name for an account receivable (page 656)

Do You Want More Examples?

Most problems in this book have detailed solutions. To use them as additional examples, do this: 1) Select the type of problem you want 2) Open the solution on your computer or mobile device screen (from the disc or worthyjames.com) 3) Read one item at a time and look at its answer. Take notes if needed. 4) Close the solution and work as much of the problem as you can. 5) Repeat as needed.

PRACTICE   Learning Goal 17

Solutions are in the disk at the back of the book and at: www.worthyjames.com

Learning Goal 17 is about receivables. Use these questions and problems to practice the procedures and principles in this goal.

Multiple Choice
Select the best answer.

1. When using either the aging or percentage of sales procedure, it is necessary to have an allowance account because:
   a. crediting Accounts Receivable might be mistaken for a write-off.
   b. the allowance account ensures proper matching.
   c. it is not possible to credit specific subsidiary accounts at the time of the estimate.
   d. it offsets the debit entry.

2. When using the aging method, the correct interpretation of the balance in the Allowance for Uncollectible Accounts is that the balance:
   a. represents the amount of expense resulting from uncollectible accounts.
   b. represents the estimated dollar amount of uncollectible accounts receivable.
   c. is the amount of accounts receivable that have been written off.
   d. is an offset to Uncollectible Accounts Expense.

3. When a business makes an entry using the direct write-off method, which of the following is true?
   a. The entry includes a credit to Accounts Receivable.
   b. The entry includes a debit to Uncollectible Accounts Expense.
   c. The entry includes a debit to Allowance for Uncollectible Accounts.
   d. Both a and b.

4. Shawnee Company shows a balance in Accounts Receivable of $48,700 and a credit balance in the Allowance for Uncollectible Accounts of $5,500. Current period receivable write-offs are $4,000. What is the net accounts receivable after the write-off?
   a. $48,700
   b. $43,200
   c. $44,700
   d. $39,200

5. If a business failed to make the period-end adjusting entry to record the estimate of uncollectible accounts, which of the following would be true?
   a. Assets would be overstated and expenses would be understated.
   b. Assets would be understated and expenses would be overstated.
   c. Assets would be understated and expenses would be understated.
   d. Assets would be overstated and expenses would be overstated.

6. A business using the allowance method writes off a $500 account receivable. Which is correct?
   a. Net income decreases $500.
   b. There is no effect on net income and no change in net accounts receivable.
   c. Net accounts receivable decreases by $500.
   d. The company records a credit to an allowance account.

7. Yakima Company uses the aging method, which indicates $2,000 of bad receivables. The allowance account currently has a $350 debit balance. Yakima Company should:
   a. credit the allowance account for $2,000.
   b. debit the allowance account for $2,000.
   c. credit the allowance account for $2,350.
   d. debit the allowance account for $2,350.

Solutions are in the disk at the back of the book and at: www.worthyjames.com

8. GAAP requires accounts receivable to be reported on the balance sheet at:
   a. historical cost.
   b. net percentage of sales.
   c. the balance in an allowance account less estimated write-offs.
   d. net realizable value.

9. Spokane Enterprises wrote off an account receivable in the amount of $450. Prior to the write-off, the Accounts Receivable account had a debit balance of $7,000, and the Allowance for Uncollectible Accounts had a credit balance of $1,000. What is the net accounts receivable (net realizable value) after the write-off ?
   a. $6,550
   b. $6,000
   c. $6,450
   d. $7,000

10. When an account receivable is written off using the direct write-off method:
    a. a debit to the Allowance for Uncollectible Accounts is recorded.
    b. a credit to the Allowance for Uncollectible Accounts is recorded.
    c. the Accounts Receivable account is debited.
    d. a debit to Uncollectible Accounts Expense is recorded.

11. Everett Company's aging of accounts receivable shows the following balances and estimated percent uncollectible at December 31:

1–30 days	31–60 days	61–90 days	Over 90 days	Total
$120,000	$45,000	$30,000	$10,000	$205,000
1%	3%	10%	60%	

The credit balance in the Allowance for Uncollectible Accounts at December 31 year end is $900. The balance in the allowance for Allowance for Uncollectible Accounts after the year-end adjusting entry will be:
    a. $11,550
    b. $10,650
    c. $12,450
    d. $900

12. For Everett Company (above), the December 31 adjusting entry will include a:
    a. debit to Uncollectible Accounts expense of $10,650.
    b. credit to Allowance for Uncollectible Accounts of $11,550.
    c. credit to Accounts Receivable of $12,450.
    d. debit to Accounts Receivable of $900.

13. The maturity value of a note is:
    a. the principal times the annual interest rate.
    b. the principal amount of the note.
    c. the principal times the annual interest rate times the number of time periods.
    d. the principal plus unpaid interest.

14. Olympia Corporation owns a $120,000, 9% note receivable dated November 1, 2017 and due on October 31, 2020. Olympia Corporation has a December 31 year end. How much interest should the company accrue at December 31, 2017?
    a. none
    b. $10,800
    c. $1,800
    d. $900

15. Bellevue, Inc. uses the allowance method to record uncollectible accounts receivable. At the beginning of the year on January 1, the Allowance for Uncollectible Accounts had a credit balance of $1,000. During the year the company recorded $3,300 of uncollectible accounts expense. The company also wrote off $3,000 of bad receivables during the year. At December 31, the balance in Accounts Receivable was $62,300. What is the net realizable value of accounts receivable on December 31?
   a. $61,000
   b. $63,600
   c. $62,300
   d. $59,300

16. At year end, a valuation adjusting entry is made for accounts receivable. According to GAAP, this entry should result in the net amount of accounts receivable being shown at what value?
   a. historical cost
   b. the collectible value
   c. the resale value
   d. the replacement cost

17. The expression "bad debts" also means:
   a. uncollectible accounts.
   b. doubtful accounts.
   c. both a and b.
   d. one of the above.

18. The direct write-off method cannot be used because it:
   a. will overstate assets on the balance sheet.
   b. does not accurately apply the matching principle.
   c. both a and b.
   d. none of the above.

Discussion Questions and Brief Exercises

1. The Allowance for Uncollectible Accounts has a credit balance of $2,300. The aging method is used and indicates a $9,100 amount of uncollectible accounts. What is the amount of the adjusting entry?

2. The Allowance for Uncollectible Accounts has a credit balance of $2,300. The percentage of sales method is used and indicates a $9,100 amount of uncollectible accounts expense. What is the amount of the adjusting entry?

3. The Allowance for Uncollectible Accounts has a debit balance of $2,300. The aging method is used and indicates a $9,100 amount of uncollectible accounts. What is the amount of the adjusting entry?

4. The Allowance for Uncollectible Accounts has a debit balance of $2,300. The percentage of sales method is used and indicates a $9,100 amount of uncollectible accounts expense. What is the amount of the adjusting entry?

5. At the start of the period, Accounts Receivable has a balance of $11,500. During the period, credit sales are $44,000 and cash sales are $10,000. Customer payments on account are $39,800. $1,000 of receivables are written off, and the estimated uncollectible accounts expense at the end of the period is 1% of credit sales. What is the balance of Accounts Receivable at the end of the period?

6. Using the same data in question 5, what is the net realizable value of Accounts Receivable at the end of the period if the Allowance for Uncollectible Accounts has a credit balance of $200 before adjustments?

7. Why does a write-off have no effect on the net realizable value of accounts receivable?

8. On May 7, a 6% simple-interest 90-day note in the amount of $4,500 is signed. The 360-day convention is used. What is the maturity value of the note?

9. Using the same data in question 7 above, what is the due date of the note?

10. What is the difference between a note receivable and an account receivable?

11. How is the allowance method different from the direct write-off method?

12. What is the meaning of a debit balance in the Allowance for Uncollectible Accounts? What is the meaning of a credit balance?

13. Does the allowance method require a specific ending balance amount in the allowance account after the adjusting entry for uncollectible accounts is made?

14. What would happen on the financial statements if a company failed to make an adjusting entry for estimated uncollectible accounts?

15. What is the correct way to record sales returns and allowances?

16. One of the WorldCom Corporation frauds consisted of increasing net income by reducing the Allowance for Uncollectible Accounts. How do you think this might have been done? How could it increase net income?

Reinforcement Problems

LG 17-1. Aging procedure calculation and journal entry. Villanova Enterprises uses the aging of accounts receivable procedure to apply the allowance method for uncollectible accounts. As of June 30, the Allowance for Uncollectible Accounts account showed an unadjusted credit balance of $370. All credit terms are 2/10, n/30, and the net credit sales for the month of June are $320,000. The company has prepared an aging schedule that has the totals you see below. For journal paper, you can use the template in the disk at the back of the book.

| | Total | Not Yet Due | Number of Days Past Due | | | |
			1–30	31–60	61–90	Over 90
	$ 47,650	$ 32,000	$ 7,050	$ 3,900	$ 3,150	$ 1,550
Estimated % Uncollectible		1%	4%	10%	30%	60%

Instructions:

a. Calculate the total estimated uncollectible amount as of June 30.
b. Round the above estimate to the nearest $100 and make the adjusting entry as of June 30.

PRACTICE   **Learning Goal 17, continued**

Solutions are in the disk at the back of the book and at: www.worthyjames.com

LG 17-2. Percent of sales procedure calculation and journal entry. In problem LG 17-1, assume that Villanova Company uses the percentage of sales procedure and estimates 1% of net credit sales as uncollectible.

Instructions:

a. Calculate the total estimated uncollectible amount as of June 30.
b. Round the estimate above to the nearest $100, and make the adjusting entry as of June 30.

LG 17-3. Identify effects of various accounts receivable events.

Instructions:

For each of the events below, indicate what the effect would be on total accounts receivable, allowance for uncollectible accounts, net realizable value, and uncollectible accounts expense. Using a separate piece of paper, indicate the effect with "+" for increase, "−" for decrease, and "NE" for no effect.

	Total Accounts Receivable	Allowance for Uncollectible Accounts	Net Realizable Value	Uncollectible Accounts Expense
Using the aging method, 2% of total accounts receivable are estimated to be uncollectible.	(Reminder: Use a separate sheet of paper to complete the table.)			
Using the percent of sales method, uncollectible accounts expense is estimated to be 1.25% of net sales.				
An account receivable is written off.				
An account receivable that was previously written off is now reinstated.				
Using the direct write-off method, an account receivable is written off.				

LG 17-4. Journal entries for different methods and allowance balances.

Instructions: Record the journal entries for each of the following independent situations. For journal paper, use the template in the disk at the back of the book or at worthyjames.com (student info.).

a. The allowance for uncollectible accounts has a $750 credit balance before adjustments. The aging schedule at June 30 year end shows an estimate of total uncollectible accounts of $5,000.
b. The allowance for uncollectible accounts has a $750 debit balance before adjustments. The aging schedule at June 30 year end shows an estimate of total uncollectible accounts of $5,000.
c. The allowance for uncollectible accounts has a $500 credit balance before adjustments. Net credit sales for the year are $90,000, and 2% of these sales are estimated as uncollectible.
d. The allowance for uncollectible accounts has a $500 debit balance before adjustments. Net credit sales for the year are $90,000, and 2% of these sales are estimated as uncollectible.

LG 17-5. Calculate allowance account balances. For each of the independent situations in problem LG 17-4, draw a T account for the Allowance for Uncollectible Accounts. Using the T accounts, show all entries in the T account and determine the ending balance for each situation.

LG 17-6. Journalize and post accounts receivable events. Presented below is the aging schedule of Turlock Company as of year end at December 31, 2017. For journal paper, use the template in the disk at the back of the book or at worthyjames.com (student info.).

Customer Name	Total	Not Yet Due	Number of Days Past Due			
			1–30	31–60	61–90	Over 90
Davis, S.	$15,000	12,000	3,000			
Lipsig, J.	47,000	20,000	10,000	17,000		
Shankar, A.	32,000				5,000	27,000
All others	410,000	288,000	41,000	32,000	39,000	10,000
	504,000	320,000	54,000	49,000	44,000	37,000
Estimated % Uncollectible		2%	4%	12%	25%	50%

At December 31, 2017, the balance in Allowance for Uncollectible Accounts before adjustment is a credit balance of $2,700.

Instructions:

a. Journalize the adjusting entry for uncollectible accounts at December 31, 2017. Draw a T account for the Allowance for Uncollectible Accounts, and show the beginning balance, the posting from the adjusting entry, and the balance after the adjusting entry.
b. On February 15 of 2018, the company decided that $15,000 of the Shankar account was uncollectible. Journalize this event and post to the allowance account.
c. On September 3, Turlock Company received a $10,000 check from Shankar. Journalize this event and post to the allowance account.
d. Assume that for the rest of the year $48,200 of accounts receivable were recorded as uncollectible and that the total estimated uncollectible accounts from the aging schedule is $29,800 as of December 31. Post the $48,200 as one entry in the allowance account. Journalize and post the year-end adjusting entry. Show the December 31, 2018, balance in the allowance account.
e. How would items a through d above be recorded if the company had been using the direct write-off method? Why is the allowance method better?

LG 17-7. Comprehensive problem. Bellarmine Associates prepares quarterly financial statements and an annual report. For the quarterly statements, Bellarmine uses the percent of sales procedure, estimating uncollectible accounts expense at 1% of net credit sales, and at December 31 year end, the company uses the aging procedure. On December 31, 2016, the adjusted trial balance includes the following: Accounts Receivable, $152,000; Allowance for Uncollectible Accounts, $4,700 credit balance. Simple interest is calculated using a 360-day year. The following selected transactions occurred during the year ended December 31, 2017:

Jan. 17   Wrote off Tyler account: $500.
March 11   Sold $7,000 of merchandise to Dinville, who signed a 90-day, 10% note. Cost of the merchandise was $5,000. Bellarmine uses the perpetual inventory system.
March 15   Received a letter from Tyler containing a $250 check and stating his intention to pay the balance in full.
March 31   Recorded uncollectible accounts expense. Credit sales for the quarter were $125,000. Recorded the accrued interest on the Dinville note, rounded to the nearest dollar.
April 20   Wrote off the Burrus account for $1,775 and Chen account for $2,950 as a compound entry.
May 23   Received $250 from Tyler.
June 9   Dinville could not pay and the note is now dishonored. The company believes that the amount due is eventually collectible.
June 30   Recorded uncollectible accounts expense. Credit sales for the quarter were $165,000.
Aug. 2   Wrote off the following accounts as a compound entry: C. Cramer $1,400; J. Seinfeld $850; G. Costanza $920.
Sept. 30   Recorded uncollectible accounts expense. Credit sales for the quarter were $180,000.
Nov. 16   Sold $20,000 of merchandise to Kessler Company, who signed a 60-day 8% note for the full amount. Cost of merchandise was $12,000.
Nov. 18   Received a check in the amount of $150 from Burrus.
Dec. 4   Wrote off the Bennis account: $1,390.
Dec. 31   Credit sales for the quarter were $190,000. An aging schedule indicates that $4,500 of accounts receivable are estimated to be uncollectible. Recorded the accrued interest on Dinville and the Kessler note rounded to the nearest dollar.

Instructions:

a. Except for the quarterly credit sales, record the transactions above in a general journal. Explanations are not required for this problem. Also draw a T account for Allowance for Uncollectible Accounts and post into the account.
b. Assume that accounts receivable collections for the year are $742,000, *not including* the cash recovered from receivables written off. Prepare a proper balance sheet presentation of the accounts and notes receivable as of December 31. (*Suggestion:* Use T accounts to keep a record of all transactions affecting both accounts receivable and notes receivable. For simplicity, you can enter the total accounts receivable collections of $742,000 as a single amount.)

PRACTICE

Learning Goal 17, continued

Solutions are in the disk at the back of the book and at: www.worthyjames.com

LG 17-8. Calculate dates and maturity values.

Maker	Origination Date	Principal	Interest Rate	Term
O'Meara	May 4, 2017	$10,000	10%	2 years
Choi	June 12	50,000	6%	3 months
Cook	September 19	80,000	12%	90 days
Agami	October 28	45,000	8%	90 days
Natenberg	July 2, 2017	20,000	10%	18 months

The interest on all the notes above is simple (non-compound) interest. For notes with terms in days, use a 360-day year. Principal and interest for all notes are due in one payment at the maturity date of each note.

Instructions:

a. Calculate the maturity date of each note.
b. Calculate the maturity value of each note. Show the interest calculation.

LG 17-9. Journalize notes receivable transactions. During the year, Hana Enterprises had the selected transactions that you see below, all of which involved notes receivable. Hana Enterprises uses a 360-day year for its interest calculations.

Instructions: Record the transactions as general journal entries.

March 14   Sold equipment at cost for $40,000 to Kapalua Corporation. The buyer paid $10,000 cash and signed a 3-year note payable to Hana Enterprises. Interest is to be paid each March 14. The note has a 9% interest rate.

April 8   Accepted a $10,000 note from Wailea Company, a customer who was unable to fully pay the balance of an account receivable. The note with interest is due in 90 days and earns interest at 10%.

June 12   Loaned $7,500 to Supplies, Inc. The loan has an 8% interest rate and is due on November 1 with interest.

July 7   Wailea Company notified Hana Enterprises that it could make only a partial payment in the amount of $5,000. Hana Enterprises agreed to accept a new 6-month note for the amount still owing on the previous note. The new note has a 12% interest rate. Interest is payable at maturity.

Aug. 20   Sold equipment at cost for $16,000 to Kahalui Bay Company. The buyer signed a 90-day note at 9% interest. Interest is payable at maturity (when the note is due).

Nov. 1   Supplies, Inc. defaulted on the payment due today. Hana Enterprises anticipated that the amount will ultimately be collectible because Supplies, Inc. continues to operate.

Nov. 18   Kahalui Bay Company paid the amount owing in full.

Dec. 31   Recorded all necessary adjusting entries. (Calculate interest in days and round to the nearest dollar.)

LG 17-10. Prepare Financial Statements. (Periodic adjusting inventory method, no income tax.)

The completed worksheet for Zhang Trading Company is shown below. Of the wages expense, 20% is for marketing and sales activities, and 50% of the supplies are used for advertising. The note receivable is for 5 years, with the principal paid at $500 per month.

Instructions:

a. Prepare a multiple-step income statement showing cost of goods sold detail.
b. Prepare a balance sheet.
c. Identify the item appearing on both statements.

LG 17-10, *continued*

Account Titles	Trial Balance Dr.	Trial Balance Cr.	Adjustments Dr.	Adjustments Cr.	Adjusted Trial Balance Dr.	Adjusted Trial Balance Cr.	Income Statement Dr.	Income Statement Cr.	Balance Sheet Dr.	Balance Sheet Cr.
Zhang Trading Company, Inc.										
Worksheet										
For the Year Ended January 31, 2017										
Cash	98,390				98,390				98,390	
Accounts Receivable	55,750				55,750				55,750	
Less: Allowance for										
Uncollectible Accounts		400		(f) 2,100		2,500				2,500
Merchandise Inventory	47,300		(e) 39,700	(d) 47,300	39,700				39,700	
Supplies	6,450			(b) 700	5,750				5,750	
Prepaid Insurance	2,950			(c) 2,000	950				950	
Notes Receivable	30,000				30,000				30,000	
Office Equipment	15,500				15,500				15,500	
Accumulated Depreciation—										
Office Equipment		10,250		(a) 500		10,750				10,750
Store Equipment	125,300				125,300				125,300	
Accumulated Depreciation—										
Store Equipment		95,600		(a) 5,500		101,100				101,100
Accounts Payable		51,300				51,300				51,300
Unearned Revenue		750				750				750
Common Stock		5,000				5,000				5,000
Retained Earnings		62,900				62,900				62,900
Dividends	18,000				18,000				18,000	
Sales		561,090				561,090		561,090		
Sales Returns and										
Allowances	2,500				2,500		2,500			
Sales Discounts	3,250				3,250		3,250			
Merchandise Purchases	284,800				284,800		284,800			
Purchase Discounts		800				800		800		
Purchase Returns/Allow.		900				900		900		
Freight-out	1,100				1,100		1,100			
Uncollectible Acct. Expense			(f) 2,100		2,100		2,100			
Insurance Expense	2,300		(c) 2,000		4,300		4,300			
Salaries & Wages Expense	75,500				75,500		75,500			
Rent Expense	21,900				21,900		21,900			
Interest Revenue		3,740				3,740		3,740		
Utilities Expense	1,740				1,740		1,740			
Totals	792,730	792,730								
Income Summary			(d) 47,300	(e) 39,700	47,300	39,700	47,300	39,700		
Supplies expense			(b) 700		700		700			
Depreciation expense			(a) 6,000		6,000		6,000			
Totals			97,800	97,800	840,530	840,530	451,190	606,230	389,340	234,300
Net Income							155,040			155,040
Totals							606,230	606,230	389,340	389,340

LG 17-11. Prepare Financial Statements. (Perpetual inventory method, no income tax.) The completed worksheet for Zhang Trading Company is shown below. Of the wages expense, 20% is for marketing and sales activities, and 50% of the supplies are used for advertising. The note receivable is for 5 years, with the principal paid at $500 per month.

Instructions:

a. Prepare a multiple-step income statement.
b. Prepare a balance sheet.

	Trial Balance		Adjustments		Adjusted Trial Balance		Income Statement		Balance Sheet	
Account Titles	Dr.	Cr.	Dr.	Cr.	Dr.	Cr.	Dr.	Cr.	Dr.	Cr.
Cash	98,390				98,390				98,390	
Accounts Receivable	55,750				55,750				55,750	
Less: Allowance for										
Uncollectible Accounts		400		(f) 2,100		2,500				2,500
Merchandise Inventory	39,900			(g) 200	39,700				39,700	
Supplies	6,450			(b) 700	5,750				5,750	
Prepaid Insurance	2,950			(c) 2,000	950				950	
Notes Receivable	30,000				30,000				30,000	
Office Equipment	15,500				15,500				15,500	
Accumulated Depreciation—										
Office Equipment		10,250		(a) 500		10,750				10,750
Store Equipment	125,300				125,300				125,300	
Accumulated Depreciation—										
Store Equipment		95,600		(a) 5,500		101,100				101,100
Accounts Payable		51,300				51,300				51,300
Unearned Revenue		750				750				750
Common Stock		5,000				5,000				5,000
Retained Earnings		62,900				62,900				62,900
Dividends	18,000				18,000				18,000	
Sales		561,090				561,090		561,090		
Sales Returns and										
Allowances	2,500				2,500		2,500			
Sales Discounts	3,250				3,250		3,250			
Cost of Goods Sold	290,500		200		290,700		290,700			
Freight-out	1,100				1,100		1,100			
Uncollectible Acct. Expense			(f) 2,100		2,100		2,100			
Insurance Expense	2,300		(c) 2,000		4,300		4,300			
Salaries & Wages Expense	75,500				75,500		75,500			
Rent Expense	21,900				21,900		21,900			
Interest Revenue		3,740				3,740		3,740		
Utilities Expense	1,740				1,740		1,740			
Totals	791,030	791,030								
Supplies expense			(b) 700		700		700			
Depreciation expense			(a) 6,000		6,000		6,000			
Totals			11,000	11,000	799,130	799,130	409,790	564,830	389,340	234,300
Net Income							155,040			155,040
Totals							564,830	564,830	389,340	389,340

Zhang Trading Company, Inc. — Worksheet — For the Year Ended January 31, 2017

Instructor-Assigned Problems

If you are using this book in a class, these review problems may be assigned by your instructor for homework, group assignments, class work, or other activities. Only your instructor has the solutions.

IA 17-1. Journalize and post accounts receivable events. The aging schedule of Champaign Company as of year end at December 31, 2017 is presented below.

Customer Name	Total	Not Yet Due	Number of Days Past Due			
			1–30	31–60	61–90	Over 90
Bruckner, P.	$27,000	22,000	5,000			
Ichiro, O.	13,800	9,200		4,600		
Pollock, G.	21,000		3,000			18,000
All others	356,200	250,100	44,100	32,000	8,000	22,000
	418,000	281,300	52,100	36,600	8,000	40,000
Estimated % Uncollectible		2%	4%	10%	20%	50%

At December 31, 2017 the balance in Allowance for Uncollectible Accounts before adjustment is a credit balance of $1,500.

Instructions:

a. Make the necessary journal entries that are related to accounts receivable. Enter page number as 25.

b. On March 12 of 2018, the company decided that $18,000 of the Pollock account was uncollectible. Journalize this event and post to the allowance account.

c. On July 9, Champaign Company received a $15,000 check from Pollock. Journalize this event and post to the allowance account.

d. During the remainder of the year, $40,500 of accounts receivable were recorded as uncollectible. The total estimated uncollectible accounts from the aging schedule as of December 31, 2018 is $34,000. Post the $40,500 as one entry in the allowance account. Then journalize and post the year-end adjusting entry. Show the December 31, 2018 balance in the allowance account.

IA 17-2. Journalize accounts receivable transactions; post to ledger account. The June 30 adjusted trial balance of Pomona Company Inc., which reports at a calendar year end, includes the following:

Accounts receivable..$786,500
Allowance for uncollectible accounts (credit balance)...17,200

The company uses 3% of sales as it's uncollectible receivable estimate at the end of each quarter. At year-end, it adjusts the allowance balance to uncollectible accounts as estimated by using the aging method.

Instructions:

a. Make the necessary journal entries that are related to accounts receivable. Page number is 25.

b. Open a ledger account for Allowance for Uncollectible Accounts, Account #112, and post into the account as necessary, maintaining a current account balance.

c. Show how accounts receivable would be reported on the December 31 balance sheet.

IA 17-2, *Continued*

Aug. 9	Wrote off the following accounts in a single compound entry: Ames: $4,200; Ellery Co.: $1,549; Williams: $3,864.
Sept. 30	Recorded uncollectible accounts expense on $390,000 of sales on account.
Nov. 4	Wrote off the following accounts in a single compound entry: Johns Co. : $6,850; Kendrick Corp.: $7,100
Dec. 12	Received check from Ellery Co. and recovered the amount due in full.
Dec. 31	An aging of accounts receivable indicates total estimated uncollectible accounts receivable as $18,500. The balance of accounts receivable at year-end was $724,500.

IA 17-3. **Various Receivables Transactions.** Denton Company prepares quarterly and annual financial statements. For the quarterly periods, Denton uses the percent of sales procedure, estimating uncollectible accounts expense at 1.5% of net credit sales. At December 31 year end, the company uses the aging procedure. On June 30, 2017, the adjusted trial balance included the following: Accounts Receivable, $210,000; Allowance for Uncollectible Accounts, $5,500 credit balance. Simple interest is calculated using a 360-day year. The following selected transactions occurred during the six months ended December 31, 2017:

July 8	Wrote off the following accounts as a compound entry: Frischmann for $1,100 and Tessoni for $2,600.
Aug. 19	Received a letter from Frischmann containing a $500 check and stating his intention to pay the balance in full. Reinstated the account for the full $1,100.
Sept. 30	Recorded uncollectible accounts expense. Credit sales for the quarter were $380,000.
Oct. 5	Sold $12,000 of merchandise to Lozano, who signed a 60-day, 6% note. Cost of the merchandise was $8,000. Denton Company uses the perpetual inventory method.
Oct. 29	Wrote off the Nichols account for $1,256, the Lewis account for $4,224, and the Garcia account for $1,400 as a compound entry.
Nov. 17	Received $600 from Frischmann.
Dec. 4	Lozano could not pay and the note is now dishonored. The company believes that the amount due is eventually collectible.
Dec. 16	Sold $10,000 of merchandise to Li Company, who signed a 90-day, 7% note for the full amount. Cost of the merchandise was $6,500.
Dec. 29	Received payment in full from Lozano, including accrued interest (rounded to the nearest dollar).
Dec. 31	Credit sales for the quarter were $390,000. An aging schedule indicates that $5,800 of accounts receivable are estimated to be uncollectible. Recorded the accrued interest on the Li note rounded to the nearest dollar.

Instructions:

a. Record the transactions above in a general journal. Explanations are not required. Also, draw a T account for Allowance for Uncollectible Accounts and post into the account.

b. Assume that accounts receivable collections for the six months from June 30 are $820,000, including the recorded recoveries of amounts previously written off. Prepare a proper balance sheet presentation of the accounts and notes receivable as of December 31. (*Suggestion:* Use T accounts to keep a record of accounts receivable and notes receivable. For simplicity, you can enter the total accounts receivable collections of $820,000 as a single amount.)

Solutions are in the disk at the back of the book and at: www.worthyjames.com

PRACTICE   Learning Goal 17, continued

IA 17-4 Review: Prepare financial statements. (Perpetual inventory method, no income tax.)
Use the worksheet below to prepare a multiple-step income statement, statement of retained earnings, and a balance sheet. Classify the income statement into selling and general and administrative expense. 10% of wages and benefits and 50% of travel are for sales and marketing purposes. Round to the nearest dollar.

Account Titles	Trial Balance Dr.	Trial Balance Cr.	Adjustments Dr.	Adjustments Cr.	Adjusted Trial Balance Dr.	Adjusted Trial Balance Cr.	Income Statement Dr.	Income Statement Cr.	Balance Sheet Dr.	Balance Sheet Cr.
Cash	176,440				176,440				176,440	
Accounts Receivable	97,205				97,205				97,205	
Allow. for Uncoll. Accts.		2,415		b. 2,445		4,860				4,860
Merchandise inventory	127,100				127,100				127,100	
Interest Receivable	981		c. 1,850		2,831				2,831	
Office Supplies	1,193			d. 475	718				718	
Prepaid Insurance	2,575			e. 750	1,825				1,825	
Long-Term Investments	115,500				115,500				115,500	
Office Equipment	85,000				85,000				85,000	
Accum. Dep'n.—										
Office Equipment		34,000		a. 2,125		36,125				36,125
Accounts Payable		107,404		g. 735		108,139				108,139
Bank Card Payable		4,320				4,320				4,320
Unearned Revenue		15,750	f. 4,650			11,100				11,100
Notes Payable, Long-Term		120,000				120,000				120,000
Common Stock		50,000				50,000				50,000
Retained Earnings		255,358				255,358				255,358
Dividends	45,000				45,000				45,000	
Sales Revenue		386,940		f. 4,650		391,590		391,590		
Sales Returns and Allow.	3,006				3,006		3,006			
Sales Discounts	3,145				3,145		3,145			
Cost of Goods Sold	194,129				194,129		194,129			
Building Lease Expense	45,000				45,000		45,000			
Equip. Lease Expense	2,400				2,400		2,400			
Wages and Benefits	65,323				65,323		65,323			
Advertising Expense	5,700				5,700		5,700			
Website / Internet Expense	2,400				2,400		2,400			
Travel Expense	1,252				1,252		1,252			
Supplies Expense	500		d. 475		975		975			
Insurance Expense			e. 750		750		750			
Utilities Expense	2,338		g. 735		3,073		3,073			
Uncollectible Accts. Exp.			b. 2,445		2,445		2,445			
Depreciation Expense			a. 2,125		2,125		2,125			
Interest Expense			h. 3,600		3,600		3,600			
Interest Payable				h. 3,600		3,600				3,600
Interest Revenue				c. 1,850		1,850		1,850		
Totals	976,187	976,187	16,630	16,630	986,942	986,942	335,323	393,440	651,619	593,502
Net income							58,117			58,117
Totals							393,440	393,440	651,619	651,619

Tucson Sales, Inc.
Work Sheet
For the Three Months Ended September 30, 2017

IA17-5. Comprehensive problem. Saint Cloud Company prepares quarterly financial statements and an annual report. For the quarterly statements, Saint Cloud uses the percent of sales procedure estimating uncollectible account expense at 1.5% of net credit sales and at December 31 year end, the company uses the aging procedure. On December 31, 2016, the adjusted trial balance includes the following: Accounts Receivable, $47,300; Allowance for Uncollectible Accounts, $950 credit balance. Interest is simple and is computed using a 360-day year. The following selected transactions occurred during the year ended December 31, 2017:

Jan. 14	Wrote off Donnelly account: $1,400.
Feb. 9	Received a letter from Donnelly containing a $1,000 check and stating her intention to pay the remainder in full.
March 31	Recorded uncollectible accounts expense. Credit sales for the quarter were $210,000.
April 18	Wrote off Nordquist account $1,400 and Carlson account $2,700 as a compound entry.
May 4	Received $400 from Donnelly.
June 30	Recorded uncollectible accounts expense. Credit sales for the quarter were $225,000.
July 19	Sold $15,000 of merchandise to Johnson Company, who signed a 90-day, 10% note for the full amount. Cost of the merchandise was $10,000. Saint Cloud uses a perpetual inventory system.
Aug. 22	Wrote off the following accounts as a compound entry: Kirk, $1,800; Spock $1,500; McCoy, $2,550.
Sept. 30	Recorded uncollectible accounts expense. Credit sales for the quarter were $230,000. Recorded accrued interest on note receivable rounded to the nearest dollar.
Oct. 17	Received $10,000 from Johnson Company for interest and principal and received a letter asking for a 90-day renewal for the principal still owing. Agreed to renew the note using the same terms.
Nov. 30	Received a check in the amount of $150 from Carlson.
Dec. 8	Wrote off Scott account: $2,900.
Dec. 31	Credit sales for the quarter were $310,000. An aging schedule indicates that $5,100 of accounts receivable are estimated to be uncollectible. Accrued interest on the Johnson note rounded to the nearest dollar.

Instructions:

a. Except for the quarterly credit sales, record the transactions above in a general journal. Explanations are not required for this problem. Also, draw a T account for Allowance for Uncollectible Accounts, and post into the account.

b. Assume that all accounts receivable collections for the year are $915,500, which includes those recoveries of amounts previously written off. Prepare a proper balance sheet presentation of the accounts and notes receivable as of December 31. (*Suggestion:* Use T accounts to keep a record of all transactions affecting both accounts receivable and notes receivable. For simplicity, you can enter the total accounts receivable collections of $915,500 as a single amount.)

PRACTICE   **Learning Goal 17, continued**

INTERNET EXERCISES

Use the SEC website—find and identify types of violations. Go to the Securities and Exchange Commission (SEC) homepage at www.sec.gov. Under the section titled "Divisions," click on the link for "Enforcement" and then in the search box type "AAER" (Accounting and Auditing Enforcement Release). (Use bookmark/favorites to save the location in an "Accounting References" folder.)

Instructions:

a. Scroll downward for the preceding 12 months and count the number of AAER links that represent actions by the SEC. How many do you count for only the past year? Notice that you are on a page for only "selected" items. What indication does this give you about the need for caution as an investor?

b. Do the following for the past 6 months: starting with the most recent AAER link, click each link. Look for documents that show "Other Release No. LR–." These documents ("Litigation Releases") represent lawsuits initiated by the SEC. Read the first few paragraphs of each litigation release to determine the nature of the violation (the "complaint" by the SEC). Set up a table like the one below:

AAER#/Company	Revenue	Expense	Other

Identify the type of violation as revenue, expense, or other by writing a brief description in the appropriate column.

c. Looking at your list, what are the most common categories or types of accounting fraud you encountered? In these text volumes, we have repeatedly discussed the importance of correct event analysis, consisting of the elements of classification, valuation, and timing. For the first 10 items, identify the failures in correctly applying the elements of event analysis that were connected with each fraud. How do you think the financial statements would be different if the event analysis had been proper?

d. The items you identified in items a, b, and c above are only a small sample and represent only selected SEC actions against fraudulent activities or extreme earnings management. They do not include other federal actions or state attorneys general lawsuits or other actions or sanctions. They also do not involve many lesser earnings management or ethical issues. Has this exercise changed your awareness of the amount of financial reporting issues? If so, in what way?

e. What do you think was the cause of each violation? For each violation that you identified, indicate the ethical issues that led to the violation.

Your Questions?

It is *very* important to be aware of what you need to understand better. What do you need to understand better about this learning goal? On a separate piece of paper, write the questions that you want to discuss with your classmates, instructor, or supervisor. Try to be very specific about what is bothering you, such as explanations that you do not fully understand.

<table>
<tr><td>LEARNING GOAL 18</td><td># Record, Report, and Control Merchandise Inventory</td></tr>
</table>

In this Learning Goal, you will find:

Merchandise Inventory

Cost of Inventory: Overview of the Issues

Introduction

In this learning goal we look more closely at how the cost of goods sold is calculated. At the same time, how cost of goods sold is calculated affects the cost of the remaining inventory.

The Two Factors

Two factors determine the cost of goods sold:

- When cost of goods sold is calculated
- Which costs are assigned to cost of goods sold

When It Is Calculated

As we saw in the previous learning goals, cost of goods sold can either be calculated at the end of a period for all the sales in that period, or cost of goods sold can be calculated continuously with each individual sale as it happens. Calculating cost of goods sold at the end of a period is called the *periodic system*. Calculating cost of goods sold with each sale is called the *perpetual system*. You can review these methods in the prior learning goals.

Which Costs Are Assigned to Cost of Goods Sold (Cost Flow)

After a business decides whether to use either the periodic or perpetual method, it then has to decide how the inventory cost will be assigned to cost of goods sold. The cost of the merchandise inventory available to sell is recorded by a business as it purchases the merchandise inventory. At first, most students assume that the cost of this merchandise becomes cost of goods sold in the same order that the merchandise is purchased. This is quite logical, and many businesses do use this method, called *first-in, first-out*. However, GAAP also permits other methods for assigning the cost of the merchandise into cost of goods sold.

The different cost assignment methods that we will study are called:

- FIFO (first-in, first-out)
- LIFO (last-in, first-out)
- Average cost
- Specific identification

These methods generally result in different costs being assigned to cost of goods sold.

continued ▶

Cost of Inventory: Overview of the Issues, *continued*

Unsold Inventory Is Affected

The decision as to which cost assignment method should be used affects more than just cost of goods sold. The cost of the ending inventory is also affected.

For example, suppose that the cost of the goods (merchandise) available for sale is $10,000. If $7,000 of this cost is assigned as the cost of the goods sold, then $3,000 is left as the cost of the ending inventory. On the other hand, if a different method is used and $6,000 of the merchandise cost is assigned as the cost of the goods that are sold, that will leave $4,000 for ending inventory.

Remember that the method of cost assignment affects both cost of goods sold on the income statement and the ending inventory on the balance sheet.

Coming Up

In this learning goal, we discuss inventory cost assignment for both the periodic and perpetual methods. After that, we discuss a special period-end inventory valuation method required by GAAP. We finish by discussing the effects of errors, a method to estimate ending inventory, and some weaknesses in what GAAP allows.

Assigning Costs Using the Periodic System

Overview

The Objective

Do two things:

- Determine the cost of ending inventory.
- Determine the cost of goods sold.

Overview, *continued*

Periodic System Procedure

The periodic inventory method calculates ending inventory and cost of goods sold only at the end of a period, when the inventory is counted.

Only two possible results can happen to the total cost of goods available for sale: Some of the cost goes to cost of goods sold and the remainder is assigned to ending inventory. For example, in the June data table below, the 300 units' cost of goods available for sale is $4,680 and the ending inventory is 100 units. Therefore 200 units were sold during the period. There are two possible approaches that we could use to calculate cost of goods sold and ending inventory cost:

- First assign part of the $4,680 to the 200 units sold to get cost of goods sold. Then subtract this cost from the $4,680 available to get ending inventory cost. Or:
- First assign part of the $4,680 to the 100 units of ending inventory. Then subtract this cost from the $4,680 available to get cost of goods sold.

For the periodic system, both approaches give the same answers, but the second way is faster and easier. The examples that follow use this method.

Inventory Data for the Methods Shown

Data Table

The table below shows the inventory data that is used in the examples that follow. Notice that the unit cost of the items has been changing.

| Explanation | Date | Purchases | | Total Cost |
		Units	Unit Cost	
Beginning bal.	June 1	40	$10	$ 400
Purchase	June 8	50	12	600
Purchase	June 15	130	16	2,080
Purchase	June 27	80	20	1,600
Total available		300		$4,680
Ending inventory by physical count, June 30		100		

Periodic First-In, First-Out (FIFO) Method

Method Description

FIFO, *first-in, first-out*, is a popular method for assigning costs. This method applies the matching principle by assigning the oldest merchandise costs as the first costs that flow out to cost of goods sold. Because businesses usually sell the oldest merchandise first to prevent it from deteriorating or becoming obsolete, the flow of costs allocated by FIFO to cost of goods sold generally approximates the actual physical flow of merchandise as it is sold.

As a result, the remaining costs for *ending inventory* will be *the most recent* costs. Think of the *ending inventory* costs as *LIST* (Last-In, Still-There).

Example

Because the oldest costs are assumed to flow into cost of goods sold (200 units), the *most recent costs* are assigned to the 100 units of *ending inventory*. Refer to the data on page 697.

Step	Action	Example
1	Determine cost of ending inventory.	80 units × $20 = $1,600 20 units × $16 = 320 100 units $1,920
2	Determine cost of goods sold.	$4,680 − $1,920 = $2,760

Analysis

Cost is assigned to ending inventory by working back from the most recent cost layer. To assign 100 units' worth of cost, we use up all 80 units of cost in the June 27 layer and then need 20 units' more worth of cost from the next layer, which is June 15.

You can confirm the cost of goods sold by using the alternate approach of assigning costs to the 200 units *sold* in FIFO sequence and then totaling the costs: 40 units @ $10 plus 50 units @ $12 plus 110 units @ $16 = $2,760.

Periodic Last-In, First-Out (LIFO) Method

Method Description

The LIFO method, **last-in, first out**, assigns the costs of the most recent purchases to the first items sold. In other words, the most recent costs are assigned to cost of goods sold first. The remaining costs assigned to *ending inventory* will be *oldest* costs. Think of the *ending inventory* costs as FIST (First-In, Still-There). Note that this method does not follow the actual physical flow of merchandise.

Example

The most recent costs are assumed to flow into cost of goods sold (200 units), so *the oldest costs* are assigned to the 100 units of *ending inventory*.

Step	Action	Example
1	Determine cost of ending inventory.	40 units × $10 = $ 400 50 units × $12 = 600 10 units × $16 = 160 100 units $1,160
2	Determine cost of goods sold.	$4,680 − $1,160 = $3,520

Analysis

Cost is assigned to ending inventory by working up from the oldest cost layers. To assign 100 units' worth of cost, we used up all 40 units of cost in the beginning inventory. Then we used up the 50 units' worth of cost from the June 8 layer. Finally, we needed 10 more units of cost, which we took from the June 15 layer.

You can confirm the cost of goods sold by using the alternate approach of assigning costs to the 200 units *sold* in LIFO sequence and then totaling the costs: 80 units @ $20 plus 120 units @ $16 = $1,600 + $1,920 = $3,520.

Periodic Weighted Average Method

Method Description

The **weighted average method** is the simplest method. An average unit cost is calculated by dividing the total cost of goods available for sale by the total units available. This average cost is then multiplied by the units of ending inventory.

continued ▶

Periodic Weighted Average Method, *continued*

Example

The ending inventory cost is the average unit cost times the number of units of ending inventory.

Step	Action	Example
1	Determine cost of ending inventory.	$4,680/300 = $15.60 per unit (weighted average) $15.60 × 100 = $1,560
2	Determine cost of goods sold.	$4,680 – $1,560 = $3,120

Analysis

Cost is assigned to ending inventory by multiplying the weighted average cost times the ending inventory units. *Weighted average* means that the number of units at each cost level influences the final cost per unit. (You can read more about weighted and arithmetic averages in "Essential Math for Accounting." It is in the disk at the back of the book.)

You can confirm the cost of goods sold by multiplying the 200 units *sold* by the weighted average cost of $15.60 per unit.

Comparison

The following table compares the results of the three methods.

Ending Inventory:	(LIST) FIFO	(FIST) LIFO	Average
Cost of Goods Available for Sale	$4,680	$4,680	$4,680
Less: Ending Inventory	1,920	1,160	1,560
Cost of Goods Sold	$2,760	$3,520	$3,120

Analysis

Referring to the data table for these examples, you can see that prices were rising. In this environment FIFO will always give the lowest cost of goods sold and the highest ending inventory values. This is because the most recent (highest) costs are allocated to ending inventory, which results in the oldest (lowest) costs going to cost of goods sold.

LIFO gives the opposite result because the costs are allocated in the opposite order: the ending inventory receives the oldest costs, so cost of goods sold has the most recent costs.

Weighted average smooths out the costs and gives a result in between FIFO and LIFO. *If prices had been declining, the FIFO and LIFO results would have been reversed.*

Periodic Weighted Average Method, *continued*

Review of Journal Entries for Periodic System

We studied the journal entries for a periodic system in earlier goals; however, now is a good time to review the following points regarding journal entries in a periodic system:

- When a purchase is made, the purchase is recorded.
- When a sale is made, *only the sales revenue* is recorded, as follows:

Accounts Receivable	$$	
Sales		$$

- Cost of goods sold is not journalized at the time of the sale. Instead, cost of goods sold is a calculation that is done at the end of the period for all sales in the period.

Check Your Understanding Part I

Write the completed sentences on a separate piece of paper. The answers are below.

FIFO refers to · · · · · · · – · · · · · – · · · · · · · · · – out. "Out" refers to the inventory · · · · · · · that is assigned to cost of goods sold. LIFO refers to · · · · · · · · · · – · · · · · · – · · · · · · – out. Weighted average cost is calculated by dividing the total · · · · · · · of · · · · · · · · · · · · · · by the total · · · · · · · available.

FIFO always assigns the · · · · · · · (oldest/latest) cost to cost of goods sold and the · · · · · · · (oldest/latest) cost to ending inventory. LIFO always assigns the · · · · · · · (oldest/latest) cost to cost of goods sold and the · · · · · · · (oldest/latest) cost to ending inventory.

In a period of rising prices, · · · · · · · (FIFO/LIFO) will result in the highest cost of goods sold and the lowest ending inventory.

Answers

In a period of rising prices, LIFO (FIFO/LIFO) will result in the highest cost of goods sold and the lowest ending inventory.

FIFO always assigns the oldest (oldest/latest) cost to cost of goods sold and the latest (oldest/latest) cost to ending inventory. LIFO always assigns the latest (oldest/latest) cost to cost of goods sold and the oldest (oldest/latest) cost to ending inventory.

FIFO refers to first - in - first - out. "Out" refers to the inventory cost that is assigned to cost of goods sold. LIFO refers to last - in - first - out. Weighted average cost is calculated by dividing the total cost of goods available by the total units available.

Check Your Understanding Part II

Determine ending inventory cost and cost of goods sold using FIFO, LIFO, and average methods in a periodic system. Use the approach of calculating ending inventory and subtracting it from cost of goods available for sale to obtain cost of goods sold. Ending inventory is 20 units.

Beginning inventory	10 units @ $11	=	$110
Purchase #1	30 units @ $12	=	$360
Purchase #2	10 units @ $14	=	$140
Purchase #3	15 units @ $18	=	$270

Answer

Ending inventory:

FIFO: (15 units @ $18) + (5 units @ $14) = $340

LIFO: (10 units @ $11) + (10 units @ $12) = $230

Average: $880 / 65 units = $13.538; $13.538 × 20 = $271 (rounded)

	FIFO	LIFO	Average
Cost of Goods Available	$880	$880	$880
Ending Inventory	340	230	271
Cost of Goods Sold	$540	$650	$609

Specific Identification Method

Method Description

The *specific identification method* can be used whenever it is possible to identify the ending inventory units as coming from specific purchases.

Example

Assume that 10 units of ending inventory of custom furniture are identified as consisting of units from the following purchases: 1 unit of beginning inventory that costs $1,000 per unit, 3 units from a purchase that cost $1,600 per unit, and 6 units from a purchase that cost $2,000 per unit. Total cost of goods available for sale is $52,000.

Step	Action	Example
1	Determine cost of ending inventory.	1 unit × $1,000 = $ 1,000 3 units × $1,600 = 4,800 6 units × $2,000 = 12,000 Total $17,800
2	Determine cost of goods sold by subtracting ending inventory from cost of goods available.	$52,000 – $17,800 = $34,200

Analysis

The specific identification method is generally most useful if the inventory consists of easily identifiable items of high unit value. *Examples:* Expensive jewelry, art, furniture, and automobiles. Specific identification is the same for either the periodic or perpetual system.

However, for many businesses the method is impractical or very difficult to use. In situations where large amounts of identical or similar items are purchased at different costs, it becomes too difficult to identify each individual item with its specific cost. *Example:* Trying to distinguish one computer chip from a similar type computer chip.

Inventory Count

Whichever method is selected, the periodic inventory system always requires a physical inventory count. Without a count of the ending inventory, the ending inventory cost cannot be calculated.

Assigning Costs Using the Perpetual System

Overview

The Objective

Our objective is to do two things.

- Determine cost of goods sold.
- Determine the cost of the ending inventory.

Perpetual System Procedure

The perpetual inventory system maintains a continuous record of all inventory items as they are purchased and sold.

Inventory Data for Methods Shown

Data Table

The table below shows the inventory data used in the examples that follow.

| Description | Date | Purchases | | Total Cost |
		Units	Unit Cost	
Beginning bal.	June 1	40	$10	$ 400
Purchase	June 8	50	12	600
Purchase	June 15	130	16	2,080
Purchase	June 27	80	20	1,600
Total available		300		$4,680

Sales				
	June 4	20		
	June 12	45		
	June 18	15		
	June 29	120		

Perpetual First-In, First-Out (FIFO) Method

Method Description

This popular method assigns cost to cost of goods sold by assuming that the oldest costs are always the first ones allocated to the units that are sold. Businesses usually sell the oldest merchandise first to prevent it from deteriorating or becoming obsolete, so costs allocated by FIFO approximate the actual physical flow of merchandise as it is sold.

Example

The table below shows how FIFO is applied in a perpetual system.

Date	Purchase	Cost of Goods Sold	Inventory
June 1			40 units @ $10 = $400
June 4	20 units sold	20 units @ $10 = $200	20 units @ $10 = 200
June 8	50 units @ $12 = $600		20 units @ $10 = 200 50 units @ $12 = 600 $800
	45 units sold		
June 12		20 units @ $10 = $200 25 units @ $12 = 300	25 units @ $12 = $ 300
June 15	130 units @ $16 = $2,080		25 units @ $12 = $ 300 130 units @ $16 = 2,080 $2,380
	15 units sold		
June 18		15 units @ $12 = $180	10 units @ $12 = $ 120 130 units @ $16 = 2,080 $2,200
June 27	80 units @ $20 = $1,600		10 units @ $12 = $ 120 130 units @ $16 = 2,080 80 units @ $20 = 1,600 $3,800
	120 units sold		
June 29		10 units @ $12 = $ 120 110 units @ $16 = 1,760	20 units @ $16 = $ 320 80 units @ $20 = 1,600 $1,920

Analysis

For each sale, cost is assigned to cost of goods sold from the oldest cost layer available at the time of the sale. When an old layer is entirely used, the costs from the next oldest layer are used, and so on. For example, 45 units were sold on June 12, so the oldest available cost layer consisting of 20 units at $10 was used up first. Then 25 units of cost were taken from the next layer. As a result, only 25 units were left in inventory.

continued ▶

Perpetual First-In, First-Out (FIFO) Method, *continued*

Review of Journal Entries

We studied journal entries for the perpetual method in earlier learning goals about merchandising operations. However, here is a quick review using the data in the table on the previous page for June 4 through June 18. Assume a sales price of $25 per unit.

Date	Account	Post. Ref.	Dr.	Cr.
June 4	Accounts Receivable		500	
	Sales			500
	Cost of Goods Sold		200	
	Inventory			200
8	Inventory		600	
	Accounts Payable			600
12	Accounts Receivable		1,125	
	Sales			1,125
	Cost of Goods Sold		500	
	Inventory			500
15	Inventory		2,080	
	Accounts Payable			2,080
18	Accounts Receivable		375	
	Sales			375
	Cost of Goods Sold		180	
	Inventory			180

Look back at the table.

If you add beginning inventory ($400) to the total purchases ($4,280) and subtract total cost of goods sold ($2,760) you will get ending inventory of $1,920.

Perpetual Last-In, First-Out (LIFO) Method

Method Description

Perpetual LIFO is used less often than other methods due to the expense of keeping a record of many cost layers for different units. To apply perpetual LIFO, instead of using costs from the oldest layer, use the costs from the most recent layer first, with each sale.

Date	Purchase	Cost of Goods Sold	Inventory
June 1			40 units @ $10 = $400
June 4	20 units sold	20 units @ $10 = $200	20 units @ $10 = 200
June 8	50 units @ $12 = $600		20 units @ $10 = 200 50 units @ $12 = 600 $800
	45 units sold		
June 12		45 units @ $12 = $540	20 units @ $10 = $200 5 units @ $12 = 60 $260
June 15	130 units @ $16 = $2,080		20 units @ $10 = $ 200 5 units @ $12 = 60 130 units @ $16 = 2,080 $2,340
	15 units sold		
June 18		15 units @ $16 = $240	20 units @ $10 = $ 200 5 units @ $12 = 60 115 units @ $16 = 1,840 $2,100
June 27	80 units @ $20 = $1,600		20 units @ $10 = $ 200 5 units @ $12 = 60 115 units @ $16 = 1,840 80 units @ $20 = 1,600 $3,700
	120 units sold		
June 29		80 units @ $20 = $1,600 40 units @ $16 = 640	20 units @ $10 = $ 200 5 units @ $12 = 60 75 units @ $16 = 1,200 $1,460

Analysis

Cost is assigned to cost of goods sold first from the most recent cost layer available at the time of a sale. For example, on June 12 the most recent cost layer is 50 units @ $12, so all 45 units of cost were taken from this layer. As a result, 5 units of this layer are left in inventory, plus the previous 20 units.

Notice how numerous cost layers are built up and old cost layers can develop having costs that are very different (often much lower) than current costs.

Perpetual Moving Average Method

Method Description

Calculation of cost of goods sold with the ***moving average method*** is very straightforward. Simply calculate a new average cost each time there is a new purchase. This average cost is used until the next purchase. To calculate an average cost, divide the total inventory cost by the total number of units. Calculate each average to at least three places before rounding the final answer to two places.

Example

The table below shows how to apply the moving average method. Total costs are rounded to the nearest dollar.

Date	Purchase	Cost of Goods Sold	Balance
June 1			40 units @ $10 = $400
June 4		20 units @ $10 = $200	20 units @ $10 = $200
June 8	50 units @ $12 = $600		Total cost is $800 for 70 units $800/70 = $11.43/unit
June 12		45 @ $11.43 = $514	25 units @ $11.43 = $286
June 15	130 units @ $16 = $2,080		Total cost is $2,366 for 155 units $2,366/155 = $15.27/unit
June 18		15 units @ $15.27 = $229	140 units @ $15.27 = $2,138
June 27	80 units @ $20 = $1,600		Total cost is $3,738 for 220 units $3,738/220 = $16.99/unit
June 29		120 units @ $16.99 = $2,039	100 units @ $16.99 = $1,699

Effect of Discounts, Returns, and Freight-In

Purchase discounts, purchase returns and allowances, and the cost of freight-in affect the total cost of inventory and the cost per unit of inventory. In practice, accounting software factors these items into a perpetual inventory system. However, we do not include these issues in our discussion because of the details and complexities involved, allowing us to focus on the essential procedures.

TIP

What is the most popular method?

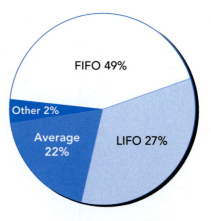

FIFO 49%

Other 2%

Average 22%

LIFO 27%

Source: Based on AICPA survey

Check Your Understanding

Determine ending inventory cost and cost of goods sold using FIFO, LIFO, and average methods in a perpetual inventory system. Use a table format as illustrated on the prior pages.

Beginning inventory	30 units @$9	=	$270
Sale	20 units		
Purchase #1	20 units @ $13	=	$260
Sale	25 units		
Purchase #2	10 units @ $14	=	$140
Sale	8 units		

Answer

Average

Purchase	C of GS	Inventory
		30 @ $9 = $270
	20 @ $9 = $180	10 @ $9 = $90
20 @ $13 = $260		30 units for $350 $350/30 = $11.667
	25 @ $11.667 = $291.67	5 @ $11.667 = $58.33
10 @ $14 = $140		15 units for $198.33 $198.33/15 = $13.222
	8 @ $13.222 = $105.78	7 @ $13.222 = $92.55

C of GS total: $577.45
Ending Inventory: $92.55

FIFO

Purchase	C of GS	Inventory
		30 @ $9 = $270
	20 @ $9 = $180	10 @ $9 = $90
20 @ $13 = $260		10 @ $9 = $90 20 @ $13 = $260
	10 @ $9 = $90 15 @ $13 = $195	5 @ $13 = $65
10 @ $14 = $140		5 @ $13 = $65 10 @ $14 = $140
	5 @ $13 = $65 3 @ $14 = $42	7 @ $14 = $98

C of GS total: $572
Ending Inventory: $98

LIFO

Purchase	C of GS	Inventory
		30 @ $9 = $270
	20 @ $9 = $180	10 @ $9 = $90
20 @ $13 = $260		10 @ $9 = $90 20 @ $13 = $260
	20 @ $13 = $260 5 @ $9 = $45	5 @ $9 = $45
10 @ $14 = $140		5 @ $9 = $45 10 @ $14 = $140
	8 @ $14 = $112	5 @ $9 = $45 2 @ $14 = $28

C of GS total: $597
Ending Inventory: $73

Comparison of FIFO, LIFO, and Moving Average

Comparison

The following table compares the results of the three methods.

	FIFO	LIFO	Average
Cost of Goods Sold	$2,760	$3,220	$2,982
Ending Inventory	1,920	1,460	1,699

Analysis

Referring to the data table for these examples, you can see that prices were rising. In this environment, FIFO always gives the lowest cost of goods sold and the highest ending inventory values. This is because the oldest (lowest) costs are allocated first to cost of goods sold, leaving the most recent costs in ending inventory.

LIFO gives the opposite result because the costs are allocated in the opposite order: with each sale, cost of goods sold is allocated to the most recent costs first.

Moving average smoothes out the costs and gives a result in between FIFO and LIFO. *Note: If prices had been declining, the FIFO and LIFO results would have been reversed.*

Inventory Count

Regardless of which method is selected, inventory is counted at least once per year to confirm the calculations. Any difference is recorded as an adjustment to cost of goods sold and inventory.

TIP

If you compare the periodic and perpetual methods, notice that the procedure for periodic is to calculate ending inventory first (at the end of the period), whereas the procedure for perpetual is to calculate cost of goods sold first, with each sale.

Did you also notice that both periodic and perpetual FIFO give the same results for cost of goods sold and ending inventory? (The other methods do not.)

A Practical Comparison of FIFO, LIFO, and Moving Average

Some Practical Issues

The table below shows some practical issues related to the use of FIFO and LIFO for either the periodic or perpetual method. Remember that prices are increasing in our examples and that decreasing prices would give opposite results when comparing FIFO and LIFO.

■ Net income effects	LIFO puts the *most current costs into cost of goods sold.* In our examples, inventory costs were increasing, so the most recent costs resulted in higher cost of goods and lower net income.
■ Balance sheet effects	FIFO puts the *most current costs into the inventory* on the balance sheet. This is because oldest costs are the first to flow into cost of goods sold. In our examples, FIFO resulted in the highest ending inventory.
■ Income tax effects	The method that produces the highest cost of goods sold results in the lowest net income and lowest taxes.
■ LIFO period-end purchases	Unfortunately, LIFO users can manipulate net income by manipulating the amount of inventory purchases at the end of a period. With LIFO, cost of goods sold receives the most recent costs first, so a higher-priced purchase at the end of the current period increases cost of goods sold. Deferring the purchase into the next period results in lower cost of goods sold for the current period. This is because older, lower costs of the period are allocated to cost of goods sold.
■ LIFO liquidation	LIFO inventory can have old cost layers—sometimes at very low cost. If prices have been increasing, and if the inventory balance decreases between the beginning and the end of a period, the old (low) costs flow into cost of goods sold, suddenly increasing net income. This is called *LIFO liquidation*.
■ Consistency	Both accounting and tax authorities require that the method selected be used consistently. A one-time change is usually permitted, provided that the effect on net income is disclosed. Any further changes require compelling evidence that financial reporting is improved by the change. However, a company may use different inventory methods for different categories of inventory, provided that the methods are used consistently.

Revaluing the Inventory

Lower of Cost or Market

Introduction

Up to now our discussion has concentrated on the GAAP rules for assigning cost to cost of goods sold and to ending inventory, using the actual (historical) cost of the items. However, after the cost has been assigned by using one of the methods we have discussed (FIFO, LIFO, average), GAAP also requires that the current value of the inventory must be checked later, at the time that the financial statements are prepared. If the current value of the items has fallen below the original transaction value, then the original value showing on the balance sheet (historical cost) must be changed (*written down*) to the new value.

Rule: Use Lower of Cost or Market

The method used to determine the inventory value is called **lower of cost or market, or LCM**. For the purposes of this method, *cost* means historical cost using one of the methods (FIFO, LIFO, average) we have discussed. *Market* means selling price ("net realizable value") for FIFO and average, and replacement cost for LIFO. Lower of cost or market (as of the balance sheet date) can be applied in two ways:

- *Item-by-item method:* This method selects the lower of cost or market for each type of inventory item. This always results in the lowest total value.
- *Major category method:* The inventory is classified into major categories of similar items. LCM is selected for the dollar total of each category.

Adjusting Journal Entry Example:

On December 31 year end, the FIFO historical cost of inventory is $100,000, but the expected selling price is $92,000. To record this decline in value, an operating expense such as *Inventory Valuation Loss* is debited for $8,000, and the Merchandise Inventory account is credited for $8,000. Instead of debiting an operating expense, some companies debit cost of goods sold.

Some Key Points

- Using LCM is an example of applying the valuation element of event analysis. Because inventory is usually such a significant asset, its loss of value can materially affect financial condition. This cannot be ignored.
- Using LCM is a departure from historical cost. When the new value is used, the historical cost is eliminated. To the extent that the original cost is changed, the matching rule is superseded by a valuation requirement.

Inventory Errors

Overview

Causes

Errors in properly assigning cost to inventory are commonly caused by:

- Incorrect count of inventory
- Incorrect unit pricing of inventory
- Failure to identify when title transfers for in-transit inventory
- Failure to identify consignment inventory
- Incorrect record-keeping

Effects

The effect of an inventory error depends on two factors:

- Whether the error is for beginning inventory or ending inventory
- Whether the error is an overstatement or understatement

Analysis

Summary of Effects

The table below summarizes the possible effects of the types of inventory errors stated above.

Beginning Inventory					
In this period . . .			In the next period . . .		
if beginning inventory is . . .	cost of goods sold will be . . .	net income will be . . .	NO EFFECT		
understated	understated	overstated			
overstated	overstated	understated			
Ending Inventory					
In this period . . .			In the next period . . .		
if ending inventory is . . .	cost of goods will be . . .	net income will be . . .	beginning inventory will be . . .	cost of goods sold will be . . .	net income will be . . .
understated	overstated	understated	understated	understated	overstated
overstated	understated	overstated	overstated	overstated	understated

continued ▶

Analysis, *continued*

How to Analyze

You can easily analyze all the effects of inventory errors by using the cost of goods sold equation (BI + net P – EI = C of GS), then subtracting cost of goods sold from sales to determine gross profit.

Examples

Assume that the numbers in the table below are correct.

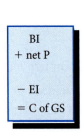

	Period 1	Period 2
Sales revenue	$20	$20
Cost of goods sold:		
Beginning inventory	3	5
Net purchases	10	10
Cost of goods available...	13	15
Less: Ending inventory...	5	2
Cost of goods sold	8	13
Gross profit	12	7

Error example 1: Beginning inventory is overstated by $3.

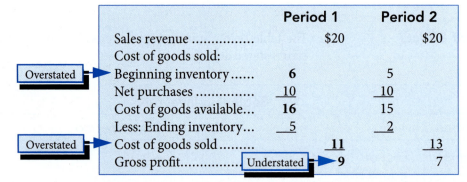

	Period 1	Period 2
Sales revenue	$20	$20
Cost of goods sold:		
Overstated → Beginning inventory	**6**	5
Net purchases	10	10
Cost of goods available...	**16**	15
Less: Ending inventory...	5	2
Overstated → Cost of goods sold	**11**	13
Gross profit ..... **Understated →**	**9**	7

Error example 2: Ending inventory is overstated by $3. The error understates cost of goods sold by $3 in the first period and then overstates cost of goods sold by the same amount in the second period. This is typical of ending inventory errors. In turn, this affects gross profit and ultimately net income.

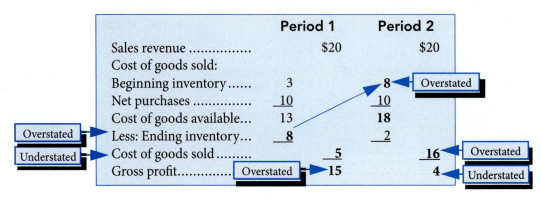

	Period 1	Period 2
Sales revenue	$20	$20
Cost of goods sold:		
Beginning inventory	3	**8** ← **Overstated**
Net purchases	10	10
Cost of goods available...	13	**18**
Overstated → Less: Ending inventory...	**8**	2
Understated → Cost of goods sold	**5**	**16** ← **Overstated**
Gross profit ..... **Overstated →**	**15**	**4** ← **Understated**

Analysis, *continued*

Errors Offset

Notice that with the ending inventory error the gross profit was overstated in the first period and understated in the second period by exactly the same amount of $3. The first period gross profit was $15 instead of $12 and the second period was $4 instead of $7.

So if the errors offset, do we care? Absolutely, yes! What has really happened is that results of two financial periods are incorrectly stated. Decisions that are based on the reported results and trends of each period could be very badly misinformed.

Estimating Inventory

Gross Profit Method

Overview

Sometimes a business finds itself in the situation of needing to estimate the value of its inventory. This usually happens when there has been a fire, theft, or other casualty loss, and the business has not maintained perpetual inventory records. A popular way of *estimating* inventory is called the *gross profit method*. This procedure uses the historical gross profit percentage to estimate the inventory. But remember—*this is only an estimating procedure* and is not acceptable for normal GAAP purposes, which require a physical count.

Example

Assume the following facts: Tallahassee Company suffered storm damage from a hurricane and lost all of its inventory. The beginning inventory was $65,000, and records show purchases of $285,000. The company has had a fairly stable historical gross profit of 30% and net sales to the date of loss were $380,000.

continued ▶

Gross Profit Method, *continued*

Procedure

The table below shows the procedure for applying the gross profit method using the information from the example above.

Step	Action	Example
1	Calculate the cost of goods available for sale.	Beginning inventory $ 65,000 Purchases 285,000 Cost of goods available $350,000
2	Calculate the historical cost of goods sold percentage.	100% − gross profit %: 100% − 30% = 70%
3	Estimate the cost of goods sold by multiplying the cost of goods sold % by net sales.	$380,000 × .7 = $266,000
4	The difference between the cost of goods available and the estimated cost of goods sold is the estimated ending inventory.	Cost of goods available $350,000 Cost of goods sold 266,000 Estimated inventory $ 84,000

Note: If the historical gross profit percentage or cost of goods sold percentage is not readily available, then it has to be calculated up to a date as close as possible to the date of the estimate.

Analysis: Income Statement View

Net sales $380,000

Beginning inventory......................... $ 65,000
Purchases 285,000
Cost of goods available for sale $350,000

Estimated ending inventory.............$ 84,000

Estimated cost of goods sold................................. $266,000
Estimated Gross profit $114,000

Internal Control for Inventory

Essential Methods

Overview

Inventory can be lost and misplaced, and some types of inventory are very attractive targets for thieves. Inventory fraud also frequently occurs as part of schemes to prepare fraudulent financial statements. This section shows some basic precautions for safeguarding and correctly reporting inventory.

Separation of Duties

The separation of duties idea concerning cash also applies here:

- Anyone with access to the accounting records should never have access to inventory. Theft of any asset can be hidden by false bookkeeping entries.
- Related purchasing activities should be done by different people. This includes ordering merchandise, receiving the merchandise, and payment.
- Related sales activities should be done by different people. This includes making the sale, shipping the inventory, billing, and cash receipts.

Physical Control

Inventory should be subject to physical safeguards and limited access, such as locked rooms, identification badges for entry, and surveillance video. In some cases, guards may be required to limit access and maintain records of access.

Perpetual Inventory System

A perpetual inventory system requires continuous record keeping of inventory and provides the best internal control. At a minimum, it should be used for all high-value items. This record keeping should include physical units, costs, full explanation of adjustments with documentation, and dates of all incoming and outgoing items.

Counting Inventory

- To prepare correct financial statements, all inventory should be counted at least one time per year to verify the amount of ending inventory.
- High-value inventory should be subject to surprise counts to verify that the amount of inventory on hand correlates to perpetual inventory records.

continued ▶

Essential Methods, *continued*

**Other Important
Controls**

- Receiving reports/purchase orders: A receiving reporting showing the number and kind of items received should be compared to the purchase order. Then, these together should be compared to the invoice before a check is written.
- Calculate cost of goods sold percentage: An unexplained increase in cost of goods sold percentage when sales prices have not decreased can indicate an inventory theft (or theft of sales cash receipts). A sudden decrease should also be checked as an indicator of inflated sales revenue or payable write-downs that reduce recorded purchases.
- A computerized system can maintain a record of inventory, identify reorder points, and record sales amounts based on predefined markup percentages.

GAAP Weakness

Comparability and Reliability

**Financial Statements
Are Not Comparable**

As you studied the different inventory costing methods, you may have been surprised by the numerous methods and the different results. In a perfect world, we would have a single "most accurate" method. Unfortunately, this is not the case. In fact, most businesses select an inventory method or a combination of methods that best meet their own purposes for either most favorable financial statement presentation or hoped-for tax savings.

This means that the matching principle is not uniformly applied to businesses with inventory.

The result is that for different businesses with significant inventory, financial statements are difficult to compare, unless a company voluntarily discloses additional inventory information. Because inventory and cost of goods sold are such significant items, this lack of comparability is a real shortcoming in GAAP. To date, the situation remains unresolved.

> *Note:* Because LIFO does not usually result in an ending inventory that is close to replacement cost, the Securities and Exchange Commission does require public companies that report using LIFO disclose the cumulative inventory value difference between LIFO and FIFO. This difference is called *LIFO reserve.* Reporting this difference also provides a means to reconcile the income difference created by LIFO and FIFO between different companies.

Comparability and Reliability, *continued*

Manipulating Financial Statements	Despite the requirement for consistent application of a method, the rules are permissive enough to allow unethical companies to "massage" numbers for their own purposes and therefore manipulate income. Some examples:

- LIFO year-end purchase decisions
- The ability to choose how the lower of cost or market rule will be applied
- The ability to decide what is "expected selling price". (LCM)

TIP

LIFO Conformity Rule: The Internal Revenue Service requires *LIFO Conformity*. If a company uses LIFO for its income tax calculation, the company must also use LIFO on the financial statements.

IFRS and GAAP	In the context of our discussion, there are several notable differences between IFRS (International Financial Reporting Standards) and GAAP.

- GAAP permits the use of LIFO and IFRS does not. IFRS limits the use of specific identification to defined identifiable circumstances.
- GAAP does not permit write-down reversals. IFRS permits reversals of write-downs if net realizable value increases.
- GAAP permits the use of different inventory methods for all types of inventory. IFRS requires the same method for inventories similar in nature and use.

Do You Want More Examples?	Most problems in this book have detailed solutions. To use them as additional examples, do this: 1) Select the type of problem you want 2) Open the solution on your computer or mobile device screen (from the disc or worthyjames.com) 3) Read one item at a time and look at its answer. Take notes if needed. 4) Close the solution and work as much of the problem as you can. 5) Repeat as needed.

QUICK REVIEW

- The cost of ending inventory and cost of goods sold can be calculated in these ways:

  - Periodic system: FIFO, LIFO, weighted average, or specific identification
  - Perpetual system: FIFO, LIFO, moving average, or specific identification

- To determine ending inventory, FIFO (first-in, first-out) assigns the first (oldest) costs to cost of goods sold; therefore, the most recent costs are assigned to ending inventory. LIFO (last-in, first-out) assigns the most recent costs to cost of goods sold; therefore, the oldest costs are assigned to ending inventory. Average methods calculate an average cost and assign this average cost to all units. Specific identification assigns specific costs to specific units.

- The periodic inventory method applies the selected calculation only at the end of an accounting period. This is normally done by: (1) assigning a cost to ending inventory and (2) subtracting the ending inventory cost from cost of goods available to determine cost of goods sold. A physical inventory count is required to apply the method.

- The perpetual method applies the selected calculation continuously during an accounting period. A physical inventory count is performed to confirm the ending inventory value.

- At the end of each period the lower of cost or market valuation rule must be applied. This rule compares the historical cost of the inventory to the selling price of the inventory and uses the lower of the two values for the balance sheet inventory value.

- Errors in beginning inventory and purchases affect only the same accounting period in which the error occurred. Errors in ending inventory affect two accounting periods—the period in which the error occurred and the next period.

- The gross profit method is used to estimate ending inventory when it cannot be counted. This is done by using an estimated gross profit percentage to determine the cost of goods sold percentage. The cost of goods sold percentage is then multiplied by net sales to determine cost of goods sold. The difference between cost of goods sold and cost of goods available is the estimated ending inventory.

VOCABULARY

First-in, first-out (FIFO): the costs of the first items acquired are considered to be the first costs that flow out to cost of goods sold (page 698)

Gross profit method: a method of estimating inventory using a historical gross profit percentage (page 721)

Last-in, first-out (LIFO): the costs of the last items acquired are considered to be the first costs that flow out to cost of goods sold (page 699)

Lower of cost or market (LCM): a valuation rule that requires inventory value to be shown on the balance sheet at the lower of cost or selling price (page 712)

Moving average method: a method that calculates inventory cost as the weighted average cost per unit for all units at the time of each purchase times the number of units acquired; used for the perpetual method (page 708)

Specific identification method: a method that identifies inventory items as coming from specific purchases (page 703)

Weighted average method: a method that calculates unit inventory cost by multiplying the quantity of units purchased times the price per unit for the units purchased and then dividing by total units purchased; used for the periodic method (page 699)

PRACTICE   Learning Goal 18

Solutions are in the disk at the back of the book and at: www.worthyjames.com

Learning Goal 18 is about recording, reporting, and controlling merchandise inventory. Use these questions to practice what you have learned.

Multiple Choice
Select the best answer.

1. In a period of rising prices:
   a. FIFO results in the highest cost of goods sold and lowest ending inventory.
   b. LIFO results in the highest cost of goods sold and highest ending inventory.
   c. FIFO results in the lowest cost of goods sold and highest ending inventory.
   d. LIFO results in the lowest cost of goods sold and highest ending inventory.

2. The lower-of-cost-or-market (LCM) rule is:
   a. a valuation rule that applies regardless of whatever cost is assigned to inventory.
   b. a valuation rule that is applied to estimate the ending inventory.
   c. a valuation rule that is used instead of FIFO, LIFO, or average methods.
   d. not a valuation rule.

3. In a period of decreasing prices:
   a. FIFO results in the highest cost of goods sold and highest ending inventory.
   b. LIFO results in the highest cost of goods sold and lowest ending inventory.
   c. FIFO results in the lowest cost of goods sold and highest ending inventory.
   d. LIFO results in the lowest cost of goods sold and highest ending inventory.

4. Freeport Enterprises had beginning inventory of $10,000, purchases of $80,000, and net sales of $100,000 with a gross profit of 30%:
   a. Cost of goods sold is $30,000.
   b. Cost of goods available for sale is $70,000.
   c. Ending inventory is $20,000.
   d. Cost of goods sold is $10,000.

5. FIFO:
   a. assigns the most recent costs to cost of goods sold.
   b. assigns the oldest costs to ending inventory.
   c. results in the lowest cost of goods sold.
   d. assigns the most recent costs to ending inventory.

6. LIFO:
   a. assigns the most recent costs to cost of goods sold.
   b. assigns the most recent costs to ending inventory.
   c. results in the highest cost of goods sold.
   d. assigns the oldest costs to cost of goods sold.

7. When costs are assigned to ending inventory:
   a. LIFO results in the most current inventory costs on the balance sheet.
   b. FIFO results in the oldest inventory costs on the balance sheet.
   c. the weighted average method results in the most accurate cost.
   d. none of the above.

8. When an error is made in the beginning inventory:
   a. if beginning inventory is overstated, cost of goods sold will be overstated.
   b. if beginning inventory is understated, cost of goods sold will be understated.
   c. if beginning inventory is understated, cost of goods sold will be overstated.
   d. both a and b are true.

9. When an error is made in the ending inventory:
   a. if ending inventory is overstated, cost of goods sold will be understated.
   b. if ending inventory is understated, cost of goods sold will be understated.
   c. if ending inventory is overstated, cost of goods sold will be overstated.
   d. both a and b are true.

10. An inventory valuation adjustment that results from using LCM is an example of:
    a. the matching principle.
    b. the revenue recognition principle.
    c. the valuation element of event analysis.
    d. the cost principle.

11. If the cost of inventory as determined by FIFO is $136,000 and the cost to replace this inventory as of the balance sheet date is $121,000:
    a. no journal entry is required.
    b. debit Inventory $15,000 and credit Inventory Valuation Loss $15,000.
    c. switch to the LIFO method.
    d. debit Inventory Valuation Loss $15,000 and credit Inventory $15,000.

12. A fire destroyed the warehouse of Nonantum Company, which uses the periodic inventory method. Up to the date of the fire, sales were $350,000, beginning inventory was $20,000, purchases were $200,000, and the historical gross profit percentage was 40%. What is the estimated inventory loss from the fire?
    a. $10,000
    b. $80,000
    c. $88,000
    d. $132,000

13. Which procedure would provide the best internal control for inventory?
    a. Use a periodic inventory system.
    b. Use a perpetual inventory system.
    c. Periodically analyze cost of goods sold to check for inventory problems.
    d. Both b and c.

14. Separation of duties in respect to inventory requires that:
    a. the accountant periodically check the inventory.
    b. related purchasing activities such as purchasing and receiving be done by one person.
    c. related sales activities such as taking orders and shipping be done by one person.
    d. none of the above.

15. Controlling the amount of purchases at the end of an accounting period makes it possible to manipulate cost of goods sold and ending inventory with which inventory method?
    a. FIFO
    b. LIFO
    c. average
    d. none of the above

16. To help remember the periodic inventory system calculations, we used these memory aids:
    a. for FIFO, LIST refers to the ending inventory costs as Last-In, Still-There whereas FIFO refers to the flow of costs into cost of goods sold.
    b. for LIFO, FIST refers to the ending inventory costs as First-In, Still-There whereas LIFO refers to the flow of costs into cost of goods sold.
    c. neither of the above is correct.
    d. both a and b are correct.

17. Iroquois Company inventory records show the following:

Item	Units	Unit Cost
Inventory, January 1	700	$4
Purchase 1	2,500	6
Purchase 2	900	7
Inventory, December 31	1,000	

What is the cost of the ending inventory using FIFO?
a. $4,600
b. $7,000
c. $6,900
d. None of the above

18. Using the information in question 17, what is the cost of ending inventory if the company uses LIFO?
a. $7,000
b. $6,700
c. $6,900
d. none of the above

19. Using the information in question 17, what is the cost of ending inventory using average cost?
a. $5,878
b. $5,667
c. $6,733
d. none of the above

20. Rocky Hill Corporation understated its ending inventory by $5,000 in 2017. The effect of this will be:
a. 2017 income overstated by $5,000 and 2018 income understated by $5,000.
b. 2017 income understated by $5,000 and 2018 income understated by $5,000.
c. 2017 income overstated by $5,000 and 2018 income overstated by $5,000.
d. 2017 income understated by $5,000 and 2018 income overstated by $5,000.

Discussion Questions and Brief Exercises

1. (a) For one type of inventory system, we calculate cost of goods sold first and then subtract that from cost of goods available to determine remaining inventory cost. (b) For another type of inventory system, we calculate ending inventory first and then subtract that amount from cost of goods available to get cost of goods sold. What are the names of these inventory systems for (a) and for (b)? Do they always result in the same answers?

2. Suppose you are the manager of a retail company and you strongly believe that there will be a long-term increase in the cost of the company's merchandise inventory. The board of directors wants you to make a presentation about what you believe are the most important issues in selecting the best inventory method. What is your analysis?

3. Trout Creek Company had $120,000 of inventory on hand at the start of the year. The net cost of inventory purchases during the year was $200,000. If the cost of goods sold during the year was $275,000, what was the cost of the ending inventory?

4. Contrast the effects of a calculation error in beginning inventory or purchases to the effects of a calculation error in ending inventory.

5. Historical cost is an important accounting principle. How is historical cost determined for merchandise inventory?

6. What is the LIFO conformity requirement?

7. Explain how the averaging method is different between the periodic system and the perpetual system.

8. The ending inventory of Baton Rouge Partners was understated by $5,000. In the current period, what effect will this have on cost of goods sold? What will be the effect on net income?

9. Tecumseh Company began the year with $185,000 of inventory. The net cost of inventory purchases during the year was $745,000, and the net sales were $1,500,000. The recent gross profit percentage has averaged 40%. Estimate the cost of the ending inventory using the gross profit method.

10. What is the objective when assigning cost to inventory, and what important accounting principles relate to this?

11. Two types of problems can arise with LIFO. These are LIFO liquidation and the use of LIFO at the end of an accounting period to manipulate income. Explain how these problems can occur.

12. The actual cost of inventory for Suwanee Company using FIFO is $10,000. The expected selling price on December 31 is $8,800. Using the lower of cost or market procedure, which amount should be reported on the December 31 Suwanee balance sheet?

13. a. Is physical goods flow the same as cost flow?
    b. Do FIFO and LIFO result in different quantities of ending inventory?
    c. Does FIFO mean that the first (oldest) costs are in ending inventory and LIFO mean that the last costs are in ending inventory?

14. For which of the following systems or methods is the physical count of inventory unnecessary or not done: periodic, perpetual, gross profit?

15. For purposes of financial reporting, can a company change inventory methods from year to year? How often can a company change methods? Can a company use different methods for different inventory types?

16. Identify and describe internal control procedures for inventory.

17. How is merchandise inventory shown on the balance sheet? Are supplementary disclosures required?

Solutions are in the disk at the back of the book and at: www.worthyjames.com

PRACTICE Learning Goal 18, continued

Reinforcement Problems

LG 18-1. Calculate ending inventory and cost of goods sold using FIFO and LIFO and explain the differences. Orono Company's periodic system inventory records show the information that you see below. During the month, 97 units were sold.

Instructions:
a. Compute the cost of the ending inventory using periodic FIFO and LIFO.
b. Identify which method results in the highest ending inventory. Why?
c. Identify which method results in the highest cost of goods sold. Why?

Date	Item	Units	Cost per Unit	Total Cost
Sept. 1	Beginning balance	40	$5	$200
10	Purchase	20	7	140
22	Purchase	35	8	280
30	Purchase	10	9	90
Totals		105		$710

LG 18-2. Identify method: calculate inventory and cost of goods sold using FIFO, LIFO, weighted average. Shepherdstown Enterprises has the following inventory record for the month of June:

Beginning inventory: 50 units at $9	June 11: purchase 200 units at $10.50	June 20: purchase 100 units at $11.25
June 4: purchase 320 units at $9.50	June 14: purchase 100 units at $11.15	June 28: purchase 120 units at $11.20

The June 30 ending inventory balance is 180 units.

Instructions:
a. Is the company using the periodic or perpetual method? How do you know?
b. Calculate ending inventory and cost of goods sold for June using each of the following methods: FIFO, LIFO, and Weighted Average.
c. Prove the FIFO and LIFO cost of goods sold amount by a different calculation.

LG 18-3. Perpetual system: calculate FIFO, LIFO, moving average, make journal entries.

Instructions: Using the inventory information below for the Boss Boot Company, prepare a separate table like the one you see formatted below for each of the following assumptions. Also, for each method show the total cost of goods sold and the total ending inventory.

a. Perpetual FIFO is used.
b. Perpetual LIFO is used.
c. Moving average (perpetual average) is used.
d. Assume that each pair of boots sells for $175 and all sales are on account.
    Prepare journal entries using the FIFO cost table.

Inventory information:

Beginning inventory	5 pair @ $50
Purchase 1	10 pair @ $55
Sale 1	11 pair
Purchase 2	12 pair @ $65
Sale 2	10 pair
Purchase 3	8 pair @ $70
Sale 3	5 pair

Complete the table below using a separate piece of paper.

Event	Purchase	Cost of goods sold	Inventory
(Reminder: Use a separate sheet of paper to complete the table.)			

When completing the Inventory column, show the units and cost for each separate cost layer.

LG 18-4. Identify method; calculate ending inventory and cost of goods sold. Sandusky Company has the following inventory record for the month of October:

Beginning inventory (Oct. 1)	100 units @ $3.00
Purchase (Oct. 7)	1,300 units @ $3.20
Purchase (Oct. 15)	2,400 units @ $4.00
Purchase (Oct. 28)	300 units @ $4.50

During October the company sold 3,600 units of merchandise.

a. How many units should be in ending inventory on October 31?
b. Is the company using the periodic or perpetual system? How do you know?
c. Using FIFO, calculate ending inventory and cost of goods sold.
d. Using LIFO, calculate ending inventory and cost of goods sold.
e. Using average cost, calculate ending inventory and cost of goods sold.

LG 18-5. Identify possible inventory systems; use perpetual system. Dayton Wholesale Sporting Merchandise has the following inventory record of ski parkas:

Beginning inventory (June 1)	80 units @ $50
Purchase (June 9)	150 units @ $60
Sale (June 12)	120 units
Purchase (June 15)	200 units @ $65
Sale (June 29)	210 units

a. Can the company use either the periodic or perpetual system? How do you know?
b. Using perpetual FIFO, calculate ending inventory and cost of goods sold.
c. Using perpetual LIFO, calculate ending inventory and cost of goods sold.
d. Using moving average cost, calculate ending inventory and cost of goods sold.

LG 18-6. Periodic system: calculate cost of goods sold and ending inventory. Prove the answer.

Kirksville Company uses the periodic inventory system. At the beginning of the year on January 1, Kirksville had 3,500 units of inventory with a total cost of $42,000. During the year, the company made the following purchases:

Purchase 1: 7,800 units	Cost: $12.50 per unit
Purchase 2: 12,000 units	Cost: $14.00 per unit
Purchase 3: 5,000 units	Cost: $14.20 per unit

On December 31 year end, a physical count of inventory shows 7,000 units still on hand.

a. How many units were sold during the year?
b. Compute the cost of goods available for sale.
c. Compute the ending inventory using FIFO. Then compute cost of goods sold using your calculation of ending inventory.
d. Prove your answer for c by calculating cost of goods sold directly, using the units sold. Then calculate the cost of the ending inventory. Which method is easier, c or d?
e. Repeat items c and d using LIFO.

Solutions are in the disk at the back of the book and at: www.worthyjames.com

PRACTICE   Learning Goal 18, continued

LG 18-7. **Determine effects of inventory errors.** The table below shows information for the years 2016, 2017, and 2018:

	2016	2017	2018
Beginning inventory	$3,500	$8,500	$10,000
Net purchases + freight-in	21,000	19,000	28,000
Cost of goods available	24,500	27,500	38,000
Ending inventory	8,500	10,000	5,000
Cost of goods sold	16,000	17,500	33,000

The following errors have occurred:

- The ending inventory of 2016 was overstated by $2,000.
- The ending inventory of 2017 was understated by $5,000.

Instructions:

a. Determine the correct cost of goods sold for each year.
b. Show the positive or negative difference between the correct cost of goods sold and the incorrect cost of goods sold, and explain the cause of the difference.

LG 18-8. **Perpetual system: calculate inventory and cost of goods sold using various methods, prepare income statements.** The accountant at Las Cruces Company was preparing a schedule for management to show the effects of perpetual method FIFO, LIFO, and moving average. The accountant was called away for another assignment, and it is your job to complete the schedule for the month of May. Sales revenue for May is $15,000. Operating expenses are $2,500. The company pays taxes at the rate of 30%.

Date	Transaction	Cost of Goods Sold	Inventory Balance
May 1	Balance: 120 units @ $17.50	(Reminder: Use a separate sheet of paper to complete the table.)	
May 2	Sold 90 units		
May 9	Purchased 150 units @ $19.20		
May 16	Sold 50 units		
May 19	Sold 90 units		
May 27	Purchased 250 units @ $23.00		
May 28	Sold 210 units		
May 31	Purchased 125 units @ $24		
	Final Balances		

LG 18-8, *continued*

Instructions:

a. On a separate page, calculate ending inventory and cost of goods sold for May using each of the following methods: FIFO, LIFO, and moving average. Use the format above and prepare a separate schedule for each method. What ending inventory will appear on the balance sheet for each method?

b. Prepare three comparative income statements to the level of operating income, with each income statement using a different inventory costing method. The cost of goods sold section in each statement should include beginning inventory, purchases, cost of goods available, ending inventory, and costs of goods sold.

c. Which method assigns the most current cost to cost of goods sold? To ending inventory?

d. Which method most closely approximates the actual physical flow of merchandise?

e. Which method results in more additional cash? Why?

LG 18-9. Periodic system: use same data. Rework problem LG 18-8 above assuming that the company uses the periodic inventory method. Compare the results for b through e.

LG 18-10. Compare periodic FIFO and LIFO under conditions of both increasing and decreasing prices. Kearney Technology Company uses an electronic component part that has an increasing cost. Omaha Technology Company uses a component that has had a decreasing cost. The table below shows the inventory information for each company during a recent month. Both companies use the periodic method. The ending inventory for each company is 300 units.

Kearney		Omaha	
Balance	100 units @ $5.00	Balance	100 units @ $10.50
Purchase	400 units @ $6.25	Purchase	400 units @ $9.00
Purchase	500 units @ $7.50	Purchase	500 units @ $7.50
Purchase	200 units @ $9.00	Purchase	200 units @ $6.25
Purchase	200 units @ $10.50	Purchase	200 units @ $5.00

a. For Kearney Company, calculate the cost of goods sold and ending inventory by using FIFO and LIFO.

b. For Omaha Company, calculate the cost of goods sold and ending inventory by using FIFO and LIFO.

c. Compare your answers and comment on the reason for the results. What are the effects on ending inventory and cost of goods sold?

LG 18-11. Misstated inventory costs. The income statements for Scranton Company for July and August are shown below:

Scranton Company	July		August	
Sales revenue		$27,350		$23,200
Cost of goods sold:				
Beginning inventory..............	$8,900		$5,800	
Net purchases	15,750		16,150	
Cost of goods available...........	24,650		21,950	
Less: Ending inventory...........	5,800		5,800	
Cost of goods sold		18,850		16,150
Gross profit		8,500		7,050
Operating Expenses		3,700		3,450
Net Income		$4,800		$3,600

The bookkeeper of the Scranton Company accidentally entered an incorrect amount into the computer and understated the July 1 inventory by $5,800. Unfortunately, the manager also forgot to include in July 31 inventory $700 of items in transit FOB shipping point, which had transferred title to Scranton Company. What is the correct net income for each month?

LG 18-12. Identify system used, apply FIFO and LIFO, prepare income statements, analyze results. Towson Corporation's chief accountant is analyzing the possible effects of using FIFO and LIFO inventory methods. For the year ended December 31, 2017, she has gathered the following information:

Inventory, January 1................	6,500 units: $18,200
Purchase, March 11	20,000 units: 61,000
Purchase, August 23................	12,000 units: 47,400
Purchase, September 5.............	4,000 units: 16,000
Purchase, December 4	8,000 units: 32,800
2017 net sales	$297,000
2017 operating expenses	$105,800
Inventory, December 31.............	14,000 units

a. Based on the information provided, do you think the perpetual or periodic system is being used?
b. Prepare comparative income statements using FIFO and LIFO. The current tax rate is 20%.
c. Identify the reasons for the difference in gross profit and net income.
d. Will there be a difference in cash provided by operations? If so, how much and why does it happen?

Solutions are in the disk at the back of the book and at: www.worthyjames.com

PRACTICE   Learning Goal 18, continued

LG 18-13. Falsified inventory costs. An inventory record for Jones Corporation, which is desperately attempting to show more income in order to increase the price of its stock, is presented below. Because the company uses periodic LIFO, the manager intentionally changes and falsifies the invoice of the last purchase by changing the purchase date of December 23 to January 3, and she changes the receiving report to show January 10, thereby reducing the current period recorded purchases by 15,000 units. However, the merchandise is actually part of the December 31 ending inventory units. When the company's auditors, Tattered and Howe, CPAs, ask for documents, the manager produces copies of the invoices on which the dates appear to be authentic. The junior auditor does not question the use of copied documents (rather than requiring original documents).

a. Prepare both a correct and a falsified cost of goods sold calculations.
b. Explain the causes of the difference.
c. What will the effect be in the next accounting period?

Item	Unit Cost	Units (in 000's)
Beginning inventory	$5	20
Purchase	$8	30
Purchase	$9	40
Purchase	$10	50
Purchase (Dec. 31)	$11	15

The physical inventory count at December 31 is properly supervised by the auditors and is accurate. The count shows 20,000 units still on hand.

LG 18-14. Concept reinforcement. After reading this book, suppose that you decide to find a part-time accounting job to see if you can apply what you have learned. You find a job at a small, but very chic and expensive, specialty grocery store. You notice that the cost of most of the merchandise is regularly increasing, so you decide to let the owner know that LIFO in a period of rising prices will reduce net income and therefore reduce income taxes.

The owner says, "Well, I like the idea of reducing taxes, but I never liked accounting or business classes very much, so I don't remember anything about LIFO—what is it?" After you explain LIFO, she replies, "That is exactly why I decided not to waste time in school—this LIFO method is only something in a book. It has no connection to how I have to do things in the real world."

She continues, "Any store owner knows that you have to put the new items on the *back* of the shelf and push the old items out to the front of the shelf. That is first-in, first-out. What would happen to my expensive clotted creams and my other groceries if I put the new items in the front and let the old items sit in the back? No one would ever buy the older items, and they would go bad and be wasted! I'm sure your accounting teacher means well, but he doesn't understand that LIFO can never work in my business." What do you think about this?

LG 18-15. **Compare the effects of different methods.** On a separate piece of paper, enter the letter a, b, or c for each item in the table below to indicate the method described. Methods: (a) FIFO, (b) LIFO, (c) Average cost.

Description	Method
a. Highest gross profit in a period of rising prices	
b. Lowest gross profit in a period of rising prices	
c. Highest gross profit in a period of decreasing prices	
d. Lowest gross profit in a period of decreasing prices	
e. Easiest method to use	
f. Matches the physical flow of merchandise sold	
g. Matches oldest costs with current period revenue	
h. Matches most recent costs with current period revenues	
i. Results in a balance sheet inventory value with the most current costs	
j. Results in cost of goods sold with the most current costs	
k. Moderates both inventory cost and cost of goods sold; does not produce extreme results	

LG 18-16. **Estimate ending inventory.**

A fire destroyed the warehouse of Arlington Enterprises on August 8. The owner is fully insured but needs to submit an estimate to the insurance company for the cost of the inventory destroyed. The owner summarizes the information for the current year beginning January 1 as follows:

Net sales to July 31: $800,000	Purchases to July 31: $411,200	Freight-in to July 31: $3,800
January 1 inventory: 120,000	August purchases: $15,000	Aug. 1–8 freight-in: $800
July 31 inventory: 197,000	Purchase discounts to July 31: 2,000	Aug. 1–8 purchase discounts: 500

The net sales in August to the date of the fire were $32,000.

Instructions: Calculate an estimate of the value of the destroyed inventory for the insurance claim.

Instructor-Assigned Problems

If you are using this book in a class, these review problems may be assigned by your instructor for homework, group assignments, class work, or other activities. Only your instructor has the solutions.

IA 18-1. **Perpetual system: calculate inventory and cost of goods sold using various methods, prepare income statements.** The schedule below shows sales and purchases information for the month of June. Sales revenue for the month is $22,500. Operating expenses are $3,100. The income tax rate is 30%.

Date	Transaction	Cost of Goods Sold	Inventory Balance
June 1	Balance: 100 units @ $22.50	(Reminder: Use a separate sheet of paper to complete the table.)	
June 5	Sold 84 units		
June 7	Purchased 130 units @ $24		

PRACTICE **Learning Goal 18, continued**

IA 18-1, *continued*

Date	Transaction	Cost of Goods Sold	Inventory Balance
June 14	Sold 70 units	(Reminder: Use a separate sheet of paper to complete the table.)	
June 20	Purchased 215 units @ $25		
June 25	Sold 96 units		
June 27	Sold 130 units		
June 30	Purchased 120 units @ $27		
	Final Balances		

Instructions:

a. On a separate page, calculate ending inventory and cost of goods sold for June using each of the following methods: FIFO, LIFO, and moving average. (Round unit cost to three places and total cost to the nearest dollar.) Use the format above, and prepare a separate schedule for each method. What ending inventory will appear on the balance sheet for each method?

b. Prepare three comparative income statements to the level of operating income, with each income statement using a different inventory costing method. The cost of goods sold section in each statement should include beginning inventory, purchases, cost of goods available, ending inventory, and cost of goods sold.

c. Which method assigns the most current cost to cost of goods sold? To ending inventory?

d. Which method results in more additional cash? Why?

IA 18-2. **Periodic system: calculate inventory and cost of goods sold using various methods, prepare income statements.** *Instructions:* Using the same information in problem IA 18-1, do the following:

a. Calculate ending inventory and cost of goods sold for June using each of the following methods: FIFO, LIFO, and weighted average (round unit cost to three places and total cost to the nearest dollar) for a periodic inventory system. What ending inventory will appear on the balance sheet for each method?

b. Prepare three comparative income statements to the level of operating income, with each income statement using a different inventory costing method. The cost of goods sold section in each statement should include beginning inventory, purchases, cost of goods available, ending inventory, and cost of goods sold.

c. Which method assigns the most current cost to cost of goods sold? To ending inventory?

d. Which method results in more additional cash? Why?

PRACTICE   Learning Goal 18, continued

IA 18-3. **Review of perpetual and periodic, FIFO, LIFO, and average methods.** A business prepares monthly financial statements, and its inventory information for the month of November is presented here. In this problem, you can complete either or both Part I and Part II below, according to your assignment.

Inventory Information		
November		
1	Beginning inventory	20 units @ $20
5	Sale	15 units
11	Purchase	10 units @ $22
15	Sale	5 units
21	Purchase	20 units @ $25
23	Sale	18 units
27	Purchase	10 units @ $27

Part I: Periodic method calculations

Instructions:

a. Calculate cost of goods available, ending inventory, and cost of goods sold using the periodic inventory method. Prepare a comparison table in the following format:

	FIFO	LIFO	Average
Cost of Goods Available			
Less: Ending Inventory			
Cost of Goods Sold			

b. After completing the table, use the formula BI + net P – EI = C of GS to verify the cost of goods sold amount.

c. Identify the FIFO, LIFO, and average differences in cost of goods sold and ending inventory. What is the reason for the differences?

Part II: Perpetual method calculations

Instructions:

c. Use the following format to prepare a table using the perpetual inventory method for FIFO, LIFO, and average cost methods. Round average cost to three places and round final answer to nearest cent.

Date	Purchase	Cost of Goods Sold	Inventory

c. Calculate final totals for each column and use the formula BI + net P – EI = C of GS to verify the ending inventory amount.

d. Identify the FIFO, LIFO, and average differences in cost of goods sold and ending inventory. What is the reason for the differences?

e. If you completed Part I, identify and explain any differences for FIFO, LIFO, and average cost of goods sold between the perpetual and periodic methods.

PRACTICE   **Learning Goal 18, continued**

IA 18-4. **Review of perpetual and periodic, FIFO, LIFO, and average methods.** A business prepares monthly financial statements, and its inventory information for the month of November is presented here. In this problem, you can complete either or both Part I and Part II below, according to your assignment.

Inventory Information		
November		
1	Beginning inventory	20 units @ $20
5	Sale	15 units
11	Purchase	10 units @ $18
15	Sale	5 units
21	Purchase	20 units @ $15
23	Sale	18 units
27	Purchase	10 units @ $13

Part I Periodic method calculations

Instructions:

Using the inventory information in this problem, complete steps a, b, and c from IA18-3 above.

Part II Perpetual method calculations

Instructions:

Using the inventory information in this problem, complete steps c, d, and e from IA18-3 above.

Part III Analysis

Instructions:

If you completed IA18-3, compare your results in this problem to your results in IA18-3. Can you explain the differences?

IA 18-5. **Estimating inventory**

An earthquake severely damaged the storage facilities and records of Anchorage Enterprises on June 20. Inventory was last calculated and placed in secure data storage as of May 31. The company controller prepared the following information to calculate the claim to the insurance company.

a. What is the estimated cost of the destroyed inventory?
b. What would the effect be on the insurance claim if the gross profit percentage decreased? Increased?

Inventory, May 31: $875,410	June purchases: $195,400	June purchase discounts: $1,500
Average gross profit percentage January 1 to May 31: 37%	June net sales: $522,000	June freight-in: $1,200.

PRACTICE   Learning Goal 18, continued

IA18-6. Perpetual system; calculate cost of goods sold and ending inventory, prove inventory answer. Muncie Company uses the perpetual inventory system. At the beginning of the year on January 1, Muncie had 2,800 units of inventory with a total cost of $8,400. The inventory records indicate the activity for the year as follows:

Purchase 1:	4,000 units	Cost: $3.50 per unit
Sale 1:	3,000 units	
Purchase 2:	5,000 units	Cost: $5.00 per unit
Sale 2:	2,700 units	
Purchase 3:	1,000 units	Cost: $6.00 per unit
Sale 3:	4,000 units	

Instructions:

a. Calculate the cost of goods sold and ending inventory using FIFO. Prove the ending inventory amount by two calculations.

b. Calculate the cost of goods sold and ending inventory using LIFO. Prove the ending inventory amount by two calculations.

c. Calculate the cost of goods sold and ending inventory using moving average. (Round average unit cost to two decimal places.) Prove the ending inventory amount by two calculations. (There should be a rounding error of less than $10.)

INTERNET EXERCISES

Ethics — analyze cases. Go to the University of New Mexico UNM Anderson School of Management (at https://danielsethics.mgt.unm.edu/teaching-resources/highlighted-cases-and-case-studies.asp) (Daniels Fund Ethics Initiative Cases). Select a case that interests you. (Use bookmark/favorites to save the location in an Accounting References folder.)

a. Read the case, and write down your ethics commentary notes as your read the case.

b. What are the main ethical issues you identified?

c. If you are using Volume 1 in this set, apply the ethics discussion and guidelines in Learning Goal 10 to analyze the case. If you are not using Volume 1, do the following: 1) Identify the key issues from 'b' above. 2) Determine if there a moral issue of a possibly wrongful act. 3) What decisions would you make or position you would take?

d. Answer the discussion questions at the end of the case.

Your Questions?

It is *very* important to be aware of what you need to understand better. What do you need to understand better about this learning goal? On a separate piece of paper, write the questions that you want to discuss with your classmates, instructor, or supervisor. Try to be very specific about what is bothering you, such as explanations that you do not fully understand.

| LEARNING GOAL 19 | # Record, Report, and Control Fixed Assets and Intangibles |

In this Learning Goal, you will find:

Fixed Assets

Overview

Examples

The expression *fixed assets* refers to the following asset types that have a useful life of more than 1 year and are used for a productive purpose:

- *Property, plant, and equipment* are tangible assets that are used by a business. Examples are land, building, and equipment. These are also called *plant assets* or *plant and equipment*.
- *Natural resources* refers to substances that are taken from the land and consumed. Examples are oil and gas, minerals, and timber.

Non-Examples

- A business purchases some land with the intention of reselling it. The land is not currently being used as part of business operations. The land should be classified as an investment, not a fixed asset.
- A corporation purchases some stock and bonds of another corporation. The stock and bonds should be classified as investments.

Property, Plant, and Equipment Acquisition

Cost Allocation

Overview

A cash payment can be made for any of the following three reasons: to pay for an asset, to pay for an expense, or to pay a claim (creditor or owner). When long-term assets are acquired, expenditures are called **capital expenditures** (also called *capitalizing*). The discussion below shows you how to record capital expenditures for acquisition of property, plant, and equipment.

Definition

Property, plant, and equipment assets:

- are acquired for use in operations and not for resale.
- are long-term (will be used for more than a year).
- have physical substance (are tangible).

Rule: How to Record

To record the acquisition of a long-term asset, apply the GAAP historical cost rule in the following way:

As part of the asset cost, capitalize those expenditures that are normally incurred to acquire (or develop) a particular long-term asset and bring it into its initial normal operating condition.

Do not include general feasibility studies and preliminary analyses—these are operating expenses.

Examples of the Rule

- *Equipment:* The cost of equipment includes purchase price less discounts, plus sales tax and other taxes, freight costs, insurance while in transit, assembly, normal installation costs, and normal testing. Interest is not capitalized.
- *Buildings:* The cost of a purchase includes purchase price and buying costs, make-ready costs, and prior unpaid property taxes. Interest is not capitalized. Construction costs include all materials, labor, and services related to the asset.
- *Land:* The cost includes purchase price and all buying costs, unpaid property taxes, landscaping, and all costs such as razing and grading, needed to prepare the land for its intended use.
- *Land improvements:* Costs include a separate account for driveways, fences, parking lots, and any other depreciable items of limited life related to the property.
- *Construction period interest:* Interest on borrowed money used to construct an asset is capitalized for the amount paid during the construction period.

continued ▶

Cost Allocation, *continued*

Examples of the Rule,
continued

■ *Research and development:* Most research and development expenditures are required to be expensed, and they become part of operating expenses – unless the expenditures definitely create a new tangible product, at which point they are capitalized.

Lump Sum (Group)
Purchases

Assets purchased as a group should be capitalized by allocating the cost in proportion to the appraised value of each asset.

Example: Land, building, and equipment are purchased together for a single price of $2,100,000. The appraised values are: land, $750,000; building, $1,250,000; equipment, $500,000. The cost allocation is:

Land: $ 750,000/$2,500,000 × $2,100,000 = $ 630,000
Building: $1,250,000/$2,500,000 × $2,100,000 = $1,050,000
Equipment: $ 500,000/$2,500,000 × $2,100,000 = $ 420,000

Property, Plant, & Equipment Operations

Overview

Operational Expenses

Operational expenses related to plant and equipment assets generally fall into the categories of either:

1. depreciation, or
2. expenditures for repairs and maintenance.

Payments for ordinary repairs and maintenance are often referred to as **revenue expenditures**.

Operational expenses are discussed in the next sections.

Depreciation

Overview

Depreciation is caused by wear and tear and by obsolescence. On pages 47 and 139, we discussed the recording of depreciation as an application of the matching principle. Using this principle, depreciation allocates the cost of a long-term tangible asset as expense into the periods in which the asset provides benefits. An exception is land, which does not depreciate.

We also discussed a common depreciation method called *straight-line* depreciation. However, various other depreciation methods may sometimes provide a better application of the matching principle because these methods more closely follow how an asset provides its benefits. The two most frequently used of these methods are discussed below.

Double-Declining Balance (200% Declining Balance)

Calculation Method

To calculate the annual depreciation expense for all years except the final year:

- **Step 1:** Calculate the straight-line rate per year, and then double it. This is the **double-declining-balance (DDB)** rate used for each year of depreciation.
- **Step 2:** Multiply the asset's *book value* (cost minus accumulated depreciation) at the beginning of the year by the DDB rate.

To calculate the final year's annual depreciation expense, subtract any estimated residual value from the book value *at the beginning of the final year*. (This reduces the final year book value to residual value.)

continued

Double-Declining Balance (200% Declining Balance), *continued*

Example

The example below shows a DDB depreciation calculation for a $3,600 asset purchased on January 2, with a 5-year estimated life and $100 residual value.

Straight-line rate per year: $\frac{1}{5}$ = 20%. Doubled: 20% × 2 = 40%

Per-year calculation of expense (calendar year periods):

	Current Year Calculation					End of the Year	
Year	**Book Value: Start of Year**	×	**DDB Rate**	=	**Annual Expense**	**Accumulated Depreciation**	**Book Value**
2013	$3,600	×	.4	=	$1,440	$1,440	$2,160
2014	2,160	×	.4	=	864	2,304	1,296
2015	1,296	×	.4	=	518	2,822	778
2016	778	×	.4	=	311	3,133	467
2017	467		467 − 100	=	367	3,500	100

Result

Compared to straight line ($700 per year), DDB results in more depreciation expense in the first periods and less in later periods. This is called an *accelerated depreciation method*.

Change to Straight-Line

Frequently, companies will change a double-declining calculation to straight-line for the remaining years of an asset's life. In the example above, if the depreciation were switched to straight-line at the beginning of year 2016, the annual depreciation expense would be (778 − 100)/2 = 339 for years 2016 and 2017.

TIP

The double-declining-balance method is really just one (but the most popular) application of what is known as *fixed percentage on a declining balance*. For example, a different application is to use 150% declining balance. How would this be different? It's easy—instead of using 2 times (200%) the straight-line rate, you would use 1-1/2 times (150%) the straight-line rate. In the example above, the result would be 20% × 1.5 = 30% rate (instead of 40%). Generally, double-declining is the most accelerated method used.

Companies are free to develop any depreciation method they want—GAAP only requires that the method used is "systematic and rational"!

Units-of-Production Depreciation

Introduction

The *units-of-production method* calculates a fixed amount of depreciation expense per unit of output that an asset produces. This method should only be used in situations where obsolescence or the non-operating passage of time are not significant factors in the depreciation.

Calculation Method

- **Step 1:** Estimate the useful life of the asset in terms of the number of units of product or service that it can produce (units of production, or UOP).
- **Step 2:** Determine depreciation expense per unit as follows: (Cost – Residual Value)/UOP = Expense Per Unit.
- **Step 3:** At the end of each period, multiply the units produced by the expense per unit.

Example

The example below is for an aircraft jet engine purchased in 2014 with a cost of $2,500,000 and an estimated life of 100,000 operating hours. Residual value is $50,000. ($2,500,000 – $50,000)/100,000 hrs. = $24.50/hr.

| | Current Year Calculation | | | | End of the Year | |
Year	Units of Production	×	Expense Per Unit	= Annual Expense	Accumulated Depreciation	Book Value
2014	12,000 hours	×	$24.50	= $294,000	$294,000	$2,206,000
2015	5,200 hours	×	24.50	= 127,400	421,400	2,078,600
2016	25,000 hours	×	24.50	= 612,500	1,033,900	1,466,100
2017	18,700 hours	×	24.50	= 458,150	1,492,050	1,007,950

Income Tax Depreciation

Overview

Depreciation for federal income tax purposes is based on selecting a depreciation table from mandatory tables; the table to use is determined by the type of asset. This system is known as **MACRS** for *Modified Accelerated Cost Recovery System*. The system is designed to limit choices of asset life and method and thereby ensure consistency and reduce the excessive depreciation calculations that produce exaggerated tax deductions. MACRS tables generally result in accelerated depreciation, although MACRS also permits straight-line depreciation.

The calculation of depreciation expense for tax purposes is an extensive subject. You can find detailed guidance in Internal Revenue Service (IRS) Publication 946. State tax rules vary, although many states conform to IRS methods; however, you should check with your local state tax authority.

Partial Year Depreciation

Overview

If an asset is purchased or sold during the year, depreciation expense must be prorated if the depreciation is being calculated based on the passage of time. *Be extra careful to remember that this must be done for any period in which an asset is either purchased or sold.*

Double-Declining Example

Refer to the table on page 742. Assume that the asset was purchased on April 30, 2013 and the accounting period is a calendar year that ends on December 31.

- 2013 (partial year) depreciation expense: $(\$3,600 \times .4) \times \frac{8}{12} = \$960$

- 2014 depreciation expense: $(\$3,600 - \$960) \times .4 = \$1,056$

- 2015 depreciation expense: $(\$3,600 - \$2016) \times .4 = \$634$, and so on

Straight-Line Example

Refer to the table on page 742. Assume that the asset was purchased on April 30, 2013. Assume that straight-line depreciation is used and there is no residual value.

Annual depreciation expense: $(\$3,600/5) = \$720$

- 2013 (partial year) depreciation expense: $\$720 \times \frac{8}{12} = \$480$

- Future years continue on at $720 per year. The last depreciation calculation is for four months in 2018: this is $\$720 \times \frac{4}{12}$ for the first four months of 2018.

Mid-Month Methods

If an asset is purchased or sold during a month, various acceptable methods can be used for calculating depreciation for the partial month. Whatever is selected, the method should be used consistently. *Examples:*

- Record a full month's depreciation for an asset purchased on or before the 15th or disposed of after the 15th day of a month. Record no depreciation for an asset purchased after the 15th or disposed of before the 15th.
- Prorate the depreciation based on days held during the month.
- Begin depreciation on the first full month an asset is owned.
- For MACRS tax purposes, tables are provided.

Using Fully Depreciated Assets

Overview

A fully depreciated asset is an asset on which all depreciation has been taken. The asset is held for a period beyond its estimated useful life and continues to be used and to provide benefits. Until such an asset is finally disposed of, the book value of the asset (cost minus accumulated depreciation) simply remains on the books and on the balance sheet.

What If the Estimated Life Was Wrong?

If a plant asset continues to be useful beyond its estimated life, this simply means that the estimate of useful life was too low. To that extent, the depreciation expense was allocated too quickly and should have been spread over more years.

If an asset becomes unusable sooner than its estimated life, then the depreciation expense was allocated too slowly, and there will be a loss in the year when the asset is removed from the books. (See the following section on asset retirement.) It is difficult to precisely estimate an asset's useful asset life. In either case, some reasonable degree of error is normal and expected.

However, if it becomes apparent early in an asset's life that the estimated life is significantly incorrect, then the estimated life can be revised. The discussion below explains this procedure.

TIP

Can a business use different depreciation methods for different individual assets? Yes, it can. GAAP does not consider this to be a violation of the consistency principle. For example, in the same business, one truck can be depreciated using the straight-line method and another truck can be depreciated using the double-declining-balance method.

Changing the Estimated Useful Life

Overview

No one can perfectly estimate the useful life of an asset. Generally, an estimate is not changed if it appears to be reasonably close. However, if part way through an asset's use, it is clear that the estimate was materially incorrect, then the estimated life can be changed.

continued ▶

Changing the Estimated Useful Life, *continued*

Procedure

- Determine the remaining years of asset life.
- Depreciate the remaining book value (minus any residual value) over the revised remaining years of life.

Example

Equipment with a cost of $9,000 and $1,000 residual value is being depreciated by the straight-line method over a 5-year useful life, with annual depreciation expense of $1,600. After three years of use, the useful life is revised to 7 years. Therefore, remaining years of useful life are: $7 - 3 = 4$. At this point the book value is $9,000 - $4,800 = $4,200$. The revised annual depreciation is:

$$\frac{(\$4,200 - \$1,000)}{4} = \$800$$

TIP

When referring to depreciable assets, the expressions ***book value*** and ***carrying value*** both mean the same thing. They both mean asset cost minus accumulated depreciation.

Misconceptions About Depreciation

Overview

The concept of depreciation as used in accounting and finance is often misunderstood. These misunderstandings are often repeated in financial reporting and business publications.

Misconceptions About Depreciation, *continued*

Common Mistakes

The table below shows the most common misconceptions about the concept of depreciation.

Misconception	Explanation
Depreciation means a decrease in the sales value or replacement value of an asset.	This is the "everyday" or nonfinancial meaning of depreciation. In accounting, depreciation is an application of the matching principle and has nothing to do with the sales or replacement value of an asset. Depreciation means allocating the cost of a plant asset as an expense into the accounting periods in which the asset provides benefits to a business.
Depreciation is a source of cash.	Depreciation is never a source of cash. (Look at a depreciation journal entry—no cash is involved!) Depreciation is simply the using-up of a non-cash asset.
Accumulated depreciation (sometimes called *reserve for depreciation*) represents a cash fund to replace a plant asset.	Accumulated depreciation is a contra asset account that records the cumulative amount of depreciation of an asset. It does not represent cash. Any cash balances would be shown as part of the asset "cash" on the balance sheet.
The amount of depreciation recorded depends on the profitability of a business.	Depreciation is calculated in a rational and systematic manner based entirely on the best possible application of the matching principle. This is done by estimating the useful life of an asset and allocating its cost into depreciation expense during the useful life.

Check Your Understanding

Calculate the depreciation expense for the following situations.

1. A truck is purchased for $11,000 on January 2. The truck is estimated to have a 5-year useful life and $1,000 residual value. What is the depreciation expense for the year ended December 31 using the straight-line method?

2. The truck in question 1 was purchased on October 1.

3. A truck is purchased for $12,000 on January 2, 2017. The truck is estimated to have a 5-year useful life and $1,000 residual value. What is the depreciation expense for the year ended December 31, 2018, using the double-declining-balance method?

4. A truck is purchased for $12,000 on October 1, 2017. The truck is estimated to have a 5-year useful life and $1,000 residual value. What is the depreciation expense for the year ended December 31, 2018, using the double-declining-balance method?

5. A truck is purchased for $55,000 on January 2. The truck is estimated to have a useful output of 100,000 miles with $1,000 residual value. During the current year, the truck is driven for 18,000 miles. What is the depreciation expense for the year ended December 31 using the units-of-production method?

Answers

1. ($11,000 − $1,000)/5 = $2,000

2. ($11,000 − $1,000)/5 = $2,000. The truck was owned for 3 months in the current year, so the depreciation expense is prorated for 3 months: $2,000 × $\frac{3}{12}$ = $500.

3. The asset has a 5-year estimated useful life. This rate is $\frac{1}{5}$ = 20% per year. Doubling this, the double-declining rate is 40%. The 2017 depreciation expense is $12,000 × .40 = $4,800. At the end of the first year, the book value is $12,000 − $4,800 = $7,200. Therefore, the 2018 depreciation expense is $7,200 × .40 = $2,880.

4. The asset has a 5-year estimated useful life. This rate is $\frac{1}{5}$ = 20% per year. Doubling this, the double-declining rate is 40%. A full first-year depreciation expense is $12,000 × .40 = $4,800. However, the asset was owned for only three months, so the depreciation must be prorated for three months: $4,800 × $\frac{3}{12}$ = $1,200. At the end of the first year, the book value is $12,000 − $1,200 = $10,800. Therefore, the 2018 depreciation expense is $10,800 × .40 = $4,320.

5. ($55,000 − $1,000)/100,000 = $.54 per mile depreciation. 18,000 miles × $.54 = $9,720.

You can use financial statement information to get an idea of the approximate age of depreciable assets. Divide the annual depreciation expense into the accumulated depreciation. This works best if the company uses straight-line depreciation—most companies do.

Repairs and Maintenance

Normal Repairs

After an asset begins its initial operation, any expenditure that maintains the asset is an expense. This is what we usually consider to be normal maintenance such as lubrication, parts replacement, painting, and so on.

Extraordinary Repairs

You must be careful to distinguish normal maintenance from any expenditure that materially *improves the function* of the asset or materially *extends its life*. These are capital expenditures, and they are called **extraordinary repairs**. Examples are an engine replacement on a truck, replacing a roof on a building, or adding faster chips to your computer. These items are usually recorded by debiting the Accumulated Depreciation account, which increases an asset's book value. *If the expenditure extends the asset's life, the asset's new book value is depreciated over the asset's new remaining life.*

Additions and Betterments

An **addition** is an enlargement or expansion of the plant or office of a business. An example is the addition of a new room to a building. A **betterment** is an improvement in the functionality of a plant or office. An example is the addition of air conditioning or new lighting. The cost of an addition or betterment should be capitalized as a separate asset by debiting an asset account. The new asset is then depreciated over its estimated life.

Disposition

Three Disposition Methods

Overview

Plant and equipment assets can be disposed of in three basic ways. An asset can be:

- Retired (discarded)
- Sold
- Exchanged for another asset. (See Learning Goal 19 appendix)

Retired Assets

Asset Discarded

An asset is said to be retired when it is discarded (or "scrapped") because it is no longer useful. Nothing is received when the asset is given up. This can happen at any time because the asset has been used up and no longer provides any service potential or because something destroyed the asset.

continued ▶

Retired Assets, *continued*

Discarding Examples

A computer that cost $24,500 with an estimated life of 5 years is retired at the end of the fourth year. The remaining $4,900 book value is a loss.

12/31	Accumulated Depreciation—Computer	19,600	
	Loss on Retirement of Plant Assets	4,900	
	Computer		24,500

If the asset is fully depreciated (a zero book value), there would be no loss:

12/31	Accumulated Depreciation—Computer	24,500	
	Computer		24,500

Sold Assets

Rule

To record the sale of an asset, compare the asset's book value to the proceeds received. The difference is a gain or loss.

Selling Examples

The first entry below shows the computer being sold at the end of the fourth year at a sales price of $7,000. In the second example, the sales price is $4,000. The book value at the end of the fourth year is $24,500 − $19,600 = $4,900.

Gain

12/31	Cash	7,000	
	Accumulated Depreciation—Computer	19,600	
	Computer		24,500
	Gain on Sale		2,100

The book value given up: $4,900
Total effect:

$$A \uparrow \quad \downarrow \quad = \quad L \quad + \quad \uparrow SE$$
$$7,000 \quad 4,900 \qquad\qquad 2,100$$

Loss

12/31	Loss on Sale of Plant Assets	900	
	Cash	4,000	
	Accumulated Depreciation—Computer	19,600	
	Computer		24,500

The book value given up: $4,900
Total effect:

$$A \uparrow \quad \downarrow \quad = \quad L \quad + \quad \downarrow SE$$
$$4,000 \quad 4,900 \qquad\qquad 900$$

Impaired Assets

Overview and Procedure

Definition

An asset is considered to be *impaired* when it has lost an amount of its economic value that is considered to be significant. The word "impairment" is typically used in reference to valuation loss of long-term fixed assets and certain intangible assets.

Why It is Important

Impaired assets indicate a loss of value that should be recognized. This is important because: 1) Although the balance sheet is not intended to show current market values of assets (with limited exceptions), nevertheless accounting principles should not allow balance sheet values to be materially overstated, and 2) Significant value decreases create economic losses that should be recognized on the income statement.

Basic Procedure

GAAP requires the following basic impairment procedure for tangible assets and intangible assets with definite lives:

1. Management should test for impairment if it observes any indicators of possible impairment. Such indicators would include: a material decrease in the sales value of an asset, negative cash flows or operating losses, a material change in the use of an asset, or plans to dispose of an asset.

2. Test for impairment:

Step	Comment
1. Determine the current asset book value (cost – accumulated depreciation)	Book value is also sometimes called "carrying value".
2. Estimate the total (undiscounted) future cash flows from the asset including an estimated sale value.	This is an estimate and will be subjective. Some assets provide a clear source of cash flow and others do not.
3. If the estimated future cash flows are less than the asset book value, the asset is impaired.	This will require a loss to be recognized.
4. Measurement of loss: The amount of loss to record is the difference between the asset's book value and a net market value sales price ("fair value"), if lower than book value.	Example: Market value sales price: $500,000 Less: selling expenses: (10,000) Net amount: $490,000 Book value: $600,000 Impairment loss: $110,000

continued ▶

Overview and Procedure, *continued*

Example

Palo Alto Company owns equipment that produces mobile phone cases. The equipment was purchased at a cost of $150,000 two years ago and is estimted to have a 6-year useful life with straight-line depreciation expense of $25,000 per year. In the current period, management discovers that the machine has begun to operate much less efficiently and produce fewer units. This has the effect of reducing its operating cash flow to $15,000 per year for the next four years and its future estimated market value sales price to $20,000. The current fair value of the equipment is $52,000.

- Current book value: $150,000 − $50,000 = $100,000
- Undiscounted future cash flows: ($15,000 × 4) + $20,000 = $80,000
- Book value vs. cash flows: $100,000 exceeds $80,000 = Asset is impaired.
- Amount of impairement loss: $100,000 − $52,000 = $48,000

Journal entry: Record the impairment loss as follows: first eliminate accumulated depreciation (a debit). Then adjust the asset cost down to current fair value by crediting the asset for the difference between the original cost and the current market value (fair value).

Accumulated Depreciation	50,000	
Impairment Loss	48,000	
Equipment ($150,000 − $52,000)		98,000

Total effect:

$$A \uparrow \quad \downarrow \quad = \quad L \quad + \quad SE \downarrow$$
$$50{,}000 \quad 98{,}000 \qquad\qquad\qquad 48{,}000$$

Result: the asset has a "new" cost of $52,000 which becomes the basis for depreciation over the asset's remaining life. The impairment loss is permanent and a higher value cannot be restored if the asset value increases later. Notice that although a loss is recorded in the current period, future depreciation expense will be reduced because of the new lower recorded cost (minus new residual value), increasing future net income.

How to Report Impairment

An impairment loss should be reported as part of continuing operations, before tax. The clearest reporting is in the "other" section of the income statement. Footnote disclosure of the details and estimating methods is also required.

Overview and Procedure, *continued*

TIP

The valuation adjustment to record impairment is a departure from historical cost (original transaction value) that is the basic valuation rule. Conservatism in accounting usually requires that historical cost be reduced if there is a significant decrease in an asset value, which can be calculated in different ways, depending on the type of asset.

For example, in addition to an impairment loss for long-term assets, we also have seen valuation adjustments happen with the accounts receivable adjustment for uncollectible accounts, and with inventory for the lower of cost or sales value adjustment. In all these cases, there was a particular GAAP rule that required the recorded historical cost (original transaction value) be reduced under certain conditions.

Internal Control for Plant and Equipment

Essential Methods

Overview	Plant and equipment, although less subject to theft and loss than inventory, nevertheless usually has a much higher dollar value than inventory and is still subject to theft, loss, and damage. The following discussion summarizes key elements of internal control for plant and equipment.
Assign Identifying Numbers	Assign each asset a unique identifying number that is permanently affixed to the asset in a way that makes it difficult to remove. Maintain a permanent file that shows the asset names, their identifying numbers, and their locations.
Periodically Identify the Assets	Perform a physical identification of plant and equipment assets periodically. This is similar to the physical count that is performed for inventory, although the equipment count can be performed less frequently.
Safeguard the Assets	Physically safeguard valuable or easily removable assets by security devices.

Check Your Understanding

Write the completed sentences on a separate piece of paper. The answers are below.

For property, plant, and equipment, we examined the three basic topics of significance, which are
· · · · · · · ·, · · · · · · · ·, and · · · · · · · · .

To record the purchase of a property, plant, and equipment item, we should capitalize as asset cost any expenditure that is · · · · · · · · required to acquire the item and bring it into its initial · · · · · · · · operating condition.

Typical operating expenditures recorded as expenses related to property, plant, and equipment are
· · · · · · · ·, which applies the matching principle to long-term assets, and · · · · · · · · and · · · · · · · · expenses, which are required to maintain an asset in normal operating condition.

There are three ways to dispose of an asset. These are to · · · · · · · · it, to · · · · · · · · it, and to · · · · · · · · it. If there is a gain or loss on disposal, it is always the difference between the value of what is received for the asset and the · · · · · · · · · · · · · · · · · of the asset given plus cash given.

Answers

For property, plant, and equipment, we examined the three basic topics of significance, which are acquisition, operation, and disposal.

To record the purchase of a property, plant, and equipment item, we should capitalize as asset cost any expenditure that is normally required to acquire the item and bring it into its initial normal operating condition.

Typical operating expenditures recorded as expenses related to property, plant, and equipment are depreciation, which applies the matching principle to long-term assets, and repairs and maintenance expenses, which are required to maintain an asset in normal operating condition.

There are three ways to dispose of an asset. These are to discard it, to sell it, and to exchange it. If there is a gain or loss on disposal, it is always the difference between the value of what is received for the asset and the book value of the asset given plus cash given.

Natural Resources

Overview

Examples

Examples of natural resources are minerals, timber, and oil. Natural resources are long-term assets.

Acquisition and Operation

Acquisition Cost

Natural resources are long-term assets and for most natural resources all costs related to acquisition of natural resources are capitalized. *Exception:* GAAP makes an important exception for those natural resource properties that involve exploration costs, such as for oil or minerals. GAAP presently permits two opposite approaches for recording the cost of acquiring these resources. The first method (*full costs*) permits all exploration costs to be capitalized as part of the asset. This includes unsuccessful exploration. The second method (*successful efforts*) permits the unsuccessful exploration costs to be recorded as an expense, and only the successful exploration costs are recorded as part of the asset cost.

Depletion

Normally, land cost is not depreciated or ever recorded as an expense. One exception to this is loss resulting from toxic waste problems. Another important exception is **depletion**, which is the allocation of the cost of a natural resource asset over the asset's estimated amount of resources that will be removed or extracted. Depletion is similar to units-of-production depreciation.

continued

Acquisition and Operation, *continued*

Example

Mega Mineral Company purchased land for $10,000,000. The company intends to mine coal. The company estimates that the land will have no residual value due to severe environmental damage from the mining operations. The company estimates that it will extract 200,000 tons of coal from the land. In the first year, 5,000 tons are extracted and 4,000 tons are sold. Use the procedure table below to calculate depletion cost and inventory.

Step	Procedure	Example
1	Calculate cost per ton using the formula: (cost – residual value)/estimated units	$\dfrac{(\$10{,}000{,}000 - 0)}{200{,}000} = \$50$ per ton
2	Calculate total cost of extracted units.	$\$50 \times 5{,}000 = \$250{,}000$
3	Subtract the cost of unsold units to determine depletion expense.	$\$250{,}000 - (\$50 \times 1{,}000) = \$200{,}000$

Journal Entry

The journal entry below shows the depletion cost of the 5,000 tons of coal and the cost of goods sold when 4,000 tons are sold.

Coal Inventory		250,000	
Accumulated Depletion			250,000
Cost of Goods Sold		200,000	
Coal Inventory			200,000

Intangible Assets

Overview

Definition

In accounting, ***intangible asset*** has a specific meaning that refers to a long-term asset with no physical substance that is not a financial instrument. Intangible assets are usually legal rights but also include goodwill.

Examples

- ***Patent:*** The exclusive right granted by the U.S. government to manufacture and sell an invention generally for 20 years.
- ***Trademark:*** The ownership and exclusive right granted by the U.S. government to use a product-related word, description, title, or symbol for 10 years plus unlimited renewals of 10 years each. *Example:* Coca-Cola.
- ***Copyright:*** An exclusive right granted by the U.S. government to reproduce and sell a published or artistic work for the life of the creator plus 70 years.
- ***Franchise:*** A contractual agreement between an owner, called the *franchisor* and the user, called the *franchisee,* in which the franchisee pays the franchisor for the right to exclusively use the franchisor's name and sell the franchisor's products, usually within a designated geographic area.
- ***Goodwill:*** The amount paid for a business that is in excess of the fair market value of the owner's equity. This excess is attributed to *intangible* attributes (such as location or efficient employees) of the business that are expected to produce higher profits than similar businesses.
- ***Leasehold:*** The right to occupy a building or land with a long-term lease agreement.

TIP

In case you were wondering, because accounts receivable and notes receivable are legal rights to collect money, they are intangible. Prepaid expenses are also intangible assets. However, none of these qualify for the definition of *intangible* above—a receivable is a financial instrument, and prepaid expense is generally short term.

These items may be classified as "intangible" for other purposes, such as certain tax calculations.

Acquisition and Operation

Cost

- *Purchased:* Intangible assets cost money, just like tangible assets. The capitalized cost of intangible assets includes the purchase price as well as the design and registration costs (if developed). Legal fees to defend legal rights are added to the cost.

- *Developed:* Any *development* costs related to an intangible asset, such as research and development, are expensed. In this way, intangible assets cost is different from tangible assets costs, which include development and construction. (*Note:* A special rule for computer software requires expensing only until *technological feasibility* is determined to have been achieved—i.e., the point at which the software becomes a functional and marketable asset that will provide service potential.)

Amortization

Similar to the depreciation of tangible assets, the cost of an intangible asset is expensed over the life of the asset. For an intangible asset, this process is called **amortization**.

TIP

Be careful with the word *amortization*. It has other financial meanings:

1. A reduction in loan principal over a period of time
2. Spreading the cost of any expenditure over a period of time
3. Allocating a bond premium or discount over a period of time

Rule for Amortization

- If an intangible asset has a *definite legal life*, calculate amortization on a straight-line basis by dividing the cost of the intangible asset by the *shorter of* its legal life or its estimated useful life.

- If an intangible asset has an *indefinite legal life* (such as a trademark or goodwill) there is no amortization. Instead, the asset is regularly tested for loss of value, called *impairment*. If there is impairment, the asset's value is written down or written off, as described on page 751.

Example

The entry below shows an annual journal entry to amortize a patent with a cost of $255,000 and an estimated useful of 8 years. (Legal life is 20 years.)

Amortization Expense	31,875	
Patent		31,875

Financial Statement Presentation

Fixed Assets and Intangible Assets

Balance Sheet

Property, plant, and equipment and natural resources are usually shown together as a section below total long-term investments, or, if there are no long-term investments, they are shown below total current assets. Intangible assets are usually reported as a separate section under property, plant, and equipment and natural resources.

Example

Total current assets			$ XXX
Long-term investments			XXX
Property, plant, and equipment:			
Land	$950,000		
Land improvements	420,000		
Buildings	1,500,000		
Equipment	370,000		
Less: Accumulated depreciation	(715,000)		
		$2,525,000	
Mineral lands	2,100,000		
Less: Accumulated depletion	(1,500,000)		
		600,000	
Total property, plant, and equipment			3,125,000
Intangible assets			
Patents, net of accumulated amortization of $200,000			425,000

Income Statement

- Depreciation expense is an operating expense on the income statement. Depending on how the asset is used, depreciation expense is reported as part of either selling or administrative expenses.

- Depletion expense is reported as the cost of producing the product, so it is treated just like cost of goods sold for the units of resource sold.

- Amortization expense is an operating expense. It is usually reported as an administrative expense.

Note: The treatments above for depreciation and amortization are for non-manufacturing companies. In a manufacturing company, these items may also become part of inventory and cost of goods sold.

GAAP Weakness

Comparability and Reliability

Financial Statements Not Comparable

Just as with GAAP for the other non-cash assets we have studied, the available selection of different GAAP methods relating to long-term assets can create financial statements that are not comparable to each other when businesses use different methods. Some examples of the alternative rules for long-term assets are: (1) the choice of depreciation methods and (2) the *full cost* or the *successful efforts* methods for exploration expenditures.

Manipulating Financial Statements

By now you have seen that GAAP permits the use of estimates in many applications. The intent of this is to permit the flexibility that will result in more accurate financial statements reflecting the economic environment of each individual business.

The dark side of the use of estimates, however, is that unethical businesses can use estimates to manipulate financial statement reporting. Some examples are:

1. Manipulating asset valuation (impairment and exchanges)
2. Manipulating cash flow estimates (impairment and exchanges)
3. Subjectivity in applying repair and maintenance guidelines
4. Estimates of asset life and units for depreciation, amortization, and depletion

"New from accounting, sir. Two and two is four again."

Comparability and Reliability, *continued*

IFRS and GAAP

In the context of our discussion, there are several notable differences between IFRS (International Financial Reporting Standards) and GAAP.

- GAAP does not allow impairment losses to be reversed. IFRS allows later asset write-ups and write-downs based on appraised fair market value.
- GAAP generally requires intangible items to be purchased in order to be recorded as assets. IFRS allows an internally developed item to be recorded as an asset if there is a probable future benefit and the item value can be estimated.
- GAAP allows but does not require major components of an asset to be depreciated separately. IFRS requires that significant components with different lives be depreciated separately.

QUICK REVIEW

- Accounting for fixed assets involves three topics: acquisition, operation, and disposition.

- An asset is acquired and recorded at its capitalized cost, which may include various expenditures to bring the asset into normal operating condition. If several items are purchased together for one price, the items are appraised, and the purchase cost is allocated to the items based on their relative appraised values.

- Operations for plant and equipment and natural resources involves recording operating expenses such as repairs, maintenance, and depreciation and depletion expenses. It is very important to distinguish capital expenditures from operating expenses.

- Depreciation is the process of allocating to expense the capitalized cost of a plant asset over its useful life. Different depreciation methods are straight line, double-declining balance, and units of production. Tax depreciation is called MACRS.

- Depreciation can be revised. This occurs when the estimated useful life of an asset is changed or additional capital expenditures are made to an asset to improve its function or extend its life.

- Several common misunderstandings about depreciation are the beliefs that the purpose of depreciation is to record change in asset value, that depreciation is a source of cash, and that accumulated depreciation is a reserve cash fund.

- Fixed assets can be disposed of in three ways: discarded, sold, or exchanged.

- Accounting for intangible assets requires amortization of the asset cost as an operating expense. The amortization is straight-line over the asset's estimated useful life or legal life, whichever is less.

- A summary of cost allocation for fixed and intangible assets:

  - Plant and equipment → Depreciation
  - Natural resources   → Depletion
  - Intangibles   → Amortization

- On a balance sheet, plant and equipment and natural resource assets are shown as separate items under the classification of property, plant, and equipment. Intangible assets are shown as separate items under the classification of intangible assets.

VOCABULARY

Accelerated depreciation method: depreciation methods that result in greater depreciation early in an asset's life and less depreciation later in the asset's life (page 742)

Addition: a capital expenditure for an enlargement or expansion of a plant or office (page 749)

Amortization: the allocation of the cost of an intangible asset into expense over its estimated useful life (page 758)

Betterment: a capital expenditure that is an improvement in the functionality of a plant or office (page 749)

Book value: asset cost minus accumulated depreciation (page 746)

Capital expenditure: an expenditure to purchase, develop, or improve an asset (page 739)

Carrying value: an expression that means the same as book value (page 746)

Copyright: the exclusive right granted by the U.S. government to reproduce and sell a published or artistic work for a period of the life of the creator plus 70 years (see page 757)

Depletion: the allocation of the cost of a natural resource into expense over its estimated useful life (page 755)

Double-declining-balance (DDB) method: an accelerated depreciation method (page 741)

Extraordinary repair: a major repair that extends a plant asset's life or improves its functionality and is treated as a capital expenditure (page 749)

Franchise: the exclusive right to use another's name and sell another's products (page 757)

Goodwill: the amount paid for a business that is in excess of the fair market value of the owner's equity (page 757)

Impaired asset: an asset that it has lost a significant amount of its economic value (page 751)

Intangible assets: long-term assets with no physical substance (page 757)

Leasehold: the right to occupy a building or land with a long-term lease agreement (page 757)

MACRS: a depreciation method required for income tax calculation (page 743)

Natural resources: substances that are taken from the land and consumed (see page 738)

Patent: the exclusive right granted by the U.S. government to manufacture and sell an invention for 20 years (page 757)

Property, plant, and equipment: long-term tangible productive assets except natural resources (page 738)

Revenue expenditure: a payment that is an expense (page 740)

Trade-in allowance: an amount offered for an asset given in exchange for a new asset and that reduces the cash paid for the new asset (page 782)

Trademark: the ownership and exclusive right granted by the U.S. government to use a product-related word, description, title, or symbol for 10 years plus 10-year renewals (page 757)

Units-of-production of method: a depreciation method that calculates depreciation based on a fixed amount of depreciation expense per unit of output (page 743)

Learning Goal 19 is about accounting for fixed assets and intangibles. Use these questions to practice what you have learned.

Multiple Choice
Select the best answer.

1. Which of the following is correct?
   a. Record capital expenditures as expenses and revenue expenditures as assets.
   b. Record revenue expenditures as expenses and capital expenditures as assets.
   c. Capitalize expenditures.
   d. Record receipts as revenue and capitalize payments.

2. All expenditures normally required to acquire a plant asset and to put it into initial normal operating condition are:
   a. capitalized as part of the asset cost.
   b. revenue expenditures.
   c. adjustments to book value by debiting accumulated depreciation.
   d. allocated based on relative appraisal values.

3. The procedure of allocating the cost of a plant and equipment asset into expense during the accounting periods in which it provides benefits is called:
   a. depletion.
   b. allocation.
   c. depreciation.
   d. service potential.

4. The depreciable cost of newly acquired property, plant, and equipment should be:
   a. book value.
   b. cost less residual value.
   c. cost less accumulated depreciation.
   d. fair market replacement value.

5. Kingsville Enterprises purchased some equipment, a building, and a truck for $600,000. The appraised values of each item are $80,000, $650,000, and $70,000, respectively. To record the purchase, debit:
   a. Equipment $200,000; Building $200,000; Truck $200,000.
   b. Equipment $106,640; Building $866,667; Truck $93,333.
   c. Equipment $80,000; Building $650,000; Truck $70,000.
   d. Equipment $60,000; Building $487,500; Truck $52,500.

6. St. John's Company made the following expenditures while acquiring some equipment: equipment cost, $82,000; sales tax, $5,330; shipping costs, $900; uninsured damage during shipping, $1,200; installation materials costs, $2,700; employee wages for employees performing initial testing, $2,000. What is the cost of the equipment?
   a. $92,930
   b. $92,030
   c. $90,930
   d. none of the above

7. Which of the following methods always allocates an equal amount of depreciation expense each full year?
   a. straight-line
   b. double-declining balance
   c. units-of-production
   d. MACRS

8. Book value means:
   a. total accumulated depreciation.
   b. asset cost minus accumulated depreciation.
   c. the remaining undepreciated cost of an asset.
   d. both b and c; they are the same thing.

9. During the current year, Thunderbird Company purchased, for $5,000,000, land that contains an estimated 100,000 tons of bauxite mineral deposits. During the year, 20,000 tons are extracted, and 18,000 tons are sold. What is the current depletion expense for the year and the remaining inventory?
   a. $900,000 depletion expense and $100,000 remaining inventory
   b. $1,000,000 depletion expense and $100,000 of remaining inventory
   c. $100,000 depletion expense and $900,000 of remaining inventory
   d. $5,000,000 depletion expense and no remaining inventory

10. Which of the following is not an intangible asset?
    a. patent
    b. leasehold
    c. unearned revenue
    d. goodwill

11. Which of the following is true about intangible assets?
    a. Intangible assets that are purchased must be expensed in the year of acquisition.
    b. The development costs for the creation of an intangible must be expensed.
    c. The acquisition costs for tangible and intangible assets must be recorded in the same way.
    d. Intangible assets are depreciated straight-line similar to tangible assets.

12. Research and development expenditures:
    a. become part of the cost of an intangible asset.
    b. are not treated as tangible asset costs.
    c. that are related to intangible assets are recorded as expenses.
    d. may be recorded as either an expense or capitalized as part of an asset cost.

13. When a business makes an expenditure to obtain the benefits of an economic resource, that expenditure can only recorded as either:
    a. a revenue or expense.
    b. an increase in an asset or a decrease in a liability.
    c. a decrease in an asset or an increase in a liability.
    d. an asset or expense.

14. A plant and equipment asset impairment that must be recognized should be reported on the income statement as:
    a. part of "other" items.
    b. a miscellaneous expense or loss item.
    c. a non-miscellaneous operating expense.
    d. part of cost of goods sold.

Discussion Questions and Brief Exercises

1. What is the basic procedure for determining the cost of a long-term asset when it is purchased?

2. What should a business do if it is still using an asset that has been fully depreciated? What is the meaning of this situation in terms of applying the matching principle?

3. There are three basic ways to dispose of a long-term asset. What are these three ways? What is the procedure for determining gain or loss in each of these situations?

PRACTICE   Learning Goal 19, continued

Solutions are in the disk at the back of the book and at: www.worthyjames.com

4. What is the difference between normal repairs and extraordinary repairs? What are the accounting methods for recording each of these types of repairs?

5. At the beginning of the new year, Soleimani Corporation spent $15,000 to replace the operating system software in a computer system. The computer system was purchased 4 years ago, had an estimated life of 8 years, and cost $50,000. The accumulated depreciation has been calculated on a straight-line basis with no residual value. The new software will extend the useful life of the system by 4 years. Prepare the journal entries for the replacement of the software and for the current year depreciation expense.

6. What is the meaning of *depreciation*? What broad accounting principle is involved?

7. Explain the different effects that straight-line, double-declining-balance, and units-of-production depreciation methods will have on net income. If you were a manager, what would you consider when deciding which is the best method to use?

8. McCloud Company paid $100,000 for some production machinery that the management estimated would last for 6 years, with a $10,000 residual value. After 4 years of straight-line depreciation, the equipment is no longer functional or saleable and is disposed of. Prepare the general journal entry to record the disposal.

9. On January 5, Watson and Sons Partnership purchased store fixtures for $80,000. The fixtures are estimated to last for 10 years and have a $5,000 residual value. Calculate the first two year's depreciation expense using straight-line and double-declining-balance depreciation methods.

10. The management of Borczak Enterprises assembled the following information about one of their commercial rental buildings that recently appeared to have declined in value: future annual net cash flow for the next 10 years: $25,000; estimated sales value at the end of its useful life: $200,000; current book value: $550,000; current estimated net market sales price: $400,000. Determine if the building should be reported as impaired and if so, the amount of the impairment loss.

11. Tomiko Company recently incurred $2,000,000 of expenditures to develop a cell phone patent. The legal life of the patent is 20 years, and management believes that the patent will give the company an advantage over competing devices for 8 years. Record the acquisition of the patent and the first year amortization.

12. An investor is looking at the balance sheet of a company and sees accumulated depreciation in the amount of $75,000. The investor feels pleased with this because the investor now believes that the business has accumulated a $75,000 cash reserve that can be used to replace the asset when it wears out. Is this correct?

13. What is the difference between depreciation, depletion, and amortization?

14. On December 1, Billings Partnership purchased computer equipment, computer software, and production equipment is an single purchase for $5,000,000. The computer equipment was appraised at $300,000, the software at $4,500,000, and the production equipment at $1,200,000. Prepare a general journal entry to record the purchase. The partnership paid $1,000,000 cash and signed a note payable for the balance.

Solutions are in the disk at the back of the book and at: www.worthyjames.com

PRACTICE   Learning Goal 19, continued

Reinforcement Problems

LG 19-1. **Calculate purchase and construction costs of long-term assets.**

a. Wilkes-Barre Company had the expenditures that you see below related to the acquisition of some new equipment. Calculate the cost of the equipment.

Equipment price: $47,500   Installation: $2,900   1 year fire insurance: $150   Initial lubrication: $50
Shipping: $740   Shipping insurance: $300   Wages for assembly: $1,265   Sales tax: $2,375

b. Houston Fondren Associates had the expenditures that you see below related to the acquisition of a building. Calculate the cost of the building.

Property price: $752,000   Title insurance: $5,100   Past-due property tax: $8,000
Attorney's fee: $3,200   Broker's commission: $22,500   Loan interest: $2,900
Building renovation: $41,500   New furniture for building: $15,000   Security person wages: $3,200

c. Furman Enterprises owns some equipment. The book value of the equipment is $92,300, and the accumulated depreciation on the equipment is $183,600. What was the cost of the equipment, assuming no extraordinary repairs were made?

d. Statesboro Partnership is constructing a building and had the expenditures related to the construction period and the land acquisition that you see below. Identify the separate assets involved and the cost that should be recorded in each asset account.

Construction cost: $810,200   Land purchase price: $195,000   Fence around property: $15,000
Architect's fee: $20,000   Broker's commission: $5,850   Interest on construction loan: $40,500
Clearing the land: $12,500   Parking lot paving: $15,000   Building permits: $1,500
Landscaping costs: $18,000   Exterior lighting: $16,750   Current property tax: $18,000
Sidewalks: $14,500   Uninsured fire damage: $25,000 Land survey $2,950

e. Gallaudet Company purchased some equipment. The company wrote a check for $127,500 and signed a 5-year note payable for $38,000. What cost should be recorded in the Equipment account?

f. Silver City Corporation purchased land, building, and some equipment for $1,500,000. The appraised value of the assets are: land, $700,000; building, $900,000; equipment, $400,000. At what amount should each asset be debited into the accounts?

LG 19-2. **Changing depreciable life, journal entry.** Stephenville Enterprises purchased a computer system for $275,000 and is using the straight-line depreciation method with an estimated useful life of 8 years and $5,000 residual value. After using the system for 2 years, the company is now revising the estimated useful life from 8 years to 6 years. The residual value is unchanged. What will the depreciation expense be in year 3? Prepare the journal entry to record year 3 depreciation expense.

LG 19-3. **Calculate full-year deprecation using straight-line, declining balance, and units-of-production.** On January 2, 2017, Phoenix Company purchased some computer equipment for $21,000. The company estimates that the equipment will have a 5-year useful life and a residual value of $1,000. The equipment is also estimated to have 10,000 hours of potential user time.

Instructions: Complete a table formatted like the one you see below for each for each of the following assumptions:

a. The company uses straight-line depreciation.
b. The company uses double-declining-balance depreciation.
c. The company uses units-of-production depreciation, and it uses the equipment as follows: 2017, 2,000 hours; 2018, 3,500 hours; 2019, 2,500 hours; 2020, 1,500 hours; and 2021, 500 hours.

Period	Depreciation Expense	Accumulated Depreciation	Book Value
2017	(Reminder: Use a separate sheet of paper to complete the table.)		
2018			
2019			
2020			
2021			

LG 19-4. **Full and partial-year depreciation, comparison of effects of different methods.** Wabash Company purchased a truck on July 1 of 2015 at a cost of $124,000. The estimated useful life is 5 years, with a residual value of $4,000. The company uses straight line depreciation.

a. Create a table with the column headings "Depreciation Expense," "Accumulated Depreciation," and "Book Value." Calculate the amounts for these columns for each year of the truck's useful life.
b. Assume that the truck was sold for $62,000 on December 30 of 2017. Prepare a general journal entry.
c. Repeat a and b using double-declining-balance depreciation. What is the effect on annual reported expenses and on the recorded sales transaction?

LG 19-5. **Extraordinary repairs.** Oswego Company purchased a truck for $130,000. The truck is being depreciated using straight-line depreciation and an estimated useful life of 8 years, with $10,000 residual value. At the start of year 7, the company replaced the engine on the truck at a cost of $12,000. The company estimates that this will extend the life of the truck for 3 years beyond the original estimate.

a. What will the depreciation expense be in year 7?
b. What will the book value be at the end of year 7?
c. Prepare the journal entry for the engine replacement.
d. Record the depreciation expense for year 7.

LG 19-6. Full and partial years' depreciation, accumulated depreciation, and book value. In each of the situations below, assume that the policy of the business is to record a full month's depreciation expense for any asset that is owned by the 15th day of a month. No depreciation is recorded for the month for an asset that is acquired after the 15th or sold before the 15th.

Instructions: Calculate depreciation expense, accumulated depreciation, and book value for each of the years.

a. A truck was purchased on April 3, 2017 for $35,000. The estimated life of the truck is 5 years, and the estimated residual value is $1,000. Calculate the depreciation expense, accumulated depreciation, and book value for 2017, 2018, and 2019 using straight-line and double-declining-depreciation methods.

b. Office equipment was sold on January 19, 2018. The equipment was purchased on August 28 of 2016 for $27,000 and was depreciated based on a useful life of 10 years with no residual value. Calculate the depreciation expense, accumulated depreciation, and book value for 2016, 2017, and 2018 using straight-line and double-declining-depreciation methods.

c. On July 1, 2017, an old tractor was exchanged for a new tractor, which was recorded at a cost of $150,000. The new tractor is estimated to have an 8-year useful life and $10,000 of residual value. Calculate the new tractor's depreciation expense, accumulated depreciation, and book value for 2017, 2018, and 2019 using straight-line and double-declining-depreciation methods.

LG 19-7. Computations for different depreciation methods and comparison of net income and cash flow effects. Cullowhee Company purchased a large truck on January 2, 2017, at a cost of $180,000 plus 5% sales tax. The company also spent $3,000 painting a company logo design on the sides of the truck and $4,000 for heavy-load suspension equipment. The first fill-up of the fuel tank cost $90. The company estimated the truck would have a 5-year useful life, $6,000 residual value, and would provide 200,000 miles of service. The actual mileage was: year 1 (2017), 20,000 miles; years 2 and 3, 50,000 miles per year; years 4 and 5, 40,000 miles per year.

Instructions:

a. Prepare depreciation schedules for the truck that shows each of the following depreciation methods for the five years beginning on January 2, 2017: straight-line, double-declining balance, and units-of-production. Each schedule should show cost, depreciation expense for each year, accumulated depreciation at the end of each year, and book value at the end of each year.

b. In 2017, Cullowhee Company reported $585,000 of service revenue and $415,000 of operating expenses, except for the depreciation on the truck. Calculate the operating income before tax for the year 2017 for each depreciation method. Why are the income amounts different?

c. Assume that the combined income tax rate for Cullowhee Company is 40% in 2017. What effect will each of the depreciation methods have on the 2017 cash flow of the company?

d. Over the 5-year life of the truck, which method results in greatest depreciation and greatest tax savings, assuming the tax rate is constant?

LG 19-8. **Calculate and journalize acquisitions, depreciation, and disposals.** Gunnison Associates had the transactions during 2017 that you see below. The business has a December 31 year end.

Jan. 3	Purchased $10,000 of office furniture by paying $7,000 cash and recording a $3,000 account payable for the balance. The furniture is estimated to have a 10-year life with no residual value and is depreciated using the straight-line method.
June 1	Sold a copy machine for $2,100 cash. The copy machine had cost $12,500, and, as of December 31 of the prior year, the copy machine had accumulated depreciation of $11,000. The copy machine was depreciated using the units-of-production method at a rate of $.02 per copy. In the current year the machine had produced 10,800 copies.
Sept. 1	Discarded a computer that had cost $4,500 and that had $4,100 of accumulated depreciation.
Nov. 30	Sold $2,000 of the office furniture purchased on January 3 for $3,500.
Dec. 31	Purchased new video equipment for $26,500. The new equipment is estimated to have a $1,000 residual value and is depreciated using the straight-line method with a 7-year useful life.

Instructions:

a. Using a general journal, journalize the transactions above.
b. Journalize adjusting entries that are necessary as of December 31, 2017 and December 31, 2018.

LG 19-9. **Calculate and journalize asset retirements, sales, and impairment.** Pomona Enterprises owns a machine that cost $175,000 and has recorded $168,000 of accumulated depreciation.

Instructions: Using a general journal, record the disposal of the machine in each of the following independent situations:

a. The machine is retired.
b. The machine is sold for $10,000.
c. The machine is sold for $5,000.
d. The machine value is impaired. Sales price plus future cash inflows is estimated at $3,000. The asset fair value is $2,100.

Appendix to Learning Goal 19

Exchange Transactions

Overview

Basic Idea

These exchange rules affect the plant and equipment assets that we have discussed in this learning goal. These are the typical kind of assets that are exchanged. (They are often referred to as "non monetary" assets because they don't have a fixed monetary value such as cash or accounts receivable.) The manner in which exchanges of plant and equipment assets are properly recorded depends on whether or not the transactions have a material effect on the financial condition of a business. This transaction effect is called **commercial substance**.

The Meaning of Commercial Substance

Overview

Commercial substance is the terminology used to indicate a genuine, material effect on the financial condition of a business. In an exchange, if each party's economic condition changes as a result of a transaction, there is commercial substance. Commercial substance is a very useful guide in determinimg whether or not a transaction should record a genuine gain or loss, or whether the transaction is only a superficial movement of assets in which each party ends up with essentially the same thing that was given up.

The Test for Commercial Substance

An exchange transaction has commerical substance for a business if **future cash flows will change after the exchange has been completed**. In practice, this test is the most difficult part of accounting for an exchange, because it requires a careful analysis of the transaction, rather than just a procedural application of rules. Clearly, there can be subjectivity in recording exchanges. The following are basic indicators of a probable change in future cash flows:

- The *amount* of cash flow changes
- The asset uses are different
- Risk changes in some manner
- The *timing* of cash flow changes
- The asset useful lives are different

In general, when assets are different (such as land for machinery) there is commercial substance. However, even when assets are similar there can be commercial substance because of the factors above.

continued ▶

The Meaning of Commercial Substance, *continued*

Basic Procedure

The basic procedure for evaluating a nonmonetary exchange transaction is shown by the illustration below. Follow these steps:

- First determine if the transaction has commercial substance.
- Analysis: determine if there is potential gain or loss.
- Recording: record the transaction with or without gain or loss as indicated and calculate the new asset value as indicated.

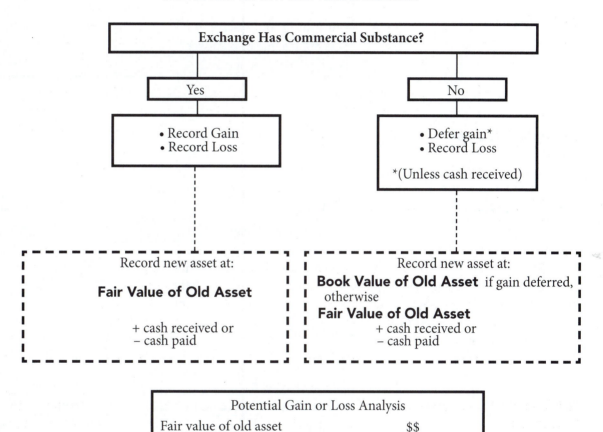

Exchanges With Commercial Substance

Overview

Exchanges with commercial substance are the most common, and the procedure is also the easiest to remember: Aways recognize gain or loss and always use fair value of the asset given (+ or − cash) to record the asset received. Whenever fair value is used and does not equal book value, a gain or loss will result. Examples:

Exchanges With Commercial Substance, *continued*

Example 1, Commercial Substance, No Cash

In an exchange transaction with commercial substance, ABC Company exchanged a truck for some machinery from XYZ Company. The truck has a book value for ABC of $25,000 (cost $40,000 – accumulated depreciation $15,000). Its fair value is $28,000. The equipment has a book value for XYZ of $34,000 (cost $50,000 – accumulated depreciation $16,000) and a fair value of $28,000.

	ABC Co.	XYZ Co.
Fair value of old asset	$28,000	$28,000
Less book value of old asset	25,000	34,000
Gain or (loss) recognized	$3,000	($6,000)

Example 1 Journal Entries

Journal entry for ABC:

Machinery	28,000	
Accumulated Depreciation—Truck	**15,000**	
Truck		**40,000**
Gain on Exchange		3,000

Total effect:
A ↑ ↓ = L + SE ↑
28,000 25,000 3,000

Journal entry for XYZ:

Truck	28,000	
Loss on Exchange	6,000	
Accumulated Depreciation—Machinery	**16,000**	
Machinery		**50,000**

Total effect:
A ↑ ↓ = L + SE ↓
28,000 34,000 6,000

Because this transaction has commercial substance, gains and losses are recorded. The cost of the new asset is the fair value of the asset exchanged to acquire it.

Example 2, Commercial Substance, With Cash

In an exchange transaction with commercial substance, DEF Company exchanged a computer for a newer computer from UVW Company. The DEF computer has a book value of $4,000 (cost $10,000 – accumulated depreciation $6,000). Its fair market value is $5,000. The newer UVW com

continued ▶

Exchanges With Commercial Substance, *continued*

Example 2, Commercial Substance, With Cash continued

puter has a book value of $20,000 (cost $21,000 – accumulated depreciation $1,000) and a fair market value of $18,000. Because of the difference in fair values, DEF pays UVW $13,000 in cash.

	DEF Co.	UVW Co.
Fair value of old asset	$5,000	$18,000
Cash paid (received)	13,000	(13,000)
Cost of new asset	$18,000	$5,000
Fair value of old asset:	$5,000	$18,000
Less book value given up:	4,000	20,000
Gain or (loss) recognized	$1,000	($2,000)

The computer cost to DEF is the $5,000 fair value of its old asset plus the $13,000 cash paid. The computer cost to UVW is the fair value of its old asset reduced by the $13,000 cash received. Gain or loss is the difference between the fair value and the book value given up for the new asset.

TIP

An alternative is to begin with book value instead of fair value. Book value of old asset + gain recognized (or – loss recognized) + cash paid (or – cash received) = cost of new asset.

You can verify each potential gain or loss by calculating the difference between the asset fair value and book value for each company.

Example 2 Journal Entries

Journal entry for DEF:

Computer (new)	18,000	
Accumulated Depreciation—Computer	**6,000**	
Computer (old)		**10,000**
Cash		13,000
Gain on Exchange		1,000

Total effect:

A ↑ ↓   = L + SE ↑
18,000 4,000   1,000
           13,000

Journal entry for UVW:

Loss on Exchange	2,000	
Cash	13,000	
Computer (new)	5,000	
Accumulated Depreciation—Computer	**1,000**	
Computer (old)		**21,000**

Total effect:

A ↑ ↓   = L + SE ↓
13,000 20,000   2,000
5,000

Exchanges With Commercial Substance, *continued*

Example 3, Commercial Substance, Trade-in Allowance

A trade-in allowance is simply a reduction in the cash payment for a new asset; therefore, this example is similar to example 2. GHI Company trades in its old Ford company car for a new Ford with a dealer list price of $42,000. The old car has a cost of $28,000 and accumulated depreciation of $25,000. The dealer offers a $2,000 trade-in allowance as fair value of the old car; therefore, GHI will pay cash of: $42,000 − $2,000 = $40,000. To the dealer the new car is inventory, and it has a cost to the dealer of $35,000.

	GHI Co.	Dealer
Fair value of old asset	$2,000	$42,000
Cash paid (received)	40,000	(40,000)
Cost of new asset	$42,000	$2,000
Fair value of old asset	$2,000	$42,000
Less book value given up: $	3,000	(35,000)
Gain or (loss) recognized	($1,000)	$7,000

Example 3 Journal Entries

Journal entry for GHI:

Loss on Exchange	1,000	
Car (New)	42,000	
Accumulated Depreciation—Car	**25,000**	
Car (Old)		**28,000**
Cash		40,000

Total effect:

A ↑ ↓ = L + SE ↓
42,000 3,000   1,000
        40,000

Journal entry for Dealer:

Used Car Inventory	2,000	
Cash	40,000	
Cost of Goods Sold	35,000	
New Car Inventory		35,000
Sales		42,000

Total effect:

A ↑ ↓ = L + SE ↓ ↑
2,000 35,000   35,000 42,000
40,000

continued ▶

Exchanges With Commercial Substance, *continued*

Determining Fair Value

It is very unlikely that any exchange would occur without total value of assets given and received being equal. Therefore, if not known, fair value of the asset given up can be determined by the fair value of the asset received, minus cash paid or plus cash received. To generalize, "fair value" means the sales price most likely to be received in an orderly market. In many situations appraisals are used to estimate fair value.

Exchanges With No Commercial Substance

Overview

Because exchange transactions that lack commercial substance do not create a material change in financial condition, the basic approach is to not recognize gains but recognize losses. This not only tends to discourage these types of transactions, but also maintains accounting conservatism. Gains are suppressed simply by recording the cost of the new asset as the book value of what was given up to acquire it. Finally, the inclusion of cash in these transactions adds an element of complexity that we will briefly discuss, but we leave comprehensive examples of this and other exchange issues to more advanced books.

Example 4, No Commercial Substance, No Cash

In a transaction with no commercial substance, IJK Company exchanged machinery for similar machinery from RST Company. The IJK machinery has a book value of $31,000 (cost $60,000 – accumulated depreciation $29,000. Its fair value is $28,000. The RST machinery has a book value of $24,000 (cost $70,000 – accumulated depreciation $46,000) and a fair value of $28,000.

Because this is an exchange with no commercial substance, we need to first check for potential gain or loss because if a potential gain exists, it will not be recognized. For IJK: potential loss is $3,000 ($28,000 – $31,000). For RST: potential gain is $4,000 ($28,000 – $24,000).

	IJK Co.	RST Co.
Fair value of old asset	**$28,000**	**$28,000**
Gain deferred		(4,000)
Cost of new asset	$28,000	$24,000

IJK has a loss, so its new asset cost is fair value of $28,000. RST does not record fair value in this non-cash exchange because it has a potential gain and there is no commercial substance. That gain is suppressed by using the $24,000 book value of its old asset as the cost of the new asset. (The reduced asset cost for RST will result in lower depreciation in future years and greater gain if the asset is later sold—so the gain is just being deferred.)

Exchanges With No Commercial Substance, *continued*

Example 4 Journal Entries

Journal entry for IJK:

Machinery (New)	28,000	
Loss on Exchange	3,000	
Accumulated Depreciation—Machinery	**29,000**	
Machinery (Old)		**60,000**

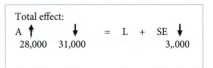

Total effect:
A ↑   ↓   = L + SE ↓
28,000   31,000   3,.000

Journal entry for RST:

Machinery (New)	24,000	
Accumulated Depreciation—Machinery	**46,000**	
Machinery (Old)		**70,000**

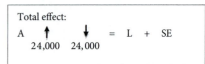

Total effect:
A   ↑   ↓   = L + SE
24,000   24,000

No Commercial Substance, With Cash

If a significant amount of cash is part of an exchange that otherwise lacks commercial substance, GAAP treats the exchange as if it has commercial substance. The cash receipt is like as sale, so fair values and gains and losses should be recorded. An exchange in which cash is 25% or more of the total fair value of the transaction is the guideline. For example, refer to example 2. Let's assume that the transaction has **no** commercial substance. The cash of $13,000 exceeds 25% of the $18,000 fair market value of the transaction, so the transaction would be recorded in the same manner as you see in example 2.

If cash is less than 25% for a transaction with no commercial substance, then the party receiving the cash recognizes a portion of the potential gain, calculated as the percentage of cash received to all value received. For example, if cash received in a transaction was $10,000 and the fair value of the asset received was $40,000 then $10,000 / ($10,000 + $40,000) = 20% of the potential gain is recognized by the recipient of the cash. The new asset cost is the book value of the asset given – cash received + gain deferred.

PRACTICE   Appendix to Learning Goal 19

Instructions: For each of the transactions below, record the journal entries for both companies. Suggestion: analyze the transaction for commercial substance and then use an analysis table as illustrated in the appendix before recording a journal entry.

LG A19-1 In a transaction with commercial substance, company A exchanged a computer for a newer computer from B Company, which needed cash. The A Company computer had a book value of $6,000 (cost $10,000 – accumulated depreciation $4,000). Its fair market value was $11,000. The newer Company B computer had a book value of $16,000 (cost $21,000 – accumulated depreciation $5,000) and a fair market value of $18,000. Because of the difference in fair values, A paid B $7,000 in cash.

LG A19-2 Company A acquired land by exchanging land purchased at a cost of $45,000 for land from Company B, with the same value, that was purchased for $19,000. An appraisal by a certified appraiser indicated a value of the Company B land at $41,000. Each company holds the land for investment. Neither company is a developer. The land exchanged is similar in use, location, and zoning.

LG A19-3 Company A exchanged store fixtures with of cost of $190,000 that had accumulated depreciation of $150,000, plus $45,000 cash for some fixtures with different display features from Company B. Company B fixtures had a cost of $89,000 and accumulated depreciation of $15,000 and fair value of $100,000.

LG A19-4 Smith Company traded in an old truck with accumulated depreciation of $38,000 for a new van with a list price of $59,000. The old truck had cost $46,000, and the dealer selling the new van gave Smith Company a $3,000 trade-in allowance for the old truck, which was its fair value. The new van dealer's cost is $50,000.

LG A19-5 Company A exchanged old air conditioning equipment with a cost of $85,000 and accumulated depreciation of $83,000 plus $110,000 cash for a different model of air conditioning equipment from Company B. The Company A air conditioner had a fair market value of $15,000. The equipment from Company B has accumulated depreciation of $106,000 and had cost $185,000.

LG A19-6 Taxi Company A exchanged a car with a fair value of $9,000 for a similar car of the same year and similar mileage with Taxi Company B. Company car A cost was $40,000 and accumulated depreciation is $35,000. Company car B cost and accumulated depreciation are $43,000 and $32,000.

<table>
<tr><td>**LEARNING GOAL 20**</td><td># Record, Report, and Control Current Liabilities and Payroll</td></tr>
</table>

In this Learning Goal, you will find:

Current Liabilities

Summary

Overview

Numerous kinds of current liabilities appear everywhere in business operations, and we have previously studied many of them. Some examples of current liabilities we have studied are:

- Accounts payable
- Short-term notes payable
- Sales tax payable
- Accrued expenses
- Unearned revenue
- Interest payable

In the discussion that follows we review some essential points and introduce you to two new concepts about current liabilities: liabilities that must be estimated and contingent liabilities

Definition

A current liability is a liability that is payable within the greater of one year or a business operating cycle. In most cases, a current liability is simply a liability due within one year.

Why There Are Current Liabilities

Current liabilities primarily result from four situations:

- Assets received but not yet paid for
- Expenses incurred but not yet paid for (accrued expenses)
- Advance payments from customers
- Debt that must be paid within a year

When a Liability Must Be Recorded (Important!)

GAAP requires that a liability be recorded whenever an obligation is created that will require using resources to eliminate that obligation.

- The obligation does not have to be a definite amount, provided that it can be reasonably estimated.
- The obligation does not have to be certain; it only needs to be probable.

Therefore a liability is not only recorded if it is certain at a definite amount, but also if it is probable and can be estimated.

Estimated Liabilities

Estimated liabilities are not in doubt; however, the amount has to be estimated. Examples of estimated (but certain) liabilities are property taxes, income taxes, and employee bonus pay.

Contingent Liabilities

Contingent Liabilities

Contingent liabilities are uncertain obligations. Whether or not a contingent liability becomes an actual liability depends upon (is "contingent" upon) another event happening or not happening. Here are some examples of contingent liabilities:

This contingent liability . . .	becomes an actual obligation when . . .
Product warranty	the customer wants a defective item repaired or replaced.
IRS audit	the IRS assesses a deficiency.
Activity impacting the environment	environmental damage has occurred.
Potentially dangerous product	damages are awarded or settlement is agreed.
Defendant in a lawsuit	the lawsuit results in damages awarded or settlement agreed.
Issuance of Coupons	a sale is made.
Guarantee a debt	the borrower does not repay the debt.
Frequent-flier miles	non-paying passengers replace paying passengers.

Not All Equally Likely

From the list above, you can see that not all contingent liabilities are equally likely. For example, a product warranty probably requires payments both in the current period and future periods for repairs or customer reimbursements. On the other hand, a loss in a lawsuit is very unpredictable.

GAAP Rule for Contingent Liabilities

Liability Situation	Rule
• Probable, can be estimated	• Increase expense/decrease revenue and increase a liability.
• Probable, cannot be estimated	• Describe in footnotes
• Reasonably probable	• Describe in footnotes
• Remote	• Disclosure not required

It is clear that these guidelines are subjective and often require considerable judgment. How probable is losing a lawsuit, having to pay environmental damages, or simply redeeming coupons or fulfilling a product warranty? Of course, many companies would prefer to record or disclose as few liabilities as possible—that is why there are GAAP requirements and auditors.

Example of Recording Contingent Liability (Expense)

Assume that a business sells $50,000 of appliances on which there is a one-year warranty. Past experience indicates that about 4% of appliances will have to be replaced within one year. The business should make the following journal entry in the same accounting period that the sale was recorded:

Warranty Expense	2,000	
Warranty Payable		2,000

Contingent Liabilities, *continued*

Example of Recording Contingent Liability (Revenue)

It is common for retail businesses to issue coupons, rebates, gift cards, and many other buyer incentives. These are all forms of contingent liabilities and they all involve allocation or reduction of revenue. Because of the different forms in which incentives can be offered, recording rules vary and again, judgment is required. For example, on May 1, repair service is offered at $500 and a discount coupon is offered to the customer on future repairs. The business estimates that the fair value of a coupon is $5. The customer uses the coupon on May 14.

May 1	Cash	500	
	Service Revenue		495
	Coupon Liability		5
May 14	Coupon Liability	5	
	Service Revenue		5

Current Portion of Long-Term Debt

Overview

Long-term liabilities are often repaid in regular installments. For example, monthly payments are made on real estate loans and car loans. Any amount of long-term loan *principal* that is payable within a year is called ***current portion of long-term debt.***

Balance Sheet Example

Suppose that in May of 2017, Middlebury Company borrows $500,000 to be repaid over five years. The loan agreement requires monthly payments of principal plus interest. Financial statements are prepared as of December 31, 2017. As of that date, the *principal* payments due within the next year are $95,000.

The balance sheet as of December 31, 2017 would show the current portion of long-term debt as a current liability. In addition, any unpaid interest accrued since the last payment date would also be a current liability. For example:

Current liabilities	
Current portion of long-term debt	$ 95,000
Interest payable	3,000
Long-term liabilities	
Note payable less current portion of $95,000	405,000

Payroll

Overview of Payroll

What Is Payroll?

The term *payroll* generally refers to the process of identifying employees, calculating the pay and payroll taxes, recording the payroll transactions, making the payments, and completing required federal and state payroll tax forms. The diagram on the next page shows you an overview of the process.

Legal Rules

This payroll topic is unique from the other topics in this book because payroll involves many federal (and state) payroll tax and income tax withholding laws, and pay rate calculation rules. Each of these legal rules imposes different requirements. So, to understand the payroll process, you will find yourself learning more than just how to properly analyze and record transactions. You will also learn about payroll laws and what is required to comply with these laws. Because each state has its own payroll laws, we focus on federal payroll requirements in this book.

Getting Help

This learning goal provides a general description of the payroll process. If you need to understand more about federal and state payroll laws and compliance requirements, or to calculate a payroll, you will need more help. Here are some suggestions for where to find more detailed information:

- **Circular E:** (Publication 15) This is a comprehensive employer resource for federal payroll rules. You can find it at the Internal Revenue Service website (www.irs.gov and ftp.irs.gov for ftp users) and you can also order it from the Internal Revenue Service Forms and Publications department by calling a local Internal Revenue Service office.
- **State Information:** With access to the Internet, you can quickly find state payroll references in several ways, including: (1) You can do an Internet search for "state of (name of state) payroll tax." (2) As of this writing, some useful websites are www.taxsites.com and the American Payroll Association site. (3) Use the reference section of a library.
- **Professional Help:** If you are in business or going into business, you *must* obtain expert professional help, because rates change and laws change and can be complex to apply. Find a CPA or an attorney who already has clients in the same type of business that you are in and who is familiar with your type of payroll and business issues. Interview several prospects, get client references, and double-check with state licensing boards.

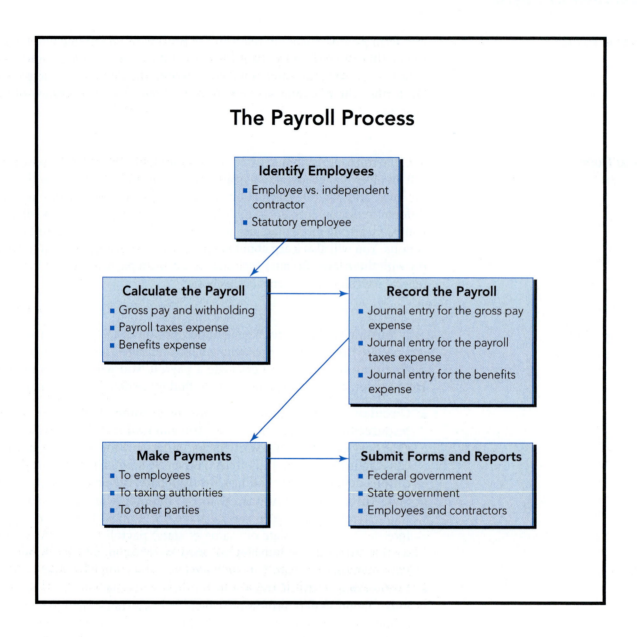

Identify Employees

Employees

Overview

Not all people who perform duties for a business are employees. It is very important to accurately identify which workers qualify as employees because the law imposes different requirements for workers who are employees and those who are not. Every business must comply with the requirements of these laws. Proper identification also reduces fraud and waste.

"Employee" Defined

The general rule (called *common law*) is that any person who performs services for a business is an **employee** if *the business controls*:

- *what* will be done, *and*
- *how* it will be done

This definition must be applied to each individual. It makes no difference what job title or name is used, frequency or means of payment, or whether the work is full time or part time.

> *Note:* A business can submit Form SS-8 to have the Internal Revenue Service determine employee status. Contact state employment offices for state rules.

Example of an Employee

Jane is a secretary at Smith Company and is given word-processing tasks to perform that include preparing management reports. Jane is expected to be at the business during certain hours and allow her manager to review and make changes in her work. She must use the business office and the computer equipment and word-processing software used by the business. Jane is an employee because the Smith Company supervises and controls *how the job is done*.

Not an Employee

Mary also performs the same type of services for Smith Company. Mary is given a management report to complete, and she completes the job from her own office, which is not at the Smith Company location. Mary uses her own equipment and software, and she completes the job during her own hours without review from Smith managers. Mary is not an employee because Smith Company does not supervise or control *how the job is done*.

Employee Identification and Internal Control, *continued*

Human Resources Department

The mandatory use of a separate human resources department acts as an internal control device to reduce the potential frauds and errors described above. In a small business that cannot afford a separate department, the owner(s) should perform most or all of these functions. An outside employee search firm or consultant can be used to assist the employer and to perform background checks of job applicants.

Employee Identification in the Human Resources Department

Summary Table

The table below summarizes the functions and procedures used for employee identification that should be done *only* by the human resources department.

Function	Procedure	Purpose
Hiring	Review job description	▪ Determine if the worker will act as employee or as independent contractor ▪ Clarify job requirements and duties
	Advertise, screen, and interview	▪ Find qualified applicants. This also helps screen out "ghost" and unneeded employees. ▪ Perform background checks
Authorizing	Complete forms that authorize employment and send forms to payroll department	▪ Prevent "ghost" employees from being placed on the payroll list ▪ Remove terminated employees from the payroll
	Issue employee badges	▪ Permit access and identification
Obtaining Data Required by Law	Obtain tax information form W-4	▪ Provide payroll withholding information
	Obtain tax information form W-9	▪ Provide contractor information
	Obtain work eligibility form I-9	▪ Identify undocumented immigrant workers

TIP

The difference between an employee and independent contractor has serious consequences. Classification as independent contractor means that payroll taxes are entirely shifted to a worker. As well, workers compensation benefits, unemployment benefits, overtime, and antidiscrimination protection do not apply. Companies that misclassify workers as independent contractors are subject to serious costs including all prior unpaid taxes, large penalties, interest, accumulated sick and vacation pay and other benefits, and medical insurance coverage.

Write the completed sentences on a separate piece of paper. The answers are below.

A person is an employee if the person or company they work for controls what work will be done and · · · · · · · · it will be done. Proprietors and partners performing their duties · · · · · · · · (are/are not) employees, whereas shareholders of a corporation who work for the business · · · · · · · · (are/are not) employees.

An · · · · · · · · · · · · · · is an individual who is in business to offer services to the public as a business. A · · · · · · · · · · · · · · · is someone who performs a particular occupation that is legally specified as an employee occupation.

"Ghost employees" and misclassification of employees · · · · · · · · (is/is not) a potentially serious internal control problem for many businesses. A key internal control device for payroll procedures is the use of a · · · · · · · · department. In a small business, the · · · · · · · · performs these duties.

"Ghost employees" and misclassification of employees is (is/is not) a potentially serious internal control problem for many businesses. A key internal control device for payroll procedures is the use of a personnel department. In a small business, the owner performs these duties.resources consumed.

An independent contractor is an individual who is in business to offer services to the public as a business. A statutory employee is someone who performs a particular occupation that is legally specified as an employee occupation.

A person is an employee if the person or company they work for controls what work will be done and how it will be done. Proprietors and partners performing their duties are not (are/are not) employees, whereas shareholders of a corporation who work for the business are (are/are not) employees.

Calculate the Payroll

Overview

Introduction

To *calculate a payroll* means to make a calculation for a specific time period of total employee expense and then to determine the payments required.

Total Expense

The total employee expense includes three basic elements:

- Gross pay expense
- Payroll taxes expense
- Benefits expense

Overview, *continued*

Payment Allocation

As each expense is calculated, the allocation of the payment for that expense is determined. The most detailed part of the payment calculation is determining how much of the gross pay will be withheld from the employee and then paid to various government taxing authorities and other third parties. Additionally, the payments required for other payroll taxes and benefits are calculated.

Not Part of Payroll

Remember that independent contractors are not employees and therefore are not part of the payroll calculation. Payments to independent contractors are recorded as separate categories of operating expenses.

Gross Pay

Identifying and Calculating Gross Pay

Definition

The term **gross pay** (sometimes called *gross earnings* or *gross wages*) means the total amount of compensation earned by an employee. This usually results in the employee receiving a paycheck. The amount earned could be for:

- **Salary:** The term *salary* generally refers to a fixed amount per period (such as annually) that is not determined by hours worked. Salaries are earned by managers, administrators, supervisors, and other professional staff.
- **Wage:** The term *wage* usually means an amount that is determined by hours worked or units of product completed (called *piecework*). Usually wages are earned by clerks and by skilled and unskilled labor.
- **Commission:** Commissions are earnings based on a percentage of sales.
- **Bonus:** Bonus earnings are extra amounts given as reward for achievement or meeting performance goals.
- **In kind:** Payment in some form of property or services (rather than money) are called *in kind* and are part of gross pay unless specifically exempted by law.

Examples of Not Gross Pay

Some examples that are *not* gross pay are:

- Amounts earned by independent contractors (because independent contractors are not employees)
- Employee business expense reimbursements under an approved plan (because approved reimbursements are exempt—they are not compensation)

Identifying and Calculating Gross Pay, *continued*

Overtime

Overtime is gross pay calculated at a higher rate per hour for those hours worked in excess of a standard daily amount of 8 hours or a weekly amount of 40 hours. Overtime is generally paid to hourly workers; an annual minimum of about $47,000 is also required for salaried workers who are not exempt from overtime. (Examples of exempt workers are professional and administrative positions, top-level managers, corporate officers, and other specified jobs.) It does not matter when or how often the worker is paid. For most workers, the minimum overtime rate is 1-1/2 times the regular pay rate per hour for time exceeding 8 hours per day or 40 hours per week. Some companies add extra overtime pay rates for work such as on Sundays or holidays, or for activities designated by union contracts.

Overtime (and minimum wage) is regulated by the federal *Fair Labor Standards Act (FLSA)*, by U.S. Department of Labor regulations and by state laws that may impose additional requirements.

Overtime Example

Dave is a wage-earning employee, and his regular rate is $18 per hour. He worked 45 hours this week, Monday through Friday. He also worked 3 hours on Saturday. His company pays twice the regular rate for weekend and holiday work. Dave's gross pay is:

40 hours × $18.00 = $720 regular
  5 hours × $27.00 =   135 overtime ($18 × 1.5 = $27)
  3 hours × $36.00 =   108 overtime ($18 × 2 = $36)
                      $963 total gross pay for the week

Withholding

Overview

Introduction

Payroll withholding means that an employer withholds (deducts) amounts from an employee's gross pay. These amounts are then paid by the employer to taxing authorities and other third parties. The amounts withheld from an employee's pay are called *payroll deductions*. The remaining amount that the employee actually receives is called *net pay*. Payroll deductions are not a tax on the employer; the employer is simply acting as a collection agent. The two categories of payroll deductions are:

- Deductions required by law
- Voluntary deductions by agreement

continued ▶

Overview, *continued*

Deductions Required by Law

The following items are imposed upon individuals classified as employees and must be deducted by the employer from employee pay:

- Employee income taxes
- Employee social security (FICA) tax
- Other state employment taxes
- Other deductions imposed by law

These amounts are calculated and withheld on a *calendar year* basis, even if the business uses a different fiscal year. The process begins each new January 1 and ends on December 31.

Voluntary Deductions by Agreement

Optional deductions may consist of many different items. Some examples are:

- Savings and stock purchase plan contributions
- Union dues
- Charitable contributions

Employee Income Tax

Overview

Federal law (and many state laws and some city laws) imposes an income tax and requires that employers withhold income tax from employee pay. For every employee, the amount of the income tax deduction each period is based on a calculation that estimates the approximate amount of annual income tax for that employee. This calculation procedure has two steps.

Step 1

Form W-4 is completed by an employee when hired (and may be revised at any time). The employer uses this form to determine employee filing status and the number of withholding allowances claimed by the employee.

Filing status refers to "single," "married," and "other." The percent income tax rate is different for each different filing status.

A ***withholding allowance*** (also called an ***exemption***) exempts a fixed amount of gross pay from income tax withholding. This is because each allowance also is a deduction on the employee's income tax return at year end. In general, each employee may claim one allowance for himself or herself, one for a spouse who does not also claim one, and one for each dependent, although more allowances are permitted if the tax return shows a material overpayment.

Employee Income Tax, *continued*

Step 2

Estimate the employee's income tax for the payroll period. The employer usually does this by referring to income tax withholding tables. This is called the ***wage-bracket method***. To determine the correct income tax withholding:

Find the table:

- Refer to the filing status for the employee (single, married, etc.).
- Select the appropriate payroll period (weekly, monthly, semi-monthly, etc.).

Use the table:

- Select the wage bracket row that includes the amount of gross wages.
- Select the column for the number of allowances.
- The amount of the withholding is where the row and column intersect.

Table

A partial federal income tax withholding table is reproduced below.

MARRIED Persons—**SEMIMONTHLY** Payroll Period										
If the wages are . . .		And the number of withholding allowances are . . .								
At least	But less than	0	1	2	3	4	5	6	7	8
		The amount of income tax to be withheld is . . .								
$1,380	$1,400	$143	$124	$105	$ 86	$ 67	$48	$36	$23	$10
1,400	1,420	146	127	108	89	70	51	38	25	12
1,420	1,440	149	130	111	92	73	53	40	27	14
1,440	1,460	152	133	114	95	76	57	42	29	16
1,460	1,480	165	136	117	98	79	60	44	31	18
1,480	1,500	158	139	120	101	82	63	46	33	20
1,500	1,520	161	142	123	104	85	66	48	35	22
1,520	1,540	164	145	126	107	88	69	50	37	24
1,540	1,560	167	148	129	110	91	72	53	39	26
1,560	1,580	170	151	132	113	94	75	56	41	28
1,580	1,600	173	154	135	116	97	78	59	43	30
1,600	1,620	176	157	138	119	100	81	62	45	32
1,620	1,640	179	160	141	122	103	84	65	47	34
1,640	1,660	182	163	144	125	106	87	68	49	36
1,660	1,680	185	166	147	128	109	90	71	52	38
1,680	1,700	188	169	150	131	112	93	74	55	40

continued ▶

Employee Income Tax, *continued*

Example

Jane Smith and John Doe are paid semi-monthly. Jane claims five exemptions and has gross wages of $1,685 for the period. The withholding for Jane is $93. John claims one exemption and has gross wages of $1,540. The withholding for John is $148.

Employee Social Security (FICA)

Overview

The *"social security tax"* is a general term and is a result of a very dramatic and difficult time in American history. This period began in 1929 with the onset of the "great depression." (The great depression is an amazing story that you should read about.) In 1935, the United States Congress enacted the Federal Insurance Contribution Act *(FICA)*. This act imposed a tax on employees (and employers) to provide workers with a guaranteed minimum amount of old age and survivor's income, and disability insurance benefits *(OASDI)*. FICA was expanded in 1965 to provide limited medical benefits for people without medical insurance *(Medicare)* generally at age 65, and who otherwise qualify for OASDI.

Wage Base and Tax Rate

A *wage base* is a maximum *calendar-year* amount of gross pay that is subject to payroll tax. Gross pay that exceeds the annual wage base is not subject to OASDI tax. **The OASDI wage base usually increases each year.** The *tax rate* is the percent that must be paid as a tax. Payroll tax is calculated individually for each employee for each payroll period by multiplying the tax rate times the amount of current period's gross pay that does not cause the cumulative gross pay to exceed the wage base.

The Social Security Tax Bases and Rates (OASDI and Medicare)

There is a separate wage base and tax rate for each part of the social security plan (FICA). For all the FICA examples in this book, **we will assume that the OASDI wage base is $130,000**. Here are the components of FICA:

- The wage base for the OASDI part is $130,000. The tax rate is 6.2%. This means that during a calendar year the first $130,000 of gross pay of each employee is subject to a 6.2% OASDI tax.
- The wage base for Medicare is unlimited. This means that all gross pay is subject to Medicare tax. The tax rate is 1.45%. (An additional surtax of .9% may apply to high-income households.)
- For wages *not* exceeding $130,000, the combined FICA rate (OASDI and Medicare) is 7.65%.

Employee Social Security (FICA), *continued*

Procedure with Examples

The table below illustrates the FICA tax calculation procedure. Suppose that a business has two employees, Adam and Amy. The business needs to calculate the individual and total social security tax for the monthly payroll period ending November 30. During the current year prior to this period, Adam had gross pay of $77,500 and Amy had $127,200. Adam's November gross pay is $5,900, and Amy's November gross pay is $7,500. Assume a $130,000 wage base.

Step 1

Subtract the cumulative gross pay from the wage base.

If the result is zero or positive, cumulative pay is still below the OASDI limit, so all of the current gross pay is taxable. Go to Step 3. **If** the result is negative, cumulative pay has exceeded the limit, and this excess is not taxable for OASDI. Some or all of the current gross pay is excluded from the OASDI tax. Go to Step 2.

Examples:

Adam		Amy	
Wage base	$130,000	Wage base	$130,000
Cumulative gross pay	83,400	Cumulative gross pay	$134,700
Go to Step 3	$46,600	Go to Step 2	($4,700)

Step 2

Offset the negative amount (the amount excluded) against the current gross pay to find the OASDI taxable portion of the current gross pay (but not less than zero). Then go to Step 3.

Examples:

Adam	Amy	
Not applicable—all current gross pay is fully taxable for FICA	Current gross pay	$7,500
	Excluded portion	(4,700)
	Taxable portion	$2,800

Step 3

IF all the current gross pay is taxable, multiply the current gross pay by the 7.65% combined rate.

IF some of the current gross pay is excluded from OASDI:

- Multiply the taxable portion of current gross pay by 6.2% (OASDI tax).
- Multiply all the current gross pay by 1.45% (Medicare tax).
- Add the results.

Examples:

Adam	Amy		
$5,900 × .0765 = $451.35	$2,800 × .062 =	$173.60	(OASDI)
	$7,500 × .0145 =	$108.75	(Medicare)
	Total	$282.35	

Other Required Withholding

Other State Taxes

Some states impose additional employment-related taxes on the wages of employees. For example, many employees in California are required to have state disability insurance payments withheld. Usually other state employment taxes are calculated in the same basic manner as social security, that is, by using a wage base amount and a tax rate. See page 791 for how to get more information on wage bases, tax rates, and other state payroll information.

> *Note:* Remember that wage bases and tax rates may change from year to year. However, the calculation method is unchanged.

Vacation Pay

For paid absences such as vacation pay, tax and other withholding is also required. However, the withholding occurs only when the vacation paycheck is prepared for the employee and not when the vacation pay expense is accrued.

Fringe Benefits

Withholding is required for any other form of compensation, such as fringe benefits that are not otherwise exempted. (Examples of benefits exempt from withholding are qualified medical and pension plan benefits.)

Other

Other required withholding is usually the result of a legal action, such as court-ordered child support. Usually these payments are a fixed amount per month.

Voluntary Deductions

Overview

Voluntary deductions are deductions that an employee and employer agree upon together by direct agreement or indirectly through a union contract. These amounts are usually a fixed amount per month.

TIP

For many people, the easiest and most reliable way to save money is by regular payroll withholding. If you work for a company that offers savings and investment plans or stock purchase plans, **take full advantage of these plans**. If you are not sure what these plans are or how to use them ("401k," "cafeteria" plans, etc.) then spend the time to buy and read some basic investing books (yes, more than one!), do Internet searches, or take a basic class to find out the facts (but do *not* pay someone to invest or trade for you.) It is important to your future that you learn to invest continuously and carefully.

Check Your Understanding

Write the completed sentences on a separate piece of paper. The answers are below.

According to the · · · · · · · · · · · · · · · Standards Act, if Judy is a wage earner and her regular rate is $15 per hour and she worked 44 hours this week, her gross pay should be $ · · · · · · · · .

To use the wage bracket method to determine income tax withholding, an employer must know the employee's · · · · · · · · status (married or single), the number of · · · · · · · · claimed on form · · · · · · · · , the gross · · · · · · · · and the appropriate payroll period.

The "social security tax" refers to the Federal Insurance Contribution Act (FICA), which provides "OASDI" benefits, which means · · · · · · · · · · · · · · · (for retirement), · · · · · · · · (for widows and orphans) and · · · · · · · · (can't work because of illness or accident) insurance. FICA also includes · · · · · · · · .

In October, Jan earned $1,750 plus a $1,000 bonus and had earned $129,150 from January through September. Dean earned $1,500 in commissions in October and had earned $91,000 from January through September. Using the wage base and tax rate in this section, calculate the "social security tax" withheld for Jan and for Dean. Jan: $· · · · · · · · Dean: $· · · · · · · ·

Answers

According to the Fair Labor Standards Act, if Judy is a wage earner and her regular rate is $15 per hour and she worked 44 hours this week, her gross pay should be $ 690. ($15 × 40) + ($15 × 1.5 × 4)

To use the wage bracket method to determine income tax withholding, an employer must know the employee's filing status (married or single), the number of exemptions (or allowances) claimed on form W - 4, the gross wages (or gross pay) and the appropriate payroll period.

The "social security tax" refers to the Federal Insurance Contribution Act (FICA) which provides "OASDI" benefits, which means Old Age (for retirement), Survivors (for widows and orphans) and Disability (can't work because of illness or accident) insurance. FICA also includes medicare.

Jan's FICA:
OASDI: $2,750 − $1,900 excluded = $850 taxable × .062 = $52.70
Medicare: $2,750 × .0145 = $39.88
Total Social Security Tax: $92.58

Dean's FICA:
$1,500 × .0765 = $114.75 (Dean's cumulative gross pay is below the limit, so the combined rate can be used.)

Notice that bonuses and commissions are fully taxable compensation for FICA.

Employer Payroll Taxes

Overview

Summary of Items

In addition to the gross pay expense, employers incur a second type of payroll expense: the employer payroll tax expenses. These payroll taxes apply directly to the employer and add to the employer's total employment costs. These payroll taxes are:

- Employer Social Security (FICA)
- Federal and State Unemployment Taxes (FUTA and SUTA)
- Other state and local payroll taxes

These are taxes that the employer pays; do not confuse them with the payroll taxes that the employee pays and that are deducted from an employee's gross pay. However, just like employee deductions, employer payroll taxes are calculated on a *calendar-year* basis.

Employer Social Security (FICA)

Calculation

The social security tax also applies to the employer. In addition to being a collection agent for the employee social security, the employer also pays an equal amount of its own social security tax. Therefore, it is a "matching" system; the employer matches the amount paid by the employee.

Example

On page 803, you saw that the total employee social security tax for the employees Adam and Amy is $733.70 ($451.35 Adam and $282.35 Amy). Therefore, the employer must also pay an additional $733.70 of social security tax. The total social security tax paid is: employees $733.70 + employer $733.70 = $1,467.40.

TIP

In 2010, the Affordable Care Act, also known as "ACA" or "Obama Care" (full name: Patient Protection and Affordable Care Act) was signed into law by President Obama. The purpose of this complex law is to provide medical care insurance coverage to those people without medical insurance, usually because they do not work for an employer who provides medical insurance, or because they cannot afford to pay for medical insurance, or because they do not qualify for medicare.

Among the features of this law is an additional Medicare tax on workers in high-income households, but not employers. As well, a tax is imposed on individuals above certain income amounts if they do not have medical insurance coverage. Employers are also subject to other tax provisions.

Passage of this complex law created many new benefits as well as wide-ranging effects; also, changes are likely for both economic and political reasons. As an employee or an employer, continued study and awareness of this law would be prudent.

Employer Social Security (FICA), *continued*

Self-Employment Tax

Even though a self-employed person (sole proprietor) is never considered to be an employee of his or her own business, the individual is nevertheless required to pay both the employee and employer social security tax. This is called **self-employment tax**. It is calculated as part of an individual's annual income tax return and applies to self-employment income from an unincorporated business. Taxable self-employment income is net income × .9235 (to adjust net income down by the FICA tax expense deduction an employer ordinarily would receive within the FICA wage base). If the taxable self-employment income is not greater than the annual FICA wage base (which we use here as $130,000) the tax rate is 15.3% (7.65% × 2). It is 2.9% (1.45% × 2) above the annual wage base. (A .9% surtax may also apply to high-income households.)

Example: Bill's business had net income of $150,000 for the current year. Therefore self-employment taxable income is $150,000 × .9235 = $138,525. However, this is greater than the $130,000 wage base limit, so Bill's self-employment tax is ($130,000 × .153) + ($8,525 × .029) = $20,137.

Example: Bill's business had net income of $130,000 for the current year. Therefore Bill's self-employment taxable income is $120,055. His self-employment tax is $120,055 × .153 = $18,368.

Unemployment Taxes

Overview

Another part of the social security laws is the Federal Unemployment Tax Act *(FUTA)*. This law provides unemployment benefits to workers who lose jobs even though the workers are able and qualified. The annual FUTA wage base is the first $7,000 of gross pay (for each employee) and the FUTA tax rate is 6%. However, the law allows a credit against this rate up to 5.4% for businesses in states that impose a state unemployment tax. Most states impose a 5.4% rate, so the actual FUTA rate paid is usually .6% in most cases.

All states also have state unemployment tax acts *(SUTA)*. Like the federal law, these acts provide for unemployment benefits. The minimum annual SUTA wage base is the first $7,000 of gross pay, although many states have set a higher amount; the basic tax rate is 5.4%. However, in many states the percentage rate can change *for individual employers* as it is adjusted up or down based on the stability of the employment history for a particular business.

We will use the $7,000 wage base and the 5.4% rate in all our SUTA calculations, and $7,000 and .6% for all our FUTA calculations.

continued ▶

Unemployment Taxes, *continued*

Example: FUTA and SUTA Calculation Procedure

Assume that a business has three employees: John, Bill, and Mary. From January 1 to March 31 John had total gross pay of $5,100, Bill had $6,500 and Mary had $7,200. John's April gross pay is $1,700, Bill's is $1,700 and Mary's April gross pay is $3,150. The table below shows the three calculation steps to calculate FUTA and SUTA for the April payroll.

Step 1

For each employee, subtract the cumulative gross pay from the wage base.

If the result is **zero or positive**, cumulative pay is still below the limit, so all of the current gross pay is taxable. Go to Step 3. **If** the result is **negative**, cumulative pay has exceeded the limit and this excess is not taxable. Some or all of the current gross pay is excluded. Go to Step 2.

Example:

John		Bill	
Wage base	$7,000	Wage base	$7,000
Cumulative gross pay	6,800	Cumulative gross pay	8,200
Go to Step 3	$200	Go to Step 2	($1,200)

Mary	
Wage base	$7,000
Cumulative gross pay	10,350
Go to Step 2	($3,350)

Step 2

Offset the negative amount (the amount excluded) against the current gross pay to find the taxable portion of the current gross pay (but not less than zero). Then go to Step 3.

Example:

FUTA	SUTA
John: not applicable—all taxable	John: not applicable—all taxable
Bill: $1,700 – $1,200 = $500 taxable	Bill: $1,700 – $1,200 = $500 taxable
Mary: $3,150 – $3,350 = $0 taxable	Mary: $3,150 – $3,350 = $0 taxable

Step 3

Multiply the taxable portion of the current gross pay times the tax rate, and add the results.

Example:

FUTA	SUTA
John: $1,700 × .006 = $10.20	John: $1,700 × .054 = $91.80
Bill: $500 × .006 = $3.00	Bill: $500 × .054 = $27.00
Mary: $0 × .006 = –0–	Mary: $0 × .054 = –0–
Total FUTA tax $13.20	Total SUTA tax $118.80

Employer Benefits Expense

Overview

Summary

In addition to the gross pay and the employer payroll taxes, employers may also incur a third type of payroll expense. This expense is generally called *benefits expense* or *fringe benefits*. This refers to additional compensation that is paid by the employer for the benefit of the employees. There are numerous kinds of benefits; some of the more important ones are explained here. Unless otherwise indicated, you can assume that these benefits are part of plans that qualify as tax-free and are therefore not subject to withholding.

Important Benefit Types

Insurance

- Medical insurance: This refers to a medical insurance plan that pays all or most of the cost of employee medical bills. Medical insurance has become the single most important benefit to employees because of the high cost of medical care.
- Life insurance: This insurance makes a cash payment (usually to a designated family member) in the case of the death of the insured employee. Life insurance above a certain limit is taxable to the employee and requires withholding.

The employer receives bills directly from the insurance companies and makes payments directly to the companies. The employer records these payments as operating expenses.

Pension Plan

A pension plan is an arrangement in which the employer provides for payments to employees after they retire. While an employee is still actively employed, the employer makes regular payments to a **plan administrator**. A plan administrator is a company that specializes in designing qualified pension plans and supervising the administration and investments of the plan. When an employee retires, the administrator makes payments to the employee.

The employer makes payments directly to the plan administrator, and these payments are recorded as an operating expense. However, the amount of the expense and the amount of employer liability may be subject to further calculations; this is a topic for more advanced accounting courses.

continued ▶

Important Benefit Types, *continued*

Vacation Pay

The expense for paid absences such as vacation pay is accrued each payroll period. This is because employees usually earn vacation pay as they work, but it is not actually paid until some later date.

Vacation Pay Liability is accrued and credited every payroll period. As each employee takes time off and is paid, Vacation Pay Liability is debited and Cash is credited. Vacation pay is subject to required withholding and employer payroll taxes at the time of payment.

Vacation Pay Example

Santa Rosa Company gives each employee two weeks of paid vacation per year. Therefore, the cost of 2 weeks of vacation is spread over the 50 weeks worked, or 4% per week. The gross wages for the current week are $12,000. The journal entry to record the vacation pay accrual is:

Vacation Pay Expense	480	
Vacation Pay Liability		480

Suppose that during that same week, some employees took time off and collected $650 of vacation pay. The journal entry is:

Vacation Pay Liability	650	
FICA, taxes, etc.		100
Cash		550

Note: Employer payroll taxes on vacation pay can be recorded in the year in which the liability is established or in the year paid. We omit this issue in our discussion.

Workers' Compensation Insurance

Workers' compensation insurance provides a period of income replacement for a worker who is disabled or injured on the job and as a result cannot perform his or her regular duties. Most states require that an employer pay for workers' compensation insurance at a designated minimum level or have adequate funds to make benefit payments. Premium payments to an insurance company for this coverage are an employment-related expense of a business.

Internal Control for Payroll Calculation

Overview

In the previous section about employee identification, we discussed the importance of applying internal control. We continue here with internal control as it applies to the payroll calculation.

Internal Control for Payroll Calculation, *continued*

Separation of Duties

In larger companies, the responsibility of the payroll *calculation* is assigned to a separate department, called the *payroll department*. This department calculates the payroll for employees identified by the human resources department at the pay rate indicated. Only the human resources department can authorize individuals as employees, authorize or change their rate of pay, and notify them of termination. Human resources provides new or changed information to the payroll department, which returns a signed confirmation. In turn, the payroll department is the only department authorized to perform the payroll calculations.

In smaller companies, the bookkeeper can perform payroll calculations based on the employee information provided by the owner, who in effect becomes the "human resources department."

Time Cards

Companies that have many wage employees often use time cards and a time clock. Each employee is assigned a card and must enter the card in the time clock to record his or her time of arrival and departure on the card. A security person often supervises to verify that only one card per employee is actually used. The payroll department then uses the hours on the time cards to record the hours worked and to calculate the gross pay.

Calculation Check and Payment

Payroll documentation and calculations should always be reviewed by a supervisor not involved with the calculations. This duty should be rotated. Payment is made by the treasurer after approval. In a small business, the owner performs these duties.

Record the Payroll

Overview

Four Basic Parts

The process of recording the payroll involves four basic parts:

- Record the gross wages expense.
- Record the employer payroll taxes expense.
- Record the benefits expense.
- Update each employee's earnings record.

Summarize Information

As a preliminary step to starting the process, the employer must first summarize and organize the payroll information. This is usually accomplished by using a ***payroll register*** (also called a payroll record or payroll journal, although it is not a journal or a ledger). A payroll register is an informal summary tool that is used each payroll period to show the individual and total amounts of gross earnings, deductions, and net pay for that particular payroll period.

The Payroll Register Illustrated

Example   On this page and the next page is an example of a completed payroll register.

Payroll Register for the

Employee Name	Total Hours	Earnings 1		Current Gross	Year to Date Gross 2	Current Gross Taxable for . . . 3	
		Regular	Over-time	Current Gross	Year to Date Gross	FUTA/SUTA	OASDI
Acevedo, Baxter	40	600.00		600.00	7,200.00	400.00	600.00
Dunwitty, Betty	40	720.00		720.00	7,920.00	–0–	720.00
Heintz, Marilyn	44	600.00	90.00	690.00	7,150.00	540.00	690.00
Onishi, James		800.00		800.00	8,800.00	–0–	800.00
Sanders, Emily	40	480.00		480.00	5,350.00	480.00	480.00
Van Arsdale, Robert	42	720.00	54.00	774.00	7,900.00	–0–	774.00
Washington, Ellie		900.00		900.00	9,900.00	–0–	900.00
Totals		4,820.00	144.00	4,964.00	54,220.00	1,420.00	4,964.00

Detailed Explanation   Each of the following items relates to highlighted items in the reference boxes shown on the illustrated payroll register.

1. **Earnings:** For wage employees, earnings are calculated at an hourly rate; for salaried employees (Onishi and Washington), earnings are a fixed amount. Gross earnings in the current period includes both the regular and overtime pay. For example, Marilyn Heintz earned $600 regular pay, so her regular rate must be $600/40 = $15 per hour. Therefore, her overtime rate is $15 × 1.5 = $22.50 per hour. Because she worked 4 hours in excess of 40, she earns overtime of $22.50 × 4 = $90.

2. **Year to date gross:** This is an optional column that helps identify the cumulative amount of employee gross pay that includes the current payroll. Cumulative amounts are part of each employee's individual earnings record.

3. **Current gross taxable for FUTA/SUTA and OASDI:** This is the amount of the gross pay in the current period that is subject to these taxes. *Example:* The FUTA/SUTA limit is $7,000. Baxter Acevedo's current period gross pay is $600 and this amount exceeded the limit by $200. This means that only $400 of his current gross pay ($600 – $200) is subject to FUTA/SUTA taxes. The OASDI limit of $130,000 is much greater than his cumulative gross pay, so it is easy to see that all of his current gross pay is taxable for OASDI.

The Payroll Register Illustrated, *continued*

Week Ended March 14, 2017

		Deductions				Payment		Acct. Debited	
Federal Inc. Tax	State Inc. Tax	OASDI/ Medicare	Health Insurance	Union Dues	Total	Net Pay	Ck. #	Office Salaries	Wages
89.00	18.00	45.90	12.00	5.25	170.15	429.85	857		600.00
108.00	22.00	55.08	9.00	5.25	199.33	520.67	858		720.00
104.00	21.00	52.79	15.00	5.25	198.04	491.96	859		690.00
120.00	24.00	61.20	11.00	–0–	216.20	583.80	860	800.00	
48.00	10.00	36.72	18.00	5.25	117.97	362.03	861		480.00
116.00	23.00	59.21	12.00	5.25	215.46	558.54	862		774.00
180.00	30.00	68.85	10.00	–0–	288.85	611.15	863	900.00	
765.00	148.00	379.75	87.00	26.25	1,406.00	3,558.00		1,700.00	3,264.00

Detailed Explanation (continued)

4. **Deductions:** These are the withholding deductions for each employee. For example, Baxter Acevedo has a total of $170.15 of deductions, consisting of federal and state income taxes, FICA, health insurance contributions, and union dues.

5. **Net Pay:** This shows the net amount of pay each employee will receive and, when paid, the check number of the payroll check written to the employee. Net pay is current gross pay minus the total deductions.

6. **Account debited:** These columns classify the gross wage expense. In this case, gross wages are classified as either office salaries or wages. Different companies use different classifications.

Register Format

The payroll register can vary somewhat in format. Some companies use a completely separate payroll register, whereas others make it part of their cash payments journal. Also, the column titles vary somewhat. Some formats include a column on the left side for the gross amount of accrued vacation pay being used and an "other" column in the deductions section for miscellaneous deductions.

Journal Entry for the Gross Pay Expense

Overview

The first step in recording payroll is the journal entry for the gross pay expense. This journal entry consists of recording the current gross pay, the related deductions, and the net pay. *The payroll register totals are the sources of information for this journal entry.* Refer to the payroll register on the preceding pages.

Example

The example below shows a journal entry for the gross pay expense. The total debits to office salaries and wages is $4,964, which is the total of the gross pay column, classified by type of pay. The credit to Wages Payable is the total of the net pay column, and the other payables are totals of deductions columns.

March 14	Office Salaries Expense	1,700.00	
	Wages Expense	3,264.00	
	Federal Income Tax Payable		765.00
	State Income Tax Payable		148.00
	FICA Payable		379.75
	Health Insurance Payable		87.00
	Union Dues Payable		26.25
	Salaries and Wages Payable		3,558.00

Withholding Liabilities

Notice that all the withholding deductions are recorded as credits to various liabilities. All of these are current liabilities. The employer is simply acting as a collection agent and is obligated to remit the amounts withheld to other parties in a timely manner. For example, the federal income tax and FICA withheld must be paid to the United States Treasury Department within a prescribed period of time.

Journal Entry for the Employer Payroll Tax Expense

Overview

The second step in recording payroll is the journal entry for the employer payroll tax expense. This journal entry consists of recording the employer FUTA, SUTA, and FICA payroll taxes, plus any other state payroll taxes, if applicable. The dollar amounts subject to these taxes are the totals shown in the payroll register in "current gross taxable for . . ." columns. Remember that these taxes only apply to the employer; the employees make no payments.

Journal Entry for the Employer Payroll Tax Expense, *continued*

Example

The example below shows a journal entry for the employer payroll tax expense. FUTA is .006 × $1,420 = $8.52; SUTA is .054 × $1,420 = $76.68; FICA/Medicare is the same as the employee withholding = $379.75.

March 14	Payroll Tax Expense	464.95	
	FICA Payable		379.75
	FUTA Payable		8.52
	SUTA Payable		76.68

Journal Entry for the Benefits Expense

Overview

If the employer provides benefits, then the third step in recording payroll is the journal entry for the benefits expense. This journal entry consists of accruing the expense and liability for each type of benefit.

Example

The example below shows a journal entry for benefits expense consisting of vacation pay, health insurance, and pension plan expenses.

March 14	Vacation Pay Expense	225.00	
	Medical Benefits Expense	350.00	
	Pension Benefits Expense	150.00	
	Vacation Pay Payable		225.00
	Health Insurance Payable		350.00
	Pension Plan Payable		150.00

What Is Total Payroll Cost?

The total cost of a payroll is the gross pay expense, the employer payroll tax expense, and the benefits expense. For the three examples above, this is: $4,964.00 + $464.95 + $725.00 = $6,153.95.

Employee Earnings Records

Overview

Every employer is required by law to maintain a permanent record of the wages and withholding for each employee. The primary purpose of these earnings records is to provide the information necessary to report the annual gross pay and withholding to each employee at year end on form **W-2**. Employees use the W-2 information for preparing their income tax returns as well as for other purposes, such as loan applications. The employer must also provide the same information to government taxing authorities.

continued ▶

Employee Earnings Records, *continued*

Example

The example below is a partial employee *earnings record* that shows information for the month of March. Notice that the record is updated after each payroll period. The source of the data is the payroll register. Think of each record as a subsidiary ledger for each employee's earnings history.

The example you see here has a cumulative gross pay column so the wage base limits can be identified. It also provides information for required quarterly payroll reports.

Tropics Travel Company
Employee Earnings Record
For the Year 2017

Employee: Van Arsdale, Robert
S.S.#: 123-45-6789
Employment Date: July 11, 2013
Termination Date:
Address: 80 Sunshine Ct, Denver, CO 80229

Filing Status: Single
Exemptions: 1

Pay Rate: $18 hourly
Job Title: Staff Assistant

2017 Week Ended	Total Hrs.	Earnings				Deductions							Check No.
		Reg. Pay	O.T. Pay	Gross Pay	Cum. Gross Pay	Fed. Income Tax	State Income Tax	OASDI/ Medcr.	Health Ins.	Union Dues	Total	Net	
3/7	40	720.00		720.00	7,126.00	108.00	22.00	55.08	12.00	5.25	202.33	517.67	755
3/14	42	720.00	54.00	774.00	7,900.00	116.00	23.00	59.21	12.00	5.25	215.46	558.54	862
3/21	44	720.00	108.00	828.00	8,728.00	133.00	26.00	63.34	12.00	5.25	239.59	588.41	912
3/28	43	720.00	81.00	801.00	9,529.00	129.00	25.00	61.28	12.00	5.25	232.53	568.47	988
March		2,880.00	243.00	3,123.00		486.00	96.00	238.91	48.00	21.00	889.91	2,233.09	
Third Quarter		8,750.00	810.00	9,560.00		1,590.00	312.00	731.34	144.00	63.00	2,840.34	6,719.66	

Note: The source of this information is the payroll register. For example, the March 14 (highlighted) entry comes from the March 14 payroll register example.

Reconciling the Payroll Register and Employee Pay Records

Each payroll period, the payroll department must reconcile the totals on the payroll register to the total amounts on the employee earnings records. For example, if the gross pay on the payroll register is $4,964.00, then adding up the gross pay shown on each of the employee earnings records for all the employees should also result in a total of $4,964.00. This reconciliation is also done for each deduction item and net pay. A computerized payroll system should perform this function automatically.

Make Payments

Overview

Introduction

After the payroll is calculated and approved, payroll checks are prepared, signed, and distributed. However, payroll-related payments involve more than just payments to employees. This section explains the payment process.

Payments to Whom?

Payroll-related payments are made to the following parties:

- Employees
- Government taxing authorities
- Benefits providers
- Other designated recipients

Payments to Employees

Journal Entry

The journal entry to record payment to employees is shown below:

March 13	Salaries and Wages Payable	3,558.00	
	Cash		3,558.00

Payroll Checks

The credit to cash represents the total of all the payroll checks that employees receive. This is the total net pay. Most companies use special checks for payroll. Each check has a detachable portion called a ***statement of earnings*** that shows the gross pay, withholding, and net pay for the period that corresponds to the amount of the check received by an employee. The source of this information is the payroll register. Before the check is cashed, the statement of earnings should be detached and filed by the employee.

Electronic Funds Transfer

Many employees ask their employers to have the net pay automatically deposited in the employee's checking account. This results in a quicker deposit and eliminates the risk of losing the check. The employee still receives a statement of earnings with each payroll.

Payments to Taxing Authorities

Journal Entry

The journal entry to record payment to taxing authorities is shown below. This entry has two components. The example you see below consists of:

- Payment of the withholding liability for federal and state income tax and FICA/Medicare (see also page 802).
- Payment of the employer payroll tax liability (see also page 806).

Notice that the employer portion of FICA/Medicare is part of the $759.50 debit that includes both employee and employer portions of $379.75 each.

March 19	Federal Income Tax Payable	765.00	
	State Income Tax Payable	148.00	
	FICA Payable	759.50	
	SUTA Payable	76.68	
	FUTA Payable	8.52	
	Cash		1,757.70

Note: In practice, some of these liabilities might be paid on different dates. In that case, there would be a series of journal entries, each debiting some liabilities and crediting cash.

Payroll Deposit Deadlines

Taxing authorities have strict payment deadlines for when the employer must make payroll deposits. Depending on the size of the payroll and kind of tax, payment deadlines range from quarterly to semi-weekly (the bigger the payroll, the quicker the deadline). Internal Revenue Service Publication 15 has details.

If payment deadlines are not met, significant late payment penalties will be imposed.

Note: The government considers its receipts from the employer's payroll tax deposits as an important source of cash flow. It takes the obligation to make these deposits very seriously. When I was in school, I had a part-time bookkeeping job for a small business that was constantly late with payroll deposits and that had ignored a catch-up payment agreement with the IRS. I returned from lunch one day to find two IRS agents changing the lock on the door (after seizing the assets).

How Payments Are Made

EFT: All employers must use an electronic funds transfer system (EFT) to automatically transfer payroll deposits to designated government accounts. This system is free and is called "EFTPS."

Payments to Other Parties

Overview

In general, payments to third parties are made according to the contractual agreement with each party. An exception is court-ordered withholding such as wage garnishments for child support, which have fixed payment dates.

Journal Entry

Journal entries to record payment to third parties are shown below:

March 25	Health Insurance Payable	350.00	
	Cash		350.00
March 31	Pension Plan Payable	150.00	
	Cash		150.00

Internal Control for Payroll Payments

Payroll Checks

Payroll checks should be prepared by one department and signed and distributed by another department, after the payroll calculation has been reviewed, with supporting documentation. For example, the payroll department prepares the payroll checks and employer deposit checks, but the treasurer or chief financial officer signs and distributes the checks. In a small business, the *owner* should:

- Review the checks for accuracy and for hours worked
- Sign and distribute the checks

In a larger business, the signed checks are sent directly to employees from the treasurer's office or employees must present identification to receive their paychecks. This helps reduce the problem of payment to fictitious employees.

- Payroll data: All data changes in employee status, wage rates, or withholding must originate with human resources (or owner) and be sent to the payroll department.

continued ▶

Internal Control for Payroll Payments, *continued*

Payroll Bank Accounts	For reasons of efficiency, companies with many employees keep one or even two separate payroll bank accounts. Not having a large number of payroll checks in the regular checking account makes it much easier to reconcile the account. Also, because many payroll checks may be outstanding at the end of a month, using two payroll accounts allows checks to clear from one account while the other is being used. This makes it easy to reconcile the account that is not being used during the current month.

Independent Payroll Services

Many companies use independent payroll preparation services (also called ***payroll processing centers***). These services are independent businesses that specialize in payroll processing. Banks also offer these services. Such services are especially helpful for small- to moderate-sized companies. The use of an independent payroll service substantially reduces employee labor time, reduces the cost of computerized systems, and can improve internal control by reducing manual calculation errors and employee collusion.

The general procedure is for the company to provide the payroll service with basic employee payroll information and hours worked. The payroll service, using its own computer system, then performs all calculations, prepares checks, prepares required reports, and maintains payroll records. As well, it provides the information that the company uses for journal entries.

However, outside payroll processing calculations must also be checked for accuracy. This is especially true of the withholding and payroll tax expense calculations. If an outside service is used to make payments, it is particularly important to regularly verify that the correct payments have been made. Finally, funds should not leave a company's accounts until payment is actually necessary.

Voucher System

If a voucher system is being used (see Learning Goal 16) the supervisor of the payroll department, after payroll calculations have been checked, prepares a voucher for the total amount of the net pay for the period. This voucher will be recorded in the accounting department as a debit to Salaries and Wages Payable and a credit to Vouchers Payable.

Similarly, a voucher will be prepared for each of the other liability payments, and the accounting department will debit the liability and credit Vouchers Payable.

Check Your Understanding

Write the completed sentences on a separate piece of paper. The answers are below.

In addition to gross pay, employers have at least one other type of payroll expense: employer payroll taxes. Three employer payroll taxes are · · · · · · · ·, · · · · · · · ·, and · · · · · · · · (use the abbreviated names).

An important internal control procedure is to · · · · · · · · (combine/separate) the payroll calculation functions and the other payroll functions. It is generally · · · · · · · · (necessary/unnecessary) to require a rotating review of all payroll calculations by different supervisors or in a small business, by the · · · · · · · ·.

If the wage base is $7,000 how much of each the following employee's current period wages would be subject to tax?

1. Cornejo: Prior cumulative wages: $3,500. Current period wages: $1,450. Taxable: · · · · · · · ·
2. Halliday: Prior cumulative wages: $5,100. Current period wages: $2,000. Taxable: · · · · · · · ·
3. Roche: Prior cumulative wages: $7,900. Current period wages: $ 1,300. Taxable: · · · · · · · ·

Answers

In addition to gross pay, employers have at least one other type of payroll expense: employer payroll taxes. Three employer payroll taxes are FICA, FUTA, and SUTA (use the abbreviated names).

An important internal control procedure is to separate (combine/separate) the payroll calculation functions and the other payroll functions. It is generally necessary (necessary/unnecessary) to require a rotating review of all payroll calculations by different supervisors, or in a small business, by the owner.

1. Cornejo: Taxable: $1,450
2. Halliday: Taxable: $1,900
3. Roche: Taxable: –0–

Submit Required Forms and Reports

Key Items

Overview

Most forms and reports are prepared to comply with the requirements of government taxing authorities. Government taxing authorities want to maintain close control over cash flow from payroll deposits, and therefore require frequent reports. Substantial penalties are imposed if the reports are not submitted in a timely manner.

Other required reports are those that must be provided to employees

Government Reporting

The table below summarizes the key reports that are required to be sent to taxing authorities. See irs.gov for a full federal reports list. State forms vary. The frequency refers to a calendar year basis.

Form/Report	Frequency	What For
Form 941/Employer's Federal Payroll Tax Return	Quarterly	Reports the liability and withholding for federal income tax, employer/employee OASDI, and Medicare
Form XXX/Employer's State Payroll Tax Return	Quarterly	Reports the liability and withholding for state income tax, SUTA, and other state taxes
Form 940/Employer's Federal Unemployment Tax Return	Annual (year end)	Reports the liability and withholding for FUTA
Form W-2 (copies)/Employee Wage and Tax Statement	Annual (year end)	Reports an employee's gross pay and taxable pay and withholding for the year; sent to federal, state, and local taxing authorities
Form W-3/Transmittal form	Annual (year end)	Summary federal transmittal form that must accompany the copies of the W-2 and 1099 (below)
Forms 1095 (copies) Employee medical coverage	Annual (year end)	Forms required for some businesses by the Affordable Care Act
Form 1099 (copies)/ Non-Employee Compensation Statement	Annual (year end)	Reports a *non-employee's* compensation and withholding; sent to federal, state, and local taxing authorities

Internet Use

The Internal Revenue Service permits Internet reporting for Forms 941 and 940 by payroll services and professional practitioners qualified under the *e-filing* system. This reporting works with most payroll software and is also integrated with a payment procedure. The use of Internet reporting and paying is likely to grow in the future.

Key Items, *continued*

Employee Reporting

- Each employee must receive a *Form W-2* at year end. This shows the employee's gross pay and withholding. This information is required to complete individual tax returns.
- Employers that maintain pension plans and other benefit plans should also provide a summary report to employees at year end.

Non-Employee Reporting

Each independent contractor must receive a *Form 1099-MISC* that reports total compensation and withholding. The form is required for each provider of services of $600 or more.

The Use of Computers in Payroll

Overview

Introduction

Because of detailed calculations and potentially large amounts of data, payroll procedures are an excellent application for the use of a computer. In fact, one of the first computer applications that a small business wants to use is often the preparation of payroll (for businesses that do not use an independent payroll service).

What a Computerized Payroll System Does

A fully integrated computerized payroll system performs the following functions:

- Maintains a database of employee information and current payroll tax rates, wage bases, and other information needed for calculations
- Performs all payroll calculations
- Prints payroll checks
- Performs accounting and record-keeping functions
- Prints all payroll forms and tax returns
- Provides management with summary analysis reports

Input Is Required

Of course, the computer system cannot perform these payroll functions unless data are entered into the computer. For example, hours worked by employees must be calculated and recorded for each payroll period, and then they must be entered into the computer with employee identification codes. Additionally, the database of employee information frequently must be updated, and entering this information is not an automated procedure.

The journal entries created by the payroll software should interface with the general ledger software, so these entries are recorded with a single command.

continued ▶

Overview, *continued*

Hidden Costs

A computerized payroll system has numerous hidden costs; therefore, the volume of calculations and reports should be large enough to create a time savings that offsets the other hidden costs. Some of these costs are:

- Substantial training and practice time is required to understand and efficiently operate a computerized accounting system.
- Annual updates of payroll software are required.
- Recurring updates of employee database information are required.
- Software support services from the vendor may be an additional charge.
- Special payroll forms are required.
- Upgrades of computer hardware will be needed, particularly if the size of the software program increases.

Internal Control Issues

Computerized payroll systems create special internal control issues. The primary concerns are about access and separation of duties.

- Because a single payroll computer module can perform virtually all the payroll functions, one person with access to the payroll program can essentially control all payroll functions.
- Pay rates and critical data can be altered, and unauthorized program changes can be made. This means that overpayments as well as fictitious employees can easily be created.
- Small- to moderate-sized business are particularly vulnerable because only one or two people regularly use the computer accounting system.

Financial Statement Presentation of Payroll Items

Key Points

Income Statement

Payroll-related expenses such as gross pay expense, employer payroll tax expense, and benefits expense are operating expenses on the income statement.

Key Points, *continued*

Balance Sheet

The balance sheet shows payroll liabilities as current liabilities. This includes:

- Salaries and Wages Payable: This is the net pay owing to employees at the end of a completed payroll period (see journal entry on page 814.) This account also shows accrued wages for a partial payroll period (see below).
- FICA/FUTA/SUTA Payable: These are the employer and/or employee withheld payroll taxes that are still undeposited, from completed payroll periods (not the cumulative totals for the year). These accounts are also used for the same liabilities resulting from payroll tax expense accruals for a partial payroll period (see below).
- Other: These are liabilities to pension and benefit plans and other third parties.

Period-End Accruals

- Gross pay accrual: The matching principle requires that the wages, salaries, and other compensation expense that have been incurred at the end of an accounting period, but not yet paid, must be accrued.
- Payroll tax expense accrual: Because payroll tax expenses are incurred at the same time as gross pay expense, employer payroll taxes should be accrued. *Example:* A fiscal year ends on June 30. The current payroll period will not end until July 5; however, as of June 30, $4,800 of employee earnings have been earned for the time worked. The wages expense should be accrued and the employer payroll tax should be accrued on this as follows:

Payroll Tax Expense	465	
FICA Payable		367
SUTA Payable		88
FUTA Payable		10

Note: Some companies save time and do not accrue payroll tax expense because payroll taxes are not a liability until the employees are paid. This is a violation of the matching principle for an expense resulting in a probable liability.

Withholding on Accruals

It is not necessary to identify employee withholding in the situation above. This only needs to be done at the end of a completed payroll period when employees are paid. Expenses are accrued, but withholding is not recorded until employees can access payment.

QUICK REVIEW

- Current liabilities are obligations that require the use of company resources within a year.

- Included in current liabilities are liabilities that must be estimated, probable (contingent) liabilities, and current portion of long-term debt.

- The payroll process consists of five elements:

  1. Identify employees.
  2. Calculate the payroll.
  3. Record the payment.
  4. Make payments.
  5. Submit forms and reports.

- Identifying workers as employees or not employees is a critical first step in the payroll process; this requires internal control procedures to prevent fraud and employee/contractor misclassification errors.

- Calculating the payroll involves three basic elements:

  1. Gross pay expense and withholding
  2. Payroll taxes expense
  3. Benefits expense

- Four types of withholding deductions from gross pay are required:

  1. Income tax: Usually determined by using withholding tables.
  2. Social security tax: Calculated by using a wage base limit and a tax rate for OASDI and no wage limit and a different rate for Medicare.
  3. State unemployment tax: set by each state, generally using a wage base and tax rate method
  4. Any other deductions imposed by law

- Employer payroll tax expense always includes FICA, FUTA, and SUTA

- A payroll register is often used to organize the calculations, and employee earnings records are required by law. This is used as a source when payroll is recorded.

- Payroll tax deposit and tax return filing have deadlines specified by law, and there are significant penalties for noncompliance.

- Internal control is an essential part of the payroll calculation.

- Payroll tax liability appears as a current liability on the balance sheet.

VOCABULARY

Bonus: extra gross pay given as a reward for achievement or meeting goals (page 798)

Commission: gross pay determined as a percentage of sales dollars (page 798)

Contingent liability: a liability that is created only if another event happens first (page 789)

Current portion of long-term debt: the amount of principal payments of a long-term loan that are payable within a year (page 790)

Earnings Record: a legally required record of employee gross pay, withholding, and net pay that must be maintained by an employer for each employee (page 816)

Employee: any person who performs services for a business if the business can control what work will be done and how it will be done (page 793)

Exemption: another name for withholding allowance (page 800)

Fair Labor Standards Act (FLSA): A federal law that governs working conditions for wage earners and sets standards for overtime pay and minimum wage (page 799)

FICA: Federal Insurance Contribution Act that created social security (page 802)

Filing status: marital status that determines the applicable income tax rate (page 800)

VOCABULARY

Form W-2: an employee wage and tax statement that shows annual gross pay and withholding; must be provided to each employee at calendar year end (page 823)

Form W-4: a federal form that indicates employee filing status and withholding allowances (page 800)

Form 1099-MISC: a federal form that reports total compensation and withholding for independent contractors (page 823)

FUTA: Federal Unemployment Tax Act; imposes a tax on employers that provides for payments to unemployed employees (page 807)

Gross pay: the total compensation received by an employee (page 798)

In kind: payment made in the form of property or services value and not cash (page 798)

Independent contractor: an individual who is in business to offer services to the public and who is not an employee (page 794)

Medicare: medical insurance for uninsured workers financed by social security tax (page 802)

Net pay: gross pay minus deductions; the amount of cash received by an employee (page 799)

Payroll: the process of (1) identifying employees, (2) calculating pay and payroll taxes, (3) recording payroll transactions, (4) making payments, and (5) completing payroll reporting forms (page 791)

Payroll deduction: an amount deducted from gross pay by the employer (page 799)

Payroll processing center: an independent business that specializes in payroll processing and record-keeping services (page 820)

Payroll register: an accounting worksheet used to organize and summarize payroll information each payroll period (page 811)

OASDI: old age, survivor's, and disability insurance financed by social security tax (page 802)

Plan Administrator: a company that designs and administers pension plans (page 809)

Salary: a fixed amount of gross pay per period not dependent upon hours worked (page 798)

Self-employment tax: the combined employee/employer FICA amount that must be paid by a self-employed individual (page 807)

Social security tax: a general term describing a tax on employees and employers to provide old age, survivor's, and disability insurance benefits and medicare (page 802)

Statement of earnings: a detachable portion of a payroll check that shows gross pay, deductions, and net pay (page 817)

Statutory employee: a worker who is not an employee under common law but who is designated as an employee by statute (page 795)

SUTA: State Unemployment Tax Act of any state; imposes a tax on employers that provides for payments to unemployed employees (page 807)

Tax rate: the percent of tax (page 802)

Wage: gross pay determined by hours worked or units completed (page 798)

Wage base: a fixed annual calendar year amount of gross pay subject to payroll tax (page 802)

Wage-bracket method: a common method of calculating income tax withholding (page 801)

Withholding allowance: a fixed amount allowed for each employee, the employee's spouse, and each dependent; used to exempt that amount of wages from income tax withholding (page 800)

Learning Goal 20 is about recording, reporting, and controlling current liabilities and payroll. Use these questions and problems to practice what you have just read.

Note: For these questions and problems assume the following: OASDI, wage base of $130,000 and a rate of 6.2%; Medicare, no limit and a rate of 1.45%; SUTA and FUTA, wage base of $7,000 with rates of 5.4% and .6%, respectively.

Multiple Choice
Select the best answer.

1. Jeffery is paid at the rate of $20 per hour. This week he worked 46 hours. Under the FLSA rules what is his total gross pay?
   a. $920
   b. $1,040
   c. $1,380
   d. $980
2. Employer payroll taxes do not include which of the following?
   a. FICA
   b. FUTA
   c. SUTA
   d. income tax
3. Which of the following is an essential internal control procedure for payroll?
   a. Separate the human resources activities from payroll calculation activities.
   b. Require the payroll department to sign all payroll checks.
   c. Install a computerized accounting payroll system.
   d. Use a payroll register.
4. Good internal control requires that who of the following should distribute paychecks?
   a. payroll department
   b. human resources department
   c. treasurer or chief financial officer's office
   d. the immediate supervisor
5. Which of the following is not a deduction from an employee's gross pay?
   a. FICA
   b. FUTA
   c. SUTA
   d. both b and c
6. Joe is married with three small children. If his wife does not work or works and does not claim an exemption, Joe should claim:
   a. 6 exemptions.
   b. 5 exemptions.
   c. 3 exemptions.
   d. 2 exemptions.
7. Which of the following is not a current liability?
   a. advance payment from a customer
   b. wages payable
   c. possible loss in a lawsuit
   d. any liability that must be estimated

8. Mary's proprietorship business had net income of $170,000 last year. What was Mary's self-employment tax?
   a. $26,010
   b. $30,940
   c. $20,673
   d. None of the above

9. Which item is paid both by the employer and the employee?
   a. income tax withholding
   b. FUTA
   c. FICA
   d. SUTA

10. The three different journal entries required to record total payroll expenses will show:
    a. gross pay expense, independent contractor expense, benefits expense.
    b. gross pay expense, payroll deposits expense, payroll processing service expense.
    c. gross pay expense, payroll tax expense, benefits expense.
    d. net pay expense, payroll tax expense, income tax expense.

11. In regard to payroll liabilities presented on the balance sheet:
    a. employer payroll tax deposit liability may be shown as a long-term liability.
    b. wages payable may sometimes be a long-term liability.
    c. employee withholding liabilities should be accrued at the end of an accounting period.
    d. payroll liabilities are always current liabilities.

12. Which of the following should *not* be accrued at the end of an accounting period?
    a. employer payroll tax expense
    b. salaries and wages expense
    c. employee withholding
    d. employee benefits

13. Who is not an employee?
    a. Janet in the sales department who is paid on a commission basis.
    b. Bob in the human resources office who sometimes takes work home with him.
    c. The owner of a corporation who performs regular duties for the company.
    d. John, the computer consultant, who has worked every day for the last month at the same company but also works for other clients.

14. At year end:
    a. an employee receives a W-2 form, and an independent contractor receives a 1099-MISC form.
    b. both an employee and an independent contractor must receive a W-2.
    c. an employee receives a W-4, and an independent contractor receives a 1099-MISC.
    d. none of the above.

15. Which of the following does *not* determine the amount of income tax withholding?
    a. gross pay per pay period
    b. withholding allowances claimed
    c. the cumulative amount of gross pay
    d. being married or single

16. If Gloria earned $180 of overtime pay and worked 5 hours of overtime for the week, what was her total regular pay?
    a. $900
    b. $960
    c. $1,440
    d. Some other amount

PRACTICE   **Learning Goal 20, continued**   *Solutions are in the disk at the back of the book and at: www.worthyjames.com*

17. Roland earned $135,000 for the current year. The amount of his FICA withholding should be:
a. $8,032.50
b. $7,191.00
c. $9,262.50
d. some other amount

18. Which of the following is a payroll internal control weakness?
a. Payroll preparation is separated from employee hiring and personnel activities.
b. Two bank accounts are used: one for payroll and one for other operations.
c. The supervisor must submit time cards and hand out payroll checks.
d. None of the above.

Discussion Questions and Brief Exercises

1. Cupertino Enterprises purchased $400,000 of electronics equipment and signed a 3-year note payable.
a. At year-end, $85,000 of the note principal and $15,000 of interest would be due within one year. Prepare the year-end journal entry and show how the liability would be reported on the balance sheet.
b. Identify four causes of current liabilities and give one example of each.

2. Anne-Marie is married with two dependent children, and her husband is self-employed. She is paid semi-monthly, and her gross pay this period was $1,600. What is her income tax withholding? (Use the withholding table on page 801.)

3. What is the difference between an employee and an independent contractor?

4. What is the difference between forms W-2 and W-4? What information does each contain?

5. What is an employee earnings record? Why is it necessary and how is it used?

6. What is FICA? Who pays FICA?

7. What are FUTA and SUTA? Who pays FUTA and SUTA?

8. When an employer withholds federal income tax and state income from a paycheck, are those withholding items expenses for the employer?

9. A business allows employees to earn 1.5 days of paid vacation for each month worked. If the business has 30 employees and the average daily pay during the month is $170, what is the vacation pay that should be accrued for the month. What would the journal entry be?

10. What is the difference between a payroll register and an employee earnings record?

11. Describe important internal control procedures designed to safeguard the payroll process.

12. In January, Dave had gross pay for the month of $4,500. Therefore, his employer's January SUTA tax liability is: ($7,000 − $4,500) = $3,500. So, $3,500 × .054 = $189 tax liability. Correct?

13. What is the FLSA? How does it affect an employee's gross pay?

14. Andy's hourly pay rate is $20 per hour, and he receives an overtime rate of $30 per hour. During the current pay period he worked 48 hours. His federal income tax withholding is $220, and his wages are subject to FICA tax. Calculate Andy's gross and net pay. Explain your calculations.

15. What are the three categories of payroll-related expense items that an employer pays?

16. Identify the five elements in the sequence of the payroll process.

17. For the current month, the gross wages expense of Potomac Company is $30,000. Assume that all of the employee wages are taxable for FICA, SUTA, and FUTA. Calculate the employer payroll tax expense, and prepare the journal entry for the employer payroll tax.

18. Chi-Ming earned gross salary for the year of $134,000. During the year, $32,000 of federal income tax and $6,500 of state income tax were withheld. $1,800 of medical insurance premiums were withheld. The employer pays 50% of medical insurance. Prepare a single journal entry that records Chi-Ming's gross wages, withholding, and net pay for the year. Also prepare a journal entry that records the employer's payroll tax expense and benefits expense.

Reinforcement Problems

LG 20-1. Calculate missing items, prepare payroll journal entries. The payroll records of Ogden Company show the following information for the month of January:

Instructions:

a. Calculate the missing amounts in the table.
b. Prepare the payroll journal entries using the completed table.

Item	Employee Earnings Items	Amount
a.	Regular pay	$30,000
b.	Overtime pay	18,000
c.	Total gross pay	?
d.	Federal income tax withheld	6,800
e.	State income tax withheld	900
f.	FICA tax	?
g.	Charitable contribution withholding	1,000
h.	Net pay	?
	Employer Payroll Tax and Benefit Items	
i.	SUTA tax	?
j.	FUTA tax	?
k.	Medical insurance	$2,500
l.	Retirement plans	750
m.	Total employer payroll tax and benefit items	?

LG 20-2. Prepare payroll journal entries. New Orleans Company pays employees monthly and incurred employee wages expense of $70,000 for the month of August. Federal tax withholding is $9,800, and state income tax withholding is $2,870. Two of the employees have exceeded the FICA wage base limits, so $4,000 of the gross pay is not subject to OASDI. Only $15,000 of the gross pay is subject to the federal and state unemployment tax. The company also incurs a monthly expense for employee benefits as follows: health insurance, $2,200; life insurance, $200; pension plan benefits, 3.5% of gross pay. Union dues withheld are $220.

Instructions: Record all necessary payroll journal entries as of August 31.

LG 20-3. Social Security tax calculations. In October, Evelyn earned $4,750 and Sue earned $2,800. From January through September, Evelyn had earned $126,500 and Sue had earned $104,100.

Instructions: Calculate the following:

a. the October amount of FICA (social security tax) withholding for Evelyn and Sue
b. the total amount of FICA tax for both employees from January through October

LG 20-4. Journal entries and accruals.

a. Kenai Company has a weekly payroll period. The current weekly payroll period has just ended on Friday, October 12. The table below shows current employee payroll information for the week ended Friday, October 12.

Employee Name	Current Hours	Rate	Federal Income Tax	Prior Cum. Earnings
Bishop	40	$30/hr	$255	$67,300
Chignik	44	25/hr	190	59,200
Peters	40	40/hr	310	6,200
Sagamore	Salary	2,400/week	672	129,200

b. Talkeetna Partnership has a weekly payroll period. The accounting year end of October 31 is on a Wednesday. The weekly payroll period will end on Friday, November 2. The table below shows you current employee payroll information for the three days ended Wednesday, October 31.

Employee Name	Current Hours	Rate	Federal Income Tax	Prior Cum. Earnings
Abrams	24	$20/hour	$80	$6,000
Cantwell	24	45/hour	88	129,600
Tok	Salary	3,000/week	335	141,000
Wenham	20	35/hour	90	6,900

Instructions: Prepare the necessary weekly journal entries for each company.

LG 20-5. Identify various liabilities.

For each of the items listed below, indicate if the item should appear on the balance sheet as a liability.

a. Unpaid wages at year end, but before the end of the payroll period
b. Income tax withholding in item a above
c. Income tax withholding at the end of a payroll period
d. Warranty expense that has to be estimated
e. 3 months' rent paid in advance by a tenant
f. Possible loss of plant assets located in a foreign company because of foreign government expropriation
g. The amount of a 10-year loan that is payable within a year
h. The amount of a 10-year loan that is payable after one year
i. Possible loss from a loan guarantee in which our company must pay if the borrower does not pay
j. 6-month magazine subscription payments received from customers
k. Employer payroll taxes at year end, but before the end of the payroll period
l. Employee bonus pay for all employees entitled to receive bonuses based on various factors
m. Coupons given to customers (Coupon value may be used for future purchases.)

LG 20-6. Calculate the Social Security Withholding. Use a separate piece of paper to complete the following table:

Cumulative Gross Pay Through November 30	Current Gross Pay: December	Cumulative Gross Pay Year To Date	Current Gross Pay Subject to OASDI Tax	Current Gross Pay Subject to Medicare Tax	December OASDI Withheld	December Medicare Withheld
$44,300	$3,750					
$124,150	$7,200					
$130,700	$3,550					
$127,900	$5,200					

LG 20-7. Gross pay journal entry. The following account titles and amounts are from a payroll journal entry on May 15 and are shown in no particular order. All withheld amounts are shown. Prepare a general journal entry. Recreate the complete journal entry.

Sales Salary Expense: $5,150   FICA Payable: $620   Federal Income Tax Payable: $1,400
State Income Tax Payable: $410   Union Dues Payable: $125   Office Wages Expense: $3,330

PRACTICE   Learning Goal 20, continued

Solutions are in the disk at the back of the book and at: www.worthyjames.com

LG 20-8. **Gross and net pay calculation.** Don Suzuki works as floor salesperson in a custom furniture store. Don earns a base monthly salary of $1,000 plus a 10% sales commission. During March his total sales were $21,500 dollars. Don's federal income tax withholding has been averaging 15% of gross pay, and state withholding has been averaging 3%. His prior gross pay for the year is $6,100. He contributes $50 per month to a qualified savings plan by automatic payroll withholding. Compute Don's gross and net pay for March.

LG 20-9. **Journal entries.** Using the information in problem LG 20-8 above, prepare the general journal entries to record the employer's gross pay expense and payroll tax expense at the end of the March payroll period.

LG 20-10. **Payroll register, journal entries.** Napa Vineyard Enterprises provides you with the payroll information for the week ended November 8, which you see presented in the table below.

Instructions:

a. On separate piece of paper, prepare a payroll register. Use the payroll register on pages 812 and 813 as your model.
b. Prepare the proper general journal entries.

Employee Name	Current Hours/ Ck. #	Weekly Rate	Federal Income Tax	State Income Tax	Health Insurance	Prior Cum. Earnings
Evans	41/704	$800	$120	$25	$28	$6,600
Griffin	Salary/705	3,100	470	110	28	128,550
Klosterman	40/706	1,000	240	44	28	48,000
Theriault	40/707	760	155	38	28	6,770
Walzak	45/708	880	210	50	28	35,800

Other Information: The company contributes to the employee health insurance plan at a cost of $100 per employee per week and pays for group term life insurance at a cost of $10 per employee per week. Wage employees work in sales, salaried employees are office employees. Use 5.4% as the SUTA rate and .6% for the FUTA rate.

LG 20-11. **Record payroll entries.** The accountant for Providence Enterprises assembled the following payroll information for the month ended March 31:

Sales wages expense	$168,000
Administrative salary expense	325,000
Sales commissions expense	112,000
Employee withholding:	
Federal income tax	134,200
State income tax	18,300
FICA (combined OASDI/Medicare)	38,240
Medical insurance premiums	12,200
Gross wages subject to FUTA/SUTA	80,000
Employer medical insurance payable	35,800
Worker's compensation insurance	24,400

LG 20-11, *continued*

Instructions:

a. Prepare a general journal entry that records the employee payroll for the month ended March 31.
b. Prepare an adjusting journal entry to accrue Providence Enterprise's related payroll expenses as of March 31.

LG 20-12. Payroll entries; various calculations. Santa Rosa Enterprises pays its employees on a biweekly basis. The table below shows employee wage and withholding information for the period. The employer pays 80% of medical insurance premiums and employees pay 20%. Employees earn the required time and one-half rate for hours worked in excess of 40 hours per week. The employees also receive two weeks of paid vacation per year. One employee, Walker, not shown in the table below, received $2,000 of vacation pay during the current period. Walker's prior cumulative earnings were $44,000. Walker withholds $350 of Federal income tax and $100 of state income tax and pays $35 of health insurance premiums per biweekly period.

Instructions: Record the payroll entries for the current biweekly payroll period. Record Walker separately.

Employee Name	Current Hours	Biweekly Rate	Federal Income Tax	State Income Tax	Health Insurance	Prior Cum. Earnings
Chen	82	$1,200	$220	$ 25	$35	$ 5,000
Grossman	Salary	3,300	500	140	45	127,700
Moss	80	2,000	280	50	40	48,000
Siler	88	1,600	160	48	40	6,700
Zhang	80	1,200	200	22	35	29,800

LG 20-13. Calculate gross and net pay; record payroll entries. Abner Watson earns regular pay of $1,200 per week plus time and one-half (1.5) for weekly hours in excess of 40 hours per week. His federal income tax withholding is at the rate of 20%. There is no state income tax. Watson pays court-ordered child support of $200 per week. His employer pays SUTA taxes at the rate of 5.4%, and FUTA taxes at the rate of .6%. During the week ending May 10, Watson worked 46 hours. His cumulative year-to-date pay prior to the current week is $6,400. The employer also contributes to a medical plan at the rate of 3% of gross pay.

Instructions:

a. Calculate Watson's gross pay and net pay for the week.
b. Prepare a general journal entry to record each of the following for the employer:

- Watson's wages expense, withholding, and net pay
- The employer's payroll tax expense
- The employer's benefits expense
- The cash payment to Watson on May 12
- The cash payment to pay all payroll taxes on May 15

Solutions are in the disk at the back of the book and at: www.worthyjames.com

PRACTICE   Learning Goal 20, continued

LG 20-14. Challenging problem: complete the payroll register and review all payroll calculations. A payroll register for the semi-monthly period (assume 80 hours) ended November 12, 20XX is presented below.

Instructions: Make a copy of each of the payroll register pages and complete the register by entering a correct amount in each empty box.

| Employee Name | Tot. Hrs. | Earnings | | | | Current Gross Taxable for . . . | |
		Regular	Overtime	Current Gross	YTD Gross	FUTA/ SUTA	FICA (OASDI)
Curtis, R.	80	3,200	–0–	3,200	44,500		
Fisher, Y.	85		120		4,100		
McLeod, S.			–0–		133,100		
Slocum, P.			–0–				1,300
Teruya, M.	84				49,600		
Total	—						

Payroll Register for the Semi-Monthly

Other information:

1. Fisher is married and claims 3 exemptions. Teruya is married and claims 4 exemptions. You can use the income tax withholding table on page 801 to calculate income tax withholding.
2. The FICA tax rate is 7.65%, consisting of 6.2% for OASDI and 1.45% for Medicare. The OASDI portion wage base is $120,000. The FUTA/SUTA wage base is $7,000. The SUTA rate is 5.4% and the FUTA rate is .6%.
3. The state income tax rate is 4% of gross wages.
4. McLeod and Slocum are administrative employees that are paid salaries. The other employees are in sales and paid at hourly rates.
5. Overtime hours are paid at a rate of one and one-half times the regular rate for time worked in excess of 80 hours for the period.
6. Employees contribute to the health insurance plan at the rate of 1% of their regular gross pay.

LG 20-14, *continued*

Period Ended November 12, 20XX

| | Deductions | | | | | Payment | | | |
Fed. Inc. Tax	State Inc. Tax	OASDI/ Medicare	Health Insurance	Total	Net Pay	Ck. #	Admin. Salaries	Sales Wages
440.00						250		
						251		
652.50	300.00					252		
895.00		150.20	48.00			253		
			15.20			254		
						—		

LG 20-15. Identifying forms and reports. On a separate piece of paper, complete the information in the empty spaces in the table below.

Form/Report	Frequency	What For
(Reminder: Use a separate sheet of paper to complete the table.)		Reports the liability and withholding for federal income tax, employer/employee FICA, and Medicare
		Reports the liability and withholding for state income tax, SUTA, and other state taxes
		Reports the liability and withholding for FUTA
		Reports the employee gross pay and withholding for the year; sent to federal, state, and local taxing authorities
		Summary federal transmittal form that must accompany the copies of the W-2 and 1099
		Reports a *non-employee's* compensation and withholding; sent to federal, state, and local taxing authorities

PRACTICE   Learning Goal 20, continued

Instructor-Assigned Problems

If you are using this book in a class, these review problems may be assigned by your instructor for homework, group assignments, class work, or other activities. Only your instructor has the solutions.

IA 20-1. Record payroll entries. The accountant for Gatlinburg Company assembled the payroll information that you see below for the end of the current payroll period ended May 31.

Instructions:

a. Prepare a general journal entry to record the employee payroll for the period. (For journal paper, you can make copies from the general journal template in the disk at the back of the book.)

b. Prepare an adjusting journal entry to accrue related payroll expenses as of the end of the period.

General and administrative wages	$383,700
Sales salaries	92,000
Sales commissions	245,000
Employee withholding:	
Federal income tax	154,800
State income tax	15,500
FICA (combined OASDI/Medicare)	53,100
Medical insurance premiums	17,900
Gross wages subject to FUTA/SUTA	110,000
Employer medical insurance payments	51,600
Worker's compensation insurance	49,800

IA 20-2. Payroll register, journal entries. Whittier Corporation has assembled the payroll data for the week ended October 17, which you see in the table below.

Instructions:

a. On separate piece of paper, prepare a payroll register. Use the payroll register on pages 812 and 813 as your model.

b. Prepare the correct general journal entries. (For journal paper, make copies from the general journal template in the disk at the back of the book.)

Employee Name	Current Hours/ Ck. #	Weekly Rate	Federal Income Tax	State Income Tax	Health Insurance	Prior Cum. Earnings
Barbaria	40/486	$1,200	$240	$36	$35	$ 6,200
Johnson	44/487	1,600	320	48	35	65,500
Ling	Salary/488	3,200	575	70	35	128,400
Singh	48/489	1,400	280	42	40	58,800
Ventura	40/490	1,300	150	26	20	3,700

Other Information: The company contributes to the employee health insurance plan at a cost of $120 per employee per payroll period and pays for group term life insurance at a cost of $10 per employee per payroll period. Wage employees work in manufacturing; salaried employees are office employees.

PRACTICE   Learning Goal 20, continued

IA 20-3. Review and record various current liability events. Bill Smith is the sole stockholder in his auto parts business, Smith Parts and Services, Inc., and is one of the four employees of the corporation. The transactions below all involve current liability events during December. Fiscal year-end is December 31. The current payroll period ends in December.

Instructions: Indicate how each event should be treated, including required journal entries.

4   Received a notice that the prior year corporate income tax return is being audited.

7   Received notice from a bank that a $50,000 note payable that the business had guaranteed for a long-time regular business customer is now in default. The customer has said that it can begin making payments again soon, but is not sure when.

16   Taxable sales for the first two weeks are $250,000. The sales tax rate is 6%.

17   The company made sales in the amount of $30,000 that included coupons valued at $4,500.

19   For some products, the business must fulfill a 1-year warranty obligation to replace the products at no charge. The amount of these products sold in December that will be under warranty is $75,000. The average rate of warranty use is 5% of sales and cost of goods sold averages 70%.

21   Received $1,500 in advance payments from customers.

27   The business is a defendant in a hazardous product lawsuit. The attorney advises that the outcome is uncertain; some defendants in similar circumstances have been assessed large amounts of damages.

31   Unpaid wages at year-end are $25,000. All employees except one have earned cumulative wages for the year of less than $130,000 and all except one more than $10,000. Bill Smith had earned $129,000 before the current payroll period, and earned $2,500 in the current payroll period. A new employee hired in November has earned $3,000 before the current period and $1,500 in the current period.

IA 20-4. Payroll calculations for employee and employer. At November 30 of the current year, Cheyenne Miller had earned $107,250 regular gross pay. In December, she received her regular gross pay plus an additional year-end bonus of $18,000. During the full year, her monthly income tax withholding was as follows: federal income tax: $1,950; state income tax: $500. Additional withholding on her bonus was federal: $4,000; state: $1,600. In addition, she authorized the following monthly withholding amounts: medical insurance contribution: $200; life insurance: $15; retirement plan: $500; animal welfare charity: $20.

Her employer incurred payroll tax expenses at the normal rates. In addition the employer incurred the following additional costs: matching medical insurance contribution: $200; vacation pay at 6% of gross regular monthly wages.

Instructions:

a. Record the employer's journal entry for December as if Cheyenne Miller is the only employee.

b. Calculate her gross pay and withholding for the full year.

c. Calculate the total employer cost for the year.

d. Calculate the percentage of her total gross pay that was withheld for both income and payroll tax.

PRACTICE   Learning Goal 20, continued

IA20-5 Reporting different types of current liabilities. We have seen that depending on circumstances, an actual or potential current liability could be classified as follows:

Liability	Potential Liability
• Actual obligation at a definite amount	• Contingent obligation at a definite amount
• Actual obligation that can be estimated	• Contingent obligation that can be estimated
• Actual obligation that cannot be estimated	• Contingent obligation that cannot be estimated

Instructions: For each of the independent situations below, explain the reporting requirement at the time financial statements are issued.

1) Sales tax is collected from customers.

2) Products are sold with a two-year warranty.

3) An advance payment is received from a customer.

4) A company is a defendant is a lawsuit

5) A company has operations in another country with a government that dislikes foreign companies.

6) The property tax bill for the coming year has not yet been received.

7) A loan guarantee

8) A company does not purchase flood insurance.

9) A retail store offers coupons to customers.

10) An airline offers frequent-flier miles.

11) A company that is a defendant in a lawsuit has lost the lawsuit, but the judgment is still pending.

12) An employee earned $128,000 year to date; at May 31 month-end $3,000 of current wages are earned but not paid.

INTERNET EXERCISES

Use the IRS website/research payroll taxes; research your own state payroll taxes.

a. Go the Internal Revenue Service (IRS. website at www.irs.gov) for the link to Publication 15 (Circular E). Using Publication 15 and 15A, locate the IRS rules for identifying an independent contractor. How many factors are involved in determining who is an independent contractor? Next, use Publication 15 to answer this question: "Do employment taxes have to be withheld from the gross wages of family employees working in a family business?"

b. Locate form 941 (Employer's Quarterly Federal Tax Return). Which line shows the total income tax withholding liability? Which line shows total FICA tax liability?

c. Do an Internet search to find out what payroll taxes are required to be paid in your state. You can begin with a state government home page (which sometimes has "starting a new business" information) or the state Department of Employment. Who pays these payroll taxes—the employer? Or are they withheld from the employee? For each type of tax, what are tax rates and the amount of income subject to the tax? (Use bookmark/favorites to save the locations in an "Accounting References" folder.)

Analyze and Plan Cash Flow

OVERVIEW

What this section does

This section explains how to create and use the fourth major financial statement, the statement of cash flows. In addition, this section explains how to develop a basic cash budget in order to plan cash flow.

LEARNING GOALS

LEARNING GOAL AND BOOK APPENDIX

LEARNING GOAL 21

BOOK APPENDIX 1
www.worthyjames.com
(student info.)

Appendix 1: The Cash Budget
Located in disk and at worthyjames.com (student info.)

LEARNING GOAL 21	**Prepare and Analyze a Statement of Cash Flows**

In this learning goal, you will find:

Overview of the Statement of Cash Flows

Prepare a Statement of Cash Flows: Indirect Method

Prepare Operating Activities Using the Direct Method

What Does It All Say?

Worksheet Supplement

Overview of the Statement of Cash Flows

What is It?

An Essential Financial Statement

GAAP (generally accepted accounting principles) require the presentation of a statement of cash flows along with the balance sheet, income statement, and statement of retained earnings/stockholders' equity (or owner's equity for a proprietorship). The statement of cash flows is the fourth essential financial statement.

What Does It Do?

Analysis of Cash

The *statement of cash flows* reports the following information:

- The cash balance at the beginning of the current period
- Why cash increased or decreased during the period
- The cash balance at the end of the current period.

The statement of cash flows is a link between balance sheets. The statement of cash flows explains the difference between the cash balance on the balance sheet at the end of the prior period and the cash balance on the balance sheet at the end of the current period. The statement of cash flows is usually prepared for the same period of time as the income statement.

The income statement and cash flow statement both show change and are dated for the same period of time. What is the difference between them? The purpose of the cash flow statement is to report only why cash increased or decreased. It contains only transactions that involve cash. The purpose of the income statement is to report income or loss; in other words, why the entire net worth of a business (stockholders' or owner's equity) changed as a result of all revenue and expense transactions, which may or may not involve cash.

Why Is It Important?

Cash is King

Cash is the most essential asset for business survival and a key asset for business success. Cash is used to pay debts, to pay expenses, to stay competitive, and to grow and take advantage of business opportunities as they occur. If a business cannot properly manage its cash, it will not continue to exist.

continued ▶

Why Is It Important?, *continued*

Who Uses the Information

Detailed information that explains the sources and uses of cash is valuable in many ways. Some of these are:

- Management uses cash flow information for analysis of the most recent changes in cash. The statement shows the effects that operations, long-term asset changes, and changes in debt and equity have had on cash flow. This information is used to modify operations and strategies. The statement of cash flows works best when it is used with a cash budget, which is a detailed cash planning device.
- Creditors use cash flow information when deciding if it is prudent to sell on account or to make loans. Cash flow affects the ability to repay debt.
- Investors use cash flow information to evaluate a company before making an investment decision. For example, it is possible that a company could show net income and at the same time be using up cash so quickly that it is in danger of going out of business if it cannot pay creditors or replace inventory.

What We Will Do

The statement of cash flows is one of the three essential tools needed to fully control cash. The first tool that we discussed in Learning Goal 16 is internal control, which is needed to protect cash from theft and mismanagement. The statement of cash flows provides a second resource: It is a management-level device that is used to explain and analyze the sources and uses of cash. The third tool, cash budgeting, is a planning tool that is explained in Appendix 1 to this book.

In this learning goal, we will discuss how a statement of cash flow explains changes in cash; then, we will learn how to apply this knowledge to prepare and analyze a statement of cash flows. Preparation of the statement will give you a deeper understanding of its meaning and how it can be used.

How the Statement of Cash Flows Classifies Cash

Overview

The statement of cash flows classifies cash into three categories:

- Operating activities
- Investing activities
- Financing activities

The statement explains the overall change in cash by reporting the cash inflows (cash receipts coming in) and cash outflows (cash payments going out) for each of these three categories.

How the Statement of Cash Flows Classifies Cash, *continued*

Operating Activities

The operating activities section is the most important part of the statement of cash flows and appears at the top of the statement. Operating activities shows the cash inflows and outflows connected to the everyday business operations involving revenues and expenses, as well as any any short-term investment trading. Operating activities are imporant because for the most part they are the regular, recurring business operations that continue into the future.

Operating activities typically involve the following types of transactions:

Inflows:

- Cash received from customers
- Cash received from interest and dividends
- Cash received from short-term investment trading

Outflows:

- Cash paid for operating expenses and for taxes
- Cash paid for current assets and to pay current liabilities
- Cash paid for interest on debts
- Cash paid for short-term investment trading

Transactions that are classified as operating activities are the types of transactions that are reported on the income statement and that affect current assets and current liabilities. The statement of cash flows converts these transactions into their cash inflows and cash outflows.

Investing Activities

The investing activities section reports the cash inflows and outflows related to long-term assets such as plant and equipment, notes receivable, and long-term investments. On the statement of cash flows, it appears after the operating activities section.

Investing activities include the following types of transactions:

Inflows:

- Cash received from the sale of property
- Cash received from collecting loan principal payments
- Cash received from the sale of long-term investments

Outflows:

- Cash paid for purchasing property, plant, and equipment
- Cash paid when making a long-term loan (being a lender)
- Cash paid when making long-term investments

In general, investing activities involve those transactions that affect long-term assets on the balance sheet.

continued ▶

How the Statement of Cash Flows Classifies Cash, *continued*

Financing Activities

The financing activities section reports cash inflows and outflows related to transactions that involve financing a business. "Financing" a business means obtaining and repaying cash from lenders or investors.

Financing activities include the following types of transactions:

Inflows:

- Cash received from borrowing money by issuing long-term notes or bonds
- Cash received from issuing stock

Outflows:

- Cash paid to repay long long-term debt (notes and bonds)
- Cash paid to acquire treasury stock
- Dividend payments to stockholders

In general, financing activities are those transactions that affect the long-term liability and stockholders' (or owner's) equity section of the balance sheet.

TIP

Intererest income and interest expense and dividend income are related to debt and to investments, so it may seem inconsistent that they are classified as operating activities. They are part of operating activities because they appear on the income statement.

What It Looks Like

Overview

This is a diagram of a statement of cash flows format:

Cash flows from operating activities		
Indirect or direct format here		
Net cash provided (used) by operating activities		$$
Cash flows from investing activities		
List each item here...	$$	
	$$	
Net cash provided (used) by investing activities		$$
Cash flows from financing activities		
List each item here...	$$	
	$$	
Net cash provided (used) by financing activities.		$$
Net increase (decrease) in cash		$$
Beginning cash balance.		$$
Ending cash balance.		$$

Indirect and Direct Formats

There is one more format consideration. The *operating activities section* can be presented either in a format that is called the **indirect method** or the **direct method**. Each format has advantages and disadvantages. We will study both formats, beginning with the indirect method. These methods do not affect the investing or financing activities sections.

Here is an illustration of the basic format for the **indirect method**. Net income is entered first. Then all positive and negative adjustments are made to net income to convert it into cash flow from operating activities.

Cash flow from operating activities		
Net income		$$
Adjustments		
Add: Adjustment items providing cash or not using cash		
List each type of increase adjustment...	$$	
	$$	
Total increases		$$
Subtract: Adjustment items not providing cash or using cash		
List each type of decrease adjustment...	$$	
	$$	
Total decreases		($$)
Net cash provided (used) by operating activities		$$

Note: There can be some small variations in how adjustments are shown. For example, rather than grouping increases and decreases as you see here, some formats will show all the adjustments in no particular order or other presentations will combine certain items. The results are the same.

Check Your Understanding

For each item list below, place an 'X' in the appropriate column to classify the item as part of an operating, investing, or financing activity.

	Item	Operating	Investing	Financing
1	Net income			
2	Issuance of stock			
3	Increase or decrease in accounts payable			
4	Gain on sale of land			
5	Supplies expense			
6	Sale of equipment			
7	Borrowing money			
8	Unearned revenue			
9	Repay a long-term loan			
10	Dividends paid			
11	Dividends received			
12	Buying inventory on account			
13	Increase or decrease in accounts receivable			
14	Interest earned			
15	Loaning money			

Answers

Notice that all the items that involve current assets and current liabilities and that are part of everyday operations are always operating activities.

	Item	Operating	Investing	Financing
1	Net income	X		
2	Issuance of stock			X
3	Increase or decrease in accounts payable	X		
4	Gain on sale of land		X	
5	Supplies expense	X		
6	Sale of equipment		X	
7	Borrowing money			X
8	Increase or decrease in unearned revenue	X		
9	Repay a long-term loan			X
10	Dividends paid			X
11	Dividends received	X		
12	Buying inventory on account	X		
13	Increase or decrease in accounts receivable	X		
14	Interest earned	X		
15	Loaning money		X	

Prepare a Statement of Cash Flows: Indirect Method

Procedure Overview and Continuing Example

Procedure to Follow

Step 1: Prepare a blank statement. You will fill this in as you complete the steps.

Step 2: Operating activities: Enter net income and adjust for income statement items that are always non-cash, and for gains and losses.

Step 3: Operating activities: Analyze the change in each non-cash current asset and current liability account. Enter results into appropriate location in the operating activities section.

Step 4: Investing and financing activities: Analyze the changes in the remaining balance sheet accounts plus any additional information, and enter results into the investing and financing activity sections as appropriate.

Step 5: Complete the statement by totaling the amounts and making a final check for noncash investing and financing activities.

Step #1: Prepare the Blank Form

Format a Blank Page

Use a blank page to set up the sections of a statement of cash flows as you see in the illustration on the top of page 847. Use a full page. Operating activities will use the indirect method format shown on the bottom of the page. Check your format by referring to the completed statement illustration on page 861.

Step #2: Operating Activities: Income Statement Accounts

Net Income, Depreciation, Other Gains or Losses

1) **Net income/loss** is the starting point. Refer to the 2017 Executive Enterprises income statement on page 850. Enter $71,000 net income in operating activties as the first item. All the adjustments in the operating activities section will convert this accrual basis net income into cash basis.

2) **Items that are always non-cash:** Because **depreciation** reduced net income but did not use cash, the amount must be added back to cancel out the deduction and convert to a cash basis. We enter $12,000 as a positive adjustment for depreciation. The same kind of adjustment is made for similar non-cash items such as **amortization** and **depletion.**

3) **Gains and losses** must also be canceled out; therefore gains would be a negative adjustment and losses would be a positive adjustment. This is done for two reasons: first, a gain or a loss does not correctly show cash flow and

continued ▶

Step #2: Operating Activities: Income Statement Accounts, *continued*

second, disposals of assets belong in the investment activities section of the cash flow statement. Enter a $5,000 negative adjustment for the gain.

To confirm that you correctly entered these adjustments, look at the completed statement of cash flows on page 861.

Executive Enterprises, Inc.
Comparative Income Statements
Years Ended December 31

($ in 000s)		2017		2016
Net sales..........................		$1,248		$1,285
Cost of goods sold		881		910
Gross profit		367		375
Operating expenses				
Salaries and wages expense............	$196		$188	
Depreciation expense	12		10	
Travel expense	14		19	
Various combined operating expenses ...	23		22	
Total operating expenses.............		245		239
Operating income		122		136
Other gain or loss, revenue or expense				
Gain on sale of equipment	5		-0-	
Interest expense	(11)		(9)	
Total other.........................		(6)		(9)
Income before tax......................		116		127
Income tax............................		45		38
Net income		$71		$89

TIP

Recall that for a business to comply with generally accepted accounting principles, an income statement such as you see above must be prepared using the accrual basis. This means that revenues are recorded when they are earned. Cash receipts do not affect when revenue is recorded. Likewise, expenses are recorded when they are incurred. Cash payments do not affect when expenses are recorded. The result is that the net income is not the same thing as cash from operating activities.

When we prepare an operating activities section, we are using adjustments that cancel out the effects of accrual basis. The adjustments convert accrual basis net income into cash flow from operating activities, which we can also call a cash basis.

Executive Enterprises, Inc.
Comparative Balance Sheets
December 31

($ in 000s)	2017	2016	Increase/*Decrease*
Assets			
Current assets			
Cash	**$128**	**$114**	14 increase
Accounts receivable	187	168	19 increase
Merchandise inventory	240	279	39 *decrease*
Prepaid travel	28	14	14 increase
Supplies	5	8	3 *decrease*
Total current assets	588	583	
Long-term investments	6	-	6 increase
Property, plant, and equipment			
Fixtures and equipment	422	310	112 increase
Less: accumulated depreciation	(158)	(150)	8 increase
Land	18	11	7 increase
Total Property, plant, and equipment	282	171	
Total assets	$876	$754	
Liabilities and Stockholders' Equity			
Current liabilities			
Accounts payable	$159	$151	8 increase
Short-term vendor notes payable	24	25	1 *decrease*
Income taxes payable	23	33	10 *decrease*
Total current liabilities	206	209	
Long-term liabilities			
Notes payable	157	126	31 increase
Bonds payable	7	-0-	7 increase
Total long-term liabilities	164	126	
Total liabilities	370	335	
Stockholders' equity			
Common stock, no par, 20,000 shares	295	240	55 increase
Retained earnings	211	179	32 increase
Total stockholders' equity	506	419	
Total liabilities and stockholders' equity	$876	$754	

Additional information:

- Sales are on account.
- During the year the company purchased $125,000 of printing equipment.
- During the year the company issued bonds for the purchase land.
- The long term notes payable is for a bank loan.
- The short term note payable is for a vendor (supplier) loan for an inventory purchase.

continued ▶

Step #3: Operating Activities: Current Assets & Liabilities

Overview

Current asset and current liability accounts occur as a result of business operations. Therefore, changes in these account balances affect the cash flow from operating activies. Except for the cash account (which is what we are analyzing) the process is to work our way down the current assets and liabilities of a balance sheet, identifying the change in each account to see how it affects cash flow. Refer to the balance sheets on page 851. We begin with the accounts receivable $19,000 increase.

Accounts Receivable

A net increase in a current asset always creates a negative adjustment to net income to convert it to cash basis. In the example below, we see that Accounts Receivable increased by $19,000. This means that not all of the sales were collected in cash. The sales on account *increased net income*, but *did not increase cash by the same amount*; some sales are still receivable.

Here are two quick methods to help you analyze an account:

1) *T accounts method:* If we look for a moment only at beginning and ending balances of Accounts Receivable (left side below) we see that the account balance has a net (meaning entire or final) increase of $19,000. This indicates that not all the sales revenue has been collected in cash, even though the sales increased net income. On the statement of cash flows, enter a $19,000 negative adjustment to net income for this difference.

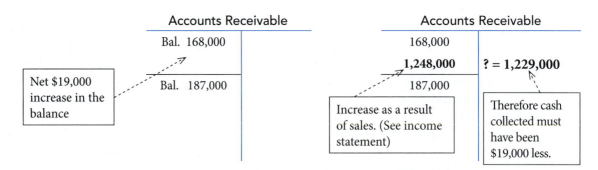

2) *Visualize journal entry method:* A simple method is to visualize a journal entry that would make Accounts Receivable show a net increase of $19,000. This avoids the details of the debits and credits to the account. Then check to see if an increase or decrease to cash is part of the entry. To make Accounts Receivable increase by $19,000 the entry would be:

Accounts Receivable	19,000	
Sales		19,000

continued ▶

Step #3: Operating Activities: Current Assets & Liabilities, *continued*

You can see from the journal entry that an increase in the Accounts Receivable balance was the result of Sales on account. There is no cash in this entry—the sales increased accounts receivable, not cash. However, the sales did increase net income. Therefore again we see that net income must be reduced by $19,000 to convert it to a *cash basis*. There is a $19,000 negative adjustment to operating cash flow (see page 861).

Merchandise Inventory

A net decrease in a current asset always creates a positive adjustment to net income. A decrease in merchandise inventory means that some inventory was used up, creating an expense and reducing net income. However, this is an expense that did not use cash. Let's visualize a journal entry that would show a net decrease in inventory:

Cost of Goods Sold	39,000	
Merchandise Inventory		39,000

We see that an expense is created, but no cash is used, so there would have been a decrease to net income without the use of cash. To convert net income to a *cash basis*, a positive adjustment of $39,000 is needed to cancel out the noncash expense. To confirm your adjustment, refer to the cash flow statement on page 861.

Prepaid Expenses

A net increase in a current asset always creates a negative adjustment to net income. A different example is prepaid expense. Again, refer to the balance sheets on page 851. An increase in a prepaid expense balance indicates that there was a use of cash to acquire the prepaid item. We have learned that in proper accrual accounting, payment to acquire an asset (the prepaid item) does not create an expense and does not affect net income, even though cash is used. Let's visualize a journal entry that would show a net increase in the Prepaid Expense account:

Prepaid Travel	14,000	
Cash		14,000

We see that cash is used, but no expense is recorded, so there was no decrease in net income. However, to convert net income to a *cash basis*, a negative adjustment to net income of $14,000 is needed to account for the use of the cash. To confirm your adjustment, look at the statement of cash flows on page 861.

continued ▶

Step #3: Operating Activities: Current Assets & Liabilities, *continued*

Supplies

A net decrease in a current asset always creates a positive adjustment to net income. The balance sheets show a $3,000 decrease in supplies. A decrease in supplies means that some supplies were used up, creating an expense and reducing net income. However, this is an expense that did not use cash. Let's visualize a journal entry that would show a net decrease in supplies:

Supplies Expense	3,000	
Supplies		3,000

We see that an expense is created, but no cash is used, so there would have been a decrease to net income without the use of cash. To show net income *on a cash basis*, make a positive adjustment to net income of $3,000 to cancel out the noncash expense. To verify this, look at the statement of cash flows on page 861.

Accounts Payable

A net increase in a current liability always creates a positive adjustment to net income. The balance sheets show an $8,000 increase in Accounts Payable. An increase in a liability means that some kind of payment has been deferred. If the liability involves an expense, that was an expense that did not use cash. Let's visualize a journal entry that would show an increase in Accounts Payable for any expense:

xxx Expense	8,000	
Accounts Payable		8,000

We see that an expense is recorded, but no cash is used, so there would have been a decrease to net income without the use of cash. To convert net income to a cash basis, make a positive adjustment of $8,000 to cancel out the noncash expense. To confirm your adjustment, look at the statement of cash flows on page 861.

> *Note:* It is also possible that an increase in accounts payable is related to an asset increase rather than an expense—for example, the purchase of inventory or a prepaid item. However, all the adjustments will still be correct. This is because although the asset increase created a negative adjustment we now know that the asset increase did not actually use cash, because we see the accounts payable increase. The accounts payable positive adjustment simply offsets the asset negative adjustment, resulting in no net change in cash, which would be correct. At the same time, all the account changes have been identified and accounted for.

Step #3: Operating Activities: Current Assets & Liabilities, *continued*

**Notes Payable
(Short-Term)**

A net decrease in a current liability always creates a negative adjustment to net income. This is because a current liability is decreased by using cash. However, paying a liability is not an expense and therefore does not reduce net income. Let's visualize a journal entry that would show a net decrease in current Notes Payable:

Notes Payable	1,000	
Cash		1,000

We see that the liability decreases as cash is used to pay it, but no expense is recorded. To convert net income *to a cash basis*, a negative adjustment of $1,000 is needed to record the cash expenditure that did not reduce net income.

Another important point to keep in mind with current liabilities: The current liability must be owed to a vendor or supplier as the result of everyday operations that consume goods or services. If that is not the case, such as borrowing cash for another purpose, the change in the liability is not from an operating activity. The liability change becomes an adjustment as a financing activity (see below).

In this case, the additional information discloses that the short-term loan relates to an inventory purchase, so it is therefore part of operating activities.

Income Taxes Payable

A net decrease in a current liability always creates a negative adjustment to net income. This is because a current liability is decreased by using cash; however, paying a liability is not recorded as an expense and does not reduce net income. Let's visualize a journal entry that would show a net decrease in Income Taxes Payable:

Income Taxes Payable	10,000	
Cash		10,000

We see that there is a net reduction in the liability because cash was used to pay it. On the income statement, $45,000 of income tax expense has been recorded; however, an *additional* $10,000 of cash was used in order to reduce the taxes payable balance from $33,000 to $23,000. To confirm your adjustment, look at the statement of cash flows on page 861.

continued ▶

Step #3: Operating Activities: Current Assets & Liabilities, *continued*

Summary

We have now reviewed each current asset and current liability, and completed our analysis of all the operating activity adjustments. Our results show a total of $62,000 positive adjustments and $49,000 negative adjustments, and a net cash increase from operating activities of $84,000. (Refer to the statement of cash flows.)

Summary of Adjustments to Net Income for Operating Activities– Indirect Method			
Source	**Item**	**Positive Adjustment**	**Negative Adjustment**
Income statement	Gains		✗
	Losses	✗	
	Depreciation	✗	
Balance sheet: current assets and liabilities	Increase in a current asset (except cash)		✗
	Decrease in a current asset (except cash)	✗	
	Increase in a current liability	✗	
	Decrease in a current liability		✗

Notice that if all current assets (excluding cash) increase more than current liabilities, there would be greater negative adjustments than positive adjustments, and a net decrease in cash flow. If all current assets decrease more than current liabilities, there would be greater positive adjustments than negative adjustments and a net increase in cash flow. The relationship is illustrated by the arrows in the table above.

Check Your Understanding

For each separate question number below, use the account balances from the May and June balance sheets to determine the positive or negative adjustment to net income for each individual account. Then show the combined positive or negative net adjustment for both accounts. Use this format:

Account	Net Change	Individual Adjustment	Net Adjustment

		Balances	
Account		**June 30**	**May 31**
1) Accounts Receivable		$25,000	$14,000
Merchandise Inventory		58,000	72,000
2) Prepaid Rent		15,000	12,000
Accounts Payable		40,000	45,000
3) Accounts Receivable		31,000	35,000
Unearned Revenue		12,000	18,000
4) Merchandise Inventory		44,000	40,000
Accounts Payable		33,000	29,000
5) Wages Payable		37,000	30,000
Income Tax Payable		22,000	20,000
6) Total current assets (except cash)		240,000	170,000
Total current liabilities		188,000	148,000

Answers

Account	Net change	Individual Adjustment	Net Adjustment
1) Accounts Receivable	$11,000	($11,000)	$3,000
Merchandise Inventory	(14,000)	14,000	
2) Prepaid Rent	3,000	(3,000)	(8,000)
Accounts Payable	(5,000)	(5,000)	
3) Accounts Receivable	(4,000)	4,000	(2,000)
Unearned Revenue	(6,000)	(6,000)	
4) Merchandise Inventory	4,000	(4,000)	-0-
Accounts Payable	4,000	4,000	
5) Wages Payable	7,000	7,000	9,000
Income Tax Payable	2,000	2,000	
6) Total current assets	70,000	(70,000)	(30,000)
Total current liabilities	40,000	40,000	

Step #4: Investing & Financing Activities

Overview	We now analyze all the remaining account changes on the balance sheet. Changes in long-term assets are classified as investing activities and the changes in long-term liabilities and stockholders' equity are financing activities. (Review pages 845–846.)

Fixtures and Equipment	This account requires especially careful analysis, because several kinds of events can affect the account balance. Purchases, sales, and accumulated depreciation can all affect a long-term asset.

One good way to deal with this account or any other depreciable asset is to first calculate beginning and ending *book value*. Asset book value is the asset cost balance minus its accumulated depreciation. We call this "net" fixtures and equipment. We then use a simple equation to analyze possible changes between beginning and ending net amounts. |

Fixtures and Equipment, Net *Example:*	We use the following equation and enter whatever values we know. The amounts are from the Executive Enterprises, Inc. income statement and balance sheets (pages 850–851) and any additional information available.

$$
\begin{array}{ccccccccc}
\text{Beginning} & & \text{Cost of} & & \text{Book Value} & & & & \text{Ending} \\
\text{Bal., Net} & + & \text{Assets} & - & \text{of Assets} & - & \text{Depreciation} & = & \text{Bal., Net} \\
\text{(book value)} & & \text{Purchased} & & \text{Disposed} & & \text{Expense} & & \text{(book value)} \\
\$160{,}000 & + & \$125{,}000 & - & X & - & \$12{,}000 & = & \$264{,}000
\end{array}
$$

Book value, beginning and ending: fixtures and equipment balances minus accumulated depreciation balances on the 2016 and 2017 balance sheets.
Cost of assets purchased: given as $125,000.
Book Value of Assets Disposed: no information given
Depreciation expense: on the income statement as $12,000.

Solving for *X*, the book value of the assets sold is $9,000. However, the amount of cash received is the sales price, not book value (and not gain or loss). The formula for determining sales price is:

$$
\begin{array}{ccccccc}
\text{Book Value} & & \text{Gain} & & & & \\
\text{of Asset} & + & \text{On} & \text{OR} - & \frac{\text{Loss}}{\text{On Sale}} & = & \frac{\text{Sales}}{\text{Price}} \\
\text{Disposed} & & \text{Sale} & & & & \\
\$9{,}000 & + & \$5{,}000 & & \text{----} & = & \$14{,}000
\end{array}
$$

Fixtures and Equipment Result	■ Investing activites is decreased by $125,000 for the equipment purchase. ■ Investing activities is increased by $14,000 proceeds from the equipment sale. (See income statement for gain on sale.) To confirm the adjustment on your statement of cash flows, look at the completed statement of cash flows on page 861.

Step #4: Investing & Financing Activities, *continued*

TIP

- The missing data for the first equation will always be either the cost of assets purchased or the book value of the assets sold. All the other data are on the financial statements or available from other sources.
- Remember that for depreciable assets, gain or loss is the difference between book value and sales price, not cost and sales price. Notice that both of the above formulas can determine book value of disposed assets if the other data is known.

Land

Land increased by $7,000. However, there is additional information concerning the land. It was acquired by issuing $7,000 of bonds (creating a $7,000 long-term liability). When a fixed asset increases as the result of debt increase, this is a ***noncash investing and financing activity***. There is no net effect on cash. Disclosure is required on the statement of cash flows as you see on page 861.

Notes Payable (Long-Term)

The $31,000 increase in Notes Payable is a financing activity because it was for the purpose of borrowing cash, and not part of operations. It is a source of financing for the business. (Note that decreasing the account by repayment would also be a financing activity, but would be a use of cash.) Bonds payable are also a long term liability and would be treated in a similar manner as the notes payable (except for non-cash transactions).

Common Stock

The $55,000 increase in Common Stock is a source of cash provided by investors. It is a source of financing for the business, and classified as a financing activity. If outstanding common stock were to change for other reasons, more information would be required to analyze the transaction.

Retained Earnings

Various transactions can affect retained earnings. The most common ones that we will discuss here are net income or net loss and dividends. Net income increases retained earnings and net loss decreases retained earnings. Dividends also decrease retained earnings. For our example, there is no data about dividends; however, an analysis of the retained earnings account can provide that information, as follows:

Beginning retained earnings	+	Net income	–	Dividends	=	Ending retained earnings
$179,000	+	$71,000	–	X	=	$211,000
				X	=	$39,000

continued ▶

Step #4: Investing & Financing Activities, *continued*

Note that net income has already been accounted for, because it is the starting point for operating cash flow. Here we are only analyzing retained earnings. The above information is also in a statement of retained earnings, if available.

Review: Non-Cash Investing and Financing Activities

Some investing and financing transactions do not involve cash. Examples are:

- Issuing debt (notes or bonds) to purchase assets
- Issuing stock to purchase assets
- Conversion of debt into stock
- Exchange of one asset for another

These transactions must be disclosed at the bottom of the statement of cash flows. They are called ***non-cash investing and financing activities***. See the statement of cash flows on page 861. Alternatively, they may be disclosed in footnotes, although in this text you should disclose these items on the statement of cash flows.

Review: Investing and Financing Activities

For investing activities: Long-term asset increases are a use of cash; decreases are a source of cash. *For financing activitities:* Long-term liability and stockholders's equity increases are a source of cash; decreases are a use of cash.

Step #5: Complete the Statement

Total the Amounts and Do a Final Check

After you have analyzed all the accounts, total the amounts in the statement of cash flows to determine the net change in cash. Combine this with the beginning cash balance at the start of the period to obtain the ending cash balance. Make a final check for any noncash investing and financing activities.

TIP

Be sure to check that the beginning cash balance and ending cash balance on the statement of cash flows are exactly the same as the cash balance showing on the balance sheet for end of the prior period and the end of the current period.

Step #5: Complete the Statement, *continued*

Executive Enterprises, Inc.
Statement of Cash Flows
For the Year Ended December 31, 2017

($ in 000s)

Cash flows from operating activities

Net income (loss)		$71
Add: adjustment items providing cash or not using cash		
Depreciation expense	$12	
Decrease in supplies.	3	
Decrease in merchandise inventory	39	
Increase in accounts payable	8	62
Subtract: adjustment items not providing cash or using cash		
Gain on sale of equipment	5	
Increase in accounts receivable	19	
Increase in prepaid travel	14	
Decrease in short-term vendor notes payable	1	
Decrease in income taxes payable	10	(49)
Net cash provided by operating activities.		84

Cash flows from investing activities

Purchase of long-term investments.	(6)	
Sale of equipment.	14	
Purchase of equipment	(125)	
Net cash used by investing activities.		(117)

Cash flows from financing activities

Borrowing cash with long-term loan	31	
Issuance of common stock	55	
Cash dividends paid.	(39)	
Net cash provided by financing activities.		47
Net increase in cash		14
Beginning cash balance.		114
Ending cash balance.		$128

Noncash investing and financing activity

Issued bonds in exchange for land.		$7

More Condensed Adjustments

This statement of cash flows is prepared in detail to show the effect of each adjustment. In practice, the adjustments, particularly to operating cash flow, may be more condensed. For example, instead of listing individual positive and negative adjustment items for operating activities, a single positive amount of $62,000 and a single negative amount of $49,000 might be shown as adjustments to net income, or even condensed further into a single positive amount of $13,000. Disclosures can vary.

Check Your Understanding

Each question number involves accounts for determining cash flow from either investing or financing activities. For each separate question number below, use the account balances from the balance sheet and/or income statement to calculate the cash flow. Identify the cash flow as an investing or financing activity.

Account	Balances October 31	Balances September 30
1) Long-term notes receivable...............	$90,000	$150,000
2) Long-term notes payable..................	100,000	120,000
3) Common stock........................	1,000,000	880,000
4) Equipment*...........................	215,000	239,000
Accumulated depreciation—equipment	38,000	36,000
Depreciation expense—equipment	9,000	
Gain on sale of equipment................	5,000	
* Equipment account indicates no purchases.		
5) Fixtures**.............................	75,000	62,000
Accumulated depreciation—fixtures	20,000	17,000
Depreciation expense—fixtures	7,000	
Gain on sale of fixtures....................	4,000	
** Fixtures were sold for $12,000		

Answers

Item	Cash Flow	Type
1) Long-term notes receivable	$60,000	Investing
2) Long-term notes payable	(20,000)	Financing
3) Common stock	120,000	Financing
4) Equipment (sales proceeds)	22,000	Investing
$203,000 + 0 - X - 9,000 = 177,000;$		
$X = 17,000; 17,000 + 5,000 = 22,000$		
5) Fixtures ($12,000 sales - $25,000 purchases)	(13,000)	Investing
$45,000 + X - 8,000* - 7,000 = 55,000;$		
$X = 25,000$ fixtures purchased		
*12,000 sales price - 4,000 gain on sale = 8,000 book value of asset sold		

Prepare Operating Activities Using the Direct Method

Overview

As indicated earlier, the direct method is an alternative approach for presenting the cash flow from operating activities. Its final result is a cash flow from operating activities that is exactly the same amount as the indirect method. The direct method does not affect either investing or financing activities.

Instead of making cash flow adjustments to net income, the direct method begins at the top of the income statement and moves down line-by-line. The method converts each income statement line item into a cash basis amount, and shows cash inflows or cash outflows *for each income statement item.*

Step 1: Prepare a blank statement of cash flows. You will fill this in as you complete the steps.
Step 2: Convert revenue items into cash collections.
Step 3: Convert cost of goods sold (if any) into vendors (suppliers) payments.
Step 4: Convert all remaining expenses into their cash payments. (Depreciation, gains and losses are excluded from operating activities.)

Step #1: Prepare the Blank Form

Prepare a Blank Form

Prepare a blank statement of cash flows form with headings as you see in the illustration below. You will complete this form as you do your analysis. Use an income statement and comparative balance sheet as your source of data. Here, we are using the Executive Enterterprises, Inc. income statement and balance sheet. Refer to pages 850 and 851.

---

xxxx.
Statement of Cash Flows
For the xxxxx

Receipts
   Collections from customers . . . .
   Receipts from xxx. . . . .
     Total receipts . . . .   _____
Payments   _____
   Merchandise inventory . . . .
   Operating expenditures *(show individually or in total)* . . . . . .
   Other . . . .
   Interest. . . . .
   Income tax . . . .   _____
     Total payments. . . . .
Net cash provided (used) by operating activities. . . . .   _____

Step #2: Conversion of Revenues Into Cash Receipts

Use the table below

As we know, revenue on an accrual basis is not the same as cash receipts from customers. Two balance sheet categories potentially change sales and other revenues into cash collections: receivables and unearned/deferred revenue. Refer to the income statement on page 850 and the balance sheets on page 851.

Step 1: Indentify sales or other revenue (income statement): $1,248,000

Step 2: Identify any current asset/liability adjustments (balance sheet): $19,000

Result: $1,248,000 sales − $19,000 receivable increase = $1,229,000 cash receipts.

Analysis: Accounts receivable increased, so $19,000 of sales has not yet been collected in cash. There are no advance payments (unearned revenue/deferred revenue) from customers or other sources. An increase in an advance payment indicates an increase in cash that does not appear on the income statement. A decrease in an advance payment results in revenue when the service or product is provided. It reduces a liability, and does not provide cash.

Summary of Adjustments for Cash Collections		
Cash Collections Adjustments (Cash Inflow)		
Income Statement (Revenue Item)	Current Asset Adjustments	Current Liability Adjustments
Sales	+ Decrease in accounts receivable − Increase in accounts receivable	+ Increase in unearned revenue − Decrease in unearned revenue
Interest Revenue	+ Decrease in interest receivable − Increase in interest receivable	+ Increase in deferred interest revenue − Decrease in deferred interest revenue
Dividends Revenue	+ Decrease in dividends receivable − Increase in dividends receivable	
Summary: Decreases in receivables and increases in liabilities = increase *inflow*. Increases in receivables and decreases in liabilities = decrease *inflow*.		

Effect of Cash Sales

Cash sales are part of cash collections from customers. Cash sales are already included in the total sales amount, therefore no special calculation is necessary for cash sales; in other words, you only need to adjust sales as you see in the table above. However, keep in mind that when there are cash sales the total credit to accounts receivable will not represent the total collections from customers.

Step #3: Conversion of Cost of Goods Sold Into Cash Payments to Suppliers

Use The Table Below

Cost of goods is a non-cash expense. It is the amount of merchandise used up when sold to customers. To convert cost of goods sold into cash payments we first need to determine the amount of purchases and then determine how much of the purchases were paid for. In practice, this would require an analysis of accounts payable to determine the payables related to merchandise purchases; here, we will simply assume that all accounts payable were related to merchandise purchases.

Step 1) **Purchases**: Merchandise purchased: $881,000 – $39,000 = $842,000.

Analysis: Cost of goods sold of $881,000 minus the decrease in inventory of $39,000 equals purchases of $842,000. (Inventory decreased because more was needed than was purchased.)

Step 2) **Purchases payments**: $842,000 – $8,000 + $1,000 = $835,000

Of the $842,000 purchased, $7,000 has not yet been paid for as follows: Accounts Payable has increased by $8,000; however, $1,000 has been paid on the vendor Notes Payable for inventory (that liability decreased).

Merchandise Payment Adjustments (Cash **Outflow**)		
Income Statement	Determine Purchases: (Current Assets)	Determine Payments for Purchases: (Current Liabilities)
Cost of Goods Sold	+ Increase in merchandise inventory − Decrease in merchandise inventory	+ Decrease in accounts payable/vendor notes payable* − Increase in accounts payable/vendor notes payable*

*Payables related to merchandise purchases

Step #4: Conversion of Remaining Expenses to Cash Payments

Use The Table Below

To keep our example as clear as possible, any other operating expenses that are not specifically named as operating expenses are included in the total of "various other operating expenses." These are all calculations of cash outflows.

- Salaries and wages expense: No payables, so no adjustment is needed.
- Depreciation expense: This is excluded – cash is never paid for depreciation.
- Travel expense: $14,000 + $14,000 prepaid increase = $28,000
- Various other operating expenses: $23,000 – $3,000 supplies decrease = $20,000.

continued ▶

Step #4: Conversion of Remaining Expenses to Cash Payments, *continued*

■ Interest expense: There are no prepaid or payables for this account, therefore no adjustment is needed.

■ Income tax expense: $45,000 + $10,000 decrease in tax payable = $55,000.

We have now accounted for:

■ all income statement items, adjusted by
■ all changes in non-cash current assets and current liabilities.

Operating Expense and Other Income Statement Adjustments (Cash **Outflows**)		
Income Statement	Current Assets	Current Liabilities
Operating Expenses	+ Increase in a prepaid or other current asset related to the expense – Decrease in a prepaid or other current asset related to the expense	+ Decrease in a related current liability – Increase in a related current liability
Excluded	Depreciation*: Exclude – always a non-cash expense Gains and losses: Exclude – part of investing activities calculation	
Summary: Look at non-cash current assets and current liabilities. Increases in assets and decreases in liabilities increase *outflow*. Decreases in assets and increases in liabilities decrease *outflow*.		

*and other non-cash expenses such as amortization and depletion

TIP

Remember that with the direct method for operating activities, we are calculating the total inflow (cash receipts) or outflow (cash payments) separately for each income statement item. This is different than the indirect method, in which the adjustments convert net income into the operating cash flow. Of course, both methods result in the same final amount of operating cash flow.

Step #5: Complete the Statement

Overview

An example of the completed operating activities section for Executive Entereprises, Inc. using the direct method format is shown below. If effect, we have converted an accrual basis income statement into cash basis.

The investing and financing activities sections of the complete statement of cash flows are the same as previously illustrated on page 861 and explained on pages 858 to 860.

Executive Enterprises, Inc.
Statement of Operating Cash Flow
For the Year Ended December 31, 2017

Receipts		
Collections from customers.........................		$1,229,000
Payments		
Merchandise inventory..........................	$(835,000)	
Salaries and wages..............................	(196,000)	
Travel	(28,000)	
Other operating expenditures.....................	(20,000)	
Interest	(11,000)	
Income tax.....................................	(55,000)	
Total payments		(1,145,000)
Net cash provided by operating activities.....		$84,000

Calculations Summary

- Collections from customers: $1,248,000 – $19,000 = $1,229,000
- Merchandise inventory: $881,000 – $39,000 – $8,000 + $1,000 = $835,000
- Salaries and wages: $196,000 (no adjustment)
- Travel: $14,000 + $14,000 = $28,000
- Other payments: $23,000 – $3,000 = $20,000
- Interest $11,000 (no adjustment)
- Income tax $45,000 + $10,000 = $55,000

(Refer to the Executive Enterprises, Inc. income statement and balance sheet on pages 850 and 851 for your source data.)

Reconciliation

In practice, GAAP requires that when the direct method is used, the indirect method be presented in a separate schedule to reconcile net income with cash flow from operating activities.

For each separate question number below, use the information to calculate the required item.

	Balance Sheet		Required Item
	January 31	February 28	
1) Sales revenue for the month is $289,500.			
▪ Accounts receivable	$74,000	$77,500	Collections from customers
▪ Unearned revenue	2,000	8,000	
2) Cost of goods sold for the month is $188,000.			
▪ Merchandise inventory	126,100	144,900	Cash payments for merchandise inventory
▪ Accounts payable	85,500	95,300	
3) Insurance expense for the month is $4,500.			
▪ Prepaid insurance	1,250	950	Cash payments for insurance
4) Income tax expense for the month is $8,000.			
▪ Prepaid income tax	7,500	9,200	Cash payments for income tax

Answers

1) Cash collections from customers $289,500 − $3,500 + $6,000 = $292,000

2) Cash payments for merchandise $188,000 + $18,800 − $9,800 = $197,000

3) Cash payments for insurance $4,500 − $300 = $4,200

4) Cash payments for income tax $8,000 + $1,700 = $9,700

What Does It All Say?

Using the Statement of Cash Flows

Overview

In addition to assessing the size and type of individual activities presented on the statement of cash flows, there are several other valuable procedures that can be used to enhance the usefulness of the statement. These procedures are: 1) Comparing cash flows to income, 2) Calculating free cash flow 3) Applying ratio analysis.

Compare to Income Statement

If you compare the Executive Enterprises, Inc. statement of cash flows to the income statement you can quickly see that net income is not the same as cash flow. The 2017 net income is $71,000 while the operating cash flow is $84,000 and the net increase in cash is only $14,000. This reminds us that cash flow and income are different concepts. Cash flow is the change in cash. Net income (or loss) is the change in total wealth that results from running the business.

Analyze Operating Income and Operating Cash Flow

Usually the most imporant analysis is an evaluation of operations, because operations is the central, ongoing, business activity. The statement of cash flows can help us with this. We will analyze key accounts and adjustments that identify significant changes. Refer to the indirect method cash flow statement on page 861.

- Compare the change in accounts receivable to the change in sales revenue: Accounts receivable increased by $19,000; therefore, this amount of sales revenue has not been collected in cash. However, sales actually declined by $37,000. We would normally expect accounts receivable to change in roughly the same direction and proportion as sales. In this case, it appears that the business may be having some trouble collecting timely payments from customers.
- Analyze the changes in inventory and accounts payable: There was a large decrease in inventory ($39,000) as well as an increase in accounts payable of $8,000. This indicates that the business is limiting its inventory purchases and slowing the amount of cash payments to vendors, probably as a result of the slowing sales revenue. It would be more troubling if inventory were increasing as sales were decreasing; however, that is not happening here.
- Other significant changes: The company paid $14,000 that increased the Prepaid Travel account. Does this indicate a planned greater sales and marketing effort? Income tax payable decreased $10,000, probably as a result of payment required related to last year's greater net income. There is no unearned revenue and no significant changes in any other current liabilties.

continued ▶

Using the Statement of Cash Flows, *continued*

- Over several periods, the *ratio of cash flow from operating activities to operating income* should change and be in roughly the same direction and proportion as operating income. If this is not the case, particularly if operating income is increasing while operating cash flow is not, detailed investigation is warranted.

Analyze Investing Activities

Investing activities was the single biggest use of cash during the period; specifically, $125,000 was spent to purchase equipment. The company is clearly expanding its capacity and/or modernizing equipment, so it must be expecting an improvement in sales. The evidence that sales have in fact decreased during this same period may be a cause for concern.

Analyze Financing Activities

Significant financing activities consisted of the following items:

- Cash from borrowing: $31,000
- Cash from issuing stock: $55,000.

The company is clearly obtaining additional cash through debt and stock issuance. This is probably being done to help pay for the major equipment purchase. Notably, no cash was used to repay debt; there was a net increase in long-term debt.

- Dividends: Despite the large equpment purchase the company is still able to pay dividends to stockholders, without decreasing its cash balance.

Non-Cash Activities

The company also incurred additional debt by issuing bonds for the purchase of land in the amount of $7,000. No net change in cash occurred from this transaction.

Other Analytical Tools

- **Free cash flow:** Although there are various definitions, free cash flow is typically defined as cash flow from operating activities minus net plant and equipment purchases. Many analysts also subtract dividends, which we will do here.

This definition means that free cash flow is the cash created from operations that still remains after what is spent to acquire the necessary up-to-date plant and equipment, and to make dividend payments. This means that free cash flow is the cash available to make debt and other fixed payments, to take advantage of new opportunities, or to increase dividends. For Executive Enterprises, Inc. free cash flow is:

Operating Cash Flow	−	Capital Expenditures	−	Dividends	=	Free Cash Flow
$84,000	−	$111,000*	−	$39,000	=	$(66,000)

* $125,000 − $14,000 = $111,000. See statement of cash flows investing activities.

Using the Statement of Cash Flows, *continued*

This company has a negative free cash flow! How is that possible and what does it indicate? This has happened because the operating cash flow is not sufficient to provide the amount necessary for capital expenditures and the dividends expected by shareholders. As indicated by the financing activities section of the cash flow statement, the company had to borrow money and sell stock to meet most of its large cash requirements. Negative free cash flow should not happen often. It occurred this year primarily because of an unusual amount of spending on equipment—it is important for a business to have modern plant and equipment.

- **Ratio analysis:** Ratio analysis is an important tool for the analysis of financial statements (see volume 1). Some of the ratios relate to cash flow:

Cash flow to debt ratio: This is an indicator of the ability to repay debt using only operatating cash flow. This is calculated as: (cash from operating activities)/(average total liabilities).

For Executive Enterprises, Inc. in 2017: 84/(370 + 335)/2 = .238. This is a general indicator that if operating cash flow were to continue at the current rate, all the present debt could be paid in about 1/.238 = 4.2 years if the cash could be accumulated. (This can be refined to include the effect of interest and required periodic payments.) In the current year, the company has not been able to accumulate operating cash flow.

Cash basis times-interest-earned: This is an indicator of debt interest coverage. The formulat is: (cash from operating activities + interest paid)/interest paid. For Executive Enterprises, Inc. in 2017: (84 + 11)/11 = 8.64. This shows that operating cash flow before interest paid is about 8.6 times the interest requirement. (This procedure also can be used to determine coverage for any fixed recurring payment.)

These two ratios indicate that if the company does not continue to make additonal large purchases or borrow large amounts, its debt appears to be quite manageable and not excessive, provided that operating cash flow remains about the same.

Cash flow per share: Similar to earnings per share, cash flow can be calcuted per outstanding share of stock. Cash flow from operating activities is probably the most useful measure; however, net cash flow or cash flow from any other activity could be used as well.

Several Time Periods

As with all other financial statement analysis, it is important that the evaluation of cash flow should be performed over several financial periods in order to obtain a representative indication and to identify trends.

continued ▶

Using the Statement of Cash Flows, *continued*

Which is Best:
Direct or Indirect?

The direct method allows a user to see each of the revenue and expense cash inflows and outflows from operations, which the indirect method does not do. However, the indirect method is useful because it: 1) Shows the difference between income and total cash flow and cash flows from each activity, and 2) Discloses changes in account balances, which is a useful part of financial analysis. 3) Often, fewer adjustments are required. For these reasons, at the present time the indirect method is much more widely used than the direct method. Of course, usage is always subject to changes in future GAAP requirements.

TIP

Future changes? Recently the Financial Accounting Standards Board has been reviewing the idea of moving interest revenue from operating activities into investing activities and interest expense into financing activities.

Ethical Issues

Overview

The following are two ethical issues to keep in mind when using the statement of cash flows:

- In general, the statement of cash flows is much less subject to interpretation and manipulation than the income statement. The income statement (which also affects the balance sheet) involves many allowable estimates and alternative methods, which the statement of cash flows does not. For that reason, the statement of cash flows can serve as a useful check on what is reported on the income statement. We did this kind of check (above) when we used several analytical methods.
- The second issue to keep in mind is that, as with any other financial report, unethical management may still attempt to manipulate the statement of cash flows in order to make it appear more favorable. The most likely method is creating a change in the classification in which a transaction is reported.

Changing
Classification

Because cash flow from operating activities is the most important part of the statement of cash flows, unethical management would attempt to inflate this area of the statement. This is done by moving positive adjustment items into operating activities, and keeping negative items in investing and financing activities.

Aside from outright fraudulent misclassification, occasionally the careful manipulation of GAAP requirements may accomplish an advantageous shift in classification. One example is reporting certain types of investment activities in securities as either operating or investing, depending on management's stated investment intention. Another is the careful selection of leasing arrangements. In these situations a close examination of footnotes, which is always a good idea, may help to reveal what is being done.

Some Calculation Shortcuts for Operating Activities

Overview

These shortcuts should be used only after you have practiced *without them*, and already understand how changes in account balances affect operating activities for both the indirect and direct methods. Also, these shortcuts are completely optional. If you don't like dealing with more procedures (cash flow rules can be confusing at first anyway), then don't use them! That is perfectly OK. Finally, you can use one or both shortcut rules, whatever works best for you.

Change in Account Balance

The shortcuts work by just calculating the change in an account balance. Then some simple rules are applied. A "change in account balance" means the following:

Ending Balance – Beginning Balance = Change in Account Balance

Indirect Method Rule

Change in Account Balance For...	Then...
Current Asset	Subtract the change
Current Liability	Add the change

Examples

Account	December 31, 2017	December 31, 2016	Change
1. Accounts Receivable	$118,500	$101, 370	$17,130
2. Prepaid Rent	26,750	31,200	−4,550
3. Accounts Payable	95,080	81,620	13,460
4. Unearned Revenue	44,100	62,300	−18,200

Adjustment examples:

1. Net Income − $17,130 = negative $17,130 adjustment
2. Net Income − (−$4,550) = positive $4,550 adjustment
3. Net Income + $13,460 = positive $13,460 adjustment
4. Net Income + (−$18,200) = negative $18,200 adjustment

Direct Method Rule

Change in Account Balance For...	Then...
Receivable or Payable	Subtract the change
Other Current Assets or Unearned Revenues	Add the change

Examples

Account	December 31, 2017	December 31, 2016	Change
1. Accounts Receivable	$118,500	$101, 370	$17,130
2. Prepaid Rent	26,750	31,200	−4,550
3. Accounts Payable	95,080	81,620	13,460
4. Unearned Revenue	62,300	44,100	−18,200

Adjustment examples:

1. Sales Revenue (cash inflows) − $17,130 = negative $17,130 adjustment
2. Rent Expense (cash outflows) + (−$4,550) = negative $4,550 adjustment
3. xxx Expense (cash outflows) − $13,460 = negative $13,460 adjustment
4. Sales Revenue (cash inflows) + $18,200 = positive $18,200 adjustment

Worksheet Supplement

Using a Worksheet: Indirect Method

Overview

A more formal way to prepare a statement of cash flows is by first using a worksheet. This method will, of course, provide exactly the same result as the methods we have used in this learning goal. However, a worksheet will be more useful in situations where it is necessary to clearly document all the adjustments, and when financial statements are larger or more complex.

Procedure for Indirect Method

Refer to the completed worksheet on page 876 for Executive Enterprises, Inc. Balance sheet account balances are entered on the top portion of the worksheet. These are entered as debit and credit account balances. Between these balances are columns for debits and credits to adjust for the total increases and decreases to each account. It is usually easiest to simply proceed down the worksheet, one account at a time, with the change in the cash balance as the last entry.

A statement of cash flows format is placed under the account balances. Notice that this section is separated into operating, investing, and financing headings, just as you would see on a statement of cash flows. Here, the indirect format is used.

The procedure is to identify the change(s) in each account and enter the change(s) as as debits or credits to the account, at the same time entering a debit or credit to the statement of cash flows format, showing the effect on cash flow. A debit adjustment to the statement of cash flows is an increase in cash, and a credit is a decrease.

Explantion of the Example

Item	Explantion of change and entries
a	Accounts receivable increased by $19,000 which is a negative adjustment (credit) to the operating activities.
b	Prepaid expenses increased by $14,000 which is a negative adjustment to operating activities.
c	Supplies decreased by $3,000 which is a positive adjustment (debit) to operating activities.
d	Merchandise inventory decreased by $39,000 which is a positive adjustment to operating activities.
e	Long-term investments increased by $6,000 which is a negative adjustment to investing activities.
f	Fixtures and equipment increased by $125,000 for the purchase of equipment which is a negative adjustment to investing activities.

Using a Worksheet: Indirect Method, *continued*

Item	Explantion of change and entries
g	Equipment with a cost of $13,000 and accumulated depreciation of $4,000 (book value of $9,000) was sold at a gain of $5,000. These combine to cause an increase in cash and a positive adjustment of $14,000 in investing activities. The gain on sale of $5,000 is a negative adjustment to operating activities because it is part of the $71,000 net income but should not be part of operating activities.
h	Accumulated depreciation increased as a result of $12,000 of depreciation expense, which is a positive adjustment to operating activities.
i	Issued bonds for the purchase of land. This is a noncash investing and financing activity.
j	Accounts payable increased by $8,000 which is a positive adjustment to operating activities.
k	Short term vendor notes payable decreased by $1,000 which is a negative adjustment to operating activities.
l	Income tax payable decreased by $10,000 which is a negative adjustment to operating activities.
m	Notes payable increased by $31,000 which is a positive adjustment to financing activities.
n	Common stock increased by $55,000 which is a positive adjustment to financing activities.
o	Retained earnings decreased by $39,000 as a result of dividends paid, which is a negative adjustment to financing activities.
p	Retained earnings increased by $71,000 as a result of net income, which is a positive adjustment to operating activities.
q	The total of all debits to the statement of cash flows is $233,000 and the total of all credits is $219,000 which indicates a net increase in cash of $14,000, entered as credit to equalize the column totals. The $14,000 is entered as the reconciling debit to the cash account.

Prepare the Statement

After the worksheet is completed prepare the statement of cash flows using the amounts from statement of cash flows section of the worksheet.

Using a Worksheet: Indirect Method, *continued*

Account Titles			Dr.		Cr.		
Indirect Method Worksheet							
Balance sheet accounts	12/31/16						12/31/17
Debit Balances							
Cash	114,000	q	*14,000*				128,000
Accounts receivable	168,000	a	19,000				187,000
Merchandise inventory	279,000			d	39,000		240,000
Prepaid expenses	14,000	b	14,000				28,000
Supplies	8,000			c	3,000		5,000
Long-term investments	-0-	e	6,000				6,000
Fixtures and equipment	310,000	f	125,000	g	13,000		422,000
Land	11,000	i	*7,000				18,000
Total	904,000						1,034,000
Credit Balances							
Accounts payable	151,000			j	8,000		159,000
Short-term vendor notes payable	25,000	k	1,000				24,000
Income taxes payable	33,000	l	10,000				23,000
Notes payable	126,000			m	31,000		157,000
Bonds payable	-0-			i	*7,000		7,000
Accumulated depreciation	150,000	g	4,000	h	12,000		158,000
Common stock	240,000			n	55,000		295,000
Retained earnings	179,000	o	39,000	p	71,000		211,000
Total	904,000						1,034,000
Statement of Cash Flows							
Operating Activities							
Add:							
Net income		p	71,000				
Depreciation expense		h	12,000				
Decrease in supplies		c	3,000				
Decrease in merchandise inventory		d	39,000				
Increase in accounts payable		j	8,000				
Subtract:							
Gain on sale of equipment				g	5,000		
Increase in accounts receivable				a	19,000		
Increase in prepaid expenses				b	14,000		
Decrease in short-term vendor note				k	1,000		
Decrease in income taxes payable				l	10,000		
Investing Activities							
Purchase long-term investments				e	6,000		
Equipment purchase				f	125,000		
Sale of equipment		g	14,000				
Financing Activities							
Borrowing cash from note payable		m	31,000				
Sale of common stock		n	55,000	o	39,000		
Dividends paid			233,000		219,000		
				q	*14,000*		
Total			233,000		233,000		
Noncash investing and financing*	$7,000						

Using a Worksheet: Direct Method

*Procedure for
Direct Method*

Refer to the completed worksheet on page 880 for Executive Enterprises, Inc. Balance sheet account balances are entered on the top portion of the worksheet. These are entered as debit and credit account balances. Between these balances are columns for debits and credits to adjust for the total increases and decreases to each account.

The adjustments for income statement accounts are entered in the middle portion of the worksheet. A statement of cash flows format is placed under the income statement account items. Notice that the cash flow section is separated into operating, investing, and financing headings, just as you would see on a statement of cash flows formatted for the direct method. A debit adjustment to cash flows is an increase in cash and a credit adjustment to cash flows is a decrease.

The easiest procedure is to begin by entering amounts for revenue and expense items, continuing down the entire income statement one item at a time as you enter a debit or credit to cash flow. For each income statement item, also enter a debit or credit in the balance sheet section for any related account. Then enter a debit or credit in the cash flow section. When completed, all the changes in the balance sheet accounts should be accounted for, as well as the income statement accounts.

Item	Explantion of change and entries
a	Sales revenue is entered as a credit of $1,248,000 in the income statement section and this is also entered as a debit in the cash flow sections.
b	The increase in accounts receivable of $19,000 reduced collections from customers, so $19,000 is entered as a debit in the balance sheet section and a credit in the cash flow section.
c	Cost of goods sold is entered as a debit of $881,000 in the income statement section and is also entered as a credit in the cash flow section.
d	The decrease in merchandise inventory of $39,000 reduced the purchases of inventory, so $39,000 is entered as debit in the cash flow section.
e	The increase in accounts payable of $8,000 reduces payments for inventory, so the $8,000 is entered as debit in the cash flow section.
f	The decrease in short-term notes payable of $1,000 increased payments for inventory, so $1,000 is entered as credit in the cash flow section.
g	Salaries and wages expense is entered as a debit of $196,000 in the income statement section and is also entered as a credit in the cash flow section.
h	Depreciation expense is entered as a debit of $12,000 in the income statement section. This does not affect cash, but does increase accumulated depreciation.
i	Travel expense is entered as a debit of $14,000 in the income statement section and is also entered as a credit in the cash flow section.

continued ▶

Using a Worksheet: Direct Method, *continued*

Item	Explantion of change and entries
j	The increase in prepaid travel expense increased payments, so the $14,000 is entered as credit in the cash flow section for travel expense.
k	The total of various other operating expenses is entered as a debit of $23,000 in the income statement section and is also entered as a credit in the cash flow section. Supplies have also decreased by $3,000 so this is also entered as a debit to operating cash flow and a credit to supplies.
l	Gain on Sale of Equipment of $5,000 is entered as an income statement credit item and the investing activities section is debited for $5,000.
m	Interest expense is entered as a debit of $11,000 in the income statement section and is also entered as a credit in the cash flow section.
n	Income tax expense is entered as a debit of $45,000 in the income statement section and is also entered as a credit in the cash flow section.
o	The decrease in income taxes payable increased payments, so the $10,000 is entered as credit in the cash flow section for income tax expense.
xx	The final item on the income statement is net income; however, this is simply the excess of total revenues over total expenses that increases retained earnings. To complete the income statement and account for the increase in retained earnings, a debit is entered in the income statement section for $71,000 and retained earnings is credited for $71,000.
p	The increase in long-term investments increased payments, so the $6,000 is entered as credit in the cash flow section for investing activities.
q	The increase in fixtures and equipment increased payments, so the $125,000 is entered as credit in the cash flow section for investing activities.
r	The equipment sale reduced the equipment and also increased cash receipts, so $13,000 is entered as a debit as part of the cash received calculation for investing activities from the sale.
s	Accumulated depreciation decreases as a result of the equipment sold, so the accumulated depreciation is debited and investing activities from the sale is credited $4,000 as part of the cash received calculation. (The $13,000 debit and $4,000 credit represent the $9,000 cash received for the book value portion of the sale.)
t	The increase in long-term notes payable increased cash from borrowing, so the $31,000 is entered as debit in the financing activities section for income tax expense.
u	The increase in Land and Bonds Payable is a non-cash investing and financing activity. The $7,000 increases offset each other.
v	The increase in common stock increased cash, so the $55,000 is entered as debit in the financing activities section.

Using a Worksheet: Direct Method, *continued*

Item	Explantion of change and entries
w	There was a $39,000 debit to Retained Earnings for dividends paid; this is also entered as credit to financing activities.
x	The total of all debits to the statement of cash flows is $1,402,000 and the total of all credits is $1,388,000. The next amount indicates a net increase in cash of $14,000, entered as credit to equalize the column totals. The $14,000 is entered as the reconciling debit to the cash account.

Prepare the Statement

After the worksheet is completed prepare the statement of cash flows using the amounts from statement of cash flows section of the worksheet.

Practice Note

As a means of simplifying the illustration, the net change in a balance sheet account was entered as a single debit or credit whenever there was just a single change affecting the statement of cash flows. There are variations in practice. Often total debits and total credits for balance sheet accounts are entered in a worksheet. As well, income statement amounts can be entered as a single amount of net debit or credit without using a "net" column as you see in the direct method worksheet.

IFRS and GAAP

The IFRS (International Financial Reporting Standards) and GAAP statements of cash flows are similar in most respects, such as being a required statement, classification into operating, investing, and financing activities, and the use of either indirect or direct methods. A few notable differences are:

- Under IFRS interest and dividends can be classified as either operating, investing, or financing activities, provided the classification is done in a consistent manner.
- IFRS does not allow non-cash investing and financing activities to be presented as part of the statement of cash flows.
- GAAP does not require the presentation of comparative cash flow statements. (The Securities and Exchange Commission does.) IFRS requires a comparative statement for the preceding period.

Do You Want More Examples?

Most problems in this book have detailed solutions. To use them as additional examples, do this: 1) Select the type of problem you want 2) Open the solution on your computer or mobile device screen (from the disc or worthyjames.com) 3) Read one item at a time and look at its answer. Take notes if needed. 4) Close the solution and work as much of the problem as you can. 5) Repeat as needed.

Direct Method Worksheet						
Account Titles			Dr.		Cr.	
Balance sheet accounts	12/31/16					12/31/17
Debit Balances						
Cash	114,000	x	**14,000**			128,000
Accounts receivable	168,000	b	19,000			187,000
Merchandise inventory	279,000			d	39,000	240,000
Prepaid expenses	14,000	j	14,000			28,000
Supplies	8,000			k	3,000	5,000
Long-term investments	-0-	p	6,000			6,000
Fixtures and equipment	310,000	q	125,000	r	13,000	422,000
Land	11,000	u*	*7,000			18,000
Total	904,000					1,034,000
Credit Balances						
Accounts payable	151,000			e	8,000	159,000
Short-term vendor notes payable	25,000	f	1,000			24,000
Income taxes payable	33,000	o	10,000			23,000
Notes payable	126,000			t	31,000	157,000
Bonds payable	-0-			u*	*7,000	7,000
Accumulated depreciation	150,000	s	4,000	h	12,000	158,000
Common stock	240,000			v	55,000	295,000
Retained earnings	179,000	w	39,000	xx	71,000	211,000
Total	904,000					1,034,000
Income statement						
Sales				a	1,248,000	
Cost of goods sold		c	881,000			
Salaries and wages expense		g	196,000			
Depreciation expense		h	12,000			
Travel expense		i	14,000			
Various other operating expenses		k	23,000			
Gain on sale of equipment				l	5,000	
Interest expense		m	11,000			
Income tax expense		n	45,000			
Net income		xx	71,000			
Statement of Cash Flows	12/31/16					12/31/17
Operating Activities						Net
Collections from customers		a	1,248,000	b	19,000	1,229,000
Merchandise inventory		d	39,000	c	881,000	
		e	8,000	f	1,000	(835,000)
Salaries and wages				g	196,000	(196,000)
Travel				i	14,000	
				j	14,000	(28,000)
Various other		k	3,000	k	23,000	(20,000)
Interest				m	11,000	(11,000)
Income tax				n	45,000	
				o	10,000	(55,000)
Investing Activities						
Purchase long-term investments				p	6,000	(6,000)
Sale of equipment		l	5,000			
		r	13,000	s	4,000	14,000
Equipment purchase				q	125,000	(125,000)
Financing Activities						
Borrowing cash from note payable		t	31,000			31,000
Sale of common stock		v	55,000			55,000
Dividends paid				w	39,000	(39,000)
			1,402,000		1,388,000	
		x			14,000	
Noncash investing and financing*	7,000		1,402,000		1,402,000	

QUICK REVIEW

- The cash flow statement is the fourth essential financial statement after the balance sheet, income statement, and statement of stockholders' equity (or owner's equity). It is an essential report for managers, creditors, and investors because a business cannot survive and properly function without good cash management.

- A statement of cash flows classifies the changes in cash by operating activities, investing activities, and financing activities.

- Operating activities are those transactions that are involved in determining net income and that affect current assets and current liabilities. Investing activities are transactions that affect long-term assets. Financing activities are transactions that affect long-term debt and stockholders' equity.

- There are two formats for reporting operating activities. The indirect method makes adjustments to net income to convert it to a cash basis. The direct method begins with revenue and adjusts each item in the income statement into a cash basis. Both the indirect and direct methods result in the same amount of operating cash flow.

- Specific procedure steps are explained in this learning goal for the preparation of cash flow statement operating, investing, and financing activities categories.

- Analysis of a statement of cash flows consists of: 1) Review each category of cash flow and analyze significant account changes. 2) Compare cash flow to income. 3) Calculate free cash flow. 4) Use ratio analysis. 5) Make trend comparisons over several time periods.

VOCABULARY

Cash basis times -interest -earned ratio (pg. 871) An indicator of the ability to pay interest.

Cash flow to debt ratio (pg. 871) An indicator of the ability to repay debt using only operating cash flow.

Direct method (pg. 863) A method of calculating and reporting cash flow from operating activities by making adjustments to revenues and expenses.

Financing activities (pg. 846) Transactions that affect cash flow as the result of changes in long-term liabilities and stockholders' equity.

Free cash flow (pg. 870) Cash from operating activities minus capital expenditures and dividends.

Indirect method (pg. 849) A method of calculating and reporting cash flow from

operating activities by making adjustments to net income.

Investing activities (pg. 845) Transactions that affect cash flow as the result and changes in long-term assets.

Operating activities (pg. 845) Transactions that affect cash flow as the result of revenues and expenses as adjusted by changes in current assets and current liabilities.

Non-cash investing and financing activities (pg. 860) Investing and financing transactions that fully or partially offset each other and for which cash is not involved.

Statement of cash flows (pg. 843) A financial statement that reports the cash balance and changes in cash during a period and classifies the changes as operating, investing, and financing activities.

*Learning Goal 21 is about the preparation and analysis of the statement of cash flows. Use these
questions and problems to practice what you have just read.*

Multiple Choice
Select the best answer.

1. Which of the following is not true about the operating activities section?
    a. It can be presented in two different formats.
    b. It includes interest paid on loans.
    c. It includes gains and losses on sales of equipment.
    d. It is the most important part of the statement of cash flows.
2. Which of the following activities is not part of the statement of cash flows?
    a. investing
    b. financing
    c. operating
    d. financial
3. Which of the following is correct about the statement of cash flows?
    a. It is the fourth essential financial statement.
    b. It is a report that is dated for the same period as an income statement.
    c. It converts accrual basis income into cash basis income.
    d. All of the above are correct.
4. Which of the following is incorrect?
    a. The income statement reports revenues and expenses and the change in net business wealth
        (stockholders' equity) as a result of operations but the statement of cash flows does not.
    b. Items reported on one statement can affect the cash balance but items on the other will not.
    c. The income statement and statement of cash flows report for different time periods.
    d. All of the above are correct.
5. Which of the following stakeholders would generally need to use the statement of cash flows?
    a. investors
    b. managers
    c. lenders
    d. All of the above are correct.
6. Which of the following would not be reported on of a statement of cash flows?
    a. debt incurred in connection with the purchase of a long-term asset
    b. revenues and expenses
    c. cash spent to loan money to another entity
    d. cash received from the sale of an asset
7. If increases in current assets (excluding cash) are greater than increases in current liabilities,
    the effect will be
    a. a net decrease in cash flow from operating activities
    b. a net increase in cash flow from operating activities
    c. no effect on operating cash flow
    d. no effect on operating cash flow and a net increase in cash flow from financing activities
8. If decreases in current assets (excluding cash) are greater than decreases in current liabilities,
    the effect will be
    a. a net decrease in cash flow from operating activities
    b. a net increase in cash flow from operating activities
    c. no effect on operating cash flow
    d. no effect on operating cash flow and a net decrease in cash flow from financing activities

9. If McAllen Company issued $150,000 of stock in exchange for land, then
   a. financing activities would increase by $150,000.
   b. investing activities would increase by $150,000.
   c. this should not be reported on the cash flow statement.
   d. None of the above is correct.

10. Baywater Company sold land and incurred a loss of $20,000. The net effect of this transaction is
   a. a decrease in cash flow from investing activities.
   b. an increase in cash flow from investing activities.
   c. a decrease in cash flow from operating activities.
   d. an increase in cash flow from operating activities.

11. San Andreas Enterprises sold equipment with a cost of $15,000 and accumulated depreciation of $12,000 for a gain of $5,000. What is the effect on cash flow from investing activities?
   a. a decrease of $5,000
   b. a decrease of $12,000
   c. an increase of $8,000
   d. an increase of $5,000

Questions 12-15 pertain only to the indirect method.

12. Which of the following would not require a positive adjustment to net income in operating activities?
   a. an increase in accounts payable
   b. a loss from the sale of land
   c. an increase in merchandise inventory
   d. an increase in unearned revenue

13. Which of the following would not require a negative adjustment to net income in operating activities?
   a. a gain on sale of sale of equipment
   b. a loss from the sale of land
   c. an increase in accounts receivable
   d. a decrease in taxes payable

14. Net income of Atlanta Enterprises is $75,000. Depreciation expense: $3,000; increase in accounts payable: $5,000; increase in accounts receivable: $1,000. What is cash flow from operating activities?
   a. $82,000
   b. $74,000
   c. $71,000
   d. $78,000

15. If accounts receivable increase by $9,000 and accounts payable increase by $5,000 what is the net adjustment to net income?
   a. positive $4,000
   b. negative $4,000
   c. positive $14,000
   d. negative $14,000

PRACTICE   Learning Goal 21, continued

Solutions are in the disk at the back of the book and at: www.worthyjames.com

Questions 16-18 pertain only to the direct method.

16. Which of the following items would not appear on a direct method cash flow from operating activities section?
    a. gain on sale
    b. loss on sale
    c. depreciation and amortization
    d. all of the above

17. The total sales for Amherst Company are $100,000 including $10,000 of cash sales. The beginning balance of accounts receivable is $12,000 and the ending balance is $15,000. What are cash collections from customers?
    a. $10,000
    b. $97,000
    c. $103,000
    d. $100,000

18. The cost of goods sold for Calaveras Company is $90,000. Merchandise inventory increased by $10,000 and accounts payable related to the inventory increased by $4,000. What are the cash payments for merchandise inventory?
    a. $104,000
    b. $100,000
    c. $103,000
    d. $96,000

19. Which of the following methods would not be used to analyze a statement of cash flows?
    a. ratio analysis
    b. free cash flow calculation
    c. comparison of cash flows to net income
    d. All of the above are used.

20. The operating cash flow for Sonora, Inc. was $117,000 and the company spent $68,000 to purchase equipment. Dividends paid were $40,000. What is the company's free cash flow?
    a. $49,000
    b. $117,000
    c. $77,000
    d. None of the above

Discussion Questions and Brief Exercises

1. Explain the purpose of the statement of cash flows.

2. Why would you use a statement of cash flows of XYZ Company if you were:
    a) an owner or manager of XYZ Company?
    b) the loan officer of a bank to which XYZ Company has applied for a loan?
    c) a possible investor of XYZ Company?

3. What is considered to be the most important section of the statement of cash flows? Why?

Discussion Questions and Brief Exercises, *continued*

4. Why doesn't an accrual-basis income statement (properly prepared according to GAAP) show the correct amount of change in cash? Why is it necessary to make adjustments?

5. Explain the differences between the indirect method and direct method formats.

6. a) Is it possible that a company could show $100,000 of net income and also show a decrease in cash of $100,000?
   b) Is it possible that a company could show $100,000 of net loss and also show an increase in cash of $100,000?

   If your answer is yes, then specifically indicate how this could happen. If your answer is no, explain why it could not happen.

7. What are the advantages and disadvantages of the indirect method compared to the direct method?

8. How does depreciation expense affect the statement of cash flows?

9. Give at least two examples of non-cash investing and financing activities. Why is it important to disclose them? Where are they usually disclosed?

10. Indicate with an "X" in the appropriate column where each of the items below would either appear on or affect a statement of cash flows. Column headings: O: operating, I: investing, F: financing.

	Item	O	I	F
a.	A change in accounts receivable			
b.	A change in long-term notes payable			
c.	Payment of dividends			
d.	Gain on sale of land on the income statement			
e.	Purchase of equipment for cash			
f.	Interest revenue on the income statement			
g.	Interest expense on the income statement			
h.	A change in unearned revenue			

Discussion Questions and Brief Exercises, *continued*

11. Indicate with an "X" in the appropriate column where each of the items below would either appear on or affect a statement of cash flows. Column headings: O: operating, I: investing, F: financing, NC: non-cash investing and financing.

	Item	O	I	F	NC
a.	A sale of equipment				
b.	A purchase of company's own stock (treasury stock				
c.	Conversion of outstanding bonds into outstanding stock				
d.	Collection of a note receivable				
e.	Dividends paid				
f.	Dividends received				
g.	Sale of land in return for buyer's stock				
h.	Sale of long-term investment for cash				

12. Direct and indirect methods: Compare how each of the items below would be presented using the direct method and using the indirect method.

	Item
a.	Depreciation and amortization expenses
b.	Gain or loss on sale plant and equipment
c.	A change in accounts receivable
d.	A change in wages payable
e.	Cost of goods sold

13. Indirect method: Philadelphia Enterprises, Inc. recorded the following transactions during the year. Net income was $77,500. Calculate operating cash flow using the indirect format.

	Transaction	Amount
a.	Depreciation expense	$5,000
b.	Loss on sale of equipment	$1,500
c.	Increase in various accrued expense liabilities	$6,000
d.	Decrease in accounts payable	$1,600
e.	Decrease in accounts receivable	$3,900
f.	Payment of dividends	$15,000
g.	Increase in merchandise inventory	$12,000

Discussion Questions and Brief Exercises, *continued*

14. Direct method: Philadelphia Enterprises, Inc. recorded the following transactions during the year. Net sales were $740,000, cost of goods sold, $375,000 and various other operating expenses, $281,000. Calculate operating cash flow using the direct format.

	Transaction	Amount
a.	Depreciation expense	$5,000
b.	Loss on sale of equipment	$1,500
c.	Increase in various accrued expense liabilities	$6,000
d.	Decrease in accounts payable	$1,600
e.	Decrease in accounts receivable	$3,900
f.	Payment of dividends	$15,000
g.	Increase in merchandise inventory	$12,000

15. Each of the columns below contains an independent set of facts concerning equipment account balances and equipment transactions for the current accounting period. Complete the missing items in each column.

	a	b	c	d	e
Equipment, net: beginning balance	$50,000	$120,000	$88,000	$100,000	$93,000
Purchases of equipment	10,000	5,000	22,000	?	?
Book value of assets sold	?	?	?	15,000	5,000
Depreciation expense	3,000	7,000	4,500	7,000	4,000
Equipment, net: ending balance	47,000	101,000	47,000	124,000	95,000
Gain (loss) on sale	-0-	2,000	(6,000)	(13,000)	(4,500)
Cash increase (decrease) in investing activities	?	?	?	?	?

16. Which accounts need to be analyzed when completing:
    a. The investing activities section?
    b. The financing activities section?

PRACTICE   Learning Goal 21, continued

Solutions are in the disk at the back of the book and at: www.worthyjames.com

Discussion Questions and Brief Exercises, *continued*

17. Consider the following situations:
   a. Accounts receivable balance as a percentage of sales continues to increase while sales revenue remains about the same.
   b. Accounts receivable balance continues to increase while sales revenue is increasing.
   c. Accounts payable continues to increase while inventory remains about the same.
   d. Inventory is increasing as sales revenue is decreasing.

   For each of the situations above, what would be the effect on statement of cash flows? What is your opinion concerning each of these situations?

18. Wakefield Company reported the following information on its statement of cash flows:
   a. Operating cash flow: $50,000   b. Purchases of equipment: $7,000   c. cash dividends: $5,000
   Calculate the free cash flow.

19. San Fernando Company reported the following information on its annual financial statements:

   ■ Cash flow from operating activities: $140,000
   ■ Total average liabilities: $1,225,000
   ■ Purchases of equipment for cash: $36,000
   ■ Interest expense cash paid: $80,000
   ■ Cash sales of equipment: $75,000
   ■ Dividends paid: $50,000

   Calculate the following:
   a. free cash flow
   b. cash flow to debt ratio
   c. cash times-interest earned ratio

20. Indirect method. Summarized balance sheet data and additional information for Ft. Myers Co. is presented below.

	2017	2016
Current Assets		
Cash......................	$11,600	$112,900
Accounts receivable.......	21,900	26,800
Merchandise inventory.....	93,100	90,200
Prepaid insurance.........	1,500	2,500
Current Liabilities		
Accounts payable..........	15,600	22,700
Other accrued liabilities .	6,500	12,600
Unearned revenue	5,100	4,700

Additional information for 2017:

   ■ Net income: $3,500   ■ Depreciation expense: $5,100

Instructions:

Prepare the operating activities section of the statement of cash flows for the calendar year 2017 using the indirect method.

Discussion Questions and Brief Exercises, *continued*

21.   The financial statements of Torrance, Inc. are presented below.

Torrance, Inc.
Comparative Balance Sheets
December 31

	2017	2016
Assets		
Current assets		
Cash	$52,000	$22,000
Accounts receivable	30,000	28,000
Merchandise inventory	53,000	55,000
Prepaid expenses	4,000	3,000
Total current assets	139,000	108,000
Property, plant, and equipment		
Fixtures and equipment	275,000	272,000
Less: accumulated depreciation	(54,000)	(50,000)
Total property, plant, and equipment	221,000	222,000
Total assets	$360,000	$330,000
Liabilities and Stockholders' Equity		
Current liabilities		
Accounts payable	$22,000	$18,000
Income taxes payable	10,000	12,000
Total current liabilities	32,000	30,000
Long-term liabilities		
Notes payable	14,000	15,000
Total liabilities	46,000	45,000
Stockholders' equity		
Common stock	100,000	80,000
Retained earnings	214,000	205,000
Total stockholders' equity	314,000	285,000
Total liabilities and stockholders' equity	$360,000	$330,000

Torrance, Inc.
Condensed Income Statement
For the Year Ended December 31, 2017

Net sales	$412,000
Cost of goods sold	235,000
Gross profit	177,000
Operating expenses	142,000
Operating income	35,000
Other revenue or expense	
Interest earned	4,000
Income from operations before tax	39,000
Income tax expense	10,000
Net income	$29,000

Discussion Questions and Brief Exercises, *continued*

Additional information for 2017:

- Depreciation expense: $9,000 (included in operating expenses)
- Equipment was sold for $10,000 cash. The cost of the equipment was $15,000.
- Accumulated depreciation on the equipment sold is $5,000.

- All sales and merchandise inventory purchases are on account.
- Dividends of $20,000 were paid in 2017.
- Merchandise purchases are recorded in accounts payable.

Instructions:

Prepare the operating activities section of the statement of cash flows for the calendar year 2017 using the indirect method.

---

22. Use the information presented in exercise 21 (above) to prepare a statement of cash flows for Torrance, Inc. using the direct method.

---

23. Challenging question: If you have studied both the direct and indirect methods, can you explain the following similarities and differences for how adjustments are made to operating activities?

   a. For both the direct and indirect methods, increases in receivables are negative adjustments and decreases in receivables are positive adjustments.

   b. For the direct method, increases in payables are negative adjustments and decreases are positive adjustments. However, for the indirect method, increases in payables are positive adjustments and decreases in payables are negative adjustments.

   c. For the indirect method, depreciation expense is a positive adjustment. For the direct method, there is no adjustment for depreciation expense.

---

24. Prior to completing year-end financial reports, a company president instructs the chief financial   officer to report a $100,000 payment on a short-term vendor loan, used to purchase merchandise   inventory and supplies, as a decrease in long-term notes payable on the statement of cash flows. The company president justifies this by saying: "Debt is debt, it makes no real difference. We paid the debt, that's what matters. If we can make our financial statement look a little better, we aren't hurting anybody." What are the specific effects of this action? Your comments?

Reinforcement Problems

LG 21-1. Cash flow classification of transactions

During 2017 Longwood Inc. recorded events that you see below. Each of the column titles below refer to a section of a statement of cash flows. Column headings: O: operating, I: investing, F: financing, NC: non-cash investing and financing.

	Event	O	I	F	NC
1.	Interest expense of $4,00				
2.	A decrease in wages payable of $3,500				
3.	Cash sales of $61,000				
4.	Conversion of $100,000 of bonds into common stock				
5.	Cash payment of dividends of $50,000				
6.	An increase in accounts receivable of $20,000				
7.	An increase in accounts payable of $15,00				
8.	A purchase of $30,000 of land by issuing stock				
9.	Cash receipts of dividends of $5,00				
10.	A sale of equipment at no gain or loss: book value is $2,000				
11.	Gain on sale of equipment: $900				
12.	Interest revenue of $50				
13.	Payment of loan principal of $10,000				
14.	Made a long-term loan to a customer: $25,000				
15.	An increase in prepaid rent of $10,000				

Instructions: For each of the listed events, place an "X" in the appropriate column to indicate the classification of an adjustment.

LG 21-2. Indirect method: Prepare a statement of cash flows.

Summarized balance sheet data and additional information for Fresno Consulting Services, Inc. as of June 30 are presented below.

	2017	2016
Current Assets		
Cash	$198,700	$21,000
Accounts receivable	45,200	41,100
Prepaid tax	6,400	6,800
Current Liabilities		
Accounts payable	39,200	33,800
Other accrued liabilities	9,500	10,600
Unearned revenue	1,300	2,100

LG 21-2, *continued*

Additional information for the year ending June 30, 2017:

- Net income $35,200
- Long-term note payable
  issued for cash loan 25,000
- Issuance of common stock for cash . . . 125,000
- Operating expenses excluding
  depreciation and tax expense 781,000

- Depreciation expense $2,500
- Purchase of equipment for cash 9,800
- Sales revenue. 823,700
- Tax expense. 5,000

Instructions:

a. Prepare a statement of cash flows for the year ended December 31, 2017 using the indirect method for operating activities. Accounts payable and accrued liabilities result from various operating expenses. (Use whatever information you think is necessary for the operating activities section.)
b. Evaluate the sources and uses of cash on the statement of cash flows.

LG 21-3. Direct method: Prepare a statement of cash flows.

Instructions:

a. Using the information presented in LG21-2, prepare a statement of cash flows for the year ended June 30, 2017 using the direct method for operating activities. (Use whatever information you think is necessary for the operating activities section.)
b. Evaluate the sources and uses of cash on the statement of cash flows.

LG 21-4. Indirect method: Prepare a statement of cash flows. The financial statements of Norwalk, Inc. are presented below.

Norwalk, Inc. Condensed Income Statement For the Year Ended December 31, 2017		
Net sales		$1,330,000
Cost of goods sold.		774,000
Gross profit		556,000
Depreciation expense	$32,000	
Operating expenses, excluding depreciation	414,000	446,000
Operating income		110,000
Other revenue and gains		
Interest expense.	(4,000)	
Gain on sale.	7,000	3,000
Income from operations before tax		113,000
Income tax expense.		24,000
Net income.		$89,000

LG 21-4, *continued*

Norwalk, Inc. Comparative Balance Sheets December 31		
	2017	**2016**
Assets		
Current assets		
Cash	$103,000	$128,000
Accounts receivable	221,000	197,000
Merchandise inventory	347,000	325,000
Total current assets.	671,000	650,000
Property, plant, and equipment		
Fixtures and equipment.	853,000	849,000
Less: accumulated depreciation	(472,000)	(455,000)
Total property, plant, and equipment	381,000	394,000
Total assets	$1,052,000	$1,044,000
Liabilities and Stockholders' Equity		
Current liabilities		
Accounts payable	$189,000	$181,000
Income taxes payable	28,000	31,000
Total current liabilities.	217,000	212,000
Long-term liabilities		
Notes payable	25,000	150,000
Total liabilities	242,000	362,000
Stockholders' equity		
Common stock	323,000	234,000
Retained earnings.	487,000	448,000
Total stockholders' equity	810,000	682,000
Total liabilities and stockholders' equity	$1,052,000	$1,044,000

Additional information for 2017:

- Equipment was sold for $22,000 cash. The cost of the equipment was $30,000.
- Accumulated depreciation on the equipment sold is $15,000.
- $34,000 of equipment was purchased.

- All sales and merchandise inventory purchases are on account.
- Merchandise purchases are recorded in accounts payable.

Instructions:

a. For the statement of cash flows, prepare the operating activities section of the statement of cash flows for the calendar year 2017 using the indirect method.

b. What is the difference between operating cash flow and net income? What is the difference between the net change in cash and net income?

c. What were the main sources of cash and uses of cash during the year?

PRACTICE   Learning Goal 21, continued

Solutions are in the disk at the back of the book and at: www.worthyjames.com

LG 21-5. **Direct method: Prepare a statement of cash flows.**

Instructions:

a. Using the information presented in LG21-4, prepare a statement of cash flows using the direct method for operating activities.
b. What is the difference between operating cash flow and net income? What is the difference between the net change in cash and net income?
c. Excluding net income, what were the largest sources of cash and uses of cash during the year?

LG 21-6. **Indirect method: Prepare a statement of cash flows**

For the calendar year 2017, selected account transactions for Milton Company, Inc. are summarized in the T accounts below. All merchandise purchases are made on account ("Mdse. Purchases"). All annual expenses except for cost of sales and depreciation are in the Combined Expenses account.

Cash

Jan. 1	Bal.	38,000	
	Receipts	327,000	
	Payments		313,000
Dec. 31	Bal.	52,000	

Accounts Receivable

Jan. 1	Bal.	94,000	
	Sales	303,000	
	Collections		325,000
Dec. 31	Bal.	72,000	

Merchandise Inventory

Jan. 1	Bal.	89,000	
	Purchases	156,000	
	Cost of sales		121,000
Dec. 31	Bal.	124,000	

Accounts Payable

Jan. 1	Bal.		56,000
	Mdse. Purchases		156,000
	Payments	159,000	
Dec. 31	Bal.		53,000

Combined Accrued Expenses Payable

Jan. 1	Bal.		14,000
	Expenses incurred		109,000
	Payments	113,000	
Dec. 31	Bal.		10,000

Equipment

Jan. 1	Bal.	235,000	
	Purchases	26,000	
	Sale		15,000
Dec. 31	Bal.	246,000	

Sales Revenue

Jan. 1	Bal.		-0-
	Annual sales		303,000
Dec. 31	Bal.		303,000

Combined Expenses

Jan. 1	Bal.	-0-	
	Incurred during year	109,000	
Dec. 31	Bal.	109,000	

LG 21-6, *continued*

	Accumulated Depreciation-Equipment				Retained Earnings		
Jan. 1	Bal.		162,000	Jan. 1	Bal.		172,000
	Equipment sale	9,000			Dividends	15,000	
	Depreciation		28,000		Net income		41,000
Dec. 31	Bal.		181,000	Dec. 31	Bal.		198,000

	Loss on Sale	
Jan. 1	Bal.	-0-
	Equipment sale	4,000
Dec. 31	Bal.	4,000

Instructions: Using the information that you see in the T accounts:

1. Prepare an income statement for the year ended December 31, 2017. (Omit income tax.)
2. Prepare a statement of cash flows for Milton Company, Inc. for the year ended December 31, 2017. Use the indirect method.

LG 21-7. **Direct method: Prepare a statement of cash flows.**

Instructions: Using the information presented in LG21-6,

1. Prepare an income statement for the year ended December 31, 2017. (Omit income tax.)
2. Prepare a statement of cash flows for Milton Company, Inc. for the year ended December 31, 2017. Use the direct method.

LG 21-8. Indirect method: Prepare a statement of cash flows. The financial statements of Bangor Enterprises, Inc. are presented below.

Bangor Enterprises, Inc.
Condensed Income Statement
For the Year Ended June 30, 2017

Net sales....................................		$2,850,700
Cost of goods sold		1,944,200
Gross profit		906,500
Depreciation expense.........................	$31,800	
Rent expense.................................	57,000	
Various combined operating expenses	824,900	
Total operating expenses.....................		913,700
Operating income		(7,200)
Other revenues and expenses and losses		
Interest earned	1,800	
Interest expense	(20,700)	
Loss on equipment sale.....................	(7,600)	(26,500)
Net loss.....................................		$(33,700)

Bangor Enterprises, Inc.
Comparative Balance Sheets
June 30

	2017	2016
Assets		
Current assets		
Cash.....................................	$119,600	$91,200
Accounts receivable.........................	86,300	114,700
Merchandise inventory	246,200	248,100
Prepaid rent	6,000	5,500
Total current assets	458,100	459,500
Property, plant, and equipment		
Land.....................................	175,000	50,000
Fixtures and equipment	858,900	865,900
Less: accumulated depreciation	(606,900)	(585,200)
Total property, plant, and equipment	427,000	330,700
Total assets	$885,100	$790,200
Liabilities and Stockholders' Equity		
Current liabilities		
Accounts payable	$133,900	$121,100
Interest payable..........................	10,300	9,500
Accrued expenses payable	180,300	186,200
Total current liabilities	324,500	316,800
Long-term liabilities		
Bonds payable............................	295,000	245,000
Total liabilities	619,500	561,800
Stockholders' equity		
Common stock...........................	230,900	150,000
Retained earnings	34,700	78,400
Total stockholders' equity................	265,600	228,400
Total liabilities and stockholders' equity	$885,100	$790,200

LG 21-8, *continued*

Additional information for 2017:

- Equipment was sold for $32,500 cash. *Hint:* You should determine the book value of the equipment sold.
- Land was acquired by issuing $50,000 of bonds and paying cash for the balance of the cost.

- All merchandise purchases are on account, recorded in accounts payable.
- Combined operating expenses exclude depreciation and rent expense.

Instructions:
   a. Prepare a statement of cash flows for the year ended June 30, 2017 using the indirect method.
   b. Analyze the statement of cash flows.

LG 21-9. Direct method: Prepare a statement of cash flows.

Instructions:
   a. Use the information presented in LG21-8, to prepare a statement of cash flows for the year ended June 30, 2017 using the direct method for operating activities.
   b. Evaluate the sources and uses of cash on the statement of cash flows.

LG 21-10. Indirect method: Prepare a statement of cash flows, various notes receivable. The financial statements of Sacramento Co., Inc. are presented below.

Sacramento Co., Inc. Comparative Balance Sheets December 31		
	2017	**2016**
Assets		
Current assets		
Cash	$77,480	$53,290
Accounts receivable......................	61,320	72,660
Notes receivable	19,100	29,100
Merchandise inventory....................	158,400	154,120
Prepaid insurance	4,560	3,350
Total current assets	320,860	312,520
Long-term assets		
Notes receivable.........................	210,350	185,200
Equipment...............................	510,700	485,700
Less: accumulated depreciation.............	(226,000)	(196,500)
Total long-term assets...................	495,050	474,400
Total assets...........................	$815,910	$786,920

LG 21-10, *continued*

Sacramento Co., Inc.
Comparative Balance Sheets
December 31

	2017	2016
Liabilities and Stockholders' Equity		
Current liabilities		
Accounts payable	$73,350	$61,280
Accrued expenses payable	31,480	41,080
Unearned revenue	8,500	12,000
Total current liabilities	113,330	114,360
Long-term liabilities		
Bonds payable	-0-	100,000
Notes payable	172,060	286,400
Total liabilities	285,390	500,760
Stockholders' equity		
Common stock	250,000	50,000
Retained earnings	280,520	236,160
Total stockholders' equity	530,520	286,160
Total liabilities and stockholders' equity	$815,910	$786,920

Sacramento Co., Inc.
Condensed Income Statement
For the Year Ended December 31, 2017

Net sales		$834,500
Cost of goods sold		470,730
Gross profit		363,770
Depreciation expense	$35,200	
Various combined operating expenses	125,890	
Total operating expenses		161,090
Operating income		202,680
Other expense and gains and losses		
Interest expense	(22,170)	
Interest earned	11,830	
Loss on equipment sales	(4,500)	(14,840)
Income from operations before tax		187,840
Income tax expense		43,480
Net income		$144,360

LG 21-10, *continued*

Additional information for 2017:

- Short-term notes receivable arise from sales to customers in which Sacramento Co. provides short-term financing . Long-term notes receivable are long-term investments.
- Equipment was sold for $14,800 cash at a loss of $4,500. Equipment was also purchased during the year. *Hint:* you should determine the book value of the equipment sold.

- All merchandise purchases are on account, recorded in accounts payable.
- Combined operating expenses exclude depreciation.
- $100,000 of convertible bonds were exchanged for common stock.

a. Prepare a statement of cash flows for the year ended December 31, 2017 using the indirect method. (**Note: a worksheet is included in the solution if you wish to use a worksheet approach as part of the preparation.**)
b. Analyze the statement of cash flows.

LG 21-11. Direct method: Prepare a statement of cash flows.

Instructions:

a. Use the information presented in LG21-10, to prepare a statement of cash flows for the calendar year 2017 using the direct method for operating activities. (**Note: a worksheet is included in the solution if you wish to use a worksheet approach as part of the preparation.**)
b. Analyze the statement of cash flows.

Solutions are in the disk at the back of the book and at: www.worthyjames.com

LG 21-12. Indirect method: Prepare a statement of cash flows, two depreciable asset items, treasury stock sale. The financial statements of Omaha, Inc. are presented below.

Omaha, Inc. Comparative Balance Sheets December 31	2017	2016
Assets		
Current assets		
Cash...................................	$39,520	$58,610
Accounts receivable......................	77,010	61,990
Merchandise inventory....................	245,620	234,150
Prepaid travel...........................	2,690	4,800
Total current assets.....................	364,840	359,550
Property, plant, and equipment		
Automotive equipment....................	212,490	195,350
Less: accumulated depreciation- automotive...	(184,330)	(177,500)
Plant equipment.........................	253,130	275,920
Less: accumulated depreciation- plant........	(187,380)	(200,210)
Total property, plant, and equipment.......	93,910	93,560
Total assets.........................	$458,750	$453,110
Liabilities and Stockholders' Equity		
Current liabilities		
Accounts payable.........................	$51,290	$57,460
Accrued expenses payable.................	99,470	110,080
Unearned revenue........................	7,500	5,000
Total current liabilities..................	158,260	172,540
Long-term liabilities		
Notes payable...........................	10,830	28,500
Total liabilities........................	169,090	201,040
Stockholders' equity		
Common stock............................	170,000	170,000
Retained earnings	119,660	90,070
Less: 400 shares treasury stock at cost.........	-0-	(8,000)
Total stockholders' equity.................	289,660	252,070
Total liabilities and stockholders' equity	$458,750	$453,110

LG 21-12, *continued*

Omaha, Inc.
Condensed Income Statement
For the Year Ended December 31, 2017

Net sales....................................		$941,320
Cost of goods sold		611,880
Gross profit		329,440
Depreciation expense.........................	$20,250	
Travel	32,420	
Various combined operating expenses	221,560	
Total operating expenses......................		
Operating income		274,230
Other revenues and expenses and losses		55,210
Interest earned	1,000	
Interest expense	(2,350)	
Gain on equipment sales......................	3,180	1,830
Income from operations before tax...........		57,040
Income tax expense		14,250
Net income		$42,790

The president of Omaha, Inc. has come to you, the chief financial officer, with a question. She says to you: "Our revenue and net income increased this year, but we have had a substantial decline in cash. I don't understand it. We even sold some of our equipment, sold all the treasury stock, reduced liabilities, and still the cash balance decreased. How could this happen?"

Additional information for 2017:

- Automotive equipment was both purchased and sold during the year. The equipment was sold for $12,000 at a gain of $5,100. *Hint:* you should determine the book value of the equipment sold.
- Plant equipment was also both purchased and sold during the year. The cost of purchases was $12,210.
- Depreciation was recorded as $14,930 for automotive and $5,320 for plant equipment.

- All merchandise purchases are on account, recorded in accounts payable.
- All of the treasury stock was sold at a price of $12 per share. Any difference between cost and sales price is recorded in the retained earnings account.
- Combined operating expenses exclude depreciation.

Instructions:

a. Prepare a statement of cash flows for the year ended December 31, 2017 using the indirect method. (**Note: a worksheet is included in the solution if you wish to use a worksheet approach as part of the preparation**.)

b. Prepare a brief explanation for the company president.

LG 21-13. Direct method: Prepare a statement of cash flows.

Instructions:

a. Use the information presented in LG21-12, to prepare a statement of cash flows for the calendar year 2017 using the direct method for operating activities. (**Note: a worksheet is included in the solution if you wish to use a worksheet approach as part of the preparation.**)

b. Prepare a brief explanation for the company president.

PRACTICE   Learning Goal 21, continued

Instructor-Assigned Problems

If you are using this book in a class, these review problems may be assigned by your instructor for homework, group assignments, class work, or other activities. Only your instructor has the solutions.

IA 21-1. Cash flow classification of transactions

During 2017 Longwood Inc. recorded events that you see below. Each of the column titles below refer to a section of a statement of cash flows. Column headings: O: operating, I: investing, F: financing, NC: non-cash investing and financing.

	Event	O	I	F	NC
1.	Interest revenue of $230				
2.	Cash receipts of dividends of $7,500				
3.	Payment of loan principal of $5,000				
4.	Borrowed $34,000				
5.	Depreciation expense of $12,000				
6.	An increase in accounts payable of $11,200				
7.	Conversion of $50,000 of bonds into common stock				
8.	A exchange of $50,000 of land for common stock				
9.	A decrease in accounts payable of $18,500				
10.	Interest expense of $3,10				
11.	Repayment of a loan of $10,000				
12.	An increase in accounts receivable of $19,500				
13.	A decrease in prepaid rent of $4,700				
14.	Purchased a note receivable $12,000				
15.	Sold equipment costing $10,000 at a loss for $3,500				

Instructions:

a. For each of the listed events, place an "X" in the appropriate column to indicate the classification of an adjustment.
b. After completing the table, indicate which adjustment items are not actual increases or decreases to cash, and why an adjustment is required.

IA 21-2. Indirect method: Prepare a statement of cash flows.

Summarized balance sheet data and additional information for El Paso Service Company, Inc. as of December 31 are presented below.

	2017	2016
Current Assets		
Cash	$334,900	$104,100
Accounts receivable	39,600	44,800
Prepaid tax	4,100	7,200
Current Liabilities		
Accounts payable	26,400	28,500
Other accrued liabilities	7,400	5,700
Unearned revenue	2,300	5,100

PRACTICE   **Learning Goal 21, continued**

IA 21-2, *continued*

Additional information for the year ending December 31, 2017:

- Net income $80,600
- Long-term note payable issued
  for cash loan 40,000
- Issuance of common stock for cash... 115,000
- Operating expenses excluding
  depreciation and tax expense 701,200

- Depreciation expense $5,100
- Purchase of equipment for cash 15,000
- Sales revenue..................... 791,400
- Tax expense....................... 4,500

Instructions:

a. Prepare a statement of cash flows for the year ended December 31, 2017 using the indirect method for operating activities. Accounts payable and accrued liabilities result from various operating expenses. (Use whatever information you think is necessary for the operating activities section.)

b. Evaluate the sources and uses of cash on the cash flow statement using the tools from this Learning Goal.

IA 21-3. Direct method: Prepare a statement of cash flows.

Instructions:

a. Use the information presented in IA21-2, to prepare a statement of cash flows for the calendar year 2017 using the direct method for operating activities.

b. Evaluate the sources and uses of cash on the cash flow statement using the tools from this Learning Goal.

IA 21-4. Indirect method: Prepare a statement of cash flows.

- The financial statements of Yonkers, Inc. are presented below.

Yonkers, Inc.
Comparative Balance Sheets
December 31

	2017	2016
Assets		
Current assets		
Cash.....................................	$71,200	$88,600
Accounts receivable.........................	315,500	297,900
Merchandise inventory.......................	438,900	425,400
Total current assets	825,600	811,900
Property, plant, and equipment		
Fixtures and equipment	1,865,500	1,749,500
Less: accumulated depreciation..............	(391,500)	(375,300)
Total property, plant, and equipment........	1,474,000	1,374,200
Total assets	$2,299,600	$2,186,100

IA 21-4, *continued*

Yonkers, Inc.
Comparative Balance Sheets
December 31

	2017	2016
Liabilities and Stockholders' Equity		
Current liabilities		
Accounts payable	$410,700	$401,200
Income taxes payable.	3,800	8,100
Total current liabilities	414,500	409,300
Long-term liabilities		
Notes payable	324,600	275,000
Total liabilities	739,100	684,300
Stockholders' equity		
Common stock.	500,000	450,000
Retained earnings	1,060,500	1,051,800
Total stockholders' equity.	1,560,500	1,501,800
Total liabilities and stockholders' equity	$2,299,600	$2,186,100

Additional information for 2017:

- Equipment costing $34,000 was sold for $31,500 cash.
- $150,000 of equipment was purchased.

- All sales and merchandise inventory purchases are on account.
- Merchandise purchases are recorded in accounts payable

Yonkers, Inc.
Condensed Income Statement
For the Year Ended December 31, 2017

Net sales.		$2,273,300
Cost of goods sold		1,728,100
Gross profit		545,200
Depreciation expense.	$22,400	
Operating expenses, excluding depreciation	486,900	509,300
Operating income		35,900
Other revenue and gains		
Interest expense	(14,600)	
Gain on sale	3,700	(10,900)
Income from operations before tax		25,000
Income tax expense		3,800
Net income		$21,200

PRACTICE   **Learning Goal 21, continued**

IA 21-**4**, *continued*

Instructions:

a. **Pre**pare a 2017 statement of cash flows using the indirect method for operating activities.
b. **W**hat is the difference between operating cash flow and net income? What is the difference be**t**ween the net change in cash and net income?
c. **W**hat were the main sources of cash and uses of cash during the year?

IA 21-**5**. **Direct method: Prepare a statement of cash flows.**

Instructions:

a. **Us**e the information presented in IA21-4, to prepare a statement of cash flows for the cal**e**ndar year 2017 using the direct method for operating activities.
b. **W**hat is the difference between operating cash flow and net income? What is the difference be**t**ween the net change in cash and net income?
c. **W**hat were the main sources of cash and uses of cash during the year?

IA 21-**6**. **Indirect method: Calculate statement of cash flows.** The financial statements of Albu**qu**erque Enterprises, Inc. are presented below.

Albuquerque Enterprises, Inc.
Condensed Income Statement
For the Year Ended June 30, 2017

Net sales....................................		$728,500
Cost of goods sold		435,200
Gross profit		293,300
Depreciation expense........................	$32,100	
Rent expense................................	18,000	
Various combined operating expenses	240,600	
Total operating expenses.....................		290,700
Operating income		2,600
Other revenues and expenses and losses		
Interest earned	700	
Interest expense	(4,900)	
Loss on equipment sale......................	(12,000)	(16,200)
Net loss.....................................		$(13,600)

PRACTICE   Learning Goal 21, continued

IA 21-8, *continued*

Atlanta Enterprises Inc.
Condensed Income Statement
For the Year Ended December 31, 2017

Net sales......................................		$2,890,300
Cost of goods sold		1,580,950
Gross profit		1,309,350
Depreciation expense...........................	$65,900	
Various combined operating expenses	751,320	
Total operating expenses....................		817,220
Operating income		492,130
Other revenue and expense and losses		
Interest expense	(58,430)	
Interest earned	23,370	
Loss on equipment sales	(15,480)	(50,540)
Income from operations before tax..........		441,590
Income tax expense.......................		145,700
Net income		$295,890

Additional information for 2017:

- Short-term notes receivable arise from sales to customers in which the company provides short-term financing . Long-term notes receivable are long-term investments.
- Equipment was sold for $33,500 cash at a loss of $5,700. Equipment was also purchased during the year.
- Combined operating expenses exclude depreciation.

- All merchandise purchases are on account, recorded in accounts payable.
- Investors exchanged $150,000 of convertible bonds for common stock of the same value.
- At the end of 2016 the company held 500 shares of treasury stock. 400 of these shares were reissued in 2017 for $17 per share. Any difference between treasury stock and issue price is recorded in retained earnings.

a. Prepare a statement of cash flows for the year ended December 31, 2017 using the indirect method.
b. Use a worksheet to assist in your preparation of the statement of cash flows.
c. Analyze the statement of cash flows.

IA 21-9. Direct method: Prepare a statement of cash flows.

Instructions:

a. Using the information from IA21-8, prepare a statement of cash flows for the year ended June 30, 2017 using the indirect method for operating activities.
b. Use a worksheet to assist in your preparation of the statement of cash flows.
c. Analyze the statement of cash flows.

PRACTICE   Learning Goal 21, continued

IA 21-7. **Direct method: Prepare a statement of cash flows.**

Instructions:

a. Using the information from IA21-6, prepare a statement of cash flows for the year ended June 30, 2017 using the indirect method for operating activities..
b. Analyze the statement of cash flows.

IA 21-8. **Indirect method: Prepare a statement of cash flows.** The financial statements of Atlanta Enterprises Inc. are presented below.

Atlanta Enterprises Inc. Comparative Balance Sheets December 31		
	2017	**2016**
Assets		
Current assets		
Cash	$268,230	$186,850
Accounts receivable	111,580	101,320
Notes receivable	48,300	50,000
Merchandise inventory	213,100	215,060
Prepaid insurance.	3,650	2,800
Total current assets.	644,860	556,030
Long-term assets		
Notes receivable	252,000	275,000
Equipment	991,530	781,230
Less: accumulated depreciation	(308,600)	(254,500)
Total long-term assets	934,930	801,730
Total assets	$1,579,790	$1,357,760
Liabilities and Stockholders' Equity		
Current liabilities		
Accounts payable	$81,530	$77,450
Accrued expenses payable.	162,070	166,910
Unearned revenue.	7,100	12,500
Total current liabilities.	250,700	256,860
Long-term liabilities		
Bonds payable.	50,000	200,000
Notes payable	91,000	165,500
Total liabilities	391,700	622,360
Stockholders' equity		
Common stock	510,000	310,000
Retained earnings.	680,090	435,400
Less: treasury stock at cost.	(2,000)	(10,000)
Total stockholders' equity	1,188,090	735,400
Total liabilities and stockholders' equity	$1,579,790	$1,357,760

PRACTICE Learning Goal 21, continued

IA 21-8, *continued*

Atlanta Enterprises Inc.
Condensed Income Statement
For the Year Ended December 31, 2017

Net sales.....................................		$2,890,300
Cost of goods sold		1,580,950
Gross profit		1,309,350
Depreciation expense.........................	$65,900	
Various combined operating expenses	751,320	
Total operating expenses....................		817,220
Operating income		492,130
Other revenue and expense and losses		
Interest expense	(58,430)	
Interest earned	23,370	
Loss on equipment sales	(15,480)	(50,540)
Income from operations before tax..........		441,590
Income tax expense.........................		145,700
Net income		$295,890

Additional information for 2017:

- Short-term notes receivable arise from sales to customers in which the company provides short-term financing . Long-term notes receivable are long-term investments.
- Equipment was sold for $33,500 cash at a loss of $5,700. Equipment was also purchased during the year.
- Combined operating expenses exclude depreciation.

- All merchandise purchases are on account, recorded in accounts payable.
- Investors exchanged $150,000 of convertible bonds for common stock of the same value.
- At the end of 2016 the company held 500 shares of treasury stock. 400 of these shares were reissued in 2017 for $17 per share. Any difference between treasury stock and issue price is recorded in retained earnings.

a. Prepare a statement of cash flows for the year ended December 31, 2017 using the indirect method.
b. Use a worksheet to assist in your preparation of the statement of cash flows.
c. Analyze the statement of cash flows.

IA 21-9. Direct method: Prepare a statement of cash flows.

Instructions:

a. Using the information from IA21-8, prepare a statement of cash flows for the year ended June 30, 2017 using the indirect method for operating activities.
b. Use a worksheet to assist in your preparation of the statement of cash flows.
c. Analyze the statement of cash flows.

PRACTICE   Learning Goal 21, continued

IA 21-10. Ethical issue: fraudulent misclassifications

Bill Ames, the owner of Ames Company, understands accounting and has made the following fraudulent changes in his statement of cash flows before showing it to potential investors, who do not understand accounting. Indicate the effects of each change on the statement of cash flows and why it is being done.

1) A $12,000 increase in accounts receivable is reported as an increase long-term investments.
2) A $25,000 increase in long-term notes payable is reported as an increase in accounts payable.
3) A $4,000 gain on sale of equipment is reported as sales revenue.
4) A $10,000 decrease in a short-term vendor note payable is shown as a decrease in long-term notes payable.
5) $25,000 of operating expenses are reported as equipment purchases instead of expenses.

Your Questions?

It is *very* important to be aware of what you need to understand better. What do you need to understand better about this learning goal? On a separate piece of paper, write the questions that you want to discuss with your classmates, instructor, or supervisor. Try to be very specific about what is bothering you, such as explanations that you do not fully understand.

Long-Term Liabilities

Glossary

Accelerated depreciation method: depreciation methods that result in greater depreciation early in an asset's life and less depreciation later in the asset's life (page 742)

Account form: a form of the balance sheet in which all the assets are placed on the left side of a page and the equity claims are placed on the right side (page 227, 232)

Account receivable: an asset that is the right to collect money, usually as the result of a sale to a customer; payment usually in 30–60 days. (page 656)

Accounting information system: another term for accounting system. (page 510)

Accounting periods: fixed periods of time for which a company prepares financial statements. (page 7)

Accrual: a transaction in which either a revenue is earned or an expense is incurred which has not been recorded, and no cash or other assets are received, paid or, used. (page 150)

Accrual adjustment: an adjusting entry that is used to record an accrued revenue or expense that that has not yet been recorded at the end of an accounting period. (page 150)

Accrual basis accounting: the method of accounting that records the effects of all transactions (both cash and noncash) by applying the revenue recognition and matching principles. (page 18)

Accrued expense: an expense that has been incurred but is unpaid. (page 167)

Accrued liability: another term used for accrued expense. (page 167)

Accrued revenue: a revenue that has been earned but cash has not been received. (page 150)

Aging schedule: a classification of receivables by age. (page 661)

Allowance: a reduction in the amount owed a seller without returning merchandise. (page 352, 447)

Allowance account: an account that acts as an offset to another account. (page 662)

Amortization: the allocation of the cost of an intangible asset into expense over the asset's estimated useful life; also, systematic reduction in the principal of a loan. (page 758)

Bank Reconciliation: an analysis that compares the cash balance shown in a customer's records to the cash balance shown on a bank statement and explains all the differences. (page 586)

Beginning inventory: the cost of the inventory on hand as of the start of the first day of a new accounting period. (page 314)

Betterment: a capital expenditure that is an improvement in the functionality of a plant or office. (page 749)

Bill of lading: an agreement with a shipper that contains a detailed description of amount and type of items that are shipped, and may include the cost of shipping. Also see *freight bill*. (page 356, 450)

Blank endorsement: a type of check endorsement requiring only the signature of the current owner of the check, and that transfers ownership to whoever physically holds the check. (page 584)

Bond: a long-term obligation issued by a corporation, government entity, or school district to the public in order to obtain cash. (Appendix 2)

Bond (insurance bond): an insurance policy for employee theft. (page 617)

Book value: cost of an asset minus its accumulated depreciation; also, stockholders' equity. (page 47)

Bounced check: a slang expression referring to a bad check that is deposited and later is subtracted from the depositor's account balance because of payor's insufficient funds. (page 589)

Calendar year period: A fiscal year that begins on January 1 ends on December 31. (page 10)

Capital expenditure: an expenditure to purchase, develop, or improve an asset. (page 739)

Carrying value: an expression that means the same thing as asset book value. (page 47)

Cash basis accounting: the method of accounting that records only cash transactions, and records all receipts as revenue and all payments as expenses. (page 23)

Cash discount: another name for purchase discount. (page 337, 443)

Cash payments journal: a journal used to record only transactions for cash payment. (page 534)

Cash receipts journal: a journal used to record only transaction for receipt of cash. (page 532)

Chain discount: multiple trade discounts on the same sale. (page 334)

Check: a document given by a maker to a payee that directs the maker's bank to pay a specified amount to the payee. (page 582)

Check authorization (approval) form: Another name for a voucher. (page 607)

Check endorsement: a signed notation on the back of a check that transfer legal ownership of the check to another party, and therefore the right to receive payment. (page 584)

Check register: in a voucher system, a special journal that records cash payments. (page 609)

Classified balance sheet: a balance sheet in which the accounts are grouped into significant or meaningful categories. (page 229)

Cleared (canceled) check: a check that has been paid and stamped to indicate payment. (page 583)

Closing entry: journal entry that is part of the closing process. (Learning Goal 8, 12, 14)

Closing process ("closing the books"): transferring temporary account balances into permanent accounts; generally, revenue, expense, and dividends (or drawing) closed into an equity account. (Learning Goal 8)

Collusion: two or more persons acting together to commit a fraud. (page 581)

Commercial substance: a genuine or actual effect on the financial condition of a business as a result of a transaction. (page 778)

Compensating balance: a minimum cash balance that must be maintained. (page 42, App.2)

Consignment: merchandise that a business agrees to hold, but not own, while being offered for sale. (page 461, 482)

Contingent liability: a liability that is created only if another event happens first. (page 789)

Contra asset: an account that is an offset against the balance of another account. (page 47, 141)

Controlling account: any ledger account that has a subsidiary ledger (page 513)

Copyright: the exclusive right granted by the U.S. government to reproduce and sell a published or artistic work generally for a period of the life of the creator plus 70 years. (page 757)

Cost of goods available for sale: cost of beginning inventory plus net purchases and freight-in. (page 345, 357)

Cost of goods sold: an expense that is the cost of the merchandise that was sold. (page 312, 439)

Credit memorandum: a document issued by the seller of merchandise to inform the buyer of a credit to the accounts receivable. (page 336, 445)

Credit terms: the specified manner of payment that is agreed upon between buyer and seller. (page 326, 442)

Current assets: cash and other assets that can be expected to be turned into cash or used up instead of spending cash, all as part of normal operations, within one year of the balance sheet date or the operating cycle of the business, whichever is longer. (page 230)

Current liabilities: liabilities that require payment within one year of the balance sheet date or the operating cycle of the business, whichever is longer. (page 231)

Current portion of long-term debt: the amount of principal payments of a long-term debt that are payable within a year or the operating cycle, whichever is longer. (page 231, 790)

Debit memorandum: a document issued by a buyer to inform the seller of a debit to accounts payable. (page 353, 449)

Debt covenants: requirements and restrictions imposed by lenders as a condition of a loan.

Deferred expense: another name for prepaid expense. (page 44)

Deferred revenue: another name for unearned revenue. (page 106)

Deliverables: the specific services or products that will be provided. (page 94)

Depletion: the allocation of the cost of natural resource into expense over its estimated useful life. (page 755)

Depreciation: the process of allocating the cost of plant and equipment assets into expense during their estimated useful lives, in a systematic and rational manner. (page 136)

Direct write-off method: a procedure that records uncollectible accounts receivable without the use of an estimate an period-end adjustment. (page 668)

Discount period: the days allowed by a seller in which a buyer can pay and receive a discount. (page 326)

Dishonored note: a note that is not paid when due. (page 674)

Double-declining balance method: a method of accelerated depreciation. (page 741)

Drawer (or Payor): other names for the maker of a check. (page 582)

Earnings record: a legally required record of employee gross pay, withholding, and net pay that must be maintained by an employer. (page 816)

Electronic data integration (EDI): sharing accounting and production information on the Internet. (page 512)

Employee: generally any person who performs services for a business if the business controls what work will be done and how it will be done. (page 793)

Encryption: software code that prevents unauthorized reading of data. (page 615)

Expense: a decrease in stockholders' (or owner's) equity that results from consuming resources in regular business operations. (page 12)

Expired cost: another name for expense. (page 12)

Extraordinary repair: a major repair that extends a plant asset's life or improves its function and is treated as a capital expenditure. (page 749)

Factor: a company that specializes in buying accounts receivable. (page 669)

Fair Labor Standards Act (FLSA): A federal law that governs working conditions and sets standards for overtime pay and minimum wage rate. (page 799)

FICA: Federal Insurance Contribution Act of 1935, which created Social Security. (page 802)

Filing status: marital status, which is part of the calculation to determine income tax rate. (page 800)

Financing activities: a category on a statement of cash flows for cash receipts and payments related to borrowing and stockholders' equity. (page 846)

Firewalls: computer code that prevents unauthorized access to computer systems. (page 615)

First-in, first-out (FIFO): the costs of the first items acquired are considered to be the first costs that become expense. (page 705)

Fiscal year: any consecutive 12-month period of business activity. (page 9)

Fixed assets: another name for property, plant, and equipment. (page 738)

FOB: "Free on board". Refers to the location up to which the buyer is not responsible for shipping costs; the point at which ownership and risk of loss transfers to buyer. (page 451)

Franchise: an agreement that gives an exclusive right to use another's name and sell another's product. (page 757)

Free cash flow: cash flow from operating activities minus capital expenditures and dividends. (page 870)

Freight bill: an invoice from a shipping company that shows cost of shipping and sometimes additional information. (page 450)

Freight-in: a buyer's payment for shipping or delivery cost of merchandise delivered. (page 354, 449)

Freight-out: a seller's payment for shipping or delivery cost of merchandise delivered. (page 337, 449)

FUTA: Federal Unemployment Tax Act; imposes a tax on employers for an assistance program for unemployed workers. (page 807)

Gain: an incidental increase in stockholders' equity that is not part of normal sales or an investment. (page 256)

General ledger package: a computerized accounting system that is not custom-designed. (page 546)

Goodwill: the amount paid for a business that is in excess of the business fair market value of the equity. (page 757)

Gross margin: another term for gross profit. (page 312)

Gross method: a method of recording an account payable at the gross amount, before any discounts. (page 441)

Gross pay: total compensation received by an employee. (page 798)

Gross profit method: a method of estimating inventory using an historical gross profit percentage. (page 715)

Hot check: slang term for a fraudulent check. (page 589)

Impaired asset: an asset that has lost a significant amount of economic value, as determined by a specific calculation procedure, and which requires a journal entry to record a loss. (page 751)

Imprest system: a petty cash system in which the completed petty cash vouchers plus remaining cash must equal the total amount of the petty cash fund. (page 601)

In-kind: Compensation made in the form of property or services. (page 798)

Income summary: an account often used in the closing process to summarize revenues and expenses. (page 261)

Independent contractor: an individual who is in business to offer services to the public, not as an employee. (page 794)

Installment receivable: an account receivable paid in regular payments. (page 656)

Intangible: not having physical substance. (page 231)

Interest receivable: a payee's right to collect unpaid interest. (page 656)

Interim statements: financial statement prepared more often than annually. (page 10)

Internal control: the policies, procedures, and organizational design used for the purpose of safeguarding assets. (page 580)

Inventory shrinkage: an unidentified loss of inventory. (page 360, 461)

Investing activities: a category on a statement of cash flows for cash receipts and payments related to investments, lending, and transactions of long-term assets. (page 845)

Invoice: a bill showing amount due. (page 348)

Invoice price: the cost of a purchase, as shown on an invoice. (page 334)

Last-in, first-out (LIFO): the costs of the last items acquired are considered to be the first costs that become expense. (page 699)

Leasehold: the right to occupy property with a long-term lease. (page 757)

Liquid assets: another name for current assets; also, cash, receivables, and short-term investments.

List price: the price at which merchandise is offered for sale. (page 334)

Lock box: a bank collection service. (page 614)

Long-term liabilities: debts that require payment after one year from the balance sheet date or the operating cycle of the business, whichever is longer. (page 231)

Loss: an incidental decrease in stockholders' equity that is not part of normal sales or an investment. (page 256)

Lower of cost or market (LCM): a valuation rule that requires inventory value to be shown on a balance at the lowest of two values. (page 712)

MACRS: Modified Accelerated Cost Recovery System; a depreciation method specified for income tax purposes. (page 743)

Matching principle: an accrual-basis accounting rule that directs accountants to record expenses in the period in which the expenses helped produce revenues regardless of when cash is paid. (page 18)

Maturity date: the date on which a loan becomes due. (page 656)

Medicare: a federal medical insurance plan generally for persons over 65. (page 802)

Moving average method: a method that recalculates an average when new data becomes available or when time passes. (page 699, 708)

Multiple-step income statement: a detailed income statement format that classifies expenses and calculates net income in several steps. (page 392, 477)

Net accounts receivable: the balance in accounts receivable minus the balance in the related allowance for uncollectible accounts. (page 659)

Net method: recording accounts payable at the gross amount minus the potential discount. (page 441)

Net pay: gross pay minus withholding. (page 813)

Net realizable value: the estimated collectible amount of an asset. (page 659)

Net sales: gross sales minus sales discounts and sales returns and allowances. (page 323, 439)

Non-operating: a term that refers to revenues and gains or expenses and losses that do not occur as part of normal business operations to create and sell goods and services. (page 394)

Notes receivable: an asset that is the right to collect money resulting from a promissory note. (page 230)

OASDI: "Old Age, Survivors, and Disability Insurance" that is a federal program financed by the social security tax; often referred to as "social security". (page 802)

Operating activities: The section on a statement of cash flows showing cash inflow and outflow resulting from recurring business operations. (Page 845)

Operating cycle: the process in which cash is spent to create goods or services, sales are made, and cash is collected from customers. (page 230)

Operations: the business activities that create and sell something of value; the main purpose of business activities. (page 11)

Over and short: an account used to record small, unexplained cash differences, generally used in retail sales. (page 604)

Patent: an exclusive right granted by the federal government to manufacture and sell an invention, generally for 20 years. (page 757)

Payee: the party designated on a check or promissory note to receive payment. (page 582)

Payroll: a general term that refers to the steps involved in identifying and paying employees and recording the related transactions; also used as a reference to the cost of paying employees. (page 791)

Periodic inventory method: a method that determines ending inventory and cost of goods sold by periodically counting the inventory. (page 313)

Periodicity assumption: the assumption that the life of a business is divided into regular, fixed time intervals. (page 8)

Petty cash fund: a small fund of currency and coin kept on the business premises for minor cash expenditures. (page 601)

Petty cash voucher: a voucher that authorizes a petty cash payment. (page 602)

Physical inventory: counting inventory by inspection. (page 710)

Plan administrator: a company that designs and administers pension plans (page 809)

Plant and equipment: tangible assets used in production generally having life longer than a year. (page 738)

Post-closing trial balance: a trial balance that is prepared after the closing process is complete. (page 2)

Prepaid expense: an advance payment for a future expense that is recorded as an asset at the time of payment. (page 44, 71)

Principal: the amount of money borrowed and owed as stated in a promissory note. (page 672)

Promissory note: a written unconditional promise to pay an amount of money.

Property, plant, and equipment: tangible assets, including land, used in production generally having life longer than a year. (page 738)

Purchases: the cost of merchandise purchased. (page 341, 441)

Purchase discount: a discount received by the buyer for early payment within a specified discount period. (page 337, 443)

Purchase order: a formal written purchase request sent to a vendor. (page 348)

Purchase requisition: a formal written request within in an organization to purchase an item. (page 348)

Purchase returns and allowances: an account used by a buyer to record the cost of merchandise that is returned to a seller or reduced in price by the seller after purchase. (page 352, 447)

Purchases journal: a journal used to record only transactions that involve purchases on account. (page 522)

Receiving report: a written verification of the type, amount, and condition of items received. (page 608)

Recognize: to record a transaction, particularly a revenue or an expense. (page 17)

Reconciled (or adjusted or true) cash balance: a bank reconciliation balance that shows the same final cash balance for both the bank and the account holder. (page 587)

Remittance slip: the part of a bill that is returned with a payment. (page 613)

Report form: a balance sheet format in which assets are placed at the top of a page and liabilities and stockholders' (or owner's) equity are underneath. (page 232)

Residual value: the remaining value of a depreciable asset at the end of its useful life. (page 137)

Restricted cash: a cash balance that may be used only for a specific purpose. (page 579)

Restrictive endorsement: the safest type of check endorsement that restricts transfer only to the named party. (page 584)

Return to maker (RTM) check: a general expression that describes a check that will not be paid (a "bad check") for a variety of possible reasons. (page 589)

Revenue: an increase in stockholders' (or owner's) equity that results from a sale of product or services. (page 11)

Revenue expenditure: another term for expense. (page 740)

Revenue recognition principle: an accrual-basis accounting rule that directs accountants to record revenue in the period when it is earned (when a sale is made) regardless of when cash is received. (page 18)

Salary: a fixed amount of gross per period that does depend on hours worked. (page 798)

Sales discount: a discount offered by a seller to encourage quick payment. (page 327, 453)

Sales invoice: a bill sent by a seller to the buyer. (page 348)

Sales journal: a journal used to record only transactions that involve sales on account. (page 526)

Sales returns and allowances: an account used by a seller to record the cost of merchandise that is returned to the seller or a reduction in price allowed by the seller. (page 335, 454)

Sales tax: a tax collected by sellers and then remitted to a state or local taxing authority as a percentage of the dollar amount of taxable sales. (page 338, 457)

Salvage value: another name for residual value. (page 137)

Self-employment tax: the combined employee/employer FICA amount that must be paid by a self-employed person. (page 807)

Service potential: the benefits or utility provided by an asset.

Simple interest: interest calculated only on principal, excluding any prior interest. (page 672)

Single-step income statement: an income statement format in which net income can always be calculated in one step. (page 395, 480)

Social security tax: a tax paid by both employee and employer that provides social security benefits. (page 802)

Solvency: the ability to pay debts as they become due.

Special journal: a journal that records only specified types of similar transactions. (page 518)

Specific identification method: a method that calculates cost of goods sold by identifying inventory items from specific purchases. (page 703)

Statutory employee: a worker who is not an employee under common law but who is designated as an employee by statute. (page 795)

Straight-line depreciation: a method that allocates an equal amount of depreciation expense into each equal period of an asset's life. (page 139)

Subsidiary ledger: a separate ledger that contains individual accounts totaling to the amount of a single account in the general ledger called a controlling account. (page 513)

SUTA: State Unemployment Tax Act; imposes a tax on employers for an assistance program for unemployed workers. (page 807)

Tangible asset: an asset that has physical substance. (page 138)

Time-period assumption: another name for the periodicity assumption. (page 8)

Trade discount: a percentage reduction in list price. (page 334)

Trade receivable: another name for account receivable. (page 656)

Trade-in allowance: an amount allowed by a seller for an asset received in exchange for the asset being sold, which reduces the amount of cash paid by the buyer. (page 782)

Trademark: the ownership and exclusive right granted by the federal government to use a product-related word, description, title, or symbol for 10 years plus 10-year renewals. (page 757)

Transportation-in: another term for freight-in. (page 354, 449)

Unearned discount: a discount taken by a customer that pays after the discount period. (page 331)

Units-of-production method: a method that calculates depreciation based on a fixed amount of depreciation expense per unit of output. (page 743)

Useful life: an estimated period of time for which an asset will provide benefits. (page 138)

Voucher: a document that authorizes a cash payment by providing assurance of a transaction's authenticity. (page 607)

Wage base: a calendar year specified amount of gross pay subject to payroll tax. (page 802)

Wholesale: a business that sells goods to customers who are other merchants or manufacturers. (page 308)

Worksheet: an informal document that is used to organize information from accounting records, usually for the purpose of preparing financial statements or making projections. (page 205)

Checklist for Computerized Accounting Software Functions and Features

Overview

The list of items that follows is a general review of commonly used elements of computerized accounting systems. This should provide an overview of many of the system features that businesses consider important. However, it is unlikely that any list will fully apply to a given business—*some items may be irrelevant whereas the needs of a particular business might require items that are not even listed.* Also, for any list, it is a good idea to assign priorities to the individual items. For example, on a scale of 1 to 5, assign a "1" to items that are most important and assign a "5" to items that are least important. Finally, important preliminary work must be done. This may modify the checklist.

Important Preliminary Work

Analyze Information Needs

Without question, analysis of information needs is the key step in the process of developing any accounting system. Specialists can be hired for larger or complex businesses. For a small business, all that is required is a notebook and careful observation of daily activities for several accounting periods:

- What kinds of transactions occur and what accounts are affected?
- What kind of information is frequently needed or important to have?
- What kinds of financial and tax reports are required?
- What kinds of analytical reports for management would be important?
- Are any of the above likely to change? What would create changes?
- What level of security is needed?

Consult a Professional

Even when a business does not plan to purchase an expensive system, the cost of consulting a professional is often a wise investment. The best choice is a person who is very familiar with computerized accounting systems as well as the type and size of business for which the system would be used. CPAs can often provide these resources. Other possibilities are college professors or consultants. Getting good suggestions can save time, develop very useful information, and avoid future problems.

Other Research

- Take a class. The teacher and students can be good contacts.
- Do more reading. Many books and trade magazines discuss the business and accounting applications of computers.
- Talk with someone who uses a computerized accounting system.
- Scan internet information and contact online user groups.

Checklist

Scope

The checklist below is intended to apply to a low- to moderate-priced modular accounting software system. This could mean prices in the range of about $200 to $7,500 depending on modules used and individual needs.

General Features and Considerations

- Operating system supported
- Server system supported
- Capacity of existing computer system?
- Multiple simultaneous users (optimum number?)
- Installation cost
- Training availability and its cost: this can be a *significant addition to system cost* but is very important if the system is to be fully utilized. Are third-party books and references available at the local computer store? College courses?
- Vendor support after installation
- Context-sensitive help during use of system
- Upgrade and update methods and cost
- Source code access (program changes)
- Security: (a) multi-level passwords, (b) file and ledger locks, (c) master file changes report, (d) mandatory transaction printing—no transaction can be deleted, (e) automatic reports of user-defined transaction types ("suspicious" or incorrect entries), (f) Internet security features, (g) other security features.
  Remember that internal control is a very important part of an accounting system and that a computerized system can be especially vulnerable.
- Database software—which type? Scalable?

- Ability to customize screens and reports
- Backup and file recovery features
- Data entry time-saving features: this is very important, especially as volume of activity increases or if customer, vendor, or employee data files are frequently updated. For example, entering a customer name automatically fills in all customer information (also called "auto fill"); can use "hot" keys for repetitive functions.
- Transaction volume: count the number of customers, vendors, inventory items and employees you have or are likely to have. Verify with vendor (and confirm with others if possible) that the software can handle these numbers. Also keep in mind the ability of your computer to process the data at adequate speeds.
- What are limits on character field lengths in account names, data entry fields, and descriptions?
- Imports/exports data from/to other software
- Supports programs such as spreadsheets and word processing
- Drill-down from many screens to locate transactions
- Supports bar code scanning for data entry
- Internet capabilities
- Demos with *all reports* to evaluate before you buy
- Warranties

General Ledger Module and General Bookkeeping Features

- Chart of accounts: (a) can be user defined, (b) chart of accounts template available, (c) limit on the number of accounts? (d) sub-accounts are available for subsidiary accounts, departments, etc.—how many levels of sub-accounts? (e) pop-up chart of accounts if needed for reference
- No unbalanced entries default
- Automatic recurring transactions available
- Adjustment to prior periods OK
- Closing entries—both permanent and temporary
- Automatic reversing entries can be created
- General journal is supported—other journals supported?
- General journal: (a) is viewable, (b) is fully printable, (c) allows explanations/descriptions
- Batch and real-time processing

- Check writing: (a) types of checks available, (b) manual check payments can be entered and not printed, (c) printed checks are listed, (d) can void printed checks
- Automatic functions at data entry points when modules are added (sales tax by area, price of items, cost of goods sold, reorder points, etc.)
- Compatible output forms widely available
- General ledger: (a) it is viewable, (b) detailed ledger is fully printable, (c) can select any general ledger entry and drill-down to the source transaction, (d) will support budgets and compares actual to budget for each account, (e) posting cross references are maintained between all journals and ledger
- Both cash and accrual methods supported
- Number of accounting periods maintained open
- Trial balance with worksheet

Checklist, *continued*

General Ledger Module and General Bookkeeping Features, *continued*

- Financial statements: (a) produces all GAAP-required financial statements, (b) how many periods shown for comparison? (c) many report formats available—allows customization, (d) charts and graphs with financial statements, (e) can perform designated ratio analysis, (f) budget reports, (g) produce any statement in HTML format, (h) view reports on the web?
- Which modules are supported?

- Modules are fully integrated
- User-defined accounting periods
- User-defined default settings
- Query (view) any account
- View transactions by date, date range, or account
- Batch reversing entries capability
- Can make easy corrections and manual overrides
- Electronic funds transfer

Sales/Accounts Receivable Module

Note: if a business has a significant amount of sales and purchases on account, complete and well-designed sales/accounts receivable and purchases/accounts payable modules can save enormous amounts of time. These two modules should be able to handle every possible sales or purchase transaction you might encounter. What you want to avoid is spending many hours trying to figure out how to finesse a "workaround" solution to a software shortcoming that is unable to correctly record some unusual transaction.

- Create customer master file with all customer data
- Allow user-defined default account numbers
- Allow manual change of all calculations and entries
- Create report of invoice change entries
- Maintain customer subsidiary ledger that reconciles to Accounts Receivable in general ledger
- Taxable and non-taxable sales in same invoice
- Non-sale (reimbursable charges) allowed on invoice
- Services can be entered on invoice
- Create A/R automatically from a time/billing module
- User-defined revenue accounts for different products and services
- Multiple sales tax jurisdictions calculations
- Multiple ship-to addresses
- Database supports automatic price quotes which can become invoices
- Invoices created and numbered sequentially
- Prior invoice corrections and recalculation allowed
- View and print prior invoices
- Enter and save customer information into master file directly from an invoice
- Pop-up files: (a) chart of accounts, (b) customer
- Integrate with G/L, inventory, and purchases/cash disbursements modules
- Calculate different discount types by item/customer
- Automatic calculation of extensions, discounts, totals, and tax calculations on invoice
- Allow different order types (apply to standing orders, future date, current, and backorder) and view status
- Records EFT/credit card sales
- Multiple price codes (for different customers)
- Record partial (short) payments from customers

- Automatically track and apply customer prepayments
- Record sales returns and allowances
- Create debit and credit memos (usually credit memos)
- Calculate discounts on full balance, partial payments, and payments after returns and allowances
- Automatic interest and late charge calculation option
- Record customer overpayments
- Record refunds to customers
- User-defined application of customer payments to specific invoices or account balances
- Create credit limits and account "holds"
- View and print sales journal and cash receipts journal
- View and print detailed individual customer account activity (subsidiary ledger)
- View and print invoice record by user-defined query (all, open, closed, date, customer, etc.)
- Automatic sales commission calculations and reports
- Create aging reports with user-defined aging periods
- Create taxable sales report
- Create other reports based on user-defined needs
- Print customizable customer statements
- Print customizable invoices and packing slips
- Print envelopes/mailing labels
- Integrates with A/P to create a cash budget that compares actual to budgeted. (Verify that projected cash balance results from the total of each *individual account difference*—not simply at or below budgeted total for all accounts.)
- Integrates with inventory module to set sales prices based on user-defined automatic markup calculation from inventory cost

continued ▶

Checklist, *continued*

Purchases/Accounts Payable Module

- Create vendor master file with all vendor data
- Allow user-defined default account numbers
- Maintain vendor subsidiary ledger that reconciles to Accounts Payable in general ledger
- Integrate with G/L, inventory, and sales/cash receipts modules
- Allow manual change of all calculations and entries
- Create report of manual change entries
- Record partial payments to vendor
- Record purchase returns and allowances
- Record overpayments
- Calculate discounts on full balance, partial payments, and payments after returns and allowances
- Calculate different discount types by item/vendor
- Support gross and net discount methods, or
- Gross method with lost discounts report
- Record refunds from vendor
- Create debit and credit memos (usually debit memos)
- Record purchase returns and allowances
- Record partial payments to vendor
- Record reimbursable expenses from invoice and post to A/R
- Record both inventory and non-inventory items from invoices
- Automatically track and apply prepayments to invoice payment
- Automatic form 1099 for defined vendors
- Automatic payment reminders by date/vendor
- Prepare purchase orders
- Automatic invoice from purchase order
- View all open payables and select items for payment
- Pop-up files: (a) chart of accounts, (b) vendor
- Create automatic recurring entries
- Sequential reference numbers on payment documents
- Cannot make payments on closed invoices
- Create payment "holds"
- View and print invoice record by user-defined query (all, open, paid, date, customer, etc.)
- View and print purchases journal and cash disbursements journal
- View and print vendor analysis report
- View and print detailed individual vendor account activity (subsidiary ledger)
- View and print vendor aging reports with user-defined aging periods
- View and print cash requirements report
- View and print open purchase order listing
- Create other reports based on user-defined needs
- Print envelopes/mailing labels
- Record voided checks
- Check writing by single check or by batch
- Allow manual checks to be entered without printing
- Able to print payroll checks
- All payments create an invoice record—(Invoices can be created for all payments as a kind of voucher system.)
- Payment can be made directly for non-invoice items.
- Integrates with sales module to create a cash budget that compares actual to budgeted

Inventory Module

- Create inventory master file with all inventory data
- Allow user-defined default account numbers
- Integrate with G/L, sales/cash receipts, purchases/cash payments, and payroll modules
- Flexible inventory identification codes
- Allow manual change of all calculations and entries
- Create report of manual change entries
- Different costing methods available (FIFO, LIFO, average cost, etc., on unit or other basis.)
- Calculate and record unit costs
- Able to calculate unit cost that includes discounts, freight, allowances, short and partial shipments
- Tracks purchase orders for all the above plus back orders
- Different costing methods can be used with different inventory items
- Allow inventory adjustments such as write-downs
- Allow selling price below unit cost
- Both perpetual and periodic methods available for different inventory items (A computerized system usually provides greater benefits with perpetual.)
- Calculate automatic cost of goods sold
- Calculate automatic reorder point and quantity
- New inventory items can be entered into master file directly from purchase invoices.
- Item tracking: either by serial number or SKU code
- View and print full inventory ledger and sub-ledgers (sub-ledgers are for individual types of items)
- Pop-up inventory files can locate item and quantity
- Identify overstocked items exceeding user-defined maximum
- View and print inventory sales report by item (cost, markup, sales price, gross profit on units sold, inventory turnover, etc.)
- View and print stock status report (out, understock, overstock, discontinued, other) showing units, unit and total cost, including adjustments
- Distribute cost of goods sold to jobs or departments
- View and print inventory worksheet to aid in physical inventory count
- Creates ready-to-publish Internet catalog

Checklist, *continued*

Payroll Module

- Allow user-defined default account numbers
- Integrate with G/L, sales/cash receipts, inventory and purchases/cash payments
- Allow manual change of all calculations and entries
- Create report of manual change entries
- Multi-state tax rates
- Calculate all federal and state withholding
- Unlimited user-defined withholding items
- Print payroll checks in batch or singly
- Record manual payroll checks without printing
- Reprint erroneous or voided checks
- Create detailed earnings record for each employee
- Create payroll register for each payroll period
- Journalize accrual of payroll expense items
- Produce multiple checks for special situations (bonuses, vacation pay, other)
- Record vacation pay and sick leave accrued and used
- Record various pay periods (weekly, monthly, etc.)
- Record various pay types (regular, overtime, commission, tips, and piece work)
- Record non-wage compensation
- Distribute payroll cost to jobs or departments
- Accepts on-line payroll using an outside service?

Other Types of Modules

Numerous kinds of other modules are available to add efficiency and functionality. The question is: Do they really add value that justifies the cost? Some examples:

Module	Purpose
Order entry processing	Handles many types of orders and terms, speeds up the order-entry process, and follows status of orders; retrieves orders from Internet customers
Fixed asset accounting	Keeps detailed records of fixed assets, calculates different depreciation methods, and prints detailed reports
Manufacturing accounting	At a basic level, handles job cost and process cost systems, calculating job, unit, and department costs
Contract management	Facilitates the bidding and completion of contracts consistent with compliance requirements.
Project management	Evaluates status and progress of projects including deadlines, costs, and budgets; numerous reports
Sales force management	Evaluates activity of sales force and provides detailed product and cost information to the sales force
Distributions systems management	Controls and designs optimum distribution plans for delivery, sales, and other distribution activities
Accounting software for specific business types	Designed to record and report on transactions and meet information requirements that are unique to specific types of businesses.

Subject Index

INDEX Appendix 1: The Cash Budget

Appendix 1 is located in the disk to this text attached to the inside back cover. It is also available at www.worthyjames.com (student info.)

Appendix 2 is located in the disk to this text attached to the inside back cover. It is also available at www.worthyjames.com (student info.)

Essential Math Index

The disk in the back of this book includes a comprehensive basic math review, Essential Math for Accounting, with explanations, problems, and solutions. It continues from the math review in the disk for Volume 1. This is the index for the Volume 2 math review. The table of contents for the Volume 2 math review is on the disk.